KU-454-195

Organization Theory

Cases and Applications

THIRD EDITION

Richard L. Daft
Vanderbilt University

Mark P. Sharfman
Pennsylvania State University

West Publishing Company
St. Paul New York Los Angeles San Francisco

50 W. Kellogg Boulevard
P.O. Box 64526
St. Paul, MN 55164–1003

Printed in the United States of America

Library of Congress Cataloging in
Publication Data
ISBN: 0–314–66769–5

Organization

Theory

CONTENTS

Technology

Structure

III INTERNAL ORGANIZATIONAL PROCESS *175*

Goals and Effectiveness

Control and Information

Decision Making

Conflict

IV ORGANIZATIONAL DYNAMICS *267*

Change

Organizational Culture

Power and Politics

V VIEW FROM THE TOP *361*

Preface

The purpose of this book is to provide a set of organization theory cases and exercises that are theoretically meaningful as well as relevant in their application. As an academic discipline, organization theory concepts pertain to everyday management problem solving and decision making. The challenge facing instructors in organization theory courses is to present the theoretical basis for these concepts and to demonstrate their practical application. From our own teaching experience, using challenging case problems can make the difference between a good organization theory course and a great one. By providing supplementary case materials that are both interesting and practical, this book helps the student become more competent in understanding organizations, including the factors that lead to success and failure. This third edition continues the approach we took in the first two by including materials with the following features:

1. The third edition contains approximately 40 percent new material. Because the field of organization theory changes so rapidly, it is essential that the book be kept fresh. We have selected cases and exercises to reflect the evolution of new organizational forms and new industries.
2. We continue to mix "problem oriented" cases with descriptions of interesting organizations. In many of our cases, the student is put in the role of management to answer the question "What do we do next?" Students have the opportunity to analyze the situation, evaluate alternatives, and suggest solutions. In other cases, we ask the student to evaluate the case in terms of how the organization got to where it was and what could be done to maintain or improve the firm. Both types of cases are useful for either group or individual projects.
3. We have included several cases that allow the student to integrate materials from other courses. Organizational issues are intricately tied to other phenomena in a firm. We have selected cases that allow the student to examine such issues as the relationship between strategy and structure, the costs involved in organizational change, and design and control of the production function. Se-

lecting cases that integrate organization issues with other problems in the firm provides case analyses that come closer to real management situations.

4. The cases cover the breadth of organization theory, especially topics that have emerged in recent years. We have addressed many of the traditional organization theory topics, such as environment, bureaucracy, structure, and technology. We have also included cases that reflect such emerging issues as ethics, culture, information systems, retrenchment, and turnaround. Several cases and exercises address high-growth industries, such as aerospace, biotechnology, computers, and robotics. We have also increased our coverage of the service sector, including both proprietary and nonprofit organizations. To reflect the growing internationalization of business, we have included several new cases from outside of the United States.
5. We have selected the materials for this edition because of their variety and potential interest for students. These cases reflect real people in real organizations. The most important criterion for inclusion in this edition was that the materials be well written and enjoyable. Most of the cases have been tested in the classroom before inclusion.
6. We have also made improvements to the exercise portions of the book. We have added several new exercises and made sure that more exercises can fit into a 75-minute class. We have made a major effort to insure that the exercises are meaningful and the instructions are clear. We have also included exercises that can perform double duty. They are interesting as classroom exercises and can be modified and used for diagnosis or training in organizations.
7. As always, we asked outside reviewers to evaluate the second edition prior to the release of this new edition. They suggested numerous changes, several of which we adopted. For example, we have reduced the number of cases set in universities and increased the number of cases set in nonprofit settings. We have brought a better balance to the number of cases and exercises in each section. The instructor's manual also has been improved to include more information about the integration possibilities in several of the cases.

Acknowledgments

This book, more than most books, reflects the work and influence of several people in addition to the authors. First and foremost, we must thank the case writers. They studied the organizations, wrote the cases, and gave us permission to use their work. We also must thank all of the publishers who granted us permission to use previously published materials.

We also extend our appreciation to administrators and colleagues at Texas A & M and Penn State who were helpful and supportive during the development of this third edition. Michael Hitt, Management Department head, Benton Cocanougher, dean of the College of Business at Texas A & M, and Charles Snow, Management and Organization Department head, and Jay Hammond, dean of the College of Business Administration at Penn State, have created excellent climates for research of all types and have provided some of the resources for this project. Several colleagues at Texas A & M and Penn State have provided assistance and intellectual stimulation along the way. We especially thank Jim Dean, Bill Millman, Jim Thomas, and Linda Trevino. We must give special recognition to the individuals who gave have us such painstaking reviews of the second edition. Their assistance made the creation of this new edition much easier. Our thanks go to Diane Lloyd Gillo of the University of Wisconsin—Stevens Point, Ronald Klocke of Mankato State University, Meryl Reis Louis of Boston University, Mzamo Mangaliso of the University of Massachusetts—Amherst, Carol Matteson of the University of

Maine—Augusta, John Maurer of Wayne State University, and James Swenson of Moorhead State University.

For assistance with typing, permissions, and hundreds of other details, we are indebted to Barbara Apaliski, Sandy Edkins, Judy Hackman, Jeff Knisely, Shirley Rider, Judy Sartore, and Phyllis Washburn.

We also want to thank our editors at West. Esther Craig and Dick Fenton were as wonderful as ever. Debra Aspengren in Production and Beth Kennedy in Marketing were also extremely helpful. Without the patience, wisdom, skill, and encouragement of the staff at West, this edition would have never happened.

Our final note of appreciation goes to the students and the instructors that have used the previous editions of this book. We have created this new edition for you. It is our hope that this revised edition has furthered our goal of making organization theory easily available to students and practitioners in the classroom. In business schools, our challenge is to make management education more and more relevant to practice. The comments, interest, and support for the earlier editions show that, to some degree, we have met that challenge. It is our hope that this third edition pushes us further toward that goal.

R.L.D.
M.P.S.

A General Diagnostic Model for Organizational Behavior: Applying a Congruence Perspective

Most of the job of management is the struggle to make organizations function effectively. The work of society gets done through organizations, and the function of management is to get those organizations to perform that work.

The task of getting organizations to function effectively is a difficult one, however. Understanding one individual's behavior is a challenging problem in and of itself. A group, made up of different individuals and multiple relationships among those individuals, is even more complex. Imagine, then, the mind boggling complexity inherent in a large organization made up of thousands of individuals, hundreds of groups, and relationships among individuals and groups too numerous to count.

In the face of this overwhelming complexity, organizational behavior must be managed. Ultimately the work of organizations gets done through the behavior of people, individually or collectively, on their own or in collaboration with technology. Thus, central to the management task is the management of organizational behavior. To do this, there must be the capacity to *understand* the patterns of behavior at individual, group and organizational levels, to *predict* what behavioral responses will be elicited by different managerial actions, and finally to use understanding and prediction to achieve *control*.

How can one achieve understanding, prediction, and control of organizational behavior? Given its inherent complexity and enigmatic nature, one needs tools to help unravel the mysteries, paradoxes, and apparent contradictions that present themselves in the everyday life of organizations. One kind of tool is the conceptual framework or model. A model is a theory which indicates which factors (in an organization, for example) are most critical or important. It also indicates how these factors are related, or which factors or combination of factors cause other factors to change. In a sense, then, a model is a road map that can be used to

Written by David A. Nadler and Michael L. Tushman. Published by permission of the authors, who retain all rights. A version of this paper was originally published in J. R. Hackman, E. E. Lawler, and L. W. Porter (eds.), *Perspectives on Behavior in Organizations* (New York: McGraw-Hill, 1977).

make sense of the terrain of organizational behavior.

The models we use are critical because they guide our analysis and action. In any organizational situation, problem solving involves the collection of information about the problem, the interpretation of that information to determine specific problem types and causes, and the development of action plans. The models that individuals hold influence what data they collect and what data they ignore; models guide how people attempt to analyze or interpret the data they have; finally models aid people in choosing action plans.

Indeed, anyone who has been exposed to an organization already has some sort of implicit model. People develop these road maps over time, building on their own experiences. These implicit models (they usually are not explicitly written down or stated) guide behavior (Argyris & Schon, 1974). These models also vary in quality, validity, and sophistication depending on the nature and extent of the experiences of the model builder, his or her perceptiveness, his or her ability to conceptualize and generalize from experiences, etc.

We are not solely dependent, however, on the implicit and experience based models that individuals develop. The last four decades have witnessed intense work including research and theory development related to organization behavior (see, for example, Dunnette, 1976). It is therefore possible to think about scientifically developed explicit models for the analysis of organizational behavior and for use in organizational problem solving.

This paper will present one particular research- and theory-based model. It is a general model of organizations. Rather than describing a specific phenomenon or aspect of organizational life (such as a model of motivation or a model of organizational design), it attempts to provide a framework for thinking about the organization as a total system. The major thrust of the model is that for organizations to be effective, their subparts or components must be consistently structured and managed—they must approach a state of congruence.

The paper will be organized into several sections. In the first section, we will discuss the basic view of organizations which underlies the model—systems theory. In the second section, we will present and discuss the model itself. In the third section, we will present an approach to using the model for organizational problem analysis. Finally, we will discuss some of the implications of this model for thinking about organizations.

A Basic View of Organizations

There are many different ways of thinking about organizations. Typically, when a manager is asked to "draw a picture of an organization" he/she responds with some version of a pyramidal organizational chart. The model this rendition reflects is one which views the most critical factors as the stable formal relationships among the jobs and formal work units that make up the organization. While this clearly is one way to think about organizations, it is a very limited view. It excludes factors such as leader behavior, the impact of the environment, informal relations, power distribution, etc. Such a model can only capture a small part of what goes on in an organization. It is narrow and static in perspective.

Over the past twenty years, there has been a growing consensus that a viable alternative to the static classical models of organizations is to think about organizations as social systems. This approach stems from the observation that social phenomena display many of the characteristics of natural or mechanical systems (Von Bertalanffy, 1968, Buckley, 1967). In particular, it is argued that organizations can be better understood if they are considered as dynamic and open social systems (Katz & Kahn, 1966; 1978).

What is a system? In the simplest of terms, a system is a set of interrelated elements. These

EXHIBIT 1 ■ The Basic Systems Model

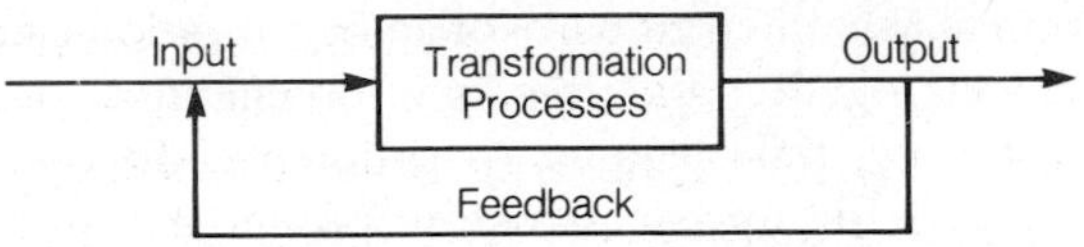

elements are related; thus change in one element may lead to changes in other elements. An *open system* is one that interacts with its environment. Thus it is more than just a set of interrelated elements. Rather, these elements make up a mechanism that takes input from the environment, subjects it to some form of transformation process, and produces output (Exhibit 1). At the most general level, it should be easy to visualize organizations as systems. Let's consider a manufacturing plant, for example. It is made up of different related components (different departments, jobs, technologies, etc). It receives input from the environment, including labor, raw material, production orders, etc., and subjects those inputs to a transformation process to produce products.

Organizations as systems display a number of basic systems characteristics. Katz and Kahn (1966; 1978) discuss these in detail, but a few of the most critical characteristics will be mentioned here. First, organizations display degrees of internal *interdependence* (Thompson, 1967). Changes in one component or subpart of an organization frequently has repercussions for other parts—the pieces are interconnected. Returning to our manufacturing plant example, if changes are made in one element (for example, the skill levels of the people hired to do jobs), other elements will be affected (the productiveness of equipment used, the speed or quality of production activities, the nature of supervision needed, etc.). Second, organizations have the capacity for *feedback* (see Exhibit 1). Feedback is information about the output of a system that can be used to control the system (Weiner, 1950). Organizations can correct errors and indeed change themselves because of this characteristic (Bauer, 1966). If, in our plant example, the plant management receives information about the declining quality of its product, it can use this information to identify factors in the system itself that contribute to this problem. It is important to note that, unlike mechanized systems, feedback information does not always lead to correction. Organizations have the potential to use feedback and be self-correcting systems, but they do not always realize this potential.

A third characteristic of organizations as systems is *equilibrium*. Organizations develop energy to move towards states of balance. When an event occurs that puts the system out of balance, it reacts and moves towards a balanced state. If one work group in our plant example were suddenly to increase its performance dramatically, it would throw the system out of balance. This group would be making increasing demands on the groups that supply it with information or materials to give it what it needs. Similarly, groups that work with the output of the high performing group would feel the pressure of work in process inventory piling up in front of them. Depending on the pay system used, other groups might feel inequity as this one group begins to earn more. We would predict that some actions would be taken to put the system back into balance. Either the rest of the plant would be changed to increase production and thus be back in balance with the single group, or (more likely) actions would be taken to get this group to modify its behavior to be consistent with the levels of performance of the rest of the system (by removing workers, limiting supplies, etc.). The point is that somehow the system would develop energy to move back towards a state of equilibrium or balance.

Fourth, open systems display *equifinality*. In other words, different system configurations can lead to the same end or lead to the same type of input-output conversion. This means there is not a universal or "one best way" to organize. Finally, open systems need to display *adaptation*. For a system to survive it must maintain a favorable balance of input or output transactions with the environment or it will run down. If our plant produces a product for which there are decreasing applications, it must adapt to the environmental changes and develop new products or ultimately the plant will simply have to close its doors. Any system therefore must adapt by changing as environmental conditions change. The consequences of not adapting to the environment can be seen in the demise of many once prosperous organizations (such as the eastern railroads) which did not alter in response to environmental changes.

Thus, systems theory provides a different way of thinking about the organization, in more complex and dynamic terms. While systems theory is a valuable basic perspective on organizations, it is limited as a problem-solving tool. The reason is that as a model systems theory is too abstract to be used for day-to-day organizational behavior problem analysis. Because of the level of abstraction of systems theory, we need to develop a more specific and pragmatic model based on the concepts of the open systems paradigm.

A Congruence Model of Organizational Behavior

Given the level of abstraction of open systems theory, our job is to develop a model which reflects the basic systems concepts and characteristics, but which will also be more specific and thus more usable as an analytic tool. In this section, we will describe a model which attempts to specify in more detail what are the critical inputs, what are the major outputs, and what are the transformation processes that characterize organizational functioning.

The model puts its greatest emphasis on the transformation process and in particular reflects the critical system property of interdependence. It views organizations as made up of components or parts which interact with each other. These components exist in states of relative balance, consistency, or "fit" with each other. The different parts of an organization can fit well together and thus function effectively or fit poorly, thus leading to problems, dysfunctions, or performance below potential. Given the central nature of these "fits" among components in the model, we will talk about it as a *congruence model of organizational behavior,* since effectiveness is a function of the congruence among the various components.

The concept of congruence is not a new one. Homans (1952) in his pioneering work on social processes in organizations emphasized the interaction and consistency among key elements of organizational behavior. Leavitt (1965) for example identified four major components of organization as being people, tasks, technology and structure. The model we will present here builds on these views and also draws from fit models developed and used by Seiler (1967), Lawrence and Lorsch (1969) and Lorsch and Sheldon (1972).

It is important to remember that we are concerned about modeling the *behavioral* system of the organization—the system of elements that ultimately produce patterns of behavior and thus performance of the organization. In its simplest form, we need to deal with the questions of what inputs does the system have to work with, what outputs does it need to and actually produce, and what are the major components of the transformation process, and how do these components interact with each other.

Inputs

Inputs are those factors that are, at any one point in time, the "givens" that face the organization. They are the material that the organization has to work with. There are several different types of inputs, each of which presents a different set of "givens" to the organization. (See Exhibit 2 for an overview of inputs.)

The first input is the *environment,* or all of those factors outside of the boundaries of the

EXHIBIT 2 ■ Key Organizational Inputs

Input	Environment	Resources	History	Strategy
Definition	All factors, including institutions, groups, individuals, events, etc., outside of the boundaries of the organization being analyzed, but having a potential impact on that organization.	Various assets that organization has access to, including human resources, technology, capital, information, etc., as well as less tangible resources (recognition in the market, etc.).	The patterns of past behavior, activity, and effectiveness of the organization which may have an effect on current organizational functioning.	The stream of decisions made about how organizational resources will be configured against the demands, constraints, and opportunities, within the context of history.
Critical Features of the Input for Analysis	■ What demands does the environment make on the organization? ■ Environment puts constraints on organizational action.	■ What is the relative quality of the different resources that the organization has access to? ■ To what extent are resources fixed, as opposed to flexible, in their configuration?	■ What have been the major stages or phases of development of the organization? ■ What is the current impact of historical factors such as strategic decisions, acts of key leaders, crises, core values, and norms?	■ How has the organization defined its core mission, including: ■ What markets it serves? ■ What products/services it provides to these markets? ■ On what basis does it compete? ■ What supporting strategies has the organization employed to achieve the core mission? ■ What specific objectives have been set for organizational output?

organization being examined. Every organization exists within the context of a larger environment which includes individuals, groups, other organizations and even larger social forces, all of which have a potentially powerful impact on how the organization performs (Pfeffer & Salancik, 1978). Specifically, the environment includes markets (clients or customers), suppliers, governmental and regulatory bodies, labor unions, competitors, financial institutions, special interest groups, etc. The environment is critical to organizational functioning (Aldrich & Pfeffer, 1976). In particular, for purposes of organizational analysis, the environment has three critical features. First, the environment makes demands on the organization. For example, it may require the provision of certain products or services, at certain levels of quality or quantity. Market pressures are particularly important here. Second, the environment may place constraints on organizational action. It may limit the types of kinds of activities in which an organization can engage. These constraints could range from limitations imposed by scarce capital, all the way to governmental regulatory prohibitions. Third, the environment provides opportunities which the organization can explore. In total, then, the analysis of an organization needs to consider what factors are present in the environment of the organization, and how those factors individually or in relation to each other create demands, constraints, or opportunities.

The second input is the *resources* of the organization. Any organization faces its environment with a range of different assets to which it has access and which it can employ. These include human beings, technology, capital, information, etc. Resources can also include certain less tangible assets such as the perception of the organization in the marketplace, or a positive organizational climate. A set of resources can be shaped, deployed, or configured in different ways by an organization. For analysis purposes, there are two features that are of primary interest. One aspect of resources concerns the relative quality of those resources, or what value they have in light of the nature of the environment. The second factor concerns the extent to which resources can be reconfigured, or how fixed or flexible different resources are.

The third input is the *history* of the organization. There is growing evidence that the contemporary functioning of many organizations is greatly influenced by events in the past (see Levinson, 1972; 1976). In particular, it is important to understand what have been the major stages or phases of development of the organization over time (Galbraith & Nathanson, 1978) as well as understanding what is the current impact of events that occurred in the past such as key strategic decisions that were made, the acts or behavior of key leaders in the past, the nature of past crises and the organizational responses to them, and the evolution of core values and norms of the organization.

The final input is somewhat different from the others in that it in some ways reflects some of the factors in the environment, resources, and history of the organization. The fourth input is *strategy.* We will use this term in its most global and broad context (Hofer & Schendel, 1978) to describe the whole set of decisions that are made about how the organization will configure its resources against the demands, constraints and opportunities of the environment within the context of its history. Strategy refers to the issue of matching the organization's resources to its environment, or making the fundamental decision of "what business are we in?" For analysis purposes, several aspects of strategy are important to identify (Katz, 1970). First is what is the core mission of the organization, or what has the organization defined as its basic purpose or function within the larger system or environment? The core mission includes decisions about what markets the organization will serve, what products or services it will provide to those markets, or what basis it will use to compete in those markets. Second, strategy includes the specific supporting strategies (or tactics) that the organization will employ or is employing to achieve its core mission. Third is the specific performance or output objectives that have been established.

Strategy is perhaps the most important single input for the organization (see discussion in Nadler, Hackman & Lawler, 1979). On one hand, strategic decisions implicitly determine what is the nature of the work that the organization should be doing, or the tasks that it should perform. On the other hand, strategic decisions, and particularly decisions about objectives, serve as the basis for determining what the outputs of the system should be. Based on strategy, one can determine what is the desired or intended output of the system.

In summary, there are three basic inputs: environment, resources, and history, and a

EXHIBIT 3 ■ Key Organizational Outputs

ORGANIZATIONAL FUNCTIONING
- Goal Attainment
- Resource Utilization
- Adaptability

GROUP/UNIT FUNCTIONING INDIVIDUAL FUNCTIONING
- Behavior
- Affective Reactions

fourth input, strategy, which reflects how the organization chooses to respond to or deal with those other inputs. Strategy is critical because it determines the work that the organization should be performing and it defines the nature of desired organizational outputs.

Outputs

Outputs describe what the organization produces, how it performs, or globally, how effective it is. There has been a lot of discussion about what makes for an effective organization (see Steers, 1978; Goodman & Pennings, 1978; Van de Ven & Ferry, 1980). For our purposes, however, it is possible to identify a number of key indicators of organizational output. First, we need to think about system output at different levels (see Exhibit 3). Obviously we can think about the output that the system itself produces, but we also need to think about the various other types of output that contribute to organizational performance, such as the functioning of groups or units within the organization as well as the functioning of individual organization members.

At the organizational level, three factors are important to keep in mind in evaluating organizational performance. The first factor is goal attainment, or how well the organization meets its objectives (usually determined by strategy). A second factor is resource utilization or how well the organization makes use of resources that it has available to it. The question here is not just whether the organization meets its goals, but whether it realizes all of the potential performance that is there and whether it achieves its goals by continuing to build resources or by "burning them up" in the process. A final factor is adaptability, or whether the organization continues to position itself in a favorable position vis-a-vis its environment—whether it is capable of changing and adapting to environmental changes.

Obviously, these organizational level outputs are contributed to by the functioning of groups or units (departments, divisions, or other subunits within the organization). Organizational output also is influenced by individual behavior, and certain individual level outputs (affective reactions such as satisfaction, stress, or experienced quality of working life) may be desired outputs in and of themselves.

The Organization as a Transformation Process

So far, we have defined the nature of inputs and outputs for the organizational system. This approach leads us towards thinking about the transformation process. The question that any manager faces, given an environment, a set of resources, and history, is "How do I take a strategy and implement it to produce effective organizational, group/unit, and individual performance?"

In our framework, the means for implementing strategies, or the transformation mechanism in the system is *the organization.* We therefore think about the organization and its major component parts as the fundamental means for transforming energy and information from inputs into outputs (see Exhibit 4). The question then is what are the key components of the organization, and what is the critical dynamic which describes how those components interact with each other to perform the transformation function?

Organizational Components

There are many different ways of thinking about what makes up an organization. At this point in the development of a science of organizations, we probably do not know what is the one right

EXHIBIT 4 ■ The Organization as a Transformation Process

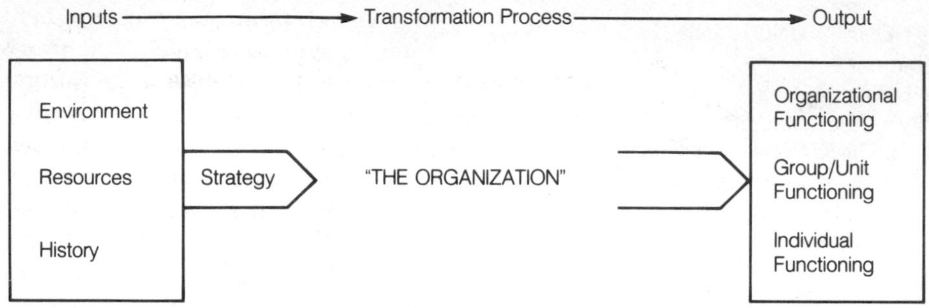

or best way to describe the different components of an organization. The question then is to find approaches for describing organizations that are useful, help to simplify complex phenomena, and help to identify patterns in what may at first blush seem to be random sets of activity. The particular approach here views organizations as composed of four major components: (1) the task, (2) the individuals, (3) the formal organizational arrangements, and (4) the informal organization. We will discuss each one of these individually. (See Exhibit 5 for overviews of these components.)

The first component is the *task* of the organization. The task is defined as the basic or inherent work to be done by the organization and its subunits. The task (or tasks) is the activity the organization is engaged in, particularly in light of its strategy. The emphasis is on the specific work activities or functions that need to be done, and their inherent characteristics (as opposed to characteristics of the work created by how the work is organized or structured in this particular organization at this particular time). Analysis of the task would include a description of the basic work flows and functions, with attention to the characteristics of those work flows such as the knowledge or skill demands made by the work, the kinds of rewards the work inherently provides to those who do it, the degree of uncertainty associated with the work, and the specific constraints inherent in the work (such as critical time demands, cost constraints, etc.) The task is the starting point for the analysis, since the assumption is that a primary (although not the only) reason for the organization's existence is to perform the task consistent with strategy. As we will see, the assessment of the adequacy of other components will be dependent to a large degree on an understanding of the nature of the tasks to be performed.

A second component of organizations concerns the *individuals* who perform organizational tasks. The issue here is identifying the nature and characteristics of the individuals that the organization currently has as members. The most critical aspects to consider include the nature of individual knowledge and skills, the different needs or preferences that individuals have, the perceptions or expectancies that they develop, and other background factors (such as demographics) that may be potential influences on individual behavior.

The third component is the *formal organizational arrangements.* These include the range of structures, processes, methods, procedures, etc., that are explicitly and formally developed to get individuals to perform tasks consistent with organizational strategy. Organizational arrangements is a very broad term which includes a number of different specific factors. One factor of organizational arrangements is organization design, how jobs are grouped together into units, the internal structure of those units, and the various coordination and control mechanisms used to link those units together (see Galbraith, 1977; Nadler,

EXHIBIT 5 ■ Key Organizational Components

Component	Task	Individual	Formal Organizational Arrangements	Informal Organization
Definition	The basic and inherent work to be done by the organization and its parts.	The characteristics of individuals in the organization.	The various structures, processes, methods, etc., that are formally created to get individuals to perform tasks.	The emerging arrangements, including structures, processes, relationships, etc.
Critical Features of Each Comonent	■ The types of skill and knowledge demands the work poses. ■ The types of rewards the work inherently can provide. ■ The degree of uncertainty associated with the work, including such factors as interdependence, routineness, etc. ■ The constraints on performance demands inherent in the work (given a strategy).	■ Knowledge and skills individuals have. ■ Individual needs and preferences. ■ Perceptions and expectancies. ■ Background factors.	■ Organization design, including grouping of functions, structure of subunits, and coordination and control mechanisms. ■ Job design. ■ Work environment. ■ Human resource management systems.	■ Leader behavior. ■ Intragroup relations. ■ Intergroup relations. ■ Informal working arrangements. ■ Communication and influence patterns.

Hackman & Lawler, 1979). A second factor in organizational arrangements is how jobs are designed (Hackman & Oldham, 1980) within the context of organizational designs. A third factor is the work environment, which includes a number of factors which characterize the immediate environment in which work is done, such as the physical working environment, the work resources made available to performers, etc. A final factor includes the various formal systems for attracting, placing, developing, and evaluating human resources in the organization.

Together, these factors combine to create the set of organizational arrangements. It is important to remember that these are the formal arrangements, formal in that they are explicitly designed and specified, usually in writing.

The final component is the *informal organization.* In any organization, while there is a set of formal organizational arrangements, over time another set of arrangements tends to develop or emerge. These arrangements are usually implicit and not written down anywhere, but they influence a good deal of behavior. For lack of a better term, these arrangements are frequently referred to as the informal organization and they include the different structures, processes, arrangements, etc., that emerge over time. These arrangements sometimes arise to complement the formal organizational arrangements by providing structures to aid work where none exist. In other situations they may arise in reaction to the formal structure, to protect individuals from it. It may therefore either aid or hinder organizational performance.

A number of aspects of the informal organization have a particularly critical effect on behavior and thus need to be considered. The behavior of leaders (as opposed to the formal creation of leader positions) is an important feature of the informal organization, as are the patterns of relationships that develop both within and between groups. In addition, there are different types of informal working arrangements (including rules, procedures, methods, etc.) that develop. Finally, there are the various communication and influence patterns that combine to create the informal organization design (Tushman, 1977).

Organizations can therefore be thought of as a set of components, the task, the individuals, the organizational arrangements, and the informal organization. In any system, however, the critical question is not what the components are, but rather the nature of their interaction. The question in this model is, then, what is the dynamic of the relationship among the components? To deal with this issue, we need to return to the concept of congruence or fit.

The Concept of Congruence

Between each pair of inputs, there exists in any organization a relative degree of congruence, consistency, or "fit." Specifically, the congruence between two components is defined as follows:

the degree to which the needs, demands, goals, objectives and/or structures of one component are consistent with the needs, demands, goals, objectives and/or structures of another component.

Congruence, therefore, is a measure of the goodness of fit between pairs of components. For example, consider two components, the task and the individual. At the simplest level, the task can be thought of as inherently presenting some demands to individuals who would perform it (i.e., skill/knowledge demands). At the same time, the set of individuals available to do the tasks have certain characteristics (i.e., levels of skill and knowledge). Obviously, when the individual's knowledge and skill match the knowledge and skill demanded by the task, performance will be more effective.

Obviously, even the individual-task congruence relationship encompasses more factors than just knowledge and skill. Similarly, each congruence relationship in the model has its own specific characteristics. At the same time, in each relationship, there also is research and theory which can guide the assessment of fit. An overview of the critical elements of each congruence relationship is provided in Exhibit 6.

The Congruence Hypothesis

Just as each pair of components has a degree of high or low congruence, so does the aggregate model, or whole organization, display a relatively high or low level of system congruence. The basic hypothesis of the model builds on this total state of congruence and is as follows:

other things being equal, the greater the total degree of congruence or fit between the various components, the more effective will be the organization, effectiveness being defined as the degree to which actual organization outputs at individual, group, and organizational levels are similar to expected outputs, as specified by strategy.

The basic dynamic of congruence thus views the organization as being more effective when its pieces fit together. If we also consider ques-

EXHIBIT 6 ■ Definitions of Fits

Fit	The Issues
Individual-organization	To what extent individual needs are met by the organizational arrangements. To what extent individuals hold clear or distorted perceptions of organizational structures, the convergence of individual and organizational goals.
Individual-task	To what extent the needs of individuals are met by the tasks. To what extent individuals have skills and abilities to meet task demands.
Individual-informal organization	To what extent individual needs are met by the informal organization. To what extent does the informal organization make use of individual resources, consistent with informal goals.
Task-organization	Whether the organizational arrangements are adequate to meet the demands of the task, whether organizational arrangements tend to motivate behavior consistent with task demands.
Task-informal organization	Whether the informal organization structure facilitates task performance, whether it hinders or promotes meeting the demands of the task.
Organization-informal organization	Whether the goals, rewards, and structures of the informal organization are consistent with those of the formal organization.

tions of strategy, the argument expands to include the fit between the organization and its larger environment. An organization will be most effective when its strategy is consistent with the larger environment (in light of organizational resources and history) and when the organizational components are congruent with the tasks to be done to implement that strategy.

One important implication of the congruence hypotheses is that organizational problem analysis (or diagnosis) involves description of the system, identification of problems, and analysis of fits to determine the causes of problems. The model also implies that different configurations of the key components can be used to gain outputs (consistent with the systems characteristic of equifinality). Therefore, the question is not finding the "one best way" of managing, but of determining effective combinations of components that will lead to congruent fits among them.

The process of diagnosing fits and identifying combinations of components to produce congruence is not necessarily intuitive. A number of situations which lead to congruence have been defined in the research literature. Thus, in many cases, fit is something that can be defined, measured, and even quantified. There is, therefore, an empirical and theoretical basis for making assessment of fit. In most cases, the theory provides considerable guidance about what leads to congruent relationships (although in some areas the research is more definitive and helpful than others). The implication is that the manager who is attempting to diagnose behavior needs to become familiar with critical aspects of relevant organizational behavior models or theories so that he or she can evaluate the nature of fits in a particular system.

The congruence model is thus a general organizing framework. The organizational analyst will need other, more specific "sub models" to define high and low congruence. Examples of such submodels that might be used in the context of this general diagnostic model would be (1) Job Characteristics model (Hackman & Oldham, 1980) to assess and explain the fit between individuals and tasks as well as the fit between individuals and organizational arrange-

EXHIBIT 7 ▪ A Congruence Model for Organizational Analysis

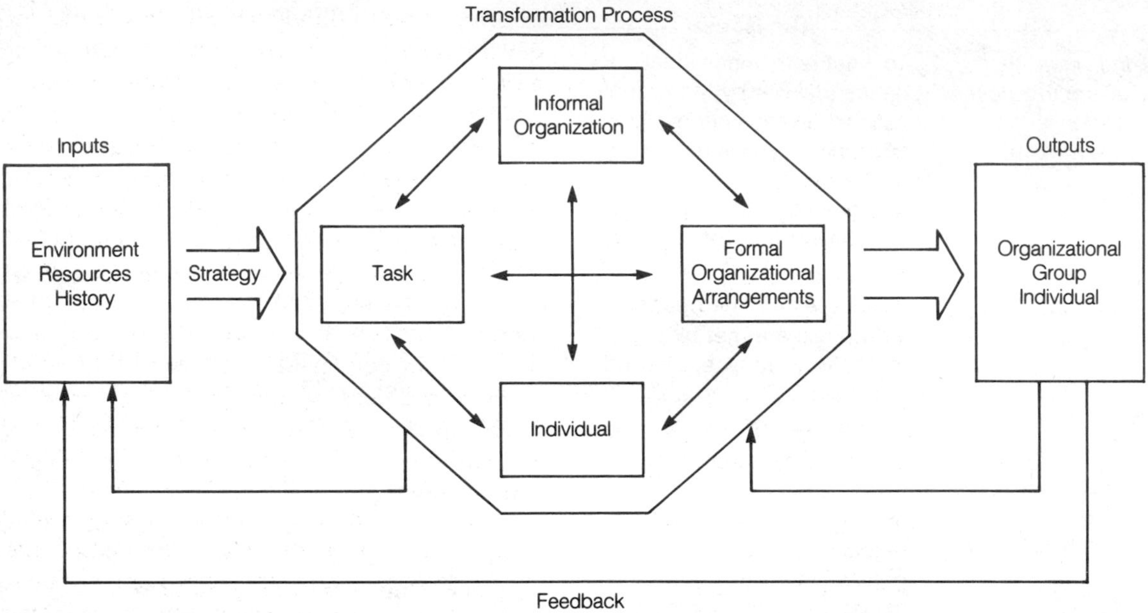

ments (job design); (2) Expectancy Theory models of motivation (Vroom, 1964; Lawler, 1973) to explain the fit between individuals and the other three components; (3) the Information Processing model of organizational design (Galbraith, 1973; Tushman & Nadler, 1978) to explain the task-formal organization and task-informal organization fits; or (4) an Organizational Climate model (Litwin & Stringer, 1968) to explain the fit between the informal organization and the other components. These models and theories are listed as illustrations of how more specific models can be used in the context of the general model. Obviously, those mentioned above are just a sampling of possible tools that could be used.

In summary, then, we have described a general model for the analysis of organizations (see Exhibit 7). The organization is seen as a system which takes inputs and transforms them into outputs. At the core of the model, the transformation process is the organization, seen as composed of four basic components. The critical dynamic is the fit or congruence among the components. We now turn our attention to the pragmatic question of how to use this model for analyzing organizational problems.

A Process for Organizational Problem Analysis

The conditions that face organizations are frequently changing, and as a consequence, managers are required to continually engage in problem identification and problem solving activities (Schein, 1970). To do this, managers must be involved in gathering data on the performance of their organizations, comparing these data to desired performance levels, identifying the causes of problems, developing and choosing action plans, and finally implementing and evaluating these action plans. These phases can be viewed as a generic problem solving process. For long-term organizational viability, some sort of problem-solving process needs to continually be in operation (Schein, 1970; Weick, 1969).

EXHIBIT 8 ■ BASIC PROBLEM ANALYSIS STEPS USING THE CONGRUENCE MODEL

Step	Explanation
1. *Identify symptoms*	List data indicating possible existence of problems.
2. *Specify inputs*	Identify the system. Determine nature of environment, resources, and history. Identify critical aspects of strategy.
3. *Identify outputs*	Identify data that defines the nature of outputs at various levels (individual, group/unit, organization). Should include: Desired outputs (from strategy), Actual outputs being obtained.
4. *Identify problems*	Identify areas where there are significant and meaningful differences between desired and actual outputs. To the extent possible, identify penalties, i.e., specific costs (actual and opportunity costs) associated with each problem.
5. *Describe components of the organization*	Describe basic nature of each of the four components with emphasis on their critical features.
6. *Assessment of congruence (fits)*	Do analysis to determine relative congruence among components (draw on submodels as needed).
7. *Generate hypotheses to identify causes*	Analyze to associate fit with specific problems.
8. *Identify action steps*	Indicate what possible actions might deal with causes of problems.

Experience with using the congruence model for organizations to do problem analysis in actual organizational settings has led to the development of an approach to using the model, based on the generic problem solving processes described above (see Exhibit 8). In this section, we will walk through this process, describing the different steps in the process and discussing how the model can be used at each stage. There are eight specific steps in the problem analysis process, and each one will be described separately.

1. *Identify symptoms:* In any situation there is initial information that presents itself as indications that problems may exist. We can think of this information as symptomatic data. These data tell us that a problem might exist, but they do not usually indicate what the problem is or what the causes are. Symptomatic data are important to note, however, since the symptoms or problems that present themselves may be important indicators of where to look for more complete data.
2. *Specify inputs:* Having noted the symptoms, the starting point for analysis is to identify the system and the environment in which it functions. This means collecting data about the nature of environment, the type of resources the organization has, and the critical aspects of its history. Input analysis also involves identifying what the strategy of the organization is, including its core mission, supporting strategies, and objectives.
3. *Identify outputs:* The third step is an analysis of the outputs of the organization at the individual, group, and organizational level. Output analysis actually involves two elements. The first is to define what is the desired, or planned output. This usually can be obtained from an analysis of strategy which should explicitly or implicitly define what the organization is attempting to achieve in terms of output or performance indicators. The second is to collect data that would indicate what type of output the organization is actually achieving.

4. *Identify problems:* Symptoms indicate the possibility of problems. For our purposes, we will define problems as the differences between expected output and actual output. A problem exists when a significant and meaningful difference is observed between output (at any level) that is desired or planned and the output that is actually being obtained. Thus problems would be discrepancies (actual vs. expected) of organizational performance, group functioning, and individual behavior or affective reactions. These data thus tell us that problems exist, but they do not specify what the causes are.

   Where data are available, it is frequently useful to also identify what are the costs associated with the problems, or the *penalties* that the organization incurs by not fixing the problem. Penalties might be actual costs (increased expenses, etc.) or opportunity costs, such as revenue that could be realized if the problem were not there.
5. *Describe organizational components:* The next step begins analysis to determine the causes of problems. Data are collected about the nature of each of the four major organizational components, including information about the component and its critical features in this organization.
6. *Assess congruence (fits):* Using the data collected in step 5 as well as applicable submodels or theories, an assessment is made of the positive or negative fit between each of the pairs of components.
7. *Generate hypotheses about problem causes:* Having described the components and assessed congruence, the next step is to link together the congruence analysis with the problem identification (step 4). Given the analysis, which poor fits seem to be associated with or account for the output problems that have been identified? The patterns of congruence and incongruence which appear to cause the patterns of problems are determined.
8. *Identify action steps:* The final step in problem analysis is to identify possible action steps. These steps might range from specific changes to deal with relatively obvious problem causes on one hand, to additional data collection to test the hypotheses developed concerning relatively more complex problems and causes.

In addition to these eight steps identified, some further steps need to be kept in mind. Having identified possible actions, problem solving involves making predictions about the consequence of those actions, choosing particular action steps, implementing those action steps, and evaluating the impact of those actions. In each case, it is, of course, important to have a general diagnostic framework to monitor what the effects of actions are.

The congruence model and this problem analysis process outline are tools for structuring and dealing with the complex reality of organizations. Given the indeterminate nature of social systems, there is no one best way of handling a particular situation. The model and the process do, however, facilitate one in collecting data, analyzing the meaning of that data, and making decisions about possible action. If these tools have merit, then it is up to the manager to use them along with his or her intuitive sense (based on experience) to make the appropriate set of diagnostic, evaluative, and action decisions over time.

Future Directions

The model that we have presented here reflects a particular way of thinking about organizations. If that perspective has merit, then it may make sense to think about the possible extensions of that model as a tool to think about more complex problems or to structure more complex situations. A number of directions for further thought, research, and theory development are as follows:

1. *Organizational change:* The issue of organizational change has received a good deal of attention from managers and academics alike. The question is how to implement

organizational changes effectively. Much talk has centered on the lack of a general model of organizational change. In one sense, however, it is hard to think about a general model of organizational change in the absence of a general model of organizations. The congruence perspective outlined here may provide some guidance and direction towards the development of a more integrated perspective on the processes of organizational change. Initial work in that area (Nadler, 1981) is encouraging in terms of the applicability of the congruence model to the change issue.

2. *Organizational development over time:* There has been a growing realization that organizations grow and develop over time, that they face different types of crises, evolve through different stages, and develop along some predictable line (see, for example, Greiner, 1972; Galbraith and Nathanson, 1978). A model of organizations such as the one presented here might be a tool for developing a typology of growth patterns by indicating what are the different configurations of task, individual, organizational arrangements and informal organizations that might be most appropriate for organizations in different environments and at different stages of development.

3. *Organizational pathology:* Organizational problem solving ultimately requires some sense of what types of problems may be encountered and kinds of patterns of causes one might expect. It is reasonable to assume that most problems that organizations encounter are not wholly unique, but rather predictable problems that one might expect. The view, often heard, that "our problems are unique" reflects in part the fact that there is no framework of organizational pathology. The question is, are there certain basic "illnesses" which organizations suffer? Can a framework of organizational pathology, similar to the physician's framework of medical pathology be developed? The lack of a pathology framework in turn reflects that lack of a basic functional model of organizations. Again, development of a congruence perspective might be able to provide a common language to use for the identification of general pathological patterns of organizational functioning.

4. *Organizational solution types:* Closely linked to the problem of pathology is the problem of treatment, intervention, or solutions to organizational problems. Again, there is a lack of a general framework to consider the nature of organizational interventions. In this case, too, the congruence model could have value as a means for conceptualizing and ultimately describing the different intervention options available in response to problems (see one attempt at this in Nadler & Tichy, 1980).

Summary

This paper has presented a general approach for thinking about organizational functioning and a process for using a model to analyze organizational problems. This particular model is one way of thinking about organizations. It clearly is not the only model, nor can we claim that it definitively is the best model. It is one tool, however, that appears to be useful for structuring the complexity of organizational life, and helping managers in creating, maintaining, and developing effective organizations.

References

Aldrich, H. E., & Pfeffer, J. Environments of organizations. *Annual Review of Sociology,* 1976, 2, 79–105.

Argyris, C., & Schon, D. A. *Theory in practice.* San Francisco: Jossey-Bass, 1974.

Bauer, R. A. Detection and anticipation of impact: The nature of the task. In R. A. Bauer (Ed.), *Social indicators,* pp. 1–67. Boston: M.I.T. Press, 1966.

Buckley, W. *Sociology and modern systems theory.* Englewood Cliffs, N.J.: Prentice-Hall, 1967.

Dunnette, M. D. *Handbook of industrial and organizational psychology.* Chicago: Rand-McNally, 1976.

Galbraith, J. R. *Designing complex organizations.* Reading, Mass.: Addison-Wesley, 1973.

______, *Organization design.* Reading, Mass.: Addison-Wesley, 1977.

______, & Nathanson, D. A. *Strategy implementation: The role of structure and process.* St Paul, Minn.: West, 1978.

Goodman, P. S., & Pennings, J. M. *New perspectives on organizational effectiveness.* San Francisco: Jossey-Bass, 1977.

Greiner, L. E. Evolution and revolution as organizations grow. *Harvard Business Review,* 1972.

Hackman, J. R., & Oldham, G. A. *Work redesign.* Reading, Mass.: Addison-Wesley, 1979.

Hofer, C. W., & Schendel, D. *Strategy formulation: Analytical concepts.* St. Paul, Minn.: West, 1978.

Homans, G. C. *The human group.* New York: Harcourt Brace Jovanovich, 1950.

Katz, D., & Kahn, R. L. *The social psychology of organizations,* New York: Wiley, 1966, 2d ed., 1978.

Katz, R. L. *Cases and concepts in corporate strategy.* Englewood Cliffs, N.J.: Prentice-Hall, 1970.

Lawler, E. E. *Motivation in work organizations.* Belmont, Calif.: Wadsworth, 1973.

Lawrence, P. R., & Lorsch, J. W. *Developing organizations: Diagnosis and action.* Reading, Mass.: Addison-Wesley, 1969.

Leavitt, H. J. Applied organization change in industry. In J. G. March (Ed.), *Handbook of organizations,* pp. 1144–1170. Chicago: Rand-McNally, 1965.

Levinson, H. *Organizational diagnosis.* Cambridge, Mass.: Harvard, 1972.

______, *Psychological man.* Cambridge, Mass.: Levinson Institute, 1976.

Litwin, G. H., & Stringer, R. A. *Motivation and organizational climate.* Boston: Harvard University Graduate School of Business Administration, 1968.

Lorsch, J. W., & Sheldon, A. The individual in the organization: A systems view. In J. W. Lorsch and P. R. Lawrence (Eds.), *Managing group and intergroup relations.* Homewood, Ill.: Irwin-Dorsey, 1972.

Nadler, D. A. An integrative theory of organizational change. *Journal of Applied Behavioral Science,* 1981 in press).

______, & Tichy, N. M. The limitations of traditional intervention technology in health care organizations. In N. Margulies & J. A. Adams, *Organization development in health care organizations.* Reading, Mass.: Addison-Wesley, 1980.

______, Hackman, J. R., & Lawler, E. E. *Managing organizational behavior.* Boston: Little, Brown, 1979.

Salancik, G. R., & Pfeffer, J. *The external control of organizations.* New York: Wiley, 1978.

Schein, E. H. *Organizational psychology.* Englewood Cliffs, N.J.: Prentice-Hall, 1970.

Seiler, J. A. *Systems analysis in organizational behavior.* Homewood, Ill.: Irwin-Dorsey, 1967.

Steers, R. M. *Organizational effectiveness: A behavioral view.* Pacific Palisades, Calif.: Goodyear, 1977.

Thompson, J. D. *Organizations in action.* New York: McGraw-Hill, 1967.

Tushman, M. L. A political approach to organizations: A review and rationale. *Academy of Management Review,* 1977, 2, 206–216.

Van de Ven, A., & Ferry, D. *Organizational assessment.* New York: Wiley Interscience, 1980.

Von Bertalanffy, L. *General systems theory: Foundations, development applications* (Rev. ed.). New York: Braziller, 1968.

Vroom, V. H. *Work and motivation.* New York: Wiley, 1964.

Weick, K. E. *The social psychology of organizing.* Reading, Mass.: Addison-Wesley, 1969.

Wiener, N. *The human use of human beings: Cybernetics and society.* Boston: Houghton Mifflin, 1950.-

Organization Theory

Cases and Applications

THIRD EDITION

I

OPEN SYSTEMS

Environment

Organizations as Systems

1

All The President's Men

John Henry is usually an optimist, but on the afternoon of March 4, 1986, his mood was as bleak as the late-winter Washington weather. He had just left a boisterous hearing on Capitol Hill, and the realization was sinking in that his company, then only five years old, might die long before it could ever bring a product to market.

Henry had known from the start that biotechnology was a tough business. The science was exotic. Technological dead ends would appear frequently. The burn rate of his venture capital would be be high. At best, profits were a decade away. Still, by 1986 Crop Genetics International was looking at a promising future. Henry's "gene jockeys" were developing a plant vaccine that could, if it worked as planned, eventually replace many chemical pesticides.

Henry was pursuing the same kind of radical change in farming as had his distant ancestor Cyrus McCormick, who invented the reaping machine in 1831 and commercialized it by founding International Harvester Corp. McCormick had carried the industrial revolution to the farm; now, Henry was helping to usher in the next great wave of change through biotechnology.

The newer technology, though, was charged with the kind of danger and controversy that had never touched McCormick's invention. The reaper was a mechanical device that greatly increased the productivity of human labor; Henry's product is a biological agent that carries the seeds of both growth and destruction. And it is that very real threat of destruction—what unintended perils might arise from the release of new biological agents into the environment?—that has raised public concern to such a pitch that it could bring down Henry's company.

It didn't help that the biotech industry was shooting itself in the foot. The hearing that day had been called by the oversight subcommittee of the House Science, Space and Technology

Committee to investigate a company named Advanced Genetic Sciences Inc. (AGS). In November 1985 AGS had been granted the first permit from the Environmental Protection Agency for a test "release" of a genetically engineered organism contained in a product called Frostban, which gave strawberries greater resistance to frost damage.

But *The Washington Post* had reported that, long before acquiring its EPA approval, AGS had injected the test bacterium into more than 45 fruit trees on the rooftop of its Oakland, Calif., headquarters. When the news broke, the EPA suspended AGS's license and levied a $20,000 fine. (The Frostban tests were later conducted by scientists in protective suits and masks.) The incident crystallized public suspicion that biotech companies were dangerously out of control, ethically dubious, and poorly regulated. Could they, as some critics warned, unleash some deadly new organism, an Adromeda strain?

John Henry was hardly an innocent in the Byzantine drama of Washington politics. He had spent three years on the staff of the Senate Foreign Relations Committee after graduating from Harvard College in 1971. But he wasn't prepared for the spectacle that unfolded before him in the hearing room that March day. The place was jammed with environmental activists, EPA officials, and journalists, and the atmosphere was chaotic.

Medical biotech is regulated by the Food and Drug Administration. But the EPA was trying to cope with the agricultural side of the industry with regulations aimed at chemicals; it had not devised any long-term policy for the release of new life forms into the environment.

By the time the hearing ended, some members of Congress were talking about creating a brand-new regulatory system for agricultural biotech. Crop Genetics might not survive several years in regulatory limbo. With a dwindling supply of venture capital and a business plan that allowed no time to spare, Henry reckoned he could be bankrupt before his technology ever got out of the gate. "My overwhelming feeling as I left that hearing was fear," he recalls. "Everything we had worked for since 1981 could go down the tubes."

It was then that Henry decided on an unusual strategy. By and large, U.S. industry and the regulatory system regard each other with mutual hostility. But Henry decided to consider the EPA not an adversary but a partner; environmental activists were to be regarded as "a fourth branch of government." Government relations would become just another business discipline, like marketing or research. And the dominant discipline at that: for the foreseeable future, government relations would be the business of Crop Genetics.

Three weeks after the hearing, Henry walked into the Washington office of a Seattle-based law firm called Perkins Coie to see William D. Ruckelshaus.

Ruckelshaus is a veteran on the Washington scene. He has been EPA administrator twice, first in 1970, when the agency was new, and again in 1983, when it was struggling to regain credibility in the wake of the Rita Lavelle perjury trials. In between, he was deputy U.S. attorney general. In March 1986 he was back in private life. Henry figured if anyone understood the regulatory *zeitgeist,* had stature and credibility, and knew how to deal with the government, that person was Bill Ruckelshaus.

Philip Angell, who had served as Ruckelshaus's chief of staff at the EPA, was a consultant to Perkins Coie. As a confidant of his old boss, he attended that first meeting. "Henry believed very deeply in what he was doing, and he asked us how to deal with a regulatory situation that was fraught with emotionalism," says Angell.

Ruckelshaus and Angell concluded that what Henry needed was good advice on sidestepping the political perils befalling other biotech outfits. They decided to put together a brain trust of Washington wise men.

In the annals of entrepreneurship, this may have been the most high-powered advisory panel ever assembled. Henry recruited Douglas M. Costle, who had headed the EPA in the Carter Administration. Ruckelshaus brought in Robert M. Teeter, a prominent Republican pollster who in 1988 would become co-chairman of the George Bush Presidential transition team. And he enlisted his old Justice Department boss, former attorney general Elliot L. Richardson, who has held a record number of Cabinet posts—Defense, Commerce, and Health, Education and Welfare.

It might seem odd that a small company with no profits could attract such heavy-gauge talent, but there was a certain logic to it. Ruckelshaus, for instance, had been a director of Monsanto Co., a chemical industry giant. Richardson, for his part, was intrigued by the idea that the plant vaccine could trim the use of chemical pesticides, a leading cause of groundwater pollution, food contamination, and bird kills. (Some 1.4 billion pounds of chemicals are dumped on U.S. farms every year, twice the amount applied just 25 years ago.) Crop Genetics paid the members $1,000 for each of the formal brainstorming sessions the committee held and gave them stock options in the company.

Henry required their advice to achieve one clear strategic objective. Because his plant vaccine is designed to kill insects, it is classified as an insecticide. And he could not conduct the first, all-important field trial without an experimental-use permit from the EPA. It was absolutely critical that the company get that permit and do its test on time.

The test was scheduled for summer 1988. The company planned to conduct it on just an acre of corn at its farm on Maryland's Chesapeake Bay. A second round of tests the following summer, to be held in the Midwest, would be far more extensive. Both field trials would have to succeed before the EPA would register the product and sales could begin. Henry aimed to introduce his product in the fall of 1991 in the United States and France, Europe's largest corn producer, envisioning a market of about $100 million. He planned to market it for use on the world's three major crops: first corn, then rice and wheat.

The EPA requires pesticide tests that prove safety. In this case, the safety question centered on the difficult issue of "spread." Could the organism move from target plants to other plants?

Henry was reasonably sure they could not. After all, his biopesticidal vaccine grew inside the plant. An organism that operated inside plants was containable, at least in theory. And anyway, lab tests showed that the microbe could survive only in the sap of living plants. Outside, in soil or water, it died.

Furthermore, the biopesticide in question is a benign, naturally occurring organism called Bt that has been used for decades with no ill effects on mammals, fish, birds, or nontargeted insects. What made the new product unique—and patentable—was its delivery system. The company had found an obscure type of bacterium called an endophyte. Lab work showed that it could be made to multiply through cell division inside more than 80 kinds of plants, from pansies to pumpkins. By splicing a single Bt gene into this endophyte, Crop Genetics scientists could "grow" pesticides inside plants—something nobody had ever attempted before.

Henry believed that farmers would clamor for the product. After all, chemical pesticides affect farmers more than anyone else. They contaminate the water they drink and the air they breathe. This new product promised to be safer and less expensive. And consumers would approve because it would solve the problem of pesticide residue on fruits and vegetables.

"The beauty of the system is that it requires virtually no manufacturing," says Peter Carlson, Crop Genetics' cofounder and chief scientist. "We enjoy a huge material advantage over chemical insecticides. Once our product is inside a plant, it acts like a tiny microbial factory, manufacturing pesticides around the clock. Only 20 pounds will stop the European corn borer—our first target pest—from damaging Iowa's 10-million-acre corn crop."

The corn borer, the nation's greatest uncontrolled corn pest, infests more than half of

America's 70 million acres of corn, inflicting some $400 million in damage every year. Acting like a biological Roto-Rooter, it eats its way up and down the stalk until the plant grows so weak it simply blows over in the wind. For Crop Genetics, a vaccine for corn was to be just the beginning. But in the spring of 1986, the company's fate hinged on one thing: obtaining the EPA permit to conduct that field test. "Without that," Henry says, "we were dead meat."

There was, however, an interesting political wrinkle at work. Given the electrified atmosphere surrounding biotech, the EPA was unlikely to issue the permit without the approval of the country's main environmental groups. For Henry, the uncertainty was nerve-racking. Political risks were piling up on top of scientific risks. It was a hell of a way to have to run a business.

The essence of our strategy was 'no surprises to anybody,'" Angell recalls. "We wanted to involve all the pertinent people as early as possible, to touch every base in sight. We wanted to contact anyone who could conceivably be interested in this experiment—to tell them who we were and what the company was doing."

And always there was an eye to the inevitability that sooner or later, Jeremy Rifkin and his Foundation on Economic Trends would take a lively interest in the company's plans. Rifkin was not to be taken lightly. Through sheer force of personality and a charismatic stage presence, he had made himself a force to be reckoned with in biotech.

Working through the courts, Rifkin had stalled the Frostban tests for several years. Later, by threatening to sue the EPA, he had caused the agency to reject a permit application from Monsanto. Rifkin was waging biotech battles nationwide, with an opposition to the new science that amounted to a crusade. He almost certainly could be counted on to fight Crop Genetics.

Richardson, though, was not intimidated. "The most effective way to deal with the Rifkins of this world is to be in a situation in which you're hiding nothing, to be prepared to answer any fair questions," he says. "And if people then attack you in some way that seems to call your good faith into question, they weaken their own position, not yours." He advised a policy of maximum disclosure of the company's work.

In the summer of 1986, the federal government decided that it wouldn't need a new law for biotech—the threat that had lingered after that congressional hearing in March. Instead, it devised the so-called "combined coordinated framework for biotechnology." The idea was to ensure that existing regulatory standards meshed, to present a unified federal approach.

This was a welcome development. Instead of operating on uncertain regulatory terrain, Henry knew the rules. But as it turned out, the new system placed yet another hurdle in his path. He was no longer dealing with just the EPA. He now had to obtain a separate test permit from the U.S. Department of Agriculture's Animal and Plant Health Inspection Service (APHIS).

Henry accepted this burden with equanimity. "You can't have a wild reaction to regulation," he says. "You have to take the world as you find it, and make it work for you. That is the tremendous insight that Bill Ruckelshaus and Elliot Richardson helped me with."

For openers, he sent his top scientists down to EPA headquarters to meet with the agency's pesticide specialists, the people who actually made the decisions. This was in mid-1986, more than a year before the company applied for its first permit.

"We explained our technology and asked them to tell us what the safety issues were," he says. "We did the lab tests, and then went back to them. Each time, we narrowed the areas of concern about our biopesticide. Does it spread? Is it harmful? Is it in the food? We entered a process of first getting a consensus on the issues, and then going out to get the data they wanted."

Next Henry turned his attention to politicians and environmental activists in Maryland, where the test would be held. It was critical to have local opinion makers on his side to offset the not-in-my-backyard syndrome. To orchestrate this delicate operation he brought in yet another high-powered advisor, Russell "Tim" Baker Jr.

Baker, a product of Harvard Law School, had been a partner in the Baltimore firm of Piper & Marbury. In 1986 he had narrowly lost a bid to become attorney general of Maryland. A Democrat, he had enjoyed unanimous support from the state's environmental groups, for whom he'd done a great deal of pro bono legal work. He also had strong connections in state politics, stemming from eight years as a federal prosecutor, including four as U.S. Attorney for Maryland.

After the election, Baker had worked with two of the venture capital firms backing Crop Genetics. Once he understood that the new technology could help eliminate chemical pesticides, he applied himself fervently to the company's cause.

"John asked me to take him around and introduce him to a series of groups," he says. "We wanted everybody to know about us before they read about us in *The Washington Post.* We were afraid the reporters would quote Rifkin saying how horrible this project was. So we talked to community associations and PTAs. We held a town meeting. We talked to local politicians, people in the governor's office, the state's U.S. senators and representatives—some 40 politicians in all. We explained that the technology was safe, that they shouldn't be worried. Their eyes just glazed over.

"But in talking to friends, I happened to point out that if this technology works, it's going to replace pesticides, which is one of the largest unsolved problems in the pollution of the Chesapeake Bay. John had been hesitant about bringing this up for fear of arousing the competitive juices of the chemical giants. But when you talk about eliminating chemical pesticides, you're hitting apple pie and motherhood. So we quickly started including that in our presentation."

On a Saturday morning in early December 1987 Baker made his major strategic move. He appeared at a meeting at the Baltimore home of Ajax Eastman, a prominent environmentalist and member of the Maryland Conservation Council. Among the more than 50 guests were leaders of the local chapters of the Sierra Club, the Nature Conservancy, and others.

"I knew this was the group that would be Rifkin's natural allies," Baker says. "Our strategy all along had been to isolate Rifkin. I knew that if this group analyzed this technology objectively, they would not ally with him on this one."

For this presentation, Baker brought in Peter Carlson, the mastermind behind the new product. Carlson, a former college professor, is as much a salesman as a scientist when he speaks, taking off his jacket, pacing around, gesturing emphatically. At first the audience was skeptical. For 90 minutes, Carlson explained the plant-vaccine technology. Even as he spoke, Baker could sense attitudes changing. He knew things were looking up when Malcolm E. King, founder of a national conservation outfit called Save Our Streams, asked the first question. He wanted to know how he could buy some Crop Genetics stock.

When it came to the national environmental groups, the company employed a similar strategy. Three of the most prominent organizations concerned with biotechnology—the National Wildlife Federation, the Environmental Defense Fund, and the National Audubon Society—had been heavily funded by the Joyce Foundation of Chicago to analyze the implications of biotech for the Farm Belt. National Wildlife, which received $210,000 over three years, had gone further, establishing the National Biotechnology Policy Center to study the new industry.

Center director Margaret Mellon, an attorney and molecular biologist Ph.D., sums up the concerns. "Society must identify the environmental problems raised by biotechnology before they occur, not after," she says. "Otherwise, we could confront in 50 years the biotech equivalents of hazardous-waste dumps, greenhouse gases, and pesticides that persist in the environment and devastate wildlife."

In keeping with Richardson's advice of "maximum disclosure," Henry dispatched Carlson to these three groups and had him bring a 500-page document that described the company's work in mind-boggling detail. It paid off. The Audubon Society praised the company, telling the EPA that "such openness and cooperation are rare, and reflect well upon the company's sensitivity to environmental and public concerns."

All this was taking an enormous amount of Henry's time and energy. On the one hand, he had the normal challenges of managing a growing company—he was up to almost 100 employees. On the other, several tough scientific problems still had to be solved, a big technological gamble. As he puts it, "I had to move a lot of pieces down the chessboard at the same time." And if the EPA refused to grant the permit, it was checkmate.

He had, however, anticipated these demands and had styled his management structure accordingly. "I have things pretty well staffed, so I'm not needed day to day," he says. "I can go where the problems are. I have really talented people, and I delegate."

But there was no denying that lobbying was complicating progress on one vital front. For the field trial, the company planned to inject each corn plant with the recombinant microbe. For commercial use, however, the organism will have to be inoculated into seed corn, a process that requires new technology.

Crop Genetics would need seed-company partners to help invent and install seed-inoculation machines; no such machines existed. But, as Henry says, "It would have been absurd to ask seed companies to team up with us for that kind of work if we couldn't successfully launch even this small-scale test." So this fundamental component of the business—marketing and distribution—had to be put on hold.

Money, at least, wasn't a pressing problem. True, Henry had spent almost $14 million in venture capital. But early in 1987 the company had gone public. Ruckelshaus had spoken on the company's behalf to investors in New York City. Richardson appeared when the road show played in Switzerland. With their help, the offering brought in $23 million, enough to fuel the firm for two more years.

But Henry, who had spent two years as a Wall Street securities lawyer, was already planning a second offering for 1988. And he knew that if his permit application failed, he could forget that.

Honing yet another prong in his offensive, Henry emphasized the public interest. On Richardson's counsel, he approached the Agricultural Research Service (ARS), a prestigious test facility of the Department of Agriculture. Scientists at the ARS-operated experimental farm in Beltsville, Md., agreed to collaborate with the company in testing the vaccine by planting an acre of test corn.

The collaboration benefited Crop Genetics. ARS had special labs and expertise that the company lacked. The government scientists would publish their studies, which Henry hoped would augment the company's own test analysis. Teaming up with ARS would also give him the imprimatur of government sanction and help expedite the APHIS permit. It was a brilliant move.

In December 1987 Crop Genetics formally filed its permit application with the EPA, a massive document three inches thick and crammed with scientific data.

Waiting for the permit was not uneventful. In March, all hell broke loose because of a mistake of the company's making.

The company's PR firm, Fenton Communications, Inc., issued a press release inviting Washington reporters to a breakfast briefing at the Hay-Adams Hotel featuring Henry, Carlson, and Elliot Richardson, by now a director. The idea was to explain the company's work so that when the permit was issued, the press would have the background. It seemed harmless.

But David Fenton, seeking a sexy angle, couldn't resist inserting this little nugget: "The principal chemical pesticide now used against the European corn borer is Furadan, which a recent EPA study said could be responsible for as many as 2.4 million deaths of birds nationwide [including] as many as 13 bald eagle deaths since 1985 in the Chesapeake Bay area, where the national bird has been making a comeback."

Now as it happened, Furadan was manufactured by FMC Corp., which was represented in Washington by Harold Himmelman, one of the country's top pesticide lawyers. In fact, he was the very same attorney Henry had hired a year earlier to represent Crop Genetics before the EPA. FMC was not amused by Fenton's "chemical bashing," and in the dustup that ensued, Himmelman dropped Crop Genetics in favor of his much larger client.

"Here it was March, less than two months before what we viewed as the climactic lawsuit with Rifkin that we'd have to win fast, and there we were without a law firm," says Tim Baker. "It was like the eighth inning and the team quits. John told me, 'Go out and find a new team, we're up next.' "

Baker frantically began interviewing law firms. Oddly enough, he was on good terms with Himmelman. They had been classmates and lacrosse teammates at Williams College in the 1960s. And Himmelman recommended that Baker try the law firm of Weil, Gotshal, & Manges, where he met Jim Davis, a young partner.

Davis turned out to be yet another Washington insider who could make water flow uphill. Not only did he have a scientific background—a Ph.D in chemistry from California Institute of Technology—but he also had spent two years as special assistant to John Moore, then the EPA's assistant administrator for pesticides and toxic substances. Davis knew the EPA, biotech, and regulatory nuances like nobody's business. Baker signed him up immediately. (Henry later hired him as general in-house counsel.)

In April the three major environmental groups submitted to the EPA their comments concerning the permit application. Not one of them would fight it. Only Rifkin weighed in with an opposing view, arguing that the delivery microbe is known to cause a stunting disease that could spread to other plants.

"Spread" was something that had also troubled Rebecca Goldburg of the Environmental Defense Fund. "I'm concerned that it might infect wild plants," she says. "I don't want to make wild plants resistant to the insects that feed on them. I mean, wild plants are the basis of the food chain." Still, given the containment procedures the company planned for its field test, she felt confident that spread would, if anything, be minimal.

As the action moved into May, Davis went into crash mode to prepare for a Rifkin legal challenge. If Rifkin sued the EPA for issuing a permit, the Justice Department would represent the agency. But Baker was skeptical. "Having been a deputy assistant attorney general there, I knew the department could get itself fouled up," he says. "I didn't want to count on them to carry the load. I thought we should get ready ourselves."

By mid-May the Crop Genetics team was set for combat. "If Rifkin sued, he'd run into a buzz saw," Baker says. "We were prepared to fight in state court or federal court. We tried to figure out every angle Rifkin might use to come after us, then have a strategy ready for it. If he filed, we'd file our papers the next day.

"We couldn't afford to lose any time. Rifkin couldn't beat us on the merits, but he wouldn't have to. All he'd have to do was get some judge confused long enough and it would end up being mid-July—it would be too late to plant the test crop."

In late May the EPA and APHIS issued the two experimental-use permits. It was an event of such moment that it made the "CBS Evening News." Crop Genetics was the only biotech firm in the country to have made it through the first round of regulatory hoops without being delayed or stalled.

Rifkin didn't sue. He and his staff attorney, Andrew Kimbrell, concluded that they didn't have much of a case after all—not this time, anyway. But that didn't soften the blow when John Henry opened the legal bills: Baker's came to $50,000.

"The cost of this thing was just incredible," Baker says. "And how do you price all the time that John Henry and Peter Carlson put in, and their scientists? It turned out that we could afford it, and we did everything right. We had played error-free ball, and we were lucky. But what happens to a company that isn't lucky, or doesn't play it so well?"

At this writing, in December, Crop Genetics has harvested its test corn and is compiling the results. Mind you, all this had nothing to do with proving that the product will work. It was only to show that the microbes didn't spread into surrounding plants. So far, says Henry, "things look good."

Already, he is preparing another application to conduct large-scale field tests next summer in the Midwest with his four new seed-company partners. They include DeKalb-Pfizer Genetics, the second-largest producer and marketer of field-corn seed in the world, and Rogers Brothers, the largest sweet corn-seed company. Those tests, Henry hopes, will demonstrate that the product's delivery system works.

The only thing he knows for sure is that this time around the action will be more bruising. "We'll be there for this one," says Andrew Kimbrell, Rifkin's attorney. Rifkin himself pledges that the first company that tries to test recombinant microbes on a large scale will face "years of battle in the courts and in Congress."

The big environmental groups also will be much more aggressive next time. "We thought there was very little risk associated with a small-scale test of this organism," says Margaret Mellon. "We based that largely on the containment features. But we are not as sanguine about the large-scale use of the product."

John Henry waxes whimsical about all this. "Sometimes I wonder why I ever got into such a complicated business," he muses. But he knows why—a huge new market beckons, just as it did for his ancestor, Cyrus McCormick. Still, he says, "It's a long, long march."

2

First National City Bank

The First National City Bank was founded in 1955 by William Jacks, who owned a controlling interest in the bank. His family had been in banking for many years, and he saw this as an opportunity to apply his banking and management experience to his own bank. The bank was located in a rapidly growing urban area in Arizona. During the initial years, First National City Bank concentrated on two goals: attracting and retaining depositors through personal service, and establishing a reputation as a safe and solid financial institution. The goals were successful, and the bank grew to $475 million in assets by 1974.

During the late 1970s, the bank's growth slowed, and Bill Jacks and the bank experienced some reversals. Two new branch locations were closed because they could not show a profit. One of the branches was located in a nearby city that had a large population of ethnic and minority people. The other branch had been located near a major university where most of the residents were college students. In both cases, the First National City branches seemed unable to attract depositors and borrowers from their local areas. The Bank did not have a positive reputation with those population segments, and did not seem to have the flexibility or types of service desired by potential customers.

By 1978, Bill Jacks began to replace some middle managers, hoping to bring in new energy and fresh ideas. Bill Jacks still believed that a bank succeeded because of its safety as a financial institution, and because it established personal relationships with middle class customers. He passed this philosophy and other management ideas on to the new managers. He stressed a traditional management structure, including centralized decision making and standardized procedures. All branch banks were encouraged to offer the same services, and many decisions were passed up the hierarchy to the top. Vertical communication and "following the rules" were deemed a safe and responsible management approach for a community bank.

As the new managers gained experience in the bank, they began to propose changes. One branch manager suggested that each of the branch locations establish an advisory board. The purpose of the advisory board would be to select people from the surrounding community to serve on a committee that would serve as a liaison between the community and First National City Bank and make recommendations to management. The advisory boards would be composed of the bank manager, Bill Jacks, and important people from the local area, such as business people, women, minority group members, or college students. The manager who proposed the idea argued that advisory board members could counsel prospective customers about bank services and in general provide good information to the bank manager and promote good will for the bank.

Another new manager proposed that the bank engage in more advertising and public relations. She argued that bank employees should become more involved in community groups, such as the Chamber of Commerce and United Way. She also argued that the bank should make a contribution to the State Association of Bankers to support lobbyists working at the state capitol to increase the interest rate ceilings, and to support lobbyists working in Washington to influence bank regulation.

As Bill Jacks considered these and other proposals, deregulation of banks became a hot topic in Washington. Deregulation had been successful in other industries, and President Carter signed into law the Depository Institutions Deregulation Act of 1980. President Reagan encouraged continued deregulation through the Depository Institutions Act of 1982. These changes dramatically affected the industry climate of banks. New powers were given to thrift institutions—credit unions, savings and loan associations—to compete directly with banks in business and consumer lending, retirement annuities, and other services. Deregulation also gave banks the freedom to become financial supermarkets and provide services such as the sale of stocks and bonds, to offer high interest rates, and to charge for services. The new regulations seemed to favor large banks because interstate banking and bank holding companies were possible.

Bill Jacks and the other managers were very uncertain about the impact of deregulation on First National City Bank. A bank consultant was hired to assess the impact of deregulation on First National City's strategy. The consultant said that as deregulation was implemented over the next three years, the bank will need, "a strong commitment to the development and delivery of new products. Moreover, customer loyalty will fade and price competition combined with technological advances and internal efficiencies will be essential for maintaining and increasing a customer base."

A university professor conducted a survey of successful community banks to learn how they were coping with deregulation. The survey found that successful banks were making changes in four areas: (1) asset-liability management, (2) cost control, (3) marketing, (4) pricing and non-interest income. Better asset-liability management in many banks was accomplished through a new asset-liability committee that helped the bank make a transition to variable-rate loans, make loans according to profit margin, and explore new investment opportunities. Cost control was accomplished through technology and data processing, such as automated tellers and the automatic transfer of funds. New marketing techniques included market segmentation and the packaging of new products for each segment. Money market accounts, discount brokerage services, increased advertising, retirement accounts, and other marketing ideas were being adopted. Important new income was also being derived from non-interest sources for successful community banks. Seventy-five percent of the banks increased fees for returned checks, overdrafts and checking account services. Fees were also increased for routine balance inquiries and saving accounts.

In January of 1983, Bill Jacks felt overwhelmed, and wondered whether he was up to managing the bank. The bank had grown little over five years, and was losing market share to other, often recently established banks. Two of the newer managers quit out of frustration over not having impact on bank policy. The impact of bank deregulation was difficult to anticipate, and he was not sure how the bank should respond. Two of the brightest young managers in the bank had been to see him about a change in management structure and approach. They encouraged the creation of several internal committees to study the problems and to coordinate the needs of each department and branch. They also suggested the bank begin planning for the addition of new departments that would be responsible for new electronic technology, new services, and stronger advertising. "The banking industry is becoming more complex and it's changing rapidly," one manager argued, "and if we don't adapt to it we will be left behind." Bill Jacks also thought back to earlier proposals, such as for advisory boards, on which he had not acted. Could the bank afford to invest in advertising, lobbying, new technology, and new departments? Would customers pay fees for services that had been provided free? Should the bank provide non-banking services? Could all of these activities be coordinated when things change so quickly? If he was unable to resolve these problems, Bill Jacks thought the best thing might be to retire and perhaps sell his interest in the bank to someone else.

3

Death of a Computer

Almost immediately, people at Texas Instruments were calling it Black Friday. Early in the afternoon of October 28, 1983, the rumors began to fly, and at the company's Lubbock-based consumer products group, the rest of the day was chaotic. Middle managers called employees in, a few at a time, to tell them that yes, it was true and there was nothing that could be done, and then everyone in Lubbock was on the phone to friends at all the other TI facilities, and by four o'clock, when the official corporate announcement was released to the press, there wasn't a soul at the company who hadn't heard the bad news. Texas Instruments, the company that had put more computers into American homes than anyone else, was pulling out of the home computer business.

Who could have imagined that it would end this way? Only a year earlier the consumer products group had been the toast of Texas Instruments, and the TI home computer, the 99/4A, its biggest success. Back then, TI people talked about the 99/4A with awe. It was destined to dominate the home computer business, they said. It was going to reach $1 billion in sales. It was going to be the biggest winner in the history of the company. Back then, TI assembly lines in Lubbock were cranking out five thousand computers a day, and that still didn't keep up with the demand.

The TI Culture

The microprocessor is one of the great inventions of the age, as seminal a step in the development of the modern computer as the invention of the silicon chip was in the late fifties. The silicon chip made it possible to put complicated electronic circuitry on a tiny piece of silicon; the microprocessor made it possible to compress an entire computer onto a chip not much larger than a postage stamp. Today there are any number of microprocessors inside a personal computer (different chips control the graphics and the memory and so on), but the central microprocessor, called the CPU, is the computer's brain, the thing that reads the bits of information sent to it.

Although selling consumer items like pocket calculators and computers is what gives Texas Instruments visibility, the company's biggest profits have always been made in less glamorous ways, chief among them the manufacture of silicon chips, which it sells in huge lots, at low prices, to other companies. Getting the volume up and the price down has always been the linchpin of TI's sales strategy. And so it was with microprocessors. Although TI did not invent the microprocessor—the credit for that goes to a Silicon Valley company named Intel—the company quickly asserted its superiority in the marketplace with its first chip, introduced in 1974, a four-bit chip called the TMS 1000. (The term "four bits" means that the circuitry can handle four bits of information at once. It is a measure of complexity and also of speed; an eight-bit chip can work twice as fast as a four-bit chip.) The TMS 1000 soon became the most ubiquitous chip in the business, used in video games, calculators, microwave ovens, and hundreds of other electronic products; to date, more than 100 million TMS 1000's have been sold.

TI's second-generation microprocessor was the 9900, but though it was a quantum leap technologically, it was a flop in the marketplace. It failed in part because it was too far ahead of the field; while Intel and everyone else were just beginning to make eight-bit microprocessors, TI leapfrogged them and made the sixteen-bit 9900. The idea was that the 9900 would make the eight-bit competition instantly obsolete and this new TI microprocessor, like the TMS 1000 before it, would become the industry standard. Instead, the industry flocked to the eight-bit microprocessors and left the 9900 dying on the vine. But to back down and build eight-bit microprocessors like everyone else was an abhorrent idea for TI, a company where managerial decisions are shaped by an internal framework that is a culture all its own.

TI is run by engineers for engineers. Both Mark Shepherd and J. Fred Bucy began their TI careers as engineers, and almost all of its top managers have engineering backgrounds. Thus, they understand the needs of engineers—the need for autonomy, for instance. Despite the company's size, the TI chain of command is quite short, and Bucy and Shepherd try not to get in the way of managers who are doing well. The company never skimps on its research and development budget, no matter what its cash-flow needs might be. R & D, which is what engineers live for, is at the heart of Texas Instruments' technological success.

But engineers have other, psychic needs, and these too have become a part of the TI culture. One is the desire to accomplish things oneself, from scratch, rather than using existing products. At TI this frame of mind has led to an obsessive dislike of—and even contempt for—other companies' products. A former TI employee remembers once suggesting in a meeting that a computer design might be improved with a common eight-bit microprocessor called the Z-80. Fred Bucy flung a book listing the different TI chips in the direction of the man and said huffily, "Show me where it's listed here." End of discussion.

Given that corporate culture, there wasn't much doubt that TI would stand by its own microprocessor, the 9900, rather than conform to a marketplace that wanted eight bits instead of sixteen. Conforming would be an admission of defeat. The preferred solution was to find an internal use for the 9900 that would make it profitable. One possibility was to build a consumer product, a computer, that would be driven by the 9900 microprocessor. It was a classic Texas Instruments solution—TI divisions have always been able to post profits by selling components to other TI divisions—but it also meant that TI would be building a computer to fit its microprocessor rather than the other way around. Though no one could know it at the time, the TI culture had just led the company into its first big home computer mistake.

The TI machine was going to be the first computer designed for Everyman. Did Everyman need—or even want—a computer in his home? That was impossible to say, since no such product existed and since most Americans had no feel for how a computer might be useful. That's what made the venture so risky. In the late seventies computers still seemed exotic. Yet TI was unperturbed by the prospect of trying to create a market from scratch. After all, hadn't the company created the market for the pocket calculator? Hadn't it made digital watches popular? Hadn't it taken a dozen other inventions and turned them into commercial successes? The feeling at TI was that it had a knack for consumer electronics and that its knack would come to the fore again, with the home computer. TI would put out a computer that was just powerful enough to entice the average person to take the plunge—no word processing, but plenty of educational programs for the kids—yet inexpensive enough that the plunge wouldn't break the bank. On the basis of price alone, TI thought, the machine would sell. Convincing people that they needed it could come later.

It wasn't long before events began to conspire against the consumer division's carefully laid plans. First, the man who had devised the strategy quit in frustration over the problems he faced in Lubbock—particularly the inability to hire the outside engineers he thought he needed. Then his chief supporter back in the Dallas headquarters took an overseas assignment.

To make matters even more complicated, there was another management shuffle in 1978, and the man put in charge of developing the home computer was an engineer whose previous job had been to design the expensive business computer. He didn't see the home computer in quite the same way that his predecessor had, and by the time he finished tinkering with the design, it was no longer a $400 machine but an $1150 machine. Then, although TI had announced that the computer would be ready by the middle of 1979, the engineers didn't shake all the bugs out of the system until the first few months of 1980, thus missing an opportunity to cash in on the 1979 Christmas season. And finally, when the new 99/4 hit the computer stores, it turned out that the average American had no idea what to do with a home computer and wasn't interested in paying $1150 for one. To the great dismay of everyone at Texas Instruments, the 99/4, four years and $10 million or so in the making, was a bomb.

The keyboard is what computer people most remember about the TI 99/4 home computer. The keyboard somehow became the symbol for everything that was wrong with the machine. It was not modeled after a typewriter, as most personal computer keyboards were. Instead, it looked like an elongated calculator keyboard, with stubby little keys that popped through the plastic casing. TI had chosen a calculator keyboard because most of the engineers who developed the 99/4 had cut their teeth on calculators; that was the technology they knew best and could produce most inexpensively. But a short time before the 99/4 came out, another company had put a calculator keyboard on a personal computer. The keyboard was widely criticized, and out of that experience grew a belief that calculator keyboards wouldn't cut it. Texas Instruments, so intent on putting out its own product, scarcely noticed.

The lesson of the calculator keyboard was not that it was an engineering mistake—at bottom, it really didn't matter what kind of keyboard you used—but that it was a *marketing* mistake. And the same applied to other facets of the machine. Using the 9900 microprocessor, for instance, was good for the Texas Instruments division that made the chip, but it caused far more problems than it was worth. Because TI's chip division had to make a profit despite the low demand, the cost to the consumer division was very high—about $20 a unit compared to about $4 for most of the popular eight-bit microprocessors. Because it had been designed for industrial uses, it did not adapt well to a consumer system; the advantage of having a sixteen-bit microprocessor was negated by the circuitous way programs had to be written for it. And because nobody else in the industry was using it, independent software companies, the third-party vendors, as they're called, had no incentive to write programs for it. The independents liked to write programs that could be easily adapted to different computers. They couldn't do that with the 99/4.

What's This Thing For, Anyway?

By the fall of 1980, with Texas Instruments selling fewer than a thousand computers a month, the people in the consumer products group had come to the not unexpected conclusion that it was time to go back to the drawing board. Peter Bonfield, then the head of the home computer division, felt that the most critical flaws in the 99/4 were its price and its 9900 microprocessor, so he asked his engineers to design a computer that used a different microprocessor and that cut the cost in half.

The new design had been slapped together by a small group of engineers. The engineers' new design kept the 9900 microprocessor (there wasn't any getting around that) and the main circuitry of the machine but changed the way the computer looked. Now the computer had a typewriter keyboard. The keyboard had also been separated from the screen—unbundling the system, it's called—so that the screen became optional. (The keyboard could be attached to a television set.) They also drew up proposals for cutting down the number of chips needed to run the computer, which had the effect of dramatically cutting costs.

By the summer of 1981, after months of working up prototypes, getting the kinks out of the system, and passing the various radiation tests mandated by the Federal Communications Commission, the 99/4A was ready. The basic cost of the computer to the retailer was $340—and the price to the consumer, without peripherals, was going to be $550. Don Bynum had done his job. But would it sell?

Why do you need a home computer? It is hard to imagine a more basic question, but no one in the home computer business has come up with a compelling answer. It is hard to sell a product when you can't tell people why they need it.

For years now, we've been hearing that the day will come when the computer will revolutionize the way we live. There's a feeling among computer people that they are not only on the frontier of the American economy but also on the frontier of American life itself. Scratch a computer engineer, and you'll most likely find a visionary, someone who foresees the day when computers will do everything but prepare dinner.

The man whose job it was to answer that question at TI was William J. Turner, and he was that rarest of birds at Texas Instruments, an outsider. He had been hired away from Digital Equipment Corporation, an important maker of minicomputers, in May 1980 and had been named marketing manager for TI's consumer products group. Although he had a degree in mathematics, he had gotten his job precisely because he wasn't an engineer. Turner had spent his career marketing computers. At 36, he was the same age as his counterpart in engineering, Don Bynum, but he was shorter and thinner, almost completely bald, with sharp features and a sharp New England accent.

He brought to the home computer division something it hadn't had before: a sales mentality. Bill Turner was gung ho about whatever product he was selling, upbeat and enthusiastic no matter what the actual state of affairs. He was great with numbers and projections. In meetings he always had a chart that proved beyond all doubt that the home computer was about to turn the corner.

He came to his job with two crucial theories. First, he believed that you couldn't sell a home computer in a computer store. Computer stores were meant for people who already knew something about computers or who were serious enough about them to spend several thousand dollars on one. Those people were not likely to wind up buying a home computer. Turner wanted to get the 99/4A placed in the kind of retail stores that already carried the company's pocket calculator, stores like Penney's and Sears and Montgomery Ward. From the day he walked in the door, Turner spent much of his time building up this retail network, and he was good at it. Every month he would report new successes. Toys R Us had signed up; K Mart had signed up; even 7-Eleven was on the verge of signing up before the roof fell in at TI. The engineers hated the thought of their machine's being sold in stores like 7-Eleven, and they complained about it, but it was mostly their pride that was hurt. Turner was right.

Turner's second theory was that the price of the 99/4A had to be a lot lower. If the price was low enough, it wouldn't matter that the home computer was more toy than tool. People would buy it on a lark. Bill Turner wanted to sell price, and that became the cornerstone of his marketing strategy. It didn't hurt his standing in the company that he was advocating the one strategy that TI's management had always felt most comfortable with.

So in the months after the 99/4A was introduced, Turner began bringing the list price of the 99/4A down, from $550 to $450 to $375. He did this partly by making what seemed to be outrageous volume projections and then hustling up new retail outlets to absorb that volume. He also pushed Bynum's engineers to find ways to lower the cost of the machine, by simplifying the design, eliminating chips, and so on. That way the profit margin on each computer remained steady—40 per cent—while the price went down. With each new round of cost cutting, the engineers became increasingly unhappy with Turner, for they felt he was pushing them to do too much too fast. But no one could argue with the results. TI had once produced fewer than eight thousand 99/4's a month; it was now producing that many 99/4A's in a good week. That wasn't enough for the consumer products group, with its large overhead and R & D budget, to turn a profit, but it was more than enough to make people believe Turner when he pulled out his latest chart and said the 99/4A was about to take off.

By then, however, Texas Instruments was not the only company in the home computer business. Atari, the video game maker, had had a computer out for some time that was under $1000—the Atari 400. Several toy companies, particularly Mattel and Coleco, were trying to get out of video game consoles (which wouldn't have a chance if home computers really hit) and into home computers. Timex had a home computer in development, which it hoped would establish an entirely new market, the under-$100 computer. And then there was Commodore. Nine months after TI put the 99/4A on the retail shelves of America, the Commodore Corporation, of King of Prussia, Pennsylvania, introduced its first home computer. It was called the Vic 20, and it came on the market at $299.

Launching the Great Price War

Talk to anyone who ever worked on the 99/4A and you'll get the same story. The Vic 20 couldn't compare with the 99/4A. It was true. While the 99/4A didn't measure up to the more expensive small business computers, it looked spectacular next to the Vic 20. The Vic 20 had a measly 4K of memory, while the 99/4A had 16K. The Vic 20 used an old-style eight-bit microprocessor, while the 99/4A had the sixteen-bit 9900. The Vic 20 had only about forty chips in its entire system; the 99/4A had sixty. There was no question that the TI computer was a far more powerful, far more sophisticated system, "a Cadillac competing against Chevys," as Don Bynum used to say.

The 99/4A's advantages, however, didn't necessarily translate into sales. The computer business didn't work that way anymore and hadn't for some time—and nobody understood that better than Jack Tramiel, the president of Commodore. Although he has recently resigned from his position, Tramiel remains a near-mythic figure in the computer business. He has a reputation as a tough, driven entrepreneur who through shrewd dealing and brilliant marketing single-handedly built Commodore into a major force in the computer business. When Tramiel set out to conquer the home computer market he knew as well as anyone that the Vic 20 was no match for the TI 99/4A on the basis of performance. He also knew that the 99/4A was no match for the Vic 20 on the basis of price. Once before, Commodore had put out a product in a market where its chief competitor was TI: a line of digital watches. TI started a price war and drove Commodore out of the market. Tramiel was not about to let that happen again. No matter how low the 99/4A went in price, Tramiel's machine could go lower. It simply cost less to build.

In retrospect Bill Turner's great mistake, as big a mistake as the original decision to use the 9900 microprocessor, was creating a marketing strategy that lived and died on price alone. He had other options. He could have promoted the 99/4A's superiority to the Vic 20 and justified a higher price on that basis. He could have tried harder to answer the question of why consumers needed to buy his home computer. But it is not just in retrospect that this is obvious; it should have been clear at the time. As soon as the Vic 20 came on the market, some Texas Instruments engineers took it apart and analyzed its insides. They poked fun at what they found, but it was apparent that it was cheaper to make. The Vic 20's cost advantage was no deep, dark secret.

In meetings Turner would rage about the Vic 20, talk about "destroying Commodore," but out there on the retail shelves, it was Commodore that was winning.

And why not? Most customers didn't know the difference between eight bits and sixteen bits. Neither did most of the people working in the stores. And Texas Instruments was doing nothing to explain the difference. All the customer knew was that two computers were sitting side by side on a shelf and one cost $300 and the other less than $250. The choice seemed obvious. Even though the 99/4A was doing better than it ever had before, it was still being outsold by the Vic 20 on the order of two to one. To Turner, the situation was intolerable.

On September 1, 1982, at a time when the 99/4A was selling for about $300 and the Vic 20 for $250, Texas Instruments announced a rebate for the computer that effectively lowered the price to $199. This time there was no cost cutting by the engineers to match the price cut. The profit margin on the 99/4A was halved, but Turner wasn't worried about that. That same day Commodore dropped the price of its machine $40 to match TI's. The price war was on.

From $20 Million to $200 Million Overnight

For the next four months Turner's price strategy worked like a charm. The fall and winter of 1982 were Turner's time of triumph, for in those months the 99/4A became the machine Texas Instruments had always wanted it to be, a computer the average American would buy. Almost as soon as the price cut was announced, home computer sales rocketed, and to the people at the consumer products group—indeed, to people throughout the company—the turn of events was astonishing. Turner was suddenly a corporate superstar at TI, the marketing genius, the outsider who had shown the engineers how to sell a computer. The retail network now constituted some 12,000 stores; the 99/4A was outselling the Vic 20 three to one; and a $20 million business had become, overnight, a $200 million business. Who could argue with that? Bucy and Shepherd were happy to leave Turner alone. That was the way TI always treated its winners.

With things going so well for the 99/4A, Turner and the consumer products group made their next big mistake. They got greedy. Timex had a dinky little computer on the market that cost about $100; it wasn't much, but it was selling, and Turner decided to go after it. He had Bynum pull together some engineers, and they undertook a crash program to develop a competitive product to be called the 99/2. Several other computers were competing in the $500 to $1000 price range, and Texas Instruments had long been developing a computer for that market: the 99/8, known by the code name "Armadillo." (Commodore was developing a computer for the same market, which became the enormously successful Commodore 64.) Partly it was good marketing strategy to come in behind the original computer with a more advanced computer like the 99/8; that's the way markets evolved. But who cared if Timex was selling some $100 computer that couldn't do much? Was that really the direction in which the market was going? It seemed that Turner and Texas Instruments simply wanted it all.

TI's extraordinary fall and winter had brought forth from Bill Turner some extraordinarily optimistic forecasts for the future. According to his projections, 1983 would be the year of the home computer. Nearly seven million would be sold that year, he predicted, more than triple the two million sold in 1982. And of that seven million, he estimated—promised, actually—that three million would be sold by Texas Instruments (whereas about 500,000 had been sold in 1982). Most analysts thought those figures were way too high; they were predicting sales in the area of four million. But Turner was undeterred. The home computer revolution had begun, he said, and TI was about to take over the market. The analysts, on the other hand, said that with the price so low and the machines so limited, most people thought of the home computer as a toy, which meant that sales would always peak in the months before Christmas. To them, that timing had as much to do with TI's success in late 1982 as the price war did. Turner, in contrast, was predicting that every month from now on was going to be about twice as good as December 1982—the best month ever for the 99/4A. With Bucy and Shepherd in tow, he was going full steam ahead.

Pulling the Plug

. . . the fall came very, very quickly. In January Commodore cut the price of the Vic 20 to $125; a few weeks later TI was forced to follow suit. The inevitable had happened: the 99/4A was no longer making a profit; it was merely breaking even. But there were plenty of orders from retailers, much of it on backlog since Christmas, so Turner kept pushing the computers out.

On April 4 Commodore cut the price of the Vic 20 to $99, thus putting Turner in an untenable position. It cost more than $99 to manufacture the 99/4A. He stalled for time, announcing that TI would offer a new rebate on the home computer by June. But it wasn't good enough. Now the Vic 20 was back where it had been before the price war began—sitting next to the 99/4A on retail shelves, at a much cheaper price. At the same time, with the Vic 20 so inexpensive, the market for the Timex product dried up completely. That was the thing about the computer business; there was no telling what the market would be like by the time your product was ready. Texas Instruments quietly canceled the 99/2, the machine that was supposed to compete with Timex, before it ever came out. Now people in the consumer products group were beginning to see the handwriting on the wall.

In late April the numbers caught up with Turner. Because the consumer products group was adhering to Turner's forecast, the TI assembly lines kept pushing out computers as fast as they could. But now computers began coming back to TI. Just because a retailer had a machine on the shelves didn't mean he had actually bought it. He had the right to return it—that was the way the market had evolved. Retailers had so many TI machines that they couldn't take any more, and since the machine wasn't selling, many of them began to send some back to make room for other products. "Sales" that had been posted by Turner were revised and lowered. It wasn't going to be December all year round. Turner's optimistic projections were crashing down around him.

There was really nothing that could be done quickly. The mistakes were too big, and they had been allowed to go on too long. By the second quarter of 1983, anyone who followed American business knew the Texas Instruments home computer was in danger. It was then that Shepherd and Bucy announced that the company had lost $119 million that quarter because of the home computer.

Pulling the plug on the home computer three months later was an act of mercy—it put the home computer division out of its misery. Could the situation have been turned around eventually? Possibly. But it would have taken new products and new strategies and new approaches in the marketplace. And most of all, it would have taken time, which Texas Instruments didn't think it could afford. The stock was dropping because analysts had become so soured on the 99/4A. The losses were continuing to mount; in the third quarter TI took a $300 million bath. When Bucy and Shepherd looked into the tunnel, they could see no light. All they could see was computers and software and peripherals everywhere, and nobody who wanted to buy them. In the end, Texas Instruments was just too big and bulky, with too much overhead and too much cultural baggage to respond to a volatile market. The home computer market belonged to the nimble—to the companies that could adapt quickly, the companies that understood that marketing was everything. In that sense, perhaps TI was doomed from the start.

4

The Audubon Park Zoo: An Urban Eden

The Audubon Park Zoo was the focus of national concern in the early 1970s, with well-documented stories of animals kept in conditions that were variously termed an "animal ghetto,"[1] "the New Orleans antiquarium," and even "an animal concentration camp."[2] In 1971, the Bureau of Governmental Research recommended a $5.6 million zoo improvement plan to the Audubon Park Commission and the City Council of New Orleans. The local *Times Picayune* commented on the new zoo: "It's not going to be quite like the *Planet of the Apes* situation in which the apes caged and studied human beings but something along those broad general lines."[3] The new zoo confined people to bridges and walkways while the animals roamed amidst grass, shrubs, trees, pools, and fake rocks. The gracefully curving pathways, generously lined with luxuriant plants, gave the visitor a sense of being alone in a wilderness, although crowds of visitors might be only a few yards away.

The Decision

The Audubon Park Commission launched the $5.6-million development program, based on the Bureau of Governmental Research plan for the zoo, in March 1972. A bond issue and a property tax dedicated to the zoo were put before the voters, with renovations to begin the day following passage. The New Orleans City Planning Commission finally approved the master plan for the Audubon Park Zoo in September 1973. But the institution of the master plan was far from smooth.

The Zoo Question Goes Public

A revenue-generating proposal was put to the voters by Mayor Moon Landrieu on November 7, 1972. When it passed by an overwhelming majority, serious discussions began about what should be done. Over two dozen special interests were ultimately involved in choosing

The authors wish to acknowledge the contributions of graduate students Martha McGraw Hamilton and Debbie Longo, who aided in research and contributed many helpful suggestions in developing the case. The case was designed for classroom discussion only. It was not meant to depict effective or ineffective administration.

EXHIBIT 4-1 ■ The Audubon Park Zoo

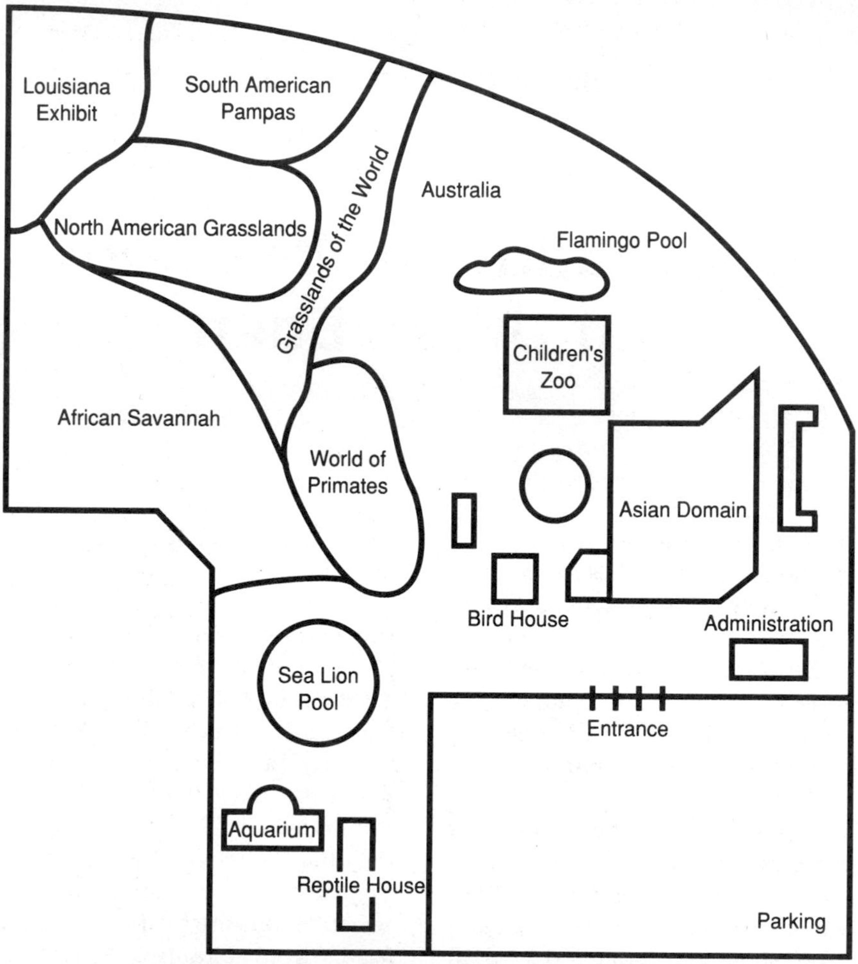

whether to renovate and expand the existing facilities or move to another site. Expansion became a major community controversy. Some residents opposed the zoo expansion, fearing that a "loss of green space" would affect the secluded character of the neighborhood. Others opposed the loss of what they saw as an attractive and educational facility.

Most of the opposition came from the zoo's affluent neighbors. Zoo Director John Moore ascribed the criticism to "a select few people who have the money and power to make a lot of noise." He went on to say that "[T]he real basis behind the problem is that the neighbors who live around the edge of the park have a selfish concern because they want the park as their private backyard."[4] Legal battles over the expansion plans continued until early 1976. At that time, the Fourth Circuit Court of Appeals ruled that the expansion was legal.[5] An out-of-court agreement with the zoo's neighbors (The Upper Audubon Association) followed shortly.

Physical Facilities

The expansion of the Audubon Park Zoo took it from 14 to 58 acres (see Exhibit 4-1). Under the master plan developed by the Bureau of Governmental Research, the zoo was laid out in geographic sections: the Asian Domain, the World of Primates, the World's Grasslands, the Savannah, the North American Prairie, the South American Pampas, and the Louisiana Swamp. Additional exhibits included the Wisner Discovery Zoo, the Sea Lion exhibit, and the Flight Cage.

Purpose of the Zoo

The main outward purpose of the Audubon Park Zoo was entertainment. Many of its promotional efforts were aimed at creating an image of the zoo as an entertaining place to visit. Obviously, such a campaign was necessary to attract visitors to the zoo. Behind the scenes, the zoo also preserved and bred many animal species, conducted research, and educated the public.

New Directions

One of the first significant changes made was the institution of an admission charge in 1972. Admission to the zoo had been free before the adoption of the renovation plan. The initial purpose behind instituting the admission charge ostensibly was to prevent vandalism,[6] but the need for additional income was also apparent. Despite the institution of and subsequent increases in admission charges, admissions increased dramatically (see Exhibit 4-2).

EXHIBIT 4-2 ■ Admissions

	Admission Charges	
Year	Adult	Child
1972	$0.75	$0.25
1978	1.00	0.50
1979	1.50	0.75
1980	2.00	1.00
1981	2.50	1.25
1982	3.00	1.50
1983	3.50	1.75
1984	4.00	2.00
1985	4.50	2.00
1986	5.00	2.50

	Admissions	
Year	Number of Paid Admissions	Number of Member Admissions
1972	163,000	
1973	310,000	
1974	345,000	
1975	324,000	
1976	381,000	
1977	502,000	
1978	456,000	
1979	561,000	
1980	707,000	
1981	741,000	
1982	740,339	78,950
1983	835,044	118,665
1984	813,025	128,538
1985	854,996	144,060
1986	915,492	187,119
1987	439,264*	93,327*

*Through the end of the second quarter.
Source: The Audubon Park Zoo

Operations

Friends of the Zoo

The Friends of the Zoo was formed in 1974 and incorporated in 1975 with 400 original members. The stated purpose of the Friends was to increase support and awareness of the Audubon Park Zoo. Initially, the Friends of the Zoo tried to increase interest and commitment to the zoo, but its activities grew dramatically over the years until it was involved in funding, operating, and governing the zoo.

The Friends of the Zoo had a 24-member governing board. Elections were held every year for six of the board members, who served staggered four-year terms. The board oversaw zoo policies and set guidelines for memberships, concessions, fund-raising, and marketing. Actual policy making and operations were controlled by the Audubon Park Commission, however, which set zoo hours, admission prices, etc.

Through its volunteer, the Friends of the Zoo staffed many of the zoo's programs. Members of the Friends of the Zoo volunteered as "edZOOcators," who were specially trained to conduct interpretive education programs, and "Zoo Area Patrollers," who provided general information about the geographic area of the zoo and helped with crowd control. Other volunteers assisted in the Commissary, Animal Health Care Center, and Wild Bird Rehabilitation Center, or helped with functions related to membership, public relations, graphics, clerical work, research, or horticulture.

Fund-Raising

The Audubon Park Zoo and the Friends of the Zoo raised funds through five major activities: Friends of the Zoo memberships, "Adopt an Animal," "Zoo-To-Do," and capital fund drives. Zoo managers from around the country came to the Audubon Park Zoo for tips on fund-raising.

■ ***Membership*** Membership in the Friends of the Zoo was open to anyone. Even though membership fees increased over the years, as summarized in Exhibit 4-3, the number of members grew steadily, from the original 400 in 1974 to 33,000 in 1987. Membership allowed free entry to the Audubon Park Zoo and many other zoos around the United States. Participation in "Zoobilation" (an annual members-only evening celebration at the zoo) and the many volunteer programs described earlier were other benefits of membership.

Increasing membership required a special approach to marketing the zoo. Chip Weigand, director of marketing for the zoo, stated,

"... [I]n marketing memberships, we try to encourage repeat visitations, the feeling that one can visit as often as one wants, the idea that the zoo changes from visit to visit and that there are good reasons to make one large payment or donation for a membership card, rather than paying for each visit. ... [T]he overwhelming factor is a good zoo that people want to visit often, so that a membership makes good economical sense."

EXHIBIT 4-3 ■ Membership Fees and Membership

Year	Family	Individual	Number of Memberships
1979	$20	$10	1,000
1980	20	10	7,000
1981	20	10	11,000
1982	25	15	18,000
1983	30	15	22,000
1984	35	20	26,000
1985	40	20	30,000
1986	45	25	32,000
1987	45	25	33,000

Source: The Audubon Park Zoo

In 1985, the zoo announced a new membership designed for businesses, the Audubon Zoo Curator Club, with four categories of membership: Bronze, $250; Silver, $500; Gold, $1,000, and Platinum, $2,500 and more.

■ ***Concessions*** The Friends of the Zoo took over the Audubon Park Zoo concessions for refreshments and gifts in 1976 through a public bidding process. The concessions were run by volunteer members of the Friends of the Zoo, and all profits went directly to the zoo. Prior to 1976, concession rentals brought in $15,000 in a good year. Profits from the operation of the concessions by the Friends of the Zoo were $400,000 a year by 1980 and were expected to be over $900,000 in 1987.

■ ***Adopt an Animal*** Zoo Parents paid a fee to "adopt" an animal, the fee varying with the animal chosen. The names of Zoo Parents were listed on a large sign inside the zoo. They also had their own annual celebration at the zoo, Zoo Parents Day.

■ ***Zoo-To-Do*** Zoo-To-Do was an annual black-tie fund-raiser with live music, food and drink, and original, high-class souvenirs, such as posters or ceramic necklaces. Admission tickets, limited to 3,000 annually, were priced starting at $100 per person. A raffle conducted in conjunction with Zoo-To-Do offered items ranging from an opportunity to be zoo curator for a day to the use of a Mercedes Benz for a year. Despite the rather stiff price, Zoo-To-Do was a sellout every year. Local restaurants and other businesses donated most of the necessary supplies, which cut the cost of the affair. In 1985, Zoo-to-Do raised almost $500,000 in one night, more money than any other nonmedical fund-raiser in the country.[7]

Advertising

The Audubon Park Zoo launched impressive marketing campaigns in the 1980s. The zoo received ADDY awards from the New Orleans Advertising Club year after year.[8] In 1986, the film *Urban Eden,* produced by Alford Advertising and Buckholtz Productions Inc. in New Orleans, finished first among 40 entries in the "documentary films, public relations" category of the 8th Annual Houston International Film Festival. The first-place Gold Award recognized the film for vividly portraying the Audubon Park Zoo as a conserving, rather than a confining, environment.

During the same year, local television affiliates of ABC, CBS, and NBC produced independent news spots on the theme: "One of the World's Greatest Zoos Is in Your Own Back Yard . . . Audubon Zoo! " Along with some innovative views of the Audubon Park Zoo being in someone's "backyard," local news anchor personalities enjoyed "monkeying around" with the animals and the zoo enjoyed some welcome free exposure.[9]

In 1986 and 1987, the zoo's advertising budgets were just over $150,000, its total public relations budgets were over $300,000, and the total marketing budgets were over $1,000,000 each year, including salaries. The marketing budgets included development or fund-raising and membership as well as public relations and advertising. Percentage breakdowns of the public relations budget for 1987 can be found in Exhibit 4-4.

EXHIBIT 4-4 ■ Public Relations and Media Budgets

Public Relations Budgets

Category	**1987 Percent**
Salaries and overtime	24.3%
Education, travel and subscriptions	1.1
Printing and duplicating	2.4
Professional services	1.5
Tourist brochures for hotel rooms	3.6
Special events	24.1
News releases	0.4
Entertainment	0.7
Photography	0.9
Miscellaneous supplies	0.6
Advertising	40.3

Media Budgets

Media	**1986 Percent**	**1987 Percent**
TV and radio	28.0%	46.3%
Special promotion contingency	32.3	13.2
Tourist publications	10.5	9.2
Streetcar and bus	6.9	7.3
Magazines	4.2	5.0
Newspaper		1.1
Production	18.1	17.8

Source: The Audubon Park Zoo

The American Association of Zoological Parks and Aquariums reported that most zoos find that the majority of their visitors live within a single population center in close proximity to the park.[10] Thus, in order to sustain attendance over the years, zoos must attract the same visitors repeatedly. A large number of the Audubon Park Zoo's promotional programs and special events were aimed at just that.

Promotional progress was slow among people outside of New Orleans. For example, Simon & Schuster, a reputed publishing firm, in its 218-page *Frommer's 1983–84 Guide to New Orleans* managed only a three-word reference to a "very nice zoo." A 1984 study found that only 36 percent of the zoo's visitors were tourists, and even this number probably included to some extent an overflow from the World's Fair.

EXHIBIT 4-5 ■ Audubon Park Zoo Promotional Programs

Title (Activity)	Month(s)
Photography contest	January
Fit for Life (aerobics)	March
Zoo-To-Do for Kids	April
Easter Family Days	April
Zoo-To-Do	May
Musical Zoo Revue (symphony concert)	May
Summer Concert Series	April to August
Breakfast with the Beasts	June
Ice Cream Sunday	June
Zoobilation (members party)	June
Play-Doh Invitational (architects compete with Play-Doh designs)	June
Teddy Bear Affair (teddy bear contests)	August
Press Party	September
Symphony Run	September
Louisiana Swamp Festival	October
Halloween	October
Beast Ballet (ballet performance)	November
Annual Essay Contest	November
Holiday Celebration	December
Annual Members' Christmas Sale	December

Source: The Audubon Park Zoo

Promotional Programs

The Audubon Park Zoo and the Friends of the Zoo conducted a multitude of very successful promotional programs. The effect was to have parties and celebrations going on continuously, attracting a variety of people to the zoo (and raising additional revenue). Exhibit 4-5 lists the major annual promotional programs conducted by the zoo.

In addition to these annual promotions, the zoo scheduled concerts of well-known musicians, such as Irma Thomas, Pete Fountain, The Monkeys, and Manhattan Transfer, and other special events throughout the year. As a result, a variety of events occurred each month.

Many educational activities were conducted all year long. These included (1) a "Junior Zoo Keeper" program for seventh and eighth graders, (2) a student-intern program for high school and college students, and (3) a Zoomobile, which took live animals to special education classes, hospitals, and homes for the elderly, among other sites.

Admission Policy

The Audubon Park Commission recommended the institution of an admission charge. Those who argued against such a charge held that it would result in an overall decline in attendance and a reduction of nongate revenues. Proponents held that gate charges would control vandalism, produce greater revenues, and result in increased public awareness and appreciation of the facility. In the early 1970s, all major international zoos charged admission, as did 73 percent of the 125 U.S. zoos.

The commission argued that there is no such thing as a free zoo; someone must pay. If the zoo is tax supported, then locals carry a disproportionate share of the cost. At the time, neighboring Jefferson Parish was growing by leaps and bounds and, it was argued, surely would bring a large, nonpaying constituency to the new zoo. Further, most zoos are tourist attractions, so tourists should pay since they contribute little to the local tax revenues.

The average yearly attendance for a zoo may be estimated by multiplying projected population figures by a "visitor generating factor." The average visitor generating factor of 14 zoos similar in size and climate to the Audubon Park Zoo was 1.34, with a rather wide range from a low of .58 in Phoenix and Miami to a high of 2.80 in Jackson, Mississippi.

Attracting More Tourists and Other Visitors

The romantic paddle wheeler *Cotton Blossom* took visitors up the Mississippi River from downtown to the zoo. The Zoo Cruise originally began at a dock in the French Quarter, but was later moved to a dock immediately adjacent to New Orleans' newest attraction, the

EXHIBIT 4-6 ■ Seven Reasons Given for Not Attending the Audubon Park Zoo

Reason (Close Ended) Characteristic	Relative Importance of Reasons Respondent Does Not Visit (in percentages)			
	Very Imp. w/ Emphasis	Very Imp. w/o Emphasis	Somewhat Important	Unimportant
The distance of the zoo's location from where you live	7	11	21	60
The *cost* of a zoo visit	4	8	22	66
Not being all that interested in zoo animals	2	12	18	67
The parking problem on weekends	7	11	19	62
The idea that you get tired of seeing the same exhibits over and over	5	18	28	49
It's too hot during the summer months	25	23	22	30
Just not having the idea occur to you	8	19	26	48

Riverwalk, on the site of the 1984 Louisiana World Exposition. Not only was the riverboat ride great fun, it also lured tourists and conventioneers from the downtown attractions of the French Quarter and the new Riverwalk to the zoo, some six miles upstream. A further attraction of the riverboat ride was a return trip on the New Orleans Streetcar, one of the few remaining trolley cars in the United States. The Zoo Cruise drew more visitors to the zoo, generated additional revenue through landing fees paid by the New Orleans Steamboat Company, and kept traffic out of uptown New Orleans.[11]

Financial

The zoo's ability to generate operating funds has been credited to the dedication of the Friends of the Zoo, continuing increases in attendance, and creative special events and programs. A history of adequate operating funds allowed the zoo to guarantee capital donors that their gifts would be used to build and maintain top-notch exhibits. See Exhibit 4-7 for sources of operating budgets over the years. The 1986 combined balance sheet and the statement of revenue and expense for the Audubon Park Commission are in Exhibits 4-8 and 4-9.

Capital Fund Drives

The Audubon Zoo Development Fund was established in 1973. Corporate/industrial support of the zoo has been very strong—many corporations have underwritten construction of zoo displays and facilities. A partial list of major corporate sponsors is in Exhibit 4-10. A sponsorship was to be for the life of the exhibit. The zoo's development department operated on a 12-percent overhead rate, which meant that 88 cents of every dollar raised went toward the projects. By 1987, the master plan for development had been 75-percent completed. The fund-raising goal for 1987 was $1.6 million.

Management

The Zoo Director

Ron Forman, Audubon Park Zoo director, was called a "zoomaster extraordinaire" and was described by the press as a "cross between Doctor Doolittle and the Wizard of Oz," as a "practical visionary," and as "serious, but with a sense of humor."[12] A native New Orleanian, Forman quit an MBA program to join the city government as an administrative assistant and found himself doing a business analysis project on the Audubon Park. Once the city was committed to a new zoo, Forman was named an assistant to the zoo director, John Moore. In early 1977, Moore gave up the battle between the "animal people" and the "people-people,"[13] and Forman took over as park and zoo director.

Forman was said to bring an MBA-meets-menagerie style to the zoo, which was responsible for transforming it from a public burden into an almost completely self-sustaining operation. The result not only benefited the citizens of the city, but also added a major tourist attraction to the economically troubled New Orleans of the 1980s.

Staffing

The zoo had two classes of employees; civil service through the Audubon Park Commission and noncivil service. The civil service employees, who included the curators and zoo keepers, were under the jurisdiction of the city civil service system. Employees who worked in public relations, advertising, concessions, fundraising, and other such activities were hired through the Friends of the Zoo and were not part of the civil service system. See Exhibit 4-11 for further data on staffing patterns.

EXHIBIT 4-7 ▪ Operating Budget

Year	Operating Budget	Gov't. Support	Self-Generated
1978	$1,700,000	$700,000	$1,000,000
1980	2,800,000	840,000	1,960,000
1986	4,469,000	460,000	4,009,000

Source: The Audubon Park Zoo

Moving Into the Future

A visitor to the new Audubon Park Zoo could quickly see why New Orleanians were so proud of their zoo. In a city that was labeled as one of the dirtiest in the nation, the zoo was virtually spotless. This environment was the result of adequate staffing and the clear pride of those who worked at the zoo and those who visited it. One of the first points made by volunteers guiding school groups was that anyone seeing a piece of trash on the ground must pick it up.[14] A 1986 city poll showed that 93 percent of the citizens surveyed approved highly of the zoo—an extremely high rating for any public facility.

Kudos came from groups outside the local area as well. Delegates from the American Association of Zoological Parks and Aquariums ranked the Audubon Park Zoo as one of the three top zoos of its size in America. In 1982, the American Association of Nurserymen gave the zoo a Special Judges Award for its use of plant materials. In 1985, the Audubon Park Zoo received the Phoenix Award from the Society of American Travel Writers for its achievements in conservation, preservation, and beautification.

By 1987, the zoo was virtually self-sufficient. Money received from government grants amounted to less than 10 percent of the budget. The master plan for the development of the zoo was 75-percent complete and the reptile exhibit was scheduled to open in the fall of 1987. The organization had expanded with a full complement of professionals and managers. (See Exhibit 4-12 for the organizational structure of the zoo.)

While the zoo made great progress in 15 years, all was not quiet on the political front. In a court battle, the city won over the state on the issue of who wielded ultimate authority over Audubon Park and Zoo. Indeed, the zoo had benefited from three friendly mayors in a row, starting with Moon Landrieu, who championed the new zoo, then Ernest "Dutch" Morial and Sidney Barthelemy, who in 1987 threw his support to both the zoo and a proposed aquarium being championed by Ron Forman.

EXHIBIT 4-8 ■ Audubon Park Commission Combined Balance Sheet, December 31, 1986

Assets	Operating Fund	Enterprise Fund	Designated Funds	Total
Current assets				
Cash - Noninterest bearing	$ 12,108	$ 0	$ 131,411	$ 143,519
- Interest-bearing	306,483	0	0	306,483
Time certificates of deposit	301,493	0	107,402	408,895
Investments	100	0	0	100
Accounts receivable:				
Friends of the Zoo, Inc.	321,774	0	1,177	322,951
Other	13,240	7,842	75,698	96,780
Due from operating fund	0	309,208	320,463	629,671
Due from enterprise fund	0	0	300,000	300,000
Due from other designated funds	0	0	66,690	66,690
Prepaid expenses	166,862	3,371	0	170,233
Total current assets	1,122,060	320,421	1,002,841	2,445,322
Fixed assets				
Equipment	0	159,455	0	159,455
Less: Accumulated depreciation	0	75,764	0	75,764
Total fixed assets	0	83,691	0	83,691
Total assets	$1,122,060	$404,112	$1,002,841	$2,529,013
Liabilities				
Cash overdraft	$ 39,700	$ 0	$ 0	$ 39,700
Accounts payable:				
City of New Orleans	267,185	0	0	267,185
Friends of the Zoo, Inc.	0	72,658	0	72,658
Other	68,805	7,099	0	75,904
Payroll taxes payable	14,337	0	0	14,337
Accrued salaries	7,973	1,579	0	9,552
Due to operating fund	0	0	46,899	46,899
Due to enterprise fund	309,208	0	0	309,208
Due to designated funds	273,564	300,000	0	573,564
Due to other designated funds	0	0	66,690	66,690
Total liabilities	980,772	381,336	113,589	1,475,697
Fund equities				
Fund balances	141,288	0	889,252	1,030,540
Retained earnings	0	22,776	0	22,776
Total fund equities	141,288	22,776	889,252	1,053,316
Total liabilities and fund equities	$1,122,060	$404,112	$1,002,841	$2,529,013

New Directions for the Zoo

Zoo Director Ron Forman demonstrated that zoos have almost unlimited potential. A 1980 *New Orleans* magazine article cited some of Forman's ideas, ranging from a safari train to a breeding center for rare animals. The latter had the added appeal of being a potential money-maker since an Asiatic lion cub, for example, sells for around $10,000. This wealth of ideas was important because expanded facilities and programs are required to maintain attendance at any public attraction. The most ambitious of

EXHIBIT 4-9 ■ Audubon Park Commission Statement of Revenue, Expenditures and Changes in Operating Fund Balance—Actual and Budgeted Year Ended December 31, 1986

	Annual Budget	Actual	% of Budget
REVENUE			
Intergovernmental			
City of New Orleans	$ 600,000	$ 450,000	75.0%
State of Louisiana	25,000	10,913	43.7
Other governmental	25,000	0	0.0
Total intergovernmental	650,000	460,913	70.9
Charges for services			
Animal rides	115,000	127,671	111.0
Binocular receipts	4,000	2,604	65.1
Education programs	10,000	930	9.3
Events	10,000	4,701	47.0
Food and drink	458,000	569,259	124.3
Gift shops	140,000	136,369	97.4
Mombasa Railroad	40,000	40,030	100.1
Race fees	30,000	30,844	102.8
Swimming Pool	17,000	15,992	94.1
Tennis	0	10,167	0.0
Train	10,000	0	0.0
Travel program	14,000	5,508	39.3
Zoo admissions	2,420,000	2,718,254	112.3
Total charges for services	3,268,000	3,662,329	112.1
Interest income	10,000	34,867	348.7
Miscellaneous			
Animal sales	10,000	38,446	384.5
Aquarium campaign	0	124	0.0
Friends of the Zoo	525,000	640,869	122.1
Miscellaneous	12,000	8,569	71.4
Riverboat	35,000	36,278	103.7
Stables	8,400	7,887	93.9
Total miscellaneous	590,400	732,173	124.0
Total revenue	4,518,400	4,890,282	108.2%
EXPENDITURES			
Personal services			
Life insurance	$ 2,000	$ 23,106	1,155.3%
Medical insurance	100,000	103,321	103.3
Pension	150,000	160,543	107.0
Payroll taxes	198,000	155,961	78.8
Salaries - regular	1,883,652	1,959,205	104.0
Salaries - overtime	59,570	61,937	104.0
Terminal leave	10,000	1,169	11.7
Uniform allowance	19,900	17,287	86.9
Workmen's compensation	50,000	38,779	77.6
Total personal services	2,473,122	2,521,308	101.9
Contractual services			
Advertising	131,200	111,863	85.3
Aquarium	90,000	248,082	275.6

	Annual Budget	Actual	% of Budget
Building repairs	5,400	18,790	348.0
Communications	100	166	166.0
Convention and travel	29,950	32,445	108.3
Delivery and parking	10,850	12,639	116.5
Dues and subscriptions	7,910	7,636	96.5
Duplicating services	14,500	5,021	34.6
Entertainment	5,800	12,350	212.9
Equipment rental	22,750	12,215	53.7
Insurance	260,000	254,079	97.7
Laboratory services	8,100	9,762	120.5
License fees	550	1,108	201.5
Minor repairs	10,300	12,265	119.1
News releases	6,000	1,551	25.9
Penguins	0	10,957	0.0
Personal contracts	46,200	0	0.0
Postage and freight	40,350	33,322	82.6
Printing	18,700	9,207	49.2
Professional services	342,890	362,050	105.6
Swimming pool	48,000	42,835	89.2
Telephone	40,000	50,634	126.6
Utilities	40,000	41,902	104.8
Vehicle repairs	10,000	12,307	103.1
Waste removal	18,800	18,011	95.3
Total contractual services	1,208,350	1,321,197	109.3
Supplies and materials			
Amphitheater	$ 3,400	$ 2,264	66.6%
Art and essay	900	518	57.6
Artifacts	1,000	0	0.0
Building supplies	57,750	63,151	109.4
Display supplies	32,100	17,172	53.5
Educational supplies	10,050	49,626	493.8
Electrical supplies	10,300	25,283	245.5
Events	50,200	45,989	91.6
Feed and forage	187,780	172,398	91.8
Fuel	38,000	23,874	62.8
Graphics supplies	4,500	8,152	131.2
Hand tools	4,000	3,120	78.0
Horticultural supplies	20,000	17,788	88.9
Hospital and laboratory supplies	15,300	13,711	89.6
Janitorial and cleaning	51,500	50,018	97.1
Junior keeper	500	817	163.4
Medical supplies	1,750	1,300	74.3
Minor equipment	28,950	30,384	105.0
Motor vehicle supplies	30,000	10,285	34.3
Office supplies	34,150	29,768	87.2
Photographic supplies	5,150	6,138	119.2
Plants, shrubs, and trees	18,300	16,574	90.6
Police supplies	1,500	3,128	208.5
Public information	0	638	0.0

	Annual Budget	Actual	% of Budget
Read the Zoo	7,000	7,675	109.6
Safari carts	3,000	1,136	37.9
Special education	10,000	12,731	127.3
Teacher in-service	6,000	2,562	42.7
Uniforms	5,060	4,329	35.6
Zoomobile	3,000	1,138	37.9
Total supplies and materials	641,140	621,667	97.0
Equipment			
Animals	$ 22,400	$ 14,359	64.1%
Automotive	40,000	56,722	141.8
Communications	1,150	847	73.7
Construction projects	50,000	32,418	64.8
Educational and recreational	0	96	0.0
General plant	7,000	5,621	80.3
Hospital and medical	4,200	2,947	70.2
Office furniture and equipment	8,500	35,897	422.3
Total equipment	133,250	148,907	111.8
Other expenditures			
Claims	12,000	10,385	86.5
Miscellaneous	1,000	19,461	1,946.1
Total other expenditures	13,000	29,846	229.6
Total expenditures	4,468,862	4,642,925	103.9
Excess of revenue over expenditures	49,538	247,357	499.3
OTHER FINANCING USES			
Operating transfers out	49,538	150,000	302.8
Excess of revenue and other financing sources over expenditures and other uses	$ 0	97,357	
OPERATING FUND BALANCE AT BEGINNING OF YEAR		43,931	
OPERATING FUND BALANCE AT END OF YEAR		$ 141,288	

Forman's ideas was for an aquarium and riverfront park to be located at the foot of Canal Street.

Although the zoo enjoyed political support in 1987, New Orleans was suffering from a high unemployment rate and a generally depressed economy resulting from the depression in the oil industry. Some economists were predicting the beginning of a gradual turnaround in 1988, but any significant improvement in the economy was forecasted to be years away. In addition, the zoo operated in a city where many attractions competed for the leisure dollar of citizens and visitors. The Audubon Park Zoo had to vie with the French Quarter, Dixieland jazz, the Superdome, and the greatest of all attractions in the city—Mardi Gras.

The New Orleans Aquarium

In 1986, Forman and a group of supporters proposed the development of an aquarium and riverfront park to the New Orleans City Council. In November 1986, the electorate voted to fund an aquarium and a riverfront park by a

EXHIBIT 4-10 ▪ Major Corporate Sponsors

Amoco Corporation
American Express
J. Aron and Company
Breaux Mart
Chevron USA, Inc.
Conoco, Inc.
Consolidated Natural Gas Corporation
D. H. Holmes, Ltd.
Dr. G. H. Tichenor Antiseptic Company
Exxon Corporation
First National Bank of Commerce
Freeport-McMoRan, Inc.
Frischhertz Electric Company
Goudchaux/Maison Blanche
Hibernia National Bank
Kentwood Spring Water
Louisiana Coca-Cola Bottling Company, Ltd.
Louisiana Land and Exploration Company
McDonald's Operations of New Orleans
William B. Reily and Company
Texaco USA
Trammell Crow Company
Wendy's of New Orleans
Whitney National Bank
Frank B. Williams and Company

Source: The Audubon Park Zoo

70-percent margin—one of the largest margins the city has ever given to any tax proposal. Forman[15] hailed this as a vote of confidence from the citizens as well as a mandate to build a world-class aquarium that would produce new jobs, stimulate the local economy, and create an educational resource.

Once the voters had approved the bond proposal, the New Orleans City Council had many decisions to make. Should the management structure of the aquarium be placed within the same organization as the Audubon Park Zoo or under a separate structure? Where should the aquarium be located and how large should it be?

A feasibility study prepared by Harrison Price Company[16] projected a probable 863,000 visitors to the aquarium by the year 1990, with 75 percent of them coming from outside the metropolitan area. The location of the new aquarium was to be adjacent to the Riverwalk, providing a logical pedestrian link between New Orleans's major attractions of the Riverwalk and the Jax Brewery, a shopping center in the French Quarter.

The aquarium would face major opposition from several groups: riverfront developers, the Vieux Carre Commission (preservationists of the old French Quarter), the Dock Board (responsible for riverfront property usage), the U.S. Park Service, and businesses from downtown and other parts of the city. Several of these groups argued that the proposed site was not safe from river accidents. One counter plan was for the aquarium to be located on the west bank of the Mississippi River. The west bank was accessible from downtown only by two major bridges and ferry boats. The east bank contained the major tourist and visitor attractions of the French Quarter, the Convention Center, the Lakefront (Lake Pontchartrain res-

EXHIBIT 4-11 ▪ Employee Structure

Year	# of Paid Employees	Number of Volunteers
1972	36	
1973	49	
1974	69	
1975	90	
1976	143	
1977	193	
1978	184	
1979	189	
1980	198	
1981	245	
1982	305	
1983	302	56
1984	419	120
1985	454	126
1986	426	250
1987	358*	287*

*Through the end of the second quarter.
Source: The Audubon Park Zoo

EXHIBIT 4-12 ■ Audubon Park Zoo Organizational Structure

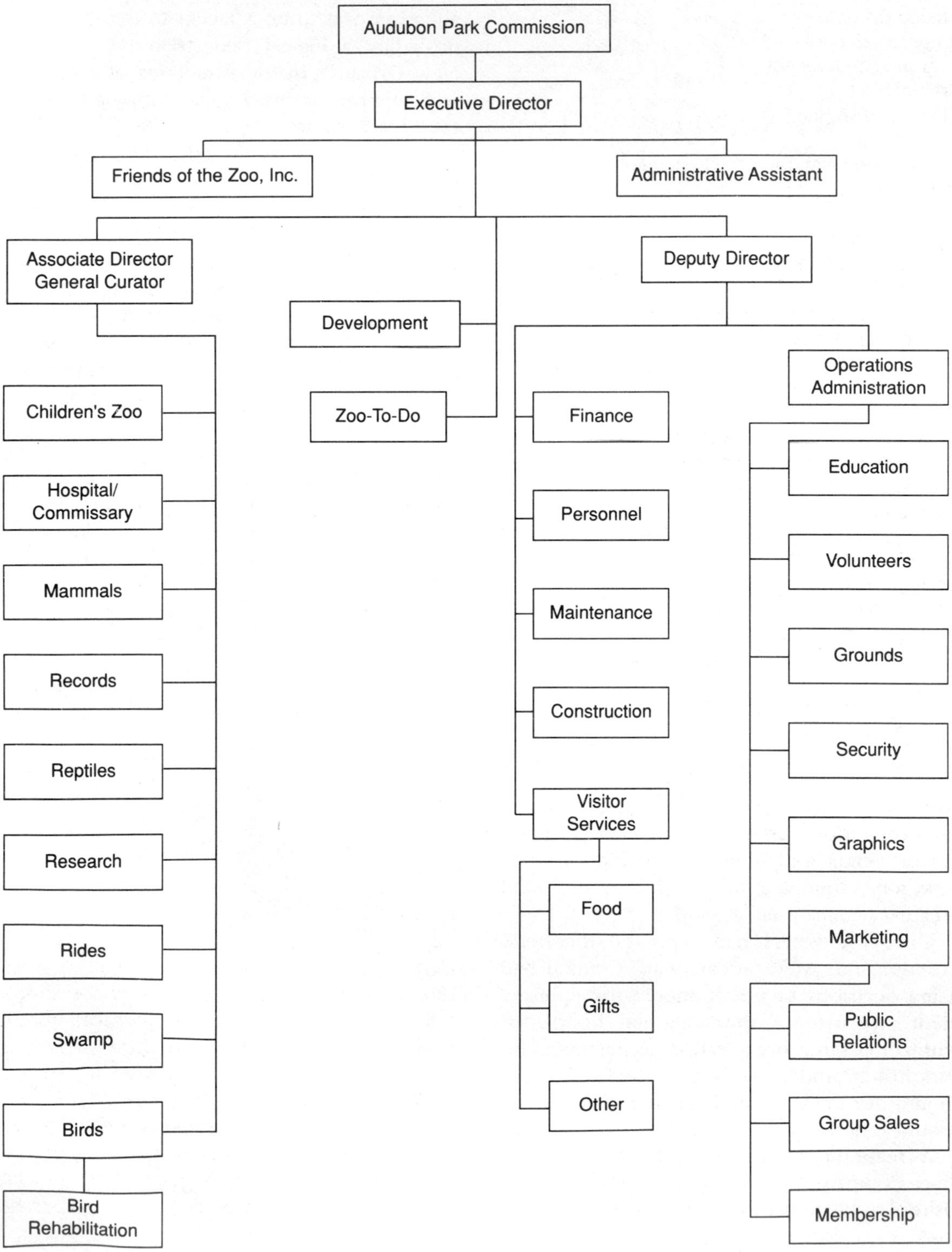

EXHIBIT 4-13 ▪ Respondent Characteristics of Zoo Visitors According to Visitation Frequency (in Percentages)

	Number of Zoo Visits Over Past Two Years			
Respondent characteristic	**Four or more**	**Two or three**	**One or none**	**Never visited zoo**
Age				
Under 27	26	35	31	9
27 to 35	55	27	15	3
36 to 45	48	32	11	9
46 to 55	18	20	37	25
Over 55	27	29	30	14
Marital status				
Married	41	28	20	11
Not married	30	34	24	13
Children at home				
Yes	46	30	15	9
No	34	28	27	12
Interest in visiting the Orleans Aquarium				
Very, with emphasis	47	26	18	9
Very, without emphasis	45	24	23	12
Somewhat	28	37	14	11
Not too	19	32	27	22
Vote intention on aquarium				
For, with emphasis	46	33	16	5
For, without emphasis	39	31	16	14
Against or don't know	11	40	32	17
Member of FOTZ				
Yes	67	24	5	4
No, but heard of it	35	30	24	12
No, and never heard of it	25	28	35	13
Would you be interested in joining FOTZ (nonmembers only)				
Very/somewhat	50	28	14	8
No/don't know	33	29	26	12

taurants and facilities), the historic Garden District, and major shopping areas. A different downtown site was pushed by an opposing political group.

Meanwhile, the Audubon Park Zoo had its own future to plan. The new physical facilities and professional care had paid off handsomely in increased attendance and new animal births. But the zoo could not expand at its existing location because of a lack of land within the city. Ron Forman and the zoo staff considered several alternatives. One was incorporating the new aquarium. Another was little "neighborhood" zoos to be located all over the city. A third was a separate breeding area to be located outside the city boundaries, where land was available. With the zoo running smoothly, the staff seemed to need new challenges to tackle and the zoo needed new facilities or programs to continue to increase attendance.

EXHIBIT 4-14 ■ Chronology of Events for the New Zoo

1972	The Audubon Zoological Society asked the Audubon Park Commission to institute an admission charge "in an amount sufficient to reduce the possibility of vandalism but not so great as to inhibit visits by family groups and less affluent members of the community" (*Times Picayune*, April 29, 1972).
1973	The City Planning Commission approved a master plan for the Audubon Park Zoo calling for $3.4 million for upgrading. Later phases called for an additional $2.1 million and were to be completed by 1978.
1974	Friends of the Zoo formed with 400 members to increase support and awareness of the zoo.
1975	Phase I renovations began: $25 million in public and private funds to expand from 14 acres to 58 acres.
1977	John Moore went to Albuquerque; Ron Forman took over as park and zoo director.
1978	Phase II began.
1980	Phase III began.
1980	First full-time education staff on duty at the zoo.
1980	Last animal removed from antiquated cage—a turning point in zoo history.
1981	Contract signed allowing New Orleans Steamboat Company to bring passengers from downtown to the zoo.
1981	Delegates from the American Association of Zoological Parks and Aquariums ranked the Audubon Park Zoo as one of the top three zoos of its size in the United States.
1981	Zoo accredited.
1982	The Audubon Park Commission reorganized under Act 352, which required the commission to contract with a nonprofit organization for the daily management of the park.

Endnotes

[1]*Times Picayune,* March 30, 1975.

[2]*Times Picayune,* January 20, 1976.

[3]Millie Ball, "The New Zoo of '82," *Dixie Magazine, Sunday Times Picayune,* June 24, 1979.

[4]*Times Picayune,* March 30, 1975.

[5]*Times Picayune,* January 20, 1976.

[6]*Times Picayune,* April 29, 1972.

[7]*Jefferson Business,* August 1985.

[8]Ibid.

[9]*Advertising Age,* March 17, 1986.

[10]Karen Sausmann (ed.). *Zoological Park and Aquarium Fundamentals,* (Wheeling, W.V.: American Association of Zoological Parks and Aquariums, 1982) 111.

[11]*Times Picayune,* November 30, 1981.

[12]Steve Brooks, "Don't Say 'No Can Do' to Audubon Zoo Chief," *Jefferson Business,* May 5, 1986.

[13]Ross Yuchey, "No Longer Is Heard a Discouraging Word at the Audubon Zoo" *New Orleans,* August 1980, 53.

[14]Yuchey, 49.

[15]*At the Zoo,* Winter 1987.

[16]Feasibility Analysis and Conceptual Planning for a Major Aquarium Attraction, prepared for the City of New Orleans, March 1985.

References

Beaulieu, Lovell. "It's All Happening at the Zoo." *The Times Picayune,* Sunday, January 28, 1978.

Ball, Millie. "The New Zoo of '82." *Dixie Magazine, Sunday Times Picayune,* June 24, 1979.

Brooks, Steve. "Don't Say 'No Can Do' to Audubon Zoo Chief." *Jefferson Business,* May 5, 1986.

Bureau of Governmental Research, City of New Orleans. *Audubon Park Zoo Study, Part I, Zoo Improvement Plan, August 1971.* New Orleans: Bureau of Governmental Research.

Bureau of Governmental Research, City of New Orleans. *Audubon Park Zoo Study, Part II, An Operational Analysis, August 1971.* New Orleans: Bureau of Governmental Research.

Donovan, S. "The Audubon Zoo: A Dream Come True." *New Orleans,* May 1986, 52–66.

Feasibility Analysis and Conceptual Planning for a Major Aquarium Attraction, prepared for the City of New Orleans, March 1985.

Forman, R., J. Logsdon, and J. Wilds. *Audubon Park: An Urban Eden.* New Orleans: The Friends of the Zoo, 1985.

Poole, Susan. *Frommer's 1983–84 Guide to New Orleans.* New York: Simon & Schuster, 1983.

Sausmann, K., ed. *Zoological Park and Aquarium Fundamentals,* Wheeling, W.V.: American Association of Zoological Parks and Aquariums, 1982.

Yuchey, R. "No Longer Is Heard a Discouraging Word at the Audubon Zoo." *New Orleans,* August 1980, 49–60.

Zuckerman, S., ed., *Great Zoos of the World.* Boulder, Colorado: Westview Press, 1980.

5

Rondell Data Corporation

"God damn it, he's done it again!"

Frank Forbus threw the stack of prints and specifications down on his desk in disgust. The Model 802 wide-band modulator, released for production the previous Thursday, had just come back to Frank's Engineering Services Department with a caustic note that began, "This one can't be produced, either. . . ." It was the fourth time Production had kicked the design back.

Frank Forbus, director of engineering for Rondell Data Corp., was normally a quiet man. But the Model 802 was stretching his patience; it was beginning to look just like other new products that had hit delays and problems in the transition from design to production during the eight months Frank had worked for Rondell. These problems were nothing new at the sprawling old Rondell factory; Frank's predecessor in the engineering job had run afoul of them too, and had finally been fired for protesting too vehemently about the other departments. But the Model 802 should have been different. Frank had met two months before (July 3, 1978) with the firm's president, Bill Hunt, and with factory superintendent Dave Schwab to smooth the way for the new modulator design. He thought back to the meeting. . . .

"Now we all know there's a tight deadline on the 802," Bill Hunt said, "and Frank's done well to ask us to talk about its introduction. I'm counting on both of you to find any snags in the system, and to work together to get that first production run out by October second. Can you do it?"

"We can do it in Production if we get a clean design two weeks from now, as scheduled," answered Dave Schwab, the grizzled factory superintendent. "Frank and I have already talked about that, of course. I'm setting aside time in the card room and the machine shop, and we'll be ready. If the design goes over schedule, though, I'll have to fill in with other runs, and it will cost us a bundle to break in for the 802. How does it look in Engineering, Frank?"

"I've just reviewed the design for the second time," Frank replied. "If Ron Porter can keep the salesmen out of our hair, and avoid any more last minute changes, we've got a shot. I've pulled the draftsmen off three other overdue jobs to get this one out. But, Dave, that means we can't spring engineers loose to confer with your production people on manufacturing problems."

"Well, Frank, most of those problems are caused by the engineers, and we need them to resolve the difficulties. We've all agreed that production bugs come from both of us bowing to sales pressure, and putting equipment into production before the designs are really ready. That's just what we're trying to avoid on the 802. But I can't have 500 people sitting on their hands waiting for an answer from your people. We'll have to have *some* engineering support."

Bill Hunt broke in, "So long as you two can talk calmly about the problem I'm confident you can resolve it. What a relief it is, Frank, to hear the way you're approaching this. With Kilmann (the previous director of engineering) this conversation would have been a shouting match. Right, Dave?" Dave nodded and smiled.

"Now there's one other thing you should both be aware of," Hunt continued. "Doc Reeves and I talked last night about a new filtering technique, one that might improve the signal-to-noise ratio of the 802 by a factor of two. There's a chance Doc can come up with it before the 802 reaches production, and if it's possible, I'd like to use the new filters. That would give us a real jump on the competition."

Four days after that meeting, Frank found that two of his key people on the 802 design had been called to Production for emergency consultation on a bug found in final assembly: two halves of a new data transmission interface wouldn't fit together because recent changes in the front end required a different chassis design for the back end.

Another week later, Doc Reeves walked into Frank's office, proud as a new parent, with the new filter design. "This won't affect the other modules of the 802 much," Doc had said. "Look, it takes three new cards, a few connectors, some changes in the wiring harness, and some new shielding, and that's all."

Frank had tried to resist the last-minute design changes, but Bill Hunt had stood firm. With a lot of overtime by the engineers and draftsmen, Engineering Services should still be able to finish the prints in time.

Two engineers and three draftsmen went onto 12-hour days to get the 802 ready, but the prints were still five days late reaching Dave Schwab. Two days later, the prints came back to Frank, heavily annotated in red. Schwab had worked all day Saturday to review the job, and had found more than a dozen discrepancies in the prints—most of them caused by the new filter design and insufficient checking time before release. Correction of those design faults had brought on a new generation of discrepancies; Schwab's cover note on the second return of the prints indicated he'd had to release the machine capacity he'd been holding for the 802. On the third iteration, Schwab committed his photo and plating capacity to another rush job. The 802 would be at least one month late getting into production. Ron Porter, Vice President for Sales, was furious. His customer needed 100 units *NOW*, he said. Rondell was the customer's only late supplier.

"Here we go again," thought Frank Forbus.

Company History

Rondell Data Corp. traced its lineage through several generations of electronics technology. Its original founder, Bob Rondell, had set the firm up in 1920 as "Rondell Equipment Co." to manufacture several electrical testing devices he had invented as an engineering faculty member at a large university. The firm branched into radio broadcasting equipment in 1947, and into data transmission equipment in the early 1960s. A well-established corps of direct sales people, mostly engineers, called on industrial, scientific and government accounts, but concentrated heavily on original equipment manufacturers. In this market, Rondell had a long-standing reputation as a source of high-quality, innovative designs. The firm's salespeople fed a continual stream of challenging problems into the Engineering Department, where the creative genius of Ed "Doc" Reeves and several dozen other engineers "converted problems to solutions" (as the sales brochure bragged). Product design formed the spearhead of Rondell's growth.

By 1978, Rondell offered a wide range of products in its two major lines. Broadcast equipment sales had benefitted from the growth of UHF TV and FM radio; it now accounted for 35% of company sales. Data transmission had blossomed, and in this field an increasing number of orders called for unique specifications, ranging from specialized display panels to entirely untried designs.

The company had grown from 100 employees in 1947 to over 800 in 1978. (Exhibit 5–1 shows the current organization chart of key employees.) Bill Hunt, who had been a student of the company's founder, had presided over most of that growth, and took great pride in preserving the "family spirit" of the old organization. Informal relationships between Rondell's veteran employees formed the backbone of the firm's day-to-day operations; all the managers relied on personal contact, and Hunt often insisted that the absence of bureaucratic red tape was a key factor in recruiting outstanding engineering talent. The personal management approach extended throughout the factory. All exempt employees were paid on a straight salary plus a share of the profits. Rondell boasted an extremely loyal group of senior employees, and very low turnover in nearly all areas of the company.

The highest turnover job in the firm was Frank Forbus's. Frank had joined Rondell in January of 1978, replacing Jim Kilmann, who had been director of engineering for only 10 months. Kilmann, in turn, had replaced Tom MacLeod, a talented engineer who had made a promising start, but had taken to drink after a year in the job. MacLeod's predecessor had been a genial old timer who retired at 70 after 30 years in charge of engineering. (Doc Reeves had refused the directorship in each of the recent changes, saying, "Hell, that's no promotion for a bench man like me. I'm no administrator.")

For several years, the firm had experienced a steadily increasing number of disputes between research, engineering, sales, and production people—disputes generally centered on the problem of new product introduction. Quarrels between departments became more numerous under MacLeod, Kilmann, and Forbus. Some managers associated those disputes with the company's recent decline in profitability—a decline that, in spite of higher sales and gross revenues, was beginning to bother people in 1977. President Bill Hunt commented:

Better cooperation, I'm sure, could increase our output by 5–10%. I'd hoped Kilmann could solve the problems, but pretty obviously he was too young, too arrogant. People like him—that conflict type of personality—bother me. I don't like strife, and with him it seemed I spent all my time smoothing out arguments. Kilmann tried to tell everyone else how to run their departments, without having his own house in order. That approach just wouldn't work, here at Rondell. Frank Forbus, now, seems much more in tune with our style of organization. I'm really hopeful now.

Still, we have just as many problems now as we did last year. Maybe even more. I hope Frank can get a handle on Engineering Services soon . . .

The Engineering Department: Research

According to the organization chart (see Exhibit 5–1), Frank Forbus was in charge of both research (really the product development function) and engineering services (which provided engineering support). To

Exhibit 5–1 ■ Rondell Data Corporation 1978 Organization Chart

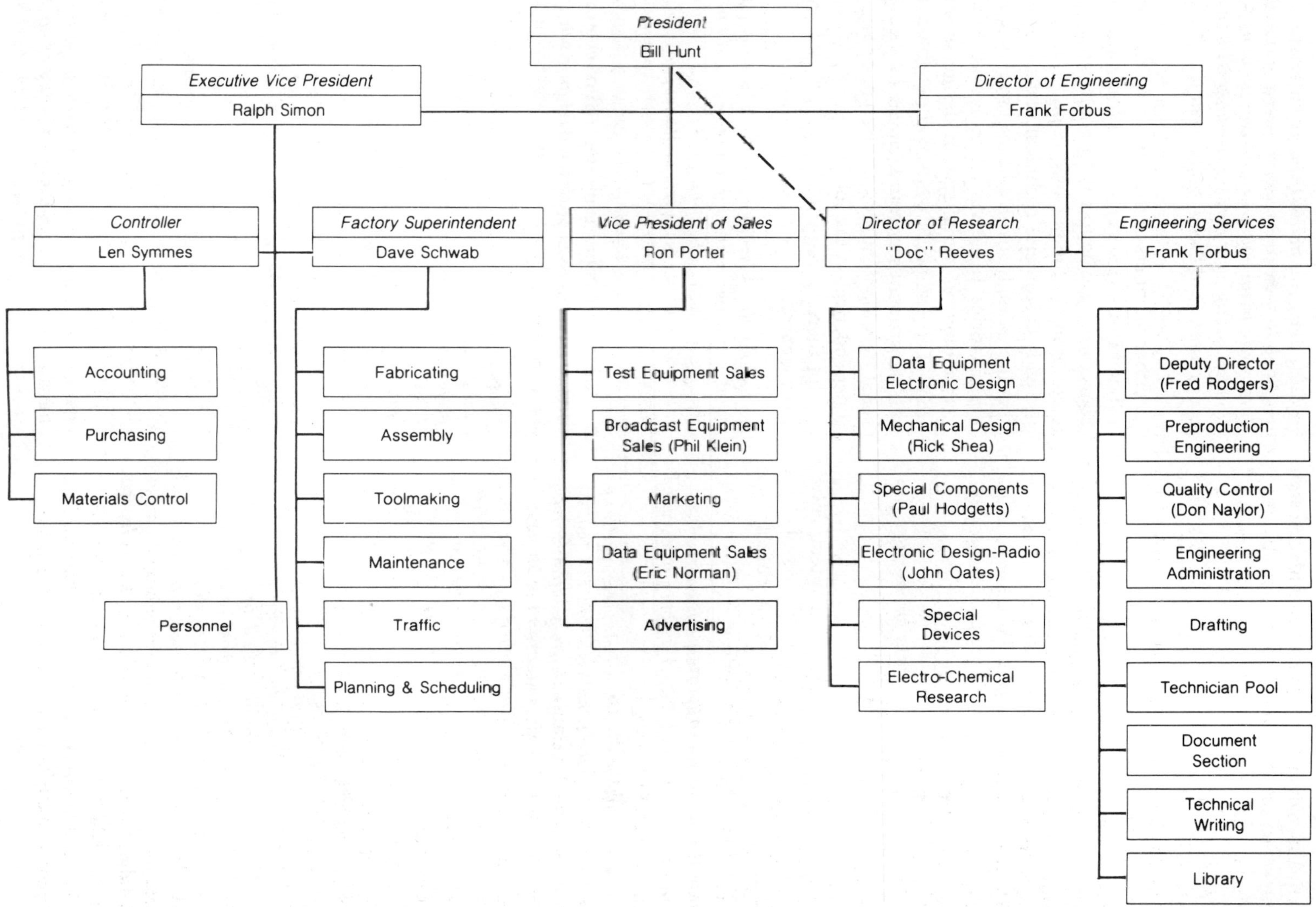

Forbus, however, the relationship with research was not so clear-cut:

Doc Reeves is one of the world's unique people, and none of us would have it any other way. He's a creative genius. Sure, the chart says he works for me, but we all know Doc does his own thing. He's not the least bit interested in management routines, and I can't count on him to take any responsibility in scheduling projects, or checking budgets, or what-have-you. But as long as Doc is director of research, you can bet this company will keep on leading the field. He has more ideas per hour than most people have per year, and he keeps the whole engineering staff fired up. Everybody loves Doc—and you can count me in on that, too. In a way, he works for me, sure. But that's not what's important.

"Doc" Reeves—unhurried, contemplative, casual, and candid—tipped his stool back against the wall of his research cubicle and talked about what *was* important:

Development engineering. That's where the company's future rests. Either we have it there, or we don't have it.

There's no kidding ourselves that we're anything but a bunch of Rube Goldbergs here. But that's where the biggest kicks come from—from solving development problems, and dreaming up new ways of doing things. That's why I so look forward to the special contracts we get involved in. We accept them not for the revenue they represent, but because they subsidize the basic development work which goes into all our basic products.

This is a fantastic place to work. I have a great crew and they can really deliver when the chips are down. Why, Bill Hunt and I (he gestured toward the neighboring cubicle, where the president's name hung over the door) are likely to find as many people here at work at ten p.m. as at three in the afternoon. The important thing here is the relationships between people; they're based on mutual respect, not on policies and procedures. Administrative red tape is a pain. It takes away from development time.

Problems? Sure, there are problems now and then. There are power interests in production, where they sometimes resist change. But I'm not a fighting man, you know. I suppose if I were, I might go in there and push my weight around a little. But I'm an engineer, and can do more for Rondell sitting right here, or working with my own people. That's what brings results.

Other members of the Research Department echoed Doc's views and added some additional sources of satisfaction with their work. They were proud of the personal contacts they built up with customers' technical staffs—contacts that increasingly involved travel to the customers' factories to serve as expert advisors in preparation of overall system design specifications. The engineers were also delighted with the department's encouragement of their personal development, continuing education, and independence on the job.

But there were problems, too. Rick Shea, of the mechanical design section, noted,

In the old days I really enjoyed the work—and the people I worked with. But now there's a lot of irritation. I don't like someone breathing down my neck. You can be hurried into jeopardizing the design.

John Oates, head of the radio electronic design section, was another designer with definite views:

Production engineering is almost nonexistent in this company. Very little is done by the preproduction section in engineering services. Frank Forbus has been trying to get preproduction into the picture, but he won't succeed because you can't start from such an ambiguous position. There have been three directors of engineering in three years. Frank can't hold his own against the others in the company. Kilmann was too aggressive. Perhaps no amount of tact would have succeeded.

Paul Hodgetts was head of special components in the R & D department. Like the rest of the department he valued bench work. But he complained of engineering services.

The services don't do things we want them to do. Instead, they tell us what they're going to do. I should probably go to Frank, but I don't get any

decisions there. I know I should go through Frank, but this holds things up, so I often go direct.

The Engineering Department: Engineering Services

The Engineering Services Department provided ancillary services to R & D, and served as liaison between engineering and the other Rondell departments. Among its main functions were drafting; management of the central technicians' pool; scheduling and expediting engineering products; documentation and publication of parts lists and engineering orders; preproduction engineering (consisting of the final integration of individual design components into mechanically compatible packages); and quality control (which included inspection of incoming parts and materials, and final inspection of subassemblies and finished equipment). Top management's description of the department included the line, "ESD is responsible for maintaining cooperation with other departments, providing services to the development engineers, and freeing more valuable people in R & D from essential activities which are diversions from and beneath their main competence.

Many of Frank Forbus's 75 employees were located in other departments. Quality control people were scattered through the manufacturing and receiving areas, and technicians worked primarily in the research area or the prototype fabrication room. The remaining ESD personnel were assigned to leftover nooks and crannies near production or engineering sections.

Frank Forbus described his position:

My biggest problem is getting acceptance from the people I work with. I've moved slowly rather than risk antagonism. I saw what happened to Kilmann, and I want to avoid that. But although his precipitate action had won over a few of the younger R & D people, he certainly didn't have the department's backing. Of course it was the resentment of other departments which eventually caused his discharge. People have been slow accepting me here. There's nothing really overt, but I get a negative reaction to my ideas.

My role in the company has never been well defined, really. It's complicated by Doc's unique position, of course, and also by the fact that ESD sort of grew by itself over the years, as the design engineers concentrated more and more on the creative parts of product development. I wish I could be more involved in the technical side. That's been my training, and it's a lot of fun. But in our setup, the technical side is the least necessary for me to be involved in.

Schwab (production head) is hard to get along with. Before I came and after Kilmann left, there were six months intervening when no one was really doing any scheduling. No work loads were figured, and unrealistic promises were made about releases. This puts us in an awkward position. We've been scheduling way beyond our capacity to manufacture or engineer.

Certain people within R & D, for instance John Oates, head of the radio electronic design section, understand scheduling well and meet project deadlines, but this is not generally true of the rest of the R & D department, especially the mechanical engineers who won't commit themselves. Most of the complaints come from sales and production department heads because items—like the 802—are going to production before they are fully developed, under pressure from sales to get out the unit, and this snags the whole process. Somehow, engineering services should be able to intervene and resolve these complaints, but I haven't made much headway so far.

I should be able to go to Hunt for help, but he's too busy most of the time, and his major interest is the design side of engineering, where he got his own start. Sometimes he talks as though he's the engineering director as well as president. I have to put my foot down; there are problems here that the front office just doesn't understand.

Sales people were often observed taking their problems directly to designers, while production frequently threw designs back at R & D, claiming they could not be produced and demanding the prompt attention of particular design engineers. The latter were frequently observed in conference with production supervisors on the assembly floor. Frank went on:

The designers seem to feel they're losing something when one of us tries to help. They feel it's a reflection on them to have someone take over what they've been doing. They seem to want to carry a project right through to the final stages, particularly the mechanical people. Consequently, engineering services people are used below their capacity to contribute and our department is denied functions it should be performing. There's not as much use made of engineering services as there should be.

Frank Forbus's technician supervisor added his comments:

Production picks out the engineer who'll be the "bum of the month." They pick on every little detail instead of using their heads and making the minor changes that have to be made. The fifteen-to-twenty-year people shouldn't have to prove their ability any more, but they spend four hours defending themselves and four hours getting the job done. I have no one to go to when I need help. Frank Forbus is afraid. I'm trying to help him but he can't help me at this time. I'm responsible for fifty people and I've got to support them.

Fred Rodgers, who Frank had brought with him to the company as an assistant gave another view of the situation:

I try to get our people in preproduction to take responsibility but they're not used to it and people in other departments don't usually see them as best qualified to solve the problem. There's a real barrier for a newcomer here. Gaining people's confidence is hard. More and more, I'm wondering whether there really is a job for me here.

(Rodgers left Rondell a month later.) Another of Forbus's subordinates gave his view:

If Doc gets a new product idea you can't argue. But he's too optimistic. He judges that others can do what he does—but there's only one Doc Reeves. We've had 900 production change orders this year—they changed 2,500 drawings. If I were in Frank's shoes I'd put my foot down on all this new development. I'd look at the reworking we're doing and get production set up the way I wanted it. Kilmann was fired when he was doing a good job. He was getting some system in the company's operations. Of course, it hurt some people. There is no denying that Doc is the most important person in the company. What gets overlooked is that Hunt is a close second, not just politically but in terms of what he contributes technically and in customer relations.

This subordinate explained that he sometimes went out into the production department but that Schwab, the production head, resented this. Personnel in production said that Kilmann had failed to show respect for oldtimers and was always meddling in other departments' business. This was why he had been fired, they contended.

Don Taylor was in charge of quality control. He commented:

I am now much more concerned with administration and less with work. It is one of the evils you get into. There is tremendous detail in this job. I listen to everyone's opinion. Everybody is important. There shouldn't be distinctions—distinctions between people. I'm not sure whether Frank has to be a fireball like Kilmann. I think the real question is whether Frank is getting the job done. I know my job is essential. I want to supply service to the more talented people and give them information so they can do their jobs better.

The Sales Department

Ron Porter was angry. His job was supposed to be selling, he said, but instead it had turned into settling disputes inside the plant and making excuses to waiting customers. He jabbed a finger toward his desk:

You see that telephone? I'm actually afraid nowadays to hear it ring. Three times out of five, it will be a customer who's hurting because we've failed to deliver on schedule. The other two calls will be from production or ESD, telling me some schedule has slipped again.

The Model 802 is typical. Absolutely typical. We padded the delivery date by six weeks, to allow for contingencies. Within two months the slack had evaporated. Now it looks like we'll be lucky to ship it before Christmas. (It was now November 28.) We're ruining our reputation in the market. Why, just last week one of our best customers—people we've worked with for 15 years—tried to hang a penalty clause on their latest order.

We shouldn't have to be after the engineers all the time. They should be able to see what problems they create without our telling them.

Phil Klein, head of broadcast sales under Porter, noted that many sales decisions were made by top management. Sales was understaffed, he thought, and had never really been able to get on top of the job.

We have grown further and further away from engineering. The director of engineering does not pass on the information that we give him. We need better relationships there. It is very difficult for us to talk to customers about development problems without technical help. We need each other. The whole of engineering is now too isolated from the outside world. The morale of ESD is very low. They're in a bad spot—they're not well organized.

People don't take much to outsiders here. Much of this is because the expectation is built up by top management that jobs will be filled from the bottom. So it's really tough when an outsider like Frank comes it.

Eric Norman, order and pricing coordinator for data equipment, talked about his own relationships with the production department:

Actually, I get along with them fairly well. Oh, things could be better, of course, if they were more cooperative generally. They always seem to say, "It's my bat and my ball, and we're playing by my rules." People are afraid to make production mad; there's a lot of power in there. But you've got to understand that production has its own set of problems. And nobody in Rondell is working any harder than Dave Schwab to try to straighten things out.

The Production Department

Dave Schwab had joined Rondell just after the Korean War, in which he had seen combat duty (at the Yalu River) and intelligence duty at Pyong Yang. Both experiences had been useful in his first year of civilian employment at Rondell's: the wartime factory superintendent and several middle managers had been, apparently, indulging in highly questionable side deals with Rondell's suppliers. Dave Schwab had gathered evidence, revealed the situation to Bill Hunt, and had stood by the president in the ensuing unsavory situation. Seven months after joining the company, Dave was named Factory Superintendent.

His first move had been to replace the fallen managers with a new team from outside. This group did not share the traditional Rondell emphasis on informality and friendly personal relationships, and had worked long and hard to install systematic manufacturing methods and procedures. Before the reorganization, production had controlled purchasing, stock control, and final quality control (where final assembly of products in cabinets was accomplished). Because of the wartime events, management decided on a check-and-balance system of organization and removed these three departments from production jurisdiction. The new production managers felt they had been unjustly penalized by this organization, particularly since they had uncovered the behavior that was detrimental to the company in the first place.

By 1978, the production department had grown to 500 employees, of whom 60% worked in the assembly area—an unusually pleasant environment that had been commended by *Factory* magazine for its colorful decoration, cleanliness, and low noise level. An additional 30% of the work force, mostly skilled machinists, staffed the finishing and fabrication department. About 60 others performed scheduling, supervisory, and maintenance duties. Production workers were nonunion, hourly-paid, and participated in both the liberal profit-sharing program and the stock purchase plan. Morale in production was traditionally high, and turnover was extremely low.

Dave Schwab commented:

To be efficient, production has to be a self-contained department. We have to control what comes into the department and what goes out. That's why purchasing, inventory control, and quality ought to run out of this office. We'd eliminate a lot of problems with better control there. Why, even Don Naylor in QC, would rather work for me than for ESD; he's said so himself. We understand his problems better.

The other departments should be self-contained, too. That's why I always avoid the underlings, and go straight to the department heads with any questions. I always go down the line.

I have to protect my people from outside disturbances. Look what would happen if I let unfinished, half-baked designs in here—there'd be chaos. The bugs have to be found before the drawings go into the shop, and it seems I'm the one who has to find them. Look at the 802, for example. (Dave had spent most of Thanksgiving Day [it was now November 28] red-pencilling the latest set of prints.) ESD should have found every one of those discrepancies. They just don't check drawings properly. They change most of the things I flag, but then they fail to trace through the impact of those changes on the rest of the design. I shouldn't have to do that.

And those engineers are tolerance crazy. They want everything to a millionth of an inch. I'm the only one in the company who's had any experience with actually machining things to a millionth of an inch. We make sure that the things that engineers say on their drawings actually have to be that way and whether they're obtainable from the kind of raw material we buy.

That shouldn't be production's responsibility, but I have to do it. Accepting bad prints wouldn't let us ship the order any quicker. We'd only make a lot of junk that had to be reworked. And that would take even longer.

This way, I get to be known as the bad guy, but I guess that's just part of the job. (He paused with a wry smile). Of course, what really gets them is that I don't even have a degree.

Dave had fewer bones to pick with the sales department because, he said, they trusted him.

When we give Ron Porter a shipping date, he knows the equipment will be shipped then.

You've got to recognize, though, that all of our new product problems stem from sales making absurd commitments on equipment that hasn't been fully developed. That always means trouble. Unfortunately, Hunt always backs sales up, even when they're wrong. He always favors them over us.

Ralph Simon, age 65, executive vice president of the company, had direct responsibility for Rondell's production department. He said:

There shouldn't really be a dividing of departments among top management in the company. The president should be czar over all. The production people ask me to do something for them, and I really can't do it. It creates bad feelings between engineering and production, this special attention that they [R & D] get from Bill. But then Hunt likes to dabble in design. Schwab feels that production is treated like a poor relation.

The Executive Committee

At the executive committee meeting of December 6, it was duly recorded that Dave Schwab had accepted the prints and specifications for the Model 802 modulator, and had set Friday, December 29, as the shipping date for the first 10 pieces. Bill Hunt, in the chairperson's role, shook his head and changed the subject quickly when Frank tried to open the agenda to a discussion of interdepartmental coordination.

The executive committee itself was a brainchild of Rondell's controller, Len Symmes, who was well aware of the disputes that plagued the company. Symmes had convinced Bill Hunt and Ralph Simon to meet every two weeks with their department heads, and the meetings were formalized with Hunt, Simon, Ron Porter, Dave Schwab, Frank Forbus, Doc Reeves, Symmes, and the personal director attending. Symmes explained his intent and the results:

Doing things collectively and informally just doesn't work as well as it used to. Things have been gradually getting worse for at least two years now. We had to start thinking in terms of formal organization relationships. I did the first organization chart, and the executive committee was my idea too—but neither idea is contributing much help, I'm afraid. It takes top management to make an organization click. The rest of us can't act much differently until the top people see the need for us to change.

I had hoped the committee especially would help get the department managers into a constructive planning process. It hasn't worked out that way because Mr. Hunt really doesn't see the need for it. He uses the meetings as a place to pass on routine information.

Merry Christmas

"Frank, I didn't know whether to tell you now, or after the holiday." It was Friday, December 22, and Frank Forbus was standing awkwardly in front of Bill Hunt's desk.

"But, I figured you'd work right through Christmas Day if we didn't have this talk, and that just wouldn't have been fair to you. I can't understand why we have such poor luck in the engineering director's job lately. And I don't think it's entirely your fault. But . . ."

Frank only heard half of Hunt's words, and said nothing in response. He'd be paid through February 28 ... He should use the time for searching . . . Hunt would help all he could . . . Jim Kilmann was supposed to be doing well at his own new job, and might need more help . . .

Frank cleaned out his desk, and numbly started home. The electronic carillon near his house was playing a Christmas carol. Frank thought again of Hunt's rationale: conflict still plagued Rondell—and Frank had not made it go away. Maybe somebody else could do it.

"And what did Santa Claus bring you, Frankie?" he asked himself.

"The sack. Only the empty sack."

6

Artisan Industries

Artisan Industries was a $9-million-a-year, family-run manufacturer of wooden decorative products.

It was approaching its first fall sales season since last year's successful turnaround under the direction of the new 29-year-old President, Bill Meister. Last fall had begun with a year-to-date loss of $125,000 and, through Meister's actions, had ended with a $390,000 profit. This had been the first profit in several years and capped a challenging eight months for the new president.

Meister had hired his first man while his father was still president, bringing in 27-year-old Bob Atwood from the local office of a "Big Eight" firm to begin modernizing the accounting system. On June 10, 1977, Bob was in Bill's office for further and, he hoped, final discussion of plans for this fall season. Artisan's sales were quite seasonal, and on June 10, there were about two more months during which production would exceed sales. Atwood, concerned with the company's limited capital, proposed a production plan to hold the inventory build-up to $1.6 million, or about twice the level shown on the last full computer listing.

The president, based on his feel for conditions after the successful 1976 season and viewing sales in the first weeks of 1977, believed total sales for this year would really beat Bob's estimate of the same as last year's and reach $9 million. But he would like to have stronger support for his opinions; a lot rested on this estimate. If sales were much beyond their plans he could expect to lose most of them and create difficulties with his customers. New customers might even be lost to the competition. Bill was also concerned with developing contingency plans for dealing effectively with the potential oversold condition. Besides getting more production from the plants at the last minute, there might be good ideas that involved the customers and salespeople. For example, if all orders couldn't be filled, should some be

Reprinted by permission of Frank C. Barnes, Associate Professor, University of North Carolina at Charlotte.

fully shipped and others dropped, or should all be shipped 75–95 percent complete? Overall in 1976 orders had been shipped 75 percent complete and during the peak months this had fallen to 50 percent. Partial shipments might be a way to keep everyone happy. If orders are canceled should they be the ones from the small "mom and pop" stores or the large department stores? The small stores are more dependable customers, but on the other hand large department stores systematically evaluate suppliers on their order completion history. Also the department store buyers must commit funds when they place an order, thus their resources are idle until the order is filled. There are potential benefits from good communications, for if you inform the buyer of any delay quickly he can cancel that order and order something he can get. Such sensitivity to the customer's needs could win the company many friends and aid Meister in building a desirable reputation. On the other hand, poor communication could cause the opposite. Meister wondered if there was some way to usefully involve the salespeople, many of whom had left a sales representative organization six months earlier to work solely for Artisan.

After about mid-August total annual sales were limited to what had been built up in inventory beforehand and production through mid-November. Thus holding back now put a lid on total sales for the season.

If, on the other hand, the sales plan was not reached there could also be serious consequences. Last year after the fall sales period the inventory loan had been paid off for the first time since the 1960s. This had made a very favorable impression on the lending institutions and brought a reduction in the high interest rates (from 12 percent to 10¼ percent). They considered Bill a "super-star," with his youth, professional appearance, and modern ideas, and their fears for the Artisan loan were diminishing. Trouble at this time might erase all this and suggest last year was just a fluke.

If sales didn't materialize, inventories could be held down by cutting back on production. But Bill believed the plants operate inefficiently during any cutbacks and such moves very likely saved nothing. He held a similar opinion of temporary second shifts. In many past years over-production early in the year had resulted in big layoffs in December and January and in the financial drain of carrying over large inventories. Meister was highly interested in building an effective work environment for people at Artisan, where attitudes were historically poor. The employees—workers and supervisors—had little exposure to "professional" managers and had much to learn. The long process had been begun, but a layoff now could undermine all his efforts and, he felt, lose him what little confidence and support he had been able to encourage.

The strategy for this fall was of critical importance to Bill and his hopes for Artisan and his future.

Artisan's History

Artisan Industries is the product of a classical entrepreneur—W. A. (Buddy) Meister. After a variety of attempts at self-employment, such as running a dry-cleaning shop, a food shop, and an appliance store, he began to have some success making wooden toys. One try in 1950 with his father and brothers failed, leaving Buddy with an old tin building and some worn-out equipment.

During the next few years Buddy put his efforts into making a collection of 10 to 15 toys, sold via direct mail, house-to-house, on television, and on the roadside, all without a sales representative. One day a visiting gummed-tape salesman offered to take on the line and a pattern of using outside sales reps was established.

The first attempt at a trade show was a last-minute entry into the regional gift show 40 miles away. Out of sympathy for Buddy, Artisan was allowed to pay the $25-a-week rent after the show. Buddy brought home $3,000 in sales but lacked the money to produce them until a friend offered a loan. The orders were produced in a dirt-floor barn. In the following months, Buddy and his wife drove off to other markets, showing the goods in their motel room.

In 1953, sales reached $15,000, then climbed to $30,000 in 1954, $60,000 in 1955, and $120,000 in 1956. Then in April the plant, or barn, burned down destroying everything. With hardly a delay, Buddy jumped into rebuilding and sales continued to double. In 1958, success allowed Artisan to move into a 30,000-square-foot building and continue using its two old buildings for finishing and shipping. Then in March of 1960, these two burned down. Again Buddy fought back and sales doubled into 1961. The rate of growth slowed to 50 percent in 1962.

The third and most disastrous fire occurred in February 1963. The entire main plant was burned to the ground with the exception of the new office, which stood under one foot of water and was damaged by smoke and water. The company was in the middle of manufacturing its show orders and the only thing saved was the inventory in the paint shop. All the jigs were burned, and before work could begin, new jigs and patterns had to be made. "Only the plant in Spencer, built only a year before, saved us. The entire operation, with the exception of the office, was moved to Spencer, and working three shifts, we were able to keep most of the 200 employees. Many employees worked night and day for approximately six months to help us get on our feet again." Before Christmas of 1963, the company was back in full operation in the main plant.

Sales reached $4 million in 1967 and $8 million in 1972. During that six-year span, Buddy's five children reached ages to begin full-time jobs in the company. The youngest, Bill, was last to join. Typical of the youngest, he had it best, having all the "toys" his father could provide. He attended Vanderbilt, where he majored in business administration and the "good life." But his good time was at last interrupted by graduation and retirement to Artisan.

Bill wanted no major role in the company but over the next three years found himself getting more involved. Buddy had developed no modern management systems; accounting was ineffective, sales was in the control of outside reps, manufacturing was outdated and unprofessional. The lack of order fit Buddy's style—close personal control and manipulation. As the company problems increased, family conflict intensified. Bill's older brother lost the support of his father and the support of the other side and left. Bill moved up to the role of spokesman for a change.

In early 1975, though sales were booming, the financial situation at Artisan was "tight." A second shift was in operation, though production was generally inefficient. By October, sales had slackened and in November, to hold inventories down, layoffs began. Accounts receivable were worsening and the worried bankers were forcing the company to pay off some of its $2.5 million loan. The inventory was reduced some and accounts payable were allowed to increase. In December, the plant was closed for three weeks and $100,000 in cash was raised through a warehouse sale. But in the end, 1975 closed with a loss of over a million dollars.

As 1976 began, the sales picture looked bad. Even with the large inventory there was difficulty shipping because it contained the wrong things. Since it tied up capital, production of salable items was limited. There were more layoffs and shut-downs in January. Some old suppliers cut off the company's credit. In February, under the threat of the local bank calling the loan, Bill and Bob negotiated a new loan with a New York firm. This was composed of an inventory loan with a ceiling of $500,000, an accounts receivable loan of up to $1 million, and a long-term loan on the warehouse and real estate of approximately $350,000. "The package was finalized and the funds transferred about one week prior to payment deadline with the Bank. Had we not completed the deal with the other group, there was no way we could have made the $25,000 payment," according to Bill.

As the troubles deepened in the spring, Buddy had few solutions and, worse, blocked Bill's actions. The atmosphere in the company became grim. As Bill put it: "It became a fight between who was going to make decisions about what. Through the spring the conflict between us continued at a heightened pace. The effect was that most people became very nervous because no one understood who was really in control. With the company in the financial condition it was then, the last thing it needed was a power struggle over who should be in charge. So in April I went to Buddy and explained the situation that the company needed one person who was clearly in authority and in control, that one person would be better than two, and that I felt that he should leave or I should leave. He suggested that since he had gotten there first, I should leave." Bill went to the mountains for good.

But two weeks later, under pressure from the lenders, Buddy stepped aside and Bill became the chief executive.

In May 1976 when Bill Meister became president, Artisan was in critical condition. Sales had fallen off dramatically, there had been little profit for three years, the number of employees had fallen from 600 to 370, modern management systems existed in no area of the company, and there were few qualified managers. "When I took over, sales were running 50 percent off and we could not get a line of credit through our suppliers, we were on a cash basis only, inventory was still relatively high, accounts receivable were running over 120 days, manufacturing was without anyone in charge, and the company was sustaining a loss of approximately $10,000 a week. The general situation looked pretty hopeless."

Bill Meister's First Year as President

When Bill became president in May, changes began. Although Bill controlled many of the changes, others were the result of actions by his managers or outside forces. By mid-summer of 1976, he had reestablished contact with a business professor he particularly respected at his alma mater and was in regular contact with a management professor at a local school. The small number of trained managers, their lack of experience, and the absence of cooperation among them were serious handicaps to his rebuilding effort. He hoped interaction with the professors would make up for the lack of inside managers to interact with.

Exhibit 6–1 shows the organization chart in June 1977. Buddy moved up to chairman, but remained around the office. Bill's sister Edith and Uncle Sam helped in the sales area. Another sister, Sally, worked for Bob Atwood in accounting. A new man, Will Shire, was over production, mainly Plant One. Two long-term men, Charles Scott and Jack Lander, headed the plants. Two other long-term employees were in management: Cal Robb over the computer and Richard Bare over purchasing. A young man, Richard Barnes, had been hired recently for plant engineering. Paul Morgan had been with Artisan about two years in design.

Marketing

The company was one of four making up the wooden decorative products industry. Sales were seasonal, peaking with the Christmas period. Artisan's customers were some 13,000 retail shops that were serviced by outside sales representatives. Regional market shows were an important part of the marketing activity. The product line consisted of over 1,400 items and included almost anything for the customer. The largest item was a tea-cart and the smallest a clothespin-type desk paper clip. New products were continually coming up; about 100 a year were added to the line. Practically no items were ever dropped. The top 100 products averaged 5,000 units a year. The first 25 items had double the sales units of the next group. Two hundred and fifty sold over 1,000 units. The average wholesale price was $3.75. The top item sold 31,000 units last year for about $75,000 in sales. The 200th had sales of over $10,000.

Marketing was the function where Bill wanted to spend most of his time. His father had

Exhibit 6–1 ■ Organization Chart—Artisan Industries—June 1977

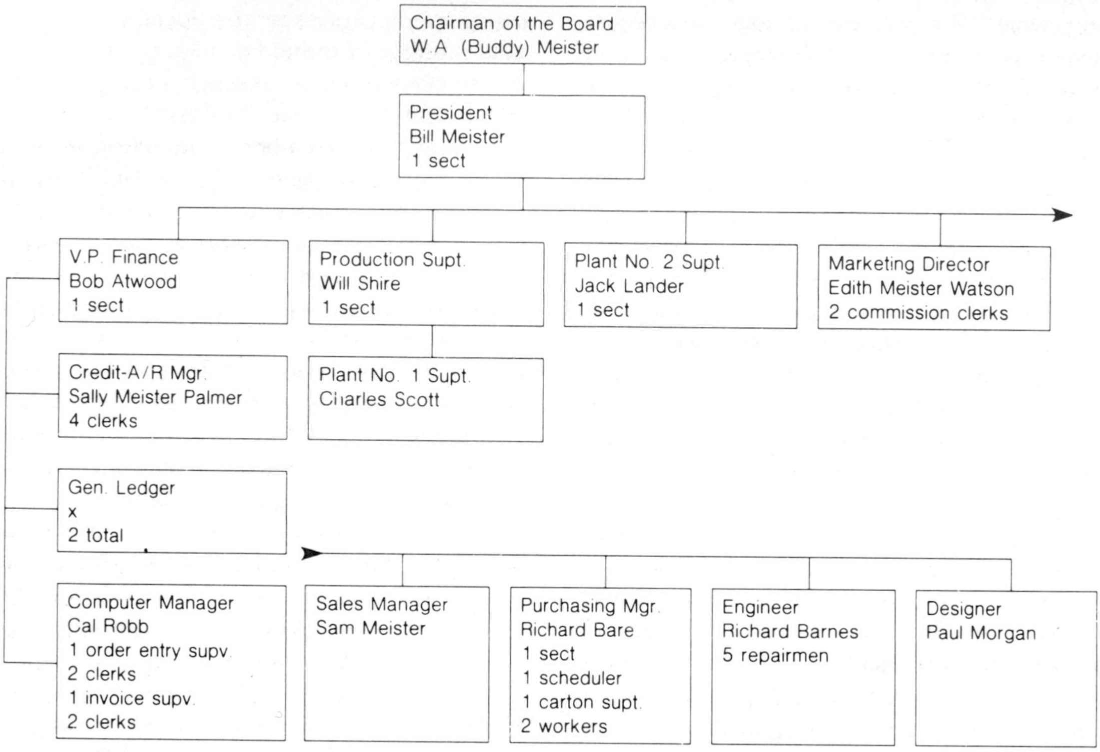

left this mainly with outsiders, but Bill was determined to put the company in charge of its own marketing. He attended all shows and found out firsthand what was going on. He felt the outside sales reps had let Artisan slide into making anything they could sell easily, regardless of costs and profits.

Bill hired a local young man with good design talent, but little experience, to set up a design department. They soon came up with a new "theme" line of items that became the talk of the industry, and Bill planned to try others. He engaged a New York advertising agency for a professional program of advertising in the trade journals and publicity in the newspapers. He produced an artistic catalog with color photographs rather than the dull listing used before.

There had been no price increases in quite a while, and with the recent inflation Atwood estimated the current sales prices would not yield a profit. In mid-October, an immediate price increase appeared imperative if 1976 was to end with a profit. But there was great concern about the advisability of such action in the middle of the major sales season. Also, waiting on new price lists to institute the increase in an ordinary manner would not accomplish a 1976 profit; orders already acknowledged or in-house but not yet acknowledged exceeded what could be shipped. In fact, as Bill, his sister Edith from sales, Bob Atwood, the computer manager, Cal Robb, and the university professor met to decide what to do, a 30-page order from one store chain for $221,000 at the old prices sat in front of them. Bob and Cal took the position that no further orders should be acknowledged until the customer had been written that prices were increased and asked to mail a reconfirmation if they still wanted the goods. Edith felt the price increase was very risky and would be very difficult to implement at this time, if even possible. But she had difficulty explaining her views and Bob, with Cal, out-talked her. Bill listened to their arguments as little was accomplished. Only when the consultant added his weight to Edith's views and pointed out the manipulation and lack of good problem solving did any practical ideas develop.

A 16 percent price increase was instituted immediately. The orders awaiting acknowledgment were examined that afternoon, and on a priority basis the salespeople were called and informed of the necessity of the increase and asked to contact their customers for immediate approval. When possible, and with moderation, orders at the new prices were given priority over those at the old prices. Within a few days, the new prices were contributing to profits.

Bill's most aggressive move was to cancel, in November 1976, the company's long agreement with E. Fudd Associates, a sales representative firm. Accounting for 60 percent of their sales, Fudd, with 50 salespeople, had handled Artisan's business in about 20 states for many years and had even lent the company money during the previous December. But Fudd was an old-style "character" much like Buddy—and Bill had been unable to systematically discuss market strategies or improvement ideas with him. Bill felt the 15 percent commission Fudd was setting could be better used as 10 percent directly to the salespeople and 5 percent in a company-controlled advertising budget.

Bill had planned to deal with E. Fudd Associates after the first of the year. It would take careful action to break with Fudd and assist any reps wishing to go independent on Artisan's line. But an accidental leak forced Bill's hand in the middle of the critical sales season. Bill did not back off but broke with Fudd immediately. Fudd countered with suits against Artisan, threats of displacing Artisan's goods with others, claims of tossing Artisan out of major regional market shows, and even withholding unpaid commissions on salespeople going with Artisan. Fudd spread rumors of Artisan's impending bankruptcy and sued any sales reps leaving him. Though there were bad moments, Bill held firm, and in a few weeks it was over. Bill had gotten all the sales personnel he wanted, he was lined up for his own space in the critical shows, and the rumors were going against Fudd.

Accounting

With the hiring of Bob Atwood in the fall of 1975, improvement in the accounting systems began, though slowly. By the spring of 1977, the outside service bureau had been replaced by a small in-house computer to handle order entry and invoicing, including an inventory listing.

The small computer system was delivered in January 1977. Prior to that, $85,000 to $100,000 a year had been spent for assistance from the service bureau. This assistance had been primarily invoicing. After orders were manually checked for accuracy and credit, they went to the service bureau where a warehouse picking ticket was prepared. Then after shipment, a form went back to initiate the invoice. Besides invoicing, they produced a monthly statement of bookings and shippings that summarized activity by item, customer, and state. The bureau was not involved with accounts receivable; aging was a manual process that took 30 days and was possibly only accurate to within $25,000. In 1975, checks had been posted, taking about three hours per day, and then forwarded directly to the lender. This had added three to four days of work for Atwood.

The computer had caused a small management crisis for Bill. Cal Robb and Bob Atwood, neither of whom had any special knowledge or experience with computers, had selected the system they wanted with no help beyond that of computer salespeople. With only verbal agreements and several contract notebooks from the supplier, they pressured Bill for his approval. When he failed to act, they saw him as dragging his feet and lacking respect for their opinions. With the counsel of the university consultant, Bill took the unpopular step of sending them back to prepare a proper proposal and timetable. In work with the vendor, several serious omissions were found and corrected, and all agreed the further documentation had been worthwhile. Bill approved the project.

The new system consisted of a 48K "small" computer with a 450-line-per-minute printer, two disc drives with two million bytes each, and seven CRTs. Monthly rental amounted to about $4,000. The software was developed in-house by Robb using basic systems supplied by the vendor at no charge. Robb was the only staff for the computer. He was 36, with a business administration degree with some concentration in accounting from a good state university. Prior to Atwood's hiring, he had been controller.

By May, inventory accounting was on the computer. The inventory listings computing EOQs were available but inaccurate. Atwood believed a couple of months of debugging was necessary before computer inventory control would be possible. The data needed for the EOQ model were all old and inaccurate; lead times, prepared by a consultant years ago, were considered by all to be way off. They and the standards hadn't been studied in five to six years. For now, Atwood felt these listings would be of some help in operating the existing production scheduling system. (EOQ stands for the Economic Order Quantity inventory model.)

By June, invoicing was fully on the computer and the lender had stopped requiring the direct mailing of the checks. About 3,000 invoices were prepared each month. The A/R systems, including statements and weekly aging of delinquent accounts, were operational, and about 2,500 statements were being prepared monthly. The controller felt both systems were running well and providing for good control. The computer supplier felt they had been lucky to get the system operational as quickly as they did. (A/R means accounts receivable, A/P means accounts payable.)

Cal expects inventory control will be on the computer by February. In another month, he will add A/P payroll and general ledger. Production control must wait on others' work and input.

Monthly preparation of financial statements had begun in January. Production costing for the statements had been based on historical indices, but Bob reported little resulting error. The statements were out, in typed form, 30 days after the close of the period.

Production

There were two plants, roughly identical and five miles apart, each with about 60,000 square feet. Kiln dry lumber, mainly high-quality Ponderosa pine, was inventoried in truck trailers and covered sheds at the rear of the plant. The lumber width, totally random, depended on the tree, and the length was from 8 to 16 feet, in multiples of two. The thickness started at the lumber mill at four, five, or six "quarter" ("quarter" meaning one-quarter inch, therefore four quarters is one inch). By the time it reached the plant, it was about an eighth of an inch less.

The rough mill foreman reviewed the batch of production orders he was given about every week and decided on the "panels" the plant would need. A panel is a sheet of wood milled to a desired thickness and with length and width at the desired dimension or some multiple. Clear panels, ones with no knots, can be made from lower grade lumber by cutting out the defects and then gluing these smaller pieces into standard panels. Artisan did no such gluing but cut high-quality, clear lumber directly to the desired length and width. The necessary panels would be made up in the rough mill from lumber or from purchased glued panels. Artisan spent about as much on purchased panels as it did on raw lumber, paying about twice as much for a square foot of panel as for a square foot of lumber. Surfacers brought the wood to the desired thickness, the finished dimension plus some excess for later sanding. Rip saws cut the lumber to needed width and cut-off saws took care of the length. About 30 people worked in this area, which had about 12 percent of the labor cost.

The plant superintendent worked with the machine room foreman to decide on the sequence in which orders would be processed. Scheduled due-dates for each department were placed on the orders in production control but they followed up on the actual flow of orders only if a crisis developed. In the machine room 22 workers (17 percent of the labor cost) shaped panels to the final form. The tools included shapers, molders, routers, and borers. Patterns and jigs lowered the skill requirements, still the highest in the plant. This part of the plant was the noisiest and dustiest.

In the third department, sanding, the parts were sanded by women working mainly at individual stations. There were 24 people here. The sanded components were moved to a nearby temporary storage area on the carts, which originated at machining. It was estimated there were six to eight wooden parts in an average item. In addition, there were purchased parts such as turnings and glass or metal parts. Sanding added about 19 percent of the direct labor to the products.

The assembly foreman kept an eye on the arrival of all parts for an order. Assembly began when all parts were available. Eighteen people assembled the items using glue, screws, nail guns, or hammer and nails. Jigs assisted the work where possible, and usually only one person worked on an order. Fourteen percent of direct labor derived from this step. Little skill was needed and dust and noise weren't a problem.

The assembled items were moved promptly to the separate finishing area. Here they were dipped by hand into stains and sprayed with several clear coats. After oven-drying they proceeded to packing. Most were packed individually into cartons made in the company's small plant. Finishing and packing employed about 50 people and accounted for 34 percent of direct labor costs. The new 60,000-square-foot finished goods warehouse was two miles away.

The labor rates ranged from $2.65 to $5.60 per hour. The average was probably $3.00, with about a dozen people making over $4.00. Factory overhead was about 60 percent of direct labor. Labor costs as a percent of the wholesale selling price ran about 20 percent; direct material, 35 percent. Variable costs totaled about 75 percent, with about another $1.8 million in total company fixed costs. There was a three-percentage-point difference between the plants in labor costs. The capacity of the plant with 150 people working was estimated to be less than $110,000 a week. Indirect labor amounted to about 12 percent of plant overhead.

Most jobs did not require high skill levels. The average jobs in the rough mill and machine room, where the skilled jobs were, required no more than five weeks to master because the person would usually already have advanced skills. Elsewhere a week was adequate. Everyone but the supervisors and workers considered the work pace quite slow.

Production Scheduling

The production control department began the scheduling process. Exhibit 6–2 outlines the production scheduling system. About every week, sometimes longer, the clerk prepared a batch of production orders for each plant. Several factors determined when a batch of orders was prepared: whether the plants said they needed more work, how sales were doing, what the situation was in the warehouse, etc. The clerk examined the "Weekly Inventory Listing" for items that appeared low and the file of "Progress Control Charts" to see if the items were already on a production order. He converted the information to an available supply in weeks and selected any with less than eight weeks. If the total of orders gotten this way did not add up to an aggregate amount he had in mind, such as $60,000 to $100,000, he went back through the lists for more things to run.

"Production Sheets," or shop orders, were prepared for each item. These contained a drawing and a list of materials and process steps. The data were already prepared and came from consultant studies several years old. The order contained a date the part was due through each department based on standard lead times, for example, one week in the rough mill, three days in machining, etc. The actual

Exhibit 6–2 ■ Production Scheduling System

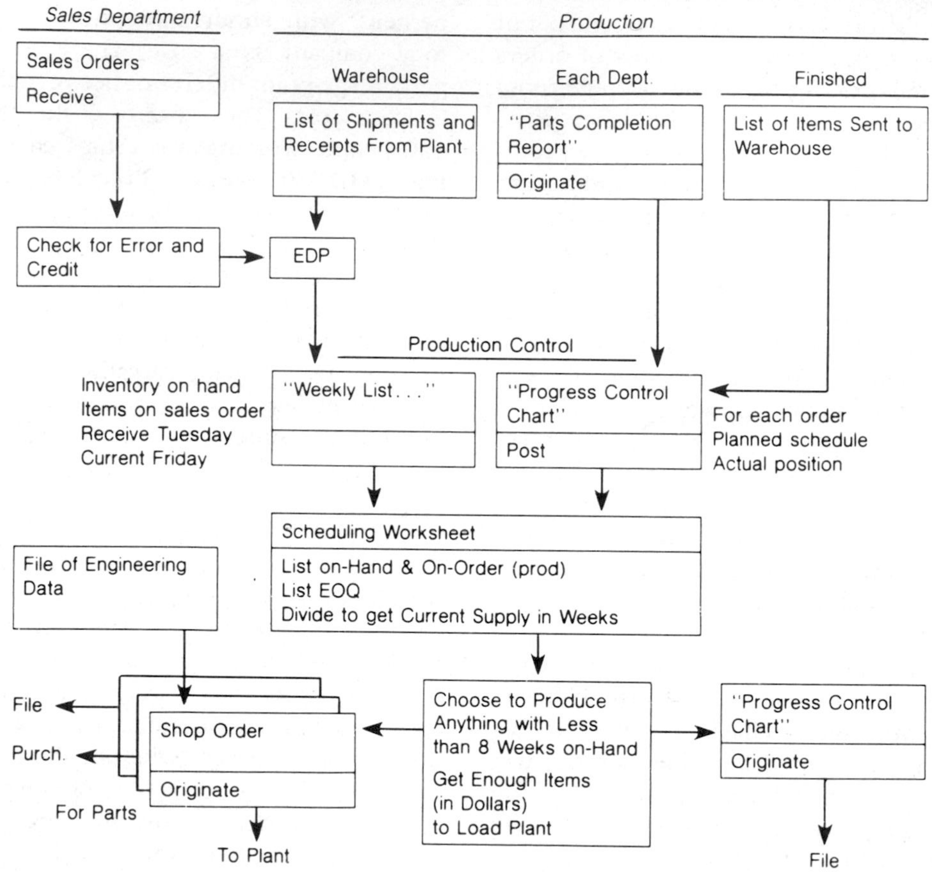

work in the plant at the time did not alter lead-times. At the same time, a "Progress Control Chart" was prepared for each order. These remained in production control to trace the flow of orders.

The batch of orders was then handed to the plant superintendent who decided exactly how the items would be run. Daily each department gave production control a "Parts Completion Report," listing production from that department—order number, part number, and number produced. The production control clerk posted this information to the "Progress Control Charts." This reporting cycle used to be every two hours. The clerk reported these charts were not actually used to control production progress; they aided in locating an order if a question arose, but one still had to go out on the floor to be sure.

A brief look at the inventory listing for December showed the first 20 items were 23 percent of the inventory value. The tenth group of 20 items was 2 percent of inventory; the cumulative value to this point was 82 percent. The fortieth item had $1,800 in inventory and the two-hundredth, $625.

Turning through the notebook for Plant One "Process Control Charts" on one day showed almost 300 open orders, perhaps 30 percent to 50 percent of them past the due date. Several items had two or even three different production orders two weeks or so apart. The order size appeared to average 200 at most. One in 10 was for more than 250 pieces. Only a couple were for 500 or more; the maximum was 1,000 pieces. The typical items appeared to contain about six parts, and each took three to five processing steps.

The engineer was trying to estimate standards for new items as they were priced. A quick look at eight of them showed a total of 1,800 minutes of set-up time for the eight and a total of 6,400 minutes per 100 units of runtime. The set-up times ranged from 100 to 250 minutes for the products, but several of the parts required no set-up in some departments and where there was set-up it amounted to 25 percent to 50 percent of the run time for 100. Many parts required less than 30 minutes of processing in a department. The lot size on these ranged from 100 to 200 units; seven were priced around $4 and one at $25.

Production Problems

Bill feels production efficiency is a major problem. In talks with machinery salespeople and other visitors to the plant over recent years, Bill has come to feel the machinery is generally appropriate. But based on guesses about his competitors, he feels his labor costs must be reduced. Earlier attempts to work with the plant superintendents and the various supervisors to systematically improve output met with no success. The supervisors had been unable to identify the needs for change in the plant or to develop the programs for bringing about improvement. To help the supervisors begin to improve their operations, a weekly production meeting was begun in June 1976. At the meeting, the supervisors were to examine the total dollar output and total labor cost for each plant for the past week, compare it to the labor percent goal of 16 percent, set by Bill, and think about what could be done to improve operations for the coming week. Data on department performance was not available. During the first several meetings, the visiting consultant had to provide direction and ideas; the plant superintendent and his supervisors volunteered no ideas about what specifically limited last week's output. Bill reported that some discussion of problems began three or four months later. It was Bill's opinion that this kind of thinking and planning was not required under his father's management. The supervisors in general felt nothing was wrong in the plant and really seemed puzzled at the thought of doing anything except continuing what they had always done.

In March 1977, after a good deal of thought and search, Bill hired two young men for the production system. One man, Will Shire, aged 28, was hired to be general superintendent over everyone in production, and the other, Richard Barnes, aged 27, was to be manufacturing engineer. It appeared the plant simply needed good management rather than any single big change that could be brought from the outside. Both of these men were young, college trained, and experienced in a wood industry.

Significant resistance from the old superintendent and most of the supervisors seemed probable. Consequently, the new men were briefed on this problem. As expected, things did not advance smoothly. Even as the new men gained familiarity with the operation, no significant changes were observed. The expected complaints and rumors were heavy, and Bill ignored them as best he could. However, after three months on the job, the complaints still persisted and, more importantly, the new superintendent did not appear to have command of the situation. He had not developed his appraisal of what needed to be done and had no comprehensive plan for improvement. Bill recently received very good evidence that Will had some major difficulties in supervising people. One of the supervisors who did not appear to be a part of the rumor campaign and was conscientiously concerned about the company gave Bill examples of the new man's mistakes. Bill felt he may have made a mistake in hiring Will.

Richard's responsibilities have also been narrowed to more technical tasks. He is supervising the five-person repair crew, engineering some of the new products, examining the procedures for producing samples of new products, and beginning to examine a major redesign of the rough-mill area.

Major Competitor's Production

The major competitor is Sand Crafters, Inc. A managerial person familiar with both operations provided these comments. Demand for Sand Crafters' products exceeded their capacity, and this, in the person's opinion, was the main reason Artisan existed. Its sales were somewhat less than Artisan's, they had no debt, and its equipment was described as new. It was located in a small community where the workers were relatively skilled for this kind of business. The work force was primarily white male. The manager characterized the Artisan worker as about two-thirds as good as Sand Crafters. The workers in the third company in the industry were rated as one-half as good. The quality of manufacture of Sand Crafters was considered first, Artisan second, and the third company a close third. Sand Crafters' weakness was in poor engineering of the products and an outdated approach to marketing. Sand Crafters schedules long runs in manufacturing with the objective of having three months' stock of top priority items. It does not use the EOQ Model because it is limited in its work-in-process space.

In describing the Artisan manufacturing system, the person noted that two-thirds of the equipment is idle at any time and that neither capacity nor optimum production mix have yet been determined. The largest run size he claimed to have seen had been 250. Setup costs he estimated to average $30. He commented that this was the least directed operation he had ever seen, with the slowest pace and the lowest level of knowledge of this type of work. He felt its employees knew only the simple way of doing the job. Only one man in the company, for example, was able to count the board feet of lumber, and there was no lumber rule in the plant. He stated that this was a skill that the smallest cabinet shop would have and that it was essential for any kind of usage control.

The Workforce

Bill was greatly interested in the newest concept of management, frequently pointing to the latest book or sending a copy of an article to his managers or anyone with whom he was interacting. The behavioral writings made a lot of sense to him, and he was very perceptive of behavioral processes in meetings or situations. The participative management systems and cooperative team environments were ones Bill wanted for Artisan. However, he recognized his managers and the work force were not ready for this yet. His managers manipulated more than cooperated, and the workers were neither skilled nor very productive. When he discussed the workers' desires with the supervisors, he was told they wanted a retirement program and higher pay, nothing else. Bill felt this was really what the supervisors themselves wanted.

As a basis for beginning change in this area, an outside consultant conducted an employee attitude survey in May 1977. All employees in the company were assisted in small groups in completing the written questionnaire. The questionnaire was designed: (1) to find out what they wanted, for example, more pay, retirement plans, more or less direction, etc.; (2) to gain insight into the probable impact of participative management moves; (3) to establish benchmarks of employee satisfaction so that changes over time could be monitored; (4) to develop an objective profile of the workers; and (5) to look for significant differences in attitudes between the various stratifications possible.

The survey included questions developed specifically for this situation as well as a highly regarded attitude instrument, the Job Descriptive Index (JDI). Although the wording is considered simple, many of the workers did not understand such words as "stimulating," "ambitious," or "fascinating," and it became necessary to read the entire questionnaire to them.

The study showed minorities accounted for 80 percent of the 300 employees; white females were the largest group at 40 percent. The work force was 58 percent female, 57 percent white, and 39 percent over 45 years old. As many people have been with the company under two years as over 10 years—24 percent. The pay was only a little above the legal minimum, but many workers felt fortunate to have their jobs.

Exhibit 6–3 ■ Summary of JDI Scores by Level (Percentile)

			Attitude toward:				
Group	**Number**	**Overall**	**Co-worker**	**Work**	**Supervision**	**Promotion**	**Pay**
(Maximum score)		25	54	54	54	27	27
Total company	318	17.4	41.2	32.3	40.4	11.1	7.1
Management	7	15.9	38.0	39.4	48.0	18.7	15.9
(%)			(35)	(60)	(70)	(80)	(55)
Office	18	16.6	45.8	36.6	47.4	6.9	7.7
(%)			(60)	(50)	(65)	(50)	(25)
Supervision	13	19.7	46.8	39.2	46.1	16.1	12.2
Plant No. 1 hourly	141	17.1	40.4	31.6	38.4	11.7	6.6
Plant No. 2 hourly	101	18.1	39.8	31.3	42.6	11.0	5.9

There did not appear to be a "morale" crisis; the five JDI measures located the company in about the middle of the norms. The supervisory group was highest in "morale," while management was lowest.

Exhibit 6–3 summarizes the Job Descriptive Index scores. The numbers in parentheses show the norms.

Employees were also questioned about a number of aspects of their work climate that could be improved. Exhibit 6–4 shows these questions.

Their expressed view of the organizational climate was relatively good. They claimed to enjoy their work, looked for ways to improve it, and felt they were expected to do a good job. They especially felt that their co-workers were good to work with and felt part of a team. They appeared to like their supervision.

Their views did not suggest need for a different manner of supervision. And they did not respond positively to the suggestions of being more in charge of themselves, did not feel strongly about having more of a say in how things are done, and did not feel there were too many rules.

The survey revealed no critical problems, differences between groups were not extreme, and the resulting view of the worker was moderate. However the workers were relatively unsophisticated, and there was concern they might not have expressed themselves on the instrument.

The Meeting with Bob on June 10

The last months of 1976 had been very good in spite of fears caused by the price increase and the changes in the sales organization and had resulted in a $390,000 profit. Bob Atwood reported that the original plan for 1977 had been for no major changes—a regrouping, doing as in late 1976, just better. However, there was no formal written plan. As actual sales in January and February ran well ahead of the prior year, production was allowed to stay higher than the plan. Bill believed Bob's estimate of sales at $6.5 million was very low. A quite conservative estimate, he felt, was $9 million. This level became accepted as the premise for production planning in the first part of the year. But March and April were disappointing and May was only fair. Bill still felt the $9 million was reasonable, as the normal retail sales patterns had been upset by inflation and the fuel crisis. But he recognized the risks and was concerned. He hoped the gift shows in July would settle what 1977 would hold.

Exhibit 6–4 ▪ Results of Attitude Survey: May 1977

What is Your Opinion on the Following Statements? Do You Agree or Disagree?	Average Employee Response
I enjoy taking the test.	3.97
My pay is fair for this kind of job.	2.26
My co-workers are good to work with.	4.14
My complaints or concerns are heard by management.	3.22
Things are getting better here.	3.45
The supervisors do a poor job.	2.35
I am fortunate to have this job.	3.95
Working conditions are bad here.	2.55
I benefit when the company succeeds.	3.11
I have all the chance I wish to improve myself.	3.19
The company is well run.	3.29
Communications are poor.	2.91
I don't get enough direction from my supervisor.	2.56
I enjoy my work.	4.13
I look for ways to improve the work I do.	4.21
I need more of a chance to manage myself.	3.11
I don't expect to be with the company long.	2.35
Morale is good here.	3.55
We all do only what it takes to get by.	2.19
I am concerned about layoffs and losing my job.	3.51
I like the way my supervisor treats me.	4.02
We need a suggestion system.	3.75
I want more opportunity for advancement.	3.86
My supervisor knows me and what I want.	3.56
We are not expected to do a very good job here.	2.01
There are too many rules.	2.58
I feel like part of a team at work.	3.82
The company and my supervisor seek my ideas.	3.06
I can influence department goals, methods, and activities.	3.01
There is too much "family" here.	2.77
This company is good for the community.	4.22

5 = Strongly agree
1 = Strongly disagree

On June 10, 1977, Bob Atwood had returned to Bill's office to press for some decision on the inventory level. He wanted Bill to pull back on plans for 1977. As sales had been slower coming in and inventories had increased more than expected, Bob had become increasingly worried. The level on the last full inventory listing prepared about six weeks before stood at $800,000 in wooden goods. The current level was nearer $1.1 million. From a financial perspective, Bob was willing to accept a level as high as $1.6 million. But this called for limiting production now. His report dated May 13 presented several alternative production levels for the fall, comparing particularly $600,000 and $720,000 per month. The advantages and disadvantages of $600,000 versus $720,000 production levels are as follows:

Advantages and Disadvantages

Advantages of $600,000 production level:

1. Reduces scope of operation to afford high degree of control.
2. Maintains positive cash flow position for remainder of year.
3. Maintains more liquid corporate position.

Disadvantages of $600,000 production level:

1. More customer dissatisfaction from possible low service level.
2. Probable lost sales if orders increase.

Advantages of $720,000 production level:

1. High service level to accounts.
2. Low probability of decrease in service if orders increase.

Disadvantages of $720,000 production level:

1. Risk of inventory buildup.
2. Risk of being in a layoff situation if orders do not increase.

He advocated a $60,000 per month level.

Bob recommended they immediately cut production and make Richard Bare, the purchasing agent, production control manager with the responsibility for guiding the controlled inventory buildup. Since the desired total inventory level of $1.6 million was twice the level shown on the last computer listing that included recommended run sizes (EOQs), he felt they could use this part of the computer system as a guide in selectively increasing the inventory. They could double either the Re-Order Points (ROPs) or the lead times in the computer, return the report, and use the new EOQs to double the inventory in a balanced form. Bob felt there had been unnecessary delay in making a decision and was impatient for Bill to put this to rest without further delay.

7

Organizational Diagnosis Questionnaire

Instructions for Use of the ODQ

Goals

I. To assist participants in understanding the process of organizational diagnosis.

II. To show participants how the various formal and informal aspects of an organization work together.

III. To provide participants with a method for understanding the functioning of the internal environment of an organization.

Group Size

May be administered individually or in small groups of six to eight. May be used with students as a training tool or as part of an organizational analysis.

Time Required

Approximately two hours.

Materials

I. A copy of the Organizational Diagnosis Questionnaire (ODQ) and score sheet for each participant.

II. A newsprint flip chart or chalk board for the instructor.

Physical Setting

A room large enough so that individuals/groups can work undisturbed. Movable chairs should be provided.

Process

Step I. Introduction (10 min.)
The instructor announces the goals of the activity, distributing copies of the ODQ, its score sheet and the associated handout. The participants are instructed to read the handout.

Step II. Overview (15 min.)
The instructor presents an overview of the Weisbord Six-Box Organizational model, provides examples, and elicits questions.

The ODQ and its introduction were prepared by Robert C. Preziosi. Reprinted from: J. William Pfeiffer & John E. Jones, (Eds.), *The 1980 Annual Handbook for Group Facilitators,* San Diego, CA: University Associates, Inc., 1980. Used with permission.

Step III. Complete the ODQ (30 min.)
Participants are told to think of an organization with which they have some knowledge. This can be a firm where they have worked, a club to which they belonged, etc. They are told to think of that organization as they respond to the items on the ODQ.

Step IV. Score the ODQ (10 min.)
After completing the ODQ, the instructor explains the scoring system, and participants score their own questionnaire.

Step V. Small Group Discussion (15 min.)
Participants are then asked to form small groups and discuss why the organizations they analyzed came out the way they did.

Step VI. Change Strategies (10 min.) (Optional)
Participants are asked to think of activities they might instigate in their organizations to change some of the negative issues that surfaced in their analysis.

Step VII. Large Group Discussion (20 min.) (Optional)
Instructor brings the entire group together and solicits volunteers to discuss the specifics of their particular organization.

Introduction to the Questionnaire

Both internal and external organization development (OD) consultants at some point in the consulting process must address the question of diagnosis. Recently the need for two levels of diagnosis, preliminary and intensive, was addressed (Lippitt & Lippitt, 1978). The purpose of the Organizational Diagnosis Questionnaire (ODQ) is to provide survey-feedback data for intensive diagnostic efforts. Use of the questionnaire eieither by itself or in conjunction with other information-collecting techniques (such as direct observation or interviewing) will provide the data needed for identifying strengths and weaknesses in the functioning of an organization and/or its subparts. The questionnaire produces data relative to informal activity.

A meaningful diagnostic effort must be based on a theory or model of organizational functioning. This makes action research possible as it facilitates problem identification, which is essential to organization development. One of the more significant models in existence is Weisbord's (1976) Six-Box Organizational Model (Exhibit 7–1). Weisbord's model establishes a systematic approach for analyzing relationships among variables that influence how an organization is managed. It provides for assessment in six areas of formal and informal activity: purposes, structure, relationships, rewards, leadership, and helpful mechanisms. The outer circle in Exhibit 7–1 determines an organizational boundary for diagnosis. This boundary clarifies the functioning of the internal environment, which is to be analyzed to the exclusion of the external environment.

The Instrument

The Organizational Diagnosis Questionnaire is based on Weisbord's practitioner-oriented theory. The ODQ generates data in each of Weisbord's suggested six areas as well as in a seventh, attitude toward change. This item was added as a helpful mechanism for the person involved in organizational diagnosis. In attempting any planned-change effort in an organization, it is wise to know how changeable an organization is. Such knowledge helps the change agent understand how to direct his efforts.

Thirty-five items compose the ODQ, five in each of the seven variables. Respondents are asked to indicate their current views of their organization on a scale of 1 to 7, with a score of 4 representing a neutral point.

Uses of the ODQ

The ODQ can be administered to a work unit, an entire organization, or a random sample of each. It might also be used to analyze staff or line functioning as well as to assess the thinking of

EXHIBIT 7–1 ■ The Six-Box Organizational Model[1]

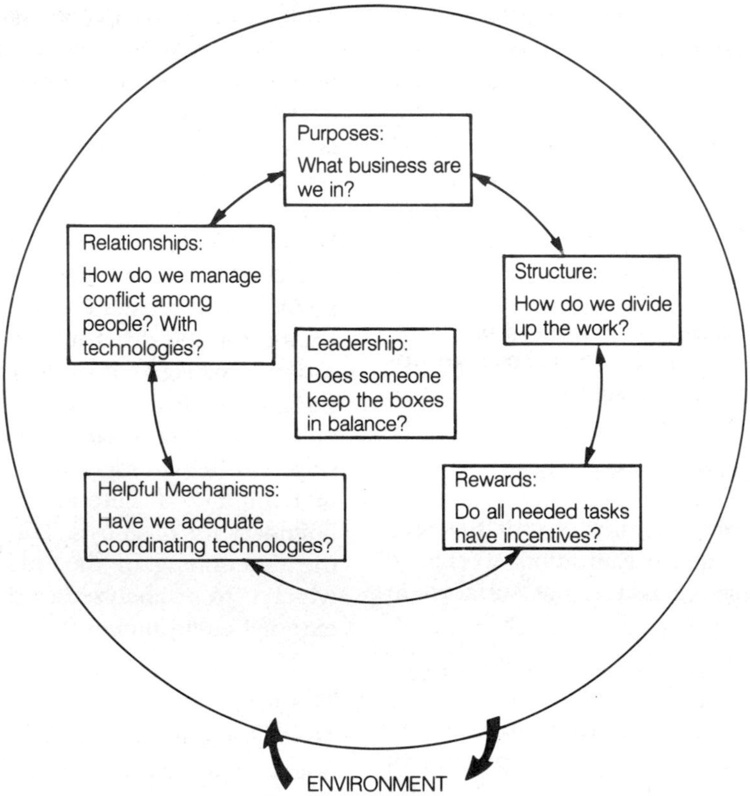
Purposes:
What business are we in?
Relationships:
How do we manage conflict among people? With technologies?
Structure:
How do we divide up the work?
Leadership:
Does someone keep the boxes in balance?
Helpful Mechanisms:
Have we adequate coordinating technologies?
Rewards:
Do all needed tasks have incentives?
ENVIRONMENT

[1]Reproduced from M. R. Weisbord, Organizational diagnosis: Six places to look for trouble with or without a theory. *Group & Organization Studies, 1976, 1* (4), 430–447, by permission of the publisher and the author.

different levels of management or supervision. It should be administered by the consultant or process facilitator in order to insure that an adequate explanation of the questionnaire and its use will be given. The consultant could also train others to administer the questionnaire.

■ ***Administration and Scoring*** The administrator of the questionnaire must emphasize to the respondents that they be open and honest. If they are not, data that yield an inaccurate assessment of the organization on any or all of the seven variables may be produced. All ODQ statements are positive and can easily be discerned as such, which may influence the manner in which the respondents react to the questionnaire.

Scoring the questionnaire may be done in more than one way. Aggregate data will be most useful; an individual's set of responses is not significant. A self-scoring sheet is provided for each individual. Individual scoring sheets could then be tabulated by the consultant, an assistant, or, for large-scale studies, a computer.

■ ***Processing the Data*** Once aggregate data have been collected, they must be processed. The first task is to prepare a bar or line graph (or any similar technique) to present the data so that they can be readily understood. The consultant-/facilitator should present the data first to the organization's president or the work unit's supervisor (whichever is applicable) to establish understanding, commitment, and support.

Next, a meeting with the work group is essential. During this meeting, the consultant/facilitator must weave a delicate balance between task and maintenance issues in order to be productive. During this meeting, a number of things take place: information is presented (feedback); information is objectively discussed; group problem solving is encouraged; brainstorming for solutions is facilitated; alternative solutions are evaluated against criteria; a solution is chosen; an action plan is developed; and a plan for future evaluation is determined. This process is presented in detail in Hausser, Pecorella, and Wissler (1977).

The ODQ produces information about the informal system. As Weisbord suggested, the formal system must be considered also. A consultant/facilitator may review an organization's charter, operations manual, personnel policies, etc. Gaps between the two systems lead to a diagnosis of what is not happening that should be happening, or vice versa.

In sum, the ODQ is useful for diagnostic efforts insofar as it provides data about people's perceptions of their organization. It is an instrument that may be used separate from or in addition to other information-collecting techniques.

References

Hausser, D. L., Pecorella, P. A. & Wissler, A. L. *Survey-guided development: A manual for consultants.* San Diego, CA: University Associates, 1977.

Lippitt, G., & Lippitt, R. *The consulting process in action.* San Diego, CA: University Associates, 1978.

Weisbord, M. R. Organizational diagnosis: Six places to look for trouble with or without a theory. *Group & Organization Studies,* 1976, 1(4), 430–447.

Organizational Diagnosis Questionnaire

From time to time organizations consider it important to analyze themselves. It is necessary to find out from the people who work in the organization what they think if the analysis is going to be of value. This questionnaire will help the organization that you work for analyze itself.

Directions: Do not put your name anywhere on this questionnaire. Please answer all thirty-five questions. *Be open and honest.* For each of the thirty-five statements, circle only *one (1)* number to indicate your thinking.

1—Agree Strongly
2—Agree
3—Agree Slightly
4—Neutral
5—Disagree Slightly
6—Disagree
7—Disagree Strongly

1. The goals of this organization are clearly stated.
   1 2 3 4 5 6 7
2. The division of labor of this organization is flexible.
   1 2 3 4 5 6 7
3. My immediate supervisor is supportive of my efforts.
   1 2 3 4 5 6 7
4. My relationship with my supervisor is a harmonious one.
   1 2 3 4 5 6 7
5. My job offers me the opportunity to grow as a person.
   1 2 3 4 5 6 7
6. My immediate supervisor has ideas that are helpful to me and my work group.
   1 2 3 4 5 6 7
7. This organization is not resistant to change.
   1 2 3 4 5 6 7
8. I am personally in agreement with the stated goals of my work unit.
   1 2 3 4 5 6 7
9. The division of labor of this organization is conducive to reaching its goals.
   1 2 3 4 5 6 7
10. The leadership norms of this organization help its progress.
    1 2 3 4 5 6 7
11. I can always talk with someone at work if I have a work-related problem.
    1 2 3 4 5 6 7
12. The pay scale and benefits of this organization treat each employee equitably.
    1 2 3 4 5 6 7
13. I have the information that I need to do a good job.
    1 2 3 4 5 6 7
14. This organization is not introducing enough new policies and procedures.
    1 2 3 4 5 6 7
15. I understand the purpose of this organization.
    1 2 3 4 5 6 7
16. The manner in which work tasks are divided is a logical one.
    1 2 3 4 5 6 7
17. This organization's leadership efforts result in the organization's fulfillment of its purposes.
    1 2 3 4 5 6 7
18. My relationships with members of my work group are friendly as well as professional.
    1 2 3 4 5 6 7
19. The opportunity for promotion exists in this organization.
    1 2 3 4 5 6 7
20. This organization has adequate mechanisms for binding itself together.
    1 2 3 4 5 6 7
21. This organization favors change.
    1 2 3 4 5 6 7

22. The priorities of this organization are understood by its employees.
    1 2 3 4 5 6 7

23. The structure of my work unit is well designed.
    1 2 3 4 5 6 7

24. It is clear to me whenever my boss is attempting to guide my work efforts.
    1 2 3 4 5 6 7

25. I have established the relationships that I need to do my job properly.
    1 2 3 4 5 6 7

26. The salary that I receive is commensurate with the job that I perform.
    1 2 3 4 5 6 7

27. Other work units are helpful to my work unit whenever assistance is requested.
    1 2 3 4 5 6 7

28. Occasionally I like to change things about my job.
    1 2 3 4 5 6 7

29. I desire less input in deciding my work-unit goals.
    1 2 3 4 5 6 7

30. The division of labor of this organization helps its efforts to reach its goals.
    1 2 3 4 5 6 7

31. I understand my boss's efforts to influence me and the other members of the work unit.
    1 2 3 4 5 6 7

32. There is no evidence of unresolved conflict in this organization.
    1 2 3 4 5 6 7

33. All tasks to be accomplished are associated with incentives.
    1 2 3 4 5 6 7

34. This organization's planning and control efforts are helpful to its growth and development.
    1 2 3 4 5 6 7

35. This organization has the ability to change.
    1 2 3 4 5 6 7

ODQ Scoring Sheet

Instructions: Transfer the numbers you circled on the questionnaire to the blanks below, add each column, and divide each sum by five. This will give you comparable scores for each of the seven areas.

■ ***Purposes***

1 ________
8 ________
15 ________
22 ________
29 ________
Total ________
Average ________

■ ***Structure***

2 ________
9 ________
16 ________
23 ________
30 ________
Total ________
Average ________

■ ***Leadership***

3 ________
10 ________
17 ________
24 ________
31 ________
Total ________
Average ________

■ ***Relationships***

4 ________
11 ________
18 ________
25 ________
32 ________
Total ________
Average ________

■ ***Rewards***

5 ________
12 ________
19 ________
26 ________
33 ________
Total ________
Average ________

■ ***Helpful Mechanisms***

6 ________
13 ________
20 ________
27 ________
34 ________
Total ________
Average ________

■ ***Attitude Toward Change***

7 ________
14 ________
21 ________
28 ________
35 ________
Total ________
Average ________

ODQ Profile and Interpretation Sheet

Instructions: Transfer your average scores from the ODQ Scoring Sheet to the appropriate boxes in the figure below. Then study the background information and interpretation suggestions that follow.

Background

The ODQ is a survey-feedback instrument designed to collect data on organizational functioning. It measures the perceptions of persons in an organization or work unit to determine areas of activity that would benefit from an organization development effort. It can be used as the sole data-collection technique or in conjunction with other techniques (interview, observation, etc.).

Weisbord's Six-Box Organizational Model (1976) is the basis for the questionnaire, which measures seven variables: purposes, structure, relationships, rewards, leadership, helpful mechanisms, and attitude toward change. The first six areas are from Weisbord's model, while the last one was added to provide the consultant/facilitator with input on readiness for change.

The instrument and the model reflect a systematic approach for analyzing relationships among variables that influence how an organization is managed. The ODQ measures the

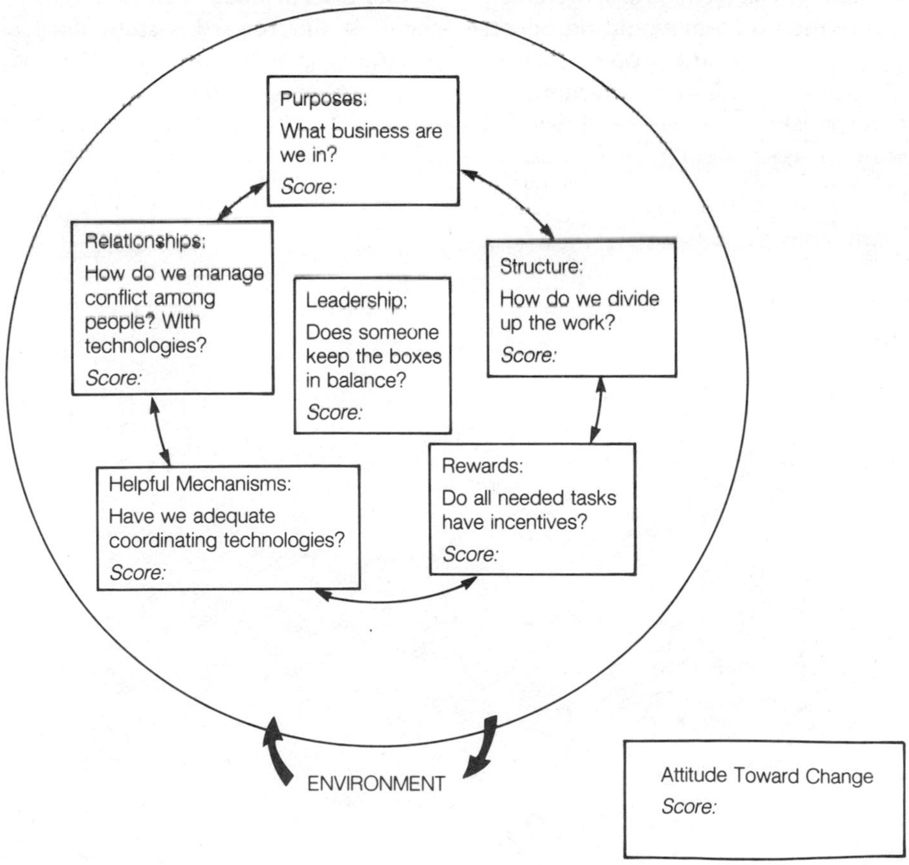
Purposes:
What business are we in?
Score:
Relationships:
How do we manage conflict among people? With technologies?
Score:
Leadership:
Does someone keep the boxes in balance?
Score:
Structure:
How do we divide up the work?
Score:
Helpful Mechanisms:
Have we adequate coordinating technologies?
Score:
Rewards:
Do all needed tasks have incentives?
Score:
ENVIRONMENT
Attitude Toward Change
Score:

informal aspects of the system. It may be necessary for the consultant/facilitator also to gather information on the formal aspects and to examine the gaps between the two.

Using the ODQ is the first step in determining appropriate interventions for organizational change efforts. Its use as a diagnostic tool can be the first step in improving an organization's or work unit's capability to serve its clientele.

Interpretation and Diagnosis

A crucial consideration is the diagnosis based upon data interpretation. The simplest diagnosis would be to assess the amount of variance for each of the seven variables in relation to a score of 4, which is the neutral point. Scores above 4 would indicate a problem with organizational functioning. The closer the score is to 7 the more severe the problem would be. Scores below 4 indicate the lack of a problem, with a score of 1 indicating optimum functioning.

Another diagnostic approach follows the same guidelines of assessment in relation to the neutral point (score) of 4. The score of each of the thirty-five items on the questionnaire can be reviewed to produce more exacting information on problematic areas. Thus diagnosis would be more precise. For example, let us suppose that the average score on item number 8 is 6.4. This would indicate not only a problem in organizational purpose, but also a more specific problem in that there is a gap between organizational and individual goals. This more precise diagnostic effort is likely to lead to a more appropriate intervention in the organization than the generalized diagnostic approach described in the preceding paragraph.

Appropriate diagnosis must address the relationships between the boxes to determine the interconnectedness of problems. For example, if there is a problem with relationships, could it be that the reward system does not reward relationship behavior? This might be the case if the average score on item 33 was well above 4 (5.5 or higher) and all the items on relationships (4, 11, 18, 25, 32) averaged above 5.5.

II

DESIGN AND STRUCTURE

Bureaucracy

Technology

Structure

8

The Clorox Company

As a part of his regular procedure for reviewing the health of the company's marketing operation, John S. Hanson, group vice president of the Clorox Company, decided to take a look at the brand management system through the eyes of an impartial outsider. How, in other words, would a nonmarketing, nonconsumer product observer see the Clorox system? How would the observations be interpreted, and what were the implications of these observations in respect to the selection of new brand managers?

To this end, an engineering manager enrolled in the Stanford Sloan Program was given permission during the spring of 1977 to interview throughout the company and to write up his impressions.

History of the Company

The Electro-Alkaline Company of Oakland, California, began commercial production of liquid chlorine bleach in 1913. The initial markets for this new product were limited to laundries, breweries, walnut wood bleachers, and municipal water companies. These companies used the product for bleaching, stain removing, deodorizing, and disinfecting. The original form of the product was a much more concentrated solution than is currently available on the retail market. In 1941, the "Clorox" brand name was registered; the company's diamond trademark was registered the following year; and in 1922, the firm changed its name to Clorox Chemical Corporation. During its first eight years of business, the company achieved distribution in the Pacific Coast states and Nevada and initiated eastern U.S. distribution with the appointment of a distributor in Philadelphia. Advertising was begun in 1925 in 20 western newspapers and four farm journals. In 1928, the company was reorganized as Clorox Chemical Company and common stock was issued for the first time. By 1939, the company operated production facilities in Oakland, Chicago, and Jersey City. By

1955, 10 additional plants were in operation around the country. In 1953, the Clorox Company initiated spot television advertising.

In 1957, the Procter & Gamble Company acquired Clorox Chemical Company, but within three months, the FTC charged Procter & Gamble with attempting to lessen competition among household bleach manufacturers. Shortly thereafter, the FTC ruled that Procter & Gamble had to divest itself of Clorox. Litigation continued until 1968, when the Supreme Court upheld the FTC ruling. Directly after the Supreme Court ruling, the Purex Corporation, manufacturer of the principal competitor of Clorox liquid bleach, filed suit against Procter & Gamble, charging that the company's acquisition of Clorox violated antitrust laws.

During 1968, Procter & Gamble divested itself of Clorox by offering for sale 15 percent of Clorox stock and subsequently offering the remaining 85 percent to Procter & Gamble shareholders on the basis of 3.85 shares of Clorox stock for each share of Procter & Gamble stock. The stock was listed on the New York Stock Exchange in August, and in January 1969, Clorox began operations as an independent company. (See Exhibit 8–1 for relevant data regarding Clorox's operations during the period 1968 to 1977.)

Product Expansion

Until 1969, the Clorox Company made and sold only one product, Clorox liquid bleach. With the exception of one unsuccessful introduction of a general-purpose household cleaning solution, Boon, in 1946, the company's new product introductions consisted of minor variations of its basic brand of liquid bleach or of package modifications.[1]

[1]The basic product was never changed, although changes in the strength of the bleach solution were attempted.

After the divestiture by Procter & Gamble, however, Clorox management began to implement a previously adopted program of growth that called for the development of: (1) a line of nonfood household products, (2) a line of specialty food products, and (3) a line of food and nonfood products for the food service industry.

The company planned to seek acquisitions to accelerate its sales and earnings growth. At the same time, it would strengthen existing brands and, over the long term, expand its business through internal development of new products.

The first step toward a broadened line of retail consumer products was the acquisition of Jiffee Chemical Corporation, manufacturer of Liquid-plumr drain opener. This was closely followed by the Acquisition of Formula 409 Spray Cleaner from Harrell International. Exhibit 8–2 presents the proliferation of Clorox-owned brands.

The expansion into the food service line began several years later. In 1972, Clorox acquired the Martin-Brower Company, a distributor of disposable packaging items, food and nonfood products, and restaurant supplies to fast-food restaurants and institutions. The Clorox Company also established the Clorox Food Service Products Division to market institutional versions of its retail brands. (See Exhibit 8–3 for Clorox performance on the three basic groups.)

As new companies were acquired, they often maintained their organizational integrity within the Clorox corporate structure. Indeed, in several instances newly acquired companies were treated as separate profit centers. The corporate organization underwent various revisions during the first few years after the Clorox divestiture from Procter & Gamble. (See Exhibit 8–4 for the current organization of the Clorox Company.)

In the 1973 annual report, Clorox President Robert Shetterly informed stockholders that he was de-emphasizing acquisitions as a means of further product expansion during the short-term and that emphasis would be placed on

Exhibit 8–1 ■ Clorox Company Performance, 1968–1977

	Year Ending June 30			
	1977	1976	1975	1974
Net sales*	$872,817.00	$822,101.00	$721,505.00	$537,601.00
Net income*	32,265.00	27,262.00	21,150.00	19,656.00
Earnings per share (primary)	1.44	1.22	0.95	0.88

*In thousands of dollars.
†Reflects two-for-one stock split effective November 1972.

utilizing internal resources for new product development. As a step toward this objective, the company moved to supplement its R&D capabilities by signing a 10-year agreement with Henkel KGaA of West Germany in 1974. Henkel is the second-largest European producer of detergents, cleaners, and related products. It subsequently acquired a minority equity position in Clorox by purchasing 20 percent of the company's outstanding shares. Under the terms of the agreement, Clorox is licensed to market Henkel-developed products on a royalty basis in the United States, Canada, and Puerto Rico and has access to Henkel technology for developing new products. Clorox agreed to pay Henkel minimum royalties of $1 million per year, beginning in 1976. These payments will be credited against future royalties earned by Henkel on products marketed by Clorox.

In the 1977 annual report, Shetterly announced that Clorox once again was looking for suitable acquisitions to build the company's business. At the same time, he said, Clorox

Exhibit 8–2 ■ Product Expansion, Clorox Company 1969–1977

Brand Name	Description	Source of Development	Year Acquired or Marketed
Liquid-plumr	Drain opener	Acquisition	1969
Clorox 2	Nonchlorine, dry oxygen bleach	Internally developed	1969
Formula 409	General-purpose household cleaner	Acquisition	1970
Formula 409	Disinfectant bathroom cleaner	Acquisition	1970
Litter Green	Cat box filler	Acquisition*	1971
BinB Mushrooms	Canned mushrooms, broiled in butter	Acquisition	1971
Kitchen Bouquet	Flavoring sauce	Acquisition	1971
Cream of Rice	Hot cereal	Acquisition	1971
Hidden Valley Ranch	Salad dressing mixes	Acquisition	1972
Kingsford	Charcoal briquettes and barbecue products	Acquisition	1973
Prime Choice	Steak sauce	Internally developed	1973
Mr. Mushroom	Mushrooms in natural cooking juices	Internally developed	1973
Cooking Ease	Natural vegetable cooking spray	Acquisition	1974
Salad Crispins	Seasoned croutons	Acquisition	1974
Soft Scrub	Mild-abrasive liquid cleanser	Internally developed	1977

*Patents and concepts for institutional products were purchased, and these were subsequently developed into consumer products.

Year Ending June 30					
1973	1972	1971	1970	1969	1968
$412,631.00	$188,203.00	$145,866.00	$98,212.00	$85,365.00	$85,854.00
26,922.00	19,252.00	15,031.00	12,010.00	11,173.00	11,411.00
1.23†	2.15	1.68	1.48	1.40	1.43

*In thousands of dollars.
†Reflects two-for-one stock split effective November 1972.

would seek opportunities to expand its liquid bleach market internationally.

Clorox ventured into the international sphere in 1973, when it set up a Canadian marketing operation that eventually would sell most of the company's retail products as well as a line of household cleaners and personal products marketed in Canada under the French Maid brand name. That same year, Clorox acquired Country Kitchen Foods, England's leading mushroom-growing and -marketing company. In 1975, the company began bleach production in its first offshore plant, in Puerto Rico. In addition, in the period between divestiture from Procter & Gamble and 1975, the company had developed export markets for liquid bleach in about 30 countries and had licenses that produced Clorox in Latin America and the Middle East.

The Brand Management System

Clorox has been a strong supporter of brand management. In 1977, the marketing operation

Exhibit 8–3 ■ Clorox Performance, 1972–1977, by Basic Lines of Business (dollars in millions)

	Year Ending June 30					
	1977	1976	1975	1974	1973	1972
Net sales:						
Retail consumer products						
Nonfood products	$342.5	$308.7	$268.1	$223.8	$225.8	$167.6
Specialty food products	63.7	59.7	56.7	44.0	25.8	20.6
Subtotal	406.2	368.4	324.8	267.8	251.6	188.2
Food service industries	466.6	453.7	396.7	269.8	161.0	—
Total	$872.8	$822.1	$721.5	$537.6	$412.6	$188.2
Income:*						
Retail consumer products	$ 74.6	$ 55.0	$ 43.4	$ 32.8	$ 46.9	$ 41.5
Food service industries	3.6	5.8	7.5	7.2	5.5	—
Total	$ 78.2	$ 60.8	$ 50.9	$ 40.0†	$ 52.4	$ 41.5

*Income before taxes on income and before allocation of corporate expenses not directly attributable to a specific line of business.
†Does not reflect one-time loss from discontinued operations.

Exhibit 8–4 ■ Clorox Company Organizational Diagram

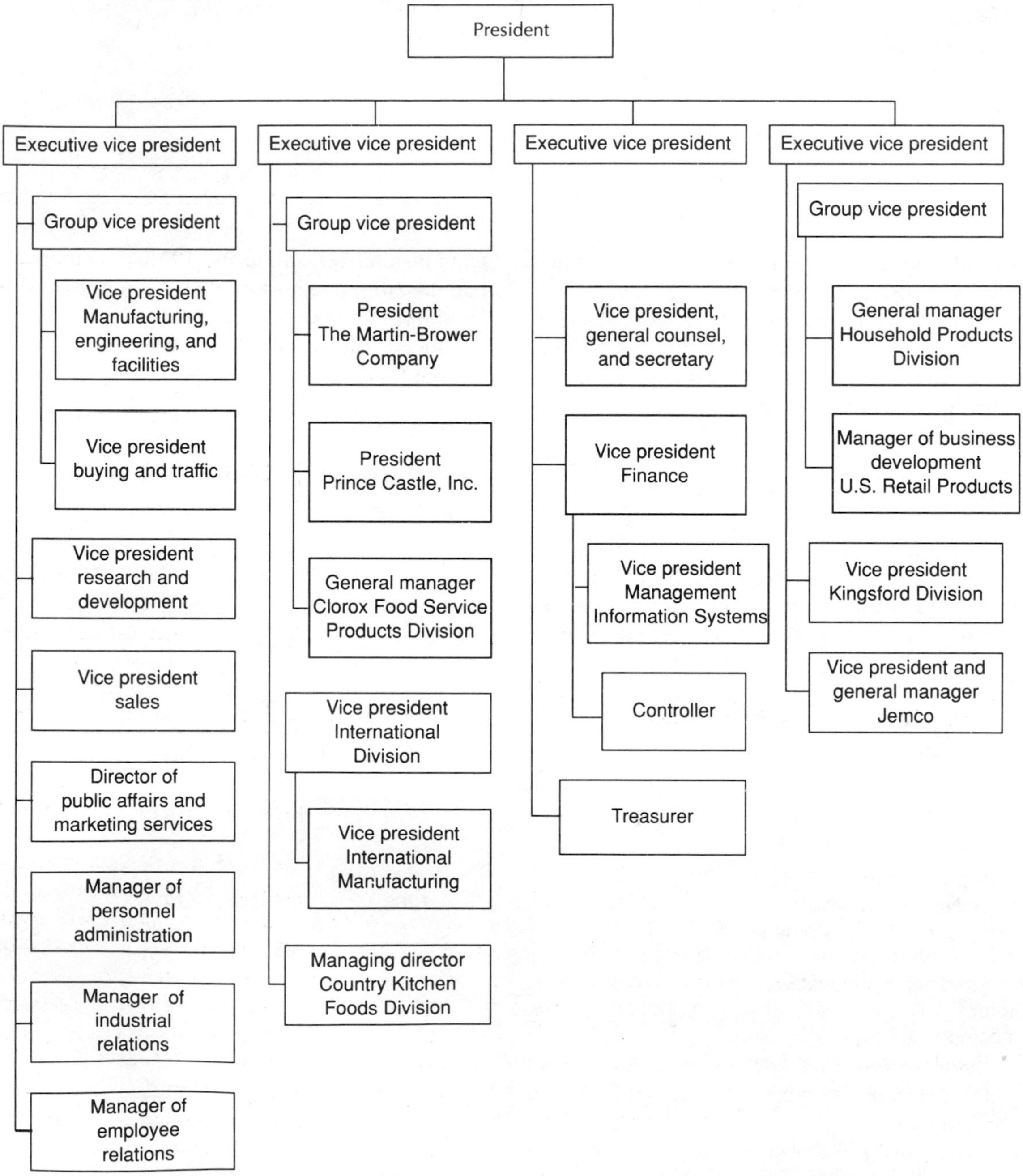

Exhibit 8–5 ■ Organization of Clorox Household Products Division

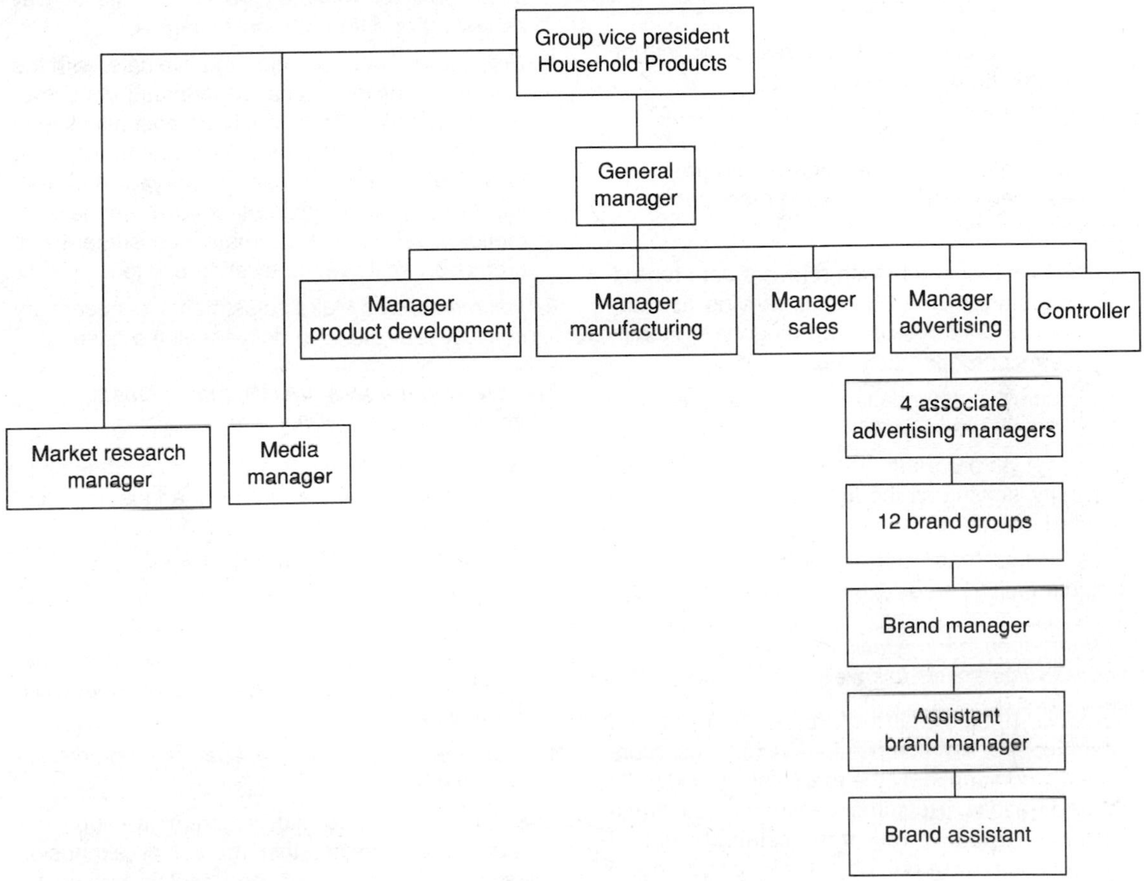

in the Household Products Division was organized as shown in Exhibit 8–5.

Although a bit unusual from an orthodox organization point of view, it is useful for the reader to think in terms of two subdivisions below general manager—"brand" and "all other." The significance of this dichotomy, which will be explained shortly, underlies the heart of the Clorox system.

There were five job levels in the brand system: brand assistant (BA), assistant brand manager (ABM), brand manager (BM), associate advertising manager (AAM), and advertising manager (AM). The focus of this case is on the brand manager and lower levels, i.e., assistant brand manager and brand assistant. (See Exhibits 8–6, 8–7, and 8–8 for relevant job descriptions.)

Although this case does not deal extensively with the AM and AAM levels of management, it is useful to know the overall roles these managers play. The AM manages all aspects of marketing, except sales execution, for the division. This manager's key objectives are not only achievement of short-term volume and profit goals but also development, testing, and expansion of new products, improved products, and line extensions. These latter goals are heavily emphasized by top management because they ensure continued corporate growth. The AAMs largely serve coordinating, controlling, training, and strategic overview roles between the AMs

Exhibit 8–6 ▪ Job Description: Clorox Brand Manager

Function. To contribute to the overall growth of Clorox through development, recommendation, and implementation of effective marketing programs capable of building brand volume, share, and profit for assigned brands. The brand manager is charged to:

a. Provide management with relevant data regarding the state of the business, serving as management's antennae in the category to identify problems and opportunities.
b. Develop recommendations which are designed to stimulate brand growth.
c. See that all programs are coordinated and run properly, serving as the focal point for all brand-related activity.
d. Ensure that brand personnel learn the skills to handle multifaceted responsibilities of the job.

The brand manager's specific marketing responsibilities are as follows:

1. *Product.* Ensure that the product and package are superior to competition within cost constraints demanded by the marketplace and profit considerations. Requires consumer usage/attitude and product research, establishment of product improvement objectives, and periodic review of progress toward these objectives.
2. *Positioning.* Position the product to maximize volume within the existing consumer and competitive environments. Periodically review marketing strategy in light of changing consumer needs, wants, and attitudes and competitive product positionings and sales. Develop and test alternative copy and promotion strategies attuned to the marketing strategy to improve the brand's overall positioning.
3. *Copy.* Ensure that copy provides the optimum selling power. Demands an ongoing effort in development and testing of new copy pools, different executional formats, and alternative copy strategies.
4. *Media.* Ensure that media plans are designed to deliver advertising in the most effective and efficient manner against the brand's target audience. Requires periodic review of target audience criterion and testing of alternative mixes of media vehicles within budget constraints, as well as testing of different media weights.
5. *Promotion.* Plan, execute, and evaluate, with the assistance of the Sales Department, consumer and trade promotions which are cost effective in increasing brand volume. Demands testing of a variety of promotions each fiscal year and testing, on a periodic basis, alternative annual promotion levels and/or alternative consumer/trade promotion splits within existing budgets.
6. *Volume control.* Make adjustments as necessary in fiscal year plans to deliver volume base.

The brand manager's specific management information responsibilities are as follows:

1. *Volume.* If fiscal year overshipment or undershipment seems obvious, inform management and recommend action.
2. *Competitive developments.* Report significant competitive activity and recommend defensive action.
3. *Product problems.* Analyze and recommend action on any product or package problems which threaten volume.
4. *Problem markets.* Identify, analyze, and propose remedial action.
5. *Schedule changes.* Advise promptly when delays from expected test market or expansion dates are encountered, and explain reason for delay.
6. *Costs/P&A.* Report significant shifts and recommend action (e.g., price increase).
7. *Governmental actions.* Report on any legislative or regulatory activities that could affect the business and recommend action.

Exhibit 8–7 ▪ Job Description: Clorox Assistant Brand Manager

Marketing responsibilities:

1. *Business building plans.* Develop, recommend, and execute those key projects which, long term, will have a major effect on the shipments/consumption of the brand. Examples of these are

the introduction of new sizes/products, major distribution building programs, or major trial-generating promotions.

2. *Copy.* Work with the brand manager in providing direction to the advertising agency in the development of new executional formats (based on current strategy) and the testing of new copy strategies/executions. Also, work with Technical and Legal to obtain copy clearance/claim/support.
3. *Media.* In conjunction with the brand manager, provide the agency with direction on new ways to more efficiently reach the brand's target audience. This may take the form of media mix tests or testing of different media levels.
4. *Product.* Ensure that a product which fulfills consumer needs and wants is marketed within cost constraints.
5. *Market research planning and analysis.* Initiate and analyze those market research projects which will yield information upon which the brand may act to improve current market position or correct an ongoing problem.
6. *Package design.* Ensure that the package in the marketplace is appealing, eye-catching, and connotes those attributes of the product most important to consumers.

Management information:

1. *Market research.* Analyzes research and recommends next steps to correct any problems or capitalize on any opportunities.
2. *Media.* Analyzes results of media testing and recommends action to be taken.
3. *Schedule changes.* Informs brand manager of delays in the progress of key projects in order that management may be apprised of the delay and the reason why.

Exhibit 8–8 ■ Job Description: Clorox Brand Assistant

Marketing responsibilities:

1. *Sales promotion.* Plans, in consultation with other Brand group members and the Sales Department, national and test promotions. Writes promotion recommendations and issues related feasibility requests and production orders. Implements consumer-oriented portions of promotions (coupon copy and media, sample drops, etc.) and oversees and/or cooperates with Sales Department in implementing trade-oriented portions of promotions (preparation of organizers, selection of salesman's incentives, etc., etc.). Controls all budgeting for promotions. Evaluates promotions.
2. *Budget administration and control.* Reviews and codes invoices. Reconciles the budget with Accounting on quarterly basis. Closes out budget with Accounting at the end of the fiscal year.
3. *Market analysis.* Analyzes Nielsen data and writes bimonthly Nielsen reports. Audits other sources of market information (monthly shipment reports, SAMI's, etc.) and writes analytical reports as necessary.
4. *Shipment estimates.* In consultation with assistant brand manager and/or brand manager, prepares monthly shipment estimate which forecasts next three months' shipments with supporting rationale.
5. *Competitive activity.* Monitors competitive activity reported by Sales (promotion and pricing activity), agency (competitive media spending), and other sources (periodicals, etc.). Writes reports on significant developments.
6. *Public relations.* Cooperates with Consumer Services in handling special consumer-oriented problems which fall outside normal Consumer Services activities. Works with Research Services (home economists) and Public Affairs on brand-related consumer information projects.

Other areas where brand assistants may contribute, depending upon individual brand assignments, are as follows:

1. *Package design.* Development of design objectives. Interfaces with package designers, marketing services, and technical staff on development, consumer testing, and feasibility determination on design. Recommendation, implementation, and evaluation of any test market.
2. *Business-building tests.* Works with assistant brand manager and/or brand manager on one or more of the following aspects of business-building tests—planning, recommendation, implementation and evaluation.

Management information—reports to brand manager on:

1. *Competitive activity.* Significant competitive developments.
2. *Budget variance.* Any variations from budget forecasts.
3. *Promotion problems.* Any problems with implementation of promotions.
4. *Consumer relations.* Any product problems which threaten volume.

---

and the BMs. They also have final decision-making authority on promotion activities within existing budgets, and they handle many of the administrative jobs in the Advertising Department.

The entry-level job was that of BA. The BA was primarily responsible for monitoring the product budget, developing sales promotion, and analyzing market information (e.g., sales data from the company's management information system, consumption data from the A. C. Nielsen Company, and additional data from other outside market research services). New projects were added as competence was gained until the BA was sent out for "sales training," a 12-week field sales assignment.

Promotion to ABM followed this selling experience. Emphasis was placed upon learning advertising copy and media, developing long-term business-building programs, and assisting and helping train the BA in the area of sales promotion. ABM was a transition job that could last from one to two and a half years, depending on the capabilities of the ABM and the needs of the company.

When the ABM was promoted to BM, he[2] was given overall marketing responsibility for one or more products, including planning, forecasting, and controlling volume and spending for these products. He also supervised ABMs and BAs. Due to rotation and normal turnover, not all brand groups were fully staffed with a BA and an ABM.

In terms of day-by-day operations, the brand management group considered the other Clorox functions as "staff" to it. Hence, the earlier reference to "brand" and "all other." Nonetheless, it must be recognized that brand had no direct authority over sales, manufacturing, market research, and product development. But it did have the responsibility to obtain from staff the inputs necessary to successful marketing. Each functional group, for this purpose, had a representative designated to deal with the brand manager. An integral part of this system of "responsibility without direct authority" was the fact that brand controlled budgets for areas such as market research and package design and represented staff's channel to top management. For example, a departmental request for information or specific action was typically directed to the brand manager who not only had to concur but was the interface with top management. Communication to top management, in other words, was generally through the brand groups. Perhaps the best summary of the brand manager's role is contained in Exhibit 8–9.

Climate

Clorox had been a Procter & Gamble (P&G) subsidiary from 1957 until separated by government order in 1969. The P&G influence pervaded Clorox. A number of top- and middle-management people had either stayed with Clorox after divestiture or had joined Clorox from Procter & Gamble. The P&G style of memo writing, job titles, and organization continued.

The brand management system had been very strong at P&G and continued to be strong at Clorox. The brand managers played a "line management" role within the marketing func-

[2]Although we use the masculine gender throughout this text rather than both masculine and feminine (e.g., he/she) to improve readability, the reader should assume that this refers to both female and male brand personnel

Exhibit 8–9 ■ Interface Matrix

Brand Manager Responsibilities	Work with These Departments	Brand Role
1. Product or package improvement	Sales, R&D, Market Research, Manufacturing, and Controller	*a.* Develop objectives for product or package development. *b.* Approve aesthetics. *c.* Develop consumer research objectives, fund research, and summarize results. *d.* Determine unit profit potential and return on investment. *e.* Recommend test market to management. *f.* Write manufacturing production orders for test market production of product. *g.* Analyze test market results and recommend national expansion.
2. Positioning	Advertising agency, Market Research, and Legal	*a.* Develop alternative positionings. *b.* Develop consumer research objectives and fund research. *c.* Analyze research results and recommend test market. *d.* Analyze test market results and recommend national expansion.
3. Copy	Advertising agency, Market Research, and Legal	*a.* Review agency copy submissions and select copy to be presented to management. *b.* Approve final production for on-air copy testing. *c.* Analyze copy test results. *d.* Recommend national airing of copy.
4. Media	Advertising agency and Media Services	*a.* Review agency media objectives and strategies and recommend alternatives. *b.* Review and modify agency media plans with help of Media Services. *c.* Forward agency media plan to management. *d.* With help of Media Services, monitor implementation of media plan.
5. Sales promotion	Sales, Manufacturing, Promotion Development, and Legal	*a.* Develop national promotion plan with help of Sales Department. *b.* Recommend plan to management. *c.* Write manufacturing production order for production of sales promotion product. *d.* Implement consumer portion of promotion (i.e., coupons, samples, etc.) and fund all trade allowances and consumer promotions.
6. Volume control	Sales	a. Monitor shipments. *b.* If undershipment of objectives seems possible, recommend remedial marketing efforts.

tion at Clorox. The reasoning for this was that the BM had direct responsibility for the most critical marketing factor—advertising—and had the broadest exposure to the operations of the company and the best overall perspective on his product and markets.

The BM was able to accomplish his goals through other people by using his control over the product budget, his position as the coordinator of all information, and his interpersonal skills. He had to be successful "at getting others to do the job."

But there was even more to the essential nature of the brand manager's job, a perspective that can only be expressed by senior management. These men looked upon brand managers as people who could be expected to ask the type of questions a top manager might ask, gather the facts necessary to make a decision, and then recommend a course of action in a very succinct memo. The net effect was that top management's job of managing the marketing of a large number of diverse brands in diverse categories became easier and more effective. The system assured that all brands, even those with small sales, were given attention and that a variety of marketing approaches designed to stimulate growth would at least be explored and recommended.

The power of the brand manager rested largely in his authority to ask questions anywhere in the company and demand carefully thought-out, responsible answers, as long as the questions and answers were limited to matters that either directly affected the consumer of his product or affected his brand's contribution margin (revenue less manufacturing and shipping costs and brokerage commission). In addition, the successful brand manager had informal authority arising from his superior knowledge vis-à-vis any functional specialist in the company of all consumer aspects of his product, and he had the power to discuss his recommendations (in writing usually) with top management.

Selection and Screening

Typically, brand assistants were recent MBAs from such schools as Stanford, Berkeley, Columbia, Northwestern, and Wharton, with minimum work experience, particularly in brand management. In recent years, Clorox had hired some graduates with advertising experience as well as some transferees from other Clorox departments, but these were exceptions. Brand managers were almost always promoted from within.

During the initial hiring process, Clorox sought individuals who were intelligent, trainable, competitive, aggressive, and hardworking. Ideal candidate qualities were generalized as: analytical ability; communication skills; the ability to plan, organize, and follow through; the ability to work well with others; leadership; resourcefulness and ingenuity; decision-making skill; drive and determination; and maturity.

Training

The introduction of the new brand assistant was strenuous. Although the initial jobs might range from planning promotions to writing market research summaries (see Exhibit 8–8), there was a lot of arduous "number crunching." Hours were long, often including weekends. There were no shortcuts or special courses and readings that could bypass this breaking-in period. Nor was there much sympathy for the neophyte. Everyone in brand had been through the same experience, recognized its necessity, and knew the work could be done. Help was mainly in the form of providing initial direction, pointing out errors, and suggesting new projects as competence increased. The newer projects were invariably more interesting and challenging, which provided additional incentive to master the earlier tasks. And as the new BAs were hired, the more mundane jobs could be passed down.

The purpose of this training was to internalize certain "first principles" which were considered necessary to maintain the brand management system:

1. *All information can be derived from numerical data.*

   Brand people have minimal contact with either customers or suppliers. Customers are normally represented by market research findings and sales results. Suppliers are represented by specific liaison people. Thus it follows that there must always be an analytic justification for a project or program. The results need to be reduced to cases of product and P&A (revenue minus all costs except advertising).

2. *Concern for mistakes.*

   Brand people are trained to be detail oriented and are concerned about not making errors. No mistake, particularly in a memo, was too small to be noticed. The feedback was intensive since memos were commented on in writing as they were passed up and down the distribution chain. If anyone found a mistake, then everyone who missed it was embarrassed.

3. *The budget is a critical device by which the brand manager exercises some basic control.*

   This first principle is a bit deceptive, however. It is true that some staff groups—Market Research, Sales Merchandising, and Package Design—are dependent upon brand for funding of projects, but it would be erroneous to conclude that brand uses the budget as a club. The range of interrelationships between brand and staff is too involved to be reduced to the single lever of money control.

4. *Career success requires the "Clorox Style."*

   The Clorox Style contributes to the climate and mystique which make brand management successful. This style includes dress, memo, format, job concept, and attitude. Memos conform to a particular writing style and format and are not supposed to exceed two pages without an attached summary. Brand people must be the resident experts on everything affecting their products. The BM thinks of himself as the general manager of a very small company. Nonetheless, brand people must maintain their aggressive, competitive attitude without hurting their relations with staff. The BA may achieve a basic competence in one to two years. This competence is recognized by the addition of more complex assignments. As his credibility and influence increase with the staff, the BA conforms more and more to the brand "image."

BMs estimate that they spend as much as 25 percent of their time training BAs and ABMs. In fact, the entire brand management system is a training program. There is no such thing as an old BM; there is no place for the person who doesn't want to be promoted.

Management Information Systems

The BM used current data almost exclusively, even though comprehensive historical files were maintained. Meetings were usually frequent and short, with only a few people present. Telephone calls were also frequent and short. Memos were passed through for comment and review by the BM. Magazines might be scanned for ideas, but they were seldom read. For many BMs, only the Nielsen chart books, the product fact book, and project folders were kept within easy reach.

Tests were used extensively to determine the accuracy of the information routinely received so that results could be optimized and problems avoided. Brand people went out into the field infrequently, yet they had a strong perception about what was happening through their tests and the management information system.

Emphasis had to be placed on the management information system because the BM changed products about every 18 months to two years and thus lost all of his personal contacts in the agency and staff groups, which tended to remain with the products.

Relationship with the "Big Five"

The five groups which brand dealt with regularly were the advertising agency, Sales, Market Research, Manufacturing, and Product Development. With each group, there were conflicts which the BM had to resolve. These conflicts might include work priorities, differences of opinion about strategy or objectives, and disagreements over project timing. Brand argued that it had the responsibility for volume and spending without explicit authority to force staff compliance. These other departments, however, saw brand as more in control due to its final authority to make recommendations to top management as well as its role in setting initial objectives. The other departments would have preferred a better understanding (by brand) of their role and problems, yet essentially believed in the brand system as the best way to run Clorox.

Rotation and Promotion

Brand people were expected to shift products about every two years. Due to attrition, new hires, and promotions, the time could vary, but it seldom exceeded two and a half years. It took a BM several months to become familiar with a new assignment and perhaps a year to implement a major strategy. Thus, the typical BM was working on his predecessor's strategy for much of his tenure.

Performance was judged on a number of bases:

1. How well did he train?
2. Did he prepare a sound annual marketing plan, and was he able to sell it to management?
3. How well did his product perform against volume objectives in the marketplace (regardless of who prepared the budget)?
4. What sort of major improvements or line extensions were proposed (though not necessarily implemented)?
5. How well did he master the Clorox Style?

This last criterion referred to the fact that Clorox used an evaluation sheet that included such factors as communication, analysis, thoroughness, prioritization, productivity, organization, leadership, work with others, responsibility, ability to accept criticism, motivation, maturity, capacity, judgment, and attitude.

Summary

Brand management at Clorox was a total system. The climate, selection, training, and promotion all tended to encourage the "best and brightest" people to dedicate themselves to making a product successful.

The people were supported by a management information system and organizational structure that allowed them to be trained on the job and to rotate from product to product at frequent intervals. The products were all marketed in a similar enough way, e.g., advertising, sales promotions, grocery store outlets, etc., that the system and organization were the same for each.

The strength of the system lay in the fact that each product had a "champion" who attempted to achieve volume and share objectives, as predicted in an annual plan. The short term was not sacrificed for the long term, since the long term generally represented the incumbent's proposed strategy and ongoing business-building tests and the short term represented his predecessor's strategy. In addition, a pool of potential general management talent was being established and utilized as managers moved up.

The Interviews

Although the general outline of the system was essentially as depicted, individual managers saw reality in slightly different ways. Therefore, it may be insightful to add depth to the description by noting a number of remarks gathered by the interviewer. Needless to say, these remarks are personal interpretations—meant to put some meat on the bones. The danger, of course, is that the reader might accept each at its face value or fail to recognize that they may appear out of context. In the writer's view, however, they are consistent with his interpretation of the "true environment." The remarks are presented in a question-and-answer format.

Question 1: You typically hire MBAs with a small amount of work experience. What do you look for, and how would you describe their jobs as BAs?

Brand Manager No. 1: I find it takes several months for a BA to become acclimated. He is usually too theoretically oriented; at this level, pragmatic application of judgment to problems is more important.

The most important thing for a BA to learn is to pay attention to details. Even typos have a dollar impact. The BA should learn to think things through comprehensively.

The BA begins working about 10 hours per day plus homework, but the times goes down as he learns his job.

All marketers are pretty much alike—aggressive, detail-minded—and that's what we look for.

Brand Manager No. 2: The biggest problem a new BA has is to learn how to juggle projects and determine priorities. Business schools teach sequential problem solving, but brand requires juggling 15 trivial things and one major one. The BA's initial problem is establishing credibility. Brand requires a mixture of talents, but no one specific personality is appropriate. Brand people do consider themselves prima donnas.

Brand Manager No. 3: The BA's problem is simply a lack of experience with the Clorox system. The system relies on numbers, and the numbers come from the BA. The BA is constantly calculating and must think in analytic terms.

The BA must work very hard, develop rapidly, and learn what brand is all about. It takes two to six months for the BA to have a good grasp of the job and become acclimated to the system. All training is on-the-job.

The BA is responsible for sales promotions and the budget. It is important for the BA to develop creative ways to solve problems.

The BA must determine what motivates people and use it.

Question 2: What is the relationship between "brand" and the "other departments"?

Brand Manager No. 1: Brand is considered with respect by the advertising agency, but brand is committed to the agency because the BM can't fire them.

Most of the people in other departments do not want to move as fast as brand. It is a problem conveying the urgency and importance of timing.

The BM is responsible for planning, and the other departments for advice and/or execution.

Knowledge is power, and the BM is the resident expert on his products.

Brand Manager No. 2: Brand is more a line than a staff function.

Brand has responsibility for achieving volume objectives and keeping profit/case close to target level, but brand has no direct authority over many other departments which impact his ability to achieve objectives. Management recognizes that sometimes performance is beyond the control of brand.

Brand doesn't have to be nice to suppliers and sometimes becomes a tyrant due to the pressure.

Brand Manager No. 3: Brand controls the money. Many other departments must rely upon brand for direction and project funding.

The advertising agency has account executives who deal with brand and the agency's creative and media departments. The agency presents a national media plan once a year. Since the budget is mainly advertising, brand and the agency write the request.

Sales promotions are originated by brand and proposed to Sales.

Brand recommends and analyzes market research and test markets. The purpose of these is to avoid "national blunders," although the risk is relatively small with ongoing products.

Question 3: What common characteristics do brand managers have?

Brand Manager No. 1: The important attributes are aggressiveness and attention to detail.

Brand Manager No. 2: The BM must have an aggressive outlook toward life, be competitive, like to win, and be action oriented.

It's important to learn to do a thorough analysis of all inputs.

Question 4: How does a brand manager spend his time?

Brand Manager No. 1: Daily activities are coordination, short questions and answers on the telephone, and commenting on memos passing through. Wide variation exists, but a day might have one hour for thinking and strategy, one hour for standard reports, one hour for the "in/out basket," two hours on the phone, one hour with subordinates, and two hours in meetings.

Dealings are mainly with the "Big Five": the account executive at the advertising agency; Sales; the Manufacturing coordinator; Market Research; and the Product Development specialists.

On the average, the BM flies to the field once every three months.

Brand's job is to study the product, determine what is needed, and prioritize projects. The budget for this is set once a year.

Brand Manager No. 2: The most important job of brand is the budget request and appropriation. Once each year, a two- to three-hour meeting is held which lays out how and why money is to be spent for the next year. During the period preceding this meeting, much of a BM's time may be spent with the agency. During the remainder of the year, the time falls off with the time spent in once-a-week meetings and telephone calls.

The second major job is the Brand Improvement Objectives meeting, which is also held once a year. Brand works with R&D to develop both short-term and long-term product development plans.

Brand strategies require one and a half to two years to implement. Long-range planning is important because few changes can be made in the short term due to long lead times in production and media planning.

Most of the BM's time is spent on specific projects.

Heavy use is made of the telephone, and many short meetings are held, usually with six people or less.

Brand has a meeting with the Product Development Center every two weeks.

Question 5: How often does a brand manager change brands?

Brand Manager No. 1: All brand people are interchangeable, although it takes about two to four months to become the most knowledgeable. You spend one to two years on a brand.

Brand Manager No. 2: Rotation is caused by promotions and departures and occurs every one and a half to two years. Continuity is provided by the staggered rotation of BAs, ABMs, and BMs. Once you rotate, you usually don't have time to find out how your old product is doing.

9

Planned Organizational Change at the U.S. Naval Air Development Center

Approximately one year after a new Technical Director (TD) was selected for the U.S. Naval Air Development Center (NADC), a new Commander (CDR) arrived. These two individuals quickly developed a good working relationship, operating as a closely knit team from then until the CDR was transferred; all decisions except those limited to military personnel or functions were made jointly, and the two men conferred frequently in their adjoining offices or while on official travel (a frequent occurrence). Within a few weeks of the CDR's arrival, they agreed that there appeared to be a number of opportunities to effect positive change to improve the effectiveness of NADC. They were convinced, however, that inappropriate change or change ineffectively implemented would cause more problems than it solved. Therefore, they needed to determine exactly where the organization was and where it needed to go before beginning any change process.

They were inclined to feel that the primary need was for the development of management skill, probably at the middle level. Consequently, they decided to procure assistance from management-development consultants who had substantial experience in organizational analysis, and who had experience with and understood the Navy laboratory system, to develop a data base. The CDR and TD provided the consultants with background information, discussed their thinking about organizational change, and passed on some of their perceptions concerning the current state of the organization. The consultants were asked to identify specific opportunities for improving managerial effectiveness at NADC and to recommend the means by which these improvements could be made. (They were not asked to identify the strengths and positive aspects of the organization.) Both the consultants and the NADC management expected a management-development seminar would be designed from the data collected.

Initial Organizational Research

The consultants proceeded to collect and analyze organizational data. They reviewed organizational charts and manuals, mission statements, work packages, information systems, and management reports; and they conducted 72 nondirective, one-hour (or longer) interviews with managers at all levels in the organization and from all the major units. All 24 members of the senior executive group were interviewed. The interviews centered on opportunities to improve organizational effectiveness. As the work progressed, it became clear that organizational structure and uncoordinated decision making were critical issues that would have to be addressed before a management-development seminar would be well received by the organization. The data fell naturally into two broad categories: external environmental factors and the evolution of NADC, and significant internal issues.

External Environmental Factors

■ ***Confederation*** Over a number of years, as pressures in the Navy mounted for consolidation, several small organizations were abolished as independent entities and their functions, together with many of their people, were physically moved to NADC. As a result, these organizations lost their former visible autonomy, although they continued to function much as they had before the move. Thus, NADC had evolved into a confederation of 16 quasi-independent entities without much coordination. This situation contributed to the formation of cliques and parochialism along historic lines. People inside NADC expressed concern over how the organization was perceived by their sponsors (the dominant one being the Naval Air Systems Command) and others in the Navy. Rumors that NADC was soon to be closed were not uncommon; morale was low.

■ ***Trends*** Significant trends were changing the fundamental tasks of NADC. The total volume of work was increasing rapidly, and the total funding of NADC had approximately doubled in real terms in the past decade. During this time period, the number of personnel at NADC actually declined, and further reductions were anticipated. Three other trends emerged from the analysis of the initial research:

- Sponsor interest was shifting from technology toward systems-type work, as evidenced by shifts in funding.
- The demands for software appeared to be increasing, whereas hardware development was decreasing.
- There was an increasing demand for work to be contracted out rather than done inside NADC due to the political desire of the administration to avoid expanding the federal bureaucracy.

The above trends were placing pressure on NADC to develop more effective ways of managing in order to increase flexibility, cooperation, and integration, and to minimize the use of resources.

The NADC responded to the trend toward systems work by establishing a dedicated organizational unit, the Systems Department, which did all of the work on the various systems. This organization resulted in a high concentration of resources in this department but few procedures or techniques for the transfer or sharing of resources between departments when this would be advantageous. The trend toward software resulted from various technical factors and resource limitations, and the demand for more software created a shortage of good software people. There were not enough people to meet the needs of the various programs, and this created pressure within NADC to cooperate and share resources. The trend toward contracting out had two different kinds of impacts. First, it was necessary to use technical personnel as contract managers; second, there was increased pressure to coordinate with other people, such as procurement and legal specialists, in an effort to integrate work. Collaboration had to be developed and conducted in a relatively parochial environment. Given their choice, the technical groups preferred to do the work themselves rather than contract out.

■ ***Manpower*** With increasing frequency, the Navy was reducing manpower ceilings, average grade levels, and the number allowed in senior grade levels, and it was also imposing a hiring freeze. The authority to classify senior positions was centralized at a level above NADC, at just the point in time where increased flexibility in position management was needed at the Center.

■ ***Conflicts*** The researchers identified three sets of perceived conflicting forces that were acting on NADC. First, the requirements for contracting out and monitoring technical progress of the contractors was perceived to interfere with the desires of NADC engineers to grow technically by performing challenging engineering tasks. Second, civilian managers viewed themselves as providing continuity and long-term technical strength, whereas the military managers were seen as transients, interested dominantly in short-term output. Finally, the CDR and TD felt split between increasing demands for internal management and the critical need to rebuild relationships with the clients and sponsors of NADC.

Significant Internal Issues

■ ***Organizational Structure*** The NADC's organization (Exhibit 9–1) had six support staff departments, four technical departments, the Systems Department, 12 staff assistants, a designated program office, a technology management office, and the Naval Air Facility–Warminster, all reporting directly to top management (the CDR/TD). The size of the organization caused a span-of-control problem, and, in addition, there were five other problems associated with the structure of the organization. First, there was evidence that the "confederated" organization performed those tasks that had been most important in the past (prior to the consolidation) rather than those tasks that were currently the most important. This situation resulted in narrow-minded thinking and empire building rather than cooperation. Second, it appeared as though many individuals did not know how major organizational units were supposed to function, especially the Systems Department, which used a form of matrix management. Third, resource allocations appeared to be based on historical growth patterns rather than the high-priority tasks assigned to the organization at that time. Fourth, many people within NADC felt that there were too many layers of management and this interfered with getting the job done and made it more difficult to communicate, let alone coordinate, across organizational lines. And, fifth, it was felt that the technical expertise of NADC was being eroded by the number of people leaving technical work for jobs in management, systems, or contract monitoring.

■ ***The Decision-Making Process*** Five difficulties in the decision-making process were particularly apparent. 1) Too many decisions were being referred to the top of the organization, resulting in top management becoming a bottleneck. The individual organizational units had not developed effective mechanisms for cooperation, and therefore issues involving two or more units were pushed up to the top for resolution. 2) Too many decisions were being referred to committees, which, because of the historical development of the Center, had overlapping responsibilities and were composed of individuals who saw their primary function as defending the position of their organizational unit rather than reaching a decision that would be good for the Center as a whole. 3) The resolution of problems by top management or

Exhibit 9–1 ■ Naval Air Development Center Organization

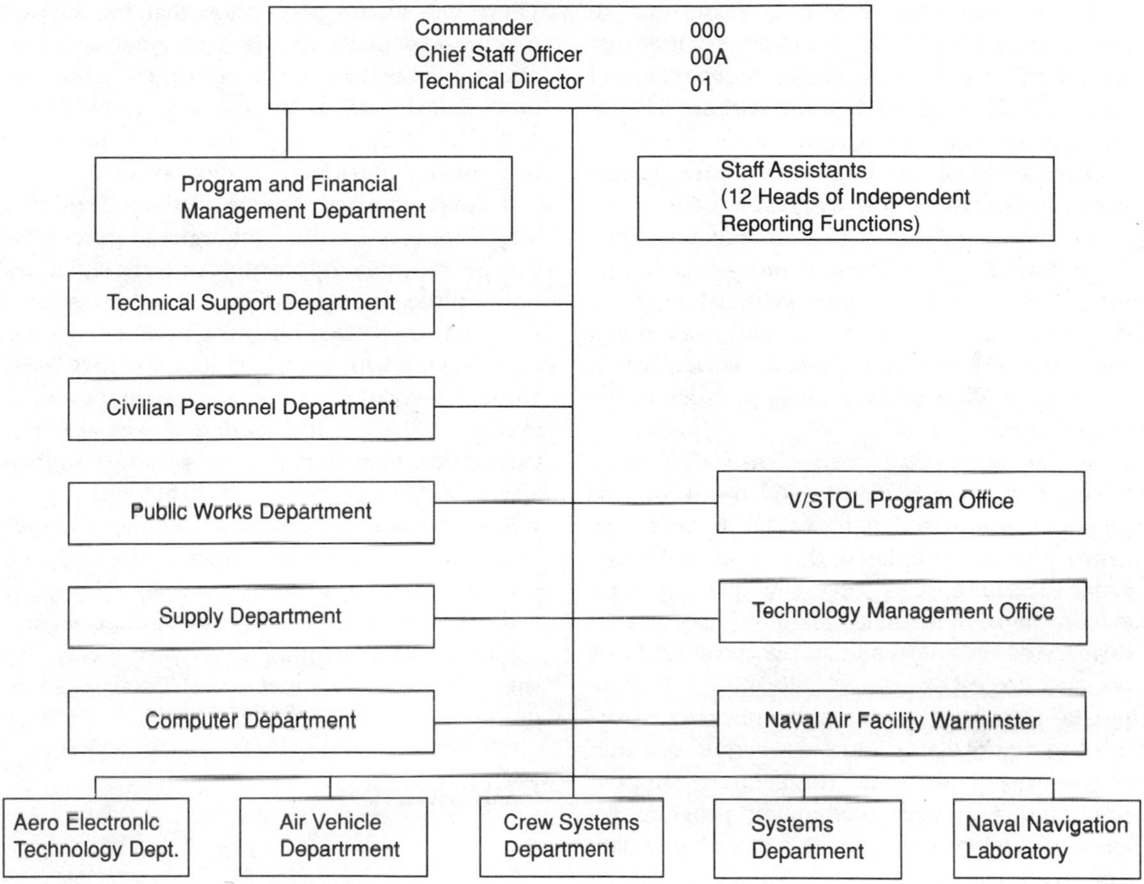

committee tended to be delayed until a crisis arose. 4) The Center management-information system was inadequate in that individual departments had evolved information systems that were useful to them but were not oriented toward generating the information necessary for Center-wide decision making. 5) Lines of responsibility and authority were felt to be unclear.

■ ***The Communication Process*** Each department's information system was different, making comparisons or integration difficult and resulting in a general lack of information about the functioning of the total organization. This situation was exacerbated by the lack of clarity in the committee decision-making process and the tendency to push things to the top of the organization, thereby overloading top management and not giving them sufficient time to communicate information down adequately. Other groups, especially support groups, tended to isolate themselves and did not communicate to those affected by their work. Hence, people at all levels felt isolated, did not know what was going on, and believed that top management was not only inaccessible but uncommunicative.

■ ***Goals, Objectives and Priorities*** Given the fragmented decision-making process and the ineffective communication system, most people in the organization had little understanding of goals, objectives, and priorities. Individual managers at all levels maintained parochial relationships with sponsors that allowed them to pull work into to the Center that interested them or their group, independent of Center goals or objectives, and without informing top management. Given a shortage of resources, especially in terms of full-time permanent employees, it was extremely difficult for top management to do overall, effective long-range planning. It seemed to many people that the Center would take on everything but get rid of nothing and that, with declining manpower, the result was self-strangulation, particularly in the areas perceived to be most important to the future of the Center.

■ ***The Planning and Control System*** Because of NADC's history and the degree to which it functioned parochially, a short-term time orientation existed that relegated long-range planning to a very low priority. The symptoms of inadequate planning and control manifested themselves in an overhead rate that seemed excessive, poor allocation of manpower resources resulting in mismatches between skills available and those required within organizational subunits, destructive competition among groups, inadequate program reviews, decisions being made without adequate information, and computer reports of questionable accuracy and timeliness.

■ ***Organizational Climate and Morale*** Morale was low, and the organizational climate was not seen as supportive. Some of the environmental trends affecting the Center were driving it in a direction that many people did not like. The increased contracting out, resulting in a need for internal contract management and decreased direct work on technological problems, was a special irritant to many people. These people were required to do work that they found inherently less satisfying, and they felt that the Center would lose its basic technological capability. Because of this shift, people perceived that there was little opportunity for technical advancement and that individuals who made sound technical contributions were not rewarded unless they were willing to leave the technology area and go into management. There was also a perception that the support people, especially in the personnel and contracting areas, had developed a "can't do" attitude, that the last reduction in force (RIF) was badly handled, and that management had failed to remove unproductive "dead wood."

■ ***Career and Development Training*** There appeared to be a widespread perception that promotional opportunities were stifled not only by the ceiling and grade-level constraints imposed on NADC, but by a number of other factors as well, including failure to remove "dead wood," favoritism, poor personnel practices, and no real technical ladder. It was also perceived that managers were not trained to manage and that they had been selected for the wrong reasons, i.e., solely on the basis of their technical ability. Top management strongly felt, however, that technical ability was and is a critical required skill for a technical manager in a research-and-development environment, but that human and conceptual skills are also required.

Conclusion

Analysis of the data collected in the initial research phase convinced the consultants and the CDR and TD that a management-development program should not be implemented until the critical issues revealed in the data had been addressed. These issues pointed to the need for significant and rather substantial changes to improve organizational effectiveness, and the CDR and TD made the decision to proceed with the necessary changes.

Planning the Change Process

The CDR and TD worked with the consultants to identify objectives of the change process, as outlined below.

Reorganize the structure and management roles to:

1. eliminate parochialism;
2. build in more effective decision-making capability, including decisions involving goals and objectives, planning, resource allocation, and evaluation of the work being done at the Center;
3. reduce the span of control to relieve top management overload; and
4. provide the structure and roles to accomplish realistic long-range planning.
5. open up communication between and among organizational units and between the CDR/TD and the rest of the organization.

The CDR, TD, and consultants agreed on several basic assumptions. First, it was assumed that a change dictated by the CDR and TD would probably be relatively ineffective. Both the CDR and TD had been involved in previous organizational change processes that had been mandated from the top with little involvement of the senior management group, and which they observed had achieved only limited success due to the significant problems of implementation. They recognized that the entire organization needed to perceive that there were significant reasons for change, that all senior managers needed to contribute their thoughts and expertise to the change process, and that all senior managers had to be committed to a different way of doing business in light of the current environment faced by the Center, as well as the environment that was likely to exist over the next several years.

Second, much was known about why people resisted change in organizations and the ways this resistance could be reduced if not eliminated. Internal and external change agents could reduce resistance. The CDR and TD were internal change agents, and the consultants needed to become external change agents. Consequently, the consultants' role needed to switch from researchers to facilitators, acting as catalysts and resource persons to help the entire management group implement the change process.

Third, although the change process should take a significant period of time, there were pressures that limited the time available:

- The Center was under pressure from higher-level Navy management to justify its very existence as an organization deserving continued support in the Naval Laboratory community.
- The Commander had only slightly more than two years left of his three-year tour and he did not want to leave the Center to a new Commander with implementation of the changes incomplete.

Finally, some major effort or step would be needed to create an atmosphere in which the managers of the Center would tend to drop their insular views of their departments and take on a Center-wide perspective. This final step seemed to be especially critical if the resource-allocation decisions required were to be made and if the Center was to develop the organizational flexibility it needed.

Implementing Change

The CDR and TD decided that a carefully planned reassignment process would be an effective first step in dealing with the narrow-minded behavior that pervaded the Center. Accordingly, they advised the top eight managers of the Center that some of them would be reassigned to head up other departments. The technical requirements of the job and their particular backgrounds would, of course, be taken into account, but because of the wide needs of the Center and the breadth of background of the managers involved, most, if not all, of the managers could expect reassignment in time. A few weeks later, three managers were reassigned. Because each of the managers could be moved, no one was secure. All of the managers perceived that their self-interest was better served now by a Center-oriented perspective rather than their former, somewhat parochial view, because if they competed with each other and developed an organization in which one unit was particularly strong and another weak, they might end up managing the weak one.

After several months, some of the executives recognized the acceleration of their own growth and became open advocates of reassignments that took into account the careful matching of technical, human, and conceptual skills with job requirements. This process was, and is, a far cry from the "musical chairs" approach to job rotation that is practiced in other parts of the Navy, and which led the NADC executives initially to resist it.

Involving Managers in the Change Process

The CDR and TD called a meeting of the top 24 managers at NADC so that the data that had been collected and analyzed by the consultants could be presented to them. The group included the eight senior department directors, their deputies, and eight others, including some staff department heads and other staff officers. More than a third of the group were Naval officers (three Captains and six Commanders). The six senior civilians were all SESs; the other civilians were GM-15s, with a few GM-14s. The group agreed with much of the data and decided to follow the consultants' recommendation for a more lengthy meeting. Approximately one month after this discussion of the research information, a three-day meeting was held offsite to examine organizational structure for NADC, particularly matrix possibilities, as well as the problems of decision making by committee. The meeting was facilitated by the consultants, and the CDR and TD adopted the role of "available resource" if requested by the group as a whole, or by any of the subgroups that were formed. In this way, the CDR and TD effectively removed themselves from the discussions in order not to inhibit their managers in a full, free, and open-ended exploration of the issues and possible improvements, while at the same time providing support and input when needed by the group or subgroups.

The charge to the group by the CDR and TD was relatively general: they were to investigate ways of improving NADC's methods of doing business, and they were to review and analyze the organizational structure to determine ways to improve its operation. The consultants acted as both facilitators and as outside experts. They focused on the process the groups were using, attempting to support open communication, and, when requested by the group or subgroups, provided outside expertise in the two areas being worked on. The group worked 15 or 16 hours a day on the two tasks derived from the research: the role of committees in the decision-making process, and the strengths and weaknesses of the matrix-type structure and its applicability to NADC.

Three different subgroups were formed, each composed of individuals who had sufficient breadth to look at the Center as a whole. Their first task was to look at matrix organizations from three different perspectives: the sponsors, the functional managers, and the top Center management. The three subgroups developed presentations of their findings and fed these back to the total group the following morning. Both the CDR and TD openly expressed their pleasure with the work of the group and their perception of its value.

The second task assigned to the subgroups was to review the functioning and utility of committees at NADC. The groups would look at three different types of decisions: strategic, operational, and tactical; and the value of committees for dealing with them. The subgroups spent the balance of the second day with this task and developed presentations to be given to the total group on the morning of the third day.

After these presentations, a general discussion about the outputs of the meeting and its value continued for some time.

Responding to the thrusts of the comments from the managers, the CDR and TD agreed that additional off-site meetings were needed to plan for the redesign of the NADC organization. The CDR and TD agreed to appoint a new ad hoc subgroup to work part-time over the next several weeks to develop a "straw-man" model organization, i.e., one that would provide the basis for further discussion and analysis in the next off-site meeting of the whole group. Certain basic boundary conditions were set for the ad hoc subgroup, but basically they were to have a free hand in developing the straw-man model.

The perceptions of the participants about the first off-site meeting were quite positive. They felt that they had begun to establish more openness, trust, and sharing of power among themselves and had made real progress in identifying opportunities for positive change.

Development of a Proposed Organization

The CDR and TD appointed eight managers to the ad hoc subgroup to develop the straw-man model organization. The eight were selected because of their ability to contribute, their status relative to the rest of the management group, and their openness and breadth of understanding. One of the facilitators was with the ad hoc subgroup at all of their meetings, helping with process problems and providing expert input and current research on organizational design.

The ad hoc subgroup met at least three times a week for over a month to develop an organization that would 1) reduce the span of control of the CDR and TD; 2) provide a matrix-type operation; 3) improve planning, decision making, and operations; and, 4) include mechanisms for conflict resolution.

Analysis of the Proposed Organization

The organization design that resulted from the meetings was presented to the management group at a second off-site meeting held six weeks after the first. The CDR, TD, and the facilitators assumed the same roles as before, but certain ground rules were imposed: the discussion would initially be limited to clarifying questions, i.e., no critical comments would be allowed until it was clear that everyone fully understood the proposal. It was also decided that the objective of the discussions was to develop an "ideal" organization; modifications addressing individual concerns would be made only after agreement had been reached on the ideal. It was hoped that this process would minimize empire building and parochialism.

After the initial clarifying discussions, three subgroups were formed to analyze the proposals at depth. These subgroups reported their conclusions to the total group, and it was clear that certain aspects of the proposal were acceptable to the entire group. These elements formed the base for an overall design. Some skepticism and hostility was evidenced by a few participants who seemed most concerned with protecting the status quo. It was decided that more intensive work needed to be done over the next two months on the structuring of the systems and functional groups.

Three new ad hoc subgroups were formed. Their tasks were to refine still further the organizational structure and to develop a plan for implementation, to be presented to the management group at a third off-site meeting. Each subgroup was assigned a part of the total organization. They hammered out the design detail for their specific segment, coordinated with the other subgroups, and developed a rough plan for implementation. The facilitators were available to meet with any or all of the three new subgroups on request, but they were less involved than previously.

A third off-site meeting was held two months later. Two of the subgroups had ironed out the details and had developed firm implementation recommendations. The subgroup working on the functional engineering and systems organizations was less clear and precise, reflecting the lingering insularity and sense of potential "loss" still in evidence in those parts of the organization. A good deal of discussion focused on the third group's report. Well into the evening, specific conclusions were finally reached by the whole group.

The CDR and TD met after the session ended to discuss the conclusions of the total group. They also interviewed individuals who would fill key roles in the new organization. The next morning, the CDR and TD shocked the management group, who had not anticipated immediate action, by abandoning the nondirective roles they had played. First, they accepted the work of the groups and stated that the new organization as designed by the group would be implemented. Then, they specified which individuals would fill key roles. This resulted in several more managers being reassigned to head up organizational elements quite different from those they had previously managed. Finally, they set a date three months away as the ideal time to implement this major organizational change. This time frame ensured a reasonable "shakedown period" before the CDR was transferred.

The balance of the discussion for this meeting focused on problems of implementation. An integrative management group was formed to deal with these specific problems. Christened the Center Management Group (CMG), it was composed of the six SES civilians and three Captains who had been in the original executive group, plus the GM-15 Controller. It was also decided that the new organization should be announced immediately, and that the CDR, TD, and the managers of the CMG would make a series of presentations to the other NADC managers. The CDR and TD accepted the responsibility for securing approval of the new organization from higher-level Naval commands.

Exhibit 9–2 shows the proposed organization that the planning group felt would overcome many of the problems noted earlier and provide a more efficient and coordinated structure. The main features of the new plan were: six line departments, four technology groups of roughly comparable size that would work on both advanced technology efforts and projects (though the projects themselves would be managed by a Command Projects Department that had the dollars and a core of managers and monitors but not the people to do the work), and a Systems Engineering group dominantly serving Command Projects in the full range of systems-engineering functions; a Planning, Assessment, and Resources group that would act as staff to the CDR and TD in these areas, making recommendations on such issues as acceptance of work by NADC, resource allocations, and an assessment of opportunities to develop new technologies or drop old ones; a Chief Staff Officer to provide day-to-day supervision of the support groups (to reduce the span of control of the CDR and TD); merger of the Naval Air Facility into NADC; and an Associate Technical Director who would be chairman of the CMG (initially referred to as the "integrator" and now also referred to as the "implementation" group) whose function would be to resolve conflicts and act as an integrator within the organization. It was not envisioned that this group would be a layer of management or would have regularly assigned duties, but rather that two or three members concerned would informally meet to resolve conflicts as they arose, keeping a Center-wide perspective. The major differences between this matrix structure (Exhibit 9–2) and the old organization (Exhibit 9–1) are in four areas: power distribution, relative balance between units, a thrust toward strengthening the functional engineering groups, and the requirement that the functional groups work for the project groups. Finally, the new organization was designed to allow for the development of centers of technical excellence that could then be used as resources in coordinated efforts for specific products.

Exhibit 9–2 ■ Proposed Organization

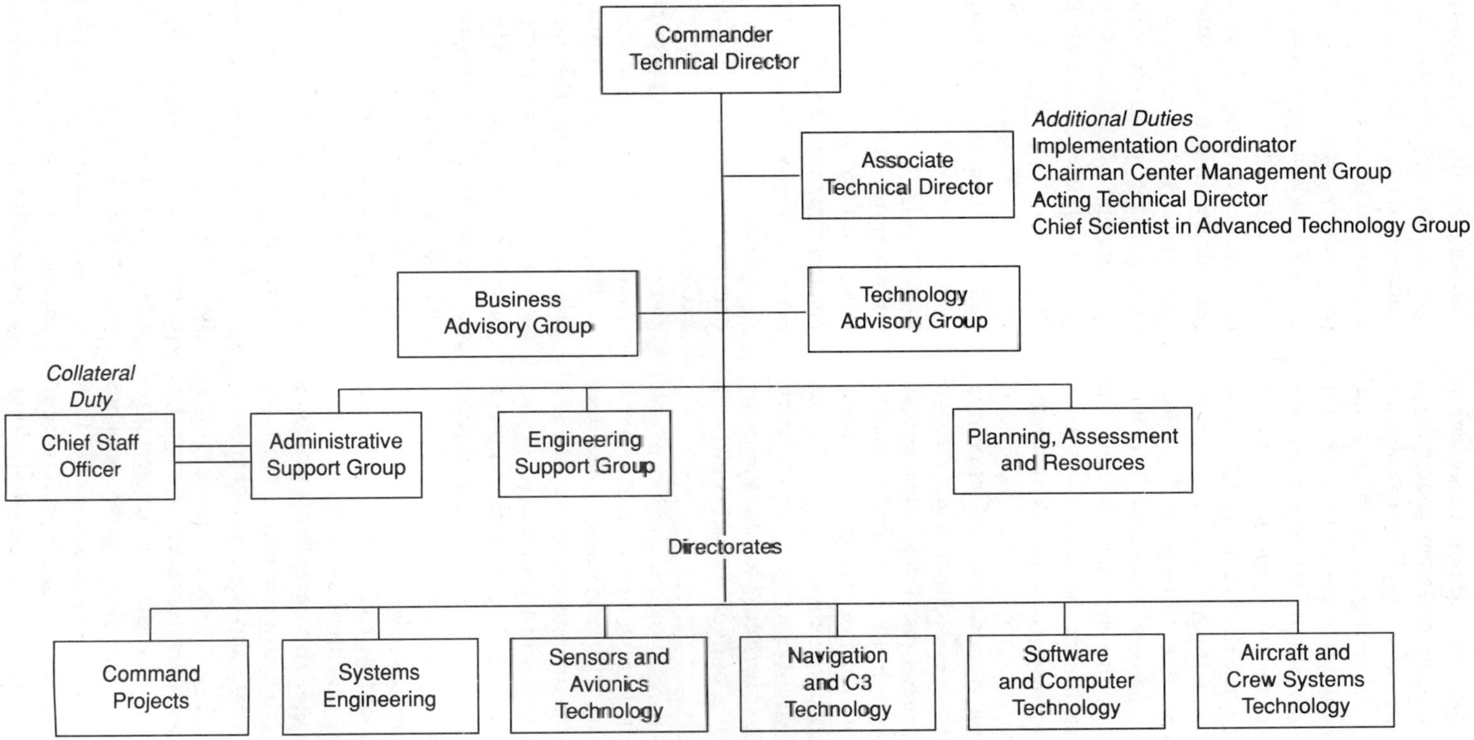

The announcement of the new organization and the presentations by NADC management to their suborganizations received mixed reactions. Many of the mid-level managers expressed their frustration at not having had any input in the reorganization and expressed considerable reservations about the proposal. Although some remained skeptical, the functional technical groups eventually became favorably disposed, whereas the systems and project groups became negatively disposed. This was not unexpected as the systems and projects groups would no longer have line authority over most of the resources necessary to get their work done.

This rebalancing of power would, of course, require much greater coordination and cooperation across organizational lines. Most people recognized the desirability of this and of sharing scarce technical talent but expressed concern over priorities and how they would be established, and also whether or not the technical groups could be "trusted" to do the work satisfactorily within budget and schedule constraints.

It became apparent to the senior people involved in the planning for reorganization that they had acquired a considerable amount of knowledge about matrix structures that the rest of the organization did not yet possess. Consequently, during an early implementation meeting of the CMG, it was decided that a short management-development program should be initiated for the next two levels of management to teach them about matrix organizations and to obtain their involvement and help in implementing the change. The consultants designed and implemented this program while remaining available to the CMG and top management as facilitators.

The management-development program began three weeks before the new organization was to be implemented. The first two sessions were devoted to matrix organizations and how they function. Three groups of 25 each were to participate. The first group consisted dominantly of those people who had done the planning for the reorganization, and the other two groups contained a total of 50 mid-level managers from all parts of the organization. At the second meeting of the third group, a number of questions were raised concerning the lack of a modus operandi. The CMG had been assigned this task along with many others but had not yet developed the guidelines for operation of the new organization.

Because the design of the management-development program called for workshop groups to be established to work on implementation problems (to be assigned by the CMG), the CDR and TD assigned the job of preparing the modus operandi to a workshop group of mid-level managers, mostly deputies of the managers serving as the CMG, and asked them to submit a draft within a week. The consultants were asked to assist. The managers on the CMG who felt they were responsible for this task apparently resented the job being given to lower-level people. They told the lower-level workshop group that their task was an academic exercise for the class only. Delays and excuses proved frustrating to the CDR and TD and to the operating groups who needed and wanted adequate guidelines.

This was the first indication that the CMG felt they "owned" the new organization, did not want to share power with lower-level managers, and, indeed, viewed the workshops as usurping their prerogatives. (The CMG refused to assign *any* implementation problem to a workshop.) The pressures on seminar participants increased when the new organization was implemented. Without the workshops to involve participants in the significant problems of implementation, some participants concluded they had higher priority uses for their time. Attendance in the management-development program declined sharply. The CMG spent a great deal of time working out the details of organizational assignments down to the lowest levels, employee by employee. Indeed, so much time was devoted to this process that other important tasks such as developing the modus operandi were not done, and a resurgence of parochialism and empire building was noted.

Meanwhile, the CDR and TD had submitted the broad plan to higher authority for approval. Only two significant changes were required in order to secure approval, both related to interpretations of regulations or law. Both the Controller and Civilian Personnel groups were set out to report directly to the CDR and TD. A great deal of time was expended in obtaining top-level approval and in "selling" the matrix concept in other parts of the Navy after approval.

The new organization was implemented as planned, on schedule. In the frequent absence of the CDR and TD, who were selling the matrix concept in order to avoid improper downgrading of personnel, the CMG began to function as a layer of management. This seems to have occurred without the people involved being conscious of it, and it led to considerable frustration on the part of the CDR and TD, as well as the members of the CMG. As a result, the CMG decided to hold its own off-site meeting to examine the way it was functioning. Two of the consultants participated in this meeting. After the meeting, additional effort was devoted to the functioning of the CMG and assessment of the new organization. This culminated in the development and use of a questionnaire to be completed by all NADC managers; the results were analyzed, and the data from this instrument, together with the CMG's output from its own analysis of its functioning, were to be presented at a larger off-site meeting of the original top management group to assess the new organization. The consultants and the CDR and TD assumed the same roles as in the earlier meetings.

Several things became obvious as a result of this meeting: the CMG viewed itself as a layer of management, managers below and above the CMG were frustrated, lower-level managers felt they had been prevented from expressing their concerns and problems with the new organization, and a number of implementation problems had not yet been resolved, including the modus operandi. At the end of this meeting, the CDR and TD stepped in and made decisions that effectively put the CMG back into the role originally intended for it, and initiated an off-site meeting of a representative group of lower-level managers so that the unresolved issues could be more thoroughly identified and corrective actions recommended. Names of nominees were to be forwarded to the CDR and TD.

Each level of management reviewed the nominees, and efforts were made to include as many as possible of those who had expressed concern or dissatisfaction. All nominees were notified that attendance was voluntary, and several chose not to participate. Some anxiety was expressed by members of the original top management group and the intervening level of management about their exclusion.

At this lower-level management meeting three weeks later, all the data then available was presented to the group. The consultants assumed the same facilitator role as before, whereas the CDR and TD made data presentations and interacted socially, then returned to NADC. The group formed workshops to define the issues and recommend actions. Presentations by each workshop group were made back at NADC several days later to the CDR and TD directly, with members of the original top management group in attendance. One recommendation was that their bosses, that is, the level between them and the top group, be included in examining the problems and reviewing the recommended actions.

The CDR and TD approved, and two weeks later another off-site meeting was held with the managers at the intervening level in attendance. The consultants again acted as facilitators, and the CDR and TD again made data presentations and interacted socially before returning to NADC. This time the group was asked not only to analyze the output of the last two meetings and develop their own output, but also to develop an action plan for approval by the CDR and TD and implementation at NADC. The group developed the action plan, and it was approved after modification.

Shortly thereafter, however, budgetary restrictions and several new tasks were imposed on NADC by the Navy. These factors necessitated a curtailment in implementing some aspects of the action plan, which created some frustrations. It also resulted in the temporary curtailment of the consultants' participation.

Six months later, most managers at NADC felt that most of the significant problems of implementing the new organization had been or were being solved and that the reputation of NADC in the eyes of higher authority had been substantially enhanced. It was also apparent that empire building and parochialism still existed, consciously or subconsciously, at very senior levels. It was suggested that another off-site meeting to reassess progress could help rebuild more effective working relationships.

At this off-site meeting, the facilitators noted considerably greater willingness for participants to be open and confrontational without being hostile. In general, roles and levels seemed to be accepted without inhibition. The group proceeded in a mature, workmanlike manner, dealt with dissent openly, examined the anxieties created by the changes, and pointed out the still-unresolved problems of the new organization, including failure to produce a modus operandi. After listening for three days, the CDR and TD again took charge and made significant decisions where conflict was still unresolved.

Postscript

After the CDR who had been involved in the change process had transferred, a period of consolidation took place. Gradually, the TD was given more and more responsibility for speical assignments that kept him away from the Center. The Associate TD (ATD) retired, and another CMG member replaced him, but the frequent absence of the TD resulted in the new ATD, who was also chairman of the CMG, managing the Center and using the CMG as a layer of management, with the Planning Assessment Resources group becoming staff to the CMG. In addition, two former CMG members left to become TDs of other Navy centers, and, of course, all military officers were changed. A new TD was appointed six months after a second new CDR was appointed. Together, they called the consultants back to review the current organization.

The consultants found that the organization was functioning with considerably greater effectiveness than prior to the reorganization, but there were significant opportunities for further improvement, as outlined below.

1. An effective, integrated, Center-oriented management-information system was still not in place and indeed looked several years away.
2. The modus operandi to document the working relationships and procedures for groups and between groups had not been developed, and no effort was being expended to do so.
3. The CMG had become a layer of management with formal weekly meetings, rather than the informal integrator and conflict-resolving group that was originally intended.
4. The CMG was perceived by some to be managing the Center, whereas the CDR and TD were seen to be focused outside the Center.
5. Parochialism, empire building, and self-interest in opposition to Center interest was still in evidence.
6. Mid-level managers appeared very concerned with improving their individual and collective management capabilities and effectiveness for the Center.
7. Managerial paperwork seemed excessive.
8. The decision-making process seemed vague.
9. The strategic-planning process seemed weak.

In short, the organization had improved somewhat, but there was a clear need for team-building activities at the senior-management level and integrated management and organizational development activities at middle-management levels to "fine-tune" the Center. Some internal team-building activities including strategic planning have been undertaken more recently. It is hoped that integrated management and organizational development activities will be undertaken soon.

10

Sigma Corporation in Iran

On the night of December 5, 1978, Alister Hunt, the country manager for Sigma Corporation in Iran, was staring out his front window toward the main street that ran by his house. It was still a sight that was new and bizarre. He was looking at a Sherman tank that had moved in during the day to protect the shah's sister, who lived next door. The shah himself often stayed at the Summer Palace within eyesight of Hunt's home. Hunt now knew the situation in Iran had become a very serious threat to Sigma's 175 employees and their 215 dependents. Seventy of those personnel were at the rest of Sigma's operations in three locations remote from Tehran, the capital. Should Hunt be concerned enough to begin pulling out his people? If he felt a major reduction in personnel was needed, how could they be sent home with little publicity and without bruising a very profitable relationship with both the U.S. and Iranian governments? According to prior agreements, only tripartite decisions could lead to such a move, and such a consensus between Iran, the U.S. government, and Sigma was unlikely at this time. Short of that, Hunt wondered what other measures could be taken to protect his people better. In other words, had his contingency planning been adequate? The lives of several hundred people depended on it.

Sigma Corporation

Founded in Cambridge, Massachusetts, in 1922 as the American Radio Corporation, a producer of radio tubes, the company adopted the Sigma name in 1925. Given the tremendous growth of the radio industry in the 1920s, Sigma was able to gain a foothold in the market in spite of the presence of larger, dominant competitors such as General Electric, Westinghouse, and its subsidiary, RCA. Sigma, however, remained a small

This case was prepared by Charles R. Kennedy, Jr., Assistant Professor at the Colgate Darden Graduate School of Business Administration.

company (total sales of $3.2 million in 1939) until the outbreak of World War II, when the company began producing military electronics, radar, and communications equipment. By 1945, total sales equaled $148 million, with all but $6 million the result of U.S. government contracts. After the war, Sigma became a leader in missile guidance systems, credited with the first mid-air interception and destruction of both aircraft and missiles. Although U.S. government contracts remained strong, the company made a conscious effort to diversify into civilian lines of business, such as industrial electronics, components, and tubes. By 1962, civilian sales exceeded $100 million and constituted 17 percent of total Sigma revenues. Sigma continued this diversification policy in the 1960s by acquiring kitchen appliance, publishing, seisomographic, and construction companies. By 1974, U.S. government contracts had fallen to 41 percent ($800 million) of total sales ($1.929 billion).

International business operations at this time were focused in three areas: Western Europe, where Sigma had been heavily involved since the late 1940s; Saudi Arabia, where a small operation had been in place since 1964; and Iran, where the first contract had been recently signed. In 1974, international sales were $530 million, or 27 percent of total sales. The lion's share of that activity was derived from NATO military contracts. Between 1974 and 1978, however, Iran came to equal Western Europe as Sigma's biggest export market; each contributed over $600 million in sales during those years. As a consequence, international revenue climbed to 34 percent of $3.24 billion in total sales by 1978.

The Iranian Operation

Sigma's involvement in Iran started at a low level in 1972, with educational systems provided to the University at Shiraz. In late 1973, however, Sigma's business in Iran expanded dramatically with the signing of a military service contract. Sigma was to provide Iran with a highly sophisticated missile-defense system called the Eagle. The equipment would be built in top-security plants in the United States, sold to the U.S. Department of Defense (DOD), and then resold to the Imperial Government of Iran. Profit margins were standard for U.S. government contracts, plus an extra 4 percent markup for the higher risks and expenses of operating in Iran. Such operations related to training programs conducted by Sigma personnel within Iran.

Over the next three years, Sigma trained 3,000 Iranian Air Force personnel at bases in the Tehran area. By 1976, Sigma had 120 employees and nearly 200 dependents in the country. Although many employees and their families suffered from culture shock, that was a common and expected reaction to a strange country. In 1976, however, the situation in Iran became especially tense and unsettling as political terrorist activity mounted dramatically; it took a decidedly anti-American business tone when two Rockwell International employees were murdered. Nevertheless, Sigma's "attrition rate," or the number of employees who quit the firm and left the country, was much lower than most other U.S. companies. During 1976, only 20 Sigma employees and their families left Iran in such a manner (17 percent of the total), half the rate in other U.S. firms, such as Bell Helicopter. Sigma's loyalty to its employees, which resulted in a very low turnover rate for the company as a whole, helped explain this record. Sigma's decision to take organized measures to protect itself during the upsurge in terrorism (defensive-driving courses, increased intelligence gathering, and contingency planning toward a pyramid communications system) also served to heighten employee morale.

During 1976, Sigma began to negotiate a new contract with Iran to provide on-the-job training in equipment maintenance. Essentially, company instructors would take the Iranian military technicians through a series of U.S. Army maintenance programs related to the Eagle missile system. The major change the new contract brought to Sigma's Iran operation was that much of the training would take place in "down-country" locations, far from the Tehran base. After several months of negotiations, the new contract was signed in July 1977. Two months later, Alister Hunt moved to Iran as Sigma's new country manager, his first such assignment overseas after many years as an engineer and administrator in Sigma's U.S. missile and antisubmarine warfare divisions.

Sigma and the 1978 Iranian Revolution

In February 1978, Sigma operations on the new contract began in earnest when the first of the additional personnel to staff the remote training sites arrived. There would eventually be five such sites staffed by 30 to 35 Sigma personnel each. The sites were located at Behbehan, Vahdati (near Ahvaz), Bushehr, Isfahan, and Chah Bahar. The Vahdati and Bushehr sites were to be staffed first, followed by Isfahan and then the others (see Exhibit 10–1).

Recruiting and staffing these positions proved to be a big problem. Every attempt was made to find single males, because no dependents were allowed at the remote training sites, but not enough were found. Married men hired for the job had their families permanently based in Tehran. All personnel at the down-country locations rotated with others at 30-day intervals.

For general management, the arrangements caused a "babysit the families" problem. Sigma handled the situation by increasing the sense of community among its employees with a company newsletter started in February and by building full recreational and (limited) housing facilities for employees—the Sigma compound. Full funding for the project was provided by the Iranian government, which technically owned the property. All in all, Sigma visibility in the country was getting appreciably higher because of the compound and because of a rising number of cars (35) and buses (eight) in the Sigma fleet. Nevertheless, life for the Sigma community was carried on in a pretty normal American way, as the June 1978 Sigma Newsletter attests (see Exhibit 10–2).

Events in Iran outside the Sigma community, however, were becoming more and more turbulent. Following the January 1978 Qom incident, when fighting between the religious community and Iranian troops resulted in dozens killed, including two mullahs (religious leaders), a cycle of religious-based violence set in. According to Shi'ite custom, ceremonies mourning the martyrs of Qom were scheduled for the fortieth day after the killings. The traditional mourning procession on February 18 took place peacefully in 15 of 16 cities. The lone but important exception was Tabriz, where rioting erupted when the provincial government closed three mosques on the day of the demonstration. Army intervention was required to squelch the rioting, which was the first sustained clash between the army and civilians since 1963. The fighting resulted in at least 26 dead and 260 wounded (opposition leaders claimed 300 killed and 700 injured). The 40-day cycle continued on March 30, but the violence really escalated in April, when there was at least one serious incident per day. In May, violence and death returned to Qom, and armored cars were deployed in Tehran for the first time. A particularly tense atmosphere existed in all major Iranian cities, especially Tehran, on June 5, the fifteenth anniversary of Ayatollah Khomeini's exile. A major clash was avoided, however, in part because of the intimidating presence of Iranian tanks in the streets for the first time.

Sigma top management reacted to these incidents with a great deal of concern. As Hunt remarked, "Religious dissent had now risen above the noise level." As a result, Sigma began implementing many of its tentative contingency plans in regard to a pyramid communications system and concrete evacuation procedures. A 200-page document was written in June and July to organize the system formally and to detail those procedures. The so-called "warden system" was the core of the communications

Exhibit 10–1 ■ Map of Iran

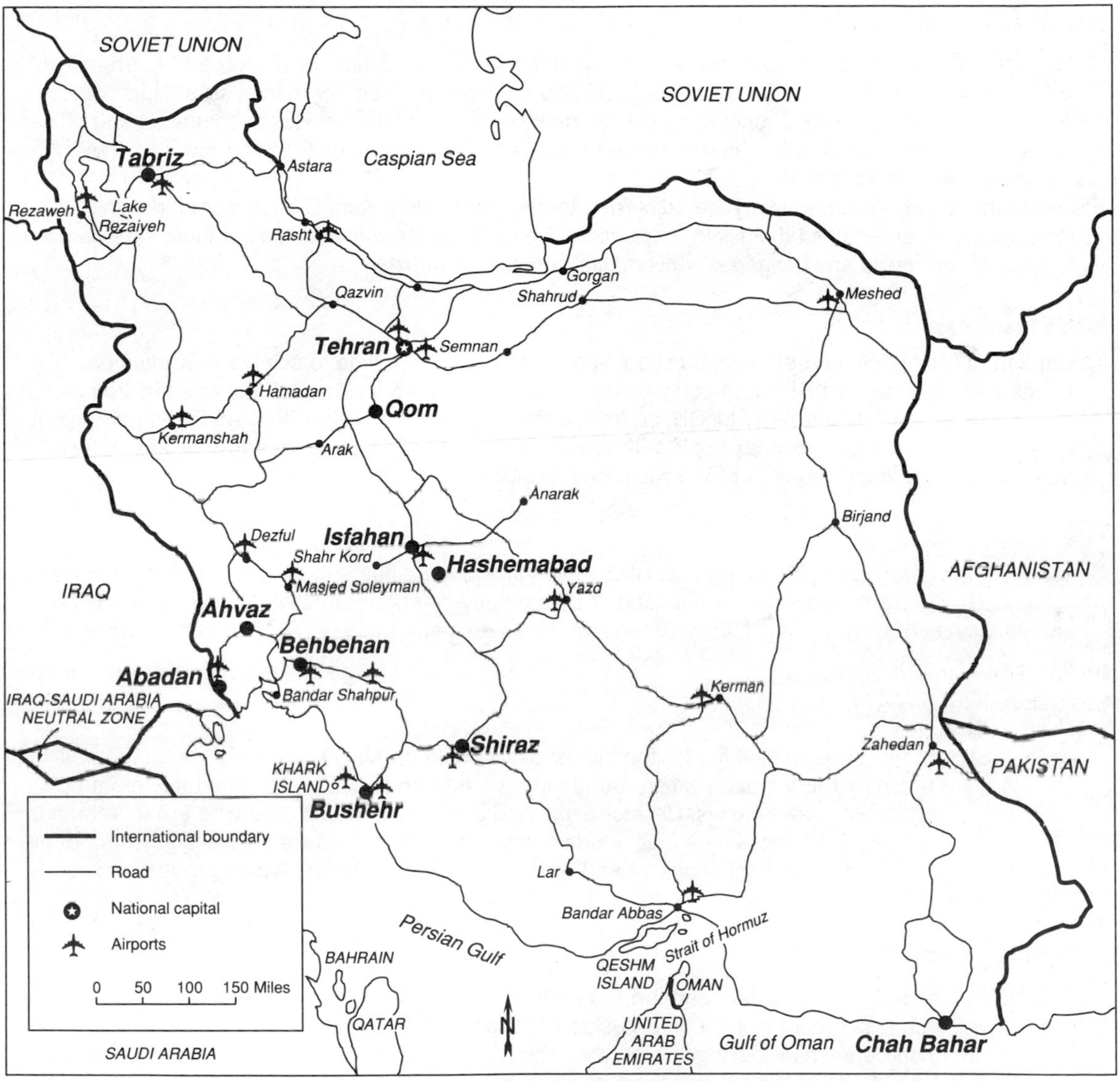

Adapted from *Iran: A Country Study*, third edition, copyright © the American University (Washington, D.C., 1978), fig. 1, p. xxviii.

system and evacuation plan. In the system, the Sigma community was divided into 12 teams, based mainly on the geographic location of residences. Each team was headed by a warden or leader who was the only member of the team with full knowledge of emergency and evacuation details. This kind of activity and planning seemed to help reduce tension and anxiety within the Sigma community, but so did the fact that a lull in the fighting and demonstrations occurred between early June and late July. As a result, the Sigma contract operations continued

Exhibit 10–2 ■ Sigma Newsletter June 1978 Tehran, Iran Volume 4, Issue 6

Sigma's Special Guests

On May 10, Sigma employees and their wives met at the recreation center for a reception to greet Paul McGrath, Sigma's program manager, and Mr. G. Burns, vice president for marketing at Huntsville, Alabama. Guests were also honored by the attendance of Major General Reisler, commanding officer of the U.S. Military mission in Iran. He spoke to Sigma families and complimented them on their successful work in Iran.

Following the guest speakers, everyone adjourned to the buffet, while Kent Griff, a member of the Bushehr team, entertained them with a selection of country-western music. Inside, there was dancing to lively taped music and congenial conversation among the guests.

Sigma Graduates

The month of May is the end of another school year, and for some, a time to celebrate graduation. Sigma proudly extends their warm congratulations to the following children who graduated from kindergarten: Peg Dill and Berry McGill, Jr. from Golestan School and Alex Jones from Piruzi School. Congratulations are also extended to our Tehran American High School graduates: Bill Mix, Steve Smith, Pat Best, and Charles Burt. We wish them the best of luck in their future endeavors.

New Arrivals

Congratulations are in order for the parents of the two youngest members of the Sigma family. Beth and Steve O'Grady are the parents of a 7-pound, 7-ounce baby boy born on May 17. The baby has been named David O'Grady. Donald Martin Greene, Jr. is the six-pound son of Dan and Bobby Greene. He was born on May 23.

Socialize

Manzarieh Scout Camp was the setting for the ladies' picnic, held on May 9. The cool, clean mountain air was quite a contrast to the usual smog found in lower Tehran. Ladies were joined this month by three brave gentlemen, Steve Ducas, Bill McKnight, and Jill Simms. Those men who are in Tehran on R & R are welcome to join these meetings. Linda Mitchell contributed a cake for the enjoyment of all. Next month, plans will be for cool drinks served at the recreation center. All ladies are encouraged to come.

Tehran Softball Season Begins

The softball season begins in Tehran, and the Sigma men in red had really been putting their all into the games. The won-loss record looks a bit one-sided at this point in the season (0–5), although improvement can be seen in every game played. The players can be proud of their batting average, which is around 500. What the players need now is a crowd of Sigma fans to root for them. Everyone interested should get in touch with Bill Mix to find out when the next game is being played. Sigma will provide transportation to the game if six or more people request it. So add your voice to the crowd and be at the next Sigma softball game!

Sigma Teens to Isfahan

Approximately 150 local students journeyed to Isfahan to entertain students of Isfahan American School. Some of the students making the trip on May 8 were four Sigma dependents. Both Susan Mix and Charles Burt made the trip as members of the jazz band, which was a real crowd pleaser drawing a standing ovation in performing an encore. It was a tired but happy group that returned to Tehran at 4:30 p.m. on May 12.

Bushehr Beach Party

April 28 was such a beautiful day at Bushehr that everyone on the Bushehr crew was in a good mood (even Charlie)! A barbeque party has been planned at the nearby beach, and Ray Walden, Kent Griff, and Dan Pool made up the advance crew to get the site ready for picking. The men left Bushehr early in the morning with two trash barrels full of supplies: one trenching tool, two Frisbees and a football. Later they were joined by Billy Smith, Fred Dean, Jerry Malory, Jim Martinez, and Felix Santiago. The food was good, the sun was hot, and lively entertainment was provided by Jim Martinez, who played the guitar while Felix Santiago did the Mexican hat dance.

That's all for now. We will be talking to you next month.

---

at an escalating pace, with the number of new personnel arriving each month increasing to around ten during July. Hunt also felt comfortable enough to allow his wife and kids to take an Iranian vacation to some down-country areas the same month. He than returned with his family to the United States in early August for a well-deserved vacation.

On August 19, however, a major turning point in the Iranian political crisis took place in Abadan. At the Rex Cinema, a fire broke out that killed over 400 people. The laxness and slow reaction of local police and firemen convinced many that SAVAK, the shah's secret police, was responsible. Suspicions were further heightened by the fact that the Abadan police chief, General Reza Razmi, had been the Qom police chief during the January rioting. The shah tried to counter the resulting countrywide protests by replacing Prime Minister Jamshid Amuzegar with Jaafar Sharif-Emmami, who was a member of the royal family's inner circle but was also the son and grandson of prestigious clerics.

The new appointment and cabinet reshuffle failed to appease the opposition. The intensity of the anti-shah movement reached a new high, and the clergy announced a mass march for September 4 and 5 to celebrate the end of Ramadan, the Moslem month of fasting. The government refused parade permits but decided to ignore the demonstrations anyway. In Tehran, demonstrators numbered over a hundred thousand each day. The clergy then called a countrywide general strike for September 7. The shah reacted by declaring martial law in 13 cities with a 10:00 p.m.-to-5:00 a.m. curfew. Public gatherings of over three people were forbidden as well. The clerics then called for anti-martial law demonstrations for September 8, a Friday and the Moslem day of worship. A bloody confrontation ensued that day, initially at Jaleh Square in south Tehran, where army units opened fire and killed at least 100 people when the crowd refused to disperse. Major riots and firefights then erupted in most parts of the city. By the end of the day, around 400 people had died and 4,000 were wounded. After "Black Friday," what had been an anti-shah protest movement appeared to have become a full-scale revolution.

The reaction within the Sigma community was one of mounting panic. Hunt rushed back to Tehran from vacation and on September 11, 1978, issued a memo to help clarify the situation and, he hoped, reduce the panic level among his people.

MEMORANDUM

TO: All Sigma Employees and Dependents
FROM: Alister Hunt
DATE: September 11, 1978
RE: Operations under Martial Law in Iran

The following guidelines are issued to help you with the present state of martial law in Tehran and other cities in Iran. As new operational procedures are developed, we will keep you informed; in the meanwhile, I urge you to monitor your radio and TV and one of the English-language newspapers for day-by-day changes in regulations.

I. Travel

Local Tehran travel via automobiles and other ground vehicles is not restricted. Common sense should be used in selecting times of travel so as not to interfere with curfew limits, presently 10:00 p.m. through 5:00 a.m. A safety factor of 30 to 45 minutes should always be allowed. Main routes should be used to the greatest extent possible. In the event you become stuck and believe that you have violated the curfew, proceed as follows:

A. If telephone communications are possible, notify by phone Bill Glade, head of Sigma security, at home or in the office and request assistance.

B. If neither time nor communications permit, present yourself to the first available policeman or soldier and request assistance. Communication may be difficult due to language problems, but don't give up; they will try to help you. You will be escorted to a precinct station or central point and communications provided. It is most important to do this *before* the curfew begins; after that, you will be arrested. Sigma does not recommend travel by train at this time for security reasons. Airline travel is unrestricted, although again somewhat flaky because of extensive rescheduling delays. Obtaining reservations for out-of-country travel are about normal, i.e., a few days. Restrictions on travel to the airport have been lifted; however, no one is allowed in the terminal without a ticket. Departure or arrival assistance can be provided to a limited extent by travel agency personnel upon request by the company during noncurfew hours. During curfew hours, Iran Air will transport via bus from the airport to in-town hotels. Taxis with special passes are permitted similar privileges. The company will escort all new arrivals in the country for the time being to minimize confusion at arrival.

C. Company buses/vehicles will continue to operate in support of travel to/from work locations, the recreational center, and the Zafar offices. Schedules have been revised and are attached to this memo. Personnel waiting to be picked up should not congregate in groups larger than two persons. Shopping transportation will continue as before, as will school buses. Mothers accompanying children to bus stops should avoid the appearance of congregating; if questioned (not likely), display the previously issued Farsi notice explaining your presence on the street.

II. Curfew

Adherence to curfew is *mandatory.* The government of Iran takes it quite seriously. Violators *will* be arrested by the authorities and should expect to be inconvenienced and/or discomforted until released. If stopped or challenged, do not resist or argue; comply with all instructions (try to smile a lot). Again, if for any unforeseen reason you are unable to reach your destination before evening curfew, go to the nearest Sigma home, police station, or government agency and communicate. Carry telephone numbers with you at all times (and a two-rial coin).

III. Emergency Assistance

Assistance in communicating in Farsi with your local police station for emergency support (ambulance, fire, other) may be obtained from the U.S. Embassy as follows:

A. Call the U.S. Embassy: 820–091 through 099.

B. Ask for the Marine duty officer.

C. State your problem and type of assistance you require.

D. Hang up and wait for a Farsi-speaking embassy employee to call you back. He/she will assist you and communicate your needs to the police precinct.

E. Call Bill Glade and advise him of the problem.

IV. Security

Martial law is imposed upon Tehran to end threats to public safety and destruction of private and public property. We expect it to be quite effective for the foreseeable future. Prudence is still required, however, and the company recommends observance of the following guidelines:

A. Stay out of southern and eastern Tehran unless absolutely necessary. This includes the bazaar and the railroad station.

B. Avoid public facilities (restaurants, theaters, movies).

C. Don't linger in stores, banks, gas stations.

D. Stay off the streets if a public demonstration or celebration is announced.

E. September 15 is the seventh day after the recent fighting occurred. It might occasion another challenge to government authority. Be aware.

F. Don't be surprised if sporadic incidents continue, particularly involving attacks on police or military personnel.

V. General

The company understands the restrictions and limits imposed on us all by the new martial law and continuing security alerts. We will attempt to deal with the problem in as many ways as we can to make the situation more pleasant. Constructive suggestions will be most welcome. In the meanwhile, stick together and help each other as you can.

Alister Hunt, Vice President, Program Manager

Throughout the remainder of September, Hunt initiated a number of crisis-management moves. Practices of the first dry runs of the emergency plan caused some updating of evacuation procedures. Flights of incoming personnel, who were numbering around ten a month in September and October, were changed to go via Athens instead of Paris so they would land in Tehran during the day, not night. A rumor-control bulletin was also developed to counter undue concern or panic. Contracts and information exchanges between Sigma, other companies, and the U.S. Embassy increased as well. An example of such activity is provided by this memo from the head of Sigma security to Hunt.

MEMORANDUM

TO: Allster Hunt
FROM: B. Glade
DATE: September 16, 1978
RE: Security Status from U.S. Embassy

Status regarding security in Tehran and other Iranian locations is as follows: Tehran—no known incidents occurred during the weekend. Expectancy is that the situation will continue to be calm and stable during the next few days. Isfahan—four significant incidents occurred in Isfahan over the weekend. All were tied to the Molotov cocktail incidents against: (1) the Ministry of Tourism, (2) two banks, and (3) Grumman motor pool. Molotovs and pipebombs were used against the Grumman motor pool on Friday. No one was injured, but a Paykan car was destroyed. Minor damage was done to other vehicles in the installation. U.S. Embassy is concerned that the American community reaction may be overly excited under the present circumstances. They also feel that the Grumman motor pool was poorly enclosed and/or secured. Note: Suggest that we discuss this with out managers so that they can with perspective counter any undue Sigma reaction. Other cities—no significant disturbances over the weekend. Travel—surface travel is still discouraged. Air travel is preferred. Response to specific questions regarding Sigma personnel traveling to Hashemabad is to travel by air to Isfahan. Hence, surface to Hashemabad base is OK so long as we comply with martial law regulations and use good judgment about leaving the base unnecessarily. Surface movement of Sigma vehicles from Tehran to Hashemabad is OK if done by an Iranian driver without passengers and the driver complies with martial law regulations. Outlook for stability in Iran under martial law still remains good. The embassy is conducting briefings as follows: bomb threat management—Monday, September 18, 1400 hours, Carvansarai lounge; general security briefing—Tuesday, September 19, 1330 hours, Carvansarai lounge; driving training—September 25, 0800 hours, American Embassy.

In general, Sigma's U.S. government contacts remained optimistic about the situation in Iran. Another source of information for Sigma had a dramatically different viewpoint, however. In late 1977, Hunt had sought and hired a local Iranian analyst who came highly recommended as "well-connected" by government sources back in the United States. Hunt only knew him as "Colonel G." and as a former Iranian police colonel. The two men arranged telephone contact numbers, and Colonel G. visited Hunt at fairly regular intervals. In on such meeting on October 24, Colonel G. assessed the situation as being very bad. He described how junior and senior high school students were joining the guerrillas, and all labor strikes were totally political now. He listed the three main opposition elements: the religious leaders, the National Front led by liberal, Western-educated professionals, and the angry and poor urban mob. Colonel G. stressed that all three elements had a strong communist presence and predicted Iran would go communist if the shah left Iran. He also predicted that Americans would increasingly become the targets of revolutionary violence. The opposition had become particularly incensed over President Carter's telephone call of support to the shah on "Black Friday."

Another meeting with Colonel G. took place on October 31. Colonel G. was extremely agitated, saying the situation had reached a "bursting point." He described the shah as alone and despondent and indicated that even the military might not back him completely. He said anything could happen in the next two months.

Colonel G.'s prediction proved accurate in a very short time. On November 5, the worst riots yet occurred in Tehran. Seventeen police stations in Tehran were attacked in a coordinated action, with two of the stations captured. At the same time, over 80 banks and hundreds of "Westernized" shops were set afire and looted, and the Ministry of Information was totally destroyed, as were all airline offices except Air France. (Khomeini lived in France.) Perhaps most frightening to some in the Sigma community, a bus of foreign-born children on their way home from school was attacked with verbal abuse and small missiles. The shah reacted to these events by replacing Prime Minister Sharif-Emmami with a new military government, led by the Iranian Army chief of staff.

Sigma reacted to these events by halting the arrival of any new personnel into Iran. Hunt also issued the following situation report, the first general release to the Sigma community since the September 11 memo. The report was issued because the panic level had reached an all-time high and guidance was needed for the difficult weeks ahead, especially for December, the religious month of Moharram.

MEMORANDUM

TO: All Sigma U.S. Personnel and Dependents
FROM: Alister Hunt, Program Manager
DATE: November 12, 1978
RE: Situation Report

Now that the turmoil of the past week has quieted, I thought it would be useful to try to put it all in perspective for you and to attempt to forecast where we go from here. Along the way I will answer some of the questions that have been put to me in the past few weeks. I realize that any prediction I make is bound to be wrong in some or many ways; however, it represents a best estimate at this time, and you should know that at least. First, the past: about 18 months ago, it became obvious that the Iranian economy was not healthy. This was obvious in different ways at different levels. At the people level, inflation in rent and food prices has stripped away any gains made by the people in the last decade. It seemed to be the cause of most of the dissatisfaction. In response to this pressure, the government of Mr. Hoveyda was changed for that of Mr. Amuzegar. He was reported to be a good manager, and his goal was to get a handle on the economy and the development program. About nine months ago, the decision was announced to liberalize the political process. This decision, coming without a guide, rapidly created chaos within the government. New parties sprang up by the dozen, and the press and other media were not able to provide any balanced coverage. The government also did not offer a transition plan. The religious leaders then became more aggressive, and the prime minister, Amuzegar, finally lost control. The pressure from the clergy led to demonstrations; the demonstrations led to bloodshed; a crisis rapidly developed late this summer. July was characterized by growing trouble in the provinces and almost total silence by the government. In August, large-scale violence broke out. The government changed to one headed by Sharif-Emmami, and large concessions were made to the Moslem clergy in hope of quieting things down. This was patently unsuccessful, and on September 8, martial law was declared in most large cities throughout the country. This action was immediately effective in restoring order in the cities. But as the opposition sensed an opportunity to gain control of the government, violence flared up in those ares not under martial law.

The new government then made several attempts to defuse the situation. Among these were televised debates of the Majlis, removal of press censorship, release of prisoners, arrests of some officials believed to be corrupt, and large wage settlements for dissatisfied government employees.

None of these actions appeared to be effective, and the pressure grew. The students appeared on the streets late in September, and demonstrations and violence returned to Iran and other large cities. While this was happening, the military showed great restraint and allowed the government to try to control the situation. It was clear that another government change was required, however, and the process of forming coalitions began. The National Front, the outlawed party of old, showed the most strength and was the best organized. Several other former leaders threw their hats in the ring. Success, however, required the coalition of a strong political force with the clergy. The shah for his part required a *constitutional* government (this had the effect of perpetuating the monarchy). Late in October, it appeared that the National Front behind Mr. Sanjabi and the clergy behind Ayatollah Khomeini would join forces. The situation in the country continued to worsen. The strikes became political, the oil fields nearly shut down, and the government revenue dropped to a trickle. Iran was close to a state of anarchy. Khomeini at that point must have sensed victory and stated that a revised constitution would be necessary. This meant the elimination of the monarchy and its replacement by the Shiite clergy at the head of the country. This was unacceptable to the shah, and at this point, he had no option left other than to install his military commanders in key government positions.

This brings us to the present—wondering where we go from here. As I see it, there are three critical periods before us.

We are in the first of these periods now, and it will last for only a week or two. During this time, the economy must restart. There will be challenges to the new government by the students, The National Front, and the clergy. But the real test will be whether everyone returns to work. If they do not, many foreigners and foreign companies will have to leave because they cannot be paid. Goods and services will become scarce, and routine operations will become difficult. This will be the economic test of the new government.

The second period or test will begin early in December and could last up to a month. I think of this as a force test. At this time, the clergy will have to make their move if they wish to fight or resist the new government with force. The logical time for this to begin will be at Ashura. The government will be well prepared then, and so I expect a challenge to be made later, say in early January. If the clergy is unsuccessful in this, I foresee an increase in acts of urban sabotage against government installations. In any event, government success is necessary here if law and order is to prevail.

The third period or test will be the most difficult. It is the political test and will occur between the New Year and July. At this time, we will find out whether a new government can be chosen through a political process or whether a military regime must remain. I have no predictions for this, but I will point out the obvious conclusion that, until we are through this period, normal conditions will not return to Iran.

While all of this is going on, the various interest groups will be jockeying for position: clergy, students, political aspirants, etc. I expect a continuing campaign to harass foreigners (us). This will take the form of warnings, threats, no service, rocks, and so forth. We can only hope that it does not become more vicious. I would like to think that these groups will lose interest in us as they become absorbed in their own future. Now for the questions:

I. Where does this leave Sigma?

We have a job to do here. We think that it is a worthwhile one and necessary to global U.S. interests, and we intend to do it. *We are not leaving, nor do we intend to send our dependents home.* The seriousness of the situation and the risks to which we are exposed here are real. They are different from those which we are used to in living and working at home. However, they are not higher in any demonstrable way. Each of us made his own decision in coming here. Each of us will have to make his own decision about staying. I sincerely hope you all see your way clear to finishing the job we have started.

II. What is Sigma doing about the situation?

We have taken several actions and have several more to take. The company in the United States monitors the political situation on a daily basis through the State Department. The company here monitors the political and security situation daily through the U.S. Embassy and the U.S. Air Force security office. In addition, we employ an analyst to interpret the meaning of our data in local terms. This does not enable us to foretell the future, but it does provide us with some lead time. We were able, for instance, on November 5 to return all of our employees to their homes several hours before the major rioting and looting occurred.

In recent weeks, I have met with either the U.S. ambassador, the U.S. military chief, or both at least once a week. This provides them with information as to what we are doing and us with information about their reactions.

The U.S. Embassy, incidentally, has received a lot of bad press lately concerning the credibility of its announcements. This is undeserved. The U.S. Embassy's job is not to protect the American community here nor to provide it with advice on how to protect themselves. Its job is to promote and implement an American policy regarding Iran, coordinate military assistance to Iran, and to establish government-to-government communication.

III. Do we have an evacuation plan?

We have developed a plan for dealing with different emergencies. This plan, among other things, provides for evacuation of employees and/or dependents should either we or the U.S. government think the situation warrants such an action. The U.S. government also has such a plan. Neither of us believes the evacuation is warranted at this time.

Many of you have asked to have the plan. I don't believe, nor does the company or the U.S. government, that releasing the plans is appropriate. The reason for this is that the plan contains much data that is private and would compromise the plan if it were to fall into the wrong hands. For example, the names, addresses, phone numbers, and map locations of each of you, your families, and your residences are contained in the plan. Pick-up points, communication methods, and travel plans are also contained.

I can tell you how the plan will be implemented, should it become necessary. (a) I will convene the emergency management team and announce the decision. (b) The warden system will be activated and be used to deliver a packet of data to each employee or family. This packet will tell you what is being done, what you can take, when you will be picked up, where you are going, and when you are going. (c) The wardens will arrange to move you to the pick-up point at the arranged time. (d) Either the U.S. government or the company will provide transportation from the pick-up points to the airport. The organization calling the action will provide transportation. In the case of a company, this transportation will be by bus or automobile. (e) After reaching the airport, you will be flown out of the country to one of three European cities. From there you will be flown to the U.S. If the U.S. government signals the evacuation, it will provide the aircraft from Iran to Europe. If Sigma signals the action, we will provide the aircraft. (f) Teams will accompany you on each leg of the journey to provide money, food, housing, and direction.

There are several other things you might like to know about the plan as it presently stands. (a) We have a military communication channel available to us if the civil system goes out between Iran and the United States. (b) We have a contract with an American fleet carrier to provide charter aircraft to us within 72 hours should we request it. (c) Personnel residing down country will be evacuated with U.S. military personnel and reunited with their families in Europe. (d) Personal belongings that you have to leave behind are insured under the provisions of our contracts. You should, of course, maintain an inventory of your personal effects, their costs, and other descriptive material (photographs for example) in a safe place. The personnel jacket or a family member in the United States should be considered a safe place. (e) Animals will not be evacuated by the U.S. Embassy.

The emergency plan has been under continuous review since early this summer. The key element of it in my opinion is communications. The warden system is the way we implement communications. We have continually exercised this system in recent months and will continue to do so. I am proud of how effective it is and can assure you from my contacts with other companies here that there is none better. There are several aspects of the plan which we are not satisfied with as yet:

(a) Our dependency on the telephone system for communication within Iran and between Tehran and down country. We have requested of the government of Iran, and I believe will shortly receive, licenses to operate our own radio communication system throughout the country. In anticipation of this, we have already ordered the necessary equipment in the United States.

(b) The transportation between Tehran and down country is dependent upon the Iranian Air Force in the event commercial facilities are not available. So far, they have taken good care of us, but in an emergency, their mission will take precedence over our needs. We have sought permission to operate charter aircrafts in and out of our training sites. Should this permission be granted, we will have much better control of personnel movement within the country (we may, for example, be able to reunite families in Tehran prior to evacuation).

(c) Transportation within Tehran is dependent upon our being able to operate vehicles, which in turn is dependent upon fuel being available. The recent strike with fuel suppliers shows us how vulnerable we are to this situation.

To counter this, we are investigating means to establish our own fuel reserves. Other actions that the company is taking or investigating include protection of work buses from flying rocks and other missiles and alternative means of transporting children to and from school. These actions are in response to concerns voiced by many of you. We have no firm answers to these items as yet.

IV. What is a low profile?

We have from time to time advised you to maintain a low profile. Some of you interpret this to mean stay at home. This is not the case. When we think you should stay at home, we will say so in plain language. Low profile means: (a) avoid such areas of the city as bazaars, mosques, universities, movie theaters, and restaurants, (b) minimize time spent in supermarkets and banks, (c) avoid large parties, public group activities, and tours.

V. What is Ashura?

The month of Moharram, which begins this year on December 2, is the period of deep mourning by Shi'ite Moslems. It commemorates the martyrdom of Hassan and Hussein, grandsons of Mohammad and second and third imams of the Shi'ites. Passion plays are given depicting the death of Hussein and mourning processions are held for the dead heroes. Two religious days occur during the Moharram: the eve of martyrdom of Imam Hussein (Tassua) and the day of his martyrdom. Both of these days are marked by increased observations of mourning. The procession of self-flagellation, where the faithful beat themselves with chains, occurs on the second day, Ashura. This period has always posed a danger to non-Moslems who happen to be in the way of the faithful, who can be in a highly emotional state and have been known to attack others who cross their paths. It is also the time when Mullahs enjoy maximum authority.

Sigma will be advising you to remain at home for three evenings prior to Ashura, the entire day and evening of Ashura, and the evening after Ashura. This advisory is traditional and has nothing to do with current events.

This has been a long and perhaps arduous message. I hope, however, it has served its purpose of imparting information. I will be happy to attempt answers to other questions of general interest as I receive them.

We are in for difficult times, times that will require innovation, imagination, and cooperation between us all if we are to accomplish our job. I, for one, enjoy the stimulation of a challenge, and am confident that together we can all come out of it proud of ourselves and proud of what we have accomplished.

Alister Hunt, Vice President

In the last two weeks of November, the situation continued to intensify. Between November 20 and December 1, at least 600 demonstrators were killed. Tanks reentered Tehran for the first time since June on November 22. And during the period of November 26 to 28, the Iranian economy came to a virtual standstill in the wake of a general strike called by Khomeini.

Besides the importance of Sigma's mission in Iran to U.S. foreign policy interests, the tripartite decision-making arrangement and the fact that 40 percent of Sigma's business was with the U.S. government dictated that the company try to find a way to cope with the situation. This task meant at least addressing deficiencies in the evacuation plan mentioned by Hunt in his November 12 memo. To correct the transportation problem within Tehran, a secret fuel dump was built in the Sigma compound and filled or topped-out during night deliveries. Additionally, since approval from the Iranian government for a Sigma communication system had not been given, Hunt and U.S.-based management decided on their own course of action: Paul McGrath, U.S. program manager for the Iran operation, and two assistants left for Tehran on December 1 to assess the situation and to smuggle 12 walkie-talkies into the country. The entire evacuation plan depended on communications with and between each warden, and frequent telephone and power outages in Tehran had made that difficult to impossible.

While Hunt was contemplating his future options that memorable day of December 5, when the crisis really came home to him and his wife with that tank outside their front door, he learned of a disturbing incident that had occurred in Bushehr the same day. Paul McGrath, while visiting the down-country site, had found his car on fire in the parking lot. The message he received was quite clear; Iran was now a very dangerous place for Sigma personnel. A U.S. government source, moreover, told Hunt that of 52,000 Americans in Iran at the beginning of the year, now only an estimated 28,000 were still in the country. Hunt somehow had to find a way to balance Sigma's business interests and obligations with the need to protect Sigma people. Corporate headquarters was obviously concerned with the situation. Paul McGrath's presence proved that. So did their weekly phone calls. Hunt's only orders were to keep the business going if at all possible. Decisions about whether business operations were untenable or too risky were basically Hunt's alone.

11

DCI

In early 1979, DCI, a major telecommunications company in the Southwest, faced a shrinking market share in certain of its product lines due to increased competition. Top management at DCI was extremely concerned over this turn of events and was certain that this trend would continue and effect many of its other products. In response, top management at DCI decided to restructure and expand their marketing management division in the hopes of regaining their dominance in the market place.

DCI's new marketing strategy revolved around new product development and technological improvements which could be used to upgrade and modify their existing products. This strategy was prompted because of the rapid influx of many new and smaller competitors into DCI's market as a result of federal deregulation. These companies had some competitive advantages over DCI. They were smaller and could respond more rapidly to changes in the market place. They were also able to exploit new technology by buying state of the art equipment from others and packaging this equipment in their own unique constellations. They were also able to vary price structure more than DCI because of lower capital investment costs.

In June 1979, the entire Marketing Management Division of DCI was expanded and restructured (see Exhibit 11–1) with many current employees promoted or transferred, and new people hired. Jim Roberts, a former marketing manager with ten years experience at DCI, was designated as Vice President and head of Corporate Marketing. Roberts quickly determined that DCI's diversity of clients required that a market segmentation strategy was necessary in order to understand and serve each major market. Therefore, a unit was created within the division to study and service the hotel/motel industry.

EXHIBIT 11–1 ▪ Partial DCI Organization Structure

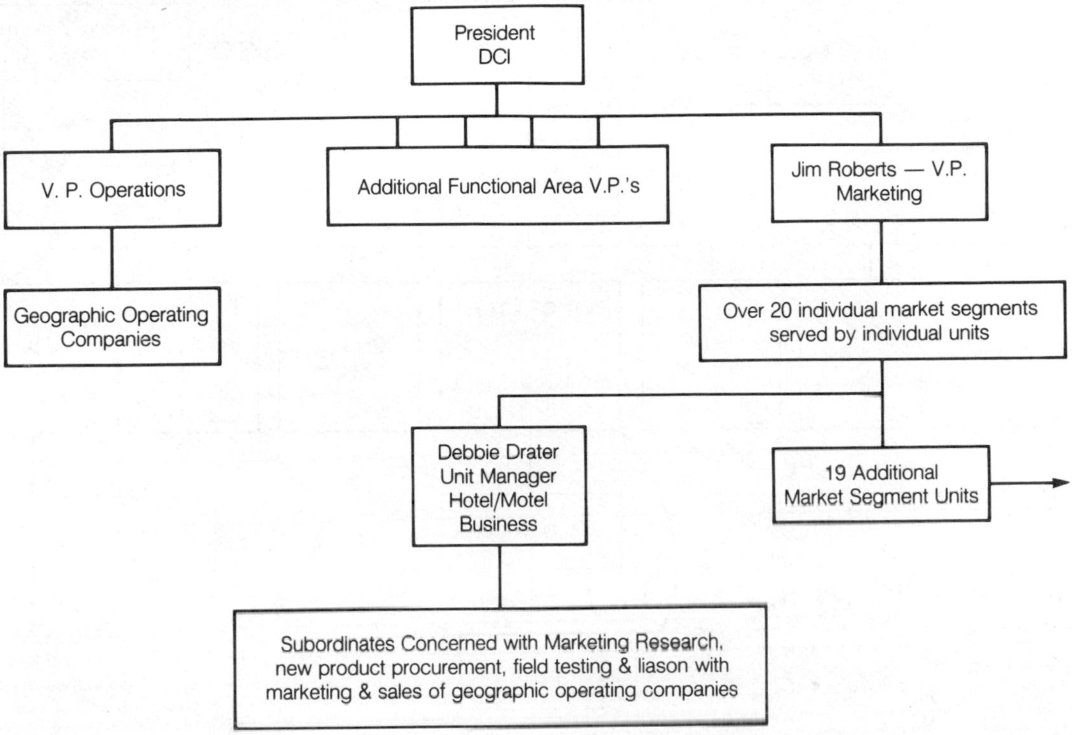

The new manager of the hotel/motel unit was Debbie Drater. Drater was hired from a high-technology non-direct competitor with a reputation for sophistication in market strategy.

In December 1979, Debbie Drater and Jim Roberts announced the development of a new product targeted specifically for the hotel/motel industry. The product was a Property Management System (PMS) designed to monitor the usual hotel/motel functions, such as check-in, check-out, housekeeping, wake-up, etc., and additionally, to perform such novel functions as local call registration, energy control in all parts of the hotel, and front desk accounting. The corporate objectives of offering such a property management system from Jim Roberts' point of view were:

a. The development of a turn-key concept in communications (i.e., one-stop shopping for all of a client's communication needs).

b. A desire to meet the needs of the hotel/motel industry.

c. An introduction of a technologically advanced product that would broaden the base of DCI's offerings.

Since the Property Management System (PMS) was new, and DCI had no experience along this line, a field trial was set up to "debug" the PMS system. From Debbie Drater's perspective, the field trial would provide the following information:

a. A data base for making appropriate changes in the product and/or the techniques of introduction.

b. The development of a marketing plan for the new system.

c. An identification of the successes and failures associated with the introduction of a new computer system.

EXHIBIT 11–2 ■ Partial Organization Chart: The Carlton

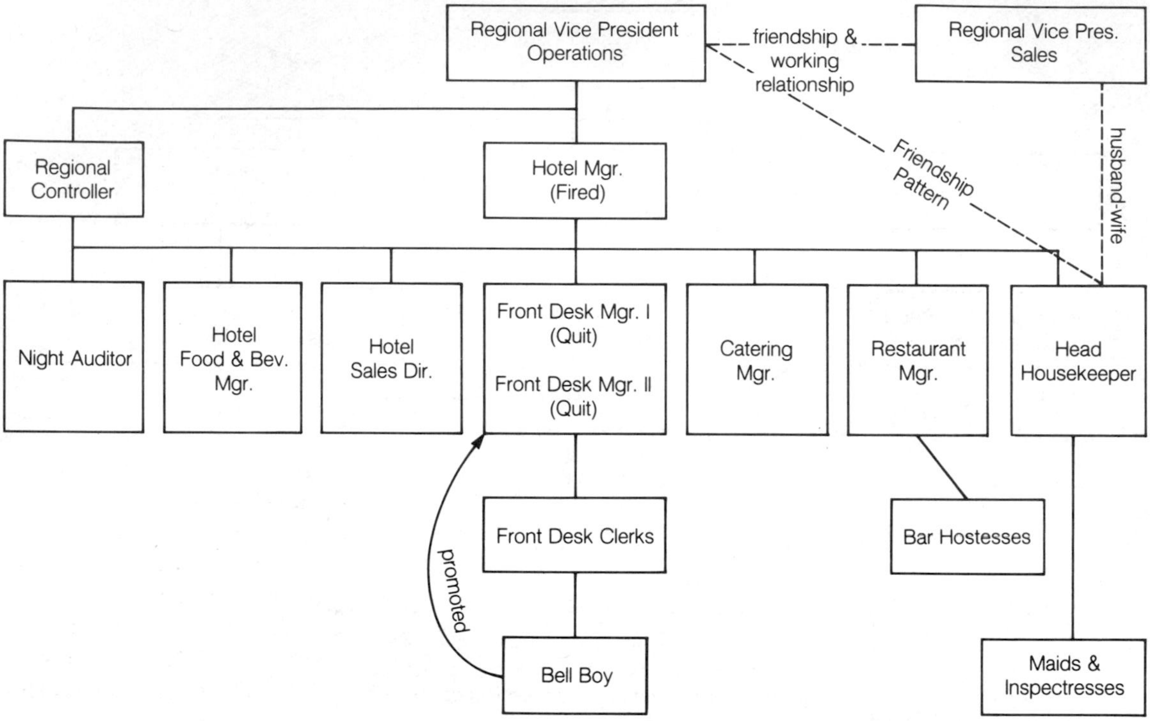

d. An assessment of the behavioral impact of a new high technology system on the hotel staff and guests.

The PMS was developed by DCI in collaboration with Techni-Lab, a computer hardware and software manufacturer, as well as one of the world's largest communications organizations. The PMS consisted of a Techni-Lab computer system integrated with standard DCI manufactured equipment.

The field trial began in February 1980 at The Carlton Hotel in San Antonio, Texas (see Exhibit 11–2). The Carlton was part of the Ripley organization, one of the world's largest hotel chains. The Carlton was chosen by DCI as its test site since its existing telecommunications equipment could adapt easily to the new technical hardware. From The Carlton's management viewpoint, the field trial allowed the hotel to test, without financial cost, an innovative system that would give the hotel a marketing edge over its competition as well as save energy at a time when energy costs were skyrocketing. The field trial at The Carlton was to take place in two phases starting in February 1980 and ending in June 1980 (see Exhibit 11–3).

The run during Phase I was not uneventful. The most serious problems were the down time during occasional "crashes" of the system and resistance of some of the hotel staff. Nevertheless, the trial was considered to be successful, and Phase II began. Unfortunately, the experience with Phase II was even more difficult.

The computer system was often down, requiring The Carlton to allow guests to leave with bills deferred for later billing because the old manual system for posting the bills had been completely removed and there was no way to extract them from the new system. Additionally, the hotel staff were not always sufficiently familiar with the operation of the system to use it effectively, and the manuals were poorly written and of little help.

EXHIBIT 11–3 ■ Field Trial at The Carlton

1. Background.

The installation took place in two phases that had the following features:

Phase I Features (February-March)

This part of the Property Management System (PMS) provides a modular computerized data collection and display system integrated with the hotel PBX to perform the following basic hotel-/motel functions:

1. *Room Status Management*
   Provides information on the status of each room in the property and assists the hotel personnel in the performance of the room management function.
2. *Housekeeping*
   Updates and displays housekeeping information to provide instantaneous status on the housekeeping conditions of the rooms in the hotel. The system also includes provisions for monitoring the assignment of maids and provides the means for reporting the housekeeping data.
3. *Automatic Wake-up*
   Operating automatically through the telephone lines, this feature will wake guests at a predesignated time with a prerecorded wake-up message.
4. *Night Audit*
   Audit displays are available for local telephone charges, wake-up summaries and house summaries to assist the night auditor in the performance of his/her functions. The audit can also be printed by the journal printer, providing hard copy.

Phase II Features (March-June)

Expansion is possible through the addition of optional features that enhance the basic system. Each of these features is modular and can be added to the system to provide additional operational and management control of the hotel/motel, such as:

1. *Guest Directory*
   A list of the current guests and their respective rooms occupied at the hotel is provided by this feature.
2. *Guest Ledger*
   The Guest Ledger/Charge Collection feature permits the collection of guest charges at revenue collection areas such as restaurant, pool, pro shop, etc., for allocation to the guest folios. This information is instantly posted electronically on the guest folio.
3. *Energy Control*
   Energy Control consists of a number of remotely located control units under control of the PMS System. The control units can turn off any power-consuming device capable of being electrically controlled. Once certain operating parameters are selected at installation, operation is completely automatic. Intervention is necessary only when the innkeeper elects to alter one of the initial operation conditions.

Even more serious were the personnel changes at The Carlton during the field trial. At the beginning of Phase II, The Carlton's manager, who was supportive and knowledgeable about the PMS, was fired. This firing occurred because the hotel was overbooked by 40 percent and several flight attendants from a large airline were among the many who could not be accommodated. Inasmuch as their airline had booked and paid for these rooms in advance, the flight attendants requested help in finding alternative arrangements. Because of a convention in town, the hotel found many unaccommodated, grumbling guests milling about the lobby. Since it was also running thin on staff, the hotel was unable to help them. The flight attendants called their airline headquarters in New York for help, reaching the vice president of personnel, who in turn called the hotel manager at 7:00 p.m. The hotel manager, who had been harassed and verbally insulted by stranded guests in the lobby, assumed that the vice president speaking to him was another flight attendant and hung up on her. She, in turn, immediately call the regional operations vice-president of the Ripley chain and demanded that the hotel manager be fired. Within a half an hour of the phone call, the hotel manager was discharged and was last seen loading his personal furniture on a rental truck the next day. Upon hearing the hotel manager was fired, the front desk manager, who was a friend of the hotel manager and also a supporter of the PMS, quit his job.

The next day, the bell captain was promoted to front desk manager and the regional operations vice-president assumed control of the day to day operations of the hotel. After two days, the newly appointed front desk manager quit, citing the pressure of the new job. He took a job in another hotel as a bellhop. One Carlton employee referred to these frequent changes as reflecting "soap opera management."

Other dynamics at The Carlton proved important. The head housekeeper of The Carlton was married to a vice president of the Ripley organization and lived on the property as did the regional operations vice president, who was now running the hotel. During Phase I, the head housekeeper was given a CRT (visual display) to allow her to enter and audit housekeeping data in the system. Noticing that she could also monitor the activity of the front desk on her CRT, she used it in her long-standing conflict with front desk personnel. She would call the front desk each time the front desk took an action she did not approve of, especially when a room was rented before she punched in that it had been completely cleaned, even though it was known to be ready. She also stormed the front desk from time to time, yelling and berating them for their incompetence.

Due to complaints from the front desk personnel, her CRT was taken away in Phase II and replaced by one with limited ability to monitor nonhousekeeping functions. She complained vociferously to her husband and the regional operations vice president. Her full-function CRT was returned the next day.

As a result of her negative feelings, she decided not to inform her maids to leave the fans of the individual room heating/airconditioning units in the "on" position. The computer system required this setting if the heating/airconditioning unit was to be controlled remotely from the front desk and thereby achieve energy savings. Further, the head housekeeper did not make an attempt to maintain the work standards of her maids, who had slowed down in anticipation of a "speed up" due to the PMS. Design of the other problems were also evident. The billing keyboard of the PMS at the front desk was the reverse of standard calculator keyboards. This resulted in slowed punching and errors when the front desk was under pressure to speed up at busy times. The night auditor/night manager who was undertrained on the system was hostile to it and bad-mouthed the system because she no longer felt important, as the system would do her auditing job. She also had fears that she might be discharged as no longer being needed. This was not true, but her fears were real to her. No one told her this was a field trial and might be a long time before a system was operational. Nor was she told that the regional operations vice president had made a commitment to DCI to keep her regardless of the system's capability, as she was needed to run the hotel at night and to use the system to prepare daily summary reports for him.

A further difficulty came about because the assignment of responsibility for maintaining the system was not clear. DCI expected their local office to provide training for the hotel staff and maintain the system with the help of Techni-Lab. The local office had received a transfer of funds from the corporate office for this purpose; however, once it was expended, the local office refused to commit its own resources to the project. Also, they lacked the expertise to deal with the frequent hardware problems. Techni-Labs was most reluctant to expend any effort to support the system as it was (unknown to DCI) in the process of phasing out of the computer business. The problems became so severe that after contact at the top levels of both companies and the commitment of more funds from DCI, the team of Techni-Lab engineers responsible for the development of the system's hardware and software were flown to San Antonio for the remainder of the field trial.

When the Techni-Lab engineers arrived at The Carlton, one hotel employee who had experienced all of the changes associated with the new PMS was heard remarking, "I don't know why everyone is so concerned with this system since it's never going to work here."

12

Acetate Department

The Acetate Department's product consisted of about twenty different kinds of viscous liquid acetate used by another department to manufacture transparent film to be left clear, or coated with photographic emulsion or iron oxide.

Before the change: The Department was located in an old four story building as in Exhibit 12–1. The work flow was as follows:

1. Twenty kinds of powder arrived daily in 50 pound paper bags. In addition, storage tanks of liquid would be filled weekly from tank trucks.
2. Two or three Acetate Helpers would jointly unload pallets of bags into the storage area using a lift truck.
3. Several times a shift, the Helpers would bring the bagged material up the elevator to the third floor where it would be temporarily stored along the walls.
4. Mixing batches was under the direction of the Group Leader and was rather like baking a cake. Following a prescribed formula, the Group Leader, Mixers and Helpers operate valves to feed in the proper solvent and manually dump in the proper weight and mixture of solid material. The glob would be mixed by giant egg beaters and heated according to the recipe.
5. When the batch was completed, it was pumped to a finished product storage tank.
6. After completing each batch, the crew would thoroughly clean the work area of dust and empty bags because cleanliness was extremely important to the finished product.

To accomplish this work, the Department was structured as in Exhibit 12–2.

The Helpers were usually young men 18–25 years of age; the Mixers 25 to 40 and the Group Leaders and Foremen 40 to 60. Foremen were on salary. Group Leaders, Mixers and Helpers on hourly pay.

From "Redesigning the Acetate Department," by David R. Hampton, Charles E. Summer, and Ross A. Webber, *Organizational Behavior and the Practice of Management* (Glenview, IL: Scott, Foresman and Company, 1982), pp. 751–755. Used with permission.

EXHIBIT 12–1 ■ Elevation View of Acetate Department Before Change

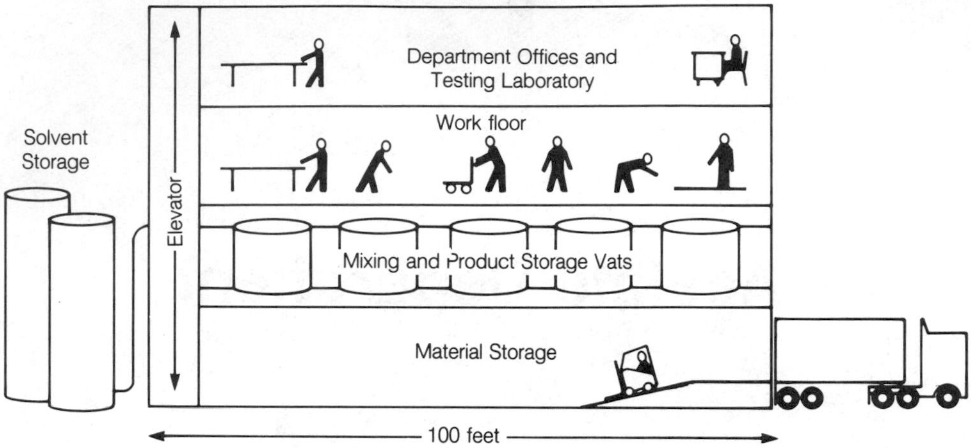

To produce 20,000,000 pounds of product per year, the Department operated 24 hours a day, 7 days a week. Four crews rotated shifts: for example, Shift Foremen A and his two Group Leaders and crews would work two weeks on the day shift 8:00 a.m. to 4:00 p.m., then two weeks on the evening shift 4:00 p.m. to midnight, then two weeks on the night shift midnight to 8:00 a.m. There were two days off between shift changes.

During a typical shift, a Group Leader and his crew would complete two or three batches. A batch would frequently be started on one shift and completed by the next shift crew. There was slightly less work on the evening and night shifts because no deliveries were made, but

EXHIBIT 12–2 ■ Organizational Chart of Acetate Department Before Change

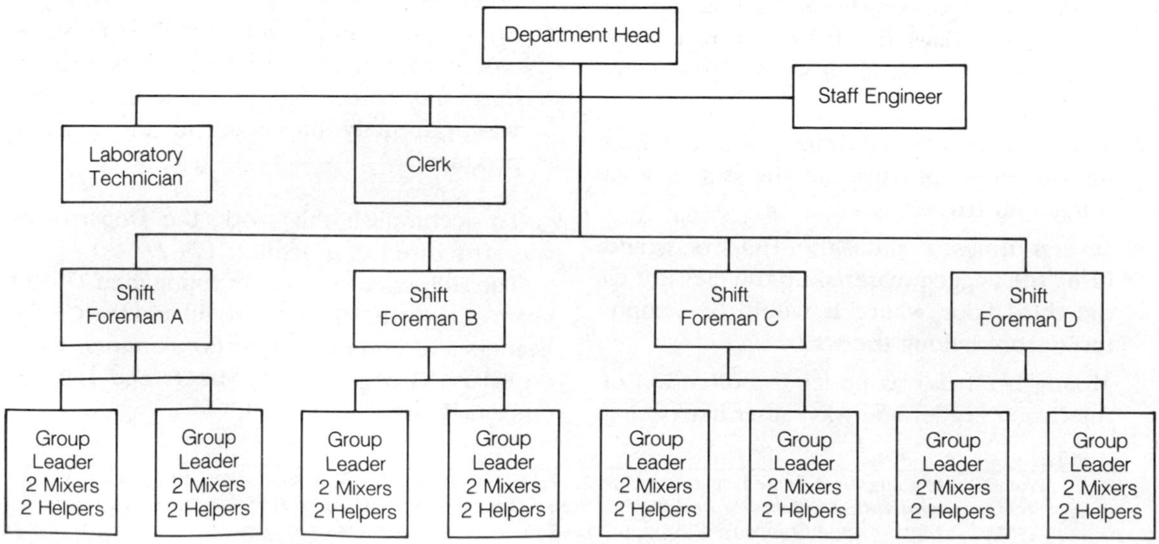

EXHIBIT 12–3 ■ Elevation View of Acetate Department After Change

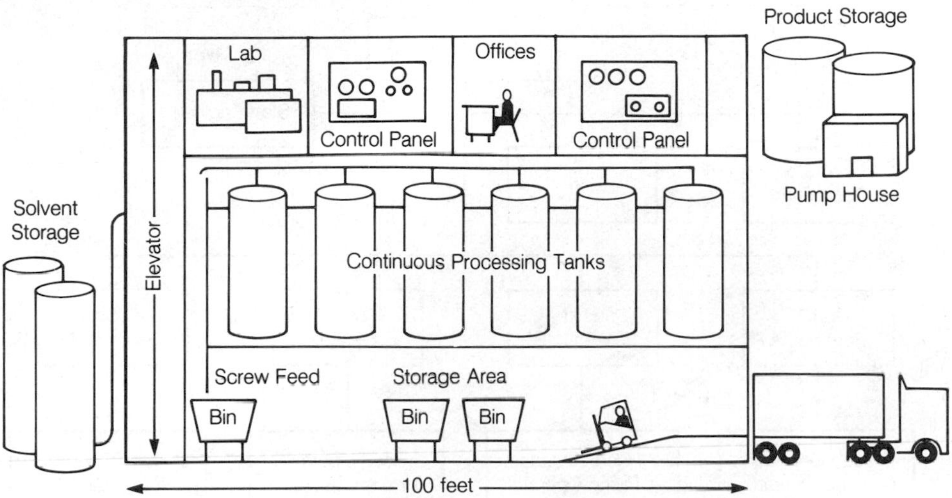

these crews engaged in a little more cleaning. The Shift Foreman would give instructions to the two Group Leaders at the beginning of each shift as to the status of batches in process, batches to be mixed, what deliveries were expected and what cleaning was to be done. Periodically throughout the shift, the Foreman would collect samples in small bottles which he would leave at the laboratory technicians' desk for testing.

The management and office staff (Department Head, Staff Engineer, Lab Technician, and Department Clerk only worked on the day shift, although if an emergency arose on the other shifts, the Foreman might call.

All in all, the Department was a pleasant place in which to work. The work floor was a little warm, but well-lighted, quiet and clean. Substantial banter and horseplay occurred when the crew wasn't actually loading batches, particularly on the nonday shifts. The men had a dartboard in the work area and competition was fierce and loud. Frequently a crew would go bowling right after work, even at 1:00 a.m., for the community's alleys were open 24 hours a day. Department turnover and absenteeism were low. Most employees spent their entire career with the Company, many in one department. The corporation was large, paternalistic, well-paying, and offered attractive fringe benefits including large, virtually automatic bonuses for all. Then came the change. . . .

The new system: To improve productivity, the Acetate Department was completely redesigned, the technology changed from batches to continuous processing. The basic building was retained, but substantially modified as in Exhibit 12–3. The modified work flow is as follows:

1. Most solid raw materials are delivered via trucks in large aluminum bins holding 500 pounds.
2. One Handler (formerly Helper) is on duty at all times in the first floor to receive raw materials and to dump the bins into the semiautomatic screw feeder.
3. The Head Operator (former Group Leader) directs the mixing operations from his control panel on the fourth floor located along one wall across from the Department Offices. The mixing is virtually an automatic operation once the solid material has been sent up the screw feed; a tape program

EXHIBIT 12–4 ▪ Organizational Chart of Acetate Department After Change

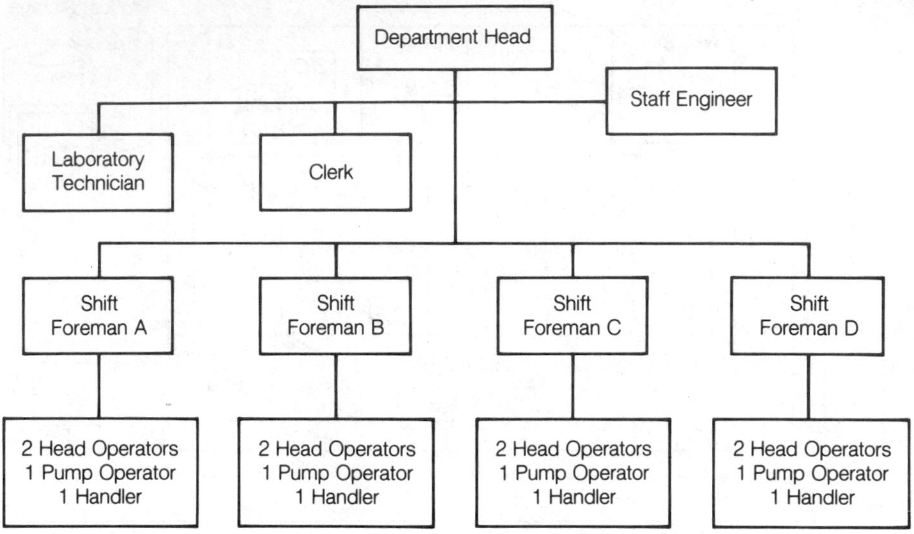

opens and closes the necessary valves to add solvent, heat, mixing, etc. Sitting at a table before his panel, the Head Operator monitors the process to see that everything is operating within specified temperatures and pressures.

This technical change allowed the Department to greatly reduce its manpower. The new structure is illustrated in Exhibit 12–4.

One new position was created, that of a pump operator who is located in a small separate shack about 300 feet from the main building. He operates pumps and valves that move the finished product among various storage tanks.

Under the new system, production capacity was increased to 25,000,000 pounds per year. All remaining employees received a 15 percent increase in pay. Former personnel not retained in the Dope Department were transferred to other departments in the company. No one was dismissed.

Unfortunately, actual output has lagged well below capacity in the several months since the construction work and technical training was completed. Actual production is virtually identical with that under the old technology. Absenteeism has increased markedly and several judgmental errors by operators have resulted in substantial losses.

13

Kalen's Supermarkets, Inc.

As ground was broken for a new Kalen's Supermarket in June 1981, the company's top management was in the process of deciding what type of checkstand equipment to buy for the store. Kalen's had installed scanning equipment in three stores in 1980 to decrease labor costs and improve their profit margins. After a year of experience, management was concerned because apparently it was not receiving the full benefits of the system. In the next three months, it intended to make a thorough evaluation of scanning in order to reach a decision for the new store.

Company Background

Kalen's Supermarkets, located in Louisville, Kentucky, was a family-run business with eleven stores in the greater Louisville area. Started by Joe Kalen in a 500-square-foot store in 1937, the business had grown to serve 5.7 million customers in 1980 with sales of over $110 million.

Kalen's success was the result of offering customers quality food at competitive prices with the best service possible. Kalen's services included courtesy clerks to carry groceries, having a qualified meat cutter on duty at all times, an easy check-cashing policy, and night stocking to avoid cluttering aisles during the day. The stores were notable for immaculate appearance, friendly employees, wide aisles, restrooms, and a delicatessen and pastry shop. Kalen's was so devoted to its customers' needs that a particular store would often carry an item even if only one customer wanted it.

The company's emphasis on customer service had paid off handsomely through the years. Despite ranking third in number of stores in

This case was prepared by Bruce A. Atherley, under the supervision of E. W. Davis, Oliver Wight Professor of Business Administration, Colgate Darden Graduate School. Names, places, and figures have been disguised.

Louisville (behind Safeway's twenty-three and A&P's fourteen), Kalen's had a 21-percent share of market, compared with Safeway's 28 percent and A&P's 14 percent. In addition, earnings after taxes had averaged 1.5 percent of sales versus the industry average of 0.87 percent.
Kalen's "people orientation" also extended to its 1,300 employees. Excellent benefits, including an annual company picnic, bonuses for full-time employees, and opportunity for advancement resulted in a low turnover rate and no employees being represented by unions.
The company was managed by James and Robert Kalen, sons of the founder. Both had attended college, and Bob had received an MBA from a well-known southeastern business school. The next level of management included a controller and eight supervisors, who were each responsible for a particular department such as meat, produce, or general merchandise. Most of the supervisors had not attended college but had worked their way up through the business, generally starting as clerks. As a group, they had approximately 150 years of experience in the grocery business.

Operations

A supermarket is a low-margin business that depends on volume to make a profit. Although Kalen's had consistently managed to achieve above-average earnings, it was always looking for opportunities to reduce costs. Out of every one dollar in sales, approximately eighty cents went towards the cost of the merchandise, ten cents to pay for labor, and eight cents for utilities, advertising, taxes, and other miscellaneous items. Thus, the two logical areas for cost control were inventory and labor.

At any time, Kalen's stores would have approximately $3.5 million tied up in merchandise, either on the shelf, in the stores' backrooms, or in the central warehouse. Inventory carrying cost was estimated at 20 percent. Since this merchandise represented a good part of their net assets, it was important that stores were not overstocked. On the other hand, not enough merchandise or the wrong mix of products would result in "stockouts," leading to lost sales and customer dissatisfaction. At each Kalen's store, the ordering function was performed by the night grocery crew that stocked the shelves. Each person in the crew was responsible for every product in one aisle of the store. Four times a week, he or she would place an order with a wholesaler based on the stock on hand and what would sell. Since the crew was, for the most part, very experienced, they generally did a good job of managing the inventory. However, as each store carried over 12,000 items, measuring the crew's performance with any precision was extremely difficult.

The second possible area for cost control was labor. At Kalen's, the greatest portion of wages, 30 percent, was paid to the people staffing the front end—that section of the store where customer purchases were totaled by cashiers and bagged by courtesy clerks. For every cashier, there were, on average, 1.5 courtesy clerks, since they had to bag and carry groceries to customer cars. In addition, a front-end manager was responsible for authorizing checks, handling customer complaints, and making sure the front end ran smoothly.

Each cashier was stationed at a checkstand about 35 inches high and eight feet long that consisted of a cash register and a conveyor belt that brought a customer's purchases to the cashier and then to the courtesy clerk. Depending on the sales volume, each store had eight to twelve checkstands.

In eight of the stores, the customer unloaded purchases onto the conveyor belt. In three stores, over-the-end (OTE) checkstands were used where the customer cart was wheeled directly to the end of the conveyor belt, the front edge of the cart was unlatched and lowered, and the checker unloaded merchandise with one hand and entered the price into the register with the other.

Cashiers used key-entry systems at eight Kalen's stores to total customer purchases. These systems consisted of a series of electronic cash registers (ECRs) linked to an in-store computer. With the exception of the newer scanning systems, the ECR link-up was the most sophisticated cash register system available. ECRs would automatically calculate and add in taxes, electronically weigh and price produce, record bottle refunds and coupons, and track sales of produce and other items through the use of a look-up code.[1] In addition, a cashier was able to enter item prices much faster than with a conventional cash register, since the ECR keyboard only had ten keys. The computer link-up allowed management to collect department and store sales daily and to monitor an individual cashier's performance in terms of speed. Kalen's had tested ECRs in 1974 and by 1978 had put them in all its stores.

Use of Scanning in Supermarkets

The factor that made the development of scanning possible was the Universal Product Code (UPC). UPC symbols were machine-readable bar codes that identified products with a ten-digit number consisting of a manufacturer code and a product code. This system of uniquely identifying products was developed by the food industry to allow the use of scanner-equipped checkstands by retailers and to provide detailed product-movement information to manufacturers.

Scanning equipment required optical scanners built into the checkstand and an in-store computer to read the UPC symbols. As a cashier passed an item over the scanner, the scanner read the code and sent it to the computer for price matching. This information was sent back to the terminal, where the price and a description of the product were printed on the sales receipt and simultaneously displayed on a view screen for the customer. One of the benefits of this system for the customer was that the register tape provided more detailed information on purchases than other systems.

Scanning was first introduced to the supermarket industry in 1972, when the Kroger Company tested a prototype system for fifteen months in a Cincinnati supermarket. Although no UPC symbols existed at that time, Kroger used similar identification markings for the test. The results, while not totally conclusive, were generally promising. The test verified that cash savings could be achieved and checker productivity improved with scanning, but several benefits, such as better inventory and management control, were difficult to quantify. Nevertheless, on the basis of the test, many people predicted that scanning would revolutionize the industry.

Several obstacles had to be overcome, however, before the new technology would become common. The most obvious was the need for food manufacturers to change their packaging to include UPC codes. Retailers felt that until 65 percent of all items were coded, scanning would not be feasible, since a cashier would have to key-enter so many uncoded prices.

In order to accomplish this task, a central agency was formed of food manufacturers, wholesalers, and retailers to administer the UPC program and to see that it became an industry standard. Despite the several billion dollars in packaging equipment costs that the manufacturers had to absorb, they went along with the program since they would ultimately get more detailed product-movement information from the program than ever before possible. Nevertheless, it was not until 1976 that 65 percent of grocery items were coded. By 1978, the percentage had risen to 80 percent, and by 1981, over 95 percent of grocery items included the UPC.[2]

[1]Instead of entering the price, the cashier would enter a two-digit code, and the computer would automatically supply the price.

[2]This figure did not include random weight items, such as meat and produce, as well as many nonfood items. Of the approximately 12,000 items carried by a typical Kalen's, only 74 percent were scannable in 1981.

Benefits of Scanning

Another problem that slowed the acceptance of scanning was the difficulty of quantifying many of the benefits of scanning, which could be divided into "hard" and "soft":

"Hard" benefits were generally related to the speed and accuracy of store operations and provided savings in operating costs, and thus, improvements in gross profit. The three principal hard benefits that could be achieved were improved checker productivity, more efficient pricing, and a reduction in merchandise shrinkage.

In the Kroger test, checker productivity had greatly improved with scanning, because the cashiers did not have to enter prices manually and because price checks were virtually eliminated.[3] Kroger found that the average time required to process an order decreased from 3.82 minutes to 2.6 minutes with scanning. In a similar study done in 1976, Giant Food, Inc. calculated that the increase in checker speed with scanning translated into a $5,112 savings per month in a $140,000 sales/week store. However, both studies compared cashier speed with scanning against cashier speed with mechanical registers. As noted earlier, ECRs also offered the potential to increase cashier speed due to the simplified keyboard. Therefore, the increase in checker productivity that could be realized from scanning depended on what type of equipment a scanner would be replacing.

A second "hard" benefit was more efficient pricing. In nonscanning stores, prices had to be applied to every item using a pricing gun to attach a gummed label. In scanning stores, prices were identified by a shelf tag that appeared underneath the product. This tag carried the name of the item, its size, price, and the unit price. The unit price was a price per standard measure that the customer could use to compare prices of different-sized items.

The only time that shelf tags had to be replaced was when they were damaged or a price changed. With item pricing, if a price changed, each item had to be taken off the shelf, the original gummed label scraped off, and the new price reapplied. Since Kalen's had price changes every week on over 400 items, shelf pricing provided a substantial labor saving.

Reduction in merchandise shrinkage, a third "hard" benefit of scanning, was principally derived from reductions in "under-ring losses," which occurred when cashiers rang up a lower-than-actual item price.

Under-ring losses were reduced in a scanning store because there were fewer opportunities for cashiers to make pricing errors. In a nonscanning store, checker errors could result in either an "over-ring" or an under-ring. Since customers would more often bring an over-ring to the attention of the checker, the result was a net under-ring loss.

The increase in pricing discipline also reduced under-rings. In a scanning store, prices were being checked constantly to ensure that the price in the computer matched the price on the shelf. Since the great majority of general price changes were increases, there were fewer incorrect prices to result in under-rings.

For example, at Dick's Supermarkets in Wisconsin, the introduction of scanners yielded an estimated 0.6 percent of sales saving in shrinkage in a $150,000 sales/week store. However, as Bill Brodbeck, vice-president of Dick's stated, "These disciplines could be put into place in a nonscanning store and the same increase in gross profit dollars would occur. The question is, will or can the average supermarket put such practices into place without being forced to do so by a scanning system?" He estimated that no more than 60 percent of the improvement possible with scanning could be achieved in a nonscanning store.

The "soft" benefits of scanning were related to improved management information and control. Three areas where the detailed information provided by scanning was useful were

[3]When an item did not have a price tag, the cashier had to wait while a clerk checked the price.

labor scheduling, checker evaluation, and merchandising.

Since scanning systems recorded the time that customer transactions took place, labor schedules for checkers and baggers could be based on the number of items purchased per time interval rather than on dollar sales. This information could improve store operations by enabling managers to eliminate extra labor during slack shopping periods and improve customer service by adding labor at peak periods. Many ECR systems were able to generate the same information, however.

Scanning could improve checker evaluations by providing scan reports on average transaction value, average customer purchase, coupon redemption, number of voids, and items scanned per minute. This information was generally used to eliminate "sweethearting," and to motivate cashiers to work faster. Sweethearting involved the cashier ringing up a lower-than-actual item price (i.e., under-ringing) or simply allowing items to pass the checkout stand undetected. Sweethearting was held in check because management could identify cashiers who consistently had a lower than average customer purchases. Motivation was often improved by instituting a cashier performance system in which cashiers received feedback on their performance and rewards were given for increasing their speed.

Problems could crop up with the measurement of performance, however, since checkers could "beat the system." For example, to increase their item count they could scan each of 24 cans in a case of soft drinks. Another problem was the definition of performance. At many supermarkets, including Kalen's, the cashiers were encouraged to know the customers on a first-name basis, which slowed them down but enhanced valuable public relations.

The third principal "soft" benefit of scanning resulted from using product-movement reports to make in-store merchandising decisions. Before scanning, retailers had to use warehouse-withdrawal information to make merchandising decisions. This information consisted of the number of cases of a given brand that were shipped to a particular store each month. While the information provided a rough guideline to the best-selling brands, it was not very precise or timely due to the effects of changing retail inventories, interstore shipments, and product promotions. Also, these warehouse figures did not include Direct Store Delivery (DSD) items.[4]

With scanners, retailers were able to find out the exact quantity sold, in units and dollars, of any UPC-coded item and could also determine the items' gross profit. This information could be used for such purposes as: (1) determining which brands should be dropped and which given more shelf space and (2) evaluating the effect of a change in location or visibility of a product category. Armed with accurate, by-brand, and timely (weekly) sales information, retailers were able to make in-store merchandising changes that had never been considered prior to scanning because of lack of information.

Despite all the benefits of scanning, retailers were slow to adopt the new technology because of the uncertainty surrounding the acceptance of the UPC code and the difficulty of quantifying the soft benefits. By 1976, only 125 supermarkets had installed scanning. Since 1976, more scanners had been installed in each year than the previous year. But by mid-1981, only 10 percent of the nation's 34,900 supermarkets had scanning.

The 1980 Decision to Install Scanning at Kalen's

Kalen's 1980 decision to install scanning equipment in three stores, two new ones and a remodeled store, had been made for three reasons. The primary reason was defensive. In

[4]DSD products, such as drinks, snacks, ice cream, and cookies, were warehoused by brokers and manufacturers and stocked on the retail shelf by salespeople.

EXHIBIT 13–1 ■ Kalen's Calculations: Scanning Payback in 1979

Additional Cost of Scanning over ECRs:	$50,000 per store
Savings: 10% at the front-end	
Front-end director labor hours/week at a $200,000/week store	1,000–1,400 hrs./week
10% reduction	100–140 hrs./week
1979 Average Wage	$3.73/hr.
1st year saving (1979)	$19,396*–$27,154
2nd year saving (1980) (assume wages increase 5%)	$20,384–$28,538
3rd year saving (1981) (assume wages increase 5%)	$21,424–$29,993

*(100 hrs./week) × (52 weeks/year) × ($3.73/hr.) = $19,396

Source: Company records.

the late 1970s, Giant Food, Inc., a 125-store chain based in Washington, D.C., had committed to install scanners in every store as soon as possible. Giant had three stores in Louisville, which Kalen's monitored closely since Giant emphasized many of the same sales features as Kalen's, such as cleanliness and customer service. Giant had stated that it would be able to lower prices as a result of scanning savings, and Kalen's was concerned about the potential impact on its business. Management thought that to delay going with scanning would mean giving up its position of leadership in providing customer value.

Another reason for going to scanning was that it appeared to be a good investment. Kalen's anticipated that scanning equipment and maintenance would cost $50,000 more per store than the type of key-entry system presently in use. Based on information from equipment vendors and other retailers, however, it estimated scanning would decrease front-end labor costs by 10 percent and payback would come in two to two and a half years (Exhibit 13–1). To be conservative, it did not consider any of the other possible savings.

The third reason for installing scanning at that time was to save money on hardware. It appeared that the technology would continue to become more expensive, so that, if Kalen's waited, the payback period would lengthen.

Kalen's Actual Scanning Experience

Kalen's actual experience with scanning was quite different from its projections. To begin with, management vastly underestimated the amount of support necessary to get the system working and keep it running smoothly. Getting price changes into the system, keeping shelf tags in the store up to date, maintaining the central item-price file in the computer, and getting the software to work properly were all tasks that turned out to be far more time consuming than originally anticipated. These tasks required the full-time services of a computer programmer, a scanning coordinator, a clerk, and a pricing specialist for each scanning store. Thus, the original $150,000 estimate of additional costs for scanning turned out to be $373,000 in the first year. In addition to the extra cost, the emphasis on simply running the system prevented Kalen's from focusing attention on gaining the expected benefits. Moreover, the number of scanning vendors continued to increase, and the scanning technology seemed to be improving. By the end of the first year, Kalen's management was very uncertain about scanning and decided to put an indefinit

EXHIBIT 13–2 ▪ Monthly Cost-Benefit Analysis: Scanning vs. ECR System

Additional Costs of Scanning (per month per store):	
Equipment rental	$1,236.90
Equipment maintenance	590.96
Pricing specialist and additional help required for changing shelf tags	1,488.00
Computer support supplied by wholesaler	400.00
Total additional costs	3,715.86
Office support required for scanning stores (fixed cost per month; will not change if additional scan stores are added)	3,848.13
Identified Benefits (per month per store):	
1 night stock clerk	1,260.00
Price change savings	506.25
Cost of labels and tags saved	249.20
Savings from elimination of yearly price checks	32.75
Total identified benefits	$2,048.20
Benefits Not Yet Calculated:	
Checker productivity	
Merchandising information	
Gross profit improvement (shrink reduction)	

Source: Company records.

hold on new scanning installations until an evaluation could be made.

Evaluation

Nelson Keegan, Kalen's controller, did a preliminary cost-benefit analysis of scanning, which is reproduced in Exhibit 13–2. His analysis identified four savings from the system:

The primary benefit came from the elimination of item pricing. Originally, management had decided to continue individual item pricing at the scanning stores because they feared adverse consumer reaction. Some consumers felt that shelf pricing was inadequate since the price in the computer could be different from the price on the shelf. These consumers were vocal enough to get laws passed in several states by 1980 that made item pricing mandatory. Kalen's wanted to remove prices but also wanted to avoid at all costs taking a position that would align it against the consumer because that would hurt its image. Since it appeared not to be realizing any front-end savings from scanning after eight months, however, it decided to remove prices in December 1982 and, by doing it quietly, suffered no adverse effect. With this move, it was able to reduce the number of men on the grocery crew who stocked and priced merchandise by one man per scanning store and also to save labor on price changes.

Another benefit resulting from dropping item pricing was an increase in pricing discipline. Because of the necessity of having a pricing specialist in each store to ensure that the shelf tags matched the prices in the computer, pricing errors were greatly reduced. Before scanning, Kalen's checked all the prices in the stores once a year and generally found about 5 percent incorrect. In the scanning stores, prices were being checked constantly and, in a recent audit, were found to be 99.2 percent correct. The increased discipline carried over to the key-entry stores as well, since the incorrect price percentage had dropped to 2 percent in recent months.

In order to determine other benefits that could be realized from scanning, Bob Kalen initiated studies in the summer of 1981 on checker productivity and merchandising benefits:

Since after a year of experience with scanning, Kalen's had seen no apparent front-end savings, a checker productivity program was initiated to raise the speed of the cashiers at the scanning stores without affecting the friendly, courteous atmosphere at the front end. At the time the program was started, cashiers at the scan stores were no faster than those at the key-entry stores, on the average. Carol Beth Martin, the training specialist assigned to the program, hypothesized three reasons for the lack of improvement of the scanning cashiers:

1) Cashiers were forced to spend time bagging when courtesy clerks were taking groceries to customer cars;
2) The older, more experienced cashiers resisted using the correct motion to scan items and tended to spend more time chatting with customers;
3) Because only 74 percent of items were scannable, the cashier's "scanning motion" was often broken.

To improve productivity, the courtesy clerk-to-cashier ratio was increased to 2 to 1 at one of the scanning stores (#92) and Carol Beth instituted a program of refresher meetings and feedback on performance to the cashiers. After three months, Carol Beth had accumulated data on cashier speed from the three scanning stores and three key-entry stores. At this point, she needed to decide if the cashiers at the scanning stores had indeed become faster and, if so, whether the increased speed would mean a decrease in labor hours.

In order to determine the extent of the merchandising benefits achievable with scanning, Bob Kalen hired an MBA summer intern to analyze the sales information generated by the three scan stores. The intern's primary objective was to quantify the benefit of using scanning sales information to make in-store merchandising changes. To accomplish the task, two controlled in-store tests were designed for flexible-bag snacks and cookies, respectively.

In the cookie area, the impetus behind the test was a merchandising idea that Bob had been reluctant to implement because of a lack of information. The idea was to create a special four-foot section in the cookie aisle that would contain reduced-price cookies. It was thought that this new section would increase total cookie sales because people would be attracted by the bargains. In a typical Kalen's, the specially priced items were spread throughout the aisle rather than grouped. If the test was successful, all eleven stores would be reset to include a special section. The results of the test are reproduced in Exhibit 13–3.

The snack test was designed to settle a continuing disagreement between Kalen's store managers about merchandising flexible-bag snacks. Several managers believed that using two secondary snack displays in the store increased total sales of snacks. Others believed that these extra displays merely transferred sales from the shelf to the displays and that no displays were required. To settle the argument and find the most profitable alternative, a controlled test was developed. The details of the test and the results are presented in Exhibit 13–4.

After analyzing the results of the two tests, Bob Kalen and the intern were still uncertain as to what dollar benefit should be ascribed to scanning. Both realized that the sales increases were not directly attributable to the scanning information, but without the information, the changes probably would not have been made. Also, Bob knew that to achieve any further

EXHIBIT 13–3 ▪ Merchandising Test: Cookies

Objective: Determine if a four-foot "special buys" section for cookies increases total cookie sales.

Test Design: The test was conducted over a two-week period, August 3 to 15, at store #91. During the two weeks, no cookie items appeared in the ad and there were no secondary cookie displays allowed in the store. For the first week, the section was left unchanged with "special buys" scattered throughout the total 48-foot cookie section. For the second week, the section was reset to include a "special buys" section where four items were prominently featured. Customer count for the store was noted.

Manufacturer	Week #1	Week #2
Murray	$ 322.58	$ 310.56
FFV	101.31	76.06
Keebler	479.45	600.85
Nabisco	823.21	863.24
MaMa	89.95	50.53
Brenner	12.46	6.23
Sunshine	193.55	228.30
Royal Crest	39.04	48.16
Archway	111.00	77.43
Fireside	25.99	10.05
Jacks	8.31	12.66
Pepperidge Farm	109.99	105.23
Salerno	15.48	0
Richfood	—	—
TOTAL	$ 2,332.32	$ 2,389.30
Customer Count	11,247	10,976

Note: Gross margin is approximately twenty-one percent for the total cookie category.
Source: Company records.

benefits would mean hiring a scan analyst to design tests and interpret the data and would also require management time if the scanning information was to be used properly.

Other benefits that had been cited by scanning-equipment manufacturers, such as the reduction in shrinkage, were impossible to measure precisely. Kalen's knew such benefits should show up in gross profit, but looking at the numbers in Exhibit 13–5, it was unsure whether scanning had made a positive contribution or not.

In addition to its own company data, Kalen's was able to get some information from other independent supermarket chains about scanning benefits. This information is presented in Exhibit 13–6.

The New Store

The new store was due to be completed in January 1982. With 33,500 square feet, it would be the largest store in the chain and was expected to relieve some of the congestion at the Masterson Avenue Kalen's (#89) located only one half mile away. The Masterson store was Kalen's leading store. In 1981, it had averaged almost $300,000 in sales each week, and its volume had grown at a rate of 25 percent each year since opening in 1975.

In the first year, Kalen's management hoped to draw $100,000 per week from the Masterson store and to generate $50,000 of additional

EXHIBIT 13–4 ■ Merchandising Test: Flexible-Bag Snacks

Objective: Determine the incremental dollar sales generated by secondary snack displays.

Test Design: The test was conducted over a two-week period, August 3 to 15, in the three scan stores. During the two weeks of the test, no snack items were advertised, since this would have invalidated the results. During the first week, all three stores sold snacks only off the shelf (no secondary displays) in order to provide comparative data. During the second week of the test, Store #88 put up two secondary displays (Frito-Lay and Wise), Store #92 put up one display (Wise), and Store #91 again had no secondary displays. To ensure that the test was not biased by business conditions, customer count was noted.

	Store #88		Store #91		Store #92	
Manufacturer	*WK#1*	*WK#2*	*WK#1*	*WK#2*	*WK#1*	*WK#2*
UTZ	$ 360.11	$ 327.67	$ 355.67	$ 400.53	$ 414.64	$ 473.87
Wise	268.37	313.28	407.72	249.21	379.69	466.40
Frito-Lay	1,410.44	1,715.85	1,657.33	1,803.50	1,377.47	1,522.05
Snyders	119.26	126.27	152.03	128.98	161.98	168.16
Charles	122.63	101.30	132.82	110.80	116.20	123.06
Gibbles	137.23	140.81	178.12	206.18	167.72	150.08
Keebler	12.75	17.00	18.70	13.60	6.80	12.75
Nabisco	96.63	87.42	112.22	59.97	97.53	108.70
Pringles	76.59	84.60	71.16	82.95	89.73	83.37
Richfood	37.05	22.44	47.50	40.84	43.70	38.23
Other	38.61	59.40	29.70	44.55	57.42	52.47
TOTAL	$2,679.67	$2,996.04	$ 3,162.97	$ 3,141.11	$2,912.88	$3,199.14
Customer count	9,443.00	9,376.00	11,247.00	10,976.00	9,282.00	9,000.00

Note: Approximate gross profit margin is 24% for snacks.
Source: Company records.

sales from competing supermarkets in the area. They estimated that because of the overcrowding at Masterson, they were losing approximately $50,000 in business each week to neighboring supermarkets, such as the Safeway store that backed up to the new store.

In deciding what type of checkstand equipment to install in the new store, Kalen's was concerned about several factors. The primary one was customer acceptance. Since it planned to draw customers from the Masterson store, Kalen's wanted to minimize the confusion for those customers switching stores. Therefore, it decided to use the checker unload system used at Masterson. Although this method was slower than customer unload, surveys done by Kalen's in 1979 had found that approximately 75 percent of customers strongly preferred the checker unload system.

With this decision made, Kalen's management had to make a decision on scanning. The Masterson store had a key-entry system, but the Safeway store had scanning and had removed item prices. In fact, in the greater Louisville area, 12 supermarkets out of a total of 90 were equipped with scanning. Despite the acceptance of scanning by most customers in Louisville, the future of shelf pricing was cloudy. The Kentucky State Legislature was soon to consider a bill that could make item pricing mandatory and thereby eliminate a large dollar savings for supermarkets.

Another issue in the checkstand decision-making process involved the merchandising

EXHIBIT 13–5 ■ Gross Profit Margins: Grocery and Frozen Food**

Store No.	1979	1980	1981
#81	17.01%	16.87%	17.37%
#82	17.19%	17.02%	17.13%
#83	16.83%	17.24%	17.35%
#84	17.90%	17.64%	17.65%
#85	17.01%	17.07%	17.06%
#86	17.56%	16.49%	17.18%
#87	17.81%	17.49%	17.66%
#88*	17.44%	17.72%	18.41%
#89	17.81%	18.68%	17.60%
#91*	17.61%	17.75%	17.51%
#92*		17.69%	18.15%
Company total	17.39%	17.45%	17.57%

Years refer to Kalen's fiscal year, which runs from August 1 to July 31. Therefore, 1979 figures are at July 31, 1979.

*Scanning stores: scanners installed spring 1980.
**Meat, produce, and general merchandise sales account for approximately 30% of sales volume. Gross profit margins for these departments are excluded since scanning has little impact on them. Data has been disguised.

benefits of scanning. The customer demographics of the new store were very similar to those at another Kalen's scan store. Since these two stores were also approximately the same size and had the same layout, Kalen's was not certain that scanning was needed at the new store to provide merchandising information.

One of the biggest questions in the checkstand decision-making process arose because of the rapidly evolving technology of the scanning equipment. In 1980, Kalen's had acquired a model 3650 programmable store system, the most advanced hardware and software package available from IBM, yet in mid-1982, a new system was due to be released that would provide 180-degree scanning capability and cost less than the old system. The new 3687 scanner would be the first to combine laser light with holography, enabling it to read UPC codes on the underside and vertical sides of items up to four and a half inches above the scanning window. While the exact price for the complete system was not known at this time, indications were that it would cost at least $12,000 less than the current 3650 programmable store system.

If purchased, a 3650 system would cost approximately $160,000 for a ten-checkstand system. However, Kalen's could lease several of the elements, which would reduce the purchase price to $120,000 and add a monthly lease payment of $1,512. Maintenance on this system would be approximately the same as with the 3687: $1,338 per month. To buy a key-entry system similar to the Masterson store's would cost approximately $75,000, while a combination purchase/lease agreement would cost $59,000 and $465 per month. Maintenance for the key-entry system would be about $730 per month.

Since Kalen's had no desire to be saddled with obsolete technology six months after the store opened, management negotiated with IBM to give them two other options. They could lease the key-entry system on a six-month renewable basis and then convert to the 3687, or they could lease the 3650 system and convert. Of course, if they did not want to convert

EXHIBIT 13–6 ▪ Other Supermarkets' Evaluation of Scanning Benefits

***DICK'S SUPERMARKETS*—Platteville, Wisconsin**
Annual savings in a $150,000 sales/week store: (compared with electronic cash registers)

Shrinkage savings	$46,800	(Estimated from improvement in gross margin)
Checker productivity	35,755	(120 hrs/wk × $5.73/hr × 52 wks)
Shelf pricing	16,788	(55 hrs/wk × $5.87/hr × 52 wks)
Price change savings	2,598	
Tracking of in-ad coupons	2,373	(7 hrs/wk manual counting × $6.52 × 52 wks)

***EASTER'S SUPERMARKETS*—Altoona, Iowa**
Annual savings in a $125,000 sales/week store (compared with electronic cash registers)

Checker productivity	$ 4,178	(16.5 hrs/wk × $4.87/hr × 52 wks)
Shrinkage savings	0	(No improvement in gross margin figures)
Shelf pricing	8,944	(43 hrs/wk × $4.00/hr × 52 wks)
Price change savings	1,820	(5 hrs/wk × $7.00/hr × 52 wks)

***GIANT FOOD, INC.*—Landover, Maryland**
Annual savings in a $140,000 sales/week store (compared with mechanical cash registers)

Checker productivity	$61,344	(Calculated on basis of hourly wage, $6.40/hr, which includes fringe benefits.)
Shelf pricing	32,940	
Reduction in under-rings	10,920	(Estimated that under-ring losses amount to 0.2% of sales and that scanning will eliminate 75% of this loss, i.e., $140,000 × 52 weeks × .002 × .75.)
Routine ordering benefit	31,766	(Not in practice yet but assumes savings of 31 hours × $8.54 × 52 wks).

when the 3687 was introduced, they could purchase either the key-entry system or the 3650.

The Decision

With the store opening only seven months away, Kalen's management needed to reach a decision. They liked the flexibility of the six-month lease arrangements but realized that they still needed to make a basic decision on whether or not to go with scanning.

James and Bob Kalen believed that the company would continue to be successful with or without scanning. However, with many of their competitors—especially the large chains—installing scanners in greater numbers, they were concerned about falling behind the industry. Already some retailers were realizing benefits from scanning in areas, such as automatic inventory reordering, scheduling stock crews, setting up new store layouts and shelf stocking patterns using the detailed product-movement data and even selling the detailed product-movement data to market research companies.

Shaw's Supermarkets, for example, a Massachusetts-based company, had set up a program making it possible for its 38 stores to restock automatically from its warehouse. As a result, inventory turnover at the stores was boosted by twenty percent. Ralph's, a supermarket chain in California, had formed a scanning analysis department in 1979 and were far ahead of the industry in terms of applications. If the national chains were able to lower their costs of doing business, Kalen's would be in trouble in future years.

On the other hand, Kalen's had to balance these purported benefits against the risks of a commitment to scanning. As Bob Kalen stated,

Our company has always been interested in new technology, but an independent really has to wait. We cannot afford to be pioneers when you are talking about spending a lot of money on equipment. We want to be progressive as a company, but we want to make sure we don't overextend ourselves, jump in, and lose everything. We are not that complicated or sophisticated an organization. Is scanning really for us?

14

The Robotics Decision

Goals

I. To help participants understand the issues involved in major technological changes.

II. To help participants understand the opposing needs of the various stakeholder groups in a technological change.

Group Size

Groups should not exceed four to six members.

Time Required

Approximately 75 minutes.

Materials

I. A copy of the Robotics Decision Case History for each participant.

II. A copy of the appropriate role play sheet for each group member.

III. Blackboard space or flipcharts and markers for each group.

Physical Setting

A room large enough so that groups can work without disturbing each other. Movable chairs should be provided.

Process

Step I. Introduction (10 min.)

The facilitator explains the purposes of the activity and leads a short discussion of the idea of stakeholders and their differing needs and agendas. Groups are given their assignment of coming up with a solution to this dilemma.

Step II. Role Play (30 min.)

Participants assume their roles and attempt to resolve the dilemma. Participants are encouraged to come to consensus about whatever choice that they make.

Step III. Processing (20 min.)

Participants are asked to identify the agenda(s)

Prepared by Mark Sharfman. "The Robotics Decision Case History" is from *The 1989 Annual: Developing Human Resources,* University Associates, Inc., San Diego, CA. Used with permission.

that they were promoting. The group should be able to answer the following questions:

1. What were the issues involved in implementing this new technology?
2. What was each participant's agenda in regard to the new technology?
3. What were the conflicting agendas and how did they conflict?
4. How did each person's agenda affect the technology change?

Step IV. Large Group Discussion (15 min.)

All of the small groups reconvene and discuss the questions in Step 3. A general discussion should include a discussion of the relationship between human resource issues and productivity/profitability issues in the adoption of new technology.

The Robotics Decision Case History

Elmire Glass and Plastics, Inc., is one of the nation's leaders in the production of glass and plastic for industrial use. The company has just received a proposal from United Robotics for the automation of its main production facility in Elmire, Pennsylvania. The change would entail full conversion from human operation to robotic production lines in the Plastic Components Division plant. This plant is the company's principal facility for the production of plastic components, which are used primarily in electronic equipment.

Elmire Glass and Plastics has been an innovator in the plastic components industry, and its components division has consistently yielded a 30-percent pre-tax return on investment. Although the demand for the company's component products appears to be strong, many of its competitors have recently switched to robotic production operations. This shift toward robotics is a source of concern to the company. Some industry analysts believe that robotics will transform the industry and will be a critical success factor in the future. Other analysts warn that robotics is a temporary solution, that it diverts attention from productivity and morale problems, and that the high capital investment required is not warranted because robotic tooling is not flexible enough to adjust to changing plastic product needs.

United Robotics claims that the pessimism of some industry analysts is totally unwarranted and that its products contain built-in design features that will ensure adaptability. The management at United argues that although the risk of obsolescence might naturally be high over a long period—say twenty years—the robotic equipment will have paid for itself five times during that period in terms of labor savings. Financial analysts at Elmire concur with this claim, estimating that the incremental rate of return from the equipment can reasonably be expected to range from 25 percent to 40 percent (pre-tax). This estimate is based on an expected capital investment of $50,000,000 and the generation of yearly savings between $12,500,000 and $20,000,000. The savings computations are based on current labor costs that will be eliminated by the changeover and do not include the cost savings due to increased efficiency. Although efficiency-related savings could be substantial, the components division at Elmire Glass and Plastics is noted to be a highly efficient operation with low defect rates and minimal employee absenteeism and turnover.

In addition to financial considerations, there are numerous other factors involved in the investment decision. This morning local representatives of the union (to which all of the company's manufacturing workers belong), met with top management. They voiced concern, resentment, and their strong opinion that even considering the robotic transition was inconsistent with Elmire's history and reputation as a family organization. They noted that although the transition might bring a substantial return in the short term, it would have an overwhelmingly negative effect on the entire company in the long term. The union leaders pointed out that other Elmire Glass and Plastics divisions, located both in Elmire, Pennsylvania, and in other locations throughout the United States, would not stand for the changeover. They noted that the interdependent divisions that make up the company rely on many unionized skilled craftsmen and technicians and that these workers would be mobilized to strike if the robotic operation were implemented. The union leaders said that the integrity of the entire company was being threatened. Interestingly, middle managers and the secretarial staff were recently overheard in the cafeteria voicing the same concern and questioning the ethics involved in the changeover.

Other pressures are being placed on the company from the local community. The town of Elmire, with a population of 50,000 and located in an already-impoverished anthracite-mining area of northeastern Pennsylvania, has been hurt recently by other plant closings. The prospect of five hundred more layoffs as well as the possibilities of strikes by other workers and layoffs from future robotic implementations are bringing many strong reactions. Several members of the town council and the Chamber of Commerce have phoned Elmire Glass and Plastics to express their concern, as have several congressional representatives and a number of local businesspeople. For the past two days, picketers from Citizens Against Corporate Irresponsibility (CACI) have been in town, organizing demonstrations in front of the components division offices and carrying signs with slogans like "Another Step Toward Greed," "Your Choice: Robots or Food for Elmire's Children," and "Robots or Responsible Management?" Although the CACI is viewed as a moderate group and advocates nonviolent protest, a number of more threatening protesters, believed to be part of an organized radical group that has used sabotage in some upstate New York manufacturing plants, jeered at managers and office employees who were entering and leaving the facility.

Three-year union contract negotiations come up for the components division in one year, just about the time the robotic operation could begin if a contract were signed now. At this point the top managers are divided regarding the best way to proceed. All agree that Elmire Glass and Plastics has survived through its years because of dedicated employees and that it has maintained a commitment to caring for its employees like family members. Layoffs have occurred in the past during difficult economic periods, but none of the magnitude of the one that would ensue with the robotic transition. The industry competition has never been so intense, and there is a fear that missing the opportunity to go with robotics and gain further competitive advantage would be disastrous and an injustice to Elmire's stockholders. A gradual transition to robotics would yield significantly lower returns in at least the next five years; also, replacements of retiring workers by automation would have its own unique set of problems, possibly acting like salt in a wound.

The need for a solution to this dilemma is critical.

15

Atlas Electronics Corporation (A)

Company History

Atlas Electronics Corporation was organized by a group of engineers and scientists who pioneered electronic research and development for the Office of Scientific Research and Development during World War II. After the war, members of this group joined together to form a private company to continue their efforts.

From the start, Atlas earned a reputation among government and corporate customers as a leader in advanced electronic techniques and systems. Its present capabilities cover a wide spectrum of electronic applications and skills, including aviation systems, radar, space payloads, communications, and electronic applications and skills, including aviation systems, radar, space payloads, communications, and electronic warfare (reconnaissance and counter- measures). Atlas has continued to distinguish itself for advances in the state-of-the-art and for superior quality on numerous prototype and initial operational equipment developed for U.S. government agencies. Fully 95% of its business is on government R & D contracts, whether directly or for prime government contractors.

Atlas's success is largely due to the competence, dedication, and stability of its staff. Of its 3,000 employees, over half have engineering or scientific degrees. Approximately 15% of these have advanced technical or M.B.A. degrees or are working toward them. The primary resource of management is the brainpower of these men, who are professional specialists in diverse fields.

Company Organization

Atlas Electronics Corporation is a typical engineering company organized along functional lines. Its Functional Engineering Departments are oriented to various technical disciplines and

This case was developed and prepared by W. R. Lockridge, C. S. Post Center, Long Island University.
Reprinted by permission.

EXHIBIT 15A–1 ■ Atlas Electronics Corporation Antenna Department

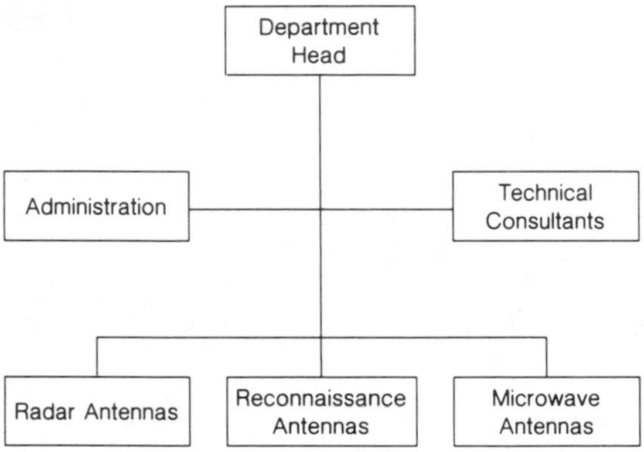

EXHIBIT 15A–2 ■ Atlas Electronics Corporation Receiver Department

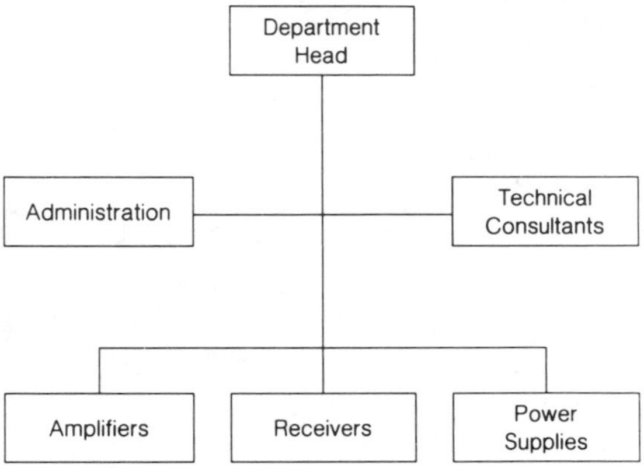

are staffed with engineers, scientists, and technicians who work on developing advanced techniques and in the support of projects.

The departmental organization structure starts with the department head and goes down the line through the section heads, group leaders, and supervisory engineers, to the scientists, engineers, and technicians who are doing the detail work. The department heads report to John Doan, executive vice-president. Communications, approvals, and directions flow through this organization in an orderly manner. Each level is under the supervision of the level above it and normally will not operate without higher level approval and direction.

Atlas had three Functional Engineering Departments: an Antenna Department, a Receiver Department, and a Data Systems Department. Each of these is responsible for developing advanced techniques, performing engineering, and for giving support to R & D projects in its technical area. The organization of each of these departments is shown in Exhibits 15A–1, 15A–2, and 15A–3.

In addition, Atlas has a Manufacturing Department (Exhibit 15A–4), which does fabrication, assembly, and testing of production units. This department also reports to John Doan. Purchasing, accounting, personnel administration, and other services are performed by various company staff departments not shown in the exhibits.

EXHIBIT 15A–3 ■ Atlas Electronics Corporation Data Systems Department

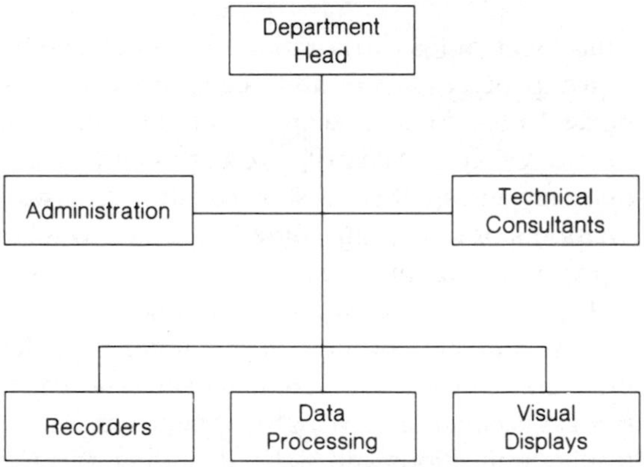

From time to time, Atlas sets up an ad hoc Project Management to handle a large R & D contract. This is a semiautonomous group consisting of a project manager and other personnel drawn from the functional organizations in the company. It has complete responsibility for meeting all the requirements of the contract, but it gets the work done in the Functional Departments. At the end of the project it is dissolved.

EXHIBIT 15A–4 ■ Atlas Electronics Corporation Manufacturing Department

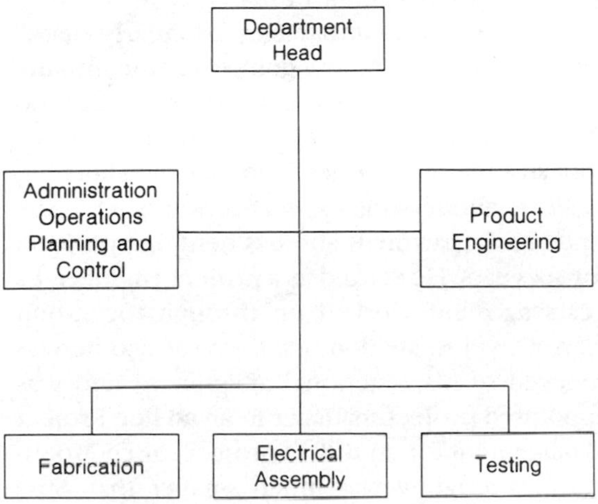

The Project Management assigns technical tasks to each supporting department to perform. To a limited extent, it is permitted to cut across organizational lines so that it can deal with the people doing the work without having to go through the whole hierarchy of their functional organizations. It handles scheduling and overall cost control; it deals with subcontractors and maintains liaison with customers; and it coordinates all the technical inputs and "hardware" from the supporting organizations into the overall system that is delivered to the customer.

The people who are transferred to the Project Management are mostly of a supervisory or senior category and report directly to the project manager. Their function is to advise him in their respective technical disciplines, to cooperate with him in managing the project, and to give "work direction"* to the personnel in the Functional Departments who are doing the work. The Project Management staff cannot directly supervise the work of the departmental personnel because these workers report in line to their department head. The department head may be on the same level or a higher level than the project manager. Consequently, the project manager has the problem of getting the utmost in effort from people who are responsible to someone else for pay raises, promotion, performance, and other aspects of line relationship.

*"Work direction": definition of the goals, specifications, and constraints (budget, schedule, etc.) for a technical task, as distinguished from detailed supervision of the work to perform it; the "what" to do, not the "how" to do it.

Spyeye Project

As the result of a successful competitive proposal, the government has awarded Atlas an R & D contract for an airborne reconnaissance system called "Spyeye." The system consists of an antenna, a receiver, an amplifier, and visual read-out equipment. This is an advanced system requiring the development of specific equipment whose performance characteristics are beyond the existing state-of-the-art. Atlas agrees to produce a prototype model in nine months. Following acceptance by the government, it agrees to produce five operational systems within another six months.

The contract is for a firm fixed price of $6 million, of which $5.6 million is the estimated target cost and $400,000 is Atlas's fee. The contract has a profit-sharing incentive whereby the government and the contractor share any cost-saving below the $5.6 million on a 90%/10% basis. It also provides penalties on the contractor for overrunning the cost, for late delivery, and for failure to meet performance specifications. The government will debit Atlas dollar-for-dollar against its fee for any cost overrun, and will assess it $200 for every day of late delivery. Various penalties, up to 20% of the fee, are provided for failure to meet technical performance specifications.

Project Support

The Spyeye project requires support from many functional areas throughout the company. It needs technical advice, engineering, and "hardware" from the reconnaissance section of the Antenna Department, the amplifier and receiver sections of the Receiver Department, the visual displays section of the Data Systems Department, and the fabrication, assembly, and testing facilities of the Manufacturing Department. (See Exhibits 15A–1 through 15A–4).

Alternatives for Project Organization

Company management has to decide whether to organize Spyeye as an ad hoc Project Management, or to handle it through one of its Functional Departments. Two men are available to lead the project, but the one selected will depend on the choice of organization. These men are Howard Datson and Burt Saunderson.

Howard Datson, 55, is head of the Receiver Department. He has been with the company since its inception and has build his department to the largest in the company. Datson and his group were responsible for numerous innovations in the receiver line and have kept the company ahead of most of its competition in that field.

Datson put in a strong plea to the president, Homer Skillton, to let the Receiver Department manage Spyeye as a project within its functional organization. "My department has been in existence since this company started," he said. "We've a well-trained staff with a lot of managerial and technical know-how. We'll have to do the bulk of the development anyhow. And I'm sure we can handle the interfaces with the other departments without any trouble."

Datson went on to express some of his personal feelings about the alternative of setting up a Project Management. "You must recognize that we've built the reputation of this company on the technical capability and quality performance of its Functional Departments. I personally dislike becoming a 'service' organization to a group who will be here today and gone tomorrow. Also, it'll probably be managed by someone who is not as technically oriented as any of our department heads.

"One thing I want to make particularly clear," he continued, "nobody's going to come into my department and tell my men how they must do their work. They report to me and my supervisors and we're the ones who call the shots."

Burt Saunderson, 45, is a section head in the Antenna Department and has held that position for six years. He started as a project engineer 12 years ago and worked up through the group leader level to section head. A year ago he was relieved of his functional assignment and was appointed project manager in an ad hoc Project Management for an B & D project called Moonglow. Moonglow was much smaller than Spyeye, but it had many of the same characteristics, such as the support from several different functional departments, a fixed price, and penalties for failure to meet cost, schedule, and performance specifications.

Saunderson and his Project Management group had successfully completed the Moonglow project. They had delivered the system on time, and the performance was satisfactory to the customer, although the equipment deviated slightly from the specification. They also had been able to increase the company's fee 1.5% by bettering the targeted cost. But Moonglow was now over and the people on it had to be reassigned.

While waiting for a new assignment, Saunderson served as bid manager on the Spyeye proposal to the government and was responsible for having come up with the reconnaissance system that the government finally bought. He felt he was the logical one to head up the Spyeye Project, if President Skillton decided to organize it as a Project Management. Accordingly, Saunderson sent a memorandum to Skillton outlining his reasons for this type of organization, which were, in essence, as follows:

1. The project involves four of the company's operating organizations. If management is

established in any one of these, the company would have the awkward situation of one Functional Department directing the activities of others who are on a parallel with itself in the company organization structure.

2. The project involves more than mere technical development. Cost, schedule, and technical performance all must be evaluated and balanced to produce the optimum overall result. A Functional Department, steeped in its own technology and hampered by its organizational structure, would lack the objectivity to view the overall project problem in perspective and to meet the ever-changing operational crises that arise from day to day.
3. The project does not involve pure research. It requires some innovation in the techniques area that can be done by the supporting Functional Departments. But someone will have to develop the overall system and that can best be done by a Project Management.
4. The project will add little to the long-range technical capability of the company. What it needs is an organization to "get the job done"—an organization that can use the technical support of the functional organizations without causing any permanent disruption in the company's organization structure.

President Skillton recognized that both men had good arguments.

Atlas Electronics Corporation (B)

Spyeye Project Management

President Skillton met with Executive Vice-President John Doan to discuss the Spyeye Project. "John, I've decided to organize Spyeye as a Project Management instead of assigning it to any of the functional departments. It's too big and too complex and it'll be in trouble from the start. I don't want to upset the stability of any department by temporarily expanding its personnel and giving it a coordinating job to handle." (See Exhibits 15B–1 and 15B–2.)

Project Manager

"But this creates some problems on which I'll need your help," he continued. "The first is the selection of a Project Manager. He's got to be at home in the front office talking about budgets, time schedules, and corporate policies and also at home in the laboratory talking about technical research and development problems. Of course, we can't expect him to double as a member of top management and a scientist equally well, but he's got to know what can be done technically and be enough of a business man to get it done within the contract."

"I'm thinking of Burt Saunderson for the job. But I'd like your opinion of him. Burt's a graduate engineer with a B.S. and M.S. in electrical engineering. From his earliest training, he's dealt with scientific analysis. He's accustomed to working objectively with tangible things. But as a project manager, he'll have to marshall pieces of preliminary or tentative information, juggle several problems at once, compromise one requirement for the benefit of another, and make decisions that are often based on experience and judgment rather than on specific knowledge."

"Another thing," Skillton continued, "as a section head, Burt's accustomed to having direct-line authority over the people in his department doing the work. They do as he says. But as a project manager, he'll have to win the cooperation of the supporting department heads and their staffs to get things done. This kind of management means dealing with human nature, and Burt will have to put a lot of emphasis on human factors to succeed."

"Well, I feel his performance on the Moonglow project shows he can do the job," Doan replied. "I'd rather have him than one of our department heads. Each of them is a professionally dedicated individual, highly skilled in the techniques of his field. What we need here is a different breed of cat—a manager who can run a business, rather than a professional who is endeavoring to optimize a technical advance."

EXHIBIT 15B–1 ■ Atlas Electronics Corporation Spyeye Project Management

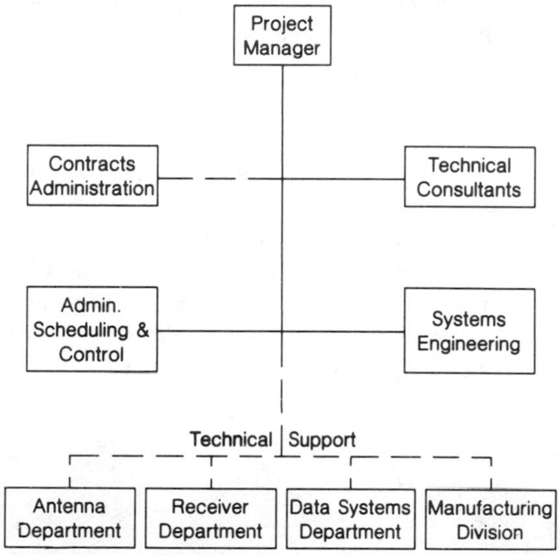

Project Manager Authority

President Skillton then raised another point. "No matter who we appoint, we've got to give him sufficient authority to get the job done. But we've a delicate situation here. We can't permit him to step in and tell a department head how to run his department. Yet we must give him sufficient status to compel their respect and cooperation. I'll have him report to you. This will place him on the same organizational level as the department heads who are supporting the Project."

"That's OK with me," Doan replied. "After all, I've other project managers reporting to me and I try to treat them and the department heads alike."

"Of course, Burt will have overall management of Spyeye and will assign technical tasks to each supporting department," Skillton continued. "But these will be in the nature of subcontracts with budgets and schedules that he'll have to negotiate with each department head and on which he'll obtain their commitment. He can tell them *what* to do, but not *how* to do it. This will keep design development in the functional departments where it belongs.

"But I'm not too happy about this arrangement," Skillton reflected, "because it gives the project manager little control. When Burt meets with a problem that requires some pressure on a supporting department, he'll have to come to you if he can't reach an agreement with the department head."

"Well, I'll have to assume that as my responsibility," Doan replied. "All the operations re-

EXHIBIT 15B–2 ▪ Atlas Electronics Corporation Spyeye Project

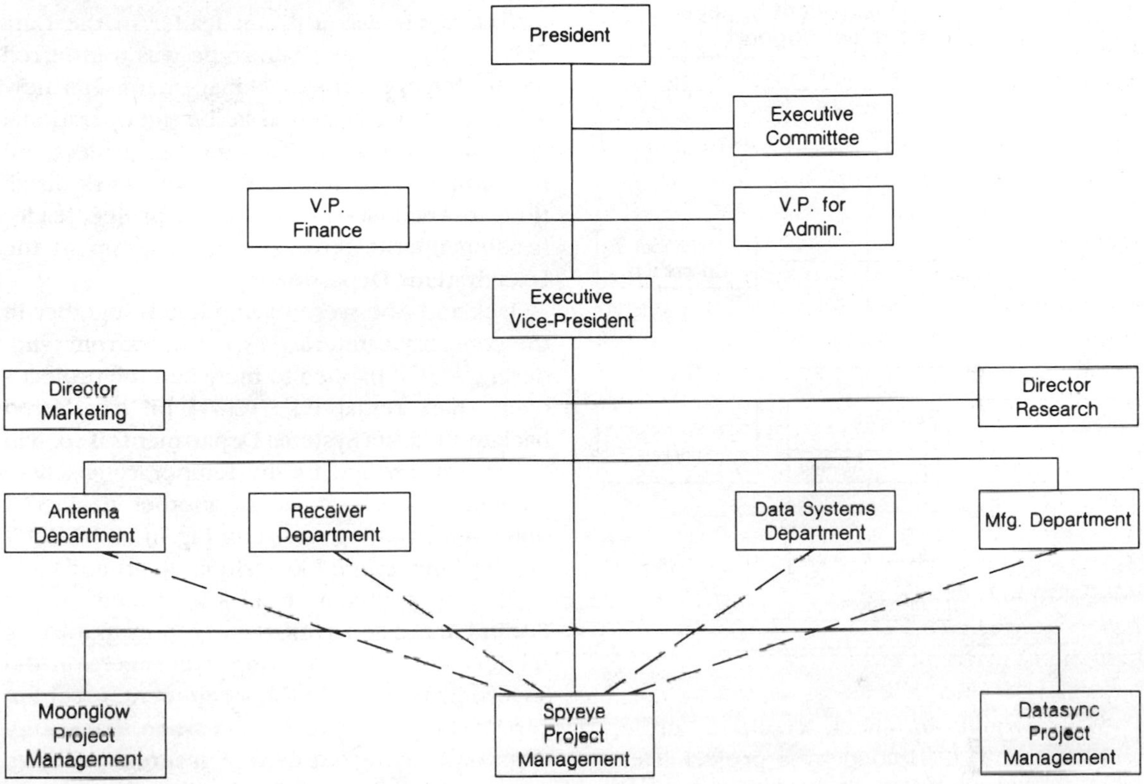

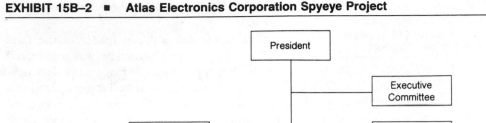

This chart indicates lines of responsibility only, not status.

port to me and it's my job to see that any conflicts are resolved in the best interest of the company."

Project Staff

"Another problem we have to consider," Skillton continued, "is how we'll staff the Spyeye Project Management. Obviously, it should be with supervisory or senior technical people from the departments skilled in the project techniques. But each of these departments needs these people in its own operations. I don't want to step in and direct any department head to transfer people to the Project Management. Burt will have to convince each department head that it's in the best interest of the company and the individual concerned to transfer him. Personally, I feel that it broadens a man's experience and capability to be assigned to a project for a while."

Project Support

President Skillton meditated for a moment and then continued, "In mulling over the problem, John, it appears to me that if we could induce each department head to set up a Spyeye Support Group as a sub-project within his own department, responsible solely for support to the Spyeye Project Management, it would overcome some of the weakness of the ad hoc organization concept.

EXHIBIT 15B–3 ■ Atlas Electronics Corporation Receiver Department Spyeye Project Support

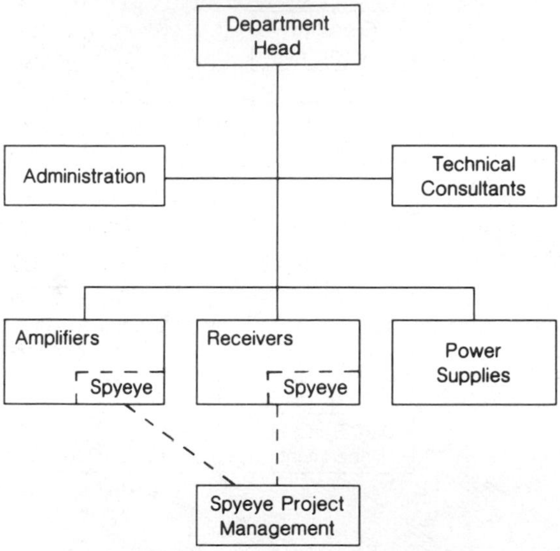

"This would, in effect, create a 'project within a project,' headed by a project leader who would take his 'work direction' from the Project Management staff rather than from his own departmental supervision. I think this would cut across the organizational lines to implement the interfaces between the Project Management and the supporting groups, and I feel it would inspire a team spirit on the project. At the same time, it would preserve the status of the functional department supervision, because detailed supervision of the work would remain with them. I want you to see if the Spyeye support can be organized in this manner," he concluded. (See Exhibit 15B–3.)

Employee Morale

Skillton and Doan had another problem that neither of them had discussed: how to maintain employee morale under the structure of "two bosses" that the Spyeye Project Management created.

Jack Davis was a group leader in the Data Systems Department before he was transferred to the Spyeye Project Management. His new assignment required that he be the operational communications link between the project and his "home" department. He gave "work direction" to Abe Marks, who was the project leader heading up the Spyeye project group in the Data Systems Department.

Jack and Abe were having lunch together in the company cafeteria. "I can't keep from wondering what'll happen to me when the project's over," Jack remarked. "Will I be transferred back to the Data Systems Department? If so, will I have lost ground by my temporary absence? Or will they assign me to another project? I don't see anything new coming in and I don't like it. Believe me, I keep looking around."

"I've my problems, too," Abe replied. "While I'm still in the department and report to Joe (his section head), I'm working exclusively on the Spyeye project. I like the assignment. I feel I'm part of the project team, and when that equipment starts flying out there, I'm sure they'll give me credit for my part. But how does this affect my status and salary?

"When it comes time for rate review," he continued, "will Joe know how I'm doing? Burt knows more about my work than Joe does. Will they talk to each other, or will I be dropped in the crack?

"I'm in another bind," Abe added. "Often I have to decide what's best for the project as against what's best for the department. Should I do what the project needs to meet its contract or be loyal to the department's policies and standards? If I 'bite the hand that feeds me' where'll I wind up?"

"I guess these are some of the risks we have to take," Jack philosophized. "Some guys prefer the challenge of strict technical development. Others want the action of a project. Personally, I feel that this project assignment will broaden my experience, or I wouldn't have taken it. But I can't help but worry about what it'll do to my future."

Burt Saunderson didn't hear this conversation, but he knew that these feelings persisted with personnel working on the project, either on his staff or in the supporting departments. He wondered how he could induce these men to keep their "eye on the ball" and devote their full effort to the project when they were worrying about their personal futures.

Performance Problem

Seven months after the project started, Saunderson noted from his progress reports that the Receiver Department still failed to meet the technical performance specification on the receiver. The specification required a band spread from 1,000–10,000 mc. The breadboard model would only operate at 1,050–9,200 mc.

Time was getting short and he had to take prompt action. Investigation disclosed that it was doubtful if the circuit, as designed by the Receiver Department, would ever meet the specification. Consequently, it did not appear advisable to spend more time on it. Saunderson's technical staff advised him that the addition of another transistor on the lower end and the substitution of a 2QXR tube for a transistor at the upper end would cure the situation. Both of these would increase the cost and the tube would change the configuration of the "black box." His project administrator advised him that the project could absorb the cost and the customer said that the slight change in the configuration was not important. But here an obstacle arose. The Receiver Department was not satisfied with the quality of the 2QXR tube and refused to use it.

Saunderson met with Datson to discuss the problem. "Howard, we've got to do something to get that receiver up to spec. Time's getting short. We'll get socked $200 a day for late delivery and they'll take a slice of our fee for failure to perform. Now, I know you hate to use the 2QXR, but it'll do the job long enough to meet the life requirements and will satisfy the customer. We've got to give somewhere or we'll be in serious trouble."

"Yeah, I know how you feel," Datson replied, "but I've got to preserve the quality reputation of the company. After all, we obtained Spyeye because of our reputation for quality as much as for our technical competence and favorable price. If I do anything to impair that image it'll only hurt us in the long run."

16

Mrs. Fields' Secret Ingredient

Part of the late Buckminster Fuller's genius was his capacity to transform a technology from the merely new to the truly useful by creating a new form to take advantage of its characteristics. Fuller's geodesic designs, for instance, endowed plastic with practical value as a building material. His structures, if not always eye-appealing, still achieved elegance—as mathematicians use the word to connote simplicity—of function. Once, reacting to someone's suggestion that a new technology be applied to an old process in a particularly awkward way, Fuller said dismissively, "That would be like putting an outboard motor on a skyscraper."

Introducing microcomputers with spreadsheet and word-processing software to a company originally designed around paper technology amounts to the same thing. If the form of the company doesn't change, the computer, like the outboard, is just a doodad. Faster long division and speedier typing don't move a company into the information age.

But Randy Fields has created something entirely new—*a* shape if not *the* shape, of business organizations to come. It gives top management a dimension of personal control over dispersed operations that small companies otherwise find impossible to achieve. It projects a founder's vision into parts of a company that have long ago outgrown his or her ability to reach in person.

In the structure that Fields is building, computers don't just speed up old administrative management processes. They alter the process. Management, in the Fields organizational paradigm, becomes less administration and more inspiration. The management hierarchy of the company *feels* almost flat.

What's the successful computer-age business going to look like in the not-very-distant future? Something like Randy Field's concept—which is, in a word, neat.

What makes it neat, right out of the oven, is where he's doing it. Randy Fields, age 40, is

Written by Tom Richman. Reprinted with permission, *Inc.* magazine, October, 1987.

married to Debbi Fields, who turns 31 this month, and together they run Mrs. Fields Cookies, of Park City, Utah. They project that by year end, their business will comprise nearly 500 company-owned stores in 37 states selling what Debbi calls a "feel-good feeling." That sounds a little hokey. A lot of her cookie talk does. "Good enough never is," she likes to remind the people around her.

But there's nothing hokey about the 18.5% that Mrs. Fields Inc. earned on cookie sales of $87 million last year, up from $72.6 million a year earlier.

Won't the cookie craze pass? people often ask Debbi. "I think that's very doubtful . . . I mean," she says, "if [they are] fresh, warm, and wonderful and make you feel good, are you going to stop buying cookies?"

Maybe not, but the trick for her and her husband is to see that people keep buying them from Mrs. Fields, not David's Cookies, Blue Chip Cookies, The Original Great Chocolate Chip Cookie, or the dozens of regional and local competitors. Keeping the cookies consistently fresh, warm, and wonderful at nearly 500 retail cookie stores spread over the United States and five other countries can't be simple or easy. Worse, keeping smiles on the faces of the nearly 4,500, mostly young, store employees—not to mention keeping them productive and honest—is a bigger chore than most companies would dare to take on alone.

Most don't; they franchise, which is one way to bring responsibility and accountability down to the store level in a far-flung, multi-store organization. For this, the franchisor trades off revenues and profits that would otherwise be his and a large measure of flexibility. Because its terms are defined by contract, the relationship between franchisor and franchisee is more static than dynamic, difficult to alter as the market and the business change.

Mrs. Fields Cookies, despite its size, has not franchised—persuasive evidence in itself that the Fieldses have built something unusual. Randy Fields believes that no other U.S. food retailer with so many outlets has dared to retain this degree of direct, day-to-day control of its stores. And Mrs. Fields Cookies does it with a headquarters staff of just 115 people. That's approximately one staffer to every five stores—piddling compared with other companies with far fewer stores to manage. When the company bought La Petite Boulangerie from PepsiCo earlier this year, for instance, the soft-drink giant had 53 headquarters staff people to administer the French bakery/sandwich shop chain's 119 stores. Randy needed just four weeks to cut the number to three people.

On paper, Mrs. Fields Cookies *looks* almost conventional. In action, however, because of the way information flows between levels, it *feels* almost flat.

On paper, between Richard Lui running the Pier 39 Mrs. Fields in San Francisco and Debbi herself in Park City, there are several apparently traditional layers of hierarchy: an area sales manager, a district sales manager, a regional director of operations, a vice-president of operations. In practice, though, Debbi is as handy to Lui—and to every other store manager—as the telephone and personal computer in the back room of his store.

On a typical morning at Pier 39, Lui unlocks the store, calls up the Day Planner program on his Tandy computer, plugs in today's sales projection (based on year-earlier sales adjusted for growth), and answers a couple of questions the program puts to him. What day of the week is it? What type of day: normal day, sale day, school day, holiday, other?

Say, for instance, it's Tuesday, a school day. The computer goes back to the Pier 39 store's hour-by-hour, product-by-product performance on the last three school-day Tuesdays. Based on what you did then, the Day Planner tells him, here's what you'll have to do today, hour by hour, product by product, to meet your sales projection. It tells him how many customers he'll need each hour and how much he'll have to sell them. It tells him how many batches of cookie dough he'll have to mix and when to mix them to meet the demand and to minimize leftovers. He could make these estimates himself if he wanted to take the time. The computer makes them for him.

Each hour, as the day progresses, Lui keeps the computer informed of his progress. Currently he enters the numbers manually, but new cash registers that automatically feed hourly data to the computer, eliminating the manual update, are already in some stores. The computer in turn revises the hourly projections and makes suggestions. The customer count is OK, it might observe, but your average check is down. Are your crew members doing enough suggestive selling? If, on the other hand, the computer indicates that the customer count is down, that may suggest the manager will want to do some sampling—chum for customers up and down the pier with a tray of free cookie pieces or try something else, whatever he likes, to lure people into the store. Sometimes, if sales are just slightly down, the machine's revised projections will actually exceed the original on the assumption that greater selling effort will more than compensate for the small deficit. On the other hand, the program isn't blind to reality. It recognizes a bad day and diminishes its hourly sales projections and baking estimates accordingly.

Hourly sales goals?

Well, when Debbi was running *her* store, *she* set hourly sales goals. Her managers should, too, she thinks. Rather than enforce the practice through dicta, Randy has embedded the notion in the software that each store manager relies on. Do managers find the machine's suggestions intrusive? Not Lui. "It's a tool for me," he says.

Several times a week, Lui talks with Debbi. Well, he doesn't exactly talk *with* her, but he hears from her. He makes a daily phone call to Park City to check his computerized PhoneMail messages, and as often as not there's something from Mrs. Fields herself. If she's upset about some problem, Lui hears her sounding upset. If it's something she's breathlessly exuberant about, which is more often the case, he gets an earful of that, too. Whether the news is good or bad, how much better to hear it from the boss herself than to get a memo in the mail next week.

By the same token, if Lui has something to say to Debbi, he uses the computer. It's right there, handy. He calls up the Form-Mail program, types his message, and the next morning it's on Debbi's desk. She promises an answer, from her or her staff, within 48 hours. On the morning I spent with her, among the dozen or so messages she got was one from the crew at a Berkeley, California, store making their case for higher wages there and another from the manager of a store in Brookline, Massachusetts, which has been struggling recently. We've finally gotten ourselves squared away, was the gist of the note, so please come visit. (Last year Debbi logged around 350,000 commercial air miles visiting stores.)

Here are some other things Lui's computer can do for him.

- ☐ Help him schedule crew. He plugs his daily sales projection for two weeks hence into a scheduling program that incorporates as its standards the times Debbi herself takes to perform the mixing, dropping, and baking chores. The program gives him back its best guess of how many people with which skill levels he'll need during which hours. A process that done manually consumed almost an hour now takes just a fraction of that time.
- ☐ Help him interview crew applicants. He calls up his interview program, seats the applicant at the keyboard, and has him or her answer a series of questions. Based on the answers given by past hirees, the machine suggests to Lui which candidates will succeed or fail. It's still his choice. And any applicant, before a hire, will still get an audition—something to see how he or she performs in public. Maybe Lui will send the hopeful out on a sampling mission.
- ☐ Help with personnel administration. Say he hires the applicant. He informs the machine, which generates a personnel folder and a payroll entry in Park City, and a few months later comes back to remind Lui that he hasn't submitted the initial evaluation (also by com-

puter), which is now slightly past due. It administers the written part of the skills test and updates the records with the results. The entire Mrs. Fields personnel manual will soon be on the computer so that 500 store managers won't forget to delete old pages and insert revised ones every time a change is made.

- Help with maintenance. A mixer isn't working, so the manager punches up the repair program on the computer. It asks him some questions, such as: is the plug in the wall? If the questions don't prompt a fix, the computer sends a repair request to Park City telling the staff there which machine is broken, its maintenance history, and which vendor to call. It sends a copy of the work order back to the store. When the work gets done, the store signs off by computer, and the vendor's bill gets paid.

That's a lot of technology applied to something as basic as a cookie store but Randy had two objectives in mind.

He wanted to keep his wife in frequent, personal, two-way contact with hundreds of managers whose stores she couldn't possibly visit often enough. "The people who work in the stores," says Debbi, "are my customers. Staying in touch with them is the most important thing I can do."

It's no accident, even if Lui isn't consciously aware of why he does what he does, that he runs his store just about the same way that Debbi ran her first one 10 years ago. Even when she isn't there, she's there—in the standards built into his scheduling program, in the hourly goals, in the sampling and suggestive selling, on the phone. The technology has "leveraged," to use Randy's term, Debbi's ability to project her influence into more stores than she could ever reach effectively without it.

Second, Randy wanted to keep store managers managing, not sweating the paperwork. "In retailing," he says, "the goal is to keep people close to people. Whatever gets in the way of that—administration, telephones, ordering, and so on—is the enemy." If an administrative chore can be automated, it should be.

Store managers benefit from a continuing exchange of information. Of course, Park City learns what every store is doing daily—from sales to staffing to training to hires to repairs—and how it uses that information we'll get to in a minute. From the store managers' perspective, however, the important thing is that the information they provide keeps coming back to them, reorganized to make it useful. The hour-by-hour sales projections and projected customer counts that managers use to pace their days reflect their own experiences. Soon, for instance, the computer will take their weekly inventory reports and sales projections and generate supply orders that managers will only have to confirm or correct—more administrative time saved. With their little computers in the back room, store managers give, but they also receive.

What technology can do for operations it can also do for administration.

"We're all driven by Randy's philosophy that he wants the organization to be as flat as possible," says Paul Quinn, the company's director of management information systems (MIS).

"There are a few things," says controller Lynn Quilter, "that Randy dislikes about growth. . . . He hates the thought of drowning in people so that he can't walk in and know exactly what each person does. . . . The second thing that drives him nuts is paper."

"The objective," says Randy, "is to leverage people—to get them to act when we have 1,000 stores the same way they acted when we had 30."

He has this theory that large organizations, organizations with lots of people, are, per se, inferior to small ones. Good people join a growing business because it offers them an opportunity to be creative. As the company grows, these people find they're tied up managing the latest hires. Creativity suffers. Entropy sets in. Randy uses technology to keep entropy at bay.

He began by automating rote clerical chores and by minimizing data-entry effort. Machines can sort and file faster than people, and sorting and filing is deadly dull work, anyway. Lately he's pushed the organization toward automated exception reporting for the same reason. Machines can compare actual results with expected results and flag the anomolies, which are all management really cares about anyway. And within a few years, Randy expects to go much further in his battle against bureaucracy by developing artificial-intelligence aids to the running of the business.

Understand that it's not equipment advances—state-of-the-art hardware—that's pushing Mrs. Fields Cookies toward management frontiers. The machines the company uses are strictly off the shelf: an IBM minicomputer connected to inexpensive personal computers. It is, instead, Randy's ability to create an elegant, functional software architecture. He has, of course, had an advantage that the leader of an older, more established company would not have. Because Mrs. Fields is still a young enough company, he doesn't have to shape his automated management system to a preexisting structure. Every new idea doesn't confront the opposition of some bureaucratic fiefdom's survival instinct. Rather, the people part and the technology part of the Fields organization are developing simultaneously, each shaped by the same philosophy.

You see this congruence at corporate headquarters and in the company's operational management organization.

Between Debbi as chief executive officer and the individual store managers is what seems on paper to be a conventional reporting structure with several layers of management. But there's an additional box on the organization chart. It's not another management layer. It transcends layers, changing the way information flows between them and even changing the functions of the layers.

The box consists of a group of seven so-called store controllers, working in Park City from the daily store reports and weekly inventory reports. They ride herd on the numbers. If a store's sales are dramatically off, the store controller covering that geographical region will be the first to know it. If there's a discrepancy between the inventory report, the daily report of batches of cookies baked, and the sales report, the controller will be the first to find it. (It is possible for a smart thief to steal judiciously for about a week from a Mrs. Fields store.) "We're a check on operations," says store controller Wendy Phelps, but she's far more than just a check. She's the other half of a manager's head.

Since she's on top of the numbers, the area, district, and regional managers don't have to be—not to the same degree, at any rate. "We want managers to be with people, not with problems," says Debbi. It's hard, Randy says, to find managers who are good with both people and numbers. People people, he thinks, should be in the field, with numbers people backing them up—but not second-guessing them. Here's where the company takes a meaningful twist.

Problems aren't reported up the organization just so solutions can flow back down. Instead, store controllers work at levels as low as they can. They go to the store manager if he's the one to fix a discrepancy, a missing report, for instance. Forget chain of command. "I'm very efficiency minded," says Randy.

So the technology gives the company an almost real-time look at the minutiae of its operations, and the organizational structure—putting function ahead of conventional protocol—keeps it from choking on this abundance of data.

Some managers would have problems with a system that operates without their daily intervention. They wouldn't be comfortable, and they wouldn't stay at Mrs. Fields. Those who do stay can manage people instead of paper.

If administrative bureaucracies can grow out of control, so can technology bureaucracies. A couple of principles, ruthlessly adhered to, keep both simple at Mrs. Fields.

The first is that if a machine can do it, a machine *should* do it. "People," says Randy, "should do only that which people can do. It's demeaning for people to do what machines can do.... Can machines manage people? No. Machines have no feelie-touchies, none of that chemistry that flows between two people."

The other rule, the one that keeps the technological monster itself in check, is that the company will have but one data base. Everything—cookie sales, payroll records, suppliers' invoices, inventory reports, utility charges—goes into the same data base. And whatever anybody needs to know has to come out of it.

Don't enforce this rule, and, says Randy, "the next thing you know you have 48 different programs that can't talk to each other." Technology grown rampant.

Having a single data base means, first, that nobody has to waste time filing triplicate forms or answering the same questions twice. "We capture the data just once," says controller Quilter.

Second, it means that the system itself can do most of the rote work that people used to do. Take orders for chocolate, for instance. The computer gets the weekly inventory report. It already knows the sales projection. So let the computer order the chocolate chips. Give the store manager a copy of the order on his screen so he can correct any errors, but why take his time to generate the order when he's got better things to do—like teaching someone to sell. Or, take it further. The machine generates the order. The supplier delivers the chips to the store and bills the corporate office. A clerk in the office now has to compare the order, the invoice, and what the store says it got. Do they all match? Yes. She tells the computer to write a check. The more stores you have, the more clerks it takes. Why not let the computer do the matching? In fact, if everything fits, why get people involved at all? Let people handle the exceptions. Now, the clerk, says MIS director Quinn, instead of a processor becomes a mini-controller, someone who uses his brain.

The ordering process doesn't happen that way yet at Mrs. Fields, although it probably will soon as Randy continues to press for more exception reporting. You can see where he's going with this concept "Eventually," he says, "even the anomolies become normal." The exceptions themselves, and a person's response to them, assume a pattern. Why not, says Randy, have the computer watch the person for a while? "Then the machine can say, 'I have found an anomoly. I've been watching you, and I think this is what you would do. Shall I do it for you, yes or no. If yes, I'll do it, follow up, and so on. If no, what do you want me to do?' " It would work for the low-level function—administering accounts payable, for instance. And it would work at higher levels as well. "If," Randy says, "I can ask the computer now where are we making the most money and where are we making the least and then make a decision about where not to build new stores, why shouldn't that sort of thing be on automatic pilot too? 'Based on performance,' it will say, 'we shouldn't be building any more stores in East Jibip. Want me to tell [real-estate manager] Mike [Murphy]?' We're six months away from being able to do that."

The ability to look at the company, which is what the data base really is, at a level of abstraction appropriate to the looker, is the third advantage of a single data base—even if it never moves into artificial-intelligence functions. It means that Debbi Fields and Richard Lui are both looking at the same world, but in ways that are meaningful to each of them.

The hurdle to be overcome before you can use technology to its best advantage—and that isn't equivalent to just hanging on outboard motor on a skyscraper, as Buckminster Fuller said—isn't technical in the hardware sense. Randy buys only what he calls plain vanilla hardware. And it isn't financial. For all its relative sophistication in computer systems, Mrs. Fields spends just 0.49% of sales on data processing, much of which is returned in higher productivity.

Much more important, Randy says, is having a consistent vision of what you want to *accomplish* with the technology. Which functions do you want to control? What do you want your organization chart to look like? In what ways do you want to leverage the CEO's vision? "Imagination. We imagine what it is we want," says

Randy. "We aren't constrained by the limits of what technology can do. We just say, 'What does your day look like? What would you *like* it to look like?' " He adds, "If you don't have your paradigm in mind, you have no way of knowing whether each little step is taking you closer to or further from your goal."

For instance, he inaugurated the daily store report with the opening of store number two in 1978. The important thing was the creation of the report—which is the fundamental data-gathering activity in the company—not its transmission mode. That can change, and has. First transmission was by Fax, then by telephone touch tone, and only recently by computer modem.

Having a consistent vision means, Randy says, that he could have described as far back as 1978, when he first began to create it, the system that exists today. But he doesn't mean the machines or how they're wired together. "MIS in this company," he says, "has always had to serve two masters. First, control. Rapid growth without control equals disaster. We needed to keep improving control over our stores. And second, information that leads to control also leads to better decision making. To the extent that the information is then provided to the store and field-management level, the decisions that are made there are better, and they are more easily made.

"That has been our consistent vision."

Postscript

Since this case was written, several things have happened at Mrs. Fields Cookies. Specifically, a *Wall Street Journal* headline of January 1, 1989, put it most succinctly: "How the Cookie Crumbled at Mrs. Fields." Several things have recently occurred at the company. During the first half of 1988, the company lost $15.1 million and was expected to report an overall larger loss for the year, compared to a $17.7 million net income in 1987. Further, the company has closed or made provisions to close 95 of its cookie stores.

Why did this rapid turnaround occur? The company suggests that a large part of the problem is the expenses incurred in combining some Mrs. Fields stores with La Petite Boulangeries (a chain of 105 French-style bakeries acquired from PepsiCo in 1987). Under the new name "Mrs. Fields Bakery Cafe," the company will operate a series of combination stores. The company argues that all of the closed stores were in areas that overlapped with proposed combination stores. These costs combined with soaring rents in many markets caused the problems. The company believes that its core business is not in trouble and that the firm will be profitable in 1989—although well below the impressive 1987 levels.

Several analysts disagree with the company's assessment. They believe many of the problems the company is experiencing stem from its change from a single-product company to a "specialty foods retailer." They argue that the firm was spread too thin in some areas and too saturated in others and did not diversify fast enough. Before the La Petite Boulangerie acquisition, there had been virtually no diversification—a dangerous choice in a trendy market like premium cookies. There is also some question of whether the management structure described in the case could keep pace with the firm's rapid growth and whether the structure was even practical when the company expanded internationally. Since the case was written, the company sold its European operations to a French firm. What else do you think might have caused problems?

17

Special Products Division of Advanced Technologies, Inc.

Introduction

Fred Hazelton spent most of the morning of May 5, 1980, preparing for a 10 o'clock meeting with his staff. The Special Products Division of Advanced Technologies, Inc., had recently received some serious complaints regarding the division's performance. Mr. Hampton, the general manager of the Special Products Division, received this negative feedback through marketing department representatives, who had recently returned from a visit to one of the division's major customers, the U.S. Air Force.

SPD had for many years been a major supplier of portable steam supply systems used for generating electric power at temporary Air Force installations. The division was organized in 1957 in response to the government's need for these types of systems. It had dominated the industry until about five years ago.

The complaints received from this major customer perplexed Mr. Hazelton. He recalled a similar episode just last month with the division's other prime customer, the Energy Research and Development Agency (ERDA). SPD had entered into a contract with ERDA in mid 1978 to design, build, and install a nuclear fusion test unit. An extremely high level of new technology dominated this project, and progress to date had been very limited. Mr. Hazelton scheduled the meeting for that morning to discuss and assess the recent complaints from their two major customers and to develop an action plan.

History of the Division

SPD was a major operating division of the Advanced Technologies Company, a worldwide firm involved primarily in the business of designing, manufacturing, and marketing both component parts and complete package energy systems. Having expertise in engineering and fabricating advanced steam supply systems, the

Prepared by Theodore T. Herbert. Used with permission.

company was approached by the Air Force in the mid 1950s concerning their possible interest in building portable units. In an agreement between the Air Force and Advanced Technologies, the division was established initially to design and fabricate five of those units. From this small beginning, SPD grew into a well-capitalized organization with unique engineering and fabrication capabilities and a strong interest in research and development.

Development of the Market and the Competitive Environment

By 1965, the division's sales to the Air Force had reached $50 million annually. Its success was boosted by the fact that no other company had shown interest in getting into the portable steam system business. SPD had developed a good rapport with the Air Force over the years, primarily because of its outstanding performance in the design, manufacture, and timely shipment of the units. For orders placed by the Air Force, SPD could essentially write its own ticket and often had significant influence on the content of the buyer's specifications. Extensive exceptions to various military specifications were requested by SPD; usually the exceptions were granted.

During the late 1960s, other companies developed the technologies and interest in the portable steam system market. The Air Force and other sources awarded several contracts, apparently for the purpose of developing the infant competition. Three competitors began to mature in the early 1970s, even though, as a result of their lack of experience in the high technology involved, their performance was not equal to SPD's. SPD still dominated the market through the mid-1970s, as contract awards were placed according to an evaluated price. That is, dependability and technical expertise were primary factors, with price being secondary. Several prototype systems were purchased, and SPD continued its dependable performance on those projects.

By 1978, however, the three new competitors had reached full maturity and were bidding on and performing successfully on Air Force and other projects. The product itself had become in general a less risky venture because of several decades of industry design, manufacturing, and plant-operating experience. The technology had stabilized, with design and manufacturing methods remaining fairly constant. Due to the basic, conservative approach encouraged by the Air Force, new design concepts were introduced only where absolutely necessary, and "tried and true" designs were used if possible.

Along with the reduced requirement for technical creativity and the stabilization of design and manufacturing techniques, the Air Force began awarding contracts based on price only. In fact, nearly 90 percent of the orders after 1975 were of a "follow on" (repeats of previously designed components) nature. As a result of changing customer needs, SPD's market share began to drop during the 1970s, accelerating during the last few years of the decade.

New Markets

In 1978, in an attempt to diversify from the Air Force steam systems market, SPD contracted with ERDA to design, build, and test a nuclear fusion reactor. This unit was to be the first test unit actually built to produce electricity in the United States and involved an intense engineering and R & D effort. Fabrication of the unit was to occur in the SPD shops, because the manufacturing and quality-control requirements were very similar to those needed by the Air Force steam systems.

The task was further complicated by a new and unfamiliar customer, necessary interfaces with other companies that served as subcontractors, and the unknowns regarding the future of fusion reactors as dictated by emerging U.S. energy practices and policy. In addition, design inexperience dictated very close coordination among engineering, manufacturing, and the customer. The new and intricate geometries anticipated from this unfamiliar type of energy source, resulting from extremely high operating temperatures and the use of advanced alloys, were likely to cause problems in the manufacturing and assembly process. Developing a design that would be acceptable to the customer and that could be built and assembled economically, and with minimal fabrication risk, requires excellent communication between departments, as well as extreme patience. Although the risks were high, Mr. Hazelton believed that successful completion of this project would give SPD a head start in fusion reactor technology.

With the recent drop in sales to the Air Force, other markets were being explored. Pressure vessels for commercial chemical processors were being considered, and in January of 1979, a chemical company ordered four hydrogenation vessels for a proposed coal liquefaction plant. These vessels were intended for high-temperature and high-pressure use, but the overall quality requirements were not as strict as those for steam systems. Design effort was minimal, with the primary objectives being economical fabrication and prompt shipment. This new product line was extremely price-competitive, but SPD saw the venture as a way to keep the shops active until the Air Force market could be regained. Administration of this new product line took a form similar to the division's established structure for other product lines.

Organization

The division is organized around functional lines, as shown in Exhibit 17–1. This organization was established by the first division manager and has changed only slightly since Mr. Hazelton took the position in 1973.

Interactions between the various departments at all levels are closely controlled by detailed procedures and work standards. Mr. Hazelton has always believed that situations should be well thought out in advance and that action plans should be available for any anticipated happening. For this reason, SPD has a four-volume set of procedures that apply to all functional departments. In addition, each member of the division must write his or her own work instruction, have it approved by the supervisor, and follow it closely. Periodic audits at all levels are performed to ensure compliance with procedures and work instructions.

Additional departmental tasks and relationships are described in the subsequent sections.

Marketing

As contracts from the Air Force are solicited, the marketing department is responsible for gathering input from all departments and assembling the company's proposal package. Specifications and other related documents pertaining to the particular project are distributed to such areas as manufacturing, engineering, quality assurance, and the contract section. Each individual department plans its execution of the task, estimates costs, and responds to the marketing department. During the early years of the division, when the portable steam system technology was new, close communications existed between the various functional departments. Plans for manufacturing, engineering, quality assurance, etc., were coordinated in the precontract stage to enhance successful overall task performance. However, as the product matured and experience was attained in all departments, less communication existed, and groups began to plan in isolation.

Engineering planning is generally the responsibility of the specific design group that is to perform the task if a contract is received. The manufacturing department, on the other hand, has a special preproduction group that plans

Exhibit 17–1 ▪ SPD Organization Chart

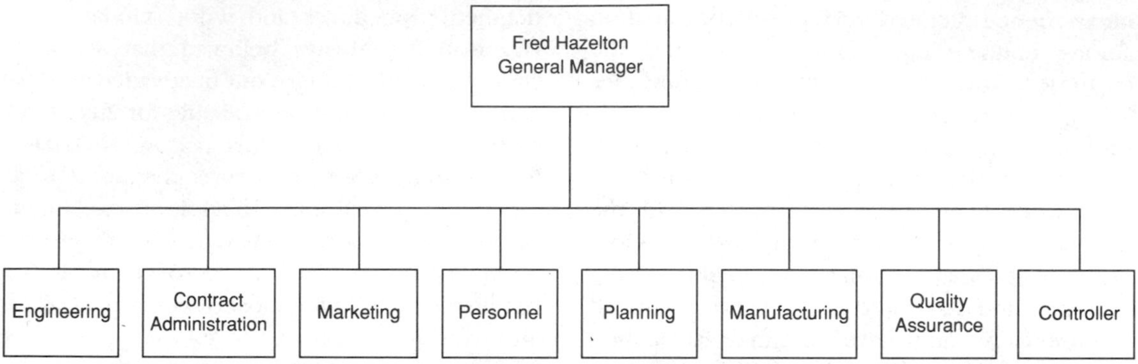

the fabrication methods, sequence, schedule, and cost estimates for all projects. It was felt by Mr. Hazelton that, because of the division's past experience, departments already had a mutual understanding of each other's problems and close coordination was no longer necessary.

The marketing department consists of 25 salaried personnel having responsibility for generating proposal packages in response to customer inquiries. For each inquiry a team from this department is formed to coordinate the proposal activity. SPD has no sales force of its own and depends on Advanced Technology's Corporate Sales Group, located at headquarters, to gather market information. Upon receipt of a contract, the marketing department's task is complete, and responsibility for performing the task is transferred to the appropriate functional areas. Recent changes in the product line—i.e., entry into the fusion reactor business—has not resulted in significant changes in the operation or organization of the division.

Project Management

The division is organized basically along functional lines, as illustrated in Exhibit 17–1. Operationally, however, each project is coordinated between function groups by a project management section. Each project management section consists of a project manager, a secretary, one or two file clerks, and a number of contract administrators. Each contract administrator is responsible for coordinating the activities of all functions necessary for accomplishing the project tasks.

Dave Roberts is a project manager responsible for three Air Force contracts. His group has one contract administrator for each of his three projects. Dale reports directly to Jim Watts, manager of the contract section shown in Exhibit 17–1. The project management group handles and coordinates all communications with the customer, including distribution of incoming mail and documents to pertinent functional groups. The project manager is basically responsible for success of the overall task.

Lateral communications occur primarily between contract administrators, engineering supervisors, process writers, and production control and quality assurance personnel assigned to the particular task. If conflicts arise, the decision-making role many times is elevated to higher levels in the hierarchy for resolution. Exhibit 17–2 illustrates the type of information flow that exists during a conflict situation.

Dale Roberts recalls several instances during his career with SPD when resolution of conflicts was not possible by "normal" lines of communication. One such incident occurred over an internal piping welding procedure for an Air Force component. The engineering supervisor demanded a high-strength weld with full non-

Exhibit 17–2 ■ Information Flow Chart

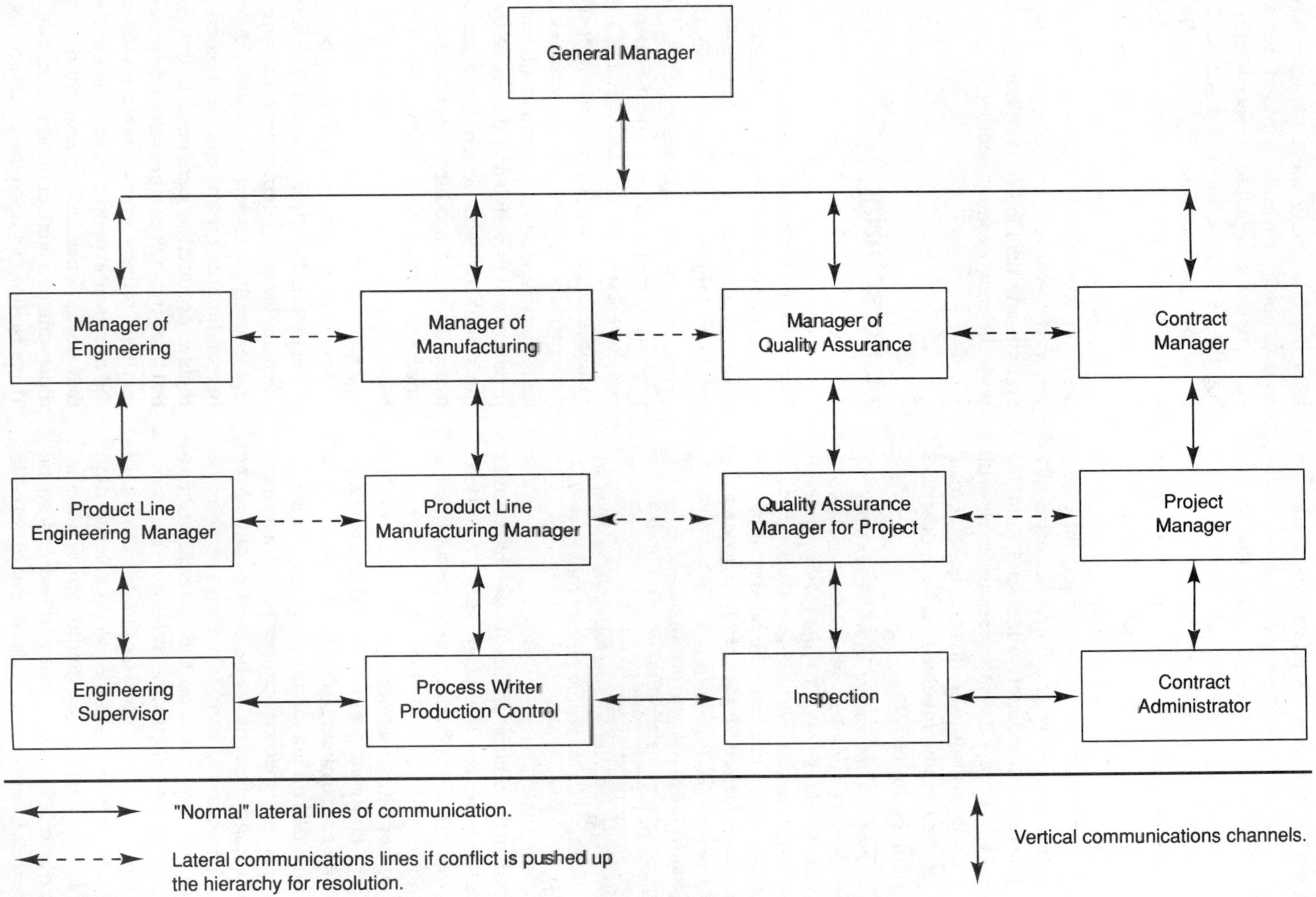

destructive examination (X-ray and penetrant testing). Manufacturing personnel, on the other hand, desired a welding method that would reduce their risk of making a bad weld, which would result in significant repair time. The quality assurance department established the rules for an acceptable result that could be nondestructively examined. Dale got involved early in this dispute as the project manager, attempting to resolve the differences speedily. He was not immediately successful, and the conflict was bumped up the various levels with limited success until the division general manager finally became involved. As Dale describes the incident, he recalls:

As it turned out, there were several acceptable alternatives. The problem was that the optimum alternative, relative to effort and risk required, was different for each department. Each functional group requested the support of its managers higher and higher in the structure to gain power in instituting its own desired method. Eventually, the problem reached the division manager, who made the final decision, to the betterment of the division as a whole. Furthermore, the decision needed to be reached very quickly, but the whole process took over a month.

Several occurrences of this nature have taken place over the last five years, and Mr. Roberts believes that SPD's performance has dropped as a result.

Another situation occurred on one of Mr. Roberts' contracts just recently that proved to be very embarrassing to SPD. A requirement was included on one particular contract for SPD to verify the material properties of a critical high-strength material to be used in one of the units. The material vendor is always responsible for performing a test on the material prior to shipment, and usually the vendor's test is dependable. However, due to the criticalness of this part, SPD was required to do a verification check in its laboratory within thirty days of material receipt. Parts were scheduled to be machined from these pieces of raw material in about two months after receipt of the material. The verification testing did not happen until after the machining was complete. Subsequent to machining, it was determined that the material was not acceptable. Responsibility for having the testing performed was traced, but no department would admit to having this responsibility. As a result, the division incurred significant additional costs and schedule delays.

Mr. Hazelton believed that the project management approach had been successful during the early years of building Air Force steam systems and decided to continue this approach with the new product ventures.

Manufacturing

The manufacturing department is responsible for economical, high-quality fabrication of the division's products on a timely basis. Often a product of this high quality requires 1½ to 2½ years to manufacture because of the many processes required and the frequent quality checks. Each major product line has a manufacturing manager who directs the efforts of several process writers, production controllers, and shop personnel. Because of the diverse products sold by SPD and the small number of units built for each design, there are normally many different products on the shop floor at one time. Production is done on a job shop basis, and careful scheduling of the various machines is necessary for effective utilization.

Preproduction planning is done by a group in the planning department, which is separate from the manufacturing department. Jobs are planned and quoted by experienced individuals in the preproduction group and are turned over to regular production personnel following a contract award. Often the scheduling and basic methods require considerable modification by the production people, many times to the extent that design changes are requested to facilitate more efficient and economical manufacturing. This situation occurs quite often on "follow-on" contracts that require very little engineering effort. Because each department operates as a cost

Exhibit 17–3 ■ SPD Engineering Organizational Chart

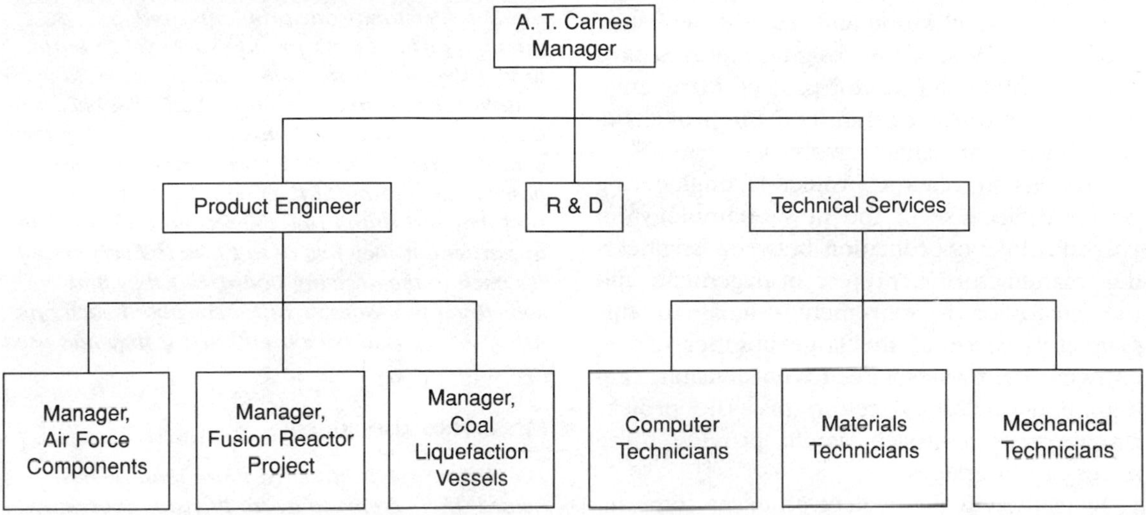

center, the number of person-hours to complete or support a project are estimated in the proposal stage. Upon contract award, the number of hours quoted are given to the cost center in the form of allocated backlog. Each cost center manager is measured by his or her backlog performance and often resists changes that cause the department more expense.

When changes in manufacturing methods are suggested, a high level of resistance sometimes errupts from other departments. Ed Brutus, a manufacturing manager for ten years in the Air Force product line, put it this way:

Preproduction people are often not as knowledgeable about current methods as they should be and do not ask our advice often enough. Every time a methods change or design change is suggested, engineering and quality assurance yell and scream to high heaven. They don't care whether we save money or not. After all, manufacturing is where this division's money is made or lost. We should get more priority when it comes to cost savings. Engineering is so conservative that they always overpenalize us anyway. When push comes to shove, they can always make the design work on paper. Manufacturing should have more authority in this division.

Engineering

The engineering department is organized into product groups, support groups, and R & D section (see Exhibit 17–3). Mr. A. T. Carnes has been manager of engineering since 1972 and holds more patents than any other employee at Advanced Technologies. Mr. Carnes has organized the engineering department in such a way as to promote a high degree of flexibility. Reorganizations are frequent to meet the needs of changing work loads. Product groups perform design and analysis in direct support of particular contracts, while support groups in the technical services section develop and update the technical tools necessary for contract work. Considerable use is made of advanced computerized analysis techniques in the Air Force and fusion reactor product groups, while engineering effort on coal liquefaction vessels is limited to manufacturing support and basic sizing using simple design rules.

Over the past years, the department has developed a great deal of technical expertise and has had the opportunity to contribute significantly to the Air Force steam system designs. Recently, however, the engineering task has been limited to analysis of customer-dictated designs, because of product stabilization and much design standardization. Most of the design challenges have come in the fusion reactor project. Many engineers have requested a transfer to this project because of the challenges involved.

The fusion reactor project is engineering centered because of the new technology involved. Close coordination between engineering, manufacturing, project management, and the customer is extremely crucial to this project because of the large number of unknowns. Mr. Carnes agreed with division General Manager Mr. Hazelton that the project management approach would provide these necessary interfaces.

Even though the project promises some future competitive advantages for SPD, it has been plagued with problems since its beginning. Engineers expecting technical challenges have found themselves reviewing specifications and writing work plans. Discouragement and frustration have occurred among the project group members because design progress has gone very slowly. Lack of agreement between engineering and manufacturing functions and the seeming inability to please the customer have resulted in further frustration, confusion, and lack of direction within the group. Mr. Carnes sizes it up this way:

Our biggest problem is that our people lack the experience necessary to handle a new technology project. The mistakes that have been made and the recent customer criticism have come as a direct result of inexperience. George [George Ward, manager of the fusion reactor group] is a heck of a leader and tries hard, but he lacks sound experience in design. For that reason, I have become intimately involved with this project. I have been helping George out lately by taking some of the load off him. I have directed the work on some key designs and have reviewed them daily. I have also begun weekly design reviews of the entire project.

Regarding the generally slow progress on the project, he said:

Other groups in this division don't pay enough attention to the engineers. Project management rarely understands our problems, and manufacturing hasn't found a way yet to build any of the designs we have come up with. Take for instance the plasma makeup nozzle. We have sent them five potential designs on this thing and they haven't agreed to any. They said there was no possible way to build the first design, and they said they just didn't like the second one. Nothing in particular, they just didn't like it. Every time, it's back to the drawing board, but they find something that doesn't suit them about each one. All of these could have been built if they had used just a little ingenuity.

Mr. Carnes also added:

The customer has hindered more than he has helped. There seems to be no pleasing those guys, especially when they don't seem to know what they want. Every time we submit a design for their review, it doesn't seem to be what they had in mind.

Conclusion

Fred Hazelton reviewed the criticisms from the Air Force one more time before the meeting began. Those comments reflecting the Air Force's image of SPD are listed below:

- Passive—not aggressive
- Not a problem-solving organization
- Pass problems back to the customer
- Defensive—will not admit poor performance
- No commitment to continued cost reduction and schedule improvement
- Customer is an opponent to be fenced with rather than satisfied

He reflected also on the lack of progress on the fusion reactor project. He wondered why SPD had lost out to competitors last year in the Air Force market. He wondered what could be done to improve SPD's performance.

18

Calgary Police Department

The function of the Calgary Police Department is to protect the life and property of the citizens and visitors to Calgary. To achieve this goal we must effectively prevent crimes, make arrests and carry out the other related aspects of police work.

Chief Rousseau (1980)

Recent History

James T. Rousseau was elected chief of police on February 2, 1962. He inaugurated a permanent recruit school. New types of radio equipment were purchased. The officers were given a much deserved day off each week. The headquarters building was redecorated to make working conditions better. The Detective Department was reorganized by division into robbery, larceny, burglary, homicide, vice, and miscellaneous squads. A wrecker was purchased to impound cars illegally parked, and a parking lot for these impounded cars was built.

In 1965, the first traffic policewomen were sworn in and given special training.

In 1966, the entire Calgary Police Department was reorganized into four divisions. These were Services, Uniform, Traffic, and Detective. Training and Detention were made separate divisions later. There was a superintendent in charge of each division.

In 1967, the County Police Department was absorbed into the Calgary Police Department. Police protection was extended to parts of the county outside the city that formerly had depended on the county police. The police department was now responsible for a geographical area almost twice as large.

Space problems were severely felt in 1971 and several departments had to be moved from headquarters. These problems were relieved in

---

The names and locations are purely fictional. The material has been adapted from "Atlanta Police Department." Permission to republish granted by Office of Justice Assistance, Research, and Statistics, U.S. Department of Justice.

1974 with the completion of a new headquarters building.

In 1973, there was a rise in racial and religious agitation. A Jewish temple was bombed and attacks against persons grew in frequency. The black civil rights and racial problem also became more significant.

The Community Environment

In 1980, the Calgary Crime Commission completed a study of the city's needs for police department services. The following are excerpts from the Crime Commission report.

Calgary's Youth

There is a serious need to focus the city's resources on the problem of preventing and controlling juvenile delinquency. We therefore recommend that the Calgary Youth Council be created as an official agency for this purpose. Membership would include the superintendent of the Calgary Public Schools, the head of the Parks Department, the chief of police, a full-time executive director, a lay chairperson, and six lay members, for a total membership of 11.

The police department should be actively involved in the formulation and implementation of a community program of delinquency prevention and control. All available public and private resources should be fully used in such a program. It also should work with the public, private, and religious agencies devoted in whole or in part to delinquency prevention and coordinate the activities of these agencies to the extent desirable. Finally, it would collect, correlate, and disseminate information, statistics, and data on the subject of juvenile delinquency and make this information available to all agencies that might benefit from it.

Police in Low-Income Areas

There is a serious lack of understanding between residents of low-income areas and the police. All available means should be used to inform every citizen of the fact that the police serve not only to arrest and punish the lawbreaker, but also to protect the average citizen in his or her day-to-day life. The Calgary Police Department should send police counselors into problem areas to hold meetings and generally to inform the public of the protective role of the police. Neighborhood committees that include a police officer trained in social problem areas should be established. Existing independent neighborhood civic associations should also be used and a police counselor stationed in each Economic Opportunity Calgary neighborhood center.

Parks

One of Calgary's most serious problems with regard to juvenile delinquency and crime is that the most congested areas of the city have the fewest recreation facilities. Parks should be built in congested high crime areas of the city. Trained supervisory personnel must be provided. Equipment should be modern. More park police should be provided so that Calgary's people can enjoy their parks. Community centers should be kept open longer during the week and on weekends, particularly during the summer.

Organized Crime

The Commission has found that organized crime exists in Calgary on a local basis. More members of the Calgary Police Department should be trained to deal with the problems of organized crime. All law enforcement agencies in the Calgary area must constantly be on the alert for encroachments of organized crime on a local or national basis.

Care of the Alcoholic

Alcoholic offenders should be identified and a concerted effort should be made to remedy their addiction, thus eliminating the expense of their continued apprehension by the police, their imprisonment, and their trial before the Municipal

Court. The Commission feels that this responsibility should belong to the City of Calgary.

Advancement

Police officers must be made secure in their jobs by an appropriate type of merit system. A cadet school for qualified high school graduates should be created, and there should be continued police training for recruit and veteran alike.

Modernization

The police department itself needs considerable modernization. The department should use all modern developments and law enforcement techniques, including such crime-fighting equipment as computers.

Police Department Study

The police department should be studied thoroughly by an independent professional agency to determine its present capabilities and its need for the immediate future. This study should evaluate and estimate Calgary's police requirements; it should appraise its organizational structure, personnel, equipment, and promotion system. On the basis of this study, there should be proposed a detailed plan of improvement to give the city and its citizens a modern police organization second to none.

Community Diversity

Different areas of the city have unique problems that do not seem to be recognized within the department. Similar services are provided throughout the city.

Present Organization Structure

In early 1980, the Calgary Police Department consisted of six divisions, each headed by a superintendent reporting to Chief Rousseau. The six divisions were: Service, Detective, Traffic, Uniform, Detention, and Training. The organization chart is shown in Exhibit 18–1.

Service Division

The Service Division, under the command of Superintendent Milton, is responsible for all the administrative aspects of the department. Superintendent Milton joined the department in 1950 and was named superintendent in 1975.

Specifically the division is charged with the compilation of criminal records (including the Royal Canadian Mounted Police reports), the transmitting and receiving of radio communications, and the telephone switchboard. The division is also responsible for all monies received by the department as well as the department's inventories, purchases, and maintenance.

The Service Division consists of the Crime Report Bureau, including Missing Persons Bureau, the Tabulation Room, and Communications. In addition, the division includes the Custodian's Office, Arsenal, and Maintenance Crew.

Detective Division

The Detective Division is headed by Superintendent Raymond Hill. Superintendent Hill joined the department in 1962 and was named Superintendent of the Detective Division in 1979.

The Detective Division is charged with the prevention of crime, the investigation of criminal offenses, the detection and arrest of criminals, and the recovery of stolen or lost property. The division consists of ten squads: Auto, Burglary, Homicide, Larceny, Robbery, Vice (includes Narcotic Investigations), Fugitive, Juvenile, Security, and Lottery. In addition, the Division includes the Identification Bureau and the General and Criminal Investigation Bureaus.

The most recent additions to the Detective Division are the Juvenile, Security, and Fugitive Squads.

The Juvenile Squad was formed in 1975 following rapid increase in the number of juve-

Exhibit 18–1. ■ Organizational Chart For The Calgary Police Department

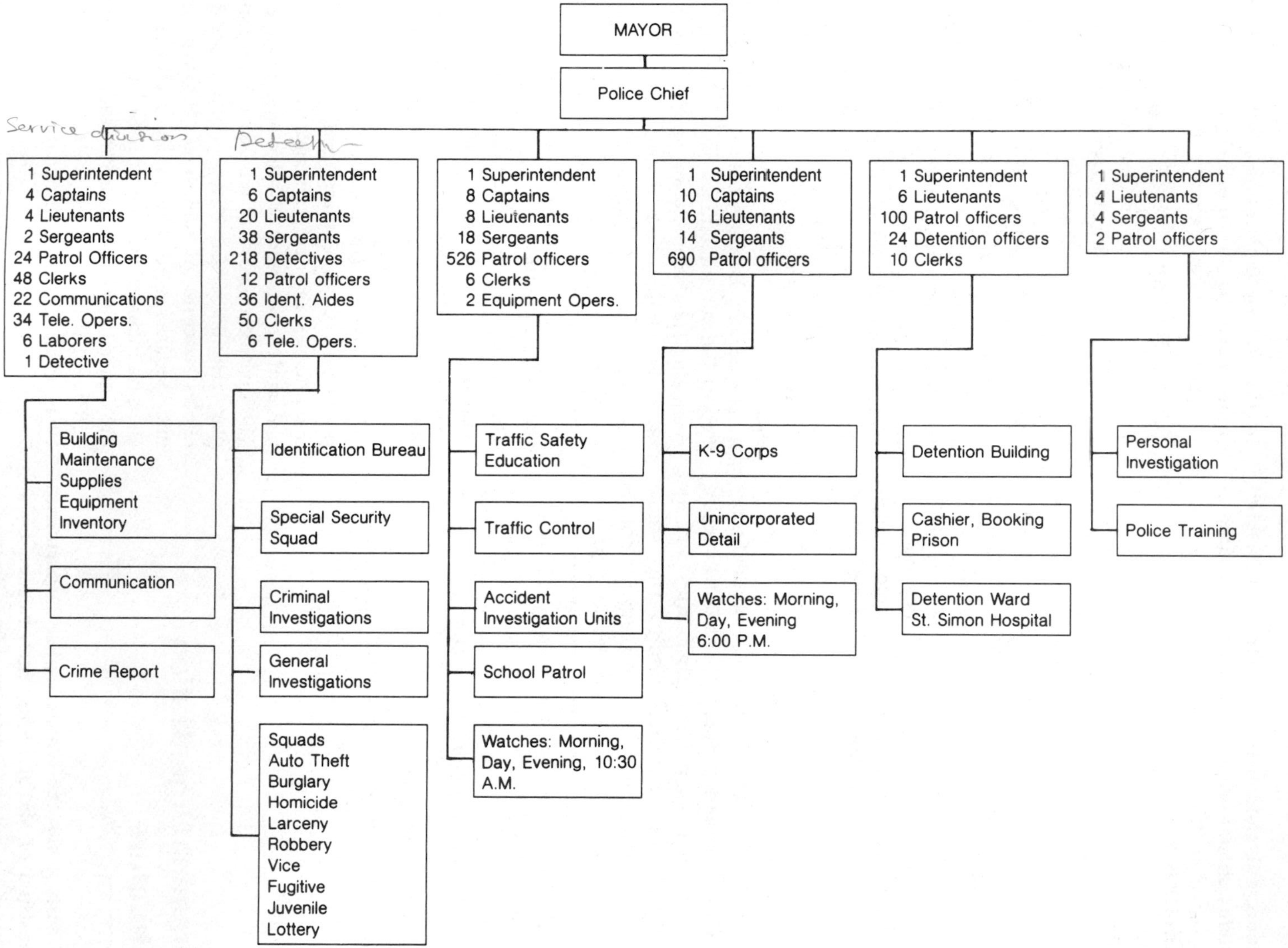

niles involved in illegal acts. The squad investigates cases in which children under 17 years of age are involved and assists other detective squads (when needed) to investigate crimes by juveniles. The division also works with the Juvenile Court authorities in the prevention of crime and rehabilitation of wayward children.

Sergeant Croy, who joined the department in 1962, heads the Juvenile Squad. Reporting to Sergeant Croy are nine persons.

The Security Squad consists of 12 officers and was formed in 1975. It operates under direct orders from the Chief of Police and the Superintendent of Detectives. The squad is charged with maintaining a constant check on the activities of subversive groups as well as keeping a check on any section of the city where racial tension exists or may start. The squad is also responsible for the safety of any visiting dignitaries (which includes working closely with other governmental agencies), investigating bombings, investigating internal problems that may arise within the department, and any other special assignments given by the Chief.

Lieutenant Madaline Barnett heads the Security Squad. Lieutenant Barnett is 32 years old. She joined the department eight years earlier as a uniformed officer patrolling a footbeat.

The Fugitive Squad was created in 1970. This squad specializes in the apprehension and prosecution of fugitives from penitentiary and justice. Lieutenant Benson heads this squad of 15 officers from Calgary plus 10 from other local jurisdictions.

Traffic Division

The Traffic Division promotes street and highway safety and the enforcement of vehicular traffic laws and regulations. In addition, the division is charged with handling large crowds who attend sports events, conventions, parades, circuses, and funerals. The Traffic Division consists of the following groups: Motorcycle, Accident Investigation, Foot Traffic, Parking Control, Radar Speed Control, and Helicopter Traffic Control. The division also includes School Police Officers, School Patrols, and the police wrecker.

Superintendent Spencer J. Lloyd heads the Traffic Division. He joined the department in 1952 and was named superintendent in 1980.

According to Chief Rousseau, if the Traffic Division can keep the number of fatalities low, the other traffic accident statistics will be reduced also. In pursuit of this goal, Chief Rousseau and Superintendent Lloyd meet weekly to discuss the current and projected traffic situation with representatives of the city, county, and provincial government agencies responsible for highways, the Calgary Safety Council, and several prominent citizens.

Uniform Division

The Uniform Division is charged with the protection of life and property, the prevention of crime, the detection and arrest of offenders, and the preservation of the public peace. Superintendent Samuel Locke is the commanding officer. He joined the department in 1949 and was named superintendent in 1966. Superintendent Locke's division consists of the following squads and bureaus: Radio Patrol; Motorcycle (nontraffic); K–9 Corps; Unincorporated Detail (see below); and Foot Patrols.

The Calgary Police Department furnishes, through the Uniform Division, services to the unincorporated area of Fulton County under a contract between the City of Calgary and Fulton County. The personnel and equipment comprising the Unincorporated Detail includes 4 captains; 2 lieutenants; 60 patrol officers; 16 patrol cars; 22 school traffic officers; and 8 motorcycles.

Detention Division

The Detention Division was established in 1973. Previously it was part of the service division. According to Chief Rousseau, during the racial problems of the early 1970's, 400 to 500 persons might be jailed at any one time. This created numerous problems that he believed could best be handled by a separate division.

Superintendent Jack Marston heads the Detention Division, which is responsible for the operations of the adjoining headquarters building and the detention ward at the Saint Simon Hospital, a large downtown public hospital. During 1980 about 155,000 people were processed by the Detention Division.

Superintendent Marston joined the department in 1955 and was named superintendent in 1966.

Training Division

The Training Division was created in 1974. Formerly it was part of the service division. The Training Division is responsible for police training and the investigation of applicants seeking to join the department. The division's commanding officer is Superintendent T. N. Danvers. He joined the force in 1950 and was appointed superintendent in 1973.

The division's principal training activity is a six-week school for new recruits conducted at least three times a year. Between 40 and 55 people attend each session, which is set up along the same lines as the RCMP's National Academy. Each session usually includes several officers from other departments, such as the airport or park police. These officers attend free of charge.

Other training activities include bi-monthly discussion by each squad of the training keys prepared by the International Association of Chiefs of Police. These meetings are conducted by lieutenants and sergeants for the officers in their squads. Periodically, written examinations are given to all officers. These papers are graded and the results recorded in each officer's personnel file.

Watch System

The Police Department operates on the watch (shift) system. The watches are:

11 P.M.-7 A.M.	Morning Watch	Traffic Division
7 A.M.-3 P.M.	Day Watch	
3 P.M.-11 P.M.	Night Watch	
10 A.M.-6 P.M.	Traffic Watch	(Intersection Control)
8-9 A.M. & 2-4 P.M.	School Patrol	
8 A.M.-4 P.M.	Office Personnel	
12 P.M.-8 A.M.	Uniform and Detective	
8 A.M.-4 P.M.		
4 P.M.-12 P.M.		

Each watch is covered by a captain from either the Uniform or Traffic Divisions, depending upon which one happens to be on duty at the time. "In this way," Chief Rousseau said, "I am able to have a superior officer responsible for whatever happens during the watch."

Districts

For patrol duty purposes, the City of Calgary is divided into four districts. Either 10 or 11 two-person patrol cars are assigned to each district during each watch. These cars are in constant radio communication with the central radio room located in the police headquarters building. Chief Rousseau referred to these patrol cars as his "mobile precincts." He believed it would take more funds to operate his department if it were organized on a precinct basis.

Strengths and Weaknesses of the Current Organization:

Interview with Chief Rousseau:

Changes in Formal Structure

At the time I took over as chief, the service office operated out of the chief's office. In line with my desire to delegate authority, I created the Service Division and moved to the service and other divisions many of the management tasks formerly carried on by the chief's office. In the process I also abolished the two Deputy Chief of Police positions. Now, in my absence, the Superintendent of the Service Division acts as Chief.

Selection and Training

When I became Chief, I took action in two areas. First, I wanted to improve the training of police officers. I realized a number of officers did not fully realize what was demanded or expected of them. Second, I wanted to strengthen the moral courage and integrity of the department. While it is not always manifest, police officers are always under scrutiny and open to accusation. It appeared to me a number of officers were overly fearful of making mistakes or being falsely accused. I set out to correct this situation through training and clear-cut policies.

Our personnel department will accept applications only if our training division says that in their opinion the applicant will make a good police officer. Once the applicant is accepted and joins the force, s/he is assigned a counselor who is either a lieutenant or sergeant. The officers are encouraged to discuss with their counselor their problems. Also, we have squad meetings periodically to discuss the things on the officers' minds. I've told the counselors that if I get any reports of misconduct involving their advisees, I want to see the counselor. I want results.

The improvements over the last 10 years have been remarkable. We now have procedures and facilities for selection, training, and continuous officer testing and development. The ability of our officers is high.

Referring to the Crime Commission Report

Now the Crime Commission has recommended we get more involved in prevention activities for juvenile and organized crime. The Mayor has told me to follow up these recommendations, but not to go over my budget allocation. In a sense our 6 P.M. detail has functioned as our crime prevention detail. Moreover, the Commission report seems to be calling for more than the normal concept of a police officer's function. How should I organize for crime prevention? How many officers should I assign to this task? What kind of officers should they be? What are some of the things these officers should be doing? These are all questions I must resolve quickly.

Other Problems

The police department is becoming very large. Size is a problem. Police officers get lost in the bureaucracy. They have trouble identifying with the purpose of the organization. I wonder if a "precinct" form of organization (self-contained area police units) would be better? In addition we have so much paperwork. Millions of pieces of paper are processed each year. No one likes it.

Coordination between divisions is poor. Each division is becoming a separate organization, doing its own business. For example, one division doesn't know what another is doing when working in schools or low-income areas. They don't communicate with one another. Other examples: a patrol officer will write up a burglary, and never hear back from the detective division. Job openings are usually filled from within the same division. Personnel rotation is poor. Police officers can spend their careers in one activity.

We would like to install a large centralized computer in the Service Division to handle paperwork and do statistical analyses. We are afraid it may be unreliable, and that it will make the Police Department more bureaucratic and impersonal. Could computers be installed in each division?

19

C & C Grocery Stores, Inc.

The first C & C grocery store was started in 1947 by Doug Cummins and his brother Bob. Both were veterans who wanted to run their own business, so they used their savings to start the small grocery store in Charlotte, North Carolina. The store was immediately successful. The location was good, and Doug Cummins had a winning personality. Store employees adopted Doug's informal style and "serve the customer" attitude. C & C's increasing circle of customers enjoyed an abundance of good meats and produce.

By 1984, C & C had over 200 stores. A standard physical layout was used for new stores. Company headquarters moved from Charlotte to Atlanta in 1975. The organization chart for C & C is shown in Exhibit 19–1. The central offices in Atlanta handled personnel, merchandising, financial, purchasing, real estate, and legal affairs for the entire chain. For management of individual stores, the organization was divided by regions. The southern, southeastern, and northeastern regions each had about seventy stores. Each region was divided into five districts of ten to fifteen stores each. A district director was responsible for supervision and coordination of activities for the ten to fifteen district stores.

Each district was divided into four lines of authority based upon functional specialty. Three of these lines reached into the stores. The produce department manager within each store reported directly to the produce specialist for the division, and the same was true for the meat department manager, who reported directly to the district meat specialist. The meat and produce managers were responsible for all activities associated with the acquisition and sale of perishable products. The store manager's responsibility included the grocery line, front-end departments, and store operations. The store manager was responsible for appearance of personnel, cleanliness, adequate check-out service, and price accuracy. A grocery manager reported to the store manager and maintained inventories and restocked shelves for grocery

EXHIBIT 19–1 ■ Organization Structure For C & C Grocery Stores, Inc.

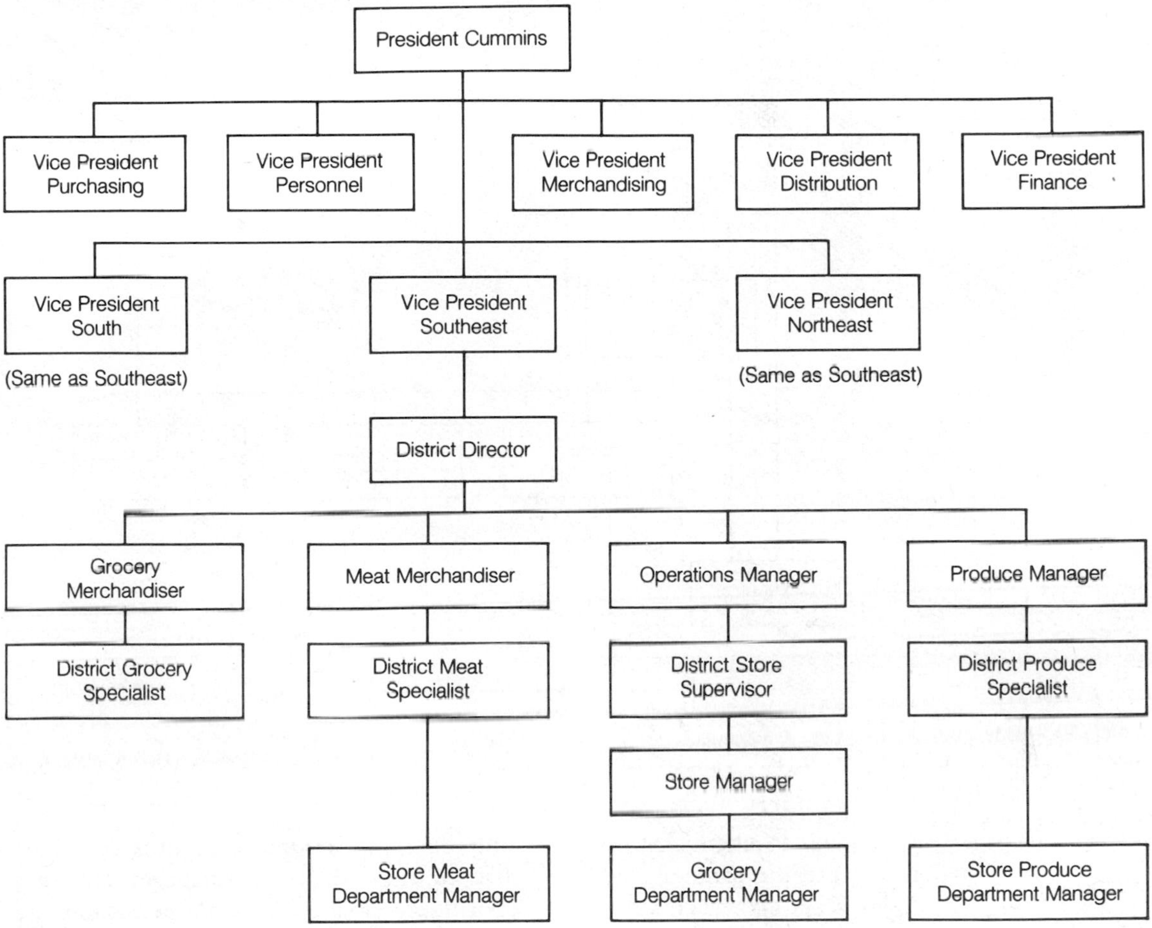

items. The district merchandising office was responsible for promotional campaigns, advertising circulars, district advertising, and for attracting customers into the stores. The grocery merchandisers were expected to coordinate their activities with each store in the district.

During the recession in 1980–81, business for the C & C chain dropped off in all regions and did not increase with the improved economic times in 1983–84. This caused concern among senior executives. They also were aware that other supermarket chains were adopting a trend toward one-stop shopping, which meant the emergence of super stores that included a pharmacy, dry goods, and groceries—almost like a department store. Executives wondered whether C & C should move in this direction and how such changes could be assimilated into the current store organization. However, the most pressing problem was how to improve business with the grocery stores they now had. A consulting team from a major university was hired to investigate store structure and operations.

The consultants visited several stores in each region, talking to about fifty managers and employees. The consultants wrote a report that pinpointed four problem areas to be addressed by store executives.

EXHIBIT 19–2 ■ Proposed Reorganization of C & C Grocery Stores, Inc.

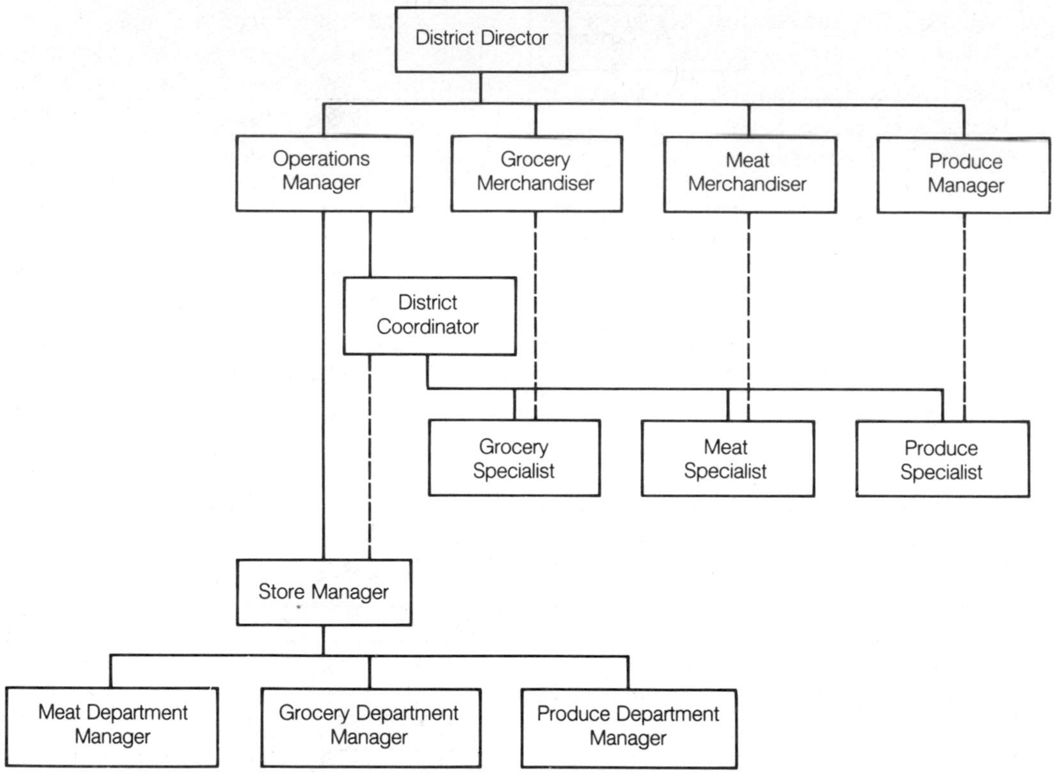

1. The chain is slow to adapt to change. Store layout and structure were the same as had been designed fifteen years ago. Each store did things the same way even though some stores were in low-income areas and other stores in suburban areas. A new grocery management system for ordering and stocking had been developed, but after two years was only partially implemented in the stores.
2. Roles of the district store supervisor and the store manager were causing dissatisfaction. The store managers wanted to learn general management skills for potential promotion into district or regional management positions. However, their jobs restricted them to operational activities and they learned little about merchandising, meat, and produce. Moreover, district store supervisors used store visits to inspect for cleanliness and adherence to operating standards rather than to train the store manager and help coordinate operations with perishable departments. Close supervision on the operational details had become the focus of operations management rather than development, training, and coordination.
3. Cooperation within stores was low and morale was poor. The informal, friendly atmosphere originally created by Doug Cummins was gone. One example of this problem occurred when the grocery merchandiser and store manager in a Louisiana store decided to promote Coke and Diet Coke as a loss leader. Thousands of cartons of Coke were brought in for the sale, but the stockroom was not prepared and did not have room. The store manager wanted to use floor area in the meat and produce sections to

display Coke cartons, but those managers refused. The produce department manager said that Diet Coke did not help his sales and it was okay with him if there was no promotion at all.

4. Long-term growth and development of the stores chain would probably require reevaluation of long-term strategy. The percent of market share going to traditional grocery stores was declining nationwide due to competition from large super stores and convenience stores. In the future, C & C might need to introduce non-food items into the stores for one-stop shopping, and add specialty sections within stores. Some stores could be limited to grocery items, but store location and marketing techniques should take advantage of the grocery emphasis.

To solve the first three problems, the consultants recommended reorganizing the district and the store structure as illustrated in Exhibit 19–2. Under this reorganization, the meat, grocery, and produce department managers would all report to the store manager. The store manager would have complete store control and would be responsible for coordination of all store activities. The district supervisor's role would be changed from supervision to training and development. The district supervisor would head a team that included himself and several meat, produce, and merchandise specialists who would visit area stores as a team to provide advice and help for the store managers and other employees. The team would act in a liaison capacity between district specialists and the stores.

The consultants were enthusiastic about the proposed structure. By removing one level of district operational supervision, store managers would have more freedom and responsibility. The district liaison team would establish a cooperative team approach to management that could be adopted within stores. The focus of store responsibility on a single manager would encourage coordination within stores, adaptation to local conditions, and provide a focus of responsibility for store-wide administrative changes.

The consultants also believe that the proposed structure could be expanded to accommodate non-grocery lines if enlarged stores were to be developed in the future. Within each store, a new department manager could be added for pharmacy, dry goods, or other major departments. The district team could be expanded to include specialists in these departments who would act as liaison for stores in the district.

III

INTERNAL ORGANIZATIONAL PROCESSES

20

Measuring Organizational Effectiveness

Organizational effectiveness is the degree to which an organization realizes its goals. Various approaches to assessing effectiveness include whether the organization achieves its goals in terms of desired levels of output; whether the organization obtains the resources necessary for high performance; and whether the internal activities and processes of the organization reflect an internal health and efficient use of resources.

The organizations listed below operate with different goals in mind and assess their effectiveness at meeting these goals in different ways. The purpose of this exercise is to illustrate the relationship between goals and effectiveness and methods for measuring effectiveness.

Step I. Determining Goals and Assessing Effectiveness (20 min.)

For each organization below list two possible goals and the approach which might be used to assess the organization's effectiveness at meeting these goals.

Step II. Small-Group Discussion (15 min.)

Working in groups of three, discuss the goals you have identified and the measures necessary to determine the effectiveness of the organization in meeting these goals.

Step III. Group Presentation (10 min.)

Each group should select from the list one organization and corresponding set of goals and effectiveness measures to share with the class. In explaining your choice, indicate why other types of measures would or would not be just as useful in measuring organizational effectiveness.

Step IV. Class Discussion (15 min.)

Review and discuss the goals and measures identified by the members of the class. The following questions may be helpful in integrating this exercise with previous class discussions regarding goals and effectiveness.

Discussion Questions

1. Did the goals and measures of effectiveness tend to be stated in quantitative or qualitative terms? Which is easier to observe?
2. Is it possible to have multiple measures for one goal? If so, give an example. Do multiple measures guarantee a better assessment of achieving goals?
3. How does efficiency relate to the goals and effectiveness measures identified by the exercise? Are there different determinations for efficiency? Such as?
4. When determining measures of effectiveness, who did you decide would be applying such measures? Top management? Employees? Customers? Does it matter?
5. In which domain is each goal? How does this translate into the measurements you selected?

	Goals	*Effectiveness Measures*
1. Automobile Manufacturer	______	______
	______	______
2. Post Office	______	______
	______	______
3. Professional Hockey Team	______	______
	______	______
4. Local Newspaper	______	______
	______	______
5. Farmer	______	______
	______	______
6. High School	______	______
	______	______
7. Labor Union	______	______
	______	______
8. Community Theater Group	______	______
	______	______
9. Local Chamber of Commerce	______	______
	______	______

21

Knox Electronics

While he was on his way to the cafeteria for lunch, Phil Chase, chief industrial engineer for Knox Electronics, was stopped by a visibly upset Scott Pagent. Scott, with four months in time study, was the newest member of the Industrial Engineering Department. He had been hired immediately upon his January 1980 graduation from Virginia Tech with a degree in industrial engineering. Just the previous month, Scott had been given the responsibility for maintaining and establishing time standards for Section 6750 of the Switches and Relays Department. The foreman for the section was John Ransom.

Scott complained:

Phil, I can't work with John Ransom. He is bucking any changes I make in his section and is encouraging the operators to take a hostile attitude towards me. I thought I was hired to bring new ideas for improving productivity, but I can't even set simple standards without his interference!

Scott Pagent's complaint was one of many that Phil had been hearing concerning the establishment of the revised work standards in the Switches and Relays Department. The department's production had dropped considerably since the introduction of the new standards six weeks previously, and the workers in that department were very unhappy. Phil wondered whether the company should stand fast behind the new standards, return to the old standards, or reach a compromise somewhere between the two extremes.

Two factors complicated the problem. First, old standards, which still covered 85 percent of the units produced in the Switches and Relays Department, had been set as far back as seven years ago using the stopwatch method. Recently, industrial engineers had restudied various jobs and set new standards using predetermined times from the Movement Time Study (MTS) Program. Management recognized that the old standards covering the various units in the Switches and Relays Department had been very loose, but the company had been reluctant to change them up until the MTS program was adopted. Second, methods changes had been instituted for the assembly of many of the relays and switches produced in the department. In many cases, these methods changes had been made simultaneously with the change in the technique used for setting the work standards. Thus, the effects of each were difficult to judge individually.

Phil explained:

I catch it from both sides. Management keeps harping about work improvements and productivity; they want the standards to be tightened. The workers, however, complain about any increase we make in the standards. Several foremen in the department are after us, too. They insist that their production will never get back to normal unless we slow down the pace of our activities of revising the old standards. I know some foremen would not care if we stayed out of the Switches and Relays Department for the next year. We industrial engineers who set the work methods and time standards are caught in the middle!

Company History

Knox Electronics was a medium-sized manufacturer of small electronics parts for sale to original equipment manufacturers, wholesalers, and large retail electronics parts dealers. The company produced over twenty-five hundred different parts such as capacitors, resistors, relays, and switches in its plant at Gambier, Ohio.

The company was founded by James Hayes in 1932 to supply relays used in telephone exchange switching equipment. From World War II up until the late 1960s, its reputation for high-quality products promoted rapid sales growth, which in turn required the company to expand production capacity. The company also diversified its product line to include a wide variety of electrical parts.

By 1970, however, overseas manufacturers were producing parts comparable in quality at lower costs, due mainly to their use of cheaper foreign labor in the construction of such hand-assembled items as switches and relays. Once its quality advantage was neutralized by these producers, Knox Electronics attempted to compete in the marketplace by lowering its selling prices. This strategy placed a severe strain on its once healthy profit margins. Several cost-reduction programs were put into action, including one for salaried employees called Foreman's Methods Improvement Program. Another, called Worker Suggestion Bonus, gave any hourly employee offering a methods improvement or any other cost-reducing suggestion 10 percent of the annual savings resulting from the suggestion. Both of these programs were successful in reducing manufacturing costs, but management now felt that even more substantial reductions were necessary in order to compete.

Approximately four hundred of the company's nine hundred employees performed some type of hand-assembly work. The majority of hand-assembly workers were women with children in school, working to supplement their husbands' incomes. Although some of the products were assembled on a line with each worker performing only one or two steps, most of the products were assembled at individual work stations.

Under the company's wage incentive plan, all hand-assembly workers were guaranteed a certain base hourly wage. Group incentives were used for line workers, but individual incentives were given for those jobs requiring complete assembly by a single worker. Production standards for the various assembly operations were pegged to the worker's base pay. For every percentage point that output exceeded standard, the worker received an equal percentage of her base pay as incentive. For example, if a worker was guaranteed \$3.50 an hour for a standard hourly production of one hundred pieces, she was still paid \$28 per day if she produced less than eight hundred pieces. If she produced sixteen hundred pieces in a day, however, she was paid $56, with $28 of this amount being the bonus or incentive compensation. Individual production records were not posted, but section production records within the various departments (i.e., switch assembly sections, relay sections) were posted weekly.

The average guaranteed hourly wage at Knox Electronics was $3.91. The average wage per hour, including incentives, however, was $5.17, which was above the community average of $4.76 per hour for workers performing similar work. During the past two-year period, management had given all employees a cost of living increase of 9 percent each year. These increases were expected to be continued.

The company was not unionized, despite repeated attempts by local union representatives. The issue had been put to a vote twice and defeated both times. Management claimed that the relatively high wages and benefits, combined with the "family-type" atmosphere of the plant, worked to keep out the union.

Time Standards at Knox Electronics

Formal industrial engineering methods, in the form of time standards, first came into use at the company in 1947. By the 1970s, the company had an industrial engineering staff of twelve men. Phil Chase described the development of standards at Knox:

The company has relied heavily on time standards since their introduction here. We depend on them for production scheduling, determination of incentive wages, making make-versus-buy analyses, and pinpointing methods improvements. Up until this year, we used the stopwatch method to determine standard times. We would make observations of a worker assembling a unit and time each element necessary for assembly. This old analysis sheet from one of the jobs in the Switches and Relays Department will illustrate what I mean. (See Exhibit 21–1.) The operator was assembling a relay spring combination used in various forms of electrical equipment while she was seated at a desk with a special fixture designed to hold four of these relays at once. The workers got each of the pieces used to assemble the spring from the raised bins on the desk behind the fixture.

As you can see, from this standard time analysis, we had six industrial engineers study two operators—Hannah Moore and Doris Crozier. The figures have been boiled down somewhat from the original observations. First of all, each analyst observed approximately one hundred assembly cycles. The figures shown here were the average times for each element in the assembly cycle. Second, since the spring assemblies were built on a four-station fixture, the original times have been divided by four. The industrial engineer who compiled this sheet took each of the six individual observations and found the average time for each element and the average time for the entire cycle (Exhibit 21–1, column 7). If only one analyst were making this study, he would have included a performance rating to adjust the time to what he considered a normal pace. In other words, if the industrial engineer felt that Hannah Moore was only working at 80 percent of the normal pace while he was timing her, he would have adjusted the times accordingly. In most time-study situations, we believe, however, that by averaging six observations on two workers, no performance rating is necessary.

The average minutes per piece total was multiplied by 115 percent to allow for delay, rest, and fatigue. These final figures (Exhibit 21–1, Column 8) gave us the standard time for each element and the total cycle. The standard for part #200280–209, operation #2 established under the stopwatch system became 74.4 pieces per hour.

All our standards were established by stopwatch until six months ago, when we began to use MTS. This is a predetermined-times system that was developed by a group of British engineers to overcome some of the difficulties usually found in the use of other predetermined-times systems like MTM. The engineers found that it was far easier to think of hand-assembly motions not in terms of distances, but in terms of limb movements.

EXHIBIT 21–1 ▪ Knox Electronics: Pile-Up Assembly Data, 200280–209 Operation #2

Department 6750	(1)	(2)	(3)	(4)	(5)	(6)	(7)	(8)
Date	5-19-74	5-19-74	5-19-74	5-19-74	5-19-74	5-19-74	Average Minute per Piece	(7) x 115% = STD. Min./Pc.
Operator Operator # Analyst	H. Moore 0654 P.B.C.	D. Crozier 0983 M.A.H.	D. Crozier 0983 K.C.O.	H. Moore 0654 P.J.D.	D. Crozier 0983 W.G.C.	H. Moore 0654 K.N.Y.		
Get & Place Bracket:	.0298	.0292	.0400	.0260	.0380	.0220	.0308	.0354
Get & Place Guide Pins:	.0440	.0564	.0542	.0502	.0420	.0440	.0484	.0557
Get & Place Bushings:	.0552	.0548	.0528	.0572	.0420	.0420	.0508	.0584
Get & Place Insulators (300 972-441)	.1092	.1242	.1296	.1476	.1440	.1500	.1338	.1539
Get & Place Spring Assembly:	.1830	.1980	.1698	.2322	.1500	.1680	.1836	.2111
Get & Place Insulators (300972-091)	.0182	.0207	.0216	.0246	.0240	.0250	.0223	.0256
Place Plate, Remove Pins- Insert Screws:	.1191	.1612	.1411	.1164	.1438	.0786	.1267	.1457
Drive Screws w/Air Driver:	.0616	.0400	.0482	.0442	.0480	.0400	.0470	.0541
Remove from Fixture, Mark, Check and Put Aside:	.0416	.0574	.0417	.0533	.0540	.0390	.0478	.0550
Machine Times	.009	.010	.011	.011	.009	.010	.010	.0115
TOTAL CYCLE	.6707	.7519	.7100	.7625	.6948	.6186	.7012	.8064

*Times are for one piece done on a four-station fixture.

.8064 std. min/pc.
1.344 hours/100 pcs.
74.4 pcs./hr.

They were able to classify six major movements which had surprisingly constant times (see Exhibit 21–2). In addition to these, they were able to identify several actions as the termination of the movements. These, too, they found, had fairly constant times. Thus, if a worker has to reach out and pick up a screw, there are only two times involved: the reach and the pick.

We found this system intriguing because it did not involve taking measurements of hand travel, etc., as is required with the Motion-Time-Measurement technique. One industrial engineer can now sit at his desk, follow a planned work method, and use the MTS predetermined times to develop a standard time for the job. That is the advantage of a predetermined-times system: you don't involve lots of engineers and you don't have to guess how fast the operator is working. We purchased the rights to use MTS from the consulting firm which suggested it to us. Six other industrial engineers and I went to their MTS training school for two weeks.

The company did put quite a bit of money into the MTS program. We felt that the savings in time required to develop standards wouldjustify the expense. One man at his desk could develop a work standard using MTS, while earlier we used six men out in the shop with stopwatches.

We welcome MTS because of its time-savings aspects. We have asked for more people in the department because we are swamped with work, but the company's current belt-tightening just won't allow us to hire any more people. We hope MTS will help us out. In addition, many of the loose production standards are being modified with MTS in an effort to boost productivity.

Six months ago, we instituted new MTS-based standards in two smaller departments with no difficulties. But this trouble we are having in the Switches and Relays Department concerns me. The old standards there were easy to beat. However, they were firm standards; they weren't something we could just walk in and change to suit ourselves, because we could not do that unless we had an obvious clerical error or methods change. Now that we have the new MTS technique we can quickly restudy an assembly procedure. If this results in a higher standard, the industrial engineer can claim a cost reduction; thus he will be saving the company money by revising a loose time standard.

Switches and Relays

John Ransom, the foreman of Section 6750 in the Switches and Relays Department, explained his view of the current difficulty:

I just don't understand what is going on! Many of the old standards for producing relays had lasted for seven years, and many of my workers were producing 150 percent of standard. Thus, they knew that eventually the standards would be tightened, but this amount of change is too much!

Well, anyway, this all started when Hannah Moore was transferred from my section to the switches section. She was barely on the job two weeks when her new foreman made a methods change by moving several of the compartments to a recessed area directly in front of the operator. This decreased the head and eye movement necessary to locate the parts and the foreman got a bonus for the methods improvement under the Methods Improvement Program. Hannah realized that the same improvement could be made on her old assembly job in my section, so she put the idea in and received a Worker Suggestion Bonus for it.

Less than a week after that methods improvement was adopted, Scott Pagent sent out a new MTS-based standard for the eight jobs affected by Hannah Moore's suggestion. Well, the women here got all upset, since most of their standards increased over 30 percent. The MTS program was new to me, and so I gave my permission for the rate increases after examining Scott's new time sheets and observing the new method of assembly; but I didn't understand those 'reference book'-produced standards. Why, Scott didn't even come out on the shop floor to observe the new methods. You can bet that I will get myself into the action the next time Pagent comes around here with his clipboard and a new MTS standard sheet for me to review.

Doris Crozier, one of the six women assigned to assembling part #200280–209, the spring combination, had this to say about the new methods and standards:

I really don't understand how they expect us to produce at the new standard of 97 pieces an hour

EXHIBIT 21–2 ■ Knox Electronics: Time Standards

Examples of Movement Time Standards (Time in Minutes)

	Allowed Time in Modules	Allowed Time in Minutes
Movement Class		
1—Finger movement only	1	.00215
2—Movement of hand from the wrist	2	.00430
3—Movement of forearm from the elbow	3	.00645
4—Movement of the entire arm (no shoulder movement)	4	.00860
5—Movement of entire arm and shoulder	5	.01075
7—Any movement longer than "5" which requires no steps or side steps	7	.01505
Action Type		
G = *Get*		
G0—Simple contact (touch)	0	0
G1—Simple grasp	1	.00215
G3—Normal get (pick up object)	3	.00645
P = *Put*		
P0—Contact put-toss-or drop	0	0
P1—Visually aided put (place)	2	.0043
P5—Specific put (more difficulty)	5	.01075
Special		
R2—Regrasp (shift fingers)	2	.0043
E2—Use eyes	2	.0043
A4—Apply pressure	4	.0086

*Any movements in parentheses are simultaneous motions and are therefore not added to total time. NOTE: Each module of time is .00215 minutes.

Illustration of the Use of MTS in Determining the New Time Standards for Assembling Spring Combination No. 200280–209

EXAMPLE: Element 2, Exhibit 6

Motion Codes	Movement Class	Action Type	Modules Allowed
2G3	2	G3	5
(R2)	This move is simultaneous and is therefore not included in time.		
2P2	2	P2	4
(2P0)	Simultaneous		
1G3	1	G3	4
(R2, 2P0)	Simultaneous		
1P2	1	P2	3
		Subtotal	16
		x frequency	4
		Total Modules	64

64 modules x .00215 minutes per module = .1376 minutes for element 2.

EXHIBIT 21–3 ▪ Knox Electronics: Hourly Employees Earnings (Sample), 1/8/80 through 1/14/80

Employee Number	Actual Hours	Incentive Pay	Premiums For Overtime	Minimum Guarantee Adjustment	Total Weekly Pay
0098	40	180.00			180.00
0158	40	204.80			204.80
0187	37.5	194.29		4.46	198.75
0311	31.9	159.50			159.50
0416	40	196.31		20.09	216.40
0635	46	285.66	18.63		285.66
0744	40	190.40			190.40
0802	40	207.49		12.11	219.60
0877	40	204.80			204.80
0983 (D. Crozier)	46	331.20	21.60		331.20
1046	46	228.62	14.95		228.62
1139	40	239.60			239.60
1265	38	186.09		3.91	190.00

when the old standard was only 74.4. This methods improvement hasn't made that big a difference! I know that some of us more experienced assemblers can often produce over standard, but not 30 percent over all the time! With the new workstation layout, I never get a chance to look up and around to speak to other girls. My husband and I are remodeling our basement into a den, and I was counting on the little bit of bonus I do make to help make the payments. I'll try my best, but I think this new standard is unreasonable!

Earnings for Doris Crozier (Employee #0983) and other workers in the Switches and Relays Department for the week of January 8, 1980 (before the methods and standards changes) are shown in Exhibit 21–3. Payroll records for the six women assembling spring combination #200280–209 showed that although their old guaranteed wage was $4.24 an hour, their actual wages averaged $5.47. For the period following the establishment of a new standard on the spring combination, however, their average wages earned were only $2.85 an hour. The company had to make up the difference to the guaranteed $4.24 an hour.

Performance Evaluation Criteria for Scott Pagent

An industrial engineer, for purposes of the annual performance-and-raise review, was judged on the following items: the standard coverage in his departments and the cost reduction that he was able to submit.

Scott, who was twenty-two, commented on his entry position in the Industrial Engineering Department:

This job is an excellent position to gain exposure to the plant's operations. As I am assigned to different areas in the plant, it allows me to see the entire manufacturing process from simple soldering to the molding of plastic parts. I see this job as a springboard, a foundation which should stand me in good stead in any attempt to get into a line management position, whether at this company or another."

Scott was aggressive, and he decided that the fastest way to gain recognition was by obtaining cost reductions. He further realized that it was easier to track loose existing standards and

EXHIBIT 21–4 ▪ Knox Electronics: Sample Productivity Report, February 11–15, 1980, Week # 567

Worker No.	ACTHR	HRSTD	STDHRS	%
0187	39.80	27.31	29.51	108
0311	40.00	39.42	37.30	95
0416	40.00	38.00	49.00	129
0744	39.80	36.52	31.20	85
0983 (D. Crozier)	40.00	34.80	58.00	166
1139	40.00	32.40	40.10	123
1591	40.00	32.00	36.00	113
1833	40.00	25.40	29.30	115

Explanation of Column Headings:
Worker No.—Individual's reporting number
ACTHR—Actual hours worked
HRSTD—Total hours worked on standard items
STDHRS—Standard hours earned
%—STDHRS/HRSTD

apply MTS to them, than to attempt the more difficult and time-consuming approach of devising new fixtures and elaborate work stations to gain a cost reduction. He therefore turned his attention to the loose standards in John Ransom's section of the Switches and Relays Department.

Scott followed a set procedure in determining standards to review. First, he looked at the weekly department production report, which gave the previous week's performance for each operator by clock number (Exhibit 21–4). If he noticed that an operator had produced a high number of standard hours while working a comparatively low number of actual hours on piece-rate work, he identified the individual by the clock number and checked if that individual worked in his area of responsibility. If the employee was assigned to John Ransom, then he obtained a copy of the job report for that person, which listed all the jobs that a worker had completed during the week. He checked this report to determine the jobs on which the employee was "beating the system." For example, Scott noted that D. Crozier, worker #0983, was working at 167 percent. He checked her job report and found that she had been on piece rate only on part #200280–209.

Next, he contacted production control about each part that raised his interest to determine how many pieces of that part were used in production the previous year and the current year to date. With this information he was able to estimate, roughly, the cost reduction that could be realized.

Finally, Scott usually observed the operator at work before he made his decision on whether or not to apply MTS to the job. If he did restudy the job using MTS and a cost reduction resulted, he submitted a cost-reduction proposal, and a revised time standard would be implemented.

Job Evaluation Criteria for John Ransom

John Ransom, age twenty-six, had been working at Knox since his graduation from high school. His first job had been in the machine shop. Tim

Jacobs, who had been responsible for the shop when John first started work, remembered him:

John is ambidextrous and smart as hell. He would give us fits in the shop. Any job that he was placed on he would bust the standard. I would go out and observe the job and convince myself that the standard was good; John would get on the job and run 200 percent. He is just one of those people who would work smart and take advantage of everything to ensure his getting a large bonus. Mind you, everything he did was near legal. In fact, I bet you he was taking home more pay in the shop than he is making on his present salary.

The manager of manufacturing, Kit Watson, primarily was looking for John to improve departmental efficiency and morale. He was hoping that, if John could accomplish these goals, the increased sales in the current year could be handled by the department without further taxing an already strained manufacturing budget.

Before being named foreman, John had spent time in production control and worked six months as a time-study man. He had recently completed the company's five-week in-house management development program.

Phil Chase's Problem

Phil Chase, after having lunch with Scott Pagent, returned to his office. He wanted all differences between John and Scott aired and settled before their dispute escalated into a confrontation between the production foremen and the industrial engineers. Phil said:

The introduction of MTS into this plant has been a full-time job for me. I believe that this system will in time improve our wage incentive plan. I have tried to spend time informing and educating the foremen and managers about the program in order to gain their acceptance. A full-blown interdepartmental squabble could seriously hurt this program.

Phil decided to set up a meeting with John and Scott in one of the conference rooms for 8:30 the next morning. Over the phone, Phil told John that the meeting would provide him with an opportunity to talk about the problems concerning standards in his section. Later, Phil wondered how easy it would be to act as a referee between the two young bucks.

Selected Comments from the Meeting

John: Scott comes into the area and resets standards. His new ones are not even reasonable. My operators are unable to even run 100 percent against his standards.... It's hurting my weekly department productivity report. Last week my department ran 84 percent, the plant average was 118 percent. ... I thought the incentive system was set up to give an operator a chance at 125 percent. ... How can I explain a low figure like this to my boss, who is expecting production from me.... I refuse to believe that my people are so bad or that I'm doing such a poor job that my department runs this low.... Look at this standard on part #200280–209, operation #2. The old standard was 74.4 pieces per hour. Scott comes in and raises it by almost one-third. Sure, you can set the standard and walk away, but I have to try and work with these people. It's hard to tell a person who is used to taking home a bonus, who considers it part of her income and sets up her budgeting accordingly, that she no longer can get it. In fact, she will have to work harder just to meet the standard. It's ridiculous, this standard is too tight and there are more like this out in the department.... Small wonder my department morale is shot to hell....I thought you guys were staff, but you walk in and work on standards at times when I'm not even in the department. Staff, hell, you have the power over the operators because you control the purse strings.

Scott: As far as part #200280–209, if you will look at the productivity report for week #567 (see Exhibit 21–4), you'll see that D. Crozier ran 166 percent on the old standards for almost five days.

I know she can make the new standard. . . . I'm doing what I was hired for. I am new here and don't have friends on the production floor who might influence my judgment. . . . The standards in your department are loose. . . . Once I set a standard, I have no authority to make sure that the proper methods are used. If an operator or foreman decides he or she doesn't like a standard, that individual can effectively undo my work. It's being in this staff position that is frustrating. I have been told by some operators in your department that you are encouraging them to drag their feet on the new standards in the hope that the vice-president of manufacturing will enter the picture on your side.

The vice-president of manufacturing, Tom Edwards, later commented on the situation:

For the past several years we have been highly concerned with our manufacturing costs. We have to meet the selling prices of our foreign and domestic competitors. The primary differential is in the cost of labor. Foreign manufacturers pay only one-third as much for their labor; therefore, we must be as productive and efficient as possible. Direct labor is now 17.6 percent of total manufacturing costs, down from 19.3 percent five years ago.

We must walk a thin line, however, because our people are not machines. We have kept the union out so far, but it gets tougher all the time. I saw the local union representative at the gate again yesterday, trying to find enough dissatisfied workers to get something going. We have tried to establish a good working relationship between labor and management. I am proud to admit that I know most of the workers here, or at least I am able to recognize them. When I walk through the plant, I like to stop and chat with different people on all levels. I think I find out the "mood" of the workers that way.

This difficulty in the Switches and Relays Department worries me. We let those loose standards exist for too long. When we tried to tighten them up, the workers complained. I hope this slowdown in production there will last only during a period of adjustment. Perhaps the new standards are too tight, but that is a decision that has to be made by industrial engineering and approved by each foreman. Though, if it does get out of hand, I'll have to step in.

22

The University Art Museum

Visitors to the campus were always shown the University Art Museum, of which the large and distinguished university was very proud. A photograph of the handsome neoclassical building that housed the Museum had long been used by the university for the cover of its brochures and catalogues.

The building, together with a substantial endowment, was given to the university around 1912 by an alumnus, the son of the university's first president, who had become very wealthy as an investment banker. He also gave the university his own small, but high quality, collections—one of Etruscan figurines, and one, unique in America, of English pre-Raphaelite paintings. He then served as the Museum's unpaid director until his death. During his tenure he brought a few additional collections to the museum, largely from other alumni of the university. Only rarely did the museum purchase anything. As a result, the museum housed several small collections of uneven quality. As long as the founder ran the museum, none of the collections was ever shown to anybody except a few members of the university's art history faculty, who were admitted as the founder's private guests.

After the founder's death, in the late 1920s, the university intended to bring in a professional museum director. Indeed, this had been part of the agreement under which the founder had given the museum. A search committee was to be appointed, but in the meantime a graduate student in art history who had shown interest in the museum and who had spent a good many hours in it, took over temporarily. At first, she did not even have a title, let alone a salary. But she stayed on acting as the museum's director and over the next 30 years was promoted in stages to that title. But from the first day, whatever her title, she was in charge. She immediately set about changing the museum altogether. She catalogued the collections. She pursued new gifts, again primarily small collections from alumni and other friends of the university. She organized fund raising for the museum. But, above all, she began to integrate the museum into the work of the university. When a space problem arose in the years immediately following World War II, Miss Kirkhoff offered the third floor of the museum to the art history faculty, which moved its offices there. She remodeled the building to include classrooms and a modern and well-appointed auditorium. She raised funds to build one of the best research and reference libraries in art history in the country. She also began to organize a series of special exhibitions built around one of the museum's own collections, complemented by loans from outside collections. For each of these exhibitions she had a distinguished member of the university's art faculty write a catalogue. These catalogues speedily became the leading scholarly texts in the fields.

Miss Kirkhoff ran the University Art Museum for almost half a century. But old age ultimately defeated her. At the age of 68 after suffering a severe stroke, she had to retire. In her letter of resignation she proudly pointed to the museum's growth and accomplishment under her stewardship. "Our endowment," she wrote, "now compares favorably with museums several times our size. We never have had to ask the university for any money other than for our share of the university's insurance policies. Our collections in the areas of our strength, while small, are of first-rate quality and importance. Above all, we are being used by more people than any museum of our size. Our lecture series, in which members of the university's art history faculty present a major subject to a university audience of students and faculty, attracts regularly three hundred to five hundred people; and if we had the seating capacity, we could easily have a larger audience. Our exhibitions are seen and studied by more visitors, most of them members of the university community, than all but the most highly publicized exhibitions in the very big museums ever draw. Above all, the courses and seminars offered in the museum have become one of the most popular and most rapidly growing educational features of the university. No other museum in this country or anywhere else," concluded Miss Kirkhoff, "has so successfully integrated art into the life of a major university and a major university into the work of a museum."

Miss Kirkhoff strongly recommended that the university bring in a professional museum director as her successor. "The museum is much too big and much too important to be entrusted to another amateur such as I was 45 years ago," she wrote. "And it needs careful thinking regarding its direction, its basis of support, and its future relationship with the university."

The university took Miss Kirkhoff's advice. A search committee was duly appointed and, after one year's work, it produced a candidate whom everybody approved. The candidate was himself a graduate of the university who had then obtained his Ph.D. in art history and in museum work from the university. Both his teaching and administrative record were sound, leading to his present museum directorship in a medium-sized city. There he converted an old, well-known, but rather sleepy museum to a lively, community-oriented museum whose exhibitions were well publicized and attracted large crowds.

The new museum director took over with great fanfare in September, 1971. Less than three years later he left—with less fanfare, but still with considerable noise. Whether he resigned or was fired was not quite clear. But that there was bitterness on both sides was only too obvious.

The new director, upon his arrival, had announced that he looked upon the museum as a "major community resource" and intended to "make the tremendous artistic and scholarly resources of the Museum fully available to the academic community as well as to the public." When he said these things in an interview with the college newspaper, everybody nodded in approval. It soon became clear that what he meant by "community resource" and what the faculty and students understood by these words were not the same. The museum had always been "open to the public" but, in practice, it was members of the college community who used the museum and attended its lectures, its exhibitions, and its frequent seminars.

The first thing the new director did, however, was to promote visits from the public schools in the area. He soon began to change the exhibition policy. Instead of organizing small shows, focused on a major collection of the museum and built around a scholarly catalogue, he began to organize "popular exhibitions" around "topics of general interest" such as "Women Artists through the Ages." He promoted these exhibitions vigorously in the newspapers, in radio and television interviews, and, above all, in the local schools. As a result, what had been a busy but quiet place was soon knee-deep in school children, taken to the museum in special buses that cluttered the access roads around the museum and throughout the campus. The faculty, which was not particularly happy with the resulting noise and confusion, became thoroughly upset when the scholarly old chairman of the art history department was mobbed by fourth-graders who sprayed him with their water pistols as he tried to push his way through the main hall to his office.

Increasingly, the new director did not design his own shows, but brought in traveling exhibitions from major museums, importing their catalogue as well rather than have his own faculty produce one.

The students too were apparently unenthusiastic after the first six or eight months, during which the new director had been somewhat of a campus hero. Attendance at the classes and seminars held in the art museum fell off sharply, as did attendance at the evening lectures. When the editor of the campus newspaper interviewed students for a story on the museum, he was told again and again that the museum had become too noisy and too "sensational" for students to enjoy the classes and to have a chance to learn.

What brought all this to a head was an Islamic art exhibit in late 1973. Since the museum had little Islamic art, nobody criticized the showing of a traveling exhibit, offered on very advantageous terms with generous financial assistance from some of the Arab governments. But then, instead of inviting one of the University's own faculty members to deliver the customary talk at the opening of the exhibit, the director brought in a cultural attache of one of the Arab embassies in Washington. The speaker, it was reported, used the occasion to deliver a violent attack on Israel and on the American policy of supporting Israel against the Arabs. A week later, the university senate decided to appoint an advisory committee, drawn mostly from members of the art history faculty, which, in the future, would have to approve all plans for exhibits and lectures. The director thereupon, in an interview with the campus newspaper, sharply attacked the faculty as "elitist" and "snobbish" and as believing that "art belongs to the rich." Six months later, in June 1974, his resignation was announced.

Under the bylaws of the university, the academic senate appoints a search committee. Normally, this is pure formality. The chairperson of the appropriate department submits the department's nominees for the committee who are approved and appointed, usually without debate. But when the academic senate early the following semester was asked to appoint the search committee, things were far from "normal". The dean who presided, sensing the tempers in the room, tried to smooth over things by saying, "Clearly, we picked the wrong person the last time. We will have to try very hard to find the right one this time."

He was immediately interrupted by an economist, known for his populism, who broke in and said, "I admit that the late director was probably not the right personality. But I strongly believe that his personality was not at the root of the problem. He tried to do what needs doing and this got him in trouble with the faculty. He tried to make our museum a community resource, to bring in the community and to make art accessible to broad masses of people, to the blacks and the Puerto Ricans, to the kids from the ghetto schools and to a lay public. And this is what we really resented. Maybe his methods were not the most tactful ones—I admit I could have done without those interviews he gave. But what he tried to do was right. We had better commit ourselves to the policy he wanted to put into effect, or else we will have deserved his attacks on us as 'elitist' and 'snobbish.' "

"This is nonsense," cut in the usually silent and polite senate member from the art history faculty. "It makes absolutely no sense for our museum to try to become the kind of community resource our late director and my distinguished colleague want it to be. First there is no need. The city has one of the world's finest and biggest museums and it does exactly that and does it very well. Secondly, we here have neither the artistic resources nor the financial resources to serve the community at large. We can do something different but equally important and indeed unique. Ours is the only museum in the country, and perhaps in the world, that is fully integrated with an academic community and truly a teaching institution. We are using it, or at least we used to until the last few unfortunate years, as a major educational resource for all our students. No other museum in the country, and as far as I know in the world, is bringing undergraduates into art the way we do. All of us, in addition to our scholarly and graduate work, teach undergraduate courses for people who are not going to be art majors or art historians. We work with the engineering students and show them what we do in our conservation and restoration work. We work with architecture students and show them the development of architecture through the ages. Above all, we work with liberal arts students, who often have had no exposure to art before they came here and who enjoy our courses all the more because they are scholarly and not just 'art appreciation.' This is unique and this is what our museum can do and should do."

"I doubt that this is really what we should be doing," commented the chairman of the mathematics department. "The museum, as far as I know, is part of the graduate faculty. It should concentrate on training art historians in its Ph.D. program, on its scholarly work, and on its research. I would strongly urge that the museum be considered an adjunct to graduate and especially to Ph.D. education, confine itself to this work, and stay out of all attempts to be 'popular,' on both campus and outside of it. The glory of the museum is the scholarly catalogues produced by our faculty, and our Ph.D. graduates who are sought after by art history faculties throughout the country. This is the museum's mission, which can only be impaired by the attempt to be 'popular,' whether with students or with the public."

"These are very interesting and important comments," said the dean, still trying to pacify. "But I think this can wait until we know who the new director is going to be. Then we should raise these questions with him."

"I beg to differ, Mr. Dean," said one of the elder statesmen of the faculty. "During the summer months, I discussed this question with an old friend and neighbor of mine in the country, the director of one of the nation's great museums. He said to me: 'You do not have a personality problem, you have a *management* problem. You have not, as a university, taken responsibility for the mission, the direction, and the objectives of your museum. Until you do this, no director can succeed. And this is *your* decision. In fact, you cannot hope to get a good man until you can tell him what your basic objectives are. If your late director is to blame—I know him and I know that he is abrasive—it is for being willing to take on a job when you, the university, had not faced up to the basic management decisions. There is no point talking about *who* should manage until it is clear *what* it is that has to be managed and for what.' "

At this point the dean realized that he had to adjourn the discussion unless he wanted the meeting to degenerate into a brawl. But he also realized that he had to identify the issues and possible decisions before the next faculty meeting a month later. Here is the list of questions he put down on paper later that evening:

1. What are the possible purposes of the University Museum:

   □ to serve as a laboratory for the graduate art-history faculty and the doctoral students in the field?

   □ to serve as major "enrichment" for the undergraduate who is not an art-history student but wants both a "liberal education" and a counter-weight to the highly bookish diet fed to him in most of our courses?

   □ to serve the metropolitan community—and especially its schools—outside the campus gates?

2. Who are or should be its customers?

   □ the graduate students in professional training to be teachers of art history?

   □ the undergraduate community—or rather, the entire college community?

   □ the metropolitan community and especially the teachers and youngsters in the public schools?

   □ any others?

3. Which of these purposes are compatible and could be served simultaneously? Which are mutually exclusive or at the very least are likely to get in each other's way?
4. What implications for the structure of the museum, the qualifications of its director, and its relationship to the university follow from each of the above purposes?
5. Do we need to find out more about the needs and wants of our various potential customers to make an intelligent policy decision? How could we go about it?

The dean distributed these questions to the members of the faculty with the request that they think them through and discuss them before the next meeting of the academic senate.

23

Reviewing Objectives and Strategies: A Planning Task for Managers

Goals

I. To review and evaluate an organization's accomplishments of the past year.

II. To clarify the organization's mission.

III. To prepare objectives and action steps for major organizational efforts in the next year.

Group Size

Eight to twelve persons who can assume the roles of the top management of an organization or organizational unit, including the chief executive officer.

Time Required

Approximately one to two hours.

Materials

I. At least six copies of the Reviewing Objectives and Strategies Sheet for each participant.

II. Newsprint and felt-tipped markers.

III. Masking tape.

Physical Setting

One large room furnished with a work table, chairs, and easel for the newsprint. Smaller rooms, furnished similarly, for individual or small-group work are helpful but not necessary.

Process

Step I. Overview (five min.)

The facilitator reviews the goals of the activity and indicates that these goals will serve as the agenda for the session and that the majority of the time will be spent on Goal III.

Step II. Review of Accomplishments (20 min.)

Explaining that planning must be based on some data, the facilitator invites the participants to review an organization's accomplishments

Prepared by Cyril Mill. Reprinted from J. William Pfeiffer and John E. Jones (eds.), *The Annual for Facilitators, Trainers and Consultants*. 1982 University Associates, Inc., San Diego, CA pp. 65–68 for the past year. This organization can be one at which a participant works; one with which participants are familiar; or one from a case. The facilitator leads the group in brainstorming answers to the question "What have they accomplished during the past year?" The facilitator may ask prodding questions during this step and/or may post a list to encourage the participants to think in terms of such things as: size, growth, profit, new organizational structures, new policies, new personnel, new technical resources, new linkages to outside groups, impact on the market or community, events (e.g., conferences), awards, and new learnings. All answers are listed on newsprint, and the list then is reviewed to eliminate redundancies and nonpertinent items. This could be done as an out-of-class assignment and reported in class.

Step III. Review of Shortcomings (20 min.)

The brainstorming procedure is repeated for the question "What have been the organization's failures or shortcomings during the past year?" This could be done as an out-of-class assignment. The list of organizational weaknesses is reviewed and narrowed down by the participants.

Step IV. Organizational Mission (30 min.)

The facilitator introduces the goal of clarifying and reaffirming the organizational mission by commenting on the following points:

1. A management team should be clear about and in agreement on the organization's mission.
2. All activities of an organization should help to achieve its mission.
3. A mission statement may be a phrase, a few sentences, or a lengthy document.

The facilitator announces that the group's task at this point is to state the organization's mission in a few sentences with which all agree. The facilitator serves as process and catalytic consultant during the group's discussion, which concludes with the writing of a mission statement on newsprint. Guidelines for the discussion may include:

1. State a *goal* rather than *operations.* A mission is more related to purpose than it is to activities.
2. A statement can be too broad or too narrow, thus limiting its usefulness. Avoid high-sounding generalities as well as specifics.
3. The statement should distinguish this organization from others.
4. Throughout the discussion, be alert to problems of interpretation or emphasis and work to clarify and rationalize these differences.

Step V. Preparing Objectives (30 min.)

The facilitator explains that the third goal, to prepare objectives and action steps for the next year, will be accomplished in two phases. In the first phase, which will take about thirty minutes, the participants will work individually on familiar material; in the second phase, the group members will work together in planning new organizational efforts.

The facilitator gives each participant six copies of the Reviewing Objectives and Strategies Sheet and instructs the participants that they may either work individually or consult freely with one another and that their task is to prepare as many objectives and strategies as they can, limiting themselves to *present operations and ongoing tasks.* The facilitator states that the emphasis of the activity is on quantity of ideas rather than on technicalities and reminds the group members that an objective is simply a statement of *intention,* whereas strategies are statements of steps that one will take to reach the objective. After thirty minutes, the participants are directed to tape their Reviewing Objectives and Strategies Sheets to newsprint sheets and to post them around the room so that everyone can walk around and read them.

Step VI. Summarization (20 min.)

The group reviews the statements, summarizing and categorizing wherever possible, and prepares an initial statement of goals and objectives.

Variations

I. If the group has difficulty in working through an issue during Step VI, the facilitator can direct the participants to form three groups and announce that the task for each group is to prepare *three* charts as follows:

1. Chart I. State the issue or the problem.
   a. What do they do well?
   b. What do they do poorly?
2. Chart II.
   a. Write a pessimistic statement that describes their approach to ________.
   b. Write an optimistic statement that describes their approach to ________.
3. Chart III.
   a. What objectives must be established to move from the pessimistic statement to the optimistic one? List three to five objectives that are clear and measurable.
   b. What strategies must be followed to accomplish each objective? List as many as are needed and indicate the resources that are needed.

II. If a block of time devoted to "thinking about the future" would be more productive than steps 5 or 6, the following procedure can be used:

1. The facilitator comments that even though the future is unpredictable, it can be useful to ask "What might happen?" and "How would they cope?"
2. The facilitator divides the participants into three groups, distributes four sheets of newsprint and felt-tipped markers to each group, and gives the following instructions: "Your group's task for the next ten minutes is to identify four significant trends, internal or external to the organization, that could have an impact within five years on the organization. Consider the four trends as future problems with which your group will have to grapple. Write a trend or problem at the top of each of the sheets of newsprint."
3. Each group is directed to give two of its newsprint sheets to each of the other groups. Each group now has four new problems with which to work. The facilitator then gives the following instructions: "Identify strategies to cope with each of the problems you have received. Be as imaginative as you wish, but do not assume that you will have unlimited resources of money or personnel. Write your solutions for each problem on the sheet of newsprint." (Forty minutes.)
4. The facilitator suggests that, as each solution is presented, the members feel free to cheer and clap to show *approval* of a solution as well as to boo and hiss to show their *disapproval*.

Reviewing Objectives and Strategies Sheet

1. Objective: (What is your intention; what do you plan to achieve? What end result do you want?)

2. Mission relationship: (What is the relationship of this objective to the organizational mission?)

3. Strategies: (What action steps will be necessary to reach the objective? If you are not the person to take these steps, identify the person who is.)

   a.

   b.

   c.

   d.

4. Who will be responsible?

5. Resources needed: (If money or people or other resources are needed for this item, indicate them here.)

24

A New Division

At the Craig Company, a new division was formed that would be responsible for the corporate mining investments overseas. The objectives were to oversee mining investments in Africa; protect the company's interests in mining investments under construction in South America; and market iron ore throughout the world, especially in the Far East and in Europe. The long-term organizational goals were to maintain or augment dividend income from the African investments that were under increasing African political pressure to reduce dividends or reinvest in Africa; to handle all legal, financial, and managerial responsibilities involved in an iron-mine investment under construction in South America; to continue to market iron ore, and to develop new markets for the ore.

Senior management decided to locate the division headquarters at the main office, in a thirty-story building located in a major international capital. The corporate offices were on floors from the sixth through the sixteenth, but because of shortage of office space, a decision was made to locate the new division on the second floor. The existing offices of the president and vice-president were on the fourteenth floor. The offices of the Market Research section, composed of five people, were on the eleventh floor; part of the Commercial staff (four people) was on the sixth floor; the Engineers (five people) and the Financial group (six individuals) were quickly moved to the second floor. The subgroups of the division were separated from each other physically by location on different floors of the building.

Since the new division was crucial to the operations of the total organization, the president was to be the chief executive officer with his vice-president assisting him. Each of the new division's separate activities was to be headed by a managing executive who would supervise the people under him. Each of these executives was to report directly to the president or, in his absence, to the vice-president.

The president determined that the prime short-term goals of the new division were to concentrate on marketing iron ore and to handle all details for the mine under construction. Management determined that a total work force of about twenty-five people would be adequate to accomplish all the work.

Before discussing the actual operation of the new division, it is necessary to make a few comments about the jobs of the president and vice-president of Craig Company. Because of the international operations of the company, both these men spent less than half their working time in their offices at corporate headquarters.

During the periods when the president and vice-president were in the office they were diligently preparing reports on their previous trips, catching up with correspondence that had accumulated during their absence, and making plans for the next trip. The periods spent in the office were short, two weeks at most, therefore both men tried to accomplish as much work as possible by giving dictation not only to their own secretaries but also to the supervisors' secretaries. The supervisors resented having their secretaries involved in this way because their own work fell behind. In order to complete the work, some overtime was required by the secretaries. The typing quality of the work for the executives was poor, because the secretaries who were enlisted often did not understand the dictation given by the officers and therefore did not type letters up to the quality standards expected by these men. The low-quality work was returned to the secretaries for retyping. Letters and reports were retyped two or three times, and occasionally some work was redone four or five times.

The executives as well as the secretaries became irritated, and such irritation manifested itself among the girls by crying, grumbling, and refusing to work overtime, and by the executives in vocal outbursts. After a few months, one excellent secretary requested a transfer. Her reason for this request was that she had never before been a secretary to several people simultaneously, and she did not intend to begin now!

All groups should have moved to the new offices in September, but the offices on the second floor required major renovation before they could be occupied. From September until January no decision was taken on the floor-plan arrangement of the new offices. The president wanted to be consulted on all phases of the layout planning. But during those months he was away on business trips about 60% of the time, so there was little opportunity to discuss with him the details of the floor plan. The vice-president traveled with the president; consequently he could not be apprised of the layout planning being done by the engineers. No other group was requested to help with the layout, or make any decision on the plan, although all groups made suggestions.

At the time the division was formed, all employees were asked by the president whether a transfer would be acceptable. If anyone refused to leave his or her existing job, no penalty was assessed. Some who were invited did not accept because they believed—or so they said—that the new organization would not afford them the best opportunities. These people were not questioned further as to the reasons for their decision. Among those who joined the group were certain individuals who were dissatisfied with their present positions and had requested transfers. There were also others who had been suggested for transfer by their superiors because of unsatisfactory performance in their present positions. A few of these were accepted because they had the talents required, even though they had not done acceptable work in other positions. One or two had a long history with the company and previously had done fine work.

One transferee, a Market Research analyst, had been transferred from two other divisions prior to joining the Overseas Investment group. In the past he had done some superb analyses, but developed a reputation for being difficult to work with. He preferred to work alone, producing volumes of work some of which proved difficult to read because of unusual grammar and syntax. His approach to a job was imaginative and considered brilliant by his co-workers. He had never been promoted to a supervisory position when younger people around him were moved up. He claimed that the other employees had taken advantage of his special knowledge and used his work to advance their own interests. After a short period of time in each division, say three months, he became increasingly close-mouthed about the work he was doing and sent progress reports and final reports of his work not to his immediate supervisor for inspection, but to the senior man of the division.

Often the supervisor objected; but the analyst continued the practice. Resentful of his behavior, the supervisor refused salary increases or job promotions for this analyst. This had been his typical history prior to entering the new division. It was hoped that by transferring him, he would find satisfaction in the job and the company would benefit from his work. In the new division he was to report to the president. His job was analyzing and reporting on potential markets. Since the president was often absent, the analyst was subjected to little supervision and was soon working on pet projects unrelated to the work of the division.

From September to January he did almost no work that could have been useful to the president, and continually irritated the Marketing personnel who requested assistance from him and were refused; moreover, he constantly criticized the work of others. Eventually there was little conversation between the analyst and the others in the division. He claimed that his reason for not complying with their requests was that the work had not been initiated by the president who was, in fact, his boss.

Operations of the New Division

Work efficiency in the new division was not high when the group was formed. Output was far less than expected. Most of the employees had not previously worked under the direction of executives; neither had the subgroups worked with their supervisors before. For some people, the type of work was different from what they had done previously. Also, employees were located on four separate floors.

Primarily the work involved calculation and accumulation of engineering, financial, and marketing data, and writing reports for the division executives and for the senior management. Advice on decisions approved or actions initiated by the division executives was relayed to the other workers vocally; however, when these men were out of the city, communication was in writing or by telephone. Frequently the executives made overseas telephone calls to keep the chief accountant, chief engineer, or other employees fully apprised of their activities.

Reports from subordinates were mailed to the executives when the latter were absent from the city. Reports from corporate headquarters were also mailed to the executives. Reports written by subordinates, however, were sent to the president and vice-president upon request and without approval of the traveling executives. Conflicts resulted when the travelers did not accept the conclusions in the reports, and in several instances subordinates were asked to retrieve the reports from the senior management so that they could be altered. The subordinates were greatly embarrassed on these occasions.

Communication between the offices in the building was accomplished almost entirely by telephone. A memorandum of instruction for normal day-to-day activity was time-wasting and unnecessary. Excessive time was consumed by the president, vice-president, and the division executives in traveling by elevator to the appropriate floors to give instructions, comment on work in process, provide trade-offs, or simply to observe what was going on. Often several trips each day were necessary for these purposes. In addition, employees were constantly traveling from floor to floor to pass on information, provide trade-offs, gossip, and report to the executives.

Telephones provided the most convenient way to communicate, but confusion and misunderstanding persisted. Errors in office correspondence and in reports to the president and vice-president became common. The uncovering of these errors resulted in anger or a feeling of frustration among the employees. Arguments between the subgroups that had cooperated to produce the reports became more frequent. Eventually the president and vice-president lost confidence in the work of the subordinates, and consequently also in the work of the division executives.

All groups attempted to take extra care to catch errors before the work left the office; yet, regardless of the amount of time devoted to eliminating errors, the instances of such errors did not diminish to any great extent. The total amount of work that would normally be expected ebbed as the writers and editors slowed in their output. Reports were produced late. A general lack of confidence in the work pervaded the entire office. The executives did not trust the subordinates, and the subordinates believed that the executives were exaggerating small errors. High-quality work, a goal of the executives and senior management, was not being produced.

Corporate management (the chairman of the board and some of the directors) also began to doubt the quality of work and pressured the president to insist on better performance from the new division. The result of this was that the president and vice-president became vocally abusive to division executives and employees, and to each other. Naturally enough, the problems continued.

As September passed into October, then November, there was a steady deterioration in work quantity and quality. Many employees spent considerable time just grousing together. The length of time spent traveling between floors to pass on information increased. One division executive began to arrive at work late and to leave early. His subordinates eased up on their work until he arrived, then slowed up again after he left. He began complaining to almost everyone who would listen. Some of his comments were, "The company has been unfair to me before on my job, and now they have shifted me to a new position where I won't be able to use my knowledge effectively." Or, "Now that I have this new job, which is a promotion, I expected to get a pay raise." Or, "The boss isn't here, and I don't know what I am supposed to do. He won't be back for a week."

In the four months that the division continued working on the four floors, morale among the employees disintegrated. A divisional esprit de corps had not developed. The few groups of three to five people who worked together on one floor developed strong subgroup strengths. They worked together all day, and even had lunch together as often as possible. Each group was composed of people who did similar work. A kind of professionalism developed among the groups, especially in their supervised relationship with the division executives.

The president was absent from the office because he had to travel, but he was also "absent" from the employees because he believed that a certain distance should be kept between the supervisor and subordinates. He disliked administrative and personnel work, and avoided these activities as often as possible. It was his intention to have the vice-president handle these functions. The vice-president had a reputation for getting along with most people and tended to supervise using the "be good" approach, but he was not in the office enough to be effective. The president was autocratic in his dealings with subordinates and disdainful of the assistantship-type function of some groups, such as the corporate Personnel Department.

At the time the new division was formed, the vice-president was requested to fill out a job description of his work in the new division. The request emanated from the corporate Personnel Department. After completing the job description form, he asked the president to evaluate it. The president signed the form with the comment that the description of work was too elaborate, but that he would sign it anyway. Some months later, when the vice-president took an action with which the president disagreed, the latter questioned why the action had been taken without requesting permission. The reply was that the decision area for that work lay with the vice-president. The vice-president reminded the president of the job description. The president then remarked that what was on the description form was for the Personnel Department, but that the form had nothing to do with what his job in the division was, so "forget the job description!"

The subgroups began to operate almost as separate companies with their own goals and objectives. After a few months, the differentiated groups increased the inter-group conflicts as trade-offs became difficult because of the physical barrier imposed by work done on separate floors. The flow of work, insufficient from the outset, decreased as conflicts increased and confusion between the groups arose. No cohesion between the subgroups existed, and inner subgroup cohesion developed to an excessive degree as the supervisors of each subgroup tended to represent only their subordinates' interests.

As this unhappy and unproductive situation wore on, top corporate management began to wonder whether the forming of the new division had been such a good idea in the first place. There was more and more talk that a complete reorganization of the new division was in the cards and, as rumor had it, "heads would roll." The president, vice-president, and division executives, feeling insecure about their jobs, were even more irritable and thus also inefficient.

25

The Bank of Boston

Introduction

The chilly February morning became colder as Bostonians heard the news reports and read the headlines: "Bank of Boston Guilty in Cash Transfer Case." In a plea bargaining arrangement with the Financial Investigation Task Force unit of the Justice Department, the bank agreed to pay a $500,000 fine after pleading guilty to federal charges of "willfully and knowingly" failing to report $1.2 billion in cash transfers with nine foreign banks. The bank had violated the Bank Secrecy Act which stipulates that all cash transfers over $10,000 made through financial institutions be reported to the Internal Revenue Service. The allegations came quickly:

- □ The bank was involved in businesses with criminal overtones.
- □ The bank laundered drug money.
- □ Bank employees were "on the take."

Less than one week later; one of the allegations appeared to be true. The bank had placed two companies controlled by a reputed organized crime figure on a list which exempted their cash transactions from being reported to the Fed.

That information started an avalanche of events. Two local communities withdrew their funds from the bank and, of greater magnitude, the city of Boston was considering withdrawing its funds. Bills to remove state money from the bank were filed in the state legislature. Both houses of Congress scheduled hearings, and approval of two pending mergers of out-of-state banks was deferred.

Stories about the bank dominated the news media until early March, when two events signified a turning point:

- □ Two other Boston banks disclosed reporting violations.
- □ Merrill Lynch announced that the bank would retain its quality rating.

This case was prepared by David Breyer, Ph.D. Assistant Professor of Management, Suffolk University, as the basis for class discussion rather than to illustrate either effective or ineffective handling of an administrative situation.

Meanwhile the congressional hearings continued; and at the bank's annual meeting, the stockholders were told that an additional $110 million transfer had not been reported. This time the cash was transported from the bank's international banking subsidiary in Miami to banks in Haiti. Despite all the troubles, the chairman of the board, William L. Brown, was able to announce to the stockholders a 70-percent projected increase in earnings.

Narrative of Events

In an effort to aid law enforcement officials in the detection of criminal, tax, and regulatory violations, Congress passed the Bank Secrecy Act in 1970. By requiring that banks report large cash transactions to the IRS, Congress intended that "money laundering" (a method by which criminals attempt to funnel illegal funds through a legal institution) be abated. Banks were given until July 1, 1972, to establish a list of customers who, in the normal course of business, have currency transactions in excess of $10,000. This "exempt" list precluded the necessity for those customers to file large currency reports. The bank complied with this request and submitted its exempt list to the government, thereby alerting the authorities to those customers normally dealing in large amounts of cash.

In 1976, the branch manager of the North End branch of the bank placed Huntington Realty Co. on the exempt list and in 1979 added Federal Investments, Inc. These companies were owned and operated by the Angiulo family, customers of the bank since 1964 and allegedly involved in organized crime in New England. The bank's records show that between 1979 and 1983 representatives of the Angiulo companies purchased with cash 163 cashier's checks totaling $2,163,457.50.

In 1980, new regulations narrowed the scope of the exempt list to operators of retail-type businesses, such as supermarkets and restaurants, whose receipts involved substantial amounts of cash. But when the bank submitted a new list, Huntington Realty and Federal Investments were still included.

In 1982, the Department of the Treasury, with help from the Organized Crime Strike Force, began investigating organized crime activities in Massachusetts. This investigation brought to light the bank's unreported overseas currency transactions completed. On June 8, 1982, investigators asked the Banking Offices Administration unit of the bank to provide additional information concerning certain customers on the exempt list. With that request, the Treasury enclosed a copy of the bank's exempt list with two types of notations:

1. check marks beside customer names requiring additional information (taxpayer number, address, etc.).
2. an X beside names of depositors that did not appear to be types of establishments that a bank is permitted to put on its exemption list without prior approval of the Treasury Department.

Because the bank's Coin and Currency Department was responsible for its own exempt list of customers (some of whom the Treasury was investigating), Banking Offices Administration referred the June letter to that department. The Coin and Currency Department did not respond to the Treasury's request until several months later.

After reviewing the information provided by the bank, the Treasury announced that several items on the list did not meet the requirements of the regulations. The Treasury requested further information which the bank supplied. Because the Treasury's request was interpreted by the bank as a request for information rather than as a request to remove the questionable customers from the list, the list remained intact at that time. However, in May 1983, the bank received subpoenas relating to its lack of compliance with the Act. At that time, the bank conducted a more thorough review of the exempt list and removed the Huntington and Federal companies.

In 1984, a grand jury probe into organized crime activities was begun in Boston. that same year, action was initiated by the Justice department's newly formed Financial Investigative Task Force, comprised of representatives from U.S. Customs, the IRS, and the Organized Crime Strike Force. As a result of both investigations, Bank of Boston on February 2, 1985, pleaded guilty to large currency reporting violations. The specific charge focused on cash transfers of $1.2 billion to Swiss banks without the filing of large currency reports. A $500,000 fine was assessed. However, given the nature of the plea, criminal overtones were unavoidable, and on February 13, local papers reported that the Angiulo businesses had been on the exempt list, thereby loosely linking the foreign cash transfers to money laundering. an onslaught of accusations followed.

William L. Brown, chairman of the bank's board of directors, called a press conference at which he blamed the violations on "systems failure" and made the point that the international money transfer business is a legitimate banking function.

Another damaging report was released on February 27: the Treasury announced that federal bank examiners had informed the bank of international reporting failures in 1982, at which time the bank had promised to take corrective action. The bank issued a swift denial, stating that the 1982 report had referred only to domestic violations, which the bank had corrected. The Treasury later retracted its statement and admitted it was mistaken. This strengthened the bank's assertion that it did not know of the international reporting violations until the summer of 1984. Nonetheless, by the end of February five independent investigations had been initiated by the following groups: the United States Senate, the United States House of Representatives, the Securities and Exchange Commission, the New England Organized Crime Strike Force, and the bank's special committee (comprised of five outside directors). The probe into reporting compliance extended even to brokerage houses, as reported in a *Boston Globe* spotlight report on money laundering channels.

Throughout this period, Chairman Brown asserted that criminal activities had not occurred at the bank; he emphasized that international transfers were legitimate and entirely unrelated to the Angiulo exemptions. He acknowledged, however, that the bank used "poor judgment" in placing the Angiulo companies on the exempt list. To restore confidence in the bank, he charged the special committee to evaluate the bank's overall state of compliance, not only with the act, but with other regulations, including Regulation E, which governs electronic funds transfers, and Truth-in-Lending.

Over the next several months, the bank continued to be the target of a highly critical media barrage which included coverage of banking activities well beyond the scope of the reporting failures. In one case, as a result of a negative news report, a pending merger with Rhode Island Hospital Trust was called into question and put on hold by the state legislature. The news media also questioned the bank's decision to relocate its credit card operation to New Hampshire.

The reporting violations became a national issue as other banks came forward with admissions of similar failures. On March 9, the Shawmut Bank of Boston made public its failure to report over $200 million of large currency transactions. Shortly thereafter, similar reports were released by Wells Fargo Bank, Chemical Bank, Bank of America, Manufacturers Hanover Bank, Irving Trust, and the Bank of New England. In all cases, officials at these banks claimed that the reporting failures were unintentional, due either to a failure to note the changes in the Bank Secrecy Act, or to a misinterpretation of those changes. The Bank of Boston was the only one to plead guilty to "willfully and knowingly" violating the regulations.

The special committee appointed by the bank's directors to conduct an internal investigation made its findings public on July 25, 1985. The report acknowledged that the "level of noncompliance at the bank with the [Bank Secrecy] Act was extensive" and that bank employees exhibited "wide-spread laxity and poor judgment." The committee concluded, however, that no one had profited from the reporting violations.

On July 28, 1985, the *Boston Globe* ran an editorial entitled "Finale at the First." The closing sentence captured the prevailing feeling among many bank employees and customers: "The First's world will never be the same as before, but it has won the right to get back to its main line of work."

The Special Committee

On February 25, 1985, the board of directors appointed a special committee to review the bank's efforts to comply with the Act. The special committee consisted of five outside directors: George R. West (chairman), chairman of the board, Allendale Mutual Insurance Company; Samuel Huntington (vice chairman), president and CEO, New England Electric System; Martin R. Allen, chairman of the board, Computervision Corporation; Thomas A. Galligan, Jr., chairman of the board, Boston Edison Company; and J. Donald Monan, S. J., president, Boston College.

The mandate of the special committee was to review the adequacy of the record compiled by management on matters relating to the reporting of large currency transactions as required by the Act; to determine who was responsible for the failures of the bank to comply with the Act; to recommend disciplinary action if deemed appropriate; and to review management's policies, procedures, and systems to ensure future regulatory compliance.

During the next four months the committee conducted a rigorous investigation which included holding over 100 interviews, reviewing files, consulting legal experts, and conducting audit tests.

The committee's findings were reported to the board of directors on June 27, 1985. The report confirmed that the level of noncompliance at the bank was extensive. Failure to comply with the act went beyond the immediate situation and extended into other operations of the bank and its affiliates. Further, when the government began its investigation, management failed to realize the seriousness of the situation or to take corrective action.

The investigation uncovered the fact that, although the requirements of the act received widespread distribution throughout the bank, there was no concerted follow-through to see that the new reporting requirements were implemented. As a result, no one caught the mistake for four years. The Coin and Currency Department which handled the cash transfers misunderstood, and therefore neglected to implement, the amended regulations. At the same time, many personnel in other departments and divisions, including Staff Services (Corporate HRD), the Law Office, and the Internal Audit Department, failed in their staff responsibilities. (Exhibit 25–1 shows the organization of the bank.) The committee found no evidence that the cash transfers involved "tainted" money.

The problems at the North End branch concerned a modification in the act which narrowed the circumstances under which domestic transactions must be reported. Prior to July 1980, the regulations provided that transactions with established customers whose business regularly involved large currency transactions could be exempted from reporting. Therefore, having the Angiulo's real estate businesses on the bank's exempt list prior to 1980 did not violate any express provision of the regulations. The amendment clearly disqualified the Angiulo businesses from the exempt list, but the manager of the North End branch kept them on the list. Although the decision to do so was questioned by the Banking Offices Administration (Retail Banking Division), it was not overruled.

Although numerous transactions went unreported and personnel in the North End branch were aware of the Angiulos' reputed ties to organized crime, there was no evidence of collusion between any employee of the bank and the Angiulos to violate any requirement

EXHIBIT 25–1 ■ Bank of Boston Corporation, 1984–85

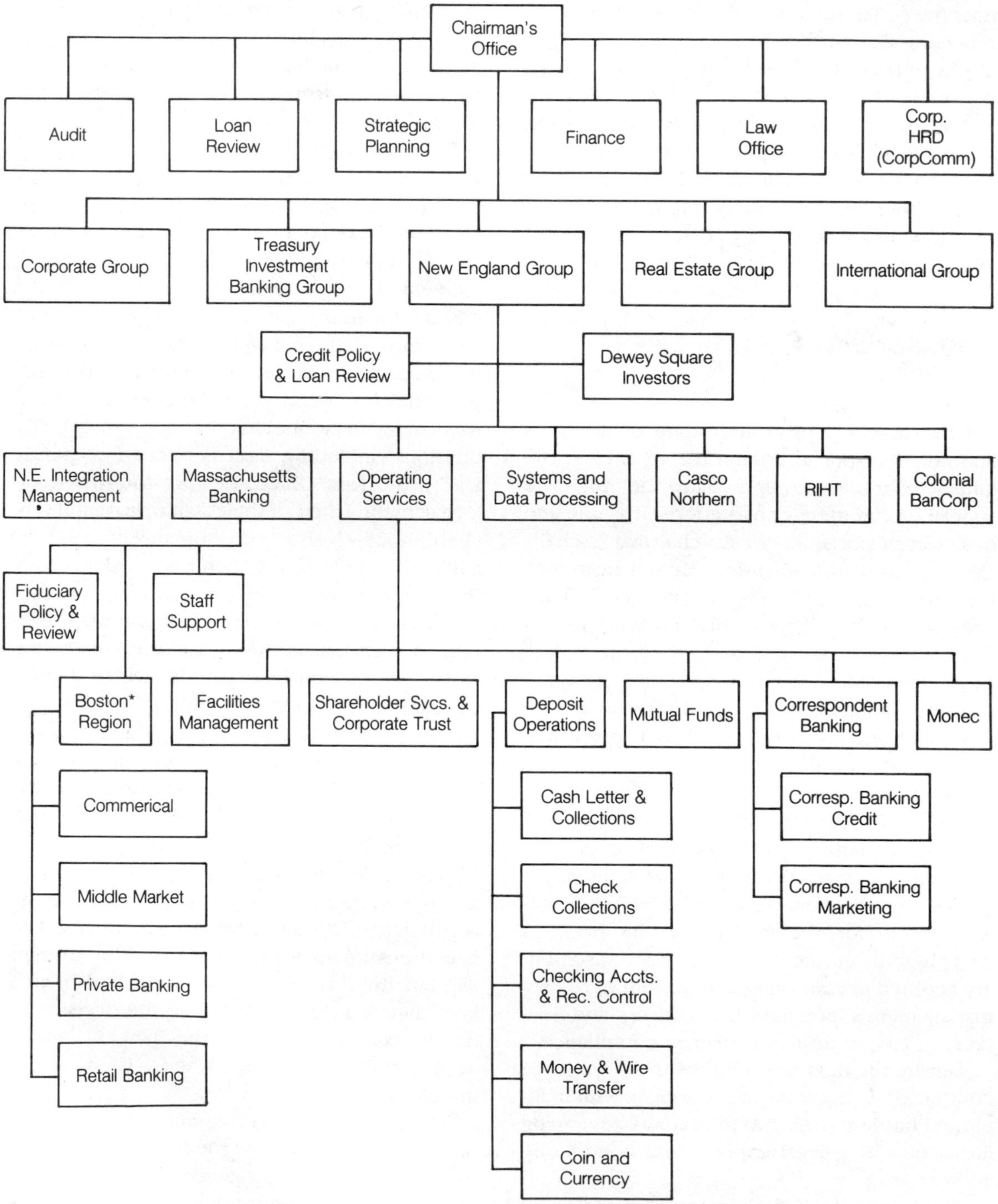

*There are seven geographic regions across the state with similar structures.

of the act. The Angiulos, like some other customers, occasionally gave small gifts to branch personnel. There was no evidence, however, that such gifts were related to the improper maintenance of their accounts on the exempt list.

Much more serious was the Bank's failure to respond promptly when a Treasury official questioned the appropriateness of certain customers on the list, including the Angiulos. Some 13 months passed before the bank responded to the Treasury, during which time the bank's Coin and Currency Department failed to report transactions for those customers.

In concluding the findings, the special committee found an unsatisfactory overall level of compliance with the act by the seven independent banks which the Bank of Boston Corporation had acquired during 1974 through 1981. Also, there was evidence of unsatisfactory compliance by the bank's Suffolk County branches and by certain branches of the Casco Northern Bank, a Maine based affiliate acquired by the bank in 1984.

Conclusion

After careful review of the special committee's report, on July 24, 1985, the bank's board of directors made public its conclusions in a news release:

The policy of the bank is and always has been to comply with all governmental regulations. Thus, the bank had written procedures regarding the Treasury department's currency reporting requirements since their inception in 1972. However, the bank failed to put in place systems and controls adequate to ensure that regulatory changes would be incorporated promptly and correctly into that policy, and to ensure that the policy would be understood and fully implemented throughout the organization. These failures led to widespread misunderstanding, and misapplication of the currency reporting requirements, especially after the change in the regulations in 1980 . . .

The Staff Services Department circulated to a number of the bank's other departments the Bulletin received by the bank in July 1980 from the Office of the Comptroller of the Currency. Neither Staff Services nor any of the recipients of the Bulletin, however, requested appropriate action by Information Systems and Services, the department which prepares and publishes the bank's operating procedures. As a consequence, the operating procedure on currency reporting which the bank had had in place since 1972 was not amended to reflect the new requirement of reporting transactions with foreign banks and the new standards for exemption for retail customers.

Even those units of the bank's operations which were in fact informed of the 1980 changes did not in all cases properly interpret and apply them. Although Banking Offices Administration sent a detailed memorandum to all branches under its jurisdiction explaining the changed standards for exempting bank customers from reporting, it did not exercise sufficient supervisory control over the exempt list to remove the ineligible customers from the list.

Similarly, as previously noted, the Coin and Currency Department of the bank received notice of the 1980 regulatory changes but failed to understand them to require reporting of tranactions with foreign banks. Because the 1980 changes were not highlighted in any subsequent operating procedure or other directives to Coin and Currency, this serious error of interpretation went uncorrected until it was discovered in mid-1984.

In addition, the bank failed to adequately audit its operating units for compliance with the act's requirements. As a result, opportunities were missed to correct the misapplication and violation of those requirements which in fact occurred. Although the bank's internal auditors conducted periodic branch audits, which included a cursory review of compliance on a periodic basis, neither the North End Branch nor Coin and Currency was audited for compliance after the change in the regulations in 1980. Moreover, even prior to 1980, the Internal Audit Department failed adequately to test the bank's administrative controls relating to compliance with currency requirements.

26

Elling Bros. Got Costs Under Control

Back in 1974, Clifford Elling discovered his company had sprung a leak. Tiny cost overruns on a $2.3-million contract were beginning to drain money out of Elling Brothers Mechanical Contractors at a rate that threatened to put the 53-year-old Somerville, N.J., firm out of business.

As Elling watched in dismay, a carefully budgeted fifteen-month job to install industrial piping turned into a financial nightmare. Day by day, design specifications changed, the price of materials shot up, and unexpected delays increased payroll costs. By 1975, when Elling Bros. closed its books on the contract, 30 months had elapsed, and the trickle of tiny overruns had become a flood. Elling's company was out $250,000 on the job—half of the privately owned company's total net worth of $500,000.

Cliff Elling decided it was time to plug the leaks on costs. He'd always taken estimates and budgets seriously; every bid was based on a meticulously prepared estimate of the materials and manpower each job would require. But budgets alone weren't enough to keep costs under control. Like any business, Elling Bros. functioned in a world of constant change. If budgets weren't updated promptly to reflect these changes, even tiny errors could multiply until they wiped out the company's profits altogether.

The problem was particularly acute in the construction industry, in which even the strongest firms typically operated with narrow profit margins and very little net worth to cushion the business against mistakes. One thing Elling did know was that there weren't any easy solutions to cost control problems, no magic wand he or a consultant could wave.

Elling Bros. wasn't prone to sloppy bookkeeping or risky ventures. The firm had been launched in 1921 by Elling's father and uncle, hardworking sons of a German immigrant farmer, who began by using the family barn as a small plumbing shop. Cliff joined the company in 1950, at age twenty-six, after a stint in the

Prepared By Matthew Berke. Reprinted with permission, *Inc.* magazine, January 1982.

Army and an M.B.A. degree from Wharton. For his first three years, he worked in the field, doing heating and plumbing work as an apprentice to the journeymen.

That fieldwork proved invaluable in giving Elling a sense of how to estimate costs and figure schedules. "Back in the '50s," he says, "there was a great lack of professionalism and training in the management aspect of construction. There was no way to become an estimator except to get a feel for the practice in the field. There was no school you could go to, no course you could take, no book you could read, to find out how long it takes to install a toilet, for instance."

As Elling worked his way up through the ranks of the family company (he became president in 1969), he learned that cost control was a subject most contractors paid lip service to, but felt very little urgency about. The 1960s in particular were "lush, plush days" for contractors, with plenty of highly profitable jobs for everyone. "If you have a budget of $850,000 for a job that pays a million," he says, "well, it's very difficult to lose money. You say, 'Why worry about all this detail? So what if I go over budget a little? I know I'm going to make money anyhow.' You worry about budgeting only when things are tight and competitive."

By the mid-1970s Elling realized that conditions in the construction industry were changing dramatically. Competition was increasing and margins were becoming tighter. Elling's own company, moreover, found itself involved in far more complex projects. Instead of standardized piping for schools and government buildings, the company was now bidding on industrial jobs that often required innovative piping systems for moving liquids and gases. "If you make 10,000 Chevies you know how much the next one will cost and how long it will take," Elling explains. "It will be pretty much like the 10,000 before it. But in these kinds of construction projects you don't have that same degree of repetition. Each job is unique."

That lesson was hammered home by the disastrous cost overruns Elling Bros. experienced on its 1973–75 contract. The budget for the job predicted a modest but acceptable gross profit for Elling Bros. but very little went according to plan. The Nixon price control program first created critical shortages of materials, then caused prices to soar after controls were lifted. The work force, supervised by unfamiliar foremen in a relatively distant part of New Jersey, was performing at only about two-thirds of expected efficiency. And dozens of changes ordered by the customer often went unbilled and unrecorded. "We weren't yet sophisticated enough to keep detailed account of them all," Elling concedes. "We didn't have the mechanism to price and record them, so we didn't get the extra money in time."

Just to survive, Elling Bros. had to cut costs quickly, and scrounge for every penny. Purchasing was rationed; only urgently needed deliveries were accepted, and only when there was money to pay for them. The top six company executives, including Elling, all took salary cuts. Bonuses and profit sharing disappeared for everyone in the office and warehouse. Though the company cut its volume of work and trimmed its fixed overhead, Elling and other stockholders had to pledge their homes and personal assets to the bank to raise operating capital. "I've always prayed a few times a day," says Elling, "but I had never prayed for the company. For the first time I started to."

Elling knew he had to go beyond emergency survival measures if he wanted to stay in business over the long haul. His financially shaky firm would have to do something more drastic than slashing overhead. Elling would have to develop a budgeting and cost-monitoring system that would blow the whistle on costs early enough to do something about them before they escalated. Most of the problems of the 1975 fiasco, he realized, could have been minimized if he'd had accurate, up-to-date information—instead of reports that were months old.

Elling huddled with his accountants and pored over books by cost-control experts. Just getting more information, he quickly realized, wasn't the answer. Elling Bros. had three purchasing agents who handled hundreds of daily

EXHIBIT 26–1 ■ Elling Bros. Cost-Control History

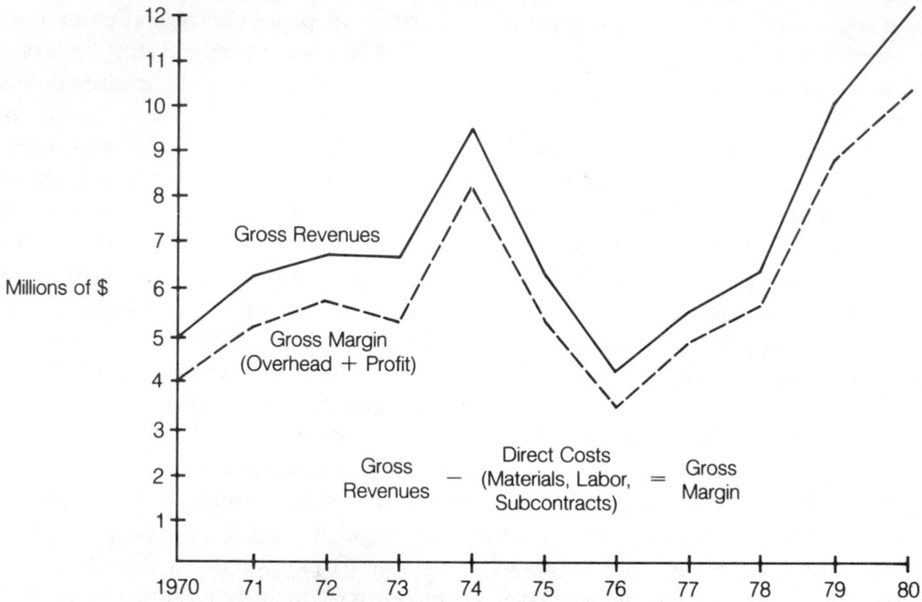

Over the last ten years, Elling Bros. has experienced wide fluctuations in its revenues from large-scale mechanical contracting projects. Most of the company's revenues are turned over quickly to pay for job-related materials, labor, and subcontracting, leaving only a narrow margin after costs to cover overhead and profit. In the early 1970s, when high-profit jobs were more plentiful, the company's gross margins were wide enough to absorb small cost overruns. But a major contract in 1973–75 almost put Elling Bros. out of business and forced the company to retrench considerably. To deal with the crisis, Cliff Elling introduced a stricter cost-monitoring system—and today, revenues and profits are both once again growing rapidly.

transactions and a labor force of seventy-five that might be employed in fifteen different locations at one time. Elling couldn't hope to keep track of the details of all this activity without drastically expanding his office staff and overhead.

Elling found the nucleus of an answer in a manual written by Jack Baker and a committee of the national Mechanical Contractors Association of America (MCAA). Baker, a contractor himself, pointed out that large, complex budgets can't be properly monitored by checking individual line items or by comparing current expenditures against the overall progress of the job. Instead, Baker suggested that budgets can be monitored by subdividing them into small, easily evaluated units and by focusing attention on those items on which costs are most likely to get out of hand.

The new cost-monitoring system Elling established for the company drew heavily on Baker's principles. Each week, a foreman and a site manager report to Elling about the progress made on well-defined stages of work at each site. Progress is measured by man-hours expended and the amount of work completed. (Most units involve fewer than one hundred hours of labor; none exceed one thousand.) Elling has his foremen and site managers send him separate opinions on each stage so he can compare reports: "You can measure a roof in square feet or a road in cubic yards of concrete. But I defy anyone to walk through a system of pipe or electrical conduits and say the job is half done or three-quarters done."

At the same time, Elling gets reports on the most cost-volatile materials that go into the job,

EXHIBIT 26–2 ■ Small Savings on Costs Add Up to Major Profits

1980 Income Statement	Elling Bros.			The Industry		
	($000)		(%)	($000)		(%)
GROSS REVENUES		12,174	100.0		10,590	100.0
Materials & equipment	3,358		27.6	3,310		31.3
Subcontracts	4,125		33.9	1,907		18.0
Job-related wages	2,100		17.2	2,929		27.6
Payroll taxes, job insurance, union benefits	680		5.6	807		7.6
Misc. direct job costs	96		0.8	290		2.7
DIRECT JOB COSTS		10,359	85.1		9,242	87.3
GROSS PROFIT		1,815	14.9		1,348	12.7
G&A expenses	999		8.2	1,186		11.2
NET INCOME (LOSS) BEFORE TAXES		726	6.0		162	1.5

In 1980, when an intensive cost-monitoring program was finally beginning to pay off for Elling Bros., the company had gross revenues of $12,174,000. An industrywide survey by the Mechanical Contractors Association of America (MCAA), published in 1980, showed that average construction revenues for member firms were about the same— $10,590,000. Elling Bros. also spent similar amounts on direct costs—85.1% of revenues compared to an industry average of 87.3%—and on G&A costs—8.2% compared to an average of 11.2%. Yet small cost savings had a dramatic effect on overall profitability. The average mechanical contracting firm earned 1.5% on its construction revenues; Elling Bros. earned four times as much, with 6.0% in pretax profits.

chiefly pipe valves and fittings, small $5 to $20 items that add up to a major proportion of job costs. Overruns are more likely to occur here, he points out, and will have the greatest long-term effect, even though individual dollar amounts are small. "You concentrate your energy where the danger is," says Elling, "as any good general will tell you."

The information from these reports goes into a small Nixdorf computer the company acquired in 1974. The computer then prints out an analysis of where Elling Bros. stands in its projections for each job—man-hours budgeted against man-hours actually spent, work accomplished, man-hours spent as a percentage of both the whole job and work accomplished, and finally, deviation from expectations, with a figure for man-hours over or under budget.

With the new monitoring system in place, Elling finally felt that he had the company's costs under control. Yet the system did not work any immediate profit magic: Elling Bros. continued to lose money. In fiscal 1971, the company had shown a respectable pretax profit of 5.5 percent on $4.8 million in revenues. By 1974, in the middle of the contract morass that taught Elling that he needed to monitor costs more carefully, pretax profit was down to 2.2 percent and by 1975, to 0.9 percent. In 1977 Elling Bros. actually lost money. "It was," Elling says, "a rather bleak picture of marginal earnings." (see Exhibit 26–1).

Yet small gains slowly began to offset the losses, and none of the losses developed into catastrophes—because they were caught early. In November 1979, for example, Elling Bros. started a job for a chemical manufacturer. By January Elling's reports showed that he was losing $1,000 a month. The reports also pinpointed the source of the losses: major overruns in labor at several job sites. Elling hopped in his car with a foreman and drove to one job site. Here he found union jurisdiction disputes over certain tasks, combined with late deliveries of critical materials. The problems were relatively easy to solve—and by the time the job was finished, in August, Elling had come out well below budget, despite his early losses.

In dozens of jobs, the cost-monitoring system brought problems to Elling's attention promptly, when dollar amounts were still small and dramatic solutions unnecessary. Says Elling, "It's really a story of what didn't happen rather than what did happen. The triumph is that we survived. It may sound ho-hum, but not if you compare it to years of losses, frustration, and cliff-hanging."

Eventually, as economic conditions in the contracting industry brightened and the company recovered its lost volume of work, Elling didn't have to be satisfied with just breaking even. In fiscal 1979 Elling Bros. turned a 2.5 percent pretax profit on $6.6 million in revenues. In 1980, revenues jumped to $10.3 million and pretax profits were 5.1 percent. And last year the company hit $12.2 million in revenues, with a 6 percent pretax profit—at a time when the industry average for mechanical contractors was only 1.5 percent profitability on revenues of $10.6 million. (See Exhibit 26–2).

"We're making more money than ever before," says Elling, "not because of fatter markups or less competition, but because we know in a timely way about any problems. The essence of good budgeting is having *timely* accounting and monitoring of changes. We have found it is critical to know where we stand, and the only way to do this is by having reasonable control over the budget and schedule.

"What you have done is constant," he adds, "but what you have to do is constantly changing. If you can imagine a football game where the goal line is changing as often as the line of scrimmage, then you can understand the kind of game we're playing."

27

Making of a Bad Cop

What makes a policeman go sour? I can tell you. I was a Denver policeman until not so long ago. Then I quit so I could hold my head up.

Don't get me wrong. I'm not trying to shift the burden of responsibility for the burglaries, break-ins, safe jobs and that sort of thing. That is bad, very bad. But I will leave it to the big shots and the newspapers and the courts to say and do what needs to be said and done about that.

My concern is about the individual officer, the ordinary, hard-working, basically honest but awfully hard-pressed guy who is really suffering now.

Young fellows don't put on those blue uniforms to be crooks. There are a lot of reasons, but for most of the guys it adds up to the fact they thought it was an honorable, decent way of making a living.

Somewhere along the line a guy's disillusioned. Along the way the pressures mount up. Somewhere along the way he may decide to quit fighting them and make the conscious decisions to try to "beat" society instead.

But long before he gets to that point, almost as soon as he dons the uniform, in fact, he is taking the first little steps down the road that does, for some, eventually lead to the penitentiary.

Let me back up a little. I want to talk about how you get to be a policeman, because this is where the trouble really starts.

Almost any able-bodied man can become a policeman in Denver. If he is within the age brackets, if he is a high school graduate, if he has no criminal record, he is a cinch.

There isn't much to getting through the screening, and some bad ones do get through. There are the usual examinations and questionnaires. Then there is the interview. A few command officers ask questions. There is a representative of civil service and a psychiatrist present.

They ask the predictable questions and just about everybody gives the predictable answers: "Why do you want to become a policeman?" "I've always wanted to be a policeman. I want

Reprinted by permission of *The Denver Post.*

to help people." Five or ten minutes and it is over.

Five or ten minutes to spot the sadist, the psychopath— or the guy with an eye for an easy buck. I guess they weed some out. Some others they get at the Police Academy. But some get through.

Along with those few bad ones, there are more good ones, and lot of average, ordinary human beings who have this in common: They want to be policemen.

The job has (or had) some glamour for the young man who likes authority, who finds appeal in making a career of public service, who is extroverted or aggressive.

Before you knock those qualities, remember two things: First, they are the same qualities we admire in a business executive. Second, if it weren't for men with these qualities, you wouldn't have any police protection.

The Police Academy is point No. 2 in my bill of particulars. It is a fine thing in a way. You meet the cream of the Police Department. Your expectations soar. You know you are going to make the grade and be a good officer. But how well are you really prepared?

There are six weeks at the academy—four weeks in my time. Six hectic weeks in which to learn all about the criminal laws you have sworn to enforce, to assimilate the rules of evidence, methods of arbitration, use of firearms, mob and riot control, first aid (including, if you please, some basic obstetrics), public relations, and so on.

There is an intangible something else that is not on the formal agenda. You begin to learn that this is a fraternity into which you are not automatically accepted by your fellows. You have to earn your way in; you have to establish that you are "all right."

And even this early there is a slight sour note. You knew, of course that you had to provide your own uniforms, your own hat, shoes, shirts, pistol and bullets out of your $393 a month.

You knew the city would generously provide you with the cloth for two pair of trousers and a uniform blouse.

What you didn't know was that you don't just choose a tailor shop for price and get the job done.

You are sent to a place by the Police Department to get the tailoring done. You pay the price even though the work may be ill-fitting. It seems a little odd to you that it is always the same establishment. But it is a small point and you have other things on your mind.

So the rookie, full of pride and high spirit, his head full of partly learned information, is turned over to a more experienced man for breaking in. He is on "probation" for six months.

The rookie knows he is being watched by all the older hands around him. He is eager to be accepted. He accepts advice gratefully.

Then he gets little signs that he has been making a good impression. It may happen like this: The older man stops at a bar, comes out with some packages of cigarets. He does this several times. He explains that this is part of the job, getting cigarets free from proprietors to resell, and that as a part of the rookie's training it is his turn to "make the butts."

So he goes into a skid-road bar and stands uncomfortably at the end waiting for the bartender to acknowledge his presence and disdainfully toss him two packages of butts.

The feeling of pride slips away and a hint of shame takes hold. But he tells himself this is unusual, that he will say nothing that will upset his probation standing. In six months, after he gets his commission, he will be the upright officer he meant to be.

One thing leads to another for the rookies. After six months they have become conditioned to accept free meals, a few packages of cigarets, turkeys at Thanksgiving, and liquor at Christmas from the respectable people in their district.

The rule book forbids all this. But it isn't enforced. It is winked at on all levels.

So the rookies say to themselves that this is OK, that this is a far cry from stealing and they still can be good policemen. Besides, they are becoming accepted as "good guys" by their fellow officers.

This becomes more and more important as the young policeman begins to sense a hostility toward him in the community. This is fostered to a degree by some of the saltier old hands in the department. But the public plays its part.

Americans are funny. They have a resentment for authority. And the policeman is authority in person. The respectable person may soon forget that a policeman found his lost youngster in the park, but he remembers that a policeman gave him a traffic ticket.

The negative aspect of the job builds up. The majority of the people he comes in contact with during his working hours are thieves, con men, narcotics addicts, and out and out nuts.

Off the job his associations narrow. Part of the time when he isn't working, he is sleeping. His waking, off-duty hours do not make him much of a neighbor. And then he wants to spend as much time as he can with his family.

Sometimes, when he tries to mix with his neighbors, he senses a kind of strain. When he is introduced to someone, it is not likely to be, "This is John Jones, my friend," or "my neighbor"; it is more likely to be, "this is John Jones. He's a policeman."

And the other fellow, he takes it up, too. He is likely to tell you that he has always supported pay increases for policemen, that he likes policemen as a whole, but that there are just a few guys in uniform he hates.

No wonder the officer begins to think of himself as a member of the smallest minority group in the community. The idea gradually sinks into him that the only people who understand him, that he can be close to, are his fellow officers.

It is in this kind of atmosphere that you can find the young policeman trying to make the grade in the fraternity. But that is not the whole story.

A policeman lives with tensions, and with fears.

Part of the tensions come from the incredible monotony. He is cooped up with another man, day after day, doing routine things over and over. The excitement that most people think of as the constant occupation of policemen is so infrequent as to come as a relief.

Part of the tensions come from the manifold fears. I don't mean that these men are cowards. This is no place for cowards. But they are human beings. And fears work on all human beings.

Paramount is the physical fear that he will get hurt to the point where he can't go on working, or the fear that he will be killed. The fear for his family.

There is the fear that he will make a wrong decision in a crucial moment, a life-and-death decision. A man has been in a fight. Should he call the paddy wagon or the ambulance? A man aims a pistol at him. Should he try to talk to him, or shoot him?

But the biggest fear he has is that he will show fear to some of his fellow officers. This is the reason he will rush heedlessly in on a cornered burglar or armed maniac if a couple of officers are present—something he wouldn't do if he were alone. He is tormented by his fears and he doesn't dare show them. He knows he has to present a cool, calm front to the public.

As a group, policemen have a very high rate of ulcers, heart attacks, suicides, and divorces. These things torment him, too. Divorce is a big problem to policemen. A man can't be a policeman for eight hours and then just turn it off and go home and be a loving father and husband—particularly if he has just had somebody die in the back of his police car.

So once again, the pressure is on him to belong, to be accepted and welcomed into the only group that knows what is going on inside him.

If the influences aren't right, he can be hooked.

So he is at the stage where he wants to be one of the guys. And then this kind of thing may happen: One night his car is sent to check on a "Code 26"—a silent burglar alarm.

The officer and his partner go in to investigate. The burglar is gone. They call the proprietor. He comes down to look things over. And maybe he says, "Boys, this is covered by insurance, so why don't you take a jacket for your wife, or a pair of shoes?" And maybe he does, maybe just because his partner does, and he says to himself, "What the hell, who has been hurt?"

Or maybe the proprietor didn't come down. But after they get back in the car his partner pulls out four $10 bills and hands him two. "Burglar got careless," says the partner.

The young officer who isn't involved soon learns that this kind of thing goes on. He even may find himself checking on a burglary call, say to a drugstore, and see some officers there eyeing him peculiarly.

Maybe at this point the young officer feels the pressure to belong so strongly that he reaches over and picks up something, cigars perhaps. Then he is "in," and the others can do what they wish.

Mind you, not all officers will do this. Somewhere along the line all of them have to make a decision, and it is at that point where the stuff they are made of shows through. But the past experience of the handouts, the official indifference to them, and the pressures and tensions of the job don't make the decision any easier.

And neither he nor the department has had any advance warning, such as might come from thorough psychiatric screening, as to what his decision will be.

Some men may go this far and no further. They might rationalize that they have not done anything that isn't really accepted by smart people in society.

This is no doubt where the hard-core guy, the one who is a thief already, steps in. A policeman is a trained observer and he is smart in back-alley psychology. This is especially true of the hard-core guy and he has been watching the young fellows come along.

When he and his cronies in a burglary ring spot a guy who may have what it takes to be one of them, they may approach him and try him out as a lookout. From then on it is just short steps to the actual participation in and planning of crimes.

Bear in mind that by this stage we have left all but a few policemen behind. But all of them figure in the story at one stage or another. And what has happened to a few could happen to others. I suppose that is the main point I am trying to make.

28

The Queen Elizabeth Hospital

The Queen Elizabeth hospital was founded in 1894 under the name of the Montreal Homeopathic Hospital (the name was changed in 1951). The hospital has been at its present location in the west end of Montreal since 1927. The catchment area consists of approximately two hundred thousand persons, the majority of whom live in middle-class residential districts. There are over 250 beds in the hospital and the number has grown only very slightly over the past ten years*.

The hospital is classified as an acute general hospital center. Most types of surgery are performed and the institution is considered to have a first-class psychiatric staff. In recent years there has been a shortage of nursing staff and psychiatric beds. The public demand for outpatient services has grown much more quickly than the hospital resources available to deal with it. For example, the total nursing staff has grown from 221 in 1972 to 232 in 1973, whereas in the same period, emergency admissions have increased over 10 percent, and the percentage increases in ambulatory visits, diagnostic radiology services, laboratory units, and social service contracts were 10 percent, 22 percent, 17 percent, and 16 percent respectively.

Of the 102 full-time members of the medical staff, 46 are directly associated with the Faculty of Medicine at McGill University as associate professors, assistant professors, lecturers, or demonstrators. The Queen Elizabeth's institutional affiliations are numerous.

In 1973, the Queen Elizabeth was requested by the provincial government to close its obstetric facilities. This case looks at the decision-making process involved in the termination of obstetric care and the conversion of facilities to other uses.

Written by Danny Miller. Reprinted with permission of the author.

*"The Hospital's aspirations are not directed to expansion but toward higher standards of performances within our resources." From *Presentation to McGill Teaching Hospital Council*, June 18, 1974, p. 4.

Key Participants and Administrative Bodies

The discussion of administrative structure will be limited to a consideration of the key entities involved in the decisions to close and transform the obstetric fracilities at the hospital. The organization chart (Exhibit 28–1) illustrates many of the important formal interrelationships in authority and accountability amongst these bodies.

The key participants in this case include:

1. *The Department of Social Affairs* of the Province of Quebec issued directives concerning the consolidation of obstetric services and the closing of facilities at the Queen Elizabeth. The resulting changes in function and budget had to be approved by this government ministry.
2. Several members of the *McGill University Faculty of Medicine* played an advisory role in the reorganization of obstetric resources among seven English-speaking hospitals in the Montreal area (including the Queen Elizabeth). Dr. Lee, the associate dean of Community Medicine, was particularly active in helping the various hospitals assess their obstetric facilities.
3. *The board of directors and the executive committee of the Council of Physicians and Dentists* in the Queen Elizabeth were responsible for ratifying the key decisions made regarding obstretrics by the committees within the hopital, within the framework, of course, of the government's directives.
4. *The executive director* of the hospital, Mr. Nixon, coordinated the various decision-making bodies, was influential in suggesting administrative procedures and committees to facilitate decision-making, and was instrumental in helping devise solutions to the transition problem. Mr. Nixon sat on the committees mentioned in (3) and (5) and reported to the board.
5. *The Property, Space Utilization, and Equipment Committee* (not shown on the organization chart) reported to both the executive committee of the Council of Physicians and Dentists and to the Board of Directors of the hospital. This committee was the most important decision-making body to deal with the problem of what to do with the obstetric facilities. The members of the committee included: the executive director (Mr. Nixon), the director of professional services (Dr. Nancekivell), the chairman of the executive committee of the Council of Physicians and Dentists, the physician in chief (Dr. Palmer), the chief of obstetrics and gynecology (Dr. Catterill), the chiefs of the other medical departments (e.g., surgery, radiology, psychiatry), the director of nursing (Miss Bryant), the nurse coordinator of the Family Medicine Unit, and the maintenance supervisor. Because he had the greatest amount of relevant expertise, Dr. Catterill was particularly active on this committee.

The Decision–Making Climate

Mr. Nixon was convinced that the decision-making approach in hospital centers should be as participative as possible and that the advice of experts was essential in making complex decisions. He maintained that because decisions in one area influence many other departments in the hospital, it was mandatory for many people to be consulted before taking action. Mr. Nixon's belief in participative decision-making set the climate in which the closing of the Obstetric Unit was carried out.

Mr. Nixon also stressed his interest in rationalizing the planning, decision-making, and transition processes in the hospital. As a senior executive with much management experience, Mr. Nixon had evolved guidelines for drafting proposals and resolving issues. He encouraged the use of cost benefit analysis, clear objectives, longer time horizons, and the generation of alternative solutions in decision-making. He also emphasized the importance of the practicality of solutions, the need to pay attention to details and potential problems in implementation, and the importance of social psychology in organizational behavior.

The Decision to Close the Obstetrics Department

The Department of Social Affairs had become increasingly concerned about the effectiveness of the obstetric units within the province. It appeared that there was an excess number of maternity beds and that infant and maternal mortality rates were unduly high. A subsequent study by the department revealed that hospitals with small obstetric units (less than one thousand deliveries per annum) had by far the highest mortality rates and were less efficient financially. The conclusion was reached that three thousand deliveries per unit would be the minimum acceptable number to yield better quality care at a lower cost. The department decided to consolidate the twenty-six obstetric units in Greater Montreal into nine to twelve centers, each having a neonatal intensive care unit.

The process was well under way by February 1973 when the deputy minister of social affairs requested the help of McGill University in examining the obstetric units of hospitals associated with McGill. Dr. Lee, the associate dean of Community Medicine at McGill, was asked to submit his recommendations on how to consolidate obstetric facilities. Seven English-language hospitals were subsequently visited and appraised by Dr. Lee, who had considerable familiarity with the problem.

Because their obstetric unit was relatively small, the Queen Elizabeth Hospital was one of the seven to be affected by the plans of the department. The number of deliveries there had declined from 1,267 to 1,182 between 1969 and 1972, and approximately 30 of the 44 beds in the Obstetrics and Gynecology area were devoted to obstetrics.

Early in March, Mr. Nixon attended a meeting with members of the McGill Faculty of Medicine (including Dr. Lee) and the administrators of the other six hospitals. The government's consolidation plans were discussed and the hospital representatives were informed that only about half of the seven hospitals would be allowed to retain their obstetric units (no names were mentioned). None of the seven hospitals handled the minimum three thousand deliveries. The reactions of the administrators were diverse; some were much against closing their units while others were receptive to the idea. Mr. Nixon adopted the latter posture.

On March 20, the bi-weekly meeting of the Property, Space Utilization, and Equipment (P.S.E.) Committee took place. Mr Nixon discussed his meeting with the representatives of McGill and the other hospitals and mentioned the department's proposed plan to close the obstetric facilities. Dr. Catterill, the chief of obstetrics and gynecology, was asked to head a committee with Mr. Nixon, Miss Bryant (the director of nursing), and Dr. Palmer (the physician in chief). The committee was to prepare recommendations on the issue for presentation to the Council of Physicians and Dentists, the hospital board, and McGill.

The executive director, most of the medical staff, and the nursing staff had long known the government's plans to consolidate obstetric facilities in the province. Thus, although no formal plans had been considered before the setting up of this committee, the hospital administration and medical personnel were aware that changes were in the wind.

On March 29, Dr. Catterill submitted a report to Mr. Nixon summarizing two options that he felt were open to the Queen Elizabeth in response to the government's directives. Exhibit 28–2 shows this report.

In late March, Dr. Catterill met with representatives from the McGill Faculty of Medicine.

EXHIBIT 28–1 ■ Queen Elizabeth Hospital of Montreal Centre, Organization and Operations Chart

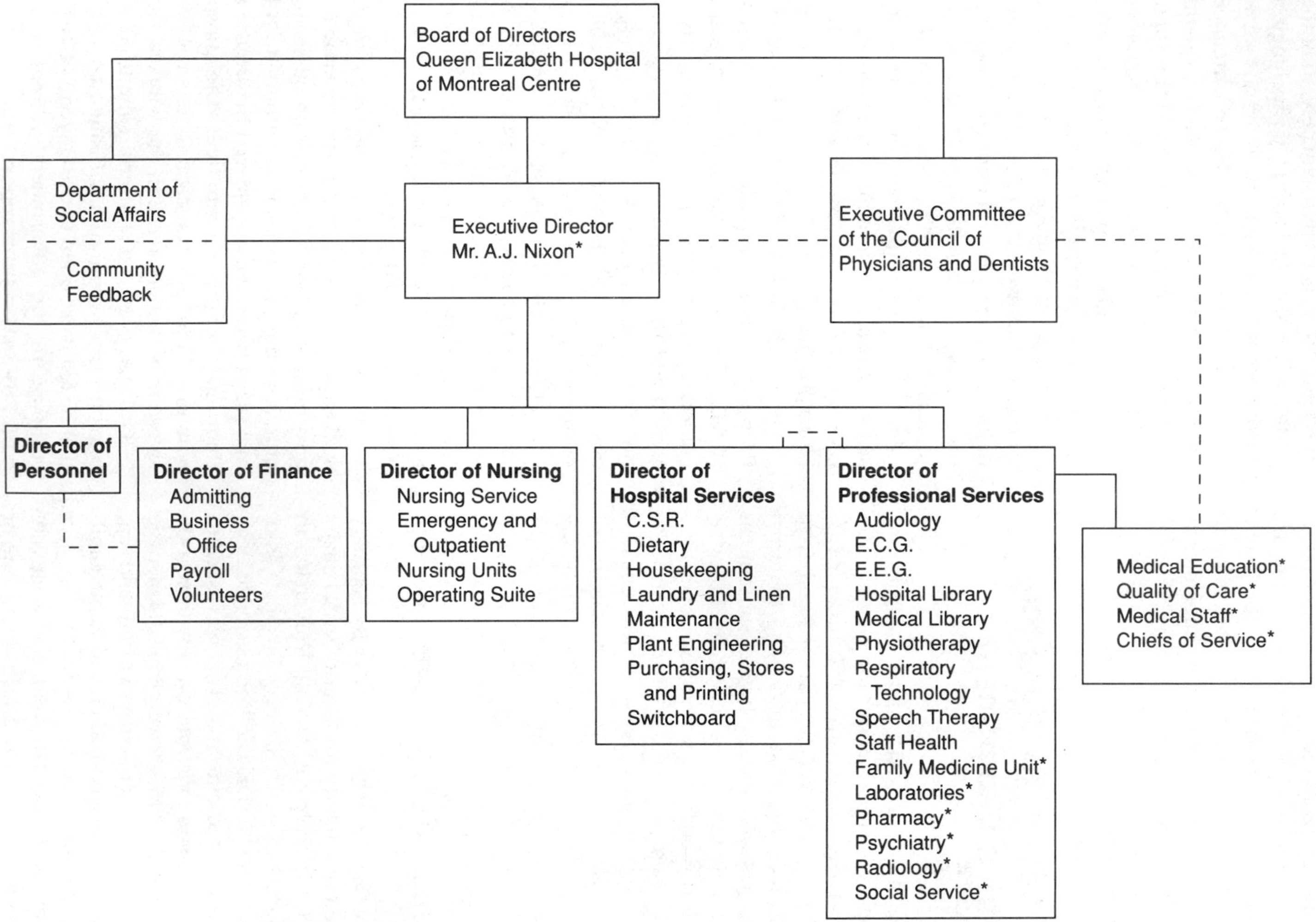

June 3, 1974.

Solid line ——— denotes direct accountability.

Broken line - - - - - denotes staff relationship (communications and advisory capacity) with no direct accountability.

*Departments that report to executive director for administrative matters.

EXHIBIT 28–2 ▪ Dr. Catterill's Report

RETAIN QUEEN ELIZABETH HOSPITAL OBSTETRICAL UNIT

Utilizations of at least 40 of the 44 beds on the present obstetrical floor at an ideal 85% occupancy rate, thus handling approximately 3,000 deliveries annually. This Unit would serve the west end of the city and could remain associated with clinics in St. Henri and Pte. St. Charles as well as Elizabeth House for unmarried girls. Neonatal problems would be handled in the Neonatal Unit of the Montreal Children's Hospital.

Difficulties:

1. There are only three delivery rooms; four would be necessary to handle this volume.
2. There are only four labor rooms; would need to increase to six or eight.
3. Lack of Recovery Room.
4. Nursery area is barely adequate.
5. Loss of present gynecology beds that are now an integral part of the obstetrical floor. This would necessitate providing gynecology facilities elsewhere.

Impression:

Our present obstetrical volume (1,200 deliveries annually) could be increased to 2,000 without major changes becoming necessary, but beyond that, the above deficiencies could create extreme problems.

DISPAND QUEEN ELIZABETH HOSPITAL OBSTETRICAL UNIT

At present there are 44 beds on the obstetrical floor, of which 15 to 18 are used for gynecology. With the loss of the Obstetrical Unit, 26 beds would be effectively freed.

Without capital outlay, the obstetrical area on the third floor could be used for:

1. *A Complete Gynecology Unit*
   The 26 beds could be available as replacements for gynecology beds closed or displaced in other hospitals as the result of enlarged obstetric units.
2. *Combined Gynecology-Surgical Specialty Unit*
   The specialty beds now on the second floor could be relocated on the obstetrical floor, thus releasing beds for the ICU and Coronary Care areas.
3. *Combined Gynecology-Urology Unit*
   Urology Unit could be relocated on the third floor, with an increase in the number of beds now allocated to Urology. This would provide a more functional Urology Unit in close association with Gynecology and provide sufficient beds for residency training in Urology.

In the above plans, the present delivery rooms would be available for minor surgical and gynecological procedures, particularly on an outpatient basis. Nurseries could be used for holding areas (Surgical Day Center).

Difficulties:

Staffing problems (Nursing and Anesthesia).

Impression:

The loss of the Obstetrical Unit would seem to be the more practical and economical plan of the two. In this way a pressing need for a Surgical Day Center area would be realized, long on the list of priorities at the Queen Elizabeth Hospital.

Respectfully submitted,
T.B. Catterill, F.R.C.O.G., F.R.C.S.(C)
Obstetrician and Gynecologist-in-Chief

His impression of the obstetrics situation is recorded in the minutes of the April 2 meeting of the P.S.E. Committee as follows:

Obstetric Beds. Dr. Catterill stated that four obstetric units of the seven in the English sector will be closed. The names of these four are not known. He was not sure whether they will be closed 3 + 1, or all four at once. The final decision will be made in July. It looks as if we well be asked to close our unit since our facilities do not seem adequate for the required number of deliveries. However, Dr. Catterill felt we could reach the minimum requirement with cramping and some reconstruction. It is undecided as to what will happen to the beds that are closed. Should this happen, gynecology may be closed out elsewhere and we then might have to increase our gynecology beds. Dr. Catterill will be meeting with Dr. Lee shortly, and will report further at our next meeting.

Discussions with Dr. Lee in early April confirmed Dr. Catterill's conclusion that the appropriate action to take would be the closure of obstetric facilities at the hospital. The board of directors were informed of this development during the month and so was the executive committee of the Council of Physicians and Dentists. Each of these bodies voiced some complaints regarding the potential loss of obstetric facilities (so did the director of nursing) but by and large they accepted the development as a fait accompli. Only token resistance was offered.

On May 3, the deputy minister of the Department of Social Affairs sent a letter to the president of the board of directors of the Queen Elizabeth requesting the hospital to close their obstetric services. (See Exhibit 28–3.)

The decision process up to this point was fairly clear cut. The government decided that obstetric resources could be more effectively allocated. McGill Faculty of Medicine personnel and several key people in the Queen Elizabeth Hospital agreed with this decision. Only a small amount of resistance to the potential closing facilities at the Queen Elizabeth was expressed by the board and the Council of Physicians and Dentists. Then a directive came from the deputy minister of Social Affairs instructing the hospital to terminate its obstetric services. Thus, although the final decision came from outside the hospital, the key parties concerned— the executive director and the obstetrician and gynecologist-in-chief—were receptive to such a decision on the basis of their own analysis. The entire sequence of events took place in less than two months.

The Decision on Resource Reallocation

The key issues after May 3 were how and when to phase out obstetrics and more importantly, how to reallocate the resources set free. Mr. Nixon stated that the key criteria were the beds of the community, and the hospital's ability to

EXHIBIT 28–3 ▪ Recommendation to Close Queen Elizabeth Hospital Obstetric Service

Mr. J.R. Houghton, President
Board of Governors
Queen Elizabeth Hospital
2100 Marlowe Avenue
Montreal, Quebec

Mr. President:

As you no doubt know, the Ministry of Social Affairs has just completed the analysis of the needs in obstetrics and postnatal sector. Following this study, the Ministry does not deem it desirable, from an economics and medical level, to maintain small obstetrics departments such as yours.

Consequently, we request you to take the necessary measures, in view of the closing of your obstetrics department around October 15, 1973.

We appreciate the quality of services rendered the population during many years and we request you to increase your services in the spheres where the needs appear to increase rapidly.

Please note that the Ministry has requested the following Hospital Centres in your region to increase the capacity of their obstetrics services: St. Mary's, Jewish General.

The Ministry is presently studying a project aimed at developing obstetrics services of the Royal Victoria Hospital. In view of the considerable time necessary for the full realization of this project, the Montreal General Hospital will continue to offer obstetrics services until it is possible for the Royal Victoria to receive a larger number of patients, in more modern quarters.

The Ministry trusts your institution will contribute important assistance to Physicians and other groups concerned, in order to facilitate the putting into effect of the changes involved by these decisions.

The Ministry personnel is disposed to meet with you to discuss dispositions relative to these changes. Dr. Stanly Knox has been assigned to act as representative of the programmation with your Board of Governors.

Please accept, Mr. President, the expression of my best regards.

JACQUES BRUNET, M.D.
Deputy Minister
cc: Dr. A. F. Nancekivell
Dr. T. B. Catterill

use existing (or retrained) personnel in the new undertaking. That is, it was agreed that any new service would have to both satisfy pressing social needs and assure complete utilization of idle resources—staff, space, beds and equipment. The facilities to be vacated upon the elimination of obstetric services consisted of three delivery rooms, four labour rooms, three nurseries, and about thirty beds.

Around the middle of May, the P.S.E. Committee began to tentatively discuss the mechanics of the phasing-out process and various suggestions were received on the alternative uses of facilities. Problems of staff training and space and bed utilization were mentioned. Since it was agreed that the committee should develop concrete plans to present to the government, all chiefs of service were asked to study the problem to present their perspectives at the next P.S.E. meeting.

At that meeting, which took place on May 28, Dr. Catterill suggested that since the Obstetrics and Gynecology issue had not been completely settled in *all* seven hospitals, plans for the reallocation of facilities on the third floor (the area of the Obstetrics Department) should be postponed until the needs of the community became better known. Dr. Palmer, physician-in-chief, though it would be best to have a plan ready to present to the Department of Social Affairs as soon as possible.

Mr. Nixon suggested that the third floor would lend itself to surgery procedures and a day care center. (This idea had been discussed several times over the past few years by surgical representatives on the Council of Physicians and Dentists.) The need for such facilities had become increasingly evident with growth of emergency and outpatient services.

Dr. Catterill suggested having Gynecology on one floor—the third—and giving up present Gynecology beds on the sixth floor to other services. He also stated that there could be room left over for a Urology ward on the third floor. The possibility of relocating Psychiatry on the third floor was considered but since this would increase its capacity by only two beds some felt such a move would not justify the cost of the relocation. The option was kept open, however.

More suggestions were offered at this meeting of May 28, but they were essentially in the same vein as above. The meeting closed without reaching any firm conclusions on the issue, although the various proposals were not fundamentally different. The P.S.E. Committee stated that it would remain open to further suggestions.

In early June, the committee decided on a closing date for Obstetric Services. October 19 was chosen after considering existing commitments to patients.

By mid July, the P.S.E. Committee had refined its ideas on the proposed use of the Obstetric facilities. Dr. Catterill's submission outlines the proposed changes in Exhibit 28–4.

On July 20, the P.S.E. Committee met to make a final decision on the matter. The resolution varied only slightly from Dr. Catterill's July 16 proposal in that it was decided to move E.N.T. (Ear, Nose and Throat, a surgical sub-specialty) to the third floor. Delivery rooms were to be used for the Surgical Day Center and thirty beds were to be devoted to Gynecology.

Mr. Nixon informed the board of these recommendations and Dr. Nancekivell (Director of Professional Services) called a meeting of the executive committee of the Council of Physicians and Dentists before the end of the month to discuss the recommendations and seek ratification.

The final decisions concerning the use of vacated obstetric services fulfilled the two original requirements: the hospital would be better able to meet community needs for emergency and outpatient surgery services, and the facilities could be adapted to this new service with minimal cost. The day care center would also reduce operating costs by eliminating the need for overnight hospital stays. Further, the additional 15 to 30 gynecology beds would help meet the increased demand that would occur with the closing of services elsewhere.

EXHIBIT 28–4 ■ Proposed Requirements and Changes for the Third Floor

1. Delivery Room area to be used as follows:
   Delivery Room 1 Minor out-patient surgery under general anaesthesia (gynecology, general surgery, etc.) cystoscopies excluded
   Delivery Room 2 Recovery Room
   Delivery Room 3 Out-patient surgery under local anesthesia (cases presently being done in Emergency area)
2. *Labor Rooms (4)* Admission area for out-patient surgery
3. *Nurseries A or B* Out-patient admission and late recovery area to replace Room 237 when 2nd floor O.R. changes are made and to relieve eventual congestion in labor room area (#2 above)

Nursery C Infertility Center - hopefully to move to larger quarters in out-patient area

4. *Obs-Gyn Bed Changes*
   1. Loss of 6 gyn beds on 6th Floor
   *2. 35 gynecology limit on 3rd Floor
   *3. Remaining 10 beds for urology (male and female)

*The present complement of gynecology beds is 21, with frequent overflow to the obstetrical area.

After October 15, there will be three further staff members requiring gynecology facilities. If one considers that 3.5 beds are required per gynecologist, we will then have to supply 9 staff members and the Infertility Center; thus the need for 35 beds.

T. B. Catterill, M.D.
July 16, 1973

Implementation

Late in the summer, Mr. Nixon began planning the implementation of the new facilities. At the P.S.E. Committee meeting of September 10, it was recommended that a committee be formed to organize the Surgical Day Care Center. The committee was comprised of the professionals most familiar with the medical requisites of such a unit.

While some members of the nursing staff were a little reluctant to change their work areas, retraining of nursing personnel in O.R. procedure went very smoothly. The director of nursing supported the changes not only because she approved of the rationalization of the city's obstetric resources, but also because she felt that the nursing services in the Queen Elizabeth's obstetric unit had been uneconomical because of the spatial layout of facilities. She suggested that the nursing staff in general were receptive to the changes because they had been advised of events at an early stage (before the government's edict arrived) and were assured in a series of group discussions (which had taken place from April to October) that individual skills and preferences would be considered in the relocation of staff.

Most of the medical specialists in Obstetrics and Gynecology were to maintain their affiliation with the Queen Elizabeth with respect to their Gynecology practices but were to start to perform deliveries at two other major hospital centers (The Royal Victoria and St. Mary's). Some of these physicians expressed remorse at having to leave the hospital for their obstetrics practice but it is believed that most did not feel seriously inconvenienced at having to do so.

On September 25, the P.S.E. Committee discussed some of the specific details which had to be settled before the day care center could open in early November. The points raised centered on the disposal of old equipment, the oxygen and suction to be installed, the precise staffing requirements, the surgical supplies re-

EXHIBIT 28–5 ■ Nixon's Report

October 22, 1973

Dr. Jacques Brunet
Deputy Minister
Ministry of Social Affairs

Dear Sir:

In accordance with your letter of May 3, the Queen Elizabeth Hospital of Montreal Center Obstetrics Department closed at 12:00 noon October 19, 1973.

The phasing-out of this Department has moved ahead as planned. The delivery room area will be used as a Day Center for elective Medical/ Surgical minor procedures.

The Gynecology Department will have access to 30 beds and the sub-specialties of Surgery will have access to the balance of 15 beds. The only expense that we will incur in this change will be the purchase of Medical/Surgical supplies for the Day Care Center, at approximate cost of $9,000.

All our Nursing Staff and other employees have been relocated satisfactorily without any disruption to their service.

The projected 1973 operating cost of our third floor including the Case Room and Delivery Room area is $427,441.

The 1974 budget estimate for the third floor including the Day Care Center is $350,225; a net saving of approximately $77,216.

We are constantly reviewing the need for beds in our Family Medicine Unit and Department of Psychiatry. Presently we are able to meet both these Departments' bed requirements, although pressure is mounting from Psychiatry for more beds.

We would appreciate receiving confirmation of these changes from your Department.

Albert J. Nixon
Executive Director

---

quired, the scheduling of personnel resources, and so forth. It was suggested that a committee be formed to look after any problems in implementing the Surgical Day Care Center. The chiefs of services were asked to nominate representatives of their departments to sit on this committee.

On October 19, 1973, the Obstetrics Department was closed. On October 22, Mr. Nixon sought confirmation for the changes from the Department of Social Affairs. (See Exhibit 28–5.)

The day care center opened, as planned, in early November 1973.

29

Company A: The CIM Decision Process

The Resurgence of Technology

Company A is a large mature corporation with several business units, all of which operate in a basic industry. In the late 1970s, a number of people within Company A began to feel that technology was not being taken seriously by the corporation. While this idea was expressed in different ways by different people, it centered around the perception that the company was overly concerned with finance and marketing, and that these disciplines had replaced technology as the driving force within the firm. "Technologists" were not occupying key vice-presidential positions, their statements were discounted, and technologically risky decisions were not being made. In the period between 1978 and 1982, a number of efforts arose spontaneously, in disparate parts of the corporation, to try to combat this trend.

Steven Robinson, at the Corporate Research Center (CRC), had become increasingly frustrated with the type of R & D planning that was going on in the business units. R & D projects were funded by the business units, and the General Managers of the business units also chaired the committees that allocated funds to research projects. Over time, it became clear that long-range, fundamental, "blue sky" projects were not getting funded. Instead, the business units were funding research which would generate quick returns in terms of existing product lines.

Robinson and others became concerned about the long-term effects of this type of planning on the corporation. In order to address the problem, an R&D planning group was formed at CRC. The focus of this group was to assist the committees in developing long-range R&D plans. They experienced some success in getting the business units to think in a more long-term and strategic manner about research.

Prepared by James Dean Jr., the Pennsylvania State University. Reprinted with permission from James W. Dean's *Deciding to Innovate: Decision Processes in the Adoption of Advanced Technology,* Copyright 1987, Ballinger Publishing Company.

At about the same time, Thomas Kidwell was transferred from CRC into corporate planning. He soon became concerned about the harm done to technology by the strategic planning process. He expressed it as follows:

Corporations, not just this one, but corporations as a whole are getting increasingly into technological and business problems because there's an inordinate financial emphasis in the strategic planning process. Strategy is more than finance. Strategy expresses itself ultimately in finance, but it does not capture technology unless it asks for a moment "What could technology substantively do for us?" You do that in the language of technology, and then, you can fold it into a financial plan. But if you don't do that carefully, you'll miss it.

While Kidwell tried to express this problem to the top management, he was unsuccessful in doing so, at least during this period. He was hampered by his place within the financial organizations, and the fact that he had three new bosses in the two years he was in the position. As Kidwell tells it, "Each time I got some awareness in the Vice President, he moved and I got a new boss." So Kidwell's message limitedly got beyond corporate planning.

The third, and probably the most significant, initiative in the resurgence of technology at Company A began in the hills outside the city where Company A's headquarters are located, on a Sunday afternoon in 1982. Geoffrey Munson, who had one year to go before retirement as Vice Chairman of Company A, was having dinner with his daughter-in-law at a local country club. He noticed at a nearby table a man who was a former vice president for a steel company. Something clicked for Munson. He said, "You know it's beginning to haunt me that those men, instead of being able to enjoy this country club, should be punished for the way they've destroyed an industry." He wondered if the management of Company A could be guilty of this as well. At that moment, he made a vow to himself that he would not be in a position to be accused of the same thing after he retired.

As a result of this experience, Munson felt that he really needed to do a better job of incorporating technology into the business plans than was being done at the time. He was thus instrumental in creating a new entity within Company A: the Strategic Technology Group. Thomas Kidwell was named Director of Strategic Technology and reported to Munson. As Kidwell describes it:

[Munson] knew he had to make it so that technology could rise to the top of the corporation without passing through finance. That meant that corporate planning and technology planning had to be parallel. I could not report into corporate planning. It had to rise to the top of the corporation in parallel.

The R&D Planning group that Robinson had started at CRC now reported to Kidwell, and their scope was broadened from R&D to include the whole corporation.

The main task of the Strategic Technology Group was to assist the business units in preparing their plans, so that they would seriously include technology. Nate Charles, who had worked in the R&D Planning group and then in Strategic Technology described the impact of the group:

It's reached a point that in the forthcoming planning cycle, when the businesses bring in their annual five year plans . . . they have been instructed by the President that they must deal explicitly with technology . . . [they must] give explicit examples of what their targets are, how much it's going to be worth once they reach those targets, and how they are going to get there. No broad brushed stuff any more. No more glib words like "we're going to put in robots" . . . He said that you've got to be much more explicit than that.

Shortly after the formation of the Strategic Technology Group, Company A's "Office of the Chairman" changed *en masse*. The former chairman retired, and was replaced as Chairman and CEO by Peter Chandler, who had been President. Geoffrey Munson also retired, and Howard Ruskin assumed roughly similar duties under the title of Executive Vice President of Science and Technology. Chandler was replaced as President by Ralph Fredericks. Paul

Jamison remained as Vice Chairman, with the financial organization reporting to him.

Howard Ruskin, the new Executive Vice President for Science and Technology, had the following comment on the situation at that time:

I would suspect that the technical effort wasn't getting the proper coordination or push; it would be pretty easy for whatever came up to be washed away.

I suggest that [when the top level changes] is the best time for change ... It is certainly a time in which you can make changes that the top guys won't block. Whether the rest of the organization will block it or not depends on how good the top guys are.

Also, it's a time that creates an awful lot of turmoil. Folks are jockeying for position ... Everyone is nervous.

Many aspects of Ruskin's sentiment were in fact borne out by subsequent developments at Company A.

With the creation of the Strategic Technology Group, and the turnover of the senior officers, the seeds which Munson and others had planted began to grow and bear fruit. First, the new Executive Committee drafted a Statement of Direction for Company A. The process by which the statement was drafted was significant because both Corporate Planning and Strategic Technology were involved. The content of the document also provided some direction for technology within the corporation:

We will strengthen our core by focusing our resources where Company A can improve our competitive advantage ... enter new areas and expand existing businesses that build upon our strengths ... In all our endeavors we will continue to be an innovative technological leader ...

While such statements can be dismissed as boilerplate, this one was taken as a serious statement about technology and competition by people within Company A. As Bruce Lindsay, the Director of Management Information Systems (MIS) put it:

I think there's a total commitment at the policy level of this company to have a rallying point ... we are going to plant a flag, we're not going to abdicate our business to foreign competition, and we're not going to sit and atrophy the way steel did. Here's where we stand and fight. That implies we're going to do things differently, because [what] steel did was a formula for disaster.

One school of thought would be that basic industry is a lousy business ... we should get out of it, let the third world have it, and start building semi-conductors or something. We've said no, we'll change, this is our business. It's going to be our business ten years from now. Instead of looking for an easy solution, we'll do what we've got to do, to be here ten years from now, and hand off a healthy company to somebody else.

Subsequent to the executive turnover and the Statement of Objectives, a number of tangible outcomes of the resurgence of technology emerged. The budget for CRC was increased, with the expectation that it would not be the first thing cut back in the event of an economic downturn. A science advisory group, consisting of top people in various fields, was formed, and its reports are presented to the Board of Directors. Another new group, called the Technology Council, was formed with Howard Ruskin as Chairman. This group includes the Director of CRC, the Vice President of Engineering, the Vice Presidents of the business units, and Kidwell. Its mission is to oversee the total portfolio of technology activity.

Thus, there have been a number of outcomes of the resurgence of technology at Company A. The outcome on which the rest of this case report will focus, however, is the development of Computer Integrated Manufacturing (CIM).

The April 1983 Meeting

The Strategic Technology Group was formed in the fall of 1982. As indicated above, its primary role was to assist the businesses in developing a technological context and strategy as an integral part of their business plans. In addition to coordinating this activity, Thomas Kidwell had taken on another task. With input from the executive level, he had developed a list of words or terms, each of which denoted a technological option which might be open to Company A. As he started his new job, he began to explore the words on his list. The word that quickly rose to the top of the list was "computer".

Kidwell had not had a great deal of prior involvement with computers and he was immediately fascinated with them. While most of the technologies he was exploring had price/performance ratios growing at a yearly rate of two or three percent, computers were growing at 25 to 100 percent, with no limit in sight.

In order to explore this technology, Kidwell and Helen Evans, a member of his group, spent the early months of 1983 visiting other firms. Many of the firms they visited, such as IBM, DEC, and GE, were both producers and users of computer equipment. Kidwell and Evans quickly noted that the emphasis on computers in the firms they visited was quite different than the emphasis at Company A: while Company A was emphasizing business applications (e.g., accounting, payroll), others were emphasizing manufacturing applications (e.g., process control), and the integration of manufacturing and business systems. They were quite struck by this discrepancy.

In order to further Company A's involvement in the technology of computers (which Kidwell had dubbed "low-cost information management"), he decided to have a meeting of those people within the firm who were most involved with computers. Three groups would be involved: MIS which is in the financial organization, the process computing group, which at this time reported to the Chief Electrical Engineer, and CRC which reported to Ruskin. The meeting was planned for April 1983.

In discussing his plans for the upcoming meeting, Kidwell indicated that he had gathered data on the wisest use of low-cost information. This broke down into two areas: the technology itself, and the organizational arrangements necessary to support it. On this latter point, he noted that, for example, Company A would need a higher ratio of engineers to accountants than was currently the case.

At this point Kidwell began what was to become a long and frustrating campaign to keep consideration of computer technology from being overwhelmed by organizational or "turf" considerations. It soon became clear that at Company A, the notion of computers, and particularly of computer integration, was intricately entangled with the notion of what organizational arrangements would support this technology.

The initial impact of this entanglement was that Kidwell was explicitly directed to exclude discussion of organization from the meeting. As Kidwell put it:

> *They told me "How can you even bring up the subject? Don't you know how sensitive it is in the organization?" So this part got killed off. Organization was illegal . . . We narrowed the subject area to say that even though we've learned some things about how the human system responds to computerization, that's not going to be dealt with in those three days at all.*

As the meeting approached, Kidwell and Evans decided that it should be limited to high-level people in the three computer-related areas. Bruce Lindsay, who had recently become Director of MIS, but had an extensive background in operations, represented the MIS group. Sanford Turner, the Chief Electrical Engineer, represented process computing. Donald Joyce, an Assistant Director at CRC, represented the computer-oriented research part of the company. Each of the three was accompanied by two others from their area. Finally, two people from the business units were present, and Kidwell and Evans participated as facilitators.

It was amazing to many in the company that the meeting could be held at all, given the fact that MIS and the process computing group had a long history of ignoring one another. They were located in two different buildings separated by a river, which was seldom crossed:

Our human system began as completely separated. Four hundred and fifty MIS people degreed in business, accounting, and computer science. One hundred fifty [in process computing] with electrical engineering degrees, and no mobility between them. Nobody from here ever went there, and nobody from there ever came here. They don't even know who each other is . . . they've never met each other before, it's a human problem. (Kidwell).

The meeting was held on April 11–13, 1983. As promised, the guidelines distributed to the participants were to "deal with what Company A should do with computers, not what organization best enables us to do it." The Company A participants spent the first one and a half days of the meeting listening to presentations made by representatives from IBM, Digital Equipment Corporation, Arthur D. Little, and General Electric. These representatives were asked to say what use a manufacturing company like Company A should be making of computers. The mechanism for doing this was to distribute 100 points among the various types of potential computer applications: business computing, office automation, CAD, process computing, and so on. Kidwell and Evans did this to allow the participants to experience directly the gap they had perceived in their visits, between Company A's (de facto) computer strategy and the thrust of state-of-the-art computing. All of the presenters stressed the need for Company A to emphasize process computing and computer integration, or CIM.

The agenda item that followed the consultants' presentations was a description of Company A's current deployment of computer resources. This presentation was made by Helen Evans, who had spent several months performing an audit of Company A's use of computers. This completed the picture of a problem with Company A's current strategy that had been begun by the consultants: while they had advised that Company A emphasize process computing and integration, Company A was placing two-thirds of its resources on business computing, one-third on manufacturing/process computing, and virtually no resources on the integration of the two.

Faced with this information, the meeting participants were next asked to enumerate potential computer strategies for Company A in the next decade, and to arrive at a consensus as to which strategies were most appropriate, and would therefore be pursued by the group. The three strategies around which consensus emerged were the idea of using computers as a tool to differentiate Company A from the competition, the need to increase computer literacy within Company A, and CIM, which quickly rose to the top of the list. The draft of the key strategies arrived at by the group at the meeting went beyond mere endorsement of CIM to advocating the immediate selection of a demonstration site:

- Formulate/implement an integrated information system for Company A . . .
- Select a location and immediately implement the integrated system (including CIM) at a plant or business unit of manageable size, such that feasibility and benefits can be effectively demonstrated.
- Recommend that the upcoming modernization embody state-of-the-art CIM . . .

So in the space of a three-day meeting, the top computer professionals within Company A came to an agreement as to computer strategies for the next decade, and how they could be initially implemented. All the participants agreed that there was a high degree of consensus on these strategies. The next major step would be to obtain approval for these strategies from the Executive Committee of the corporation.

What actually happened at the April meeting? First of all, what apparently *did not* happen is that the Company A participants learned about CIM:

Tom felt more strongly than the rest of us about the consultants being there. They didn't say anything that anyone who reads Datamation wouldn't know themselves . . . a lot of hype, no real insights (Lindsay).

Sanford Turner also noted that everyone pretty much knew what the experts were going to say. Lindsay, Turner, and Tony Joseph (a member of Turner's group) all had some previous interest/experience with CIM.

If the meeting was not primarily an educational experience for the participants, why was it universally seen as important? Several things were apparently accomplished. Sanford Turner felt that the big contributions of the meeting were the buffering of the participants from their pressing day-to-day concerns, and the establishment of a direction:

In an operating entity, the problem is today's business, and that's where you gravitate all the time. You have to get off and think about new and innovative things, which is very difficult. So we were looking for approval of a direction that would allow us to go off and worry about CIM . . . keep ourselves out of the mainstream of daily problems.

In addition, while the ideas that were presented by the consultants were not seen as a big revelation, the fact that several respected outside sources would agree did seem to have an impact. As Lindsay put it:

What they lent is a catalyst. Four different perspectives, all with a common theme, without rehearsing . . . made people feel a little bit better . . . Any one of a dozen [Company A] people could have gotten up and said it, but I don't think it would have carried the same weight.

Finally, in spite of, or perhaps because of, the proscription against discussion of organization, some organizational barriers were overcome. Bruce Lindsay commented:

I think Tom really threw a spotlight on the need to work together. You've got four computing communities in Company A: the research group, the business computing group (MIS), the process computing group, and the plants. To get anything done, those four end up having to coordinate and work together. The overlap had been minimal, and the interfacing had been only when necessary. The thing that's getting increasingly apparent to everyone is that . . . we've all got a vested interest in [CIM], let's work on it together.

Perhaps the real significance of the April meeting can best be captured by an exchange that took place between Helen Evans and Thomas Kidwell when the meeting was over. Evans told Kidwell that she was disappointed with the outcome of the meeting, because the strategies that had been adopted were obvious before the meeting took place. Kidwell responded:

Wait a minute, there's a difference between you having made up your mind [on the strategies] as a result of spending four months outside, and the corporation forming consensus and commitment around this word computers. In a sense, the meeting was to develop the backdrop, the common commitments, and the working relationships to do something about it.

Evans, after reflecting on the meeting, concluded:

Out of everything that happened out of this meeting, this was the most valuable thing. These guys closed ranks. They put away politics for a while, and said, "Hey, there's a technology out there that we ought to be grasping."

As subsequent events would show, the closed ranks, common commitments, and working relationships would be absolutely necessary to survive the challenges ahead.

The Executive Committee

Following the April meeting, the team of Sanford Turner and Bruce Lindsay, with the help of Tom Kidwell, tried to schedule a presentation before the Executive Committee, so as to obtain top-level corporate support for the computer strategies they had devised. However, the

Secretary of the Committee did not feel that this was an appropriate agenda item for the committee, so the presentation was made to only some of its members, as well as other key individuals in the senior management of Company A.

The presentation was not very well received. Descriptions of the reaction to it included "a bloody nightmare," "great abuse," "blown out of the water," and "thrown out." In fact, it did not even end with the presentation itself. As one of the presenters mentioned, "we were beat up all week long."

Why this reaction? The participants were unanimous in concluding that, once again, technology had been defeated by organization. At a time when Company A was undergoing a major push toward decentralization and business unit autonomy, the officers thought that Lindsay, Turner, and Kidwell were advocating recentralization through computers. The timing, the wording and even the identity of the presenters were all problems:

The first thing that happened was that it was a political thing. It was not a technological argument, it was an organizational argument, and this kind of slowed things down a lot. It was turf: who was going to do what . . . I think that just clouded things . . . At the time, we were doing all of this reorganization . . . and the word organization came up, and it kind of worried them (Ruskin).

The subject of centralization/decentralization had gotten confused with the subject of networking and architecture. Those of us who had considered computerization had never dealt with the question of whether or not computers should be used in a centralized or decentralized corporation . . . You can draw the corporate lines either way . . . But when we were talking about words like architecture and networking and so on, people thought that meant centralization at a time when they were trying to be decentralized (Kidwell).

At the time we did this, we were in the throes of decentralizing . . . they wanted no inference whatsoever that the integration effort was going to centralize [the corporation]. They had just committed their souls and a lot of people's livelihood [to decentralization], and they couldn't segregate the two. Maybe, if we would have had a representative from the two or three major business units with us as presenters, the officers would not have read what they read into it. But here were Bruce and I . . . both of us corporate, making this presentation on computer strategy . . . It came across that these strategies were going to be corporate mandated (Turner).

The computer spokesmen did not back down in the face of this reaction, a fact which did not go unnoticed by the senior management. They (Turner et al.) felt that there was nothing substantive in what they had heard that would change their minds, and they concluded that the problem was "basically semantics." Thus, they tried a number of related tacks to recover from the presentation debacle.

First, anything that even hinted at organizational issues was deleted. Second, they removed any language in the strategies that sounded, even remotely, like computer jargon. They were concerned that the uncertainty created by this language may have been threatening to the officers, none of whom were experienced in computing. Third, the strategies got "softened" a little.

In order to defuse any further misinterpretation of what they had in mind, Turner, Lindsay, and Kidwell held a number of one-on-one meetings with the senior officers. Kidwell met with Ruskin, his boss, as well as Jamison and Fredericks. Turner spent an hour with Chandler, at Chandler's request. Lindsay talked with his boss, Warren Ernest, Company A's Controller.

After a week or two of this sort of activity, the officers were convinced that at least Kidwell et al., did not think of this as an organizational issue. With this in mind, another meeting was scheduled to discuss the strategies. The revised strategies were explicit in their recognition of business unit autonomy:

Emphasize the technological importance of the following key elements in business unit computer strategies . . . CIM

Work with the business unit managers to select a location of manageable size and immediately begin implementing a computer integrated manufacturing system . . .

The wording changes and explanations in one-on-one meetings had the combined effect of swaying the officers: at the second meeting, the strategies were approved. With this approval, however, came more evidence of the officers' commitment to decentralization. The computer spokesmen were directed to go to the business units, and try to sell them on the strategies: "Get your story together and then go talk to the businesses. If they support it, then we support it."

The Business Units—Issues

The arena for the CIM initiative had now shifted to the business units. Rather than soliciting corporate consensus on broad strategies for computer utilization, the computer spokesmen would now have to convince the Vice Presidents/General Managers of Company A's three major business units to spend money on CIM. The next hurdle would be funding for demonstration sites, which presented a new set of issues.

One set of related issues was the long time it would take for the business unit managers to see any return, the intangibility of the short-term products of their investment, and the large amounts of money that would need to be spent. As Bruce Lindsay put it:

What's just alien to a lot of management is that we [want to spend] at one location a million and half dollars to do nothing but a general design. That still hasn't dawned on the operating folks. They expect to spend a million and a half dollars and get a 50 percent ROI next year . . . It's just how we are conditioned to go at things. I think that's one of the more fragile dimensions of the whole process. Some folks are going to spend a million and a half dollars, and what they are going to get is four thousand sheets of paper that tell them they have a real bear to take on, versus a product.

Then, you say to carry it through the detail designs, it's going to take ten years and $20 million or whatever it is. When you get into those kind of numbers, rather than being a nicety in the corner, it is going to be center stage, because now you are starting to compete with major capital. There's going to be a lot of people saying "Wait a minute. When I buy a cold mill, I know what I get. When I buy this, all I know is I got a bunch of computer types running around saying this is the right thing to do. I don't grow up with it, I don't understand it, and I'm not really sure what the hell I'm going to get out of it." I think we still have to cross that bridge before we are really off and running.

Another issue that would have to be addressed is the criteria to be used in evaluating investments in CIM. Due to intense competition for corporate capital, Company A's hurdle rate for cost reduction projects (which would include computer projects) had been increased from 50 to 100 percent. It became clear that CIM would have a very difficult time meeting these hurdle rates, so there was something of a mismatch between the computer strategy and the finance policy. It was perhaps another sign of Company A's technological resurgence that the issue was resolved in a way generally favorable to CIM:

These projects have to be justified to some extent, but there's a little bit of the rigor removed from the intensity of the justification . . . Once the corporation begins to lean toward computer integrated manufacturing, then the individual proposals have a better chance of passing the guidelines (Kidwell).

[Years ago] the technical people said we don't really need computers. You can't justify them . . . They held back the development of the computer for a long time. In these kinds of technologies, you have to get ahead, and do some degree of testing it out. Get it out of the conversational stage, get a critical mass in there, move it . . . There's hardly any way you can IE it or MBA it to really find out. You've just got to try it (Ruskin).

I'm financial and quantitative and analytical by nature, and I don't think that [ROI] is the right question to be asking. I think the question is, "Do you want to be in the business?". What does it take to be successful at that? If this is one of the things that it takes, I don't think you have an option not to do it . . .

Our controllers today have a very heavy [operations] kind of background. They use accounting as . . . one of many tools . . . It's usually false precision when you start reducing things to columns and rows anyway. They'll run through that to make sure they're in the general ballpark, but within that I think they agonize with the general manager about the market and the risk, and the technology . . . Ultimately, I don't see [the numbers] driving our decisions. I think that's very healthy (Lindsay).

A third issue that had to be addressed before CIM could proceed was, inevitably, organization. Put simply, who would do the work? The reorganization had included a substantial downsizing of corporate engineering, in which a large number of engineers had been relocated to the plants, given early retirements, or had quit. Thus, corporate handling of the projects was made difficult by a lack of engineering resources, as well as the obvious clash with the pervading spirit of decentralization.

Many felt, however, that the plants did not possess the resources to do CIM either. And, even if they did, could a truly "integrated" system be created by a set of autonomous plant-level groups? If corporate were to develop an architecture at one plant that would then be used at others, who would pay for it? And so on. Perhaps the most daunting organizational issue was the likelihood that to "create" CIM at Company A would require some combination of technical support from Electrical Engineering, MIS and CRC. This was a coalition which simply had never before existed in Company A.

To emphasize the importance of the CIM initiative, the process computing group was elevated one step in the corporation. Rather than reporting to the Chief Electrical Engineer, it now reported to the Vice President of Engineering. Sanford Turner was chosen to head this group, and, to underline the move, was given the title of General Manager.

In spite of the difficulties to be overcome, Bruce Lindsay was optimistic about the business units' response. He felt that what was most necessary was an initial success with CIM:

I would guarantee that the business and plant managers, if you demonstrate to them the ability to meaningfully change their ability to compete, they'll go through the hammers of hell with you. Their staying power is greater than that of a functional person when they believe there is something at the end of the road.

In the second half of 1983, Turner, Lindsay, and Kidwell began to approach the business units to talk about CIM.

The Business Units' Response

The Northwestern plant, which is part of the Midstream business group, had been mentioned by name in the strategies adopted at the April meeting. Those attending that meeting had felt that the size of the plant was appropriate for a demonstration project, and there was also some interest from the technologists within the plant.

In July 1984, Scott Varano, VP/GM for Midstream, approved $900 thousand to be spent on a requirements definition for CIM. This work was to be done by Sanford Turner's group, with the help of some MIS personnel, and was to be completed by late 1985 or early 1986. To date, there has been good support and enthusiasm from personnel at Northwestern. Some have credited Tony Joseph, a member of Turner's group with responsibility for Northwestern, with solidifying process computing's relationship with that plant's production management.

The response of the Downstream business unit has been more problematic. When CIM emerged from the April meeting and the Executive Committee as an area of emphasis for Company A, Downstream was already in the midst of a complete modernization effort involving three plants. The Midwestern plant was chosen as a demonstration site for CIM over the Southern plant (the other likely candidate), both because it was smaller, and because there was a greater volume of technical skill present within the plant.

Once personnel at Midwestern began to talk to Sanford Turner about how the job would be done, however, tensions arose. Midwestern has always seen themselves as an independent plant, and they felt that Turner was telling them that it would be done his way. A falling out occurred between the plant and the process computing group. The type of bond that had been formed between the corporate group and Northwestern never materialized, and the relationship came to be characterized by "a fair degree of animosity."

The culmination of this was that Midwestern decided that, rather than utilizing corporate services, they would engage an outside consultant, and hired one to begin work. This firm had never done a CIM job outside of their own facilities, and most corporate computer personnel were convinced that their approach to the Midwestern project was much too narrow. This effort is still in process at Midwestern.

The third and final business unit which showed interest in CIM was Upstream. Following the April meeting, Kidwell, Patrick Broadbent from CRC, and Michael King, the Chief EE for the business unit held a similar meeting in October, just for personnel from the business unit. Some of the same outside presenters were used. Broadbent and King both had some prior interest in CIM, and Broadbent had participated in the April meeting.

As a result of these efforts, the Upstream group approved $350 thousand for the development of some CIM capacity for the Foreign plant. This project was also to be undertaken by an outside group. Turner and others were again disappointed with the scope of the Foreign effort. It was, however, clear that the corporate group did not have the resources to pursue this project.

Ironically, the Foreign initiative in CIM had to be discontinued altogether. There was such a world oversupply of its product that, in early 1985, the Foreign plant was shut down.

Postscript

In the early months of 1985, the Science Advisory Board, which had been formed by Howard Ruskin, began to look at Company A's computer strategies. In their feedback to the company, they stressed the fragmented nature of Company A's computer initiatives, and the unevenness of the progress being made toward CIM. They described the company as "fragmented," "a set of baronies," and "lacking focus." Thomas Kidwell, who substantially agreed with the Advisory Board, said that the situation reminded him of a passage from scripture: "In those days there was no king in Israel; every man did that which was right in his own eyes" (Judges 21:25).

30

Budget Cutting: Conflict and Consensus Seeking

Goals

I. To experience the dynamics of consensus seeking in a decision-making group.

II. To provide experience in establishing priorities.

III. To explore methods for resolving conflict in decision-making groups.

IV. To examine individual ways of handling conflict in groups.

Group Size

Six members each.

Time Required

Approximately seventy-five minutes.

Materials

I. A set of six name tags labeled A, B, C, D, E, and F for each group, one for each member of the group.

II. One copy of the Budget Cutting Instruction Sheet for each participant.

III. A set of six different Budget Cutting Priorities Sheets (A, B, C, D, E, and F) for each group, one for each member of the group, corresponding to the member's name tag.

IV. One copy of the Budget Cutting Key Facts Sheet for each participant.

Physical Setting

A room large enough to accommodate a table for each group, and enough space so that the groups can work without distraction.

Process

Step I. Introduction (5 min.)

The facilitator divides the participants into groups of six members each and directs the members of each group to count off alphabetically, i.e., "A," "B," "C," etc. The facilitator

By Terry L. Maris. Reprinted from J. William Pfeiffer and John E. Jones (eds.) *The 1982 Annual for Facilitators, Trainers and Consultants*, University Associates, Inc., San Diego, pp. 35–39.

announces that each member within a group is the manager of one of six plants within a company; member A being the manager of Plant A, and so on. Name tags are distributed, and each member wears the letter designation of his or her plant. The facilitator distributes to each participant a copy of the Budget Cutting Instruction Sheet, the appropriate Budget Cutting Priorities Sheet (A, B, C, D, E, or F), and a copy of the Budget Cutting Key Facts Sheet.

Step II. Individual Preparation (15 min.)

The groups are seated at their tables, and the participants are instructed to read all their handouts and to prepare themselves to participate in a budget meeting. The facilitator answers participants' questions and ensures task clarity.

Step III. Group Discussion (30 min.)

The facilitator instructs the participants to cease their budget meeting preparations and to begin their groups' budget meetings.

Step IV. Debriefing (25 min.)

The participants are instructed to discuss their budget sessions, identifying key aspects of their groups' functioning. The following questions may be used to guide this discussion:

1. What was the general tone of the meeting?
2. What decision making processes were used?
3. Did conflict generally evolve into cooperation? What did or did not help this to happen?
4. What ways of dealing with the problem did members evidence or introduce?
5. Which methods were most effective in achieving the group's stated objective?
6. Were priorities established? How was this done?
7. Did the demand for consensus help or hinder the resolution of the problem?
8. What was the outcome of the group's deliberations?

Key aspects then are shared across groups in brief, verbal reports, and similarities are noted. These may be listed on newsprint.

Step V. Discussion (20 min.) (optional)

The participants are directed to meet again in their groups of six to discuss the following:

1. How could priorities be set most effectively in a group of this type?
2. What procedures for resolving the conflict would be most effective in a group of this type?
3. How might consensus be achieved most easily in a group of people with apparently conflicting objectives?

Variations

I. The facilitator can designate a leader or cast one participant as the president to conduct the meeting within each group.

II. Observers can be designated to record the decision-making procedures utilized in the groups.

III. The facilitator can give a brief lecturette prior to this activity on factors that influence attitudes toward consensus. Participants then can process this aspect of their behavior during the budget session.

IV. The budget meeting and/or group discussions can be videotaped and replayed for the participants' later examination.

Budget Cutting Instruction Sheet

The Ace Manufacturing Company, in which you are employed as the manager of one of six facilities (plants), *must* cut $500,000 from its budget for the next fiscal year. Although a tentative budget had been agreed to by all plant and corporate managers, this drastic adjustment now must be made because of a recent legal judgment against the company.

The president of Ace Manufacturing has called a special meeting of all plant managers; the meeting will convene soon and will last only forty-five minutes. Consistent with his style of management, the president has given you and your colleagues complete freedom to decide how the budget cuts will be allocated. His only requirement is that *all* managers *must* agree to the final decisions, whatever they may be, and that the decisions on how the cuts will be allocated must be made at today's meeting.

You and your staff have reconsidered the financial requirements for your plant and have decided that you should attempt to use this opportunity to improve the position of your plant relative to the others. In this budget meeting, you intend to see to it that your plant will receive the smallest possible budget cut, while you attempt to support the financial interests of the company as a whole and the president's request for a decision on the budget-cut allocations.

Your copy of the Budget Meeting Priorities Sheet represents the new expenditures for your plant that had been agreed to in the draft budget. You may use any or all of this information in the discussion, but you may not read verbatim from the sheet.

Budget Cutting Key Facts Sheet

The Ace Manufacturing Company has 2,446 nonunionized employees located in six plants throughout the country. All the plants produce the same product (widgets) for comparable markets. The reasons for having six geographically dispersed facilities are to minimize transportation costs and to serve regional markets better. The company has been in business for twelve years and for the past several years has held approximately 11 percent of the national market share. In the next three to five years, business is expected to expand steadily.

	Plant					
	A	B	C	D	E	F
Number of Employees:	405	399	412	395	420	415
Annual Employee Turnover (%):	15	10	13	9	12	10
Average Hourly Earnings:	$5.35	$6.40	$5.85	$6.65	$6.15	$6.50
Worker Days Lost Due to Accidents:	187	133	215	150	141	175
Annual Production (in millions):	2.315	2.107	2.410	2.110	2.323	2.349
Cost per Unit:	$5.75	$6.05	$5.65	$6.15	$5.80	$5.70
Price per Unit:	$6.05	$6.20	$5.90	$6.20	$6.00	$5.95

31

Space Support Systems, Incorporated

Space Support Systems, Incorporated (SSS) is a small but growing corporation located in Houston, Texas, adjacent to NASA's Manned Spacecraft Center. The corporation was founded four years ago with the objective of obtaining government contracts for research studies, for preliminary development in space suit technology, and for studies in other areas of environmental systems connected with space flight. At present, twenty-five people are associated with Space Support Systems.

The company was founded by its current president, Robert Samuelson, for the specific purpose of bidding on a study contract for an extravehicular hard suit (a special type of space suit) with lunar, and possibly Mars, capabilities. At the time of the company's inception, Samuelson, James R. Stone, and William Jennings comprised the entire Space Support Systems company.

Mr. Samuelson, the president, is forty-seven years old, holds a B.S.E.E. degree from a large southern state university, and prior to forming Space Support Systems, was a senior engineer with North American. He has worked for several large aircraft corporations since his graduation from college twenty-five years ago. The present venture, however, represented a technologically new slant for him.

James R. Stone, vice-president and director of Technological Research, is thirty-eight years old. He has a Ph.D. in physiology from a leading West Coast university and had, prior to the inception of Space Support Systems, taught for six years at a leading university. He also has degrees in the field of aeronautical engineering. He worked for two years in the aeronautics industry before returning to school to work toward his doctorate in aerospace applications. Dr. Stone's reputation among his colleagues in both the theoretical and creative aspects of aerospace environmental control is quite good.

EXHIBIT 31-1 ▪ Organization Chart of Space Support Systems, Incorporated

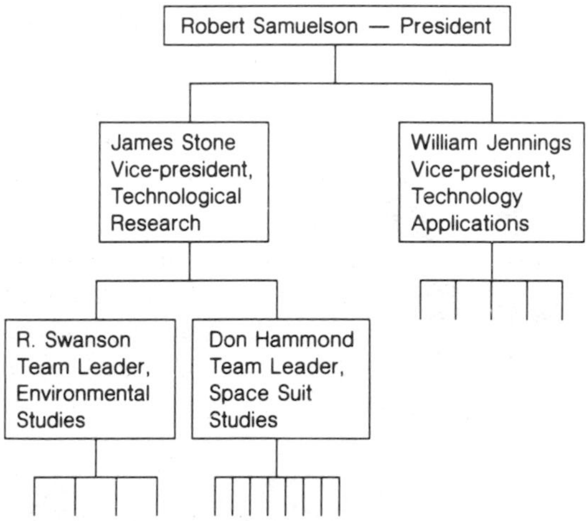

William Jennings, vice-president and director of Technology Applications, is forty-two years old. After graduating from high school, he attended college for three years before a shortage of funds forced him to quit school and seek employment in the then-lucrative aircraft industry. While in college, he majored in mechanical engineering. For three years prior to joining SSS, Mr. Jennings worked on an air force contract that involved the development of high-altitude flight suits. His particular specialty was in the development and construction of functional flight suits for initial testing, but he also showed considerable insight in new developments and changes in designs that were submitted to him prior to final construction. His reputation was such that Mr. Samuelson had been prompted to seek him out to join SSS four years ago.

The current organization chart for Space Support Systems is shown in Exhibit 31-1. There are two branches under Dr. Stone, the Environmental Studies Team and the Space Suit Studies Team. The Environmental Studies Team is primarily concerned with studies on environmental and physiological systems in spacecraft and modular structures for lunar (and other planetary) habitation. At present, there is no hardware output from the company along these lines. The team leader is Roger Swanson, and there are four men under him. Roger is thirty-three years old and has a master's degree in biology. He is highly respected by his peers and well thought of by Dr. Stone.

The Space Suit Studies Team works on study contracts investigating either hard or soft space suits used primarily for extravehicular use. Its members have also worked on suits for wear within the spacecraft. Composed of bright men, the Team is led by Don Hammond, who is twenty-eight years old and has a master's degree in physiology. He has had many opportunities to return to school to work on a Ph.D. but has elected to stay with the company each time. He is considered extremely bright and, while not as old as most of the men on his team, he is unanimously accepted as the leader. On occasion, Don and Dr. Stone have had differences of opinion and, while the two do not seem to like each other personally, they respect each other's professional abilities and qualifications.

Much of the actual management and leadership of both these teams comes from Dr. Stone. The team leaders serve as depositories for information and as spokesmen for their groups, rather than as centers of responsibility and authority. These teams are, for the most part, college-educated and well qualified technically. The average age of the fourteen men under Dr. Stone is thirty-one years and the average number of college degrees per man is 1.6.

Bill Jennings's area is responsible for actually developing and building suits for testing and presentation to NASA. This function is a logical extension of the work of the Space Suit Studies Team and requires a close coordination between the two groups. The five men under Jennings are all skilled technicians who are actually the craftsmen who build the technological systems. None of them has a college degree, although two of the men completed junior college. The average age of these men is forty-three years. They work together well and have formed a close-knit work unit. Jennings may often be found in the middle of the group working on some aspect of building mockups of functional space suits. The group is quite autonomous and functions with little direction from Mr. Samuelson.

Mr. Samuelson had never had any managerial problems in SSS that he knew of. The work had always run along fairly smoothly and, being very project-oriented, the company's employees seemed to be constantly busy with one job or another. Mr. Samuelson had to be engaged in the work of obtaining contracts and serving as a liaison with the government once a contract was secured. As a result, he knew that he might not have as thorough knowledge as he should regarding the inner workings of the SSS organization. He particularly realized that he had little feedback from personnel in the firm, but since he had experienced no apparent difficulties, he felt that all must be going well.

One afternoon, Jennings came in to see Mr. Samuelson. Jennings seemed upset and it was apparent that something was on his mind.

Samuelson: What's on your mind, Bill?

Jennings: Bob, I have worked for you for four years and I have always enjoyed my work and, in particular, working under you. But I don't think I can continue to function much longer with Jim Stone's group hanging like an albatross around my neck.

Samuelson: I don't understand. What kind of problem are we talking about?

Jennings: Well, my group does its job, and does it well; now, we could do it much better if Don Hammond, in particular, would keep his nose out and let us work once a plan is submitted to us for building. I mean—that crew from Space Suit Studies think they are supposed to supervise our work. My men are proud of their jobs and of their work. But we are going to lose some of our best guys pretty soon if this meddling isn't stopped.

Samuelson: Have you discussed this with Stone?

Jennings: No. Jim's difficult to talk to. He looks down his nose at my group because we are not eggheads. One other thing—whenever I make a change that improves the suit, Hammond's crew gets upset, particularly when it is an obvious improvement.

Samuelson: We'll straighten this problem out, Bill, I promise. But what bothers me is that your group and Don's are supposed to work together.

Jennings: Yes, I know. But it has never worked out that way. They simply look over our shoulders and don't think we are competent to work with their precious designs—even when we can make them better—which is almost always.

The conservation was terminated when Samuelson told Bill that he would look into the problem thoroughly. Bill seemed relieved that Samuelson was taking action.

The first thing the next morning, Mr. Samuelson asked Dr. Stone if he would drop by for a chat. Upon Dr. Stone's arrival Mr. Samuelson asked him to be seated and opened the conversation.

Samuelson: Jim, how are things in your area? Any problems with the X-2B suit design?

Stone: No, we are working primarily on the breastplate design right now. I think we are ahead of our target schedule.

Samuelson: Bill mentioned some friction between his men and Don Hammond's group.

Stone: *[Thinking a moment]* Well—you know we have never gotten the support and cooperation from Bill's team that we need to do our job. Don's team has to have a significant amount of cooperation from Applications in order to do its job. We need to be able to work with Bill's group, to be there to make changes and alterations as needed. Their job is to build to our specifications and let them go from there. We have to provide continuing guidance, and Bill just won't accept it. On top of all this, Bill seems intent on putting his personal touch on each piece of hardware they build.

Samuelson: I don't understand.

Stone: He makes changes on his own, which alter the specs. His group often comes up with a different product from what we asked for. We can't do anything about it because he won't allow cooperation between our groups.

Samuelson: Are his changes worthwhile?

Stone: Oh, I suppose he has some good ideas. Yes, some of his changes were very imaginative and worthwhile. But the point is that his function is to build and ours is to create designs. His suggestions are sometimes worthwhile, but he should consult me before making any changes. That's why he is there and we are here. Otherwise, why don't we simply change the structure of the organization?

Samuelson: Are there any other problems that you have experienced?

Stone: No, otherwise things are fine. All in all, we don't really have any major problems. As long as everybody does his job and stays within bounds, everything functions fine. As I said before, only when someone usurps another's authority does a problem arise.

Samuelson: Well, thanks, Jim, you've been very helpful. Do you mind if I talk with Don about this problem?

Stone: No, go right ahead.

Mr. Samuelson immediately called in Don Hammond and opened the conversation.

Samuelson: Don, I'll get right to the point. How is the working relationship between your areas and Bill's?

Hammond: What relationship? Those guys won't do anything we say. We don't get along at all.

Samuelson: Why is this?

Hammond: I don't know. Maybe it's a defense mechanism.

Samuelson: Meaning what?

Hammond: Well, Mr. Samuelson, I think they resent us because we are educated. They want to do our jobs and don't seem to realize that they are not qualified. They want to do more than build suits, they seem to want to do our design function. They just aren't qualified. I really think they resent our superior knowledge. I have tried to get Dr. Stone to talk to them or you about this, but he seemed somewhat indifferent. I guess he finally did something though. Anyway, something has got to be done. We can't do our jobs if we can't give them guidance in the building of our suits.

Samuelson: Are their changes ever worthwhile?

Hammond: No.

Samuelson: Never?

Hammond: Oh, I suppose so . . . sometimes. *[Hesitation.]* But that's not the point. It's not their job. They just aren't qualified to tinker with our designs. Don't they realize that is why we spent all those years getting our degrees? Did I waste my time? If a bunch of guys with no education can do my job, maybe I'd be better off uneducated.

Samuelson: Of course, not, Don. You and your team are top notch. But you must, by the very nature of the work, have a working relationship with Bill's group. If they can suggest improvements, all the better.

Hammond: Yes, I guess so. But we can't seem to work together. They don't clear their changes through me or Dr. Stone.

Samuelson: Well, we've never made a definite statement about the arrangement for changes, as far as I can remember.

Hammond: Mr. Samuelson, I think all their recommendations should come through me. I can then study their merits and decide on which ones should be accepted. However, they are just not qualified to design this type of equipment. They should stick to their jobs of building.

Mr. Samuelson closed the conversation by thanking Don for his frankness and promising to take action when he had all the facts.

Left alone, Robert Samuelson pondered this new turn of events. He had thought everything was just fine. The work seemed to be getting done—and now this.

He realized that after four years of the successful operation of Space Support Systems, he was faced with the first real test of his managerial abilities.

32

O Canada

Introduction

The Public Service Commission of Canada (PSC) is responsible for the provision of a comprehensive human resources management service to the fifty-two departments and agencies of the federal public service. In 1978, the commission operated through six branches. One of these, the Staff Development Branch (SDB), is the focus of the present case. The case examines the SDB in 1978 as it began to experience problems of financial restraint. The SDB was responsible for the provision of:

1. regularly scheduled courses in a variety of professional, technical, and general subjects;
2. regular and special courses for senior and executive managers;
3. specialized, custom-designed courses on a consulting basis as needed;
4. a research and development service on federal adult educational needs.

Created in 1967, the SDB had grown steadily. Its members were highly qualified professionals in their specific fields, and the SDB provided them with extensive training in adult education methods. The SDB served the federal government on a cost-recoverable basis. That is, it had to market courses and cover *all* of its costs, including overhead. Courses were sold to client departments at prices comparable to those charged for similar programs available on the open market. Prior to 1978, SDB enjoyed more business than it could handle. It had an excellent reputation, and there was no lack of funds within departmental training budgets.

In 1978, the SDB had about 250 members and was organized as shown in Exhibit 32-1. Each of the five directorates was a cost center, responsible for forecasting its own revenues

Prepared by Bonnie J. Lovelace and Royston Greenwood, Department of Organizational Analysis, Faculty of Business, University of Alberta. Used by permission. This case was prepared as a basis of classroom discussion. The events portrayed are not meant to reflect on good or bad managerial practice.

EXHIBIT 32-1 ■ Staff Development Branch

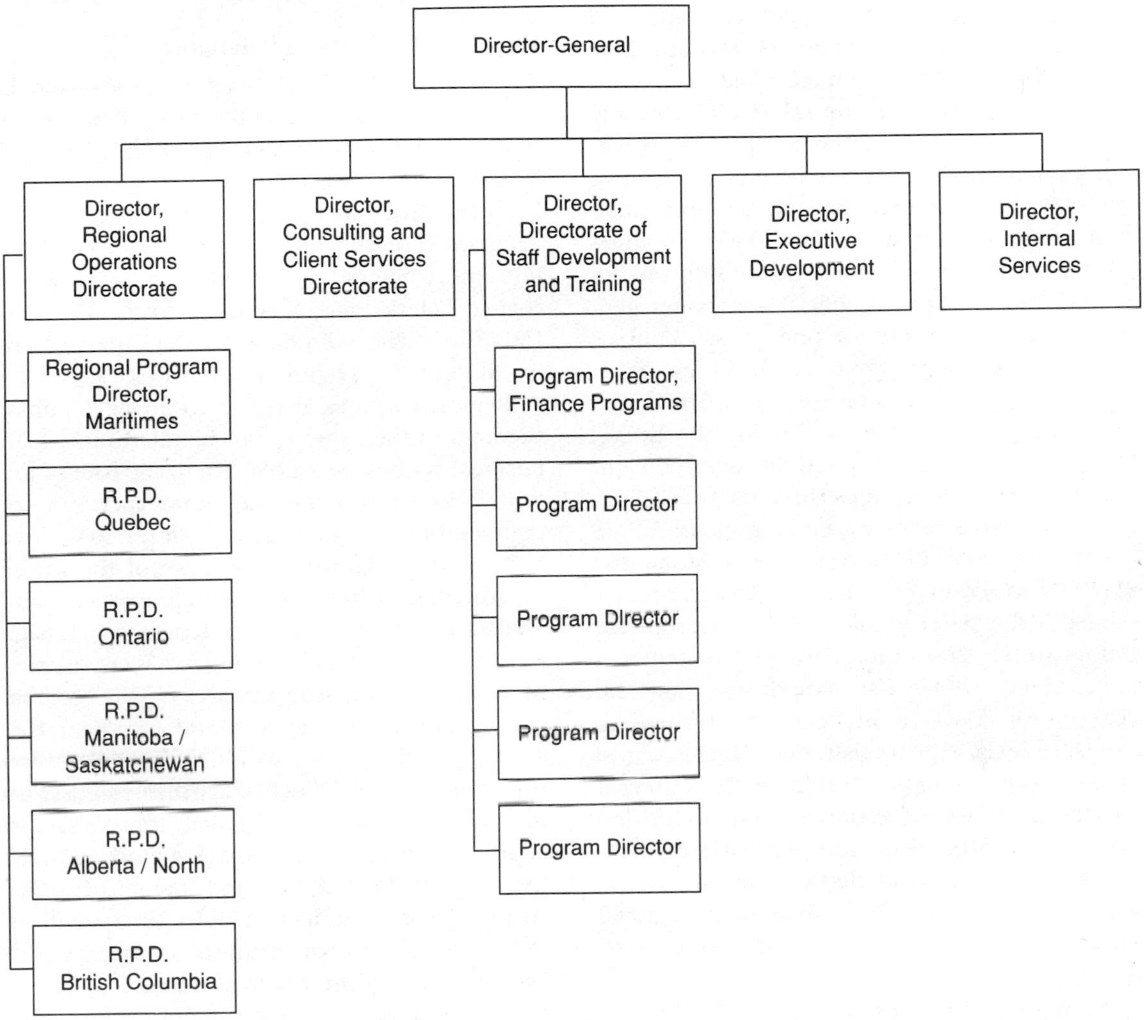

and costs. Although the SDB technically operated on a "branch break-even" basis, each directorate operated on the assumption that it should cover costs.

The two largest directorates within the branch were the Directorate of Staff Development and Training (DSDT) and the Regional Operations Directorate (ROD). These provided the bulk of the regularly scheduled courses offered by the branch. The primary division of responsibility between the DSDT and the ROD was that the DSDT serviced the Ottawa region, where the vast bulk of the public service was located, and the ROD serviced the rest of Canada. The six regional units of the ROD and the DSDT operated the same courses, but in different locations.

Directorate of Staff Development and Training

The DSDT was organized in terms of six *programs,* each headed by a program manager and staffed by up to fourteen people (including two clerks). Each program had its special field and provided a full range of courses within that field. Trainers within a program did most of their own course design and teaching and would hire outside consultants only for very special courses offered on a limited basis.

The client group of the DSDT included any public servant in the Ottawa region who was not a senior manager or an executive. The latter groups were serviced through the Executive Education Directorate. The DSDT trainers worked singly or in teams, depending on the course and their experience. Each trainer generally was responsible for one or two courses that would be taught ten to fifteen times a year.

Consulting and custom design work in the Ottawa region was not handled by the DSDT. Such work would be handled through the Consulting and Client Services Directorate (CCSD). If a client department wanted a regular course to be run in-house and for itself alone (as opposed to sending participants to the DSDT's courses), the DSDT would "sell" an appropriate trainer to the Consulting Directorate. Regional units of the ROD also could use (and be charged for) DSDT trainers.

Marketing and registration for Ottawa courses were handled through the Internal Services Directorate. Program units within the DSDT concentrated on the provision of high-quality, regularly scheduled courses in Ottawa, leasing out trainers to consulting or to regional operations when time permitted and as need demanded.[1]

Essentially, the task facing the DSDT was reasonably straightforward: develop and teach courses in one city for a very large population. The directorate was large and operated through four levels of management providing a heavy schedule of repeated courses. Each of these levels of management had controls and pressures that affected the next.

Regional Operations Division

The ROD had a small headquarters group in Ottawa, headed by the director. The six regional offices were located in Halifax, Montreal, Toronto, Winnipeg, Edmonton, and Vancouver. Each regional office was headed by a regional program director and staffed by two or three full-time trainers, supported by a secretary, a registry clerk, and a student from Waterloo University who administered the Open Learning Systems Correspondence courses.

Regional offices catered to federal public servants in the regions and handled most SDB business within their area. The basic role of the ROD was to provide the same spectrum of courses for the regions as was offered in Ottawa by the DSDT. However, because of the lower volume of demand, regional trainers were generalists and were required to teach and manage a variety of courses that in Ottawa were divided between the six program areas. The regional trainers were responsible for all administrative support services. They would design and advertise courses, prepare necessary materials, set up the classroom, teach, and assess the course. In addition, the regional trainers would administer, but not teach, a wide range of other courses. These courses would be taught by local consultants or Ottawa trainers (from DSDT) hired by the regional trainer.

The director and the trainers in the regions spent a considerable amount of time visiting clients, advertising programs, and putting out newsletters. The registry clerk spent most of her time contacting departmental training officers, looking for course participants. She also ensured that administrative letters and details were put out on time by the trainers. In addition, the trainers and director actively sought out consulting work, which they set up and discharged themselves.

The regions carried high overhead and travel expenses and had smaller clients with smaller budgets. The trainers were conscious that every

[1]The regional trainer would monitor registration, provide all the precourse counseling and advice, and administration. The Ottawa trainer could walk into a regional course ten minutes prior to commencement, secure in the knowledge that all would be in readiness. Often, the two would collaborate on some of the teaching and evaluate the course together. The regional trainer would provide all postcourse administration and follow-up.

penny counted. At the same time, quality had to be maintained. In times of trouble, most rules were set aside, and people within the regional offices worked together to generate new ideas for courses. The regional offices were small enough to encourage considerable face-to-face interaction.

Relationships between the DSDT and the regional offices of ROD were good before 1978. Many of the regional people had worked in the DSDT earlier in their careers. Two regional directors had worked through the ranks of the Otttawa division. Minor skirmishes had often occurred over the years, generally relating to problems with a few DSDT trainers who tended to head for the regions and demand that everyone from the director down should cater to their every whim. These few were well known, however, and avoided when possible. The Regional Operations Directorate, however, deliberately sought persons who preferred smaller working groups, diverse tasks, and a great deal of autonomy. The DSDT tended more towards individuals who had a particular specialty and taught it, leaving their senior managers to handle the "paperwork." There was no question that Ottawa trainers felt strong ownership of "their" courses and, given the opportunity, wanted a say in the regions. The regional people taught "everyone's" courses, depending on the schedule, and were just as happy to find local people who could do the others with a little guidance.

From Boom to Bust

Prior to the spring of 1978, the SDB had enjoyed a booming business. There was no lack of funding in departmental training budgets, and the branch had all the business it could handle. Although the economy seemed to be slumping, it did not appear serious. Rumors, however, were circulating about cutbacks as the full force of the economic downturn began to make itself felt. The Treasury Board demanded through reviews of departmental budgets, and one of the first areas cut by most departments was training. The SDB, on full cost recovery, found its market suddenly less affluent.

In June 1978, the regional directors were in Halifax for their semi-annual meeting. They usually met in one of the regions during September for a general meeting and again in January in Ottawa for a budget meeting. This year, however, they were meeting in June because a major educational conference was taking place for two days at Dalhousie University at which some of the top experts in the field were featured speakers. The regional directors had agreed with their boss, George Hudson, that they would work Sunday through Wednesday to handle regular business, leaving Thursday and Friday for the conference.

On Tuesday afternoon, the group was discussing what the ensuing months might hold. . . .

"I'm worried," mused Herb Aiken of Halifax. "My registrations are dropping off, and we're looking at cancelling courses. You know what that means; trainers sitting around on the overhead with nothing to do."

Sarah Wilson from Edmonton concurred. She had just received a telex from her office informing her that a three-day course set to start the next day had just suffered seven last-minute cancellations.

"That only leaves eight people; we can't do it, financially or pedagogically. And we've sunk training time and administrative costs into it. I'm going to have to call and tell my staff to contact the other participants and try to postpone. This is very bad for business, though, and we can't keep it up."

She left to make her call. Thomas Russell from Vancouver picked up the ball:

"The funny thing is, our clients are willing to lose the one-third late cancellation penalty, rather than pay the whole course fee. Forecasting revenues is becoming impossible, and we're barely

keeping our heads above water. Where is this taking us?"

George Hudson tried to soothe everyone's fears, saying everyone in Ottawa was still doing okay and was optimistic. The directors looked at one another, each silently thinking that it was always the regions that got hit first. It was easier for the Ottawa mandarins to make cuts where the pain wasn't staring them in the face every morning. At that moment, Sarah returned and told George there was an urgent phone call for him. He left, and the others continued to discuss the future. Hudson returned about ten minutes later, his face grim.

"There's very bad news," he said flatly. "Treasury Board issued a directive this morning stating that all nonessential training is to be reviewed and cancelled whenever possible. The phones are ringing off the wall and everything on our books is on hold until October or November."

The situation worsened during the summer. Regional trainers were out visiting their clients constantly, trying desperately to drum up business, selling a day's consulting here, working on a problem there. It was difficult. Many clients were in offices located significant distances from the regional centers. Regional directors, however, were on the rampage over travel costs and telephone bills. But, as one Toronto trainer said to her boss one day:

"A letter a day just won't do it! We need to talk to them, get them to spend whatever money they've got on our *courses, rather than buying on the private market."*

Alice Waters knew this was true, but she *had* to keep costs trimmed to the bone. The Treasury Board had told departments to trim training costs. Given their smaller budgets, many departments preferred to provide their own training or use consultants.

By late summer, a few courses were beginning to pick up registrants as people began to sort out their budgets. Some Ottawa courses were rescheduled, but there was still a lot of slack.

One morning, Sam Wisler of Winnipeg called Vancouver.

"I just had a long talk with Mike White, the Financial Management Program manager. He wants to negotiate with us about having his trainers do all the resourcing on our regional financial courses from now on. Did a lot of talking about how we should be saving branch funds by keeping the money inside wherever possible."

Thomas Russell, listening carefully, said:

"Well, in the past, we could never get their trainers, unless somebody wanted to visit his relatives and made a deal with us. All the regions hire local consultants for courses we don't teach ourselves. Saves all those travel costs. However, it's worth thinking about. What did you tell him?"

Wisler replied:

"Just that. We should all think about it. The way I see it, things are getting better, but we may never see those good times again. If we can get Programs to do some of our courses (which are the same ones being done in Ottawa), and for less than our local consultants can do it, we'll be helping each other. They've got a lot of trainers with expensive time on their hands, and we've got courses our own staff can't do, especially in EDP, Finance, and Personnel. Maybe we can help each other. I think I should talk it over with Hudson, and see about putting out a telex to all regions on it. We could discuss it on our next teleconference."

By November 1978, both Ottawa and the regions had managed to reschedule most of their courses, but at drastically reduced registration levels. This meant costs were more or less the same, but revenues were way down. Even though the branch had an official policy that break-even was calculated on the branch level, everyone knew that cost centers losing money were vulnerable. And each program, each region, was a cost center. They closed ranks. People who had worked well together for years with colleagues in the other directorate suddenly discovered negative characteristics of which they had previously been unaware. ROD jealously defended its right to hire local resources; the DSDT stubbornly insisted that course manuals were their property. Each group saw the other as untrustworthy, and open communication virtually ended. This was on everyone's mind as the regional directors held a conference by phone one morning. George Hudson opened the discussion:

"I've been getting feedback from all of you by telex on progress with Programs. My assessment so far is that they want to sell you their trainers' time to cut their overhead, and you're willing to buy it as long as charges are comparable to what it costs when you resource these programs locally. However, it appears that what they want to charge exceeds your local costs. Not only that, but each of you is negotiating separate agreements."

Thomas Russell broke in angrily:

"You can say that again. Mike White wants to send me two trainers to do the four-day "Fundamentals of Budget Formulation and Control" course, and he wants a total of nineteen days of time plus travel costs to do it. But he offered to do it for Sarah with one trainer and fewer days of time. What's going on here?"

Sarah's reply was consistent with what everyone had been experiencing.

"The month my course is scheduled is one where most of Mike's trainers are booked. He gave me whatever time was left. It seems that they want to dump all their excess time on us. Well, our budgets won't take it."

Evelyn D'anjou in Montreal continued:

"We've got to negotiate standard charges. And they must be reasonable ones, or we'll go to local, as we've always done when we had to rely on ourselves."

George Hudson, sensing that feelings were heating up and deciding a teleconference was not the best medium for this discussion, told everyone to sit back. He promised to meet with the DSDT Director, Bob Smythe, and talk things over as soon as possible.

The next day a furious Alice Waters was on the phone to George Hudson.

"Things are getting totally out of hand. I phoned Mike this morning to tell him we couldn't accept the charges he wants for our next financial course, so I had hired the Jameson people to do it. He tells me that's just fine, but all those new regulations for budgeting are being worked into the course, and his people are the only ones who can do it. And he refuses to release the new course manual because he claims it's not in its final form. George, you know we can't do outdated courses in the regions. I have to have that course book. Those manuals are branch property, not DSDT property! The Programs develop them because that's part of their responsibility, but it's policy that they must be made available to the regions, because we have to offer the same course out here. Mike as much as hinted that we will all be having trouble getting manuals for the Programs from now on. He says when things were slack over the summer, they revamped many of our courses, but the changes are still being tested. We're being blackmailed!"

Alice stopped, having run out of breath. George questioned her, giving her time to cool off a bit, but he was concerned. Alice was one of his best managers, a skilled trainer herself, and one who was more than able to negotiate solid agreements with her colleagues. If her problem-solving skills were not helping, they were in trouble.

"Have you considered training some of your own staff to do the more specialized courses, Alice? Maybe we can reduce our dependence on the Programs that way."

Alice was not mollified:

"George, you know what our trainers do. Everything . . . teach, administer, market, consult, clean up classrooms, weekends in airports. They just don't have time for more. Besides, why train them to do a course that's only offered twice a year in their own region. . . . We have others that run frequently both on our regular schedule and on an in-house basis. But the Ottawa trainers only have their one or two little courses to think about. No marketing, no consulting. Even big training centers with everything done for them! They walk out of our classrooms on Friday night and don't clean up a thing! They say that's our

job, not theirs. Well, we don't have big staffs catering to our small offices, and it's our weekend, too. But I'm getting off the topic. . . . What about those course books? I've already telexed the other regions to warn them about what's happening."

Inwardly, Hudson groaned. Every one of his directors would be up in arms by the end of the day. He promised Alice he'd go to Bob Smythe, the director of DSDT, to talk matters over, and hung up. Glancing at his telephone, he could see the lights coming on; it was starting already. Thankful it was Friday, he told his clerk to hold the calls and left to find Bob Smythe.

A half hour later, Hudson returned, and dictated a telex: everyone was to sit tight. Smythe was meeting with his managers Monday morning to discuss the matter.

The following Tuesday, Hudson picked up the teleconference phone to address his regions. He wondered how much he'd get through before the protests began.

"I just had a meeting with Bob Smythe. His managers claim we're doing outdated courses and that they should be given control of course content. They also believe we should hire their resources before any consultants, to help minimize branch downtime. Smythe agrees with them, and they're tabling the matter with the Director General at the next management committee meeting."

There was silence as the six listeners digested this news, each realizing the potential consequences. Then Sam Wisler in Winnipeg spoke angrily:

"This is incredible. They want to make money at our expense! Are we working for the same place or aren't we? What the hell is going on here? We won't let those bastards get away with this!"

Herb Aiken's language was much stronger, but the message was the same. Hudson listened to the chorus of angry voices for a while and then asked for everything in the way of financial ammunition, details of travel costs, local costs, and Programs charges. Then he ended the call.

The SDB Management Committee came to the conclusion that branch resources should be used whenever possible to teach branch courses. The regions and the Programs were instructed to work out standard charges to be used in the January budget exercise for the 1979–80 fiscal year. The point was noted that the regions had to provide up-to-date courses and, if that involved using the DSDT resources, that was the way things had to be.

In January 1979, two of the regional directors came to Ottawa to meet two representatives from the DSDT. The objective was to settle standard charges for all courses. Preparation time, teaching time, travel time, and administrative responsibilities would be fixed. Ratios were to be agreed upon and used as formulas for all courses in the future. Alice Waters and Sarah Wilson had canvassed the other regional directors on acceptable alternatives and had full authority from them to act. They had requested that the two DSDT representatives come with the same authority, as time was running out. The group met for a full day on the Monday and, by the end of it, the two regional directors were exhausted and frustrated. The DSDT representatives were demanding costly ratios, were not giving an inch, and had to take back any proposals to their own director for his approval. And he was away until Wednesday.

That night Alice and Sarah paid a late night visit to Hudson, venting their anger openly. The regions could not survive the charges being imposed by DSDT. It seemed that the SDB had some fundamental decisions to make about its internal affairs, decisions that were beyond the authority of Wilson and Waters. Those decisions had to be made before the new budgets were drafted.

Despite meeting again on Tuesday and Wednesday, the DSDT and ROD representatives failed to agree on standard charges. The matter was again put to the Management Committee. The committee reiterated its position that in-house resources had to be used and decided that the regions would have to live with the Program demands.

In March 1979, the Regional Operations Directorate tabled its budget for the 1979–80 fiscal year. It showed a substantial projected loss. The DSDT tabled its budget, showing a substantial projected profit.

Epilogue

The conflict that began between the ROD and the DSDT eventually spread to all directorates in the SDB as profits continued to decline for the next two years. The management issues were not resolved. Eventually, the director general of the SDB left to assume new responsibilities, and a new director general was appointed. He made sweeping management changes and restructured the objectives of the branch and most of its divisions. Courses were to be completely standardized, printed, and made available to all trainers. Breaking even financially became mandatory at the cost-center level (where it had always, in reality, been). The DSDT and ROD were joined together under one director. A massive study of the regions was undertaken to determine profitability in the face of continued economic problems. Eventually, all four western provinces were combined into one region for financial reporting purposes. The entire staff of the branch was technically laid off (achieved through a complicated process of wiping out everyone's position and then reinstating these positions in slightly modified form), and then all were invited to compete for any job in the "new" branch. In the face of so much uncertainty, morale had sunk and many competent people left.

Some of the outcomes described above may possibly have resulted even if the branch had been able to resolve the issue and ROD and DSDT had worked out their differences. The drastic decline in revenues would eventually have demanded changes. Nevertheless, the bitterness that arose between the two directorates provided a lesson to all managers who had been involved, and the present management holds frequent meetings where problems are aired and solved by the parties involved where possible.

However, a strong current of bitterness remained for a long time.

33

Bridging the Information Gap at Three Mile Island: Radiation Monitoring by Citizens

Introduction

Public interest in policy decisions of a complex, technical nature has grown in recent years. Formal provisions for disseminating information to the public about proposed policies are now commonplace. Because of the National Environmental Policy Act (1969) and other federal legislation, public hearings, public comment periods, and environmental impact statements have become widely adopted mechanisms for introducing and gaining public acceptance of new plans.

This paper, however, examines a situation in which these existing mechanisms for information exchange between government officials and the public were neither functional nor adequate. The issue under review was the purging of radioactive Krypton from the disabled reactor at the Three Mile Island Nuclear Generating Station (TMI), which had been the site of a serious accident one year earlier. In this case the normal public information process did not address the depth of public concern over the proposed purge and did not facilitate public understanding or acceptance of the proposed plans. Instead, the process was hampered by substantial public resistance.

In response to these circumstances, the U.S. Department of Energy (DOE) sponsored a unique project to provide citizens with information about radiation exposures and to rebuild public confidence in information supplied by government agencies. The Citizen Radiation Monitoring Program (CRMP) trained citizens to monitor, interpret, and publicize radiation levels in the community. This paper analyzes why such an intensive effort to involve citizens in disseminating public information was necessary, describes the program and its outcomes, and reflects on implications for disseminating public information on similar, complex social and technological issues in other settings.

Written by Barbara Gray Gricar and Anthony J. Baratta. Used by permission of JAI Press.

Public Concern about the Risks of Radiation Exposure

The accident at TMI in March 1979 released small but significant levels of radioactivity into the atmosphere, exposing the public to a maximum exposure of twice that of average yearly background levels. While subsequent studies identified no immediate or expected long-term physical health effects from the accident (Kemeny, 1979), they did point to both social and psychological consequences (Scranton, Note 1; Brunn, Johnson & Ziegler, Note 2; Kemeny, 1979). Overall, the personal impact of the accident, according to self-report, was moderate (Brunn, Johnson, & Ziegler, Note 2).

Removal of large quantities of radionuclides that remained after the accident requires extensive clean-up and decontamination over several years. The first major step in the clean-up was the proposed purge of the reactor building that was expected to release radioactive Krypton-85 into the atmosphere. Many residents became concerned about the risks associated with the purge. The staff of the Nuclear Regulatory Commission (NRC) had determined that the purge would increase the average yearly radiation exposure for an individual by about 1 percent and that this increase would not endanger the health and safety of the public (TMI Support Staff, Note 3). The public, however, did not totally accept this conclusion. Their concerns were exacerbated by their lack of scientific and technical knowledge about radiation and by the widely held belief that initial public reports about radiation levels during the accident were deliberately misleading. The Governor's Commission on TMI (Scranton, Note 1) attributed the psychological stress associated with the accident to the lack of credible scientific information on which residents could rely. The NRC's own special inquiry into the accident reached similar conclusions,

> *... the public misconceptions about risks ... has [sic] been due to a failure to convey credible information regarding the actual risks in an understandable fashion to the public. (Rogovin, Note 4)*

Even before the announcement of the purge, some communities near TMI had initiated inquiries about methods for monitoring radiation levels. In mid-1979, officials of Lancaster County (directly east of TMI) explored the possibility of measuring radiation levels independently of the NRC and Metropolitan Edison (the utility that operates TMI) but abandoned their efforts because costs were prohibitive. Residents of Middletown (just north of TMI) appealed to their congressman and directly to President Carter for an independent source of information about radiation levels. And another community approached the governor of Pennsylvania about a community monitoring program. Moreover, the governor's own commission (Scranton, Note 1) specifically recommended that the Pennsylvania Department of Environmental Resources (DER) design, implement, and supervise a pilot community radiation monitoring program to ensure local officials and residents quick access to information on radiation levels.

When the NRC, the EPA, and DER held public meetings to discuss the purge and its anticipated environmental impact, public opposition was fierce. Several explosive public meetings showed the serious information gap that existed, the lack of information about radiation levels and their effects, and the erosion of public confidence in information provided by the government.

Two excerpts from these meetings are illustrative:

Citizen A: I would like to ask you gentlemen personally to put a monitoring device in my yard so I can read it and we know what is going on around our neighborhood.

NRC Official: But I must also point out that there is a monitor right at the observation tower the EPA has there.

Citizen A: I don't know what it says. Nobody informs us what is going on or what the readings are.

NRC Official: Well, we will certainly provide you that information. (Three Mile Island Public Meeting, March 1980)

Citizen B: Why should we believe you when you've made such collossal mistakes already?

Citizen C: There are questions here and there are problems here that have not been faced elsewhere. . . . I've tried to believe the NRC. I've tried to believe Met Ed as best possible. When is the bottom line going to be that there will be one person that . . . won't pass the buck? When are we going to get some credibility? I want to believe you, but I do not believe you. (Three Mile Island Public Meeting, March 1980)

Ironically, communication between government officials and the public was so poor that an announcement by the NRC at one public meeting that the state and federal agencies were already pursuing a community monitoring program fell on deaf ears.

The Citizen Radiation Monitoring Program

The primary purpose of the Citizen Radiation Monitoring Program was to provide a source of accurate and credible information about radiation levels to communities within a five-mile radius of TMI. This information would permit citizens to make informed and independent judgments about the safety of radiation levels in their community and to verify radiation levels measured by existing state and federal agencies. The program was, in essence, an independent, routine surveillance program operated by local communities.

Since this program was the first of its kind, there was no precedent to follow for its design. A conceptual rationale for the design, however, was based on the premise that citizens are more likely to believe information generated by themselves or by their neighbors (subject to the same potential risks) than by government officials whose credibility is questionable, at best.

In early March 1980 the sponsoring organizations (hereafter referred to as the technical working group [TWG]) approached officials of twelve municipalities and three counties that fell within a five-mile radius of TMI to solicit their reaction to and input into the design of the program. They were asked how the program could be useful to them and how it could best be designed to ensure that timely and credible information was available to citizens. Officials were then invited to nominate four citizens from each municipality to serve as monitors. This was the first step in establishing local responsibility for the program.

The next step was to put the fifty-one citizens who were nominated through a comprehensive three-week training program. The training program was designed to provide sufficient technical background so the residents could use selected radiation detection equipment to obtain the necessary data and interpret the results. Nominees had little or no formal training in nuclear science or radiation detection. The typical individual was a high school graduate with an average of one year of college. The nominees ranged in age from early twenties to senior citizens and included teachers, secretaries, engineers, housewives, police officers, and retirees. The course included information about sources of radioactivity, how radiation affects the body, and methods of radiation detection as well as hands-on training in how to operate the monitors they would later use in the townships.

The lack of knowledge and understanding about radiation among the participants was clearly demonstrated on a number of occasions. During the first class, basic nuclear terminology related to radiation and radioactive material was defined along with the fundamentals of atomic and nuclear science. When asked by the instructor what the basic unit of activity was, less than half of the fifty-one participants knew the correct answer (a curie). Of those, only two or three demonstrated any understanding of the magnitude of one curie of activity. During another class, many of the citizens were surprised to find that commonplace household objects emitted low but measureable radiation levels.

One could argue that such comprehensive training was not required for simply taking readings. The program included enough fundamentals, however, that the participants would be conversant about radiation and could interpret their measurements to fellow citizens.

Once the training was completed, the monitors began to collect data on a regular basis using radiation detectors installed by the TWG at community-selected sites. The radiation levels were recorded on strip-chart recorders. Each day the monitors examined the charts and recorded the high, low, and average for the completed twenty-four hour period on forms developed specifically for use with the program.

The citizen monitors immediately posted a public copy of the report in their townships and reported any abnormal readings to the TWG. Later, a courier collected the reports and tapes and transmitted them to DER, who verified the readings, summarized the data from all twelve communities, and disseminated the results to the press, NRC, EPA, the local townships, and other state and federal agencies.

Reactions of the monitors and local officials and input on procedural details were continually sought during the preparatory phase through informal conversations and formally scheduled review sessions. This give and take among the TWG, the monitors, and local officials created rapport among those involved, provided input to improve the program's operation, and transferred more responsibility for the program to the communities. For example, once installation of all the monitors was completed, the class was expressly convened to critically review the procedures. Based on their first-hand experience with the system, the citizens provided a number of suggestions that led to revisions in the operating procedures. At another meeting, each community was asked to draw up and present a schedule for monitoring during and after the venting period. One community requested that a second monitoring site be established at the opposite end of their township to quell fears of residents in that area. Others agreed to exchange and compare their results. Some made tentative plans to reduce the frequency of monitoring once the venting had subsided. By mid-June, when the NRC officially approved Met Ed's request and the actual venting began, the monitors had already had one month of official monitoring experience.

Outcomes

Results of the Monitoring

When initially queried about the program, most community leaders reacted favorably to the concept, but some were skeptical about whether it could really be done. They feared that citizens could not be adequately trained to make accurate readings, that the data would be misused or reported incorrectly, and that the program would generate data that contradicted government reports. This indeed was not the case.

The citizens' readings were comparable to and in agreement with the independent measurements made by EPA. Exhibit 33-1 lists the total dose from Krypton-85 measured by the citizens. For three monitoring sites, the EPA measurements are provided for comparison.

In addition to being posted at the local monitoring sites, the citizens' data were published by the EPA concurrently with their own. Additionally, the local newspapers and TV stations carried the results during the initial days of the purge. DER and EPA received many calls from local citizens inquiring about radiation levels.

Survey of Citizen Monitors

An effort was made at the beginning and later in the program to obtain the citizens' perceptions about their own safety and about the credibility

EXHIBIT 33-1 ■ Summary of Citizen Radiation Monitoring Program (CMP) Data for the Reactor Building Purge (6/28/80–7/11/80)

CMP Station Locations				
Municipality	**Azimuth**	**Distance from TMI (mi)**	**CMP-Measured Skin Dose from Kr-85 Venting (mrem)[a]**	**EPA-Measured Skin Dose from Kr-85 Venting (mrem)**
Londonberry	40°	1	0.105	
Elizabethtown	90°	6.5	0.015	
West Donegal	100°	7	0.011	
Conoy	160°	2	0.036	0.042[b]
East Manchester	170°	7	ND	
York Haven	175°	3	0.041	
Newberry	245°	4.5	0.003	
Goldsboro	270°	1.5	0.004	0.001[b]
Fairview	285°	7	ND	
Lower Swatara	335°	2.5	0.006	
Middletown	350°	2	0.030	0.039[b]
Royalton	355°	2	0.087	

[a]The radiation units are millirem. The millirem (mrem) is a unit of radiation dose that takes into account the type of radiation, its intensity, and its biological effect. In comparison, a person receives an average skin dose of 80 mrem per year from natural background radiation.
[b]The variations show between CMP and EPA measurements are within statistical errors.

of the information they received. A ten-question survey administered on the first day of class (t_1) and again on the last day (t_2) revealed some significant differences in the citizens' attitudes.

The following sample question illustrates the format: "I feel well-informed about the progress of the clean-up activities at TMI." Responses were recorded on a five-point Likert scale varying from strongly disagree to strongly agree. Mean responses were compared using a t-test. (See Exhibit 33-2).

Generally, the results demonstrate improvements in how informed and how safe the citizen monitors felt. While the mean values of the responses to these questions only indicated they had neutral to slightly positive feelings about safety, this did represent a significant change for three questions. The responses indicated that the monitors felt better equipped to judge their own safety at the end of the course than they did when it began.

The citizens were also asked to rate (on a five-point scale ranging from 1 = excellent to 5 = bad) the quality of the information they received from eleven sources, including the NRC, Met Ed, the governor's office, the Pennsylvania Emergency Management Agency, their county officials, and the agencies represented in the TWG. The citizens rated the quality of information from Met Ed and the NRC as poor (3.6 and 3.5, respectively) and that from The Pennsylvania State University as good (1.8), with ratings of other agencies falling somewhere in between. (See Exhibit 33-3). No significant changes in these ratings were observed from the beginning (t_1) to the end of the course (t_2) with the exception of those for EPA, which improved from 2.7 to 2.2. Several explanations for this change are possible. EPA provided and serviced some of the citizens' monitors and maintained a public information center during the purge.

EXHIBIT 33-2 ■ Attitude Survey Results

Attitude Items	t_1		t_2		
	Mean	S.D.	Mean	S.D.	p[a]
1. My community is a safe place in which to live.	3.3	1.1	3.5	1.0	n.s.
2. I fell well-informed about the progress of the clean-up activities at Three Mile Island.	2.5	1.3	2.7	1.2	n.s.
3. I receive a minimum exposure to radiation every day which does not pose any hazard to my health.	3.6	1.0	3.7	1.0	n.s.
4. I have access to sufficient information from existing public and private sources to make a judgment about my safety with respect to radiation.	2.9	1.3	3.4	1.0	.01
5. Metropolitan Edison should proceed with the clean-up activities at Three Mile Island as quickly as possible, even if it means venting the Krypton gas to the atmosphere.	3.2	1.6	3.5	1.4	n.s.
6. I feel well informed about what to do in an emergency.	2.9	1.3	3.3	1.2	n.s.
7. Radiation levels in my community are currently above safe levels.	2.6	.9	2.2	1.1	.02
8. The Nuclear Regulatory Commission (NRC) should not permit Metropolitan Edison to re-open reactor #1.	3.1	1.4	2.7	1.6	n.s.
9. I currently can get accurate information about radiation levels in my community.	2.5	1.2	2.9	1.2	.03
10. Most of my friends and neighbors in my community are well informed about radiation and its effects.	1.9	.8	1.7	.8	n.s.

Note: Attitudes were measured along this continuum: 1: strongly disagree; 2: disagree; 3: neutral; 4: agree; 5: strongly agree.
[a]Significance values for two-tailed t-test.

On the second survey, an additional ten questions were asked specifically about the citizen monitoring program and about the course itself. (See Exhibit 33-4). The responses reveal that the citizens received needed information from the course and trusted those who provided the information. Moreover, they indicate that the citizens did not feel the course influenced them to either accept or reject nuclear power. This was important since the instructors took great care to guard against propaganda for or against nuclear power in order to preserve their own credibility as reasonably unbiased experts.

In open-ended questions about what they liked best and least about the course, many participants indicated that the course responded to the communities' need for information, and most believed that the material was presented objectively, as these comments by one participant suggest:

The instructors were impartial and did their best to take scientific data and bring it to the layman. I felt they did not try to influence anyone's opinion whether they were anti- or pro-nuke . . . I can live with the truth, but lies do create fear and strong distrust.

Other comments by the citizens suggest that their appetite for information about TMI and nuclear energy in general was barely whetted by the course. Many were eager for additional classes for themselves and for others in the community. One participant asserted, "Most of this material presented to the general public in a proper manner would definitely enlighten

EXHIBIT 33-3 ■ Credibility of Information Sources

Information Sources	t_1		t_2		
	Mean	S.D.	Mean	S.D.	p[a]
Pennsylvania State University (PSU)	2.0	.8	1.8	.5	n.s.
Pennsylvania Dept. of Environmental Resources (DER)	2.6	.8	2.2	1.0	n.s.
Environmental Protection Agency (EPA)	2.7	.7	2.2	.8	.05
Township Officials	2.3	1.1	2.4	.9	n.s.
County Emergency Preparedness Agency	2.6	1.2	2.7	1.0	n.s.
Department of Energy (DOE)	3.0	.7	2.8	1.1	n.s.
Pennsylvania Emergency Preparedness Agency (PEMA)	2.5	1.1	2.9	.9	n.s.
County Officials	2.8	1.0	3.0	1.0	n.s.
Gov. Thornburgh's Office	3.0	1.2	3.3	.7	n.s.
Nuclear Regulatory Commission (NRC)	3.3	1.2	3.5	1.2	n.s.
Metropolitan Edison	3.9	1.2	3.6	1.3	n.s.

Note: Respondents were asked to use this scale to rate the quality of the information that is available from each of the following sources: 1: Excellent. I trust it completely. 2: Good. I trust it most of the time. 3: Sometimes good, sometimes bad. I trust it 50 percent of the time. 4: Poor. I don't trust it much. 5: Bad. I never trust it.
[a]Significance values for two-tailed t-test.

EXHIBIT 33-4 ■ Course Evaluation

	Mean	S.D.
1. I did not learn anything in this course that I didn't already know.	1.5	.8
2. I feel better equipped to explain radiation and its effects to my neighbors than I did before the course began.	4.1	.9
3. This course provided far too much information.	2.3	1.0
4. I am well prepared to begin my job as a citizen radiation monitor in my community.	3.7	.8
5. Most of the material covered in this course was not relevant.	2.1	1.0
6. I received accurate information from the course instructors.	4.2	.6
7. This program will provide needed information to people in my community.	4.1	.6
8. My feelings about being a citizen radiation monitor are generally positive.	4.1	.6
9. I feel less secure now living near TMI than before I began the course.	2.2	1.1
10. I have been brainwashed in this course.	1.8	.83

Note: Attitudes were measured along this continuum: 1: strongly disagree; 2: disagree; 3: neutral; 4: agree; 5: strongly agree.

them, increase their confidence, and improve the general sense of security."

Overall, the survey results indicate that the program was at least moderately successful in meeting its purpose—providing an accurate and credible source of information about radiation levels to citizens around TMI. Judging the program's impact on the community at large is a difficult task for which concrete data (e.g., the number of residents who left the area during the purge) are not available. Both DER and EPA received calls from citizens either inquiring about radiation levels or expressing their support for the local monitors. In addition, the mayor of Middletown publicly credited the Citizen Monitoring Program as one of the major reasons for public acceptance of the purge.

Reference Notes

[1]Scranton, W. W. *Report on the governor's commission on Three Mile Island.* Commonwealth of Pennsylvania, February 26, 1980.

[2]Brunn, S. D., Johnson, J. H., & Ziegler, D. J. *Final report on a social survey of Three Mile Island area residents.* East Lansing, Mich.: Michigan State University, Department of Geography, August 1979.

[3]TMI Support Staff. *Environmental assessment for decontamination of the Three Mile Island unit 2 reactor building atmosphere* (NUREG-0662). Washington, D.C.: Office of Nuclear Reactor Regulation, U.S. Nuclear Regulatory Commission, March 1980.

[4]Rogovin, M. *Three Mile Island. Report to the commissioners and to the public.* Washington, D.C.: Nuclear Regulatory Commission Special Inquiry Group, January 24, 1980.

[5]Trist, E. *Referent organizations and development of interorganizational domains.* Distinguished lecture presented to the Academy of Management, Atlanta, August 9, 1979.

34

Datatrak: Dealing With Organizational Conflict

Goals

I. To illustrate the types of conflict that can arise within a work group.

II. To provide the participants with an opportunity to experience and deal with organizational conflict.

III. To help the participants to identify effective and ineffective methods of resolving conflict.

Group Size

Twenty-six to thirty participants.

Time Required

Two to two and one-half hours.

Materials

I. One copy of the Datatrak Background Sheet for each participant.

II. Seven or eight copies of the Datatrak Accounting Department Sheet (one for each of the six department members and one for each of the department's observers).

III. Six or seven copies of the Datatrak Purchasing Department Sheet (one for each of the five department members and one for each of the department's observers).

IV. Six or seven copies of the Datatrak Operations Department Sheet (one for each of the five department members and one for each of the department's observers).

V. Seven or eight copies of the Datatrak Marketing Department Sheet (one for each of the six department members and one for each of the department's observers).

VI. One copy each of the following role sheets (a different sheet for each of the twenty-two participants who are designated as department members):

1. Datatrak Accounting Role Sheets 1 through 6;

Prepared by David J. Foscue and Kenneth L. Murrell. Reprinted from: J. William Pfeiffer and Leonard D. Goodstein, (Eds.), *The 1984 Annual: Developing Human Resources,* San Diego, CA: University Associates, Inc., 1984. Used with permission.

2. Datatrak Purchasing Role Sheets 1 through 5;
3. Datatrak Operations Role Sheets 1 through 5; and
4. Datatrak Marketing Role Sheets 1 through 6.

VII. One copy of the Datatrak Observer Sheet for each observer.

VIII. A name tag for each participant. Prior to conducting the activity, the facilitator completes twenty-two of these tags with the job titles appearing on the role sheets and each of the four to eight remaining tags with the word "Observer."

Physical Setting

A room with movable chairs and plenty of space to accommodate four separate groups as well as a group-on-group configuration (see Process, Step VII).

Process

Step I. Assigning Roles

After announcing that the participants are to be involved in an activity that deals with organizational conflict, the instructor forms four groups and designates them as follows:

1. The Accounting Department (seven or eight participants);
2. The Purchasing Department (six or seven participants);
3. The Operations Department (six or seven participants); and
4. The Marketing Department (seven or eight participants).

Each group is seated at a separate table.

Step II. Distributing Background Sheets

Each participant is given a copy of the background sheet and a copy of the appropriate department sheet. The participants are instructed to read these handouts, beginning with the background sheet.

Step III. Selecting Roles

Within each department the instructor distributes the appropriate role sheets and gives each remaining member a copy of the observer sheet. All participants are asked to read their sheets, but are cautioned not to share the comments.

Step IV. Distribute Name Tags and Explain Activity

Each participant is given a name tag that identifies his or her role. The instructor has the participants put on their tags. The instructor emphasizes the importance of maintaining roles during the role play and then elicits and answers questions about the task. After telling the department managers that they have thirty minutes in which to conduct their meetings and their decisions, the instructor tells the groups to begin.

Step V. Announce Decisions

At the end of the thirty-minute period, the instructor stops the group meetings and asks the managers to spend five minutes announcing their decisions to their subordinates and explaining their rationales.

Step VI. Conclude Roles

The role plays are concluded. The observers are asked to provide their groups with feedback, and the remaining members within each group are asked to share their reactions to the feedback.

Step VII. Process Roles

The four managers are instructed to form a circle in the center of the room, and the remaining participants are asked to form a circle around the managers. The instructor leads a discussion with the managers, requesting that the remaining participants listen but not participate. The following questions form the basis of the discussion:

1. How did the details of your role affect the way in which you directed the department

meeting? How did these details affect your decision?

2. How might your decision have been different if you had not been required to play a role?
3. How did you deal with the conflicts that arose?
4. How effective were your methods for managing conflict?

Discussion Questions

After the managers have completed their discussion, the instructor leads a total-group discussion by eliciting answers to the following questions:

1. What were the consequences of your role behavior during this activity?
2. How did you feel about the constraints that your role placed on you?
3. How did the roles in your group affect the interaction of the members?
4. How might you have behaved in the same situation if you had not been required to play a role?
5. In your back-home work group, what methods does your supervisor use to manage conflict? How effective are these methods?
6. What steps can you take in the future to help to manage conflict in your own work group?

EXHIBIT 34–1 ▪ Datatrak Background Information

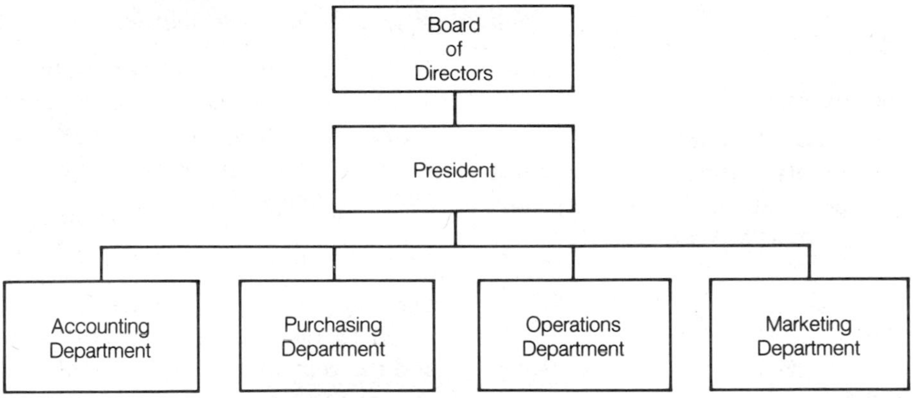

Organizational Structure

Products

Datatrak manufactures computer hardware and software designed to meet the specific needs of individual customers.

Organizational Objectives

The company's objectives are as follows:

- To manufacture computers designed to meet the specific needs of individual customers.
- To accomplish manufacturing in a manner that is cost effective to customers and that generates substantial revenue for the company and its stockholders.

Present Situation

The country is currently in the worst recession that it has ever experienced. Unemployment has reached 30 percent and is rising. The Stock market has closed each day for the past several months in a downward trend that, some economists fear, may lead to a stock-market crash.

Datatrak, your employer, is feeling the effects of the recession and is presently trying to cope with a reduction in sales and profits. An outside auditing firm has audited the company's books and determined that if the company is to survive the recession, it must reduce expenses. Consequently, the board of directors has just announced that, as a cost-reducing measure, each department must lay off one employee. Each department manager has been asked to meet with his or her subordinates in order to elicit input and opinions regarding which position should be terminated; then the manager is to make the ultimate decision. The department meetings are to take place in a few minutes.

EXHIBIT 34–2 ■ Datatrak Accounting Department Background Information

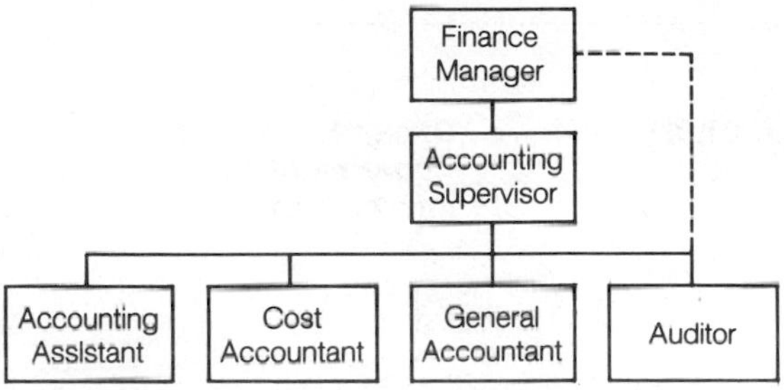

Job Descriptions

Finance Manager

Responsible for managing the Accounting Department and for presenting pertinent financial data to the president and the board of directors to facilitate timely and sound business decisions.

Accounting Supervisor

Responsible for directly supervising the accounting personnel and establishing and monitoring departmental budgets. Also responsible for other duties as assigned by management. Reports to the finance manager.

Accounting Assistant

Responsible for typing reports, providing assistance to the accountants and the auditor when necessary, and helping to put together the monthly operating report. Also performs a monthly bank reconciliation.

Cost Accountant

Responsible for accurately recording and classifying the cost of materials and properly accounting for work in progress, finished goods, and the cost of goods sold. Also responsible for providing the general accountant with this information for the preparation of the monthly operating report.

General Accountant

Responsible for preparing the balance sheet, the statement of income and retained earnings, the statement of changes in the financial position, and the monthly operating report.

Auditor

Responsible for ensuring that all departments comply with company financial policies and procedures. Also responsible for conducting periodic audits of inventories as necessary. Reports to the accounting supervisor for routine matters, but has the authority to consult the finance manager or to report directly to the president regarding significant matters.

Rumors About the Department

1. The accounting supervisor has no real work other than to report weekly to the finance manager and then to communicate the manager's wishes to others.
2. The accounting assistant habitually arrives late, frequently socializes in the other departments, and often calls in sick.
3. The cost accountant is rumored to be interviewing for positions with several competing companies.

EXHIBIT 34–3 ■ Datatrak Purchasing Department Background Information

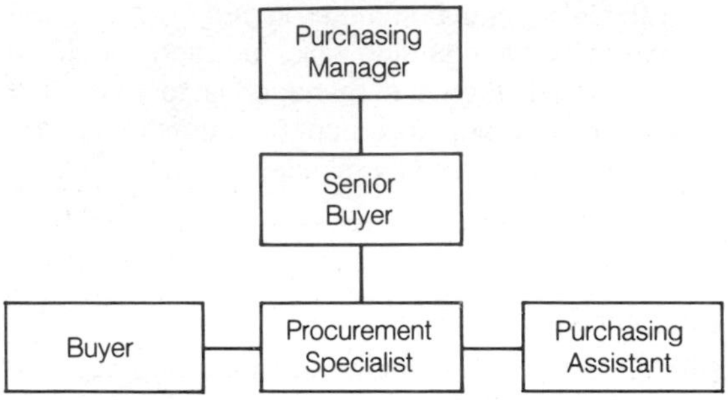

Job Descriptions

Purchasing Manager

Responsible for planning and supervising the effective procurement of materials and supplies requested by all departments within the company. Also responsible for ensuring that such items are bought after firm but fair negotiations and are delivered on a timely basis at the requested place and in excellent condition.

Senior Buyer

Responsible for planning and supervising the procurement of material and supplies requested by all departments within the company. Also responsible for ensuring that such items are bought after fair negotiations and are delivered promptly and without damage.

Buyer

Responsible for procuring materials, equipment, and services at the lowest possible cost consistent with the requirements of sound company operation. Also responsible for selecting vendors through an evaluation of price, availability, specifications, and other factors.

Procurement Specialist

Responsibilities are the same as those of the buyer.

Purchasing Assistant

Responsible for providing stenographical and other services necessary to maintain and support the functions of the Purchasing Department. Duties include transcribing material from handwritten or typed copy to final form through the use of word-processing equipment and operating terminal equipment to transmit and store textual and statistical information.

Rumors About the Department

1. The buyer is receiving kickbacks from vendors.
2. The senior buyer is eligible for early retirement, but wants to work for a few more years to build a larger retirement fund. This person frequently arrives late and leaves early, apparently without regard for the consequences.
3. Although the company has a policy against nepotism, the procurement specialist has a close relative in upper management.

EXHIBIT 34–4 ■ Datatrak Operations Department Background Information

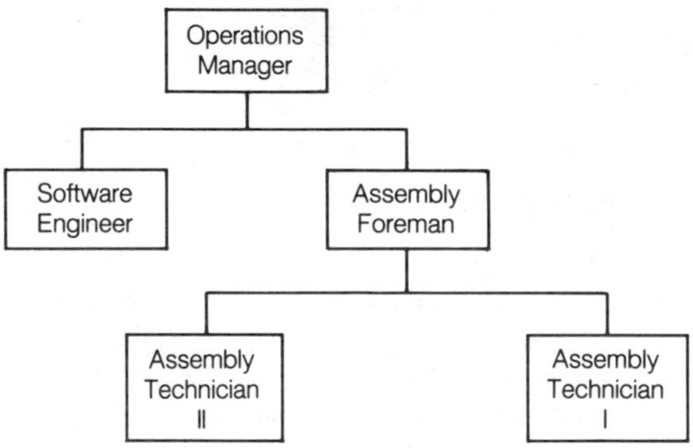

Job Descriptions

Operations Manager

Responsible for the final design, assembly, and packaging of all computer hardware and software. Also responsible for keeping assembly costs to a minimum while maintaining maximum quality and ensuring that all orders are completed on time. Supervises two people, a software engineer and an assembly foreman.

Software Engineer

Responsible for providing the software to meet each customer's needs. Also responsible for providing customers with manuals and training sessions on computer use and user language. Designs software diagnostic programs for troubleshooting the software packages. By virtue of experience and training, is the software expert in the company.

Assembly Foreman

Responsible for ensuring that computer parts are stored and assembled properly. Also responsible for checking each computer after assembly to ensure that it is operational, properly packaged, and sent to the warehouse. Makes sure that the proper tools and equipment are available to assemble each machine. Supervises assembly technicians I and II.

Assembly Technicians (I and II)

Responsible for assembling and packaging new computers and any spare parts required for existing computers, performing maintenance on tools and equipment necessary for assembling, and delivering packaged computers to the warehouse for shipping. Strong background in electronics required for both positions.

Rumors About the Department

1. The assembly foreman is given to back stabbing and to frequent verbal outbursts that upset people throughout the organization.
2. The assembly technician II is a free spirit who is often late to work and frequently calls in sick.
3. The operations manager, who was the software engineer before being promoted, spends a lot of time helping the present software engineer.

EXHIBIT 34–5 ■ Datatrak Marketing Department Background Information

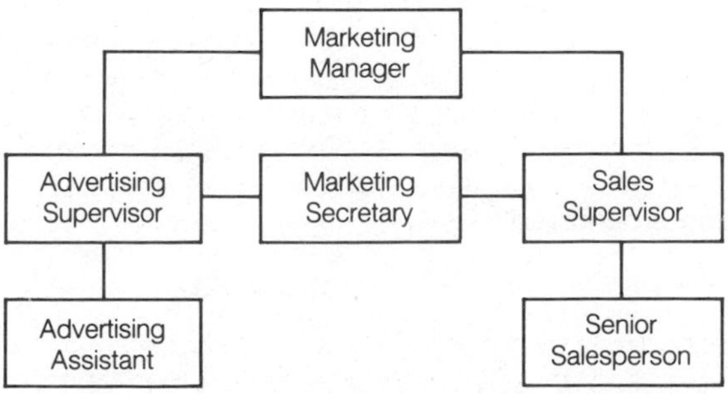

Job Descriptions

Marketing Manager

Responsible for effectively coordinating the delicate balance between the national coverage of advertising and sales. Exercises control over both the advertising supervisor and the sales supervisor in order to maintain this balance. Tasks include implementing budgets passed on by superiors, effectively reporting department sales to superiors, and informing superiors of advertising needed to maintain proper market coverage.

Advertising Supervisor

Responsible for managing all company advertising, maintaining a close relationship with the Operations Department in order to promote product lines, and advertising as effectively as possible within the limits of the budget. Works directly with the marketing manager.

Advertising Assistant

Responsible for preparing all advertising layouts and coordinating all advertising efforts with various media. Good art background required.

Marketing Secretary

Responsible for processing all paperwork for the department; answering all phone calls; and effectively managing all office equipment, such as copiers, typewriters, teletypewriter devices, and so forth.

Sales Supervisor

Responsible for setting all sales quotas, covering major accounts, and solving any and all major sales problems. Must be sensitive to market needs and must maintain a close working relationship with the Operations Department so that each sale can meet the customer's time requirements.

Senior Salesperson

Responsible for covering existing accounts in an assigned territory and acquiring enough new accounts to meet a quota.

Rumors About the Department

1. Although the company has a policy against nepotism, the sales supervisor is related to the president. Also, sales have been deteriorating since the sales supervisor has held this position.

2. The marketing manager spends many work days playing tennis.
3. The marketing manager shows favoritism toward the marketing secretary.

EXHIBIT 34–6 ■ Datatrak Observer Instructions

During the department meeting, you are to listen and observe carefully and make notes regarding answers to the following questions. After the role play has been concluded, you will be asked to share these answers with the members of your department.

1. What types of conflicts arose?

2. What methods did the manager use to manage these conflicts?

3. How did the other department members respond to these methods?

4. How did the manager gather information from the subordinates?

5. How did he or she use that information to make the ultimate decision?

6. How would you describe the mood of the department at the beginning of the meeting?

7. How did this mood change as the meeting progressed?

IV

ORGANIZATIONAL DYNAMICS

Change

Organizational Culture

Power and Politics

35

Weirton Steel Corporation

"I think it is by no means an understatement to say that the future of all companies may very well lie with how well they handle the people side of their business. And a notion that I like to keep in mind is that people must be led, and not driven."

—*Robert L. Loughhead*

At the end of March 1985, Robert Loughhead, president and CEO of Weirton Steel Corporation, sat in his office looking over the copy of preliminary first quarter results that his secretary had just left on his desk. In his mind, he began roughing out the contents of his quarterly letter to the Weirton employees. He knew that he had a number of different issues to review in this letter, several of which were related to the figures in front of him. He wanted to make sure that he presented the employees with the facts about Weirton's recent performance. But he also wanted to touch on a few things that he knew were on the employees' minds: profit-sharing, foreign competition, projections for the future.

Loughhead believed very strongly in the need for and power of open and effective communication. In speeches, he cited Lee Iacocca's words, "The ability to communicate is everything," usually adding, "and he is absolutely right." In the Hot Mill Office at Weirton, a sign read, "The greatest illusion of communications is the illusion that it has been achieved." At Weirton, a manufacturer of general steel products (located in Weirton, West Virginia, in the upper Ohio Valley), communication took on a special importance. Over the past year, Loughhead had been leading Weirton Steel from the brink of economic ruin to a level of profitability superior to that of the top American steelmakers. But Weirton's turnaround was not just a simple economic revival of an ailing corporation. It was a special case—a unique transformation of an old-style company—that involved changes in how everybody in the company thought about themselves and their jobs.

At Weirton, the phrase "people side of the business" took on new meaning, for the Weirton Steel Corporation was the nation's largest and best known 100 percent employee-owned company. Under a program known as the Employee Stock Ownership Plan (ESOP) that went into effect in January 1984, every one of the company's employees—hourly workers and managers alike—was also an owner and a stockholder of Weirton Steel. But with these titles came burdens and responsibilities as well as privileges. The key to the spiritual "New Beginning," so vaunted in press coverage of the Weirton ESOP, was to be found in the concern and personal commitment exhibited by every one of these "employee-owners."

Loughhead called this crucial component a combination of "employee participation and participative management." He explained further: "Employee participation at Weirton Steel means groups of people with common work interests being trained in problem identification, problem solving, making recommendations for solutions and getting commitments from management to implement recommendations. And what is it all about? It is about change—changing the way we do things—changing the way we treat each other and work together. It means bringing mutual respect and dignity and trust into relationships." Participative management, added Loughhead, also requires an intensely time-consuming and personal commitment on the part of top management: "Persons who lead successful companies are finding the really critical success factors are listening to employees, listening to customers, and listening to suppliers. Believe me, there is a healthy dose of change in all that."

But if active participation by employees and management was the mainspring of Weirton's recent successes, effective communication provided the key to wind it regularly. Even before the ESOP was officially underway, the new Weirton was beginning to reap benefits from a communications program that was probably one of the most comprehensive and systematic corporate communication efforts launched by an American company. The emphasis on regular information flow was in itself as radical a departure from old Weirton managerial policy as the concept of employee ownership.

Weirton under National Steel

For many years, the Weirton mill was an operating division of the National Steel Corporation, one of the United States' largest steel manufacturers, based in Pittsburgh, Pennsylvania. National Steel, like the other industry giants, had enjoyed a number of very prosperous years during the 1960s and 1970s. They got through the lean recession years by living off the profits of the fat ones. But during the early 1980s, permanent changes in the industry rendered this strategy obsolete. By the time business activity took a nosedive in the second half of 1981, steel had become a global commodity. As steel consumption dropped by 25 percent in the crippled economy, U.S. steelmakers found their business eroding even further in the face of able foreign competitors who could compete successfully both on price and quality. Domestic steel producers suffered $7 billion losses in three years.

The market for tin mill products was particularly hard hit. Even before the latest economic downturn, major changes in packaging technologies had caused demand for tin/steel cans to shrink considerably. This trend was expected to continue. National Steel produced virtually all of its tin plate at the Weirton mill, and that product made up nearly half of the plant's output. The Weirton Division had been strongly profitable for years until a gradual slide began during the late 1970s. (Exhibit 35–1 shows a statement of operations and shipments of products of 1973–1982.) This decline accelerated sharply in 1981, and the plant suffered heavy losses until becoming employee-owned.

The hostile economic climate had an acute effect on National Steel. The corporation was operating further in the red during early 1982 that it had in over fifteen years. Overexposed, National Steel began looking for a way to pare down its operations. At the time, Weirton appeared to be a large liability with little potential for improvement. On March 2, 1982, in a carefully worded surprise release, National Steel announced its intention to divest itself of the facilities at Weirton.

The news exploded upon the town of Weirton with the force of a small atomic bomb, and the shock waves spread out from there. The town drew its economic and spiritual lifeblood from the Weirton plant. Without it, said a local leader, "this place will become a ghost town." Furthermore, the Weirton mill was the primary employer in the entire region. National's decision to phase down and eventually phase out the steel-making activities would eliminate almost eight thousand jobs. The majority of these workers were facing the prospect of unemployment in a region that couldn't absorb them in new jobs. The state of West Virginia stood to lose its largest private source of tax revenues.

The way the announcement was handled by National Steel caused almost as much anger and resentment as the decision itself. While everyone had known that National, like all the other industry giants, was having difficulties with poor corporate results, the employees at Weirton had had no idea that their jobs would be cut as a consequence. The company did nothing to prepare them for the blow. The workers found out about the planned divestiture when it was announced in the media.

This closed-mouth approach to communications within the company long had been the rule rather than the exception at Weirton under National Steel. The flow of information was very restricted. In management's view, knowledge was power, and they had no interest in sharing it with the rank-and-file. Top management alone reviewed financial information. Hourly employees were told nothing about Weirton's profitability or operational performance. In fact, the workers didn't have even basic knowledge about who the plant's customers were, what Weirton steel products were used for, or why things were done the way they were. The relationship between National Steel and Weirton employees was fraught with mistrust. "There was a very deep bitterness on the shop floor," admitted one company director. The men even believed that management kept two sets of books to keep them from catching on to anything. The Independent Steelworkers Unions (ISU) received strong support from the workers, and contract negotiations were always highly adversarial. Company management had been forced over time to sweeten salary and benefits packages, which put Weirton workers considerably above the industry average.

Founding the ESOP

In the March announcement, National Steel offered only one alternative to shutting down the Weirton division: the employees could band together and buy the plant under an ESOP arrangement. Within three days, the division management and the unions had formed a joint study committee to consider the proposal. The path from this initiative to the eventual adoption of the ESOP eighteen months later surmounted many obstacles.

First, the committee hired a leading consulting firm to do a feasibility study. Its findings were not entirely encouraging. Weirton's ability to increase sales dramatically was limited by its equipment, its location, and its markets. Prices could not be raised quickly because competition from imported steel and from domestic steelmakers with excess capacity would continue to depress prices. Weirton would have to reduce costs substantially to become profitable and to have cash for capital improvements. At least one billion dollars in capital expenditures would be necessary over the next

Statements of Operations, 1973–1982 (dollars in millions)

	1973	1974	1975	1976	1977	1978	1979	1980	1981	1982
Net sales	$685	$881	$719	$884	$921	$1,088	$1,179	$1,185	$1,284	$ 904
Cost of goods sold(a)	561	717	628	799	856	962	1,046	1,053	1,133	829
Gross Profit	124	154	91	85	65	126	133	132	151	75
Operating expenses										
Mill overhead	27	31	34	35	39	43	49	54	61	61
Selling, general and administrative	19	17	17	17	20	16	18	20	22	19
Corporate expenses	5	6	6	7	7	19	21	21	21	22
Total	51	54	56	59	66	79	89	95	103	103
Net operating profit (loss)	74	110	35	25	(1)	47	44	37	48	(28)
Other income (loss)	2	1	1	1	1	1	1	3	1	(1)
Other expenses(b)										
Depreciation	22	23	25	27	26	27	28	31	32	30
Other	4	1	7	6	6	5	6	6	0	45(c)
Earnings (loss) before tax	$ 50	$ 87	$ 5	$ (6)	$(33)	$ 16	$ 11	$ 2	$ 11	$(104)

Totals may not add due to rounding.
(a) Includes inventory adjustments and amortization of blast furnace lining expense.
(b) Does not include interest expense, because National did not allocate charges for capital employed on a divisional basis.
(c) Includes non-recurring charge for write-off of coke plant.

Shipment of Products, 1973–1982 (thousands of net tons)

	1973	1974	1975	1976	1977	1978	1979	1980	1981	1982
Hot roll	310	304	189	238	206	244	266	167	178	103
Hot roll bands	40	40	31	26	31	86	87	96	86	76
Cold roll	410	431	265	365	328	372	397	269	249	143
Galvanized	541	530	282	414	402	481	478	383	430	334
Tin plate	1,240	1,271	1,011	1,032	1,078	1,037	1,008	1,063	916	767
Other	227	152	56	110	37	14	7	49	2	—
Subtotal	2,760	2,728	1,834	2,185	2,072	2,234	2,243	2,026	1,859	1,423
Inter-division sales (a)	585	379	299	345	369	526	449	357	595	169
Secondaries (b)	190	109	99	148	198	181	159	124	123	85
Total	3,534	3,217	2,231	2,678	2,640	2,941	2,852	2,507	2,577	1,678
Total excluding secondaries	3,344	3,107	2,133	2,530	2,442	2,760	2,692	2,383	2,454	1,593

(a) Sales to other National divisions.
(b) Aged or off-specification products, which are generally sold at cost.

ten years to modernize the mill facilities and allow Weirton to become fully competitive. But the consulting team concluded that the ESOP could work if Weirton could achieve a 32-percent reduction in employment costs: "an independent Weirton could be successful—but only with deep wage cuts and a better product mix."

Next, the joint committee retained an internationally known banking firm and a law firm to help structure the financing of the ESOP and assist in negotiating the terms of the buyout with National Steel. In coming to the bargaining table, National Steel technically enjoyed a position of advantage. If an agreement couldn't be reached, National would incur the cost of shutting down the plant as well as a substantial pension fund liability; Weirton stood to lose everything.

The costs of the professional services needed by the joint committee to structure the buyout were too great to be covered by the union strike fund and employee contributions. The entire community pitched in to help. A massive fund-raising campaign was run under the slogan, "Share Our New Beginning." Townspeople, businessmen, steelworkers, and their families played donkey basketball, organized fairs and art shows, ran contests and raffles—all to push their new communal dream closer to reality. A Weirton telethon on cable TV—broadcast only in the upper Ohio valley—alone netted $150,000. The cause attracted national media attention, as well as the political support necessary to obtain the tax relief and other agreements crucial to the economics of a buy out. The governor of West Virginia even opened a satellite office down the street from Weirton headquarters. Overall, the New Beginning fund drive raised more than $1.2 million to help defray the consulting and legal fees.

Ultimately, the Weirton negotiating team and National Steel arrived at a complex $386 million deal. National was to received $74 million in cash and hold two promissory notes worth $120 million, while the new Weirton Steel Corporation would assume $192 million of the old division's liabilities. Among the more important terms of the sale was National's continued responsibility for pension liabilities accrued through May 1983. One manager at National lamented that his company had been too accommodating and had "given away the store." A spokesman for Weirton limited himself to saying, "Weirton struck a hard bargain and got a good deal."

Other terms provided for the establishment of an Employee Stock Ownership Trust that would acquire 6.5 million shares of Weirton's authorized common stock in return for a $300 million note. As the Weirton Steel Corporation made annual contributions to the ESOP trust, the trust would return funds to be credited against the trust's note, thereby increasing the owners' equity in the corporation. This new equity, in turn, would be allocated to accounts established for individual employees on the basis of their salary (as a portion of total employee compensation). When all the shares were distributed, union members would control approximately 80 percent of the stock. The agreement would also required that Weirton's board have eight outside directors until 1989. As one of the architects of the deal explained: "This is not industrial democracy, it's worker capitalism. Just like any other company, stockholders do not make day-to-day decisions." Before the deal could become valid, however, a majority of Weirton's employees had to vote for acceptance of all the terms, including the ratification of a new collective bargaining agreement containing the recommended wage reductions.

The final task of the joint committee was to orchestrate the companywide voting procedures. September 23, 1983, was set as Vote Day, when Weirton's unionized employees would express their approval or disapproval of the ESOP. The timing gave the joint committee only about a month to educate the rank and file about the complex issues involved in the ESOP agreement. By now, Loughhead had been officially hired (temporarily as president of National's Weirton division until the acquisition was closed), and he played an active role in selling the deal. In a huge communications push, involving open meetings, telephone hot lines, official disclosure statements, company publications, and other supplementary material, each worker had carefully explained to him what it meant to be an owner as well as an employee.

When Vote Day arrived, much of the city gathered at the community center. The purchase agreement and new labor contract were approved by the steelworkers by a margin of 8 to 1. The whole town of Weirton celebrated with a noisy, spontaneous parade.

The New Communications Program

Now officially the CEO of the Weirton Steel Corporation, Loughhead was faced with the challenge of leading the new enterprise from mere feasibility to a concrete and successful reality. But he found that, in spite of the general jubilation over the ESOP agreement, the relationships between management and the workers were anything but ideal. Some friction and misunderstanding still remained, a troublesome legacy from the days under National.

Loughhead moved quickly to break down these barriers. One of his first major projects was a concentrated effort to improve communications. His plans included frequent interviews, regular press announcements, and corporate advertising to enhance the company's external image. But the primary focus was on radically improving internal communications. In an open letter that went to all Weirton employees even before the formal signing of the agreement with National in early January 1984, Loughhead laid out the details of the new communications program. Common to every element of this program was the underlying belief that the best employees were those who understood the company's business well and appreciated their role in it. Information was to be accurate and unvarnished. The new plant newspaper, *The Independent Weirton,* typified this philosophy: directed by a joint union-management editorial board, it went far beyond the usual limits of a plant newspaper in that the company didn't sanitize its content.

Over the course of the year, all the pieces of the new communications program were put in place. Employee reaction was extremely favorable, and feedback from the workers was plentiful. Based on these responses, the communication channels were refined and expanded. One idea, for example, led to establishing a new opportunity for communication—hourly employees began visiting customer plants to see first-hand how Weirton steel was being used and why quality concerns were of such vital importance.

Loughhead believed that direct contact between himself and the workers was an especially important component of the communications program. He realized that, as the leader of the new Weirton, his actions took on symbolic status; for the hourly worker, he personified the ideas and methods that offered Weirton its hope for the future or its link to the past. Loughhead carefully cultivated an air of approachability and candor in his weekly "face to face" meetings with employees in the various work areas. Together with the president of the labor union, he would talk about the state of the business, listen to comments by the workers, and answer questions. The atmosphere of these sessions was informal; employees found they could ask tough questions and get equally frank responses. Reactions to these meetings were extremely positive.

Since Loughhead could meet with only a relatively small part of Weirton's employees in any given week, he felt that his open letters to the other workers were practical and important extensions of this direct contact. These letters to each "employee-owner" varied in their contact from in-depth discussions of the importance of quality consciousness at Weirton to more general reviews of quarterly results. The quarterly review letter was, by now, an entrenched tradition. Loughhead aimed at fleshing out the results in a personal way for the employees— before the official news release went out to the public, or even before the results were published in *The Independent Weirton,* as was the usual practice.

December 8, 1983

Dear Fellow Employee:

In one of my recent letters, I told you that we were developing a program of employee communications that would keep *everyone* informed about what was happening in our new company. That communications program is now well along, and this is a report to you on what you may expect in the near future.

The program has been discussed with the I.S.U. and I.G.U. leadership as well as key people throughout our company. I'm happy to report that these people have been enthusiastic about the idea of increased communications and the way we plan to go about it.

Here is what is in the works:

New employee publication—This will be a monthly tabloid and will bring you a wide variety of news and opinion about all phases of Weirton Steel's activity—changes, improvements, sales success, production records, new equipment, stories about our employees, our involvement in the community, special problems we must solve—and a lot more. One special section will be employee feedback—a "man-in-the-street" feature that will carry your response to an important and timely question.

Two current publications, "Independent Weirton" and "Current Events" will become part of the new employee publication. The type of articles usually found in those publications will now be regular features in the new tabloid.

By absorbing the two publications, we'll be able to have expanded communications without greatly expanding the cost.

On-stream date: First issue in late December or early January.

Employee Mailings—This will be a series of mailings to your home on those subjects *you* want to know about. In addition, these mailings will be used to bring you news about important developments that are too "hot" to hold for an upcoming issue of the employee tabloid.

In the beginning, these mailings will come from me. Later on, you'll also be hearing from other people in our organization.

An important part of our communication program will be *your* feedback. So that you can give me your reaction *and* your ideas and opinions, almost every mailing will include a reply form. One of these reply forms is part of this mailing.

Bulletin Boards—We will have a bright, clean, well-lighted and well-maintained bulletin board in at least forty-five locations. If you would like to see a board installed where one does not now exist, let us know. (Use the appropriate space on the enclosed form.)

On-stream date: Renovation of boards to begin no later than January 1.

"Face to Face"—This part of our communication program will be a continuous series of meetings in which I'll visit work areas and office areas to give you a chance to ask questions and voice your opinions and concerns face to face. In turn, I'll try to bring you the latest news and developments at Weirton Steel.

On-stream date: Already underway; meetings have been held in the Central Machine Shop, Sheet Mill, and the Blast Furnace. A schedule of subsequent meetings is included with this mailing.

Pipeline—We're revising this telephone "hot line" to make it more useful to you and more responsive. First, we'll eliminate the one-minute "commercial" you hear when you call in. Second, we'll answer the phone "live" as often as we can (rather than use a tape recorder exclusively). Third, we'll acknowledge all calls within twenty-four hours. Fourth, we'll get back to you with answers promptly and directly.

On-stream date: "Pipeline" is now operating; by December 15 we'll be answering "live" part of the time and will acknowledge all taped calls within twenty-four hours.

Internal TV Network—We now have thirty TV monitors and the same number of tape decks throughout our facility. We believe we can add just a few more and create a "network" that will enable us to do many good things with our communications. Some examples are training, news that "won't wait," in-depth discussions of important issues by the heads of I.S.U., I.G.U. and myself, customer stories (so we can all see where and how our products are used), successful new applications—and a lot more.

On-stream date: Full network by February 28; thirty operational units by January 30.

The items above are just seven of the communication vehicles we are preparing for you; there are several more in the planning stage, and I'll be telling you about them in the coming weeks.

I can promise you one thing for certain: our communications with each other are going to be the very best they can be.

But—communications won't work if they are just one-way. And that's why we need your help. We need to know your ideas, your opinions, your concerns. The communications must be *two-way.* In other words, input form you and your fellow employees is vital.

I'll provide the means if you provide the input. We can start with the reply form and envelope enclosed with this letter; you can give me your reaction to the communications program and tell me what else you would like to hear about.

With your input and your interest, communications can be one of the driving forces behind our success. Let's make Weirton Steel not only the largest, successful employee-owned company in the world, but also the company with the best informed, most communicative employees.

Sincerely,

Robert L. Loughhead
President

Enclosures

Mr. Loughhead:

Here are my reactions to the planned program of communications at Weirton Steel:

________ I like the idea of more communications

________ I don't like the idea

Here's why:

____

____

____

I believe we can improve communications by doing the following:

____

____

____

Here are subjects I would like to know more about:

____

____

____

Here's where I think a new bulletin board should be located:

____

____

____

Name______________________________
Department______________________________
Address______________________________
City/State______________________________

____

The Quarterly Letter: March 1985

Loughhead thought he would try to present the results from the latest quarter in the context of Weirton's operations since the establishment of the ESOP at the start of 1984. (Exhibit 35–2 shows financial statements from 1984 and first quarter of 1985.) He had been generally pleased by the successes that Weirton Steel had achieved during the last year, and he knew that the workers had been pleased as well. The company's healthy performance, contrasting sharply with the losses and marginal profits under National, validated the new ways of working together and the many sacrifices that had been made. Loughhead wanted to reinforce the positive aspects of what had been accomplished, but at the same time, he aimed to present a balanced and realistic picture of exactly how far Weirton still had to go.

Weirton had slated an ambitious capital spending program that would be creating tremendous future cash flow requirements. The need to continue rebuilding and modernizing the plant was urgent. It was anticipated that another $300 million to 400 million in capital would be needed over the next five years just to stay competitive. In 1985 alone, $65 million in expenditures had been planned for pollution control, to build blast furnaces, revamp a galvanizing line, and improve a continuous casting machine. These improvements could lead to improved product capabilities and considerably lower costs, but such benefits would be realized only further down the line.

The profit-sharing mechanism, almost surely to be triggered during the 1985 fiscal year, was creating yet another strain on the corporation's cash flow. The ESOP agreement had provided for the allocation of one third of earnings to the employees in the form of cash to begin when the company's total equity exceeded the $100 million mark. Loughhead knew that the workers would be particularly interested in hearing that preparations were being made for disbursements. After sacrificing pay and benefits to get the Weirton Steel Corporation off the ground, employees were anxious to see tangible returns. Already this quarter, the company had begun to provide for the liability so that the impact would be spread over several quarters.

To meet these cash demands, Loughhead knew that earnings levels higher than those of the first quarter would have to be maintained.

EXHIBIT 35–2 ▪ Weirton Steel Corporation: Financial Statements (dollars in thousands)

Year/Quarter	1984/1	2	3	4	1985/1
Net sales	$283,127	306,276	256,110	229,614	295,562
Cost and expense	267,019	276,638	233,677	211,733	279,607
Operating profit	16,108	29,638	22,433	17,881	15,955
Interest expense	6,433	6,884	6,595	5,528	5,766
PBT	9,675	22,754	15,838	12,353	10,189
PBT (% of sales)	3.42	7.43	6.18	5.38	3.45
Tons shipped	572.7	610.8	485.2	439.0	592.4

Steel prices showed no sign of lending a hand. Selling prices remained very depressed, putting great pressure on margins. U.S. steelmakers, operating at low capacity levels, were discounting heavily in the marketplace. Import levels remained very high despite efforts by the Reagan Administration to negotiate voluntary import restraints with foreign producers. In short, Loughhead realized that, despite the uplift in the economy, competitive conditions continued to be exceptionally severe. Weirton Steel would have to look instead to stringent cost reduction measures, productivity gains, quality improvements, and higher yields as the best means for relieving the margin squeeze and freeing up additional cash.

Loughhead didn't want to forget to mention, however, that Weirton's bookings for the second quarter were good in all areas. The company had succeeded in gaining forty-eight new customers in the first quarter. Combined with the two hundred customers gained in 1984, these new clients would help keep up operating and employment levels.

36

School of Education: Case of a Contracting Organization

"How negative do you feel today, Slocum?" inquired Johnson, who was the assistant dean for programs and chairman of the reorganization committee, half in jest and half seriously of the educational administration professor. The school reorganization committee was meeting to discuss problems arising from the recent reorganization of the school.

The school had begun as a Department of Education and Psychology within a small teachers college. In 1964, Psychology became a separate department, followed in 1967 by the Elementary and Secondary Education Departments. Special Education, Educational Administration, and Counselor Education were separated out in 1970. Finally in 1973, the Student Teaching Department was formed (see Exhibit 36–1).

Dr. Anderson had been dean since 1967. Prior to that he was chairman of the Department of Education and Psychology. Having been at the university since 1948, he was now nearing retirement. A man of integrity, he was respected by most of his faculty.

The dean had tried to persuade the School of Education faculty to reorganize in 1972 and 1975. He had proposed combining the departments of Elementary Education, Secondary Education, and Student Teaching to form a Teacher Education Department. The other departments were to remain intact. Both attempts at reorganization failed in the face of considerable faculty opposition.

By 1979, when the dean made his third attempt at reorganizing the school, conditions had changed. Student credit hours (SCH) within the school had decreased by 14 percent since 1975. Full-time-equated (FTE) faculty positions had decreased 6 percent. The Department of Psychology was the only department that was growing. Their SCHs had increased 12 percent and their FTE 32 percent since 1975 (see Exhibit 36–2). If the Department of Psychology was excluded from the School of Edu-

Written by Mahmoud A. Moursi and Susan K. Smith. Reprinted with permission of Mahmoud A. Moursi, Professor, Central Michigan University.

EXHIBIT 36–1 ■ School of Education Organization Chart, August 1979

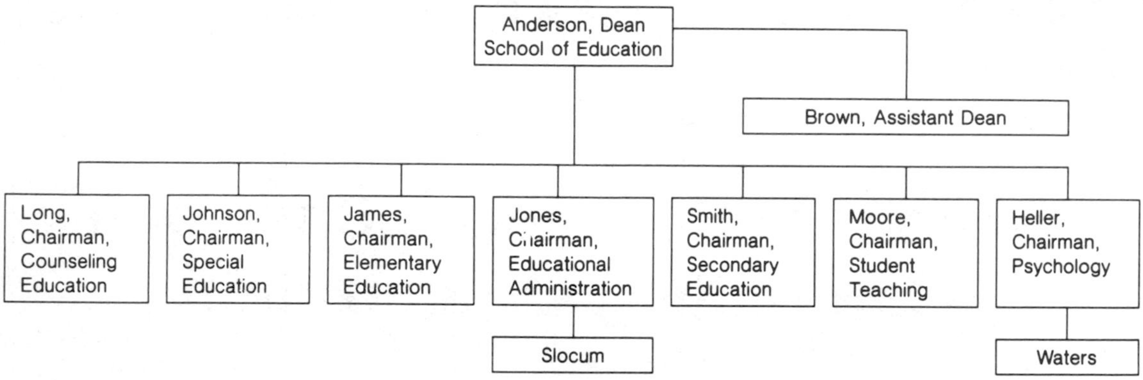

Source: Dean's Office

cation figures, the school decrease in SCH for 1975–80 was 27 percent, and the decrease in FTE was 20 percent (see Exhibit 36–3).

The provost supported the reorganization. The university had originally been a teachers college, but changes in the job market and accompanying changes in student career interests had resulted in the development of a new mission for the university. The education of teachers was no longer the basic purpose of the university. Rather, the professional education of business men and women was the university's new mission.

Since the university used a "student driven" model, declining enrollment in the School of Education had resulted in a decreased allotment of full-time-equated teaching positions to the school. Under these circumstances, contracting the organization from seven to three departments, was an appropriate response from the point of view of the Provost's office.

The decrease in FTE faculty positions was causing problems for the school since 85 percent of its faculty were tenured. Four departments, Counselor Education, Secondary Education, Elementary Education, and Educational Administration, were fully tenured. Most of the faculty had been with the school for many years (see Exhibit 36–4).

In August 1979, the dean proposed a more sweeping reorganization than he had in 1972 and 1975. Not only were Special Education, Student Teaching, Secondary Education, and Elementary Education to be combined into Teacher Education, two of the remaining three departments, Counselor Education and Educational Administration, were to be combined into Educational Services (name changed later to Counseling, Educational Administration, Library Materials, and Community Leadership). The Psychology Department, as before, was to remain untouched.

The reorganization would require some people to move to different buildings so that members of the same department could be together (see Exhibit 36–5).

An implementation committee, chaired by the dean and consisting of representatives from each of the departments, was charged with developing a proposal on which the faculty could vote on November 9.

The proposal was based on the dean's recommendation, and presented only one reorganization plan. The committee had added a transitional structure, departmental units, to the dean's proposal (see Exhibit 36–6).

The units, corresponding to the former departments, would be headed by unit coordinators. According to the proposal, the continuation of the units depended upon the departmental task forces created to develop departmental procedures. Each department

EXHIBIT 36–2 ▪ On Campus SCH[1] Production, FTE[2] Teaching Positions, 1975–1980

	1975–76	1976–77	1977–78	1978–79	1979–80	% Change 1975–80
School Education						
SCH	89,600	87,184	86,229	84,620	77,339	−14%
FTE	141.71	137.71	138.32	134.53	133.28	−6%
Dept. Counselor Education						
SCH	4,758	4,345	3,505	3,432	3,173	−33%
FTE	10.79	8.96	8.47	7.17	7.13	−34%
Dept. Elementary Education						
SCH	12,679	12,401	12,284	11,835	10,707	−16%
FTE	22.20	19.80	20.04	19.47	19.80	−11%
Dept. Educational Administration and Library Science						
SCH	6,163	4,911	5,092	4,436	3,823	−38%
FTE	10.78	11.38	11.45	10.33	10.14	−6%
Dept. Psychology						
SCH	31,065	33,422	35,689	36,318	34,560	+12%
FTE	37.01	39.92	46.19	47.61	48.92	+32%
Dept. Secondary Education						
SCH	10,324	9,696	7,903	7,623	6,715	−35%
FTE	16.70	15.37	13.10	11.79	11.64	−30%
Dept. Special Education						
SCH	7,200	6,787	6,730	6,405	5,983	−17%
FTE	10.51	10.13	9.98	10.77	10.29	−2%
Dept. Student Teaching						
SCH	17,411	15,622	14,971	14,372	12,210	−30%
FTE	33.22	31.05	28.12	26.26	24.99	−25%

[1]SCH: student credit hours
[2]FTE: full-time-equated
Source: Office of University Planning and Research

would also be directed to form a program task force charged with reviewing programs and curriculum. The task forces would have time limits within which to complete their work. In addition, an ongoing School Organization Committee would be formed and charged with resolving problems that arose out of the reorganization.

The proposal was voted upon in November and passed 61 to 27. Most of the support for the proposal came from the two departments least affected by the change: psychology and student teaching.

Psychology was not really involved since that department was not changed and members did not interact very much with the rest of the school faculty.

Student teaching consisted primarily of off-campus faculty who supervised student teachers in various locations throughout the state. As

EXHIBIT 36–3 ■ SCH[1] and FTE[2] of School of Education, Excluding Psychology Department

	1975–80					Differences:
Year	**1975–76**	**1976–77**	**1977–78**	**1978–79**	**1979–80**	**1975–80**
School SCH	89,600	87,184	86,229	84,620	77,339	−12,261
Psych SCH	31,065	33,422	35,689	36,318	34,560	+3,495
School-Psych SCH	58,535	53,762	50,540	48,302	42,779	−15,756
% Decrease, SCH	—	8%	6%	4%	11%	−27%
Psych as % of Total School SCH	35%	38%	41%	43%	45%	
School FTE	142	138	138	135	133	−9
Psych FTE	37	40	46	48	49	+12
School-Psych FTE	105	98	92	87	84	−21
% Decrease, FTE	—	7%	6%	5%	3%	−20%
Psych as % of Total School FTE	26%	29%	33%	36%	37%	

[1]Student credit hour
[2]Full-time-equated
Source: University Office of Planning & Research

a result, they were more aware of the need to update the school's curriculum and were supportive of the dean's desire to make programmatic changes in the school. They had attempted to bring about changes in curriculum themselves but had been rebuffed by the on-campus faculty.

Johnson: All right, let's get going. Last week we looked over Wells and Moody Hall to see where we could put people and I think...

Slocum: Forget it. The people in my department are not going to move out of Wells into Moody Hall. They like the offices they have now; they've been there a long time and they don't want to move in with those guys in Moody Hall. Some of them are even afraid of the rats "Psych" has over there. We didn't want to go in with Counselor Education in the first place. I've been a professor of Educational Administration throughout my career. Now I'm a professor of Counseling, Educational Administration, Library Media, and Community Leadership. The other people in my profession don't even know what that is! Another thing, we don't have anything in common with those counselors. They're all wrapped up in people and their emotions. We take a straightforward, objective view of problems. We're concerned with systems, not individuals.

Johnson: I know there are problems with putting those two departments together, but each one is too small to continue as a separate entity. With decreasing resources the Dean had to get rid of the small departments. I'll admit I thought he should have put Counselor Education in with the school psychologists in the Psychology Department. They at least have something in common.

EXHIBIT 36–4 ▪ Faculty Tenure, Fall 1980

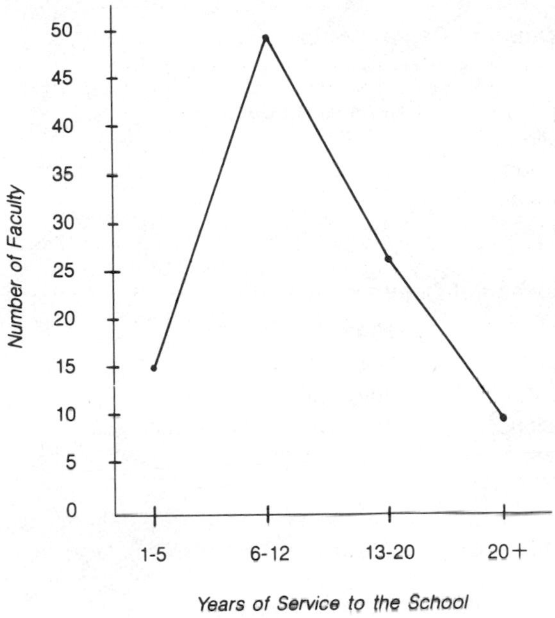

Waters: No way. The school psychologists are in my department and they wouldn't stand for it. The credentials of school psychologists and counselors are completely different. School psychologists have much more extensive training requirements than counselors. Putting those two groups together wouldn't work at all. You know, someone should have paid more attention to how this whole thing was going to come out. There is a lot more involved in change than just drawing boxes on an organization chart. This reorganization has had a big impact on people: both faculty and staff.

Johnson: Let's get back to the space problems. The dean wants Educational Administration to move into Moody and Special Education to move out of Fenwick into Wells. That way each of the departments will have all their people in the same building.

Smith: Well I hate to break this up, but I have a class at 11 and I have to get back to Wells Hall. It would sure help if we had release time to work on these committees. Some of my people are complaining about the way the departmental task forces are cutting into their class preparation time.

Johnson: OK, we'll meet again next week. Wait a minute, Smith, and I'll walk to Wells with you. I need to stop at the dean's office.

Later on their way across campus, Smith, who was chairman of the new Department of Teacher Education and former chairman of the Secondary Education Department, asked Johnson how the faculty in Special Education felt about the reorganization.

Johnson: They're very concerned. As you know, a lot of them are relatively young and new to the University. Going from a department of seven to one of fifty-six is quite a change. They are especially concerned about getting tenure. The rest of the faculty in the teacher education department don't know them very well and they are not that familiar with special education. How are the special education faculty going to be evaluated? Also, it's well known that Secondary Education has four more tenured positions than it should have according to the Provost's office, and that when people leave those positions, they won't be replaced. It looks to me as though it's going to be hard for any of my people to get tenure and if anyone has to be laid off, they'll be the first to go.

Smith: Well, I hope it doesn't come to that. Although do you realize that in 1971, 2,300 people were recommended for certification and this year we're only recommending nine hundred? What concerns me are these confounded units. Here I am, chairman of the department, and the unit coordinators are acting like department chairmen. They're signing drop and add cards, approving budgets, and recruiting staff. The units are acting just like mini-departments.

Johnson: That's because this is a year of transition. The units are supposed to fade away after this year, according to the dean. Not everyone agrees with that though.

EXHIBIT 36–5 ■ Departmental Locations

Pre-reorganization: Location of Departments

Fenwick	Wells	Moody
Psychology Special Education	Student Teaching Secondary Education Elementary Education Education Administration and Library-Media	Counseling Education

Post-reorganization: Location of Departments

Fenwick	Wells	Moody
Psychology	Teacher Education Student Teaching Secondary Education Elementary Education Special Education	C.E.A.L.M.C.L.[1] Counseling Education Educational Administration Library-Media

[1]Counseling, Educational Administration, Library Media, and Community Leadership.

Smith: That's for sure. Some of my faculty maintain these units can go on forever if the department decides to keep them. To hear them talk, there hasn't been any change at all.

Johnson: Then what's the point of the reorganization?

Smith: Beats me, but keeping these units is a neat way to finesse the reorganization.

Johnson: Why do you suppose psychology wasn't touched by any of this?

Smith: Rumor has it that the dean didn't want to do anything that might encourage them to leave the school. After all, they're the only department that's growing and if they went to Liberal Arts, we would lose a lot of FTE.

Meanwhile, two of the Counseling Education faculty were discussing the reorganization over their morning coffee.

Miller: I'm supposed to go to one of those task force meetings again this afternoon. What a waste of time!

Terry: And all for nothing, too. The only money the reorganization saves is a couple of department chairperson's salaries, and that doesn't amount to anything.

Miller: Let's face it. The real reason the dean wanted this reorganization is so that he can go out in a blaze of glory!

Terry: That's for sure. We don't have a thing in common with those guys from educational administration. I hope they never do move over here.

Later that day, Johnson, who had become the second assistant dean as a part of the reorganization, met with the dean.

Dean: How did your meeting go this morning, Mike?

Johnson: About the same. Slocum is dragging his feet and we can't seem to resolve the space issue. Educational Administration probably isn't going to move unless you tell them they must.

Dean: It's frustrating to have all this resistance. They don't seem to realize how important this is to the school. We need to cut costs and the reorganization will allow us to reduce administrative expenses. More than that, it will permit us to be more flexible. We have to expand our mission beyond that of educating the classroom teacher. We could

EXHIBIT 36–6 ■ School of Education Organization Chart, August 1980

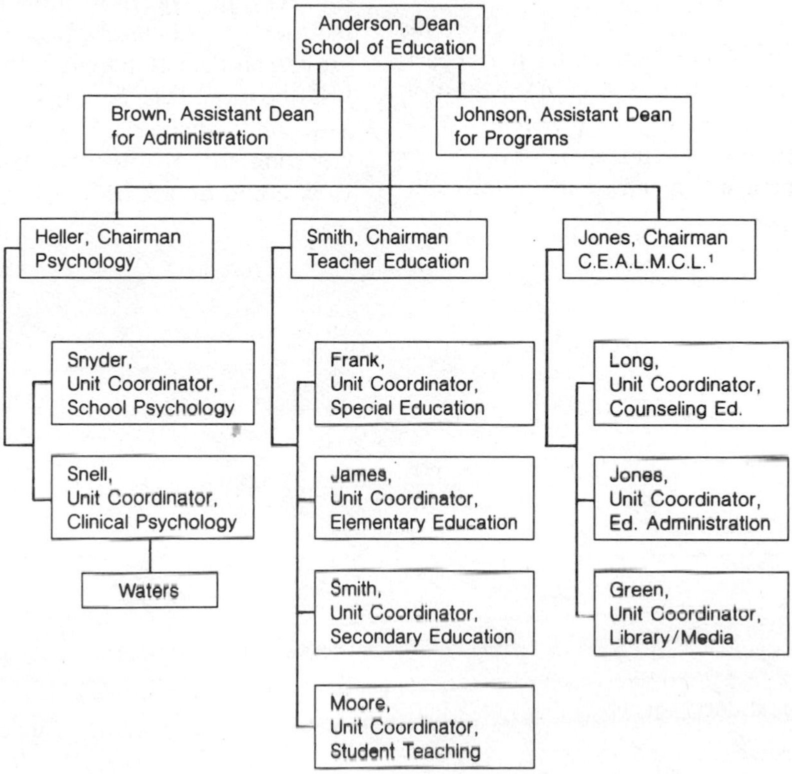

[1]Counseling, Educational Administration, Library Media, and Community Leadership.

be educating people who are training personnel outside the classroom, such as in the private sector. Also, with the emphasis on "mainstreaming" we need to have special education faculty interacting with elementary education and secondary education.

Johnson: I agree with your reasons for reorganizing, dean, but unless you take a stronger stand it's not going to happen. There are many people opposing the change, and unless you use stronger leadership, these committees are going to study it to death.

The next morning the dean met with the other assistant dean, Dr. Brown, who was also a professor of psychology.

Dean: Good morning, Louise. I wanted to speak with you about the reorganization. You talk to a lot of people. How do you think it's going?

Brown: Well, in teacher education it's beginning to come along. The chairman has a nice informal way about him that will bring those people around eventually. Jones, on the other hand, is coming on rather strongly. Most of the people in his department are maintaining their old territorial boundaries and hoping the reorganization will go away.

Dean: What do you think about the relocation of educational administration to Moody at this point?

Brown: Financially, it has to be done. We must reduce some of these administrative expenses. I hope you are successful in persuading them to move. If you force them, however, I am afraid they may bring in the faculty union.

After Dr. Brown left, the dean pondered his options. Should he continue to let the departmental task forces and School Organization Committee try to resolve the problems of the unit structure and the allocation of space, or should he play a stronger role in the process? He would be retiring in a year or two, and he wanted to accomplish the reorganization before leaving. The dean thought about how he had devoted his entire professional life to the growth and development of the school. Now he had one more task, getting the organization into a stronger position to cope with its changing environment. He needed that reorganization! How could he get it?

37

Changing a Corporate Culture: Can Johnson & Johnson Go from Band-Aids to High Tech?

On Albany Street in gritty New Brunswick, N.J., stands Johnson & Johnson's sleek new headquarters. The modernistic aluminum-and-glass structure designed by I. M. Pei stands in marked contrast to Kilmer House, the undistinguished brick building nearby that was its home from the late 1890s until last year. The new architectural face is richly symbolic, for it mirrors the more subtle changes under way within one of the most consistently successful companies in the world.

Best known to consumers for such brands as Band-Aids and Baby Shampoo, J & J has embarked on an accelerated move into far more sophisticated medical technologies. The shift poses big risks, since success depends on whether J & J can manage businesses very different from those it has dominated. And to achieve his goals, Chairman James E. Burke is tinkering in subtle but important ways with a management style and corporate culture that have long been central to the company's success.

Marketing Prowess

A good deal is at stake: In addition to its consumer brands, J & J holds powerful and profitable franchises in hospital supplies and prescription drugs. For years, these product lines have flourished under a marketing-dominated, decentralized management structure. While scores of companies are struggling to eliminate corporate bureaucracies and give power back to operations, J & J is already there.

The people running its 170 "companies" enjoy autonomy unheard of in most corporations. Most divisions have their own boards. Corporate headquarters staff is a scant 750 people. And only one management layer separates division presidents from the fourteen-member executive committee to whom they report.

It is obvious why J & J is held up as an example of decentralization's virtues. Its earnings growth in the last ten years has averaged 13 percent annually. The company says 55 percent of 1983's $6 billion in sales and much of its $489 million in earnings came from products that are No. 1 in their markets. And the resuscitation of its Tylenol pain reliever after the 1982 deaths of seven people who had taken cyanide-laced capsules, its repositioning of Baby Shampoo for the adult market, and its come-from-nowhere move to No. 2 in infants' toys demonstrate its legendary marketing prowess.

But while J & J's core businesses remain solidly profitable, Burke believes that maturing markets limit long-term growth potential. Moreover, scientific and technological advances promise to revolutionize health care. Thus, the push into technology "is absolutely critical to the future and to the present," he states flatly. Without it "we would be heading toward being just another company."

So since 1980, J & J has acquired twenty-five companies, many in promising, high-tech markets. Burke, who became CEO in 1976, has positioned J & J in products ranging from intraocular lenses and surgical lasers to magnetic-resonance scanners for diagnostic imaging.

Now, however, the longtime dominance of marketing and sales executives and the insularity of J & J's units could seriously impede the company's ability to push successfully into these new businesses and to react swiftly to changing competitive conditions in health care. Burke himself recognizes that the company's success will require greater cooperation among corporate units. And he has found that such cooperation can be hard to obtain. Former J & J executives assert, for example, that at least two key managers of J & J's Ethicon Inc., the world's largest maker of sutures, left during a struggle to persuade the unit to go along with a centralized ordering-and-distribution effort deemed critical to maintaining J & J's leading position in hospital supplies.

Learning to manage new businesses is also a major task, as evidenced by the management problems that have plagued the push into medical equipment, where losses have been heavy. One big reason for the red ink is the investment made to position companies such as Technicare Corp.—a maker of diagnostic-imaging equipment, purchased in 1979—for the long haul. The money was spent mainly to develop new products, including magnetic-resonance (MR) machines that provide strikingly clear images of the body's tissue without using radiation.

Dollars alone, however, will not solve the problems at these businesses:

Extracorporeal Inc.

Product-development problems at Extracorporeal, bought in 1978, left its dialysis equipment business with outmoded offerings when the market changed. J & J took a $38 million write-off last year and put the dialysis business on the block.

Ortho Diagnostic Systems Inc.

Organizational turmoil has hurt this maker of blood-analysis equipment and reagents. From 1977 to 1981, the marginally profitable Ortho went through four presidents. Long a leader in the field, Ortho failed to latch on to hot new technologies in the 1970s. "It was a general management and research management failure," admits executive committee member Verne M. Willaman. As a result, Ortho has been forced into an expensive catch-up effort. And although J & J denies them, rumors-persist that Ortho, too, will be sold.

Technicare Corp.

Customer relations problems stemming from reportedly overengineered products that were hard to use have hurt Technicare. It has lost $110 million since 1979, according to Larry N. Feinberg, an analyst at Dean Witter Reynolds Inc. In computer-assisted-tomography (CAT) scanners, these difficulties helped General Electric Co. to snatch the top spot away from Technicare. Some outsiders predict the same thing could happen with MR machines, which GE just started selling.

Burke acknowledges that his company's record in medical equipment is undistinguished, grading the efforts anywhere "from E-minus to A-plus." But he says: "One of the things we insist on here is that everybody understands part of their job is to fail. You don't move forward unless you make mistakes." The willingness to admit problems and try to learn from them is a J & J strength. The key question, however, is whether the company can apply the lessons to its new businesses.

More than one successful CEO has found that changing his company's mix of businesses is a lot easier than changing managers' attitudes. William T. Ylvisaker succeeded in transforming Gould Inc. into an electronics company only by replacing dozens of key managers. At Emerson Electric Co., a corporate culture that made a religion of cost-cutting and the bottom line threatens Charles F. Knight's ambitions in high tech. And Ruben F. Mettler has experienced some problems getting TRW Inc.'s divisions to share their expertise so the company can make maximum use of its considerable technological strengths.

J & J is discovering that developing and marketing high-tech equipment requires markedly different management skills than selling the products that generated its rapid growth. J & J was founded in 1885 by three Johnson brothers. But the next generation—in the person of "the General," Robert Wood Johnson—is most responsible for shaping the company into its present form. Under the General's rule from 1938 to 1963, the decentralized structure that is J & J's hallmark took shape, and the company introduced many of its most dominant products.

Pills Vs. Hardware

The General also wrote the corporate credo, which states that J & J's first responsibility is not to shareholders or employees but to "the doctors, nurses, patients, to mothers, and all others" who use its products. While many high-minded statements of corporate purpose are written and forgotten, J & J's is not.

That tradition may also explain why, despite Burke's ambitions in new technologies, virtually all of the fourteen members of J & J's executive committee have consumer-marketing or pharmaceutical backgrounds. And all have been at the company at least eleven years.

After a stint at Procter & Gamble Co., Burke joined J & J in 1953 and rose through the marketing ranks to become chairman in 1976. Initially, Burke ran the Band-Aid, dental-floss, and first-aid-kit businesses. As chairman, he personally led the marketing campaign to revive Tylenol. And colleagues say Burke foresaw the shift of emphasis in health care to early detection and prevention of illness.

Because its strength is in making and marketing consumer products, some competitors and J & J alumni doubt the company can become a leader in medical equipment. "What pill people have done well in hardware, and what hardware people have done well in pills?" asks GE's chairman, John F. Welch Jr. "The road is strewn with people who have gone far afield [from the businesses they really know]."

The lack of experience in medical equipment probably helps explain why Burke has moved cautiously in the field. At $74 million, J & J's acquisition of Technicare is its largest. And even though research-and-development spending has doubled since 1979 and will continue to rise, there is a limit to J & J's daring.

In MR scanners, for instance, GE's Welch makes no bones about his willingness to spend whatever it takes to be the leader. Technicare President Joseph G. Teague, however, says: "We don't have it as a realistic strategy to be No. 1" in the United States in several years. Matching GE's expenditures dollar for dollar, he adds, could be "frivolous and very expensive."

The questions of J & J's ability to make it in medical equipment go far beyond its financial commitment. More important is whether it has the management talent. The company's only clear high-tech success is Iolab Corp., the $50 million maker of lenses that are implanted after the surgical removal of cataracts.

Although J & J installed its own man, John R. Gilbert, as president about a year after buying Iolab, he has demonstrated a willingness to use new management approaches. He spent considerable time learning the manufacturing process, talking to physicians, and questioning the company's founders, who had left—on amicable terms. Iolab's results have been impressive: Sales have jumped nearly fivefold since the acquisition. If J & J had tried to manage Iolab like one of its more established companies, "we would have failed," concedes Herbert G. Stolzer, Gilbert's boss on J & J's executive committee.

J & J's attempts to manage other medical equipment acquisitions have not been similarly successful. Like many big companies, it has had trouble keeping the entrepreneurs who build the acquired companies. "The thinking is, perhaps understandably, 'Follow us, we have the keys to the kingdom,' " says one alumnus. J & J's financial systems and controls so bothered some managers at Extracorporeal, for instance, that they left, former J & Jers say. "That drives a lot of entrepreneurs crazy," concedes Burke.

Nothing better illustrates that the J & J system does not always contain the keys to the kingdom than its experience with Extracorporeal's dialysis business. Soon after J & J bought the company in 1978, prices for dialyzers—the filters used to clean blood—plunged as the government limited medicare reimbursements. When cost-conscious customers began reusing dialyzers, J & J found itself at a disadvantage, because competitors' products could be prepared for reuse more easily.

'Sea Change'

J & J failed to adapt. As Burke explains it, J & J is so accustomed to selling products used once—often in sterile environments—"that it was appalling to us to think that those things would become reusable."

The kind of cooperation and communication that Burke deems essential for all J & J companies also has been alien to its culture. Burke believes that sharing R & D and marketing resources is a key to speeding product development. That, he says, will enable J & J to regain share in such traditional markets as hospital supplies and to exploit new opportunities created by the movement toward preventive health care. For example, he says, combining J & J's expertise in magnetic resonance and biotechnology could revolutionize diagnostics.

But even Burke acknowledges that persuading divisions to work together has required "a sea change in attitude" for J & J managers so used to independence. One J & J unit, notes J & J President David R. Clare, even refused to take managers from other J & J companies.

Burke and Clare have moved to break down the walls. They have increased the movement of managers between companies and placed more importance on corporate-level committees whose function is to facilitate the exchange of information between companies.

But mixed signals from the top have left some divisional managers confused about just how committed to togetherness their leaders are. A case in point: Johnson & Johnson Products, which sells bandages and splints; Surgikos, a maker of surgical gowns and disinfectants; and Ethicon, the suture division, recently proposed that the three package their products in a customized surgical kit. But to their frustration, the divisions' managers have yet to secure New Brunswick's approval.

So it is no surprise that as J & J top managers preach the gospel of cooperation, some in their congregation react with more skepticism than faith. Nowhere is this more evident than in New Brunswick's tribulations in inducing its hospital-supply companies to work together—an effort one former J & J executive dubs "the company's single biggest move away from decentralization."

In a belated attempt to respond to increasing hospital cost-consciousness and the inroads American Hospital Supply Corp. has made into its business, J & J created its Hospital Services Co., which is giving volume discounts to some twenty-four hospitals on products from seven J & J companies. Crucial to making the plan pay off will be the likely development of a central, computerized ordering system that should considerably reduce customer paperwork and, finally, match what its competition created in 1976.

Less Grumbling

Some J & J managers have resisted the effort long past a sensible point. "People got fired for not supporting [Hospital Services]," says a former J & Jer who did stints in three of the companies involved. Although J & J denies this, it concedes that managers at Ethicon were resistant to change. Edward J. Hartnett, a company group chairman in New Brunswick, says, "The feeling was, 'I don't really need it.' "

Perhaps because centralization is such a sensitive issue at J & J, Burke and Clare sharply deny that Hospital Services is even a baby step in that direction. The companies involved in the effort will maintain separate sales forces—an indication that the two executives understand that instilling a cooperative spirit will take patience and time. Clare points to J & J's Absorbent Technology Group—a four-company effort to develop products for several markets—as an example of how hostility fades once a payback is evident. Clare himself had to muscle the companies into participating. But now that the group has three products under development, grumbling has diminished.

Burke and Clare have plenty of time. While some consumer markets, such as Band-Aids, are maturing, they are still solidly profitable. Indeed, J & J's 1981 withdrawal from the U.S. disposable-diaper market is the exception rather than the rule. In the last year, J & J rolled out a record six consumer products, ranging from a shampoo for the more brittle hair of women over 40 to a disposable dust cloth that eliminates the need for sprays.

J & J's record in pharmaceuticals demonstrates that there are areas of high science and technology that it indisputably knows how to manage. The $1.2 billion combined sales of its four pharmaceutical divisions make J & J the fifth-largest drug company in the United States. More than 40 percent of its R & D spending, which last year totaled $405 million, or 6.8 percent of sales, went to pharmaceuticals. Such investments already appear to be bearing fruit: J & J now has twice as many new drugs undergoing animal testing as it did five years ago.

Indeed, as significant as the internal challenges at J & J are, another important one comes from without—namely, government efforts to curtail hospital expenditures on sophisticated medical hardware. Burke argues that such hardware can identify health problems before they become catastrophic—and catastrophically expensive to treat.

But given uncertainties clouding the medical technology markets, GE's Welch cautions that the wisest strategy is simply to have "the best. There's no room for the third-best machine." In hardware, Welch scoffs that J & J is no match for GE. His advice to Burke: "People who go afar from what they know run into some ground holes." Burke's challenge is to prove J & J can climb out of them.

38

Sole Survivors

There were around 350 of them, and only one of him. But Tommy Hewitt was ready for battle.

He didn't have to wait for long. By the time he started speaking, there were plenty of angry faces among the employees of Servus Rubber Co. Most of the workers were older than the thirty-five-year-old Hewitt, and some had been making boots since before he was born. Yet here he was, an outsider dressed in khaki pants and leather moccasins, asking them to make concessions so that he and a partner could buy the company.

Drowned out at times by boos and hisses, Hewitt got only halfway through his presentation. "You're just trying to take things away from us," yelled one worker, challenging Hewitt's claim that Servus's parent company had plans to shut it down. Then came a long volley of questions. Why should we give up a week's vacation? What are you going to do with the salary you want to defer? "We can't support our families now," shouted one man. "How can we give all this up?"

Hewitt didn't get a chance to answer. "Do you want to work?" yelled the union vice-president. "We have to help them. We don't have a choice. Do you want to be out on the street?"

It was 1982, and the streets of Rock Island, Ill., were just starting to get crowded with people out of work. At International Harvester, Deere, and J. I. Case, production was shrinking. And the smaller manufacturers were losing business as subcontracting work winged overseas. Now, it was Servus's turn.

That night at the Rock Island Moose Club, a local fraternal lodge, the workers approved Hewitt's plans by a decisive vote. "It was the only future we had," says one worker, shrugging. Nobody could have predicted what the new owners had in mind. Maybe Hewitt and Michael Cappy would continue trying to compete at the low end of the market against cheap

Korean boots. Or maybe they would even padlock the factory and become a marketing group. In any case, Servus would never be an industry leader again.

Or would it?

A presidential candidate might well come to Rock Island, a living symbol of America's industrial decline, to highlight his commitment to competitiveness. On a quick tour of Servus Rubber, he might promise to fight for American jobs.

There is no kind of government intervention, though, that could have rescued a company like Servus. A tariff on Korean boots wouldn't have helped. Nor would a more favorable foreign-exchange rate. Servus fell into dire straits because it was poorly managed. Challenged by foreign competitors, the company decided to compete on the Koreans' terms. It lost touch with its market and, worse still, with its own strengths.

Servus first began drifting off course about ten years ago. Swamped by cheaper imports, the company got winded trying to match the numbers on the Koreans' price tags. It suffered steep losses. "The only question was 'When would we go?' " recalls Leon Goold, a Servus employee for thirty-five years.

Servus had seen much better days. From its 1921 beginnings, Servus had been distinguished by the quality of its boots and the splendor of its annual picnics. The all-day outings were glorious family affairs—especially packed during the 1940s, when the company employed 1,100 workers—complete with popcorn and ice cream. From Rock Island, which is about midway between Des Moines and Chicago, people had to take three buses to get to the state park in Moline, Ill. One family owned the business back then, and many families worked there: fathers brought their sons into the company to work side by side on the assembly line.

Foreign competition became a factor in the late '60s, when cheap sneakers from the Far East overran the market. Servus, which at one time was producing 25,000 tennis sneakers a day, closed its sneaker operations and successfully crept into smaller niches. It produced, for instance, a plastic galosh called the Hustler, which was popular among farmers, construction workers, and electricians. And it made special overshoes for military and industrial workers.

In 1972, the $25-million business was sold to a division of Chromalloy American Corp. Chromalloy installed new chiefs at Servus and left the strategizing to them. As the Koreans challenged more of its markets, Servus panicked. The new executives forgot what Servus did best—produce quality boots—and instead initiated a decade-long process of competing with the Koreans on price. "I don't think they even understood the reasons for Servus's success," says one observer.

To keep prices low, the company began stripping down its products. It bought rubber, zippers, buckles, and cloth from the cheapest suppliers it could find. What were once quality boots were fast becoming low-quality "me too" products. For example, the lining in one of its most popular farming boots, the Northerner, was changed to a more loosely netted fabric. That saved about $60,000 a year. At the same time, companywide returns rose to about ten percent, undoubtedly because of such problems as the netting, which tore easily. Those returns were adding substantially to shipping and labor costs; never mind the disgusted customers who left for good.

Servus stopped investing in its business. "We didn't deal with them, unless they took things away from us," says Jack Miller, the industrial-relations manager who in 1971 started as a night "cracker man" in the mill room, grinding up used rubber. Even though employees were fainting on the job, management refused to install an adequate number of fans. A minor disagreement over health insurance turned into a seven-week union strike and a one-week wildcat strike in 1978.

Equipment was also neglected. One example was the Banbury mixer, a giant machine that stirs rubber like an electric eggbeater. Servus decided not to spend $60,000 to keep an extra reconditioned body at hand. When one broke down, so did the factory.

By 1981, Servus was losing more than $1 million on $14 million in sales—and this after starting a decade earlier with a profitable company *twice* as big. No wonder; customers were fed up. "I would have bet you $1,000 that I would never buy another Servus boot," says Mary Grilliot, vice-president of Morning Pride Manufacturing Inc., which makes and distributes protective clothing for fire fighters. Customers in Servus's other markets—industrial, farming, and sporting boots—felt the same way.

A major consulting firm, called in to diagnose the company's ailment, looked at the production costs of Servus and the Koreans. It issued a half-inch-thick report. This company is terminally ill, the consultants said. Might as well shut it down. Soon, unless a buyer appeared, there would be an additional 350 unemployed people wandering the streets of Rock Island.

Michael Cappy spent about six years wandering through the corridors of corporate America—such big names as Peat, Marwick, Mitchell; Booz, Allen & Hamilton; and General Electric. At thirty-three, though, what he really wanted was to run his own manufacturing business. Tommy Hewitt, whom he had known at GE, had heard about Servus through a consultant.

So Cappy traveled to Rock Island to have a look. He met with workers and was impressed by their commitment. "They had a lot of pride," he recalls. "They talked about the history of the company, the history of the company, and the history of the company." They also voiced concerns about the *future* of the company. Chromalloy had recently liquidated a boot company it owned in Chicopee, Mass. Is the same fate in store for us? they wanted to know. Can you get us out from under them?

Maybe, Cappy thought. Back in Louisville, he and Hewitt buried themselves in industry data. Little by little, Cappy's enthusiasm grew. Here was a company that had been sorely neglected, its brands milked and run into the ground. Yet the brand names still meant something to customers. Take the Northerner line of boots, for instance. Despite being stripped of most of its value, the name still attracted customers. "That sucker deserved to be dead with what they did to it," says Cappy. "Yet it demonstrated uncanny resilience."

Servus's problem, as Cappy eventually diagnosed it, could be summed up in a word: positioning. It was competing in the wrong end of the market; it had blindly followed its Korean competitors into a market that played to the Koreans' greatest advantage, low labor costs. Servus had turned its back on its own strengths. "If the basis on which Servus competed in the marketplace was price, and there's a lot of labor content in what it makes, it doesn't take a genius to figure out that the business is going to die," Cappy says. "We found Servus playing under rules by which it could not win."

Would it be possible, he wondered, to boost the company's margins by finding small niches where customers would buy quality? Everything he read convinced him that it would be. Well, *almost* everything. Just as Cappy and Hewitt were getting close to making a deal, the consulting group's report landed with a thud across Cappy's desk. "It gave us indigestion," he recalls.

Not a chronic case, though. The report didn't change Cappy's analysis of Servus's basic strengths. It still had a solid name, some promising markets, and strong internal spirit. "Buried in every $20-million dog," Cappy says, "is a $10-million gem." And, perhaps best of all, Cappy could buy this dog at a substantial discount. CIT Commercial Finance, now a division of the New York City-based Manufacturers Hanover Corp., agreed to finance the $5.7-million buyout. The United Rubber Workers and salaried employees made some concessions that eased the bleeding. In return, Cappy gave workers about twenty percent of the business through an employee stock ownership plan. And he gave the union president a seat on the board of directors.

The first challenge was fixing the company's production and quality problems. All the marketing genius in the world wouldn't help if Servus's boots were leaking. To boost quality,

Cappy brought in consultant Behrooz Jalayer, who had recently fled Iran.

But who would run the company? For the first few months, Cappy had left most of the existing management in place, including the president that Chromalloy had installed. Jalayer contended that the president had to go, in large part because he had a terrible relationship with employees. When Jalayer started "quality sessions" between managers and workers every morning, the president hesitated to sit at the same table as the union chief. On the other hand, Hewitt argued that millions of dollars would follow the president out the door. "The more careful you want to be," Jalayer countered, "the more you are dragging your feet on the recovery of this company."

Cappy finally fired the president. The day it was announced, Servus workers went wild. Somebody took the keys to the president's company car, threw them on a table, and shouted, "Anybody want to drive the president's car?" Another employee knocked down the nameplate on his desk. Says Leon Goold, who once got into a scuffle with the president in the men's room: "There wasn't an unhappy face in the building."

Soon there was a new face in the corner office. Marc Caparrelli, the new Servus president, had spent thirteen years at Campbell Soup Co., six of them in marketing-related jobs. He and Cappy had been buddies since high school. Jalayer stayed on as a consultant, later rising to vice-president of operations and, eventually, president. All three of them own stock in Norcross Cos., the holding company that includes Servus and some ten other small businesses. Cappy owns a controlling interest in Norcross, which has revenues of nearly $135 million.

What Servus needed was "to take a consumer-marketing approach to the business," Caparrelli says. Every product is, in some ways, a consumer product. The safety director who buys a fire boot is similar in many ways to the shopper deciding on a dish-washing liquid. So, Caparrelli argued, we have to ask the same questions that a consumer marketer would ask: how can we differentiate ourselves? People purchase products that represent the best value, a mix of quality and price. How do we make ourselves a better value?

The sales staff thought that it had the answer: slash prices even more to help them open new accounts. Cappy disagreed: a price decrease, he felt, would have a negative long-term effect. Customers might try a product once, but they wouldn't stick with something inferior.

So Cappy moved ahead, positioning the company as a quality leader. Along with Hewitt, who left the company in mid-1983, he visited potential customers and assured them that Servus was returning to the topnotch quality they remembered. They played on their fond memories of the company. *You guys are still around?* the potential customers would respond, wide-eyed. Why, heck, I haven't seen a Servus sales rep in, oh, it must be *five years.*

And the salespeople brought something new with them: cut-up samples of Servus boots. We have boots, they began, with six-gauge felt lining, a high abrasion index, and total imperviousness to fatty acids. Waterproof and seamless too, with rust-resistant buckles. Never mind that other boots have some of these characteristics as well; they had never been described in such detail. "Part of what we did," says Cappy, "was to be the first to state the obvious."

The company got a surprisingly good reception. "People remembered Servus as being a good, solid company," notes Caparrelli. "Brand images die hard." If those memories weren't enough to sway them, Servus had other means. Sometimes during a visit to a potential customer, for instance, Jalayer might talk about his flight to the United States from Iran. "I get a lot of mileage out of my life story," he says. But more often he would talk about Servus: sixty-year-old company on its last legs, 350 people just barely getting by on some $6 an hour. We are trying to save these jobs, Jalayer appealed. And then there were the practical advantages of buying from Servus instead of the Koreans: you didn't have to tie up your money for nine months or take the product as is. And the new owners offered delivery within seventy-two hours.

Later, as Servus grew more surefooted, it used hardball tactics. One Servus salesman took a foreign-made boot to an independent lab. The test results showed that its steel toe crushed under the weight of seventy-five pounds, violating the federal standard. That became part of the usual pitch to customers. Servus also had tests done on a foreign fire boot. Salesmen took the less-than-impressive results to state purchasing agents and to distributors. If, heaven forbid, there's an accident, Jalayer would warn distributors, these inferior boots could land you knee-deep in liability problems. "We put a push on the liability, and that there are a lot of weirdos in this country who will sue over anything," says sales manager Julie Dolter.

By mid-1983, Servus had picked up some major accounts. A few months later, it raised prices about three percent. The company, Cappy felt, had demonstrated its commitment to quality. "You want to increase the price to be consistent with the positioning," says Cappy. "Nothing confuses a consumer more than to get something that looks like it could cost more, and doesn't." It was also consistent with the new slogan its ad agency had suggested: Servus Sets the Standard.

Servus now had a foothold. But only through innovation could the company's sales grow in mature markets.

To make that happen, Caparrelli took a cue from his former employer, Campbell Soup: wherever possible, create a flagship product. At Servus, these would be leading-edge boots that stood at the top of each line. "They create an umbrella under which the enhanced image rubs off on the other products," says Cappy, who had seen the same strategy work at General Electric. Not all consumers would be able to afford the flagship product. But they would assume that Servus brought the same know-how to its other lines of boots.

To find ripe niches, they did what any good marketers do: they got in touch with their customers. They scrutinized every possible market segment and sub-segment. The sales staff played a key role. "New-product ideas don't come from people in the labs," Cappy says.

Cappy assembled the entire sales force in Winter Park, Colorado. The first day, he listened to complaints about service, delivery, and pricing. Then he talked about his plans. "Everybody was skeptical," says Cappy. "But they can detect the difference between sincerity and BS." We've never been asked about the direction of the company, the salespeople figured, so what do we have to lose? Some came up with new products, others had ideas about material, and some contributed packaging suggestions.

Potential customers were another good source of ideas. Jalayer went to trade shows and talked with boot distributors. What niche are you after? he would ask. How do you appeal to your customers? What new products would you like to see? They were mining for sizable markets where price wasn't the decision factor.

The fire-boot market was one. Customers would happily pay for quality. And it was easy to find the nation's fire fighters. They read industry magazines and attend trade shows. Just a mildly improved fire boot, backed by targeted marketing, could create sparks. "Fire boots had gotten stagnant," says Mary Grilliot, the boot distributor. "And this is a market that will pay for an improvement, since lives are at stake." And Grilliot, who had sworn off Servus forever, was impressed. At a trade show, Jalayer dragged her to the Servus booth. There she saw a fire boot with more supple rubber, melded design lines, a beefed-up sole, and a better fit and feel. Could this be the same *Servus Rubber?*

It wasn't. But if that didn't convince her, the company's next step would. Jalayer had started thinking about how to differentiate Servus's fire boot. One night at a trade show, a customer asked him, Why isn't the lining up to the same technological level as the rest of the boot? That got Jalayer thinking, Why not create a fire boot with a flameretardant lining? Not just any flame-retardant lining, mind you, a *Kevlar-Nomex* lining. Sounds impressive, doesn't it? And that's just the point. No matter that the fire is outside the boot. Fire chiefs and safety directors appreciate technological improvements. Servus created the boot, then doubled its advertising budget for such magazines as *Fire Chief* and *Fire House*, the most efficient way of reaching the fire fighters. "We had so many calls and inquiries that it forced the distributors to start carrying this boot," says Dolter.

Servus worked hard to convince users to shell out the extra 15 percent. Jalayer sent free samples of the boots, which retail for around $80, to a number of fire chiefs to use and evaluate. The Chicago Fire Department, for example, was using Korean fire boots. When a fire fighter was injured, Jalayer used the opportunity to visit the fire chief and explain Servus's edge. He not only won him over, but the chief also agreed to recommend the Firebreaker line to suburban fire departments. Before a major trade show in 1986, Jalayer sent letters to 23,000 fire chiefs urging them to stop by and see the boot. About 4,000 visited Servus's booth during the first three days.

This year, Servus expects to sell 30 percent more fire boots than it did last year. Since 1982, sales of the fire boots have more than doubled. And among Servus's major customers is Mary Grilliot, who returned, she says, because "Servus was willing to innovate."

And not only in fire boots. Servus's line of dielectrics was very limited when Cappy bought the company. Some competitors were selling boots that could withstand 14,000 volts of electricity. Give us *something* to sell against that to the utilities, the sales staff urged Caparrelli. Sure, he said, but why would a customer switch to ours? Again, *how can we differentiate ourselves?* His solution: a boot that withstands 20,000 volts. Since 1983, sales have climbed steadily to about 10,000 pairs a year. "It's a nice margin of protection and a great selling point," says David Forsthoffer, president of Shoes & Gloves Inc., a safety-equipment distributor.

Servus added a few extra touches, as well. Based on an idea that Caparrelli got from a customer in the utility industry, Servus added a two-and-a-half-inch heel to the boots, enabling workers to climb poles more easily. The dielectric boot was in another market where quality was more important than price, and Servus could reach it through direct mail.

In some markets, Servus created a flagship boot through sheer positioning, rather than technological innovation. The three-eyelet Northerner boot, for instance, hasn't changed much in the thirty years Servus has been selling it to farmers. But the label looked slapped on, and the box featured a drawing that looked too much like pigs frolicking. Farmers are not only a price-sensitive market, but expensive to reach—and they don't like their pigs made fun of. So Caparrelli upgraded the packaging, drawing attention to the boot's benefits, and added color to a new package illustration, which now looks like a polar bear. He used point-of-purchase hangtags, with instructions for care and a two-year warranty. Inside each boot, he added an inspection tag. "It creates an image that 'these guys are really proud of this boot,'" says Cappy. "You behave like it is a superior product."

Making a superior product has its rewards. A year after Cappy took over, Servus cleared about $150,000 after having lost more than $1 million the year before. Sales reached nearly $20 million in 1986, with "substantial pretax earnings," according to the company. Employment has swelled from 350 to 500 since 1982.

How easy it is to drift back into bad habits. Servus had learned a lesson from its pursuit of the Koreans and had also rediscovered its own strengths—or *had* it?

The innovation that got the company moving again has slowed. "We're somewhat frustrated with Servus's lack of ability to develop new products," Cappy admits. Some attempts seem halfhearted. Last year, Jalayer wanted to extend the Northerner brand name into coveralls. Cappy says he agreed because Jalayer "got all hot and bothered about it." Servus sold only about 7,000 pairs in 1986, and Jalayer predicts it will sell 10,000 this year. He even talks about acquiring a coverall maker. Cappy has other ideas. "We ought to be out of that business," he snaps. "It's not even a business. It's a distraction."

Worst of all, Servus tested the low end of the market once again. In 1985, Jalayer noticed that Servus's sales of Tomahawk, an overshoe for farmers and construction workers, were only a fraction of what they had been six years before. The Korean boot makers, who were selling similar overshoes at around half the price, offered to become Servus's suppliers.

But after visiting Korea, Jalayer strolled into Caparrelli's office and announced his intention to revive Tomahawk. *Revive Tomahawk?* Don't be silly, replied Caparrelli. We can't compete on price. But maybe we could import the boots from the Koreans and market them here. No, that would damage the integrity of our own lines, countered Jalayer. What are you going to say to the union workers who don't get a change to beat the Koreans? Then Jalayer presented his own plan. Drop the price by about 20 percent, he said, and make up the margin in volume by offering it only to customers who buy at least 150 pairs. And use incremental price increases after that. Well, they finally agreed, it *would* be a great way to absorb overhead and use excess capacity.

Jalayer returned to Rock Island and plastered stickers of angry bald eagles all over the factory. "We are fighting back," they said, referring to the Korean footwear. The market responded to the drastic price cuts, and sales shot up 500 percent between 1985 and 1986. Suddenly, the Tomahawk line was becoming the company's most visible product. The local newspapers were even writing about it.

Tomahawk developed into a marketing blunder, though. The "fighting back" theme was in danger of becoming Servus's image in the marketplace. It wasn't at all consistent with the slogan Servus Sets the Standard. "The last thing I want to tell our customers is that we're fighting back," says Cappy. "Implicit in it is an admission that we got our asses kicked." Cappy was also concerned that the low-margin items of the Tomahawk line might eclipse the company's more profitable lines of boots.

If that happened, Servus could find itself back where it started. "You can be a genius in turnarounds, but if you don't follow up, it will return to worse than it was before," says Jalayer. That would be more bad news for Rock Island, where mothballed plants have become too common a sight. Since Cappy took over Servus, about 20,000 workers in the metropolitan area have lost their jobs at other companies.

All because of foreign competition, or so they think. Maybe they ought to look at Servus and think again.

39

That's Easy for You to Say

It all began on labor day weekend in 1982. Allan A. Kennedy was sitting in a low beach chair on the shore in front of his cottage on Cape Cod. Next to him was his friend and fellow consultant Tony Merlo. As they relaxed there, watching the sailboats drift across Cape Cod Bay, drinking beer, and listening to a Red Sox game on the radio, Kennedy turned to Merlo and, with the majestic eloquence suited to great undertakings, said: "Gee, Tony, you know, we ought to start some kind of business together."

This identical thought has, of course, passed between countless friends ever since the discovery of profit margins. Coming from most people, it would have fallen into the general category of loose talk. But Kennedy was not most people. For one thing, he was a thirteen-year veteran of McKinsey & Co., the management consulting firm, and partner in charge of its Boston office. More to the point, he was the co-author of a recently published book that offered a startling new perspective on corporate life—one that challenged the whole way people thought about business.

The book was entitled *Corporate Cultures,* a term that was itself new to the language, and it dealt with an aspect of business that, up to then, had been largely ignored. Broadly speaking, that aspect involved the role played by a company's values, symbols, rites, and rituals in determining its overall performance. Citing examples from some of the country's most dynamic companies, Kennedy and co-author Terrence E. Deal showed that these "cultural" factors had a major effect on the attitudes and behavior of a company's employees, and were thus of critical importance to its long-term success.

By any measure, the book was a groundbreaking work, challenging, as it did, the rational, quantitative models of corporate success that were so popular in the 1960s and '70s. But its impact had as much to do with its timing as its content. Published in June 1982, during a period of economic stagnation—with unemployment at 9.5 percent, the prime over 16 percent, and trade deficits soaring to record levels—*Corporate Cultures* offered a welcome antidote to the doom and gloom that was abroad in the land. Like *In Search of Excellence,* which appeared a few months later, it suggested that Japan was not the only nation capable of producing strong, highly motivated companies that could compete effectively in the international arena. America could produce—in fact, was already producing—its own.

What the book did not detail, however, was how corporate cultures were actually constructed. The authors could describe a particular culture and demonstrate its effects, but they offered few clues as to how a company might develop a culture in the first place. So the news that Allan Kennedy was going into business was greeted with more than passing interest among the followers of corporate culture. Here was an opportunity to find out how a living, breathing culture could be created, and the creator would be none other than the man who wrote the book.

After an extensive survey of business opportunities, Kennedy and Merlo decided to develop microcomputer software for sales and marketing management. They felt this was their most promising option, given the anticipated growth of the microcomputer market and their own experience as consultants. Acting on that assessment, they resigned from McKinsey and, in February 1983, formally launched Selkirk Associates Inc. with four of their friends.

Kennedy had lofty ambitions for Selkirk. More than a business, he saw it as a kind of laboratory for his theories. He wanted it to function as a society of professional colleagues committed to building a culture and a company that would stress collaboration, openness, decentralization, democratic decisions, respect, and trust. In this society, each individual would be encouraged to devise his or her own entrepreneurial response to the challenges of the business.

For Kennedy, this was not a long-term goal, something that would evolve naturally in the fullness of time. On the contrary, it was a pressing, immediate concern. Accordingly, he focused all his attention on creating such a culture from the start. "I spent lots of time," he says, "trying to think about what kind of values the company ought to stand for and therefore what kind of behavior I expected from people." These thoughts eventually went into a detailed statement of "core beliefs," which he reviewed and amplified with each new employee. In the same vein, Kennedy and his colleagues chose a "guiding principle," namely, a commitment to "making people more productive." They would pursue this ambition, everyone agreed, "through the products and services we offer" and "in the way we conduct our own affairs."

And, in the beginning at lest, Selkirk seemed to be everything Kennedy had hoped for. The company set up shop in Boston, in an office that consisted of a large, rectangular room, with three smaller attachments. Each morning, staff members would pile into the main room and sort themselves out by function—programmers and systems engineers by the windows; administrators in the middle; sales and marketing folk at the other end. In keeping with Kennedy's cultural precepts, there were no private offices or, indeed, any physical demarcations between functions.

It was a familial enterprise, informed with the very qualities Kennedy had laid out in his statement of core beliefs. The work was absorbing, the comradeship inspiring. Most mornings, the staff feasted on doughnuts, which they took to calling "corporate carbos," as a wordplay on "corporate cultures." They began a scrapbook as an impromptu cultural archive. Included among the memorabilia was "The Ravin'," an Edgar Allan Poe takeoff that commemorated Selkirk's first stirrings in earlier temporary headquarters:

Once upon an April morning,
  disregarding every warning,
In a Back Bay storefront,
  Selkirk software was begun:
True, it was without a toilet,
  but that didn't seem to spoil it.

To strengthen their bonds even further, the staff began to experiment with so-called rites, rituals, and ceremonies—all important elements of a corporate culture, according to Kennedy's book. Selkirk's office manager, Linda Sharkey, recalls a day, for example, when the whole company went out to Kennedy's place on Cape Cod to celebrate their common purpose with barbecues on the beach. "The sun was shining, and we were all there together," she says. "It was a beautiful day. That's the way it was. We didn't use the terms among ourselves that Allan uses in the book. With us, corporate culture was more by seeing and doing." Sharkey remembers, too, Friday afternoon luncheons of pizza or Chinese food, at which everyone in the company had a chance to talk about his or her accomplishments or problems, or simply hang out.

Kennedy was pleased with all this, as well he might be. "We were," he says, "beginning to develop a real culture."

Then the walls went up.

The problem stemmed from the situation in the big room, where the technical people were laboring feverishly to develop Selkirk's first product, while the salespeople were busy preselling it. The former desperately needed peace and quiet to concentrate on their work; the latter were a boisterous lot, fond of crowing whenever a prospect looked encouraging. In fact, the salespeople crowed so often and so loudly that the technicians complained that they were being driven to distraction. Finally, they confronted with Kennedy with the problem. Their solution, which Kennedy agreed to, was to erect five-foot-high movable partitions, separating each functional grouping from the others.

In the memory of Selkirk veterans, "the day the walls went up" lives on as a day of infamy. "It was terrible," says Sharkey. "I was embarrassed."

"It was clearly a symbol of divisiveness," says Kennedy.

"I don't know what would have been the right solution," says Reilly Hayes, Selkirk's twenty-three-year-old technical wizard, "but the wall certainly wasn't. It blocked out the windows for the other end of the room. Someone [in marketing] drew a picture of a window and taped it to the wall. The whole thing created a lot of dissension."

Indeed, the erection of the walls touched off a feud between engineering and marketing that eventually grew into "open organizational warfare," according to Kennedy. "I let the wall stand, and a competitive attitude developed where engineering started sniping at marketing. We had two armed camps that didn't trust each other."

As if that weren't bad enough, other problems were beginning to surface. For one thing, the company was obviously overstaffed, having grown from twelve people in June 1983 to twenty-five in January 1984, without any product—or sales—to show for it. "That was a big mistake," says Kennedy. "We clearly ramped up the organization too fast, particularly given the fact that we were financing ourselves. I mean, for a while, we had a burn rate of around $100,000 per month."

Even more serious, however, was the problem that emerged following the release of the company's initial product, Correspondent, in February 1984. Not that there was anything wrong with the product. It was, in fact, a fine piece of software, and it premiered to glowing reviews. Designed as a selling tool, it combined database management, calendar management, word processing, and mail merge—functions that could help customers organize their accounts, track and schedule sales calls and follow-ups, and generate correspondence. And it did all that splendidly.

The problem had to do with the price tag, a whopping $12,000 per unit. The Selkirk team members had come up with this rarefied figure, not out of greed, but out of a commitment to customer service—a goal to which they had pledged themselves as part of their cultural mission. In order to provide such service, they figured, a Selkirk representative might have to spend two or three weeks with each customer, helping to install and customize the product. Trouble was, customers weren't willing to *pay* for that service, not at $12,000 per unit anyway. After a brief flurry of interest, sales dropped off.

"We just blew it," says Kennedy. "We were arrogant about the market. We were trying to tell the market something it wasn't interested in hearing. We took an arbitrary cultural goal and tried to make it into a strategy rather than saying we're a market-driven company and we've got to find out what the market wants and supply it." Unfortunately, six months went by before Kennedy and his colleagues figured all this out and began to reduce Correspondent's price accordingly.

By then, however, Selkirk's entire sales effort was in shambles, a victim of its commitment to employee autonomy. Sales targets were seldom realized. Indeed, they were scarcely even set. At weekly meetings, salespeople would do little more than review account activity. "If a salesman said each week for three weeks in a row that he expected to close a certain account, and it never happened," says Merlo, "well, we didn't do anything about it. In any other company, he would probably have been put on probation." As it was, each of the participants entered the results of the meeting in a red-and-black ledger book and struck out once again to wander haphazardly through uncharted territory. "The mistake we made," reflects Merlo, "was using real money in a real company to test hypotheses about what sales goals should be."

Finally, in June 1984, Kennedy took action, laying off six people. In July, Correspondent's price was dropped to $4,000 per unit, but sales remained sluggish. In September, Kennedy laid off five more people, bringing the size of the staff back to twelve.

One of those laid off was the chief engineer, a close friend of Kennedy's, but a man whose departure brought an immediate ceasefire between the warring factions. That night, the remaining staff members took down the walls and stacked them neatly in the kitchenette, where they repose to this day. "We felt," says Sharkey, "like we had our little family back together again."

With morale finally rebounding, Selkirk again cut Correspondent's price in the early fall, to $1,500. This time, sales responded, and, in November, the company enjoyed its first month in the black.

But Selkirk was not yet out of the woods. What remained was for Kennedy to figure out the significance of what had happened, and to draw the appropriate conclusions. Clearly, his experiment had not turned out as he had planned. His insistence on a company without walls had led to organizational warfare. His goal of providing extraordinary service had led to a crucial pricing error. His ideal of employee autonomy had led to confusion in the sales force. In the end, he was forced to fire more than half of his staff, slash prices by 87 percent, and start over again. What did it all mean?

Merlo had one answer. "We're talking about an experiment in corporate culture failing because the business environment did not support it," he says. "The notion of corporate culture got in the way of toughminded business decisions." He also faults the emphasis on autonomy. "I don't think we had the right to be organized the way we were. I think we should have had more discipline."

Kennedy himself soon came around to a similar view. "Look in [the statement of core beliefs] and tell me what you find about the importance of performance, about measuring performance or about the idea that people must be held accountable for their performance," he says. "That stuff should have been there. I'm not discounting the importance of corporate culture, but you have to worry about the business at the same time, or you simply won't have one. Then you obviously won't *need* a culture. Where the two come together, I think, is in the cultural norms for performance, what kind of performance is expected of people. And that's a linkage that wasn't explicit in my mind three years ago. But it is now." He adds that, if the manuscript of *Corporate Cultures* were before him today, he would include a section on performance standards, measurement systems, and accountability sanctions.

On that point, he might get an argument from his co-author, Terrence Deal, a professor at Vanderbilt University and a member of Selkirk's board of directors since its inception. Deal does not disagree about the importance of discipline and performance standards, but he questions the wisdom of trying to impose them from above. The most effective performance standards, he notes, are the ones that employees recognize and accept as the product of their own commitment, and these can emerge only from the employees' experience. "One of the things that we know pretty handsomely," says Deal, "is that it's the informal performance standards that really drive a company."

In fact, Kennedy may have gotten into trouble not by doing too little, but by doing too much. Rather than letting Selkirk's culture evolve organically, he tried to impose a set of predetermined cultural values on the company, thereby retarding the growth of its own informal value system. He pursued culture as an end in itself, ignoring his own caveat, set down in his book, that "the business environment is the single greatest influence in shaping a corporate culture." Instead, he tried to shape the culture in a vacuum, without synchronizing it with the company's business goals.

In so doing, Kennedy reduced corporate culture to a formula, a collection of generic "principles." It was a cardinal error, if not an uncommon one. "There are a lot of people," says Deal, "who take our book literally and try to design a culture much as if they're trying to design an organization chart. My experience across the board has been that, as soon as people make it into a formula, they start making mistakes." By following the "formula," Kennedy wound up imposing his own set of rules on Selkirk—although not enough of them, and not the right kind, he now says. The irony is that a real corporate culture allows a company to manage itself *without* formal rules, and to manage itself better than a company that has them.

Deal makes another point. Kennedy, he observes, might be less concerned with performance today if he had not hired so many friends at the beginning. Friends are nice to have around, but it's often hard to discipline them, or subject them to a company's normal sanctions. Over the long run, Deal says, their presence at Selkirk probably undermined the development of informal performance standards.

Kennedy himself may have played a role in that, too. He estimates that, over the past year, he has spent only one day a week at Selkirk. The rest of the time he has been on the road as a consultant, using his fees to help finance the company. In all, he has sunk some $1 million of his own money into Selkirk, without which the company might not have survived. But it has come at a price. "Nobody had to pay attention to things like expenses, because there was a perception of an infinite sink of money," Kennedy says.

The danger of that perception finally came home to him last summer, when three of Selkirk's four salespeople elected to take vacations during the same month. The result was that sales for the month all but vanished. Kennedy had had enough. "I told the people here that either you sustain the company as a self-financing entity, or I will let it go under. I'm unwilling to put more money on the table."

And yet, in the end, it was hard to avoid the conclusion that a large part of Selkirk's continuing problem was Allan Kennedy himself—a thought that did not escape him. "I've got a lot to learn about running a business successfully," he says, "about doing it myself, I mean. I think I know everything about management except how to manage. I can give world-class advice on managing, but—when it comes right down to it—I take too long and fall into all the traps that I see with the managers I advise."

Whatever his shortcomings as a manager, there is one thing Kennedy can't be faulted for, and that is lack of courage. Having drawn the inevitable conclusion, he went out looking for someone who could help him do a better job of managing the company. For several months, he negotiated with the former president of a Boston-based high-tech firm, but the two of them were unable to come to terms. Instead, Kennedy has made changes at Selkirk that he hopes will achieve the same effect. In the new structure, Merlo is taking charge of the microcomputer end of the business, while Betsy Meade—a former West Coast sales representative—has responsibility for a new minicomputer version of Correspondent, to be marketed in conjunction with Prime Computer Corp. As for Kennedy, he will concern himself with external company relations, product-development strategies, and, of course, corporate culture.

Kennedy is full of optimism these days. He points out that, despite its checkered history, Selkirk has emerged with a durable product and an installed base of about 1,000 units. In addition, the company will soon be bolstered with the proceeds from a $250,000 private placement. Meanwhile, he says, some of the company's previous problems have been dealt with, thanks to the introduction of a reliable order-fulfillment process, the decision to put sales reps on a straight commission payment schedule, and the establishment of specific sales targets for at least the next two quarters. "I think we have much more focused responsibility," he says, "and much more tangible measures of success for people in their jobs."

Overall, Kennedy looks on the past three years as a learning experience. "There are times when I think I should charge up most of the zigs and the zags to sheer rank incompetence," he admits. "But then there are other times when I look back and say, 'Nobody's that smart, and you can't do everything right.' In life, you have to be willing to try things. And if something doesn't work, you have to be willing to say, 'Well, that was a dumb idea,' and then try something else." Now, he believes, he has a chance to do just that.

In the meantime, he is in the process of writing another book. He already has a proposal circulating among publishers. In his idle moments, he occasionally amuses himself by inventing titles. One of those titles speaks volumes about where he has been: *Kicking Ass and Taking Names.*

40

Lands' End

Lands' End, Inc. (LEI) was founded in 1963 by Gary C. Comer, an avid sailor and an award-winning copywriter with the advertising agency of Young & Rubican. LEI was founded to sell equipment to racing sailors by direct mail. Its unique name was the result of a mistake in its first printed mailing piece. Lands' End was meant to be Land's End, the name of a famous English seaport. The error was left uncorrected and the firm was off and running. Comer has said, "For me, Lands' End is a dream that came true. I always wanted to create a company of my own and here it is."

From its founding until 1976, LEI emphasised the sales of sailing gear while gradually adding related traditional recreational clothing and soft luggage to its product line. The clothing and luggage became so popular among the firm's upscale clientele that by 1976, LEI had shifted its focus entirely to these more popular items. In 1979, having outgrown its Chicago location, LEI moved to its current headquarters in Dodgeville, Wisconsin. The Chicago facility, which once housed the whole firm, was retained as the location of its marketing creative staff of thirty-five people.

In its first twenty-five years, Lands' End has grown to sales of over $335 million, making it one of the nation's largest merchants selling entirely through the medium of the direct mail catalog. In the five years between 1982 and 1987, LEI's sales more than tripled, and the firm set a goal of doubling fiscal 1986 sales by 1991. LEI went public in October 1986, achieving listing on the New York Stock Exchange in late 1987. LEI's 20,040,000 shares had a market value of $560 million in September, 1988. For the fiscal year ending in January 1989, Lands' End is expected to circulate 72 million catalogs, achieve sales of $388 million, and earn profits of

This case was prepared by Peter G. Goulet and Lynda L. Goulet of the University of Northern Iowa and is intended to be used as a basis for class discussion rather than to illustrate either effective or ineffective handling of an administrative situation. The authors thank Julie Coppock, a UNI graduate student, and Stephen Ashley of Blunt, Ellis, and Loewi for their help in the preparation of this case. Presented to and accepted by the refereed Midwest Society for Case Research.

$26 million, or $1.30 per share.[1] Further financial information is presented in Exhibits 40-1, 40-2, and 40-3.

Business and Customers

Lands' End is a clothing retailer serving the market by direct mail through its extensive catalog of traditional clothing and related items. The main types of products sold include men's dress shirts, slacks, ties, and accessories, as well as sport clothes, such as sweaters, shoes, jogging suits and "sweats," and a myriad of styles of knit shirts. The women's line includes similar sport clothing, as well as traditional natural-fiber shirts, skirts, and slacks, shoes, and accessories. The firm also offers a limited, but growing, line of children's clothing in styles similar to the adult lines. Finally, the firm manufactures and sells a line of soft luggage products and has recently introduced a line of linen and bedding.

The Lands' End customer is reasonably affluent. Sixty percent have incomes in excess of $35,000. Most have been to college and are employed in professional or managerial jobs. Exhibit 40-4 compares the typical Lands' End customer to its counterpart in the population as a whole. In 1986, LEI estimated that there were 23 million households in the United States that met its typical customer characteristics. Moreover, this group was growing more than three times as fast as the population as a whole. Further, it typically spends a larger proportion of its income on apparel than the average for the population.

The Direct Marketing Association (DMA) estimated that 10.1 percent of the total female population and 5.4 percent of the male population ordered at least one item of clothing from a catalog or other direct mail merchant in 1986. On average, between 9 percent and 10 percent of all the people with incomes over $30,000 made a direct mail clothing purchase. In addition, DMA has estimated that 10.7 percent of the college graduates and 10.5 percent of the professional/managerial households made such a purchase. Overall, it would appear that about 10 percent of the group Lands' End considers to be its prime customers can be expected to make a direct mail clothing purchase from some firm in a given year. Out of the base of 23 million customers, this would imply an average of 2.3 million active customers per year. In fact, LEI estimates that in the thirty-six months preceding February 1988, it had made at least one sale to 3.4 million different persons.

Industry Environment

Lands' End is part of the catalog apparel industry that accounts for approximately 10 percent of all apparel sales. Recent data for these markets is shown in Exhibit 40-5. In 1988, the firm held about a 4 percent share of the catalog apparel market, making it the seventh largest direct market or catalog apparel retailer (see Exhibit 40-6 for a list of selected competitors). This market has enjoyed recent growth of 8.6 percent per year and is expected to continue to grow at 10 percent per year through 1991. Lands' End has grown roughly two to three times as fast as the market since calendar 1985.

Though catalog retailing is expected to grow faster than retailing in general in the next three to five years, there are some clouds on the horizon. The prospects for growth have caused a sharp increase in the number of catalogs directed to the buying public. In 1985, a total of 10 billion catalogs were mailed, rising to 11.8 billion in 1987.[2] In addition, poor service on the part of some catalog merchants may help create a negative image for the segment in general. *Consumer Reports* has recently published ratings of catalog retailers to help consumers determine the relative service quality of many of the larger firms, including Lands' End. Lands' End was beaten only by L. L. Bean in these initial consumer ratings.

EXHIBIT 40-1 ▪ Lands' End Income Statements for the Fiscal Years Ended January 31 (thousands of dollars)

	1988	%	1987	%	1986	%	1985	%
Net sales	$336,291	100.0%	$265,058	100.0%	$227,160	100.0%	$172,241	100.0%
Cost of sales	190,348	56.6%	152,959	57.7%	135,678	59.7%	101,800	59.1%
Gross profit	145,943	43.4%	112,099	42.3%	91,482	40.3%	70,441	40.9%
Operating expense	104,514	31.0%	80,878	30.5%	67,781	29.9%	55,431	32.2%
Depreciation	3,185	1.0%	2,576	1.0%	1,867	.8%	1,435	.8%
Operating income	38,244	11.4%	28,645	10.8%	21,834	9.6%	13,575	7.9%
Interest expense	(1,357)	−0.4%	(1,488)	−0.6%	(1,579)	−0.7%	(1,697)	−1.0%
Other income	1,441	0.4%	1,329	0.5%	1,329	0.6%	938	0.5%
Income before tax	38,328	11.4%	28,486	10.7%	21,584	9.5%	12,816	7.4%
Income tax (1)	15,523	4.6%	13,881	5.2%	10,314	4.5%	6,076	3.5%
Net income	22,805	6.8%	14,605	5.5%	11,270	5.0%	6,740	3.9%
Per share (2)	$1.14		$0.73		$0.56			
Catalogs mailed	63.5 mil.		50.0 mil.		44.0 mil.		29.0 mil.	
Quarterly percents	Sales	Gr.Pr.	Sales	Gr.Pr.	Sales	Gr.Pr.		
Feb-Apr	18.0%	17.6%	17.8%	16.7%	19.1%	19.5%		
May-July	19.0%	18.8%	19.9%	18.7%	19.4%	18.1%		
Aug-Oct	23.8%	24.1%	24.5%	25.3%	23.7%	24.4%		
Nov-Jan	39.1%	39.4%	37.8%	39.3%	37.3%	38.0%		

Lands' End was a Sub-chapter S corporation through part of 1987. Therefore:
(1) Income taxes from 1985–1987 are estimated to reflect a normal corporate structure.
(2) Earnings per share are estimated based on shares outstanding in 1988.

EXHIBIT 40-2 ▪ Lands' End Statement of Changes in Working Capital for Fiscal Years Ended 1985-1988 (thousands of dollars)

	1988	%	1987	%	1986	%	1985	%
Sources:								
Operations (1)	$25,668		$21,804		$23,451		$14,251	
Long-term debt			264		316			
Sale of stock			22,584				520	
Fixed assets, net	776		38		243		205	
Total sources	$26,444		$44,690		$24,010		$14,976	
Uses:								
Dividends (2)	$ 4,008		$28,000		$13,775		$11,755	
Fixed assets	5,862		9,595		6,631		2,658	
Reduce long-term debt	1,918						478	
Other			40		24			
Total uses	$11,788		$37,635		$20,430		$14,891	
Net increase in working capital	$14,656		$ 7,055		$ 3,580		$ 85	

(1) Cash flow from operations consists of net income, depreciation, and additions to deferred taxes.
(2) Lands' End was a Sub-chapter S corporation through part of 1987. Therefore, dividends from 1985 to 1987 are sub-chapter S distributions.

Another threat to catalog retailers is the rising cost of shipping goods and mailing catalogs. Early in 1988, the U.S. Postal Service raised postage rates for catalogs 25 percent and UPS raised surface shipping costs as well. In addition, catalog production costs are also rising, as are catalog sizes. The typical cost for a catalog the size and quality of that published by Lands' End can run as high as $750 thousand to $800 thousand, exclusive of mailing and handling costs. A typical sixty-four-page catalog in two or four colors costs around $350 thousand to $400 thousand. To partially offset these rising costs, some catalog retailers such as Bloomingdale's, for example, have begun to sell their catalogs in major chain book stores and sell advertising space in the catalogs.

Finally, most states do not require catalog retailers to charge sales tax on catalog sales outside of the states in which the firm operates. Recently, however, states are beginning to view this practice as a significant source of lost revenue. In 1988, Iowa was added to a small, but growing list of states that will require catalog firms to remit sales tax on all purchases made from catalogs by residents of the state, regardless of where the catalog firm is located. If all states move to this type of policy, it will reduce one of the key advantages to catalog retailers and could create significant overhead expenses for keeping the records required to satisfy each state.

A segment of the direct market retailing industry outside of the catalog segment may also pose a threat to the catalog retailers. Home shopping through cable television was expected to generate an estimated $1.75 billion in sales in 1987. The companies in this segment, of which the largest is the Home Shopping Network, Inc., were estimated to have reached over 40 million households in that year. Further, though some view the cable shopping phenomenon as a fad, the DMA estimates that by 1992, this industry segment could be generating $5.6 billion in sales and be reaching nearly 80 million households. If this is true, it represents a 26-percent average annual growth rate for the period. Given the growth of retail sales in general and forecasts for direct market retailing, this would seem to be growth that could easily come at the expense of other direct marketers.

EXHIBIT 40-3 ■ Lands' End Balance Sheets for the Fiscal Years ended January 31 (thousands of dollars)

	1988	1987	1986
Current assets			
Cash & marketable securities	$ 28,175	$16,032	$ 3,578
Receivables	274	238	319
Inventories	46,444	40,091	31,057
Other	3,363	1,299	733
Total current	$ 78,256	$57,660	$35,687
Plant and equipment			
Land and buildings	15,114	13,809	9,499
Equipment	21,974	19,667	13,266
Leasehold improvements	908	661	584
Other	674		1,250
Total	38,670	34,137	24,599
Depreciation	9,947	7,315	4,758
Net fixed assets	28,723	26,822	19,841
Total assets	$106,979	$84,482	$55,528
Current liabilities			
Current portion Long-term debt	$ 1,918	$ 321	$ 193
Accounts payable	21,223	16,791	13,927
Order advances	453	449	193
Accruals	7,226	4,394	2,589
Profit sharing	2,648	1,707	830
Taxes payable	5,394	9,258	
Total current	38,860	32,920	18,002
Long-term debt	8,667	10,585	10,321
Deferred income tax	2,778	3,100	
	50,305	46,605	28,323
Stockholders' equity			
Common stock	200	100	95
Paid-in-capital	22,308	22,408	73
Retained earnings	34,166	15,369	27,037
Total equity	56,674	37,877	27,205
Total debt and owners' equity	$106,979	$84,482	$55,528

Though entry into direct marketing does not require the same level of investment required to generate similar sales in the normal retail market, the costs may still be significant. To provide sufficient service requires expertise and may involve a large equipment investment. To develop a mailing list is also important and expensive. Name rental may run anywhere from $60 to $100 per thousand names annually, or upwards of $100,000 for a million quality, proven names. As the established firms such as Lands' End and L. L. Bean become large, economies of scale and learning-curve effects may make it difficult for new firms to enter the business in all but small niche markets.

Pure catalog retailers have a number of significant advantages over conventional retailers. The most obvious of these is that they have

EXHIBIT 40-4 ■ Lands' End Customer Analysis

	Median Household Income	Women, Percent Employed	Percent Aged 25–29	Growth 25–49 $30K*	Percent Employed Profess.
LEI	$46,000	75%	69%	3.2%	70%
U.S.	24,500	< 50%	50%	< 1.0%	< 25%

*Annual growth expected from 1985–1995 for population group with incomes over $30,000 aged between 25–49.

EXHIBIT 40-5 ■ Retail Sales Data (dollars in billions)

	1985	1986	1987E	1988E	Growth Rate**
Retail sales	1374.00	1454.00	1541.00	1633.00	5.9%
Retail apparel	74.00	81.00	86.70	92.80	7.8%
Catalog sales*	26.00	27.50	29.70	32.10	7.3%
Catalog apparel*	7.50	8.20	8.90	9.60	8.6%
Lands' End	.23	.26	.34	.39	19.2%
Share catalog apparel	3.1%	3.1%	3.8%	4.1%	

*Estimated
**Average annual growth 1985–1988
Source: U.S. Commerce Department

no stores to operate and have, therefore, lower costs. Passing on some of these cost savings can create a competitive advantage. In spite of this inherent advantage, however, several of the major catalog competitors do operate store locations in addition to their catalog operation, thus offsetting the advantage. What these firms have attempted to do is improve their performance as traditional retailers by using higher profit catalog sales as an adjunct to normal store-based selling. The Limited, Eddie Bauer, Talbots, J. C. Penney, and Sears, for example, operate anywhere from several dozen to several hundred stores each.

In addition to having lower costs and prices, catalog retailers give the customer the advantage of convenience. Being able to shop through a catalog and call in an order, even in the middle of the night, may be of great benefit to households where both spouses are working outside the home, for example. Further, using a catalog means the consumer may think about the purchase and compare alternate sources without costly transportation and sales pressure. Finally, catalog shopping is also a convenience for people who live in smaller communities where a variety of upscale goods, especially, is typically not available and obtaining such goods from a conventional store would be even more inconvenient than purchasing through a catalog.

The biggest weaknesses of catalog shopping involve the inability to see an item before buying it and the cost and inconvenience of having to return an unsatisfactory purchase. In spite of these issues, however, a Gallup poll reported by the DMA in 1987 shows that two-thirds of the population would consider making a direct mail/catalog purchase even if the item were available in conventional stores.

Lands' End's Strategy

Catalog retailers must adhere to most of the principles that govern traditional store-based retailers. Merchandise must be fresh, varied, and of satisfactory quality. By maintaining itself as a retailer of traditional clothing, Lands' End does not have the concerns with fad and fashion faced by such combination in-store and direct mail retailers as the Limited and Bloomingdale's, for example. However, the firm does have to offer new merchandise regularly. Its most recent introductions have been its line of children's clothing and linens. Other featured items include its knit shirts and rugby shirts, the latter having been chosen by the U.S. National Rugby Team as its official jersey.

All Lands' End merchandise carries the firm's own private label. All catalog items except luggage are produced by outside vendors. The luggage is manufactured by the firm at its plant in West Union, Iowa. Product quality is assured by frequent inspections of goods, both at the manufacturer's facility and at the company. The firm even maintains a Lear jet to fly its staff of quality assurance personnel to the factories of domestic manufacturers to direct production according to Lands' End specifications. Further, 10 percent of every shipment received at Dodgeville is inspected to assure continuing quality. Critical products are purchased from more than one vendor, and consistency between them is maintained by strict specifications. To further assure quality and service from vendors, officers of these companies are regularly brought to Dodgeville to see the Lands' End operation.

Lands' End understands that catalog retailing is a difficult business in which to create a competitive advantage. Its catalogs, therefore, are produced with what the firm calls an "editorial" approach. Goods are not merely described in short, dry sentences. Rather, key product lines are given large half- or full-page descriptions that are designed to be interesting, appealing, and original. In addition, the catalog often contains several pages devoted to editorials, essays, and witty commentary dealing with a variety of subjects of interest to the firm's clientele. Two pages in the April 1988 issue described glass blowing. This kind of content is not unique to Lands' End. The catalog issued by the trendy Banana Republic also employs a similar approach. However, because different writers and subjects are involved in each catalog, Lands' End's catalogs can still be differentiated and are difficult to copy.

In addition, the quality and presentation of the Lands' End catalog is tightly controlled and merchandise is presented in life-style settings designed to appeal to the firm's clientele. Merchandise is grouped in "programs" to promote multiple item sales. This "magazine style" approach is further supported by the use of product teams. New items are studied by a team consisting of a writer, an artist, and a buyer to make certain that each item is presented properly in the catalog.

To interest prospective customers, Lands' End uses print advertising. The cost of this national campaign in selected upscale publications, such as the *Wall Street Journal* and the *New Yorker*, is approximately 1 percent of sales. The campaign is designed to be compatible with the firm's editorial catalog structure and contains copy in a similar style.

Lands' End considers itself a "direct merchant" and summarizes its marketing and operations strategy as:

1. Establishing a strong, unique consumer brand image.
2. Placing an emphasis on product quality and value.
3. Identifying and expanding an active customer base.
4. Creating a continuous relationship with active customers.
5. Building customer confidence and convenience through service.

Service

At least part of the success of Lands' End has been attributed to its customer-oriented marketing philosophy. This customer orientation is reflected in a number of ways. Prompt service is supported by rapid response and personal attention. The firm claims its twenty-four-hour-a-day 800 number, which is the source of 73 percent of all incoming orders, rarely requires more than two rings before it is answered. In addition, 99 percent of its orders are shipped within twenty-four hours of receipt. This level of service is facilitated by a dedicated staff, a sophisticated computerized operating system, and a distribution center just doubled in size to 275,000 square feet. The DMA reports in its 1987 survey of customer attitudes that 83 percent of all direct mail customers have some sort of complaint about direct mail purchasing. Though the most common complaints are that one cannot tell what one is likely to receive or that one will have been deceived by the merchandise, a significant percentage are either about poor service (20 percent) or inconvenience of some kind (16 percent). In addition, over half of the consumers surveyed by the DMA say they would buy more from direct marketers who provide prompt delivery.

Lands' End deals with customer complaints with the same commitment they have to customers placing orders. This is essential if the firm is to retain its strong group of dedicated customers. The DMA reports that though a high proportion of customers may have some complaint with mail order, 73 percent will remain as repeat customers if the complaint is satisfactorily handled, compared to 17 percent if it is not.

Lands' End sums up its marketing and service philosophy through its "Principles of Doing Business." These principles have been published in the catalog, annual reports, and advertising copy produced by the company.

PRINCIPLE 1. We do everything we can to make our products better. We improve material, and add back features and construction details that others have taken out over the years. We never reduce the quality of a product to make it cheaper.

PRINCIPLE 2. We price our products fairly and honestly. We do not, have not, and will not participate in the common retail practice of inflating markups to set up a future phony 'sale.'

PRINCIPLE 3. We accept any return, for any reason, at any time. Our products are guaranteed. No fine print. No arguments. We mean exactly what we say: GUARANTEED. PERIOD.

PRINCIPLE 4. We ship faster than anyone we know of. We ship items in stock the day we receive the order. At the height of the last Christmas season, the longest time an order was in the house was thirty-six hours, excepting monograms which took another twelve hours.

PRINCIPLE 5. We believe that what is best for our customer is best for all of us. Everyone here understands that concept. Our sales and service people are trained to know our products and to be friendly and helpful. They are urged to take all the time necessary to take care of you. We even pay for your call, for whatever reason you call.

PRINCIPLE 6. We are able to sell at lower prices because we have eliminated middlemen, because we don't buy branded merchandise with high protected markups, and because we have placed our contracts with manufacturers who have proved they are cost conscious and efficient.

PRINCIPLE 7. We are able to sell at lower prices because we operate efficiently. Our people are hard working, intelligent, and share in the success of the company.

PRINCIPLE 8. We are able to sell at lower prices because we support no fancy emporiums with their high overhead. Our main location is in the middle of a forty-acre cornfield in rural Wisconsin. We still operate our first location in Chicago's Near North tannery district.

Operations

The heart of any catalog retailing operation is, of course, the catalog itself. Lands' End currently mails thirteen 140-page (average) catalogs a year to its proven customers. In all, the firm circulated a total of 50 million catalogs in fiscal 1987. That number is expected to rise to 63.5 million in 1988 and 72 million in 1989, up from 18 million in 1984, the firm's most productive year in terms of sales per catalog mailed.

Another key to effective catalog retailing is the mailing list. Firms the size of Lands' End commonly maintain lists of five million or more names. LEI maintains a proprietary list of 7.8 million names. Although many catalog retailers obtain names from mailing list brokers and even competitors, Lands' End has attempted to build its list internally as much as possible as a source of competitive advantage. It has also reduced its participation in the mailing list rental market.

Catalog retailing also depends on order fulfillment and service. Merchandise is stored in and distributed from the firm's 275,000-square-foot distribution center. In spite of the size of this facility, however, it is only expected to be able to satisfy the firm's needs through 1989, when a 250,000-square-foot addition is expected to be completed. Through this center, Lands' End processed approximately 31,000 orders per day in 1987, with a high of 75,000 orders on its peak day. The center has the capacity to process 35,000 orders per nine-hour shift.

To facilitate the function of the distribution center, manage inventories, and minimize shipping costs, the firm uses an optical scanning sorting system. Orders are processed through the firm's mainframe computer system, based on three very large Series 3090 computers by IBM. Through this computer system, management can obtain real-time information on any part of its current operation status. In addition, during 1987, the firm installed a new computer-controlled garment-moving system and inseaming system as part of $6 million in capital expenditures. Finally, an automated receiving system installed during 1987 has increased the firm's receiving capacity to ten thousand boxes per day from four thousand.

Phone service is maintained through company phone centers. This service was recently enlarged by the addition of an auxillary center designed to handle seasonal overload traffic. This phone system now operates on a fiber-optic cable system to increase communication quality. Through the computer system, each operator has access to customer records and past sales history as well as a fact file on each catalog item. It is not unusual for this system to handle seventy-five calls at a time, around the clock, in normal times, with a much higher load in the Christmas season.

Though 95 percent of all sales are through the catalog and Lands' End operates no retail stores, it does maintain nine "outlet stores" at various locations in Chicago and Wisconsin. The firm also uses a "Lands' End Outlet" section in its catalog to help dispose of overstocks.

As the firm has grown, so has the number of employees. The firm now employs more than 2,200 people, with as many as 1,200 more added to handle the extra load during the busy fourth quarter. Both the founder and the current president have extensive advertising experience as well as considerable experience with the company. New additions to the list of top managers include experts in catalog merchandising, quality assurance, and other related specialties.

Lands' End realizes the importance of a quality work force. It has worked with the University of Wisconsin, Platteville, to set up an extension in Dodgeville to help workers increase their skills at company expense. Part-time workers earn full-time benefits after they work 1,040 hours in a year. All workers receive the right to an employee discount on the firm's products and share in the firm's profits. The firm also plans to provide a $5-million employee fitness center in 1988. Overall, wage levels in this industry average approximately $5.75 per hour.

Competitors

Dozens of catalog retailers sell apparel, even in the market dominated by Lands' End. However, in its specific target market, LEI has apparently become the market leader. LEI's competitors may be classified into several basic categories. There are firms, such as the J. Crew unit of

Popular Services, Inc. (men's clothing); Talbots (women's clothing), formerly owned by General Mills; and The Company Store (linens), that compete directly with a product segment served by Lands' End. Other firms, such as Hanover House, produce multiple catalogs serving a wide variety of customer product and demographic segments. Some of these segments may overlap with those served by LEI. Major retailers, such as Sears, J. C. Penney, and Spiegel, produce large, seasonal, full-line catalogs selling a wide variety of merchandise, of which apparel is only a part. These large firms, as well as other smaller catalog retailers that also operate retail stores, tend to compete more closely with traditional retailers. Exhibit 40-6 identifies a number of major catalog retailers and competitors for LEI. Exhibit 40-7 describes and contrasts several operating characteristics of LEI's closest competitors.

EXHIBIT 40-6 ▪ Direct/Catalog Sales, 1985: Largest Direct Mail/Catalog Apparel Firms

Firm	Direct/Catalog Total 1985 Sales
Fingerhut Corp./Cos.	$1,485 million
Spiegel	847 million
Sears	695 million
The Limited/Lane Bryant	612 million
J. C. Penney	510 million
New Process	330 million
Combined International	227 million
Lands' End	227 million
L. L. Bean	220 million
Hanover House	212 million
Avon Direct Response	205 million
Bear Creek	130 million
General Mills	104 million
CML Group	55 million
Popular Services	40 million

Source: *Inside the Leading Mail Order Houses,* Colorado Springs, CO: Maxwell Sroge, 1985.

Performance

Since 1984, when Lands' End achieved sales of $123.4 million and net profits of $7.3 million, the firm's sales and profits have grown at 22.2 percent and 25.6 percent annually, respectively. Sales and profit growth in the first half of fiscal 1989 were 33.7 percent and 64.6 percent higher than the same period in 1988, respectively. Gross margins have improved steadily and may be compared to a level of approximately 42.5 percent typical for apparel retailers in general. Net profit margins have also improved and may be compared to a recent level of about 3.5 percent for large retailers. The percentage of debt to equity has declined steadily throughout the period. The net profit to total assets measure of return on investment has averaged 21 percent over the last five years, compared to 4.4 percent for the nation's thirty-three largest-value retail firms (including LEI) in 1988 and approximately 7.5 percent for all retail establishments. LEI's return on stockholder's equity has averaged 40.4 percent since 1984, having earned 40.2 percent in 1988, compared to 15.4 percent for the thirty-three largest firms. Financial results for Lands' End are presented in Exhibits 40-1, 40-2, and 40-3.

Although Lands' End's recent performance is spectacular and far exceeds industry standards, it remains to be seen how long its growth and margins can be maintained. As the catalog market becomes increasingly competitive, new products and marketing methods will have to be developed.

Endnotes

[1]All financial data in this case comes from Lands' End annual reports and analytical reports prepared by Stephen Ashley of Blunt, Ellis, and Loewi, Inc. (August 4, 1987, and November 23, 1987).

[2]A. Hagedorn. " 'Tis the Season for Catalog Firms". *Wall Street Journal*, November 24, 1987, p. 6.

EXHIBIT 40-7 ▪ Lands' End Competitor Characteristics, 1985

Company	Catalog Sales ($ millions)	Catalogs Mailed (millions)	Sales per Catalog	Active Buyers (millions)	Stores and/or Notes
Lands' End	$227	44	$5.16	3.43	9 outlets
Hanover House	212	250	0.85	4.00	20 catalogs
L.L. Bean	221	68	3.25	2.15	1 store
Popular Services					
J. Crew	30	7	4.29	.45	
Cliff & Wills	10	2	5.00	.20	
CML Group	55	25	2.20	.49	5 catalogs 100 stores
General Mills (1985)					
Talbots	47	38	1.25	.47	59 stores
Eddle Bauer	57	25	2.28	.72	39 stores
General Mills (1987)					
Talbots	84	60+	<1.40	.65+	109 stores
Eddie Bauer	76	N/A	N/A	1.00	39 stores

References

Major sources of other information include:

1987 Supplement to the Fact Book. Direct Marketing Association. New York: DMA, 1987.

Inside the Leading Mail Order Houses, 3d ed. Colorado Springs, CO: Maxwell Sroge Publishing, 1987.

Lands' End Annual Reports, 1987 and 1988.

1988 Industrial Outlook. U.S. Department of Commerce.

41

Meadville State Prison

Introduction

Meadville State Prison is one of four major correctional facilities in the state. Until recently, it operated strictly in a custodial role, making very little effort to rehabilitate the inmates.

The organization of the prison consists of three departments reporting to the warden. An administrative staff, consisting of the purchasing, maintenance, health care, and recordkeeping departments, is considered as being apart from the mainstream of prison activities. A rehabilitation director heads a staff responsible for the training and counseling of inmates in preparation for their re-entry into civilian life. The deputy warden is in charge of the guards and is responsible for the security of the prison.

Meadville has experienced a change and is presently in a state of conflict. Before describing this conflict, it is essential that the personalities involved and the prior state of affairs be explored.

Background

Warden Aaron Hunsacre has been an administrator of Meadville for fifteen years, the first five of which were spent as a deputy warden and the last ten as warden.

On completing his high school education, Hunsacre immediately enlisted in the Marines, where he hoped someday to become a high ranking officer. Although he completed Officer Candidate School, he became bitter when he did not rise above the rank of major. Finally, in 1963, after thirteen years in the service, he decided to accept the deputy warden position

This case was prepared by Becky Fox, Steve Hardy, Jim Kreiner, and Kitty Putzier under the supervision of Theodore T. Herbert. The case is not intended to reflect either effective or ineffective administrative or technical practices; it was prepared for class discussion. Reprinted by permission of Theodore T. Herbert.

at Meadville. Several motives prompted his acceptance of this job, but foremost the implicit understanding that the warden's job would be his when the present holder retired in five years. The thought of being head honcho at a large prison was very appealing; he felt that the several years he had spent as an MP (military policeman) in the Marines had adequately prepared him for the position.

From this point on, events seemed to fall neatly into place for Aaron: he moved into the vacated warden's position at the end of five years and influenced the hiring of an old Marine buddy, Eugene Halter, to fill the deputy warden spot. Aaron was very content with his job, feeling that he had achieved a secure position of power and prestige in society as well as in the organization—after all, he was responsible directly to the *governor* of the state!

Aaron interpreted his job as warden as one of maintaining firm control in managing inmates. He had to punish and keep those people who threatened society out of sight. With this orientation, he hired employees who advocated strict enforcement of the rules and tolerated little misbehavior on the part of the inmates. He was very suspicious of younger, college-trained persons and held most of their theories in contempt. Whenever it could be avoided, he refused to hire college graduates.

Deputy Warden

Eugene Halter, the deputy warden, was supposed to take care of the daily operations of the prison, having the responsibility of supervising the guards who controlled the prisoners. He was to report any problems to the warden, as well as keep him informed of daily occurrences.

After Eugene had completed his stay in the Marines, he returned to school and received a two-year technical degree in criminology. It was at this point that he went to work at Meadville, a decision based on the encouragement of his friend, Aaron. He felt that this institution offered him the opportunity to rise someday to the top. Consequently, he took his job very seriously and was careful not to rock the boat in matters affecting Aaron's perceptions of the way he executed his job. After seven years with Meadville, Eugene had become Aaron's "yes man"; Eugene always avoided telling Aaron things that might upset him.

The deputy warden took his lead from Aaron and became an almost tyrannical enforcer of order. (In response to his commands, it became a standing joke for the prisoners, as well as some guards, to salute behind his back and garble his last name to sound like Heil Hitler!) The prisoners held Eugene in contempt; most of the guards regarded him with awe. It was felt that his actions to carry out his responsibilities bordered on being sadistic and that overall he was extremely power hungry.

The Captain of the Yard

Jeb Slatka was responsible for the guards and inmates in one of four sections of Meadville. He had been captain of the yard for five years, working his way up through the ranks by advancing from guard through sergeant, to watch officer, and finally to captain. He was now fifty-two with twenty-one years of service at the prison. Most of Jeb's earlier work experience had been in the military as an army noncom. After his combat tour of duty in Korea, the peacetime army no longer had an appeal for him. He had decided not to "re-up" and was looking for a job when an opening for a guard at Meadville came to his attention. The job seemed to suit his temperament, and he took it.

Jeb's office acted as the center for all yard communications. As a result of the custodial goals of the institution, primary interest was placed in the hour-by-hour reports on the location and movements of the prisoners. In addition, all orders, assignments of men, requests, and reports had to pass through his office and communications center. The line work supervisors, under these conditions, although equal in rank to the guards, had lower status and were obliged to take orders from the guards. This situation had evolved because the custodial goals of order and control were of prime importance. Meaningful work and rehabilitation were insignificant in the eyes of the warden and, therefore, to his guard staff. Other activities that might interfere even slightly with security just were not allowed.

The Guards

Although all other functions in the prison had operated under authoritarian and narrowly defined limits, much discretionary authority had been given to the guards insofar as their relationship to the prisoners was concerned. The guards had almost always been backed by their supervisors. This condition, in fact, had given the guards, as a group, more power than the line work supervisors and other rehabilitative personnel. The inmates recognized this power and considered it in all of their actions. The guards' position of power over the prisoners was enhanced by the psychological domination arising from the regimentation, frequent head counts, assemblies, and imposed silence during all supervised activities. Hence, the use of punishment was infrequent and usually unnecessary.

When imposed, punishment for control had few rules and was based on the individual guard's determination of insubordination. This created a situation wherein the accused had no rules, no forewarning, and no recourse for appeal. The uncertainty of the infliction of punishment as a means of control, not justice, produced an underlying and everpresent terror in the prisoners, especially at the lower hierarchical levels. Any of the very infrequent rewards were made only for prisoner conformity.

The Inmate Society

The authoritarian, custodial nature of the Meadville prison operation had created a no-frills environment, with few privileges available to the inmates. Under these conditions, one might have expected the men to become coequals and ready to rebel against the system at any chance. This was not the case. A highly structured inmate society, aimed at adjustment rather than rebellion, had developed. This society was led, rather surprisingly, by the least violent and aggressive men.

Although the inmate society, like the prison authorities, demanded that all prisoners be treated alike, interpersonal relations founded on dominance and subordination were the rule. The ability to exercise coercion was highly valued, not for the power, but because it was a means to achieve the goals common to all inmates: integrity and safety from official sanctions. As it currently existed, the inmate society had a static, sharply defined structure and power hierarchy aimed at attaining these goals. The society enforced member conformity through punishments usually more severe than those used by the prison officials.

When a new inmate or "fish" (just caught) arrived, he wasn't given a book of regulations defining his position. The shock of entering the prison, the capricious nature of discipline, the secrecy, and the regimentation all made the new man very dependent on any veteran inmate to whom he could attach himself. He needed an experienced man to teach him about the undefined and uncertain tolerances of the guards and to give him any insights vital for making life even the slightest bit more pleasant.

The new man was, in time, introduced to the prison grapevine. The grapevine was usually inaccurate, but it created and circulated the myths that helped to explain satisfactorily otherwise inexplicable (to the inmates) events. It helped the new men to adjust to prison life. The grapevine also helped, through the myths that held the prison officials in contempt, to create and maintain a degree of dignity and group unity.

The new, not yet accepted fish found himself lumped together at the bottom of the inmate society with those inmates whose prison jobs, behavior, or outside ties created suspicions that they might act as informers to the officials. The least a new man had to do to gain, or a current member to retain, membership in the society was to conform to the group norms. These included rejection of the outside world and to take any punishment without talking. A man who had gained seniority and the confidence of the membership and was able to explain, predict, or control in part the circumstances that others could not, would probably emerge as a leader. These leaders, because they had power, were mediators between their inmate followers and the officials. They were allowed to talk to the guards, which was not permitted for men in lower positions.

When conditions were stable, as things had been for the many years of the warden's custodial stewardship, the inmate society actually acted as a support for the authoritarian, custodial system. The inmate leaders had responsible contacts with the guards and had a voice in the assignment and distribution of privileges. This interaction between the officials and inmate leaders helped both sides achieve common, mutual goals of peace, order, and adjustment. In this way, each hierarchy was able to maintain its position of power and advantage.

The Rehabilitation Staff

The rehabilitation services department at Meadville is directed by Polly Hoover. Polly has her master's degree in social work. Before beginning graduate school, she worked for several years as a counselor in the State Detention Center for juvenile delinquents. Polly was an outstanding student during her graduate work, and at thirty-one, she is quite a bit younger than any of the previous directors. Polly has been at Meadville for almost two years now, and her staff is still making adjustments to her rehabilitation plans.

Polly is quite an idealist and believes strongly in the modern goals of therapy, treatment, education, and rehabilitation. She espouses the belief that if discipline is absolutely necessary, it must be administered in such a way as to preserve the dignity of the inmate.

The rehabilitation staff is made up of one full-time psychologist, a librarian, a part-time art instructor, two full-time vocational instructors, and another social worker (besides Polly).

Sam Fall, the prison psychologist, is fifty-three years old and quite comfortable with his position at Meadville. He is much more comfortable than he was fifteen years ago when he was still struggling to make a go of his private practice. When this position opened up twelve years ago, Sam jumped at the chance to, for once in his life, have a steady income he could count on, without the worries and responsibilities he faced when he was self-employed. Sam looked forward to spending the next twelve years waiting out his retirement.

Sam's formal responsibilities included scheduling private counseling sessions with inmates, which took up most of his time. He was also to conduct group therapy sessions, keep certain office hours for visitation by inmates, and maintain each inmate's file, updating it as to treatment and progress. He also served in an advisory capacity to the rest of the rehabilitation staff as well as the custodial staff.

The librarian, art instructor, and shop teachers were responsible for their own areas only and planned and coordinated their curricula with the advice and approval of the director. If Polly thought it necessary, Sam was called in for consultation.

The resident social worker was responsible for placing inmates in jobs within the prison in such areas as the kitchen, the laundry, and the library. He also directed prison recreational and social activities and assisted the director, Polly, in maintaining supportive relationships between prisoners and their families and friends and between prisoners and supportive volunteer organizations.

Polly was quite enthusiastic about getting outside groups more involved in the prison and trying out some of the rehabilitation techniques that she had researched during her graduate work. However, most of her staff had a less optimistic view of rehabilitation than she. Most of their efforts were directed toward keeping peace among the inmate society, rather than toward rehabilitation.

It was no secret that most of the inmates regarded the whole idea of rehabilitation as a joke. They played the game because they knew that, if they didn't, parole was a virtual impossibility. Sam Fall was not one of the most perceptive people when it came to human behavior, but even he had begun to realize that during personal counseling sessions, the inmates' responses had begun to follow predictable patterns.

Polly had become frustrated with the lack of support her rehabilitation efforts were receiving at Meadville. In fact, she was considering looking for a job elsewhere, where the attitudes of the administration were more enlightened. However, a riot at neighboring Roland State Prison brought the need for prison reform to light, and Polly felt that maybe now her ideas would be considered seriously.

The Change

The news was full of the explosive situation at Roland State. No one knew exactly how the riot started; accidently caught in the middle was a group of college freshmen from the local university who happened to be touring the facility as a field trip in psychology. Six of the group, four males and two females, had been held hostage along with four guards and a clerk from the prison's administrative staff.

The confrontation lasted for four long days with the prisoners demanding improved treatment in exchange for the hostages. The state police were prepared to attack the prisoner-controlled area and regain control by force. The fact that innocent bystanders, not a part of the prison system, were involved generated national public interest. People realized that the activities within a prison system can affect the general public and became very interested in the situation that led to the riot.

Jay Cole supplied the desired information and is considered the man most responsible for settling the riot and obtaining the release of the hostages unharmed. Cole is a local TV personality with a late-night talk show. Several months before, Cole and his station filmed a documentary on prison conditions at Roland State and conducted interviews with inmates. The show went relatively unnoticed when first aired, but during the riot the program was repeated nationwide during prime time. Cole's program and his genuine concern about prison conditions convinced a large segment of the public that reform was overdue and that the prisoners had legitimate complaints. Governor Wendell, well tuned to political pressures, saw a way to end the riot and take the initiative for reform. He selected Jay Cole to negotiate with the prisoners and offered to establish a state commission for prison reform in exchange for the hostages. The prisoners trusted Cole and agreed to the governor's terms. Cole promised the prisoners that he would keep the activities of the commission in the public eye to assure that real action would be taken.

The newly formed state commission visited Meadville and informed the warden that rehabilitation must be emphasized. A portion of the commission's findings states that:

consequently, it has been determined by our investigations that the 70 percent recidivism rate and the increase in severity of crimes committed by those released from prison indicate that prisons should take a more active part in attempting to rehabilitate inmates. Prisons must be made into something other than breeding places of hate-filled and vengeful individuals if we expect these individuals to one day re-enter our society.

The governor has also visited Warden Hunsacre and made it clear that prison reform is one of his major goals. He wants specific actions that the voter can relate to, for use in his re-election campaign next year. He reminded the warden that Jay Cole will keep this issue alive and will insist on real action, not just paper plans and programs.

The State Commission for Prison Reform presented all prison staff with a copy of the newly developed guidelines for achieving the desired changes in the state's prison system. Most of the guidelines are aimed at assuring more humane treatment of inmates and providing more opportunities for rehabilitation. The prison staff is to be responsible for maintaining a separate file on each inmate. Reports are to be filled out by both custodial and rehabilitative staff and are to be updated weekly. Each report is to include descriptions of all rehabilitation programs and efforts in which the inmate is involved, the results of the program and progress of the inmate's attitudes and behaviors, and an evaluation of custodial cooperation.

These reports are sent to the rehabilitation director, who evaluates them and summarizes the progress of the inmate population in reaching the goals set forth by the commission. These summaries will be sent to the State Commission for Prison Reform, and all inmates' files will be made available for the commission's examination.

Also, the rehabilitation staff was increased by the addition of two full-time counselors to assist in implementing the new guidelines.

Aaron realized that he had no choice other than to accommodate the wishes of the State Commission for Prison Reform. Although he felt that these new goals of the governor had their basis in political vote rallying and were not expected really to accomplish anything, he knew he would have to make a pretext of implementing them or else lose his job. He confided the following to Eugene:

Listen, I'm not about to let that Wendell and his commission come in here and tell me what to do. As far as I'm concerned, these new rehabilitation goals are nothing but a lot of hogwash! I'm only putting up with this rehabilitation director and her division because there's no way around it—but I'll tell you—they're really out in left field when it comes to understanding what a prison system is all about. They must think we're running a ______ day care center here instead of a prison. Thieves, murderers, and nogood bums!—that's what we've got here, and there's no way anyone's *going to make upstanding citizens out of that lot. Give these guys an inch and they'll take a mile. I'm sure I've made my point and you know what I mean—don't give them that first inch!*

Eugene transmitted Hunsacre's sentiments to the guards and let it be known that under no circumstances were security and control over the prisoners to be lessened. In turn, the guards were expected to remind the prisoners of exactly who was in charge and that nothing had changed.

On the other hand, Polly could not have been happier. She felt that with the governor and the commission behind her, she was finally going to have some clout in implementing her rehabilitation strategies. She expressed these beliefs in a discussion with her newly enlarged staff:

I've been waiting a long time for this kind of backing and finally we've got it. Now maybe we can make the warden see the kind of progress we can make with the prisoners if they're just treated like respectable human beings. Warden Hunsacre has told me I'm free to do whatever I want with this program and I'm sure we've got his full cooperation.

Various programs were created for the prisoners in the hopes that their self-improvement would be forthcoming. Participation in vocational education classes was encouraged, as well as participation in the formal therapy and rap sessions.

After several months of organizing and establishing these programs, Polly felt that she wasn't making as much progress as she had hoped. She felt that her social workers were facing a subverted resistance from the guards. Although the guards always seemed to listen to the rehabilitation staff, often their actions were inconsistent with the advice. Behind the staff's backs, guards apparently continued to belittle the inmates and exercise control in the way they felt necessary. The rehabilitation staff learned this through the complaints of some of the prisoners. At first, Polly could not understand why the guards were being so uncooperative, but then attributed it to laziness and unwillingness to exert the effort to interact decently with the prisoners.

The guards viewed their situation differently, as is evidenced by this conversation between two of them:

This rehabilitation stuff is for the birds. I don't know about you, but I'm getting a little tired of listening to their preaching about how we should respect these hooligans. "Try to get to know them better," they say—ha!—I know all I care to know and that's too much. I know who signs my paycheck, and if he wants the cons to toe the mark, that's what he's going to get.

Yeah. *Things ran a lot better around here before rehab got so high and mighty. These social workers are always siding with the inmates and believing their accounts over ours. You should hear some of the stories I've heard prisoners tell—sheesh! Those rehabs are a gullible bunch, they fall for any sob story.*

During the ensuing months, problems between the rehabilitation staff and the warden's group increased drastically. Minor occasions for interaction between the two groups seemed to assume more importance, and tensions increased. Guards complained that the rehabilitation staff was too lax in their dealings with the inmates, which endangered security. One guard confronted a rehabilitation teacher with the following:

Three times last week I had to confiscate weapons from inmates that they got from your class. You may think they're only harmless tools, but in the hands of most of these fellows, they're as lethal as any gun or knife. You just don't understand that these guys can't *be trusted, do you?!*

Oftentimes, a guard would, as a form of punishment, not permit a certain inmate to attend a class or self-help session. Conflicts then arose because teachers and social workers felt that the classes were too important for inmates to be arbitrarily denied.

The inmates were caught in the middle of the situation. Those in the top level of the prisoner hierarchy knew that their best course of action was to stay on the guard's best side and avoid any siding with the rehabilitation staff. Taking their cue from the façade used by the guards, those prisoners would go through the motions of "being rehabilitated," when in fact they thought it was a joke. However, in the lower echelons of the ranks of prisoners were those inmates who were trying to get the best deal for themselves by playing the staff against the guards. They could covertly "squeal" to the rehabilitation workers and gain sympathy without much fear of reprisals or sanctions from fellow inmates. It was these individuals, because they didn't conform to the main prisoner group, which wanted compliance and safety from prison sanctions, who increased the conflict between the warden and guards and the rehabilitation staff.

It became evident to Polly that the warden was not really being very cooperative in helping her to meet her rehabilitation goals. One day, the two confronted each other in the explosive argument that follows:

Polly: Listen here, Hunsacre! I get the impression you don't care at all about what I'm attempting to do with these prisoners. You tell me one thing and the next time I turn around you're doing the opposite. I can't get anywhere with your guards either, and I *need* their cooperation. It looks like I may have to go to the state commission if you don't make a few changes.

Aaron: What have I been trying to tell you all along!? Get your head out of the clouds and return to earth, will you? Don't try and put the blame on me because your program is a flop. Sometimes I think I'm the only one around here who's living in the real world. You're so blind you can't see what a mess you're making of everything. The only way to handle prisoners is with firm control and the sooner you realize that, the better off we'll all be. I wouldn't be so anxious to broadcast this mess to the commission if I were you; you just might be cutting your own throat!

42

Measuring Excellence: Applying the Lessons of Peters and Waterman

Goals

I. To help participants identify an organization's degree of excellence.*

II. To heighten the participants' awareness of the effect of management attitudes and practices within organizations.

Group Size

Six to eight individuals preferably with different degrees of work experience.

Time Required

Approximately three and one-half hours (with optional activities).

Materials

I. A copy of the Measuring Excellence Theory Sheet for each participant.

II. A copy of the Measuring Excellence Work Sheet for each participant.

III. A newsprint flip chart and a felt-tipped marker for each group.

IV. A newsprint flip chart and a felt-tipped marker for the instructor's use.

Physical Setting

A room large enough so that each group can work without disturbing the other group(s). Movable chairs should be provided.

Process

Step I. Introduction (10 min.)

The instructor announces the goals of the activity, distributes copies of the Measuring Excellence Theory Sheet, and asks the participants to read this handout.

*As defined by T. J. Peters and R. H. Waterman, Jr., in *In Search of Excellence: Lessons from America's Best-Run Companies*, Harper & Row, 1982.

Reprinted from Leonard D. Goodstein and J. William Pfeiffer, (Eds.), *The 1986 Annual: Developing Human Resources*, San Diego, CA: University Associates, Inc., 1986. Used with permission.

Step II. Overview (15 min.)

The instructor presents an overview of the eight characteristics of organizational excellence identified by Peters and Waterman, provides examples of these characteristics, and then elicits and answers questions.

Step III. Analysis (30 min.)

Each participant is asked to think of an organization with which they are familiar and to evaluate that organization in terms of the 8 basic characteristics. The participants are then told to read the instructions to the work sheet and then to complete the sheet independently. The instructor mentions that the participants' work sheets will be collected and that their responses will be discussed by the entire group, but that the participants need not put their names on their work sheets unless they wish to do so.

Step IV. Totals (15 min.)

The Instructor collects the work sheets and tallies on newsprint all participant responses to Item I.

Step V. Discussion (40 min.)

The instructor leads the entire group through a discussion of the responses to Item I. As the participants identify areas of agreement and disagreement as well as the overall levels of their responses, the instructor summarizes their findings on newsprint.

Step VI. Excellence Examples (20 min.) (optional)

The instructor reads aloud each participant's paragraph describing an example of one of the eight basics of excellence (Item II on the work sheet). After each is read, the participants are asked:

1. Which of the eight basics of excellence the incident exemplifies;
2. How frequently such incidents occur in the organization;
3. How many of the participants knew about the incident before this announcement of it; and
4. What conclusions can be drawn from this discussion of the incident.

Step VII. Excellence Omissions (20 min.) (optional)

Step VI is repeated using each participant's example of an omission of one of the basics of excellence (Item III on the work sheet).

Step VIII. Group Discussion (15 min.)

The instructor leads a discussion during which the participants determine which of the eight basics of excellence should be emphasized more strongly in organizations. As these basics are identified, the instructor lists them on newsprint.

Step IX. Action Plans (30 min.)

The instructor asks the participants to assemble into their individual groups. Each group is asked to choose one of the eight basics that requires a stronger emphasis and to devise an action plan of specific steps that an organization could take to help promote this basic. The instructor emphasizes that each plan should incorporate goals, strategies to be used, action steps to be taken to accomplish strategies, specific personnel to be responsible for the various steps, and target dates for completing the steps. Each group is given a newsprint flip chart and a felt-tipped marker and is asked to select a member to record the group's plan as it is devised.

Step X. Closure (25 min.)

The instructor reconvenes the total group and asks the participants to share their reactions to the planning phase and about the actions that they plan to take.

Measuring Excellence Theory

In their popular book entitled *In Search of Excellence: Lessons from America's Best-Run*

Companies, Peters and Waterman outline the *eight basics of excellence* that they found to be characteristic of thirty-seven of the most successful companies in the United States. These eight basics are as follows:[1]

1. **A bias for action**—a preference for doing something—anything—rather than sending a question through cycles and cycles of analyses and committee reports.
   not
   Paralysis by analysis—a preference for waiting to act until all issues and possible ramifications have been studied exhaustively.
2. **Staying close to the customer**—learning his preferences and catering to them.
   not
   Close to the organization—characterizing the customer as an intrusion into organizational functioning.
3. **Autonomy and entrepreneurship**—breaking the corporation into small companies and encouraging them to think independently and competitively.
   not
   Top-down control—concentrating control exclusively within the ranks of management and discouraging independent thinking.
4. **Productivity through people**—creating in *all* employees the awareness that their best efforts are essential and that they will share in the rewards of the company's success.
   not
   Productivity through forced labor—assuming that employees must be forced to work, cannot or will not make meaningful contributions, and should not share in the organization's success.
5. **Hands-on, value driven**—insisting that executives keep in touch with the firm's essential business.
   not
   Remote control, driven by policy manuals—allowing executives to remain in the background, removed from the firm's essential business.
6. **Stick to the knitting**—remaining with the business the company knows best.
   not
   Diversify widely—emphasizing wide diversification to achieve a synergistic effect.
7. **Simple form, lean staff**—few administrative layers, few people at the upper levels.
   not
   Complex form, top-heavy staff—a complex structure and systems, many people at the upper levels.
8. **Simultaneous loose-tight properties**—fostering a climate where there is dedication to the central values of the company combined with tolerance for all employees who accept those values.
   not
   Totalitarianism or anarchy—fostering a climate that depends on the enforcement of unbending controls or one that allows employees to pursue unbridled self-actualization.

[1] "Learn how the best-run American companies use these EIGHT BASIC PRINCIPLES to stay on top of the heap!" from *IN SEARCH OF EXCELLENCE: Lessons from America's Best-Run Companies* (Warner paperback edition) by Thomas J. Peters and Robert H. Waterman, Jr. Copyright © 1982 by Thomas J. Peters and Robert H. Waterman, Jr. Reprinted by permission of Harper & Row, Publishers, Inc.

Measuring Excellence Work Sheet

I. Indicate the degree to which each of the following eight basics of excellence is emphasized in your organization. Write "H" in each blank that corresponds to a basic that receives *heavy* emphasis, "M" in each blank that corresponds to one that receives *medium* emphasis, and "L" in each blank that corresponds to one that receives *light* emphasis.

_______ 1. A bias for action
_______ 2. Staying close to the customer
_______ 3. Autonomy and entrepreneurship
_______ 4. Productivity through people
_______ 5. Hands-on, value driven
_______ 6. Stick to the knitting
_______ 7. Simple form, lean staff
_______ 8. Simultaneous loose-tight properties

II. In the space provided below, write a paragraph describing an incident that occurred in your organization that you consider to be an *example* of one of the eight basics of excellence.

III. In the space provided below, write a paragraph describing an incident that occurred in your organization that you consider to be an *omission* of one of the eight basics of excellence.

43

Masters of Innovation

It was 1922. Minnesota Mining & Manufacturing inventor Francis G. Okie was dreaming up ways to boost sales of sandpaper, then the company's premiere product, when a novel thought struck him. Why not sell sandpaper to men as a replacement for razor blades? Why would they risk the nicks of a sharp instrument when they could rub their cheeks smooth instead?

The idea never caught on, of course. The surprise is that Okie, who continued to sand his own face, could champion such a patently wacky scheme and keep his job. But unlike most companies then—or now—3M Co. demonstrated a wide tolerance for new ideas, believing that unfettered creative thinking would pay off in the end. Indeed, Okie's hits made up for his misses: He developed a waterproof sandpaper that became a staple of the auto industry because it produced a better exterior finish and created less dust than conventional papers. It was 3M's first blockbuster.

Through the decades, 3M has managed to keep its creative spirit alive. The result is a company that spins out new products faster and better than just about anyone. It boasts an impressive catalog of more than 60,000 products, from Post-it notes to heart-lung machines. What's more, 32 percent of 3M's $10.6 billion in 1988 sales came from products introduced within the past five years. Antistatic videotape, translucent dental braces, synthetic ligaments for damaged knees, and heavy-duty reflective sheeting for construction-site signs are just a few of the highly profitable new products that contributed to record earnings of $1.15 billion in 1988.

At a time when many big U.S. corporations are trying to untangle themselves from bureaucracy, 3M stands apart as a smooth-running innovation machine. Along with a handful of other companies that might be called the Innovation Elite—Merck, Hewlett-Packard, and Rubbermaid among them (see exhibit 43–1 at the

Reprinted from the April 10, 1989 issue of *Business Week* by special permission.

end of the case)—3M is celebrated year after year in the rankings of most-respected companies. Business schools across the country make 3M a case study in new-product development, and management gurus trumpet 3M's methods. Peter Drucker's *Innovation and Entrepreneurship* is peppered with 3M tales. A star of the bestseller *In Search of Excellence,* 3M remains a favorite of co-author Thomas J. Peters. "It is far more entrepreneurial than any $10 billion company I've come across," he says, "and probably more entrepreneurial than a majority of those one-tenth its size."

The publicity has attracted representatives of dozens of companies from around the world to tour 3M headquarters near St. Paul, Minn., in search of ideas and inspiration. While such companies as Monsanto Co. and United Technologies Corp. have adopted some of 3M's methods, it's hard to emulate a culture that has been percolating since the turn of the century.

Lose Some

So how does 3M do it? One way is to encourage inventive zealots like Francis Okie. The business of innovation can be a numbers game—the more tries, the more likely there will be hits. The scarcity of corporate rules at 3M leaves room for plenty of experimentation—and failure. Okie's failure is as legendary among 3Mers as his blockbuster. Salaries and promotions are tied to the successful shepherding of new products from inception to commercialization. One big carrot: The fanatical 3Mer who champions a new product out the door then gets the chance to manage it as if it were his or her own business.

Since the bias is toward creating new products, anything that gets in the way, whether it's turf fights, overplanning, or the "not-invented-here" syndrome, is quickly stamped out. Divisions are kept small, on average about $200 million in sales, and they are expected to share knowledge and manpower. In fact, informal information-sharing sessions spring up willy-nilly at 3M—in the scores of laboratories and small meeting rooms or in the hallways. And it's not unusual for customers to be involved in these brainstorming klatches.

Peer Review

That's not to say that corporate restraint is nonexistent. 3Mers tend to be self-policing. Sure, there are financial measures that a new-product team must meet to proceed to different stages of development, but the real control lies in constant peer review and feedback.

The cultural rules work—and go a long way toward explaining why an old-line manufacturing company, whose base products are sandpaper and tape, has become a master at innovation. And a highly profitable one at that. Earnings spurted 25 percent in 1988 from a year earlier. It wasn't always so. The company hit a rocky stretch in the early 1980s. But stepped-up research spending and some skillful cost-cutting by Chairman and Chief Executive Allen F. Jacobson have revived all of 3M's critical financial ratios.

A 3M lifer and Scotch-tape veteran, Jake Jacobson took over the top job in 1985 and laid out his J-35 program. That's J as in Jake, and 35 as in 35 percent cuts in labor and manufacturing costs—to be accomplished by 1990. 3M is well on its way to reaching those goals, and the push has already improved the bottom line. Last year return on capital climbed almost three points, to 27.6 percent, and return on equity had a similar rise, to 21.6 percent. Jacobson has clamped down on costs without harming his company's ability to churn out new products one whit.

Motley Crew

3M was founded not by scientists or inventors but by a doctor, a lawyer, two railroad executives, and a meat-market manager. At the turn of the century the five Minnesotans bought a plot of heavily forested land on the frigid shores of Lake Superior, northeast of Duluth. They planned to mine corundum, an abrasive used by sandpaper manufacturers to make the paper scratchy. The five entrepreneurs drummed up new investors, bought machinery, hired workers, and started mining. Only then did they discover that their corundum, alas, wasn't corundum at all but a worthless mineral that the sandpaper industry wanted no part of.

The company tried selling its own sandpaper, using corundum shipped in from the East, but got battered by the competition. How perfect: The company that tolerates failure was founded on a colossal one. 3M was forced to innovate or die. Most of the original investors got swept out of the picture, and the remaining 3Mers set about inventing. First, the company introduced a popular abrasive cloth for metal finishing. Then Okie struck gold with his Wetordry sandpaper. They drew inspiration from William L. McKnight, who is revered to this day as the spiritual father of the company. He started out as an assistant bookkeeper and worked his way up through sales. His approach, unusual for its day, has stuck with the company. Rather than make his pitch to a company's purchasing agent, McKnight talked his way onto the factory floor to demonstrate his products to the workers who used them. After he became chairman and chief executive, he penned a manifesto that said, in part: "If management is intolerant and destructively critical when mistakes are made, I think it kills initiative."

Loyal Lifers

That kind of thinking breeds loyalty and management stability. The company rarely hires from the outside, and never at the senior level. Jacobson, 62, a chemical engineer, started out in the tape lab in 1947. And all his lieutenants are lifers, too. The turnover rate among managers and other professionals averages less than 4 percent. "It's just not possible to really understand this company until you've been around for a long while," says Jerry E. Robertson, head of the Life Sciences Sector.

Don't let 3M's dull exterior fool you. The St. Paul campus, home of company headquarters and most of the research labs, is an expanse of brick buildings with a high-rise glass tower that could have been designed by a kid with an Erector set. But inside is an army of engineers and technical experts and platoons of marketers just raring to innovate.

Here's how it typically works: A 3Mer comes up with an idea for a new product. He or she forms an action team by recruiting full-time members from technical areas, manufacturing, marketing, sales, and maybe finance. The team designs the product and figures out how to produce and market it. Then it develops new uses and line extensions. All members of the team are promoted and get raises as the project goes from hurdle to hurdle. When sales grow to \$5 million, for instance, the product's originator becomes a project manager, at \$20 million to \$30 million, a department manager, and in the \$75 million range, a division manager. There's a separate track for scientists who don't want to manage.

Many Paths

As a result, 3M is big but acts small. There are forty-two divisions, so ladders to the top are all over the place. Jacobson reached the pinnacle by cleaning up old-line operations, while his predecessor, Lewis W. Lehr, invented a surgical tape and then rode the company's burgeoning health care business all the way to the chairman's post.

So what are the corporate guidelines? A prime one is the 25-percent rule, which requires that a quarter of a division's sales come from products introduced within the past five years. Meeting the 25-percent test is a crucial yardstick at bonus time, so managers take it seriously. When Robert J. Hershock took over the occupational health division in 1982, it was utterly dependent on an aging product category, disposable face masks. By 1985, his new-product percentage had deteriorated to a mere 12 percent.

That set off alarms. He and his crew had to come up with plenty of new products—and they had to do it in eighteen to twenty-four months, half the normal time. Using technology similar to the division's facemask filters, Hershock's action teams created a bevy of products. One team came up with a sheet that drinks up the grease from microwaved bacon. Another devised a super-absorbent packing material that was widely welcomed by handlers of blood samples. The idea came from a team member who had read a newspaper article about postal workers who were panicked by the AIDS epidemic. The division's new-product sales are back above 25 percent.

Then there's the 15 percent rule. That one allows virtually anyone at the company to spend up to 15 percent of the workweek on anything he or she wants to, as long as it's product related. The practice is called "bootlegging," and its most famous innovation is the ubiquitous yellow Post-it note. Arthur L. Fry's division was busy with other projects, so he invoked the 15 percent rule to create the adhesive for Post-its. The idea came out of Fry's desire to find a way to keep the bookmark from falling out of his hymn book. Post-its are now a major 3M consumer business, with revenues estimated at as much as $300 million.

Cultural Habits

A new-product venture isn't necessarily limited by a particular market's size, either. Take Scotch tape. It was invented in 1929 for an industrial customer who used it to seal insulation in an airtight shipping package. Who could have known that it would grow into an estimated $750 million business someday?

Another recent example: The market for 3M chemist Tony F. Flannery's new product, a filter used to clean lubricants in metalworking shops, was a mere $1 million. But Flannery got the go-ahead to dabble with it anyway. He hooked up with a customer, PPG Industries Inc., which sells paint-primer systems to auto makers. The filters they were using to strain out impurities weren't doing the job. Flannery made prototypes of filter bags using a fibrous 3M material. They not only turned out to be bang-up primer filters, but the new bags are also being used to filter beer, water, edible oils, machine oil, and paint. Flannery figures that the filters could become a $20 million business in a few years.

Getting close to the customer is not just a goal at 3M—it's an ingrained cultural trait. Back in the 1920s, 3M inventor Richard G. Drew noticed that painters on automobile assembly lines had trouble keeping borders straight on the two-tone cars popular at the time. He went back to the lab and invented masking tape.

In-House Grants

Even with 3M's emphasis on innovation, new ideas do fall through the cracks. In 1983, some employees complained that worthwhile projects were still going unnoticed despite the 15 percent rule. Guaranteed free time doesn't guarantee that there will be money to build a prototype. So the company created Genesis grants, which give researchers up to $50,000 to carry their projects past the idea stage. A panel of technical experts and scientists awards as many as ninety grants each year.

One recipient was Sanford Cobb, an optics specialist at 3M. In 1983, a bulb went on in his head at a scientific conference when he ran across something called light pipe technology. Plastic is inlaid with nearly microscopic prisms so it can reflect light for long distances with little loss of energy.

Cobb knew the heavy acrylic used in the original invention was impractical because it would be difficult to mold, but he figured he could use 3M technology to make a light pipe out of a flexible plastic film. Because 3M isn't in the lighting business, though, Cobb couldn't find a division manager willing to fork over prototype money. So he applied for a Genesis grant. He got it, and made his idea work.

City Lights

3M licensed the basic technology from the inventor, and now its light pipes are used in products offered by several divisions. One use is in large highway signs. The new ones feature two 400-watt bulbs, replacing sixty to seventy fluorescent tubes. Manufacturers of explosives use light pipes to illuminate their most volatile areas. And the top of One Liberty Plaza, the new office tower dominating Philadelphia's skyline, is decorated with a light-piping design. Cobb's development is part of a major new technology program at 3M, with potential annual revenues amounting to hundreds of millions of dollars.

It's a surprise, given 3M's strong predilection toward divisional autonomy, that its technology gets spread around. But 3M is a company of backscratchers, eager to help fellow employees in the knowledge that they'll get help when they need it in return. For example, when the nonwoven-fiber experts got together with the lab folks at abrasives, the result was Scotch-Brite scrubbing sponges. A Technology Council made up of researchers from the various divisions regularly gets together to exchange information.

The result of all this interconnection is an organic system in which the whole really is greater than the sum of its parts. It's no coincidence that 3M is never mentioned as a possible breakup candidate. Bust it apart, sever the interconnections, and 3M's energy would likely die. Even if a raider decided to leave it intact, an unfamiliar hand at the helm might send the company off course. The possibility of a raid on 3M was taken a bit more seriously in the early 1980s, when financial performance slipped as the result of a strong dollar and skimping on R & D in the 1970s.

Jacobson's cost-cutting has done wonders for 3M. But his next challenge is formidable. The company's fortunes tend to track the domestic economy, so with a slowdown on the horizon, he must now find ways to spur growth. For one, he wants to expand internationally, boosting overseas sales from 42 percent of revenues to 50 percent by 1992. It may be slow going, however. Just as Jacobson was about to win a beachhead for a plethora of 3M products by buying the sponge unit of France's Chargeurs, the French government blocked the sale on antitrust grounds.

Jacobson is also starting to insist that 3M's divisions develop bigger-ticket products. The company has been taking core technologies and coming up with hundreds of variations. But those market niches can be pretty skinny—often only a few million dollars or so. Now the company's strategists are focusing on forty-five new product areas, each with $50 million in annual sales potential three to five years out. One example: A staple gun that replaces pins for broken bones. A 50-percent new-product success rate would contribute $1.2 billion in sales by 1994 from this program alone.

Sincere Flattery

Jacobson's latest achievements have yet to be reflected in 3M's stock price, which has been hovering in the 60s since the 1987 crash. Analysts are concerned that despite the company's diversification into health care, it still makes about 40 percent of its sales to the industrial sector, so it could get socked in a recession. And 3M is still considered vulnerable in floppy disks and videotape and related media, which account for about $800 million in sales. The unit has been locked in a bruising battle with the Japanese for years and lost an estimated $50 million in 1987. While those products finally became profitable in last year's fourth quarter as a result of cost-cutting and wider distribution, the area could remain a trouble spot. "It's a fragile turnaround," says analyst B. Alex Henderson at Prudential Bache Securities Inc.

Other companies would love to have 3M's problems if its successes came with them. Indeed, 3M constantly finds itself playing host to companies trying to figure out how to be more creative. Monsanto has set up a technology council modeled on 3M's, and United Technologies has embarked on an effort to share resources among its not-so-united operations. Eight years ago, Rubbermaid Inc. began insisting that 30 percent of its sales come from products developed in the previous five years.

While other companies may pick up ideas piecemeal from 3M, it would be impossible for any big corporation to swallow the concept whole. "We were fortunate enough to get the philosophy in there before we started to grow, rather than trying to create it after we got big," says Lester C. Krogh, who heads research and development. 3M has a simple formula: Find the Francis Okies, and don't get in their way. But for managers of other companies, large and small, that's often easier said than done.

EXHIBIT 43-1 ■ Corporate Innovators: How They Do It

3M Relies on a Few Simple Rules . . .

Keep divisions small. Division managers must know each staffer's first name. When a division gets too big, perhaps reaching $250 to $300 million in sales, it is split up.

Tolerate failure. By encouraging plenty of experimentation and risk-taking, there are more chances for a new-product hit. The goal: Divisions must derive 25 percent of sales from products introduced in the past five years. The target may be boosted to 30 percent.

Motivate the champions. When a 3Mer comes up with a product idea, he or she recruits an action team to develop it. Salaries and promotions are tied to the product's progress. The champion has a chance to someday run his or her own product group or division.

Stay close to the customer. Researchers, marketers, and managers visit with customers and routinely invite them to help brainstorm product ideas.

Share the wealth. Technology, wherever it's developed, belongs to everyone.

Don't kill a project. If an idea can't find a home in one of 3M's divisions, a staffer can devote 15 percent of his or her time to prove it is workable. For those who need seed money, as many as 90 Genesis grants of $50,000 are awarded each year.

. . . While Other Companies Have Their Own Approaches

RUBBERMAID Thirty percent of sales must come from products developed in the past five years. Looks for fresh design ideas anywhere; now trying to apply the Ford Taurus-style soft look to garbage cans. A recent success: stackable plastic outdoor chairs.

HEWLETT-PACKARD Researchers urged to spend 10 percent of time on own pet projects; twenty-four-hour access to labs and equipment; keeps divisions small to rally the kind of spirit that produces big winners such as its LaserJet laser printer.

DOW CORNING Forms research partnerships with its customers to develop new products such as reformulations of Armor-All car polishes and Helene Curtis hair sprays.

MERCK Gives researchers time and resources to pursue high-risk, high-payoff products. After a major scientific journal said work on anticholesterol agents like Mevacor would likely be fruitless, Merck kept at it. The drug is a potential blockbuster.

GENERAL ELECTRIC Jointly develops products with customers. Its plastics unit created with BMW the first body panels made with thermoplastics for the carmaker's Z1 two-seater.

JOHNSON & JOHNSON The freedom to fail is a built-in cultural prerogative. Lots of autonomous operating units spur innovations such as its Acuvue disposable contact lenses.

BLACK & DECKER Turnaround built partly on new-product push. Advisory councils get ideas from customers. Some new hot sellers: the Cordless Screwdriver and ThunderVolt, a cordless powertool that packs enough punch for heavy-duty construction work.

Data: Company Reports

44

Missouri Campus Bitterly Divided over How to 'Reallocate' Funds

On the campus of the University of Missouri here, the signs of spring came late and were decidedly makeshift: a white sheet bearing the spray-painted legend "SOCIAL WORK IS HERE TO STAY" draped from windows in Clark Hall; a crudely lettered placard taped to a glass door in Memorial Union defiantly announcing, "HELL NO, HOME EC WON'T GO!"

Hasty construction accounted for the home-made quality of the signs, for as the academic year drew quickly to a close, many students and faculty members were surprised to find themselves fighting for their academic lives—the survival of their programs.

In a year in which the campus has had to contend with a host of financial problems—some fabricated, critics allege—April was the cruelest month. It was on April 2 that proposals to "reallocate" nearly $12 million in operating funds over the next three years were announced. Among them were recommendations to eliminate two of the university's fourteen colleges and to reduce substantially the offerings in five others.

The ensuing controversy divided the campus. "It has set department against department and colleague against colleague," says one dean. "It's civil war, with everyone trying to gore everyone else's bull."

In mid-April, the faculty voted to call for the resignation of Chancellor Barbara S. Uehling if she did not withdraw the proposals.

By the time graduating students were preparing for last week's commencement exercises, the subject of their conversations—whether or not they had jobs—also seemed to be a prime topic of talk among many members of the faculty and staff.

What led to this course of events was a decision last summer by President James C. Olson to take action "to preserve and even enhance the quality of the university in a time of severely limited resources."

"The university has coped with ten years of inadequate funding by making cuts across the board," he says. "It became clear that a continuation of that policy was a prescription for mediocrity."

Mr. Olson announced last July that the university would attempt to save approximately $16 million over the next three years to finance pay raises as well as library, laboratory, and other improvements. He told the chancellors of the four Missouri campuses that their first priority was to be the development of an adequate compensation plan for the university staff. His plan was supported by the university's Board of Curators.

President Olson's goal is to bring salaries at the university up to the average of those at member institutions of the Big 8 and Big 10 athletic conferences—institutions that, he says, "are comparable to Missouri in mission." At the start of the 1981–82 academic year, Missouri had the lowest salary average in that comparison group, 8.9 percent below the midpoint.

Mr. Olson instructed the chancellors to find money for salary adjustments "by reducing the quantity of what you do rather than the quality."

That met with approval on the Columbia campus, where Chancellor Uehling has said "the concept of shared poverty is not viable for a competitive university," and where the faculty has been on the record for five years in opposition to across-the-board budget cuts.

The 24,000-student campus, biggest in the system, is scheduled for the largest reductions: as much as $12 million, or about 5 percent of its operating budget.

The curators adopted procedures for the "discontinuance" of program, and the university established four criteria for reviewing them: overall quality, contribution to the university's mission, need for the program, and financial considerations. Application of the criteria was left up to the individual campuses.

"On two occasions I identified to the deans the ways in which we might go about this task," says Provost Ronald F. Bunn, who is faced with reducing the budget for academic programs by $7 million.

'A Quality Matrix'

According to Mr. Bunn, most of the deans suggested that he take on the task. The Faculty Council recommended the same. "This was an administrative job," says David West, the council chairman and a professor of finance. "We wanted the administration to make its proposals, and then we'd take shots at it."

Mr. Bunn reviewed all of the campus's academic programs himself, rating them according to the four criteria established by the president. He compiled what he calls "a quality matrix," which resembles the box score of a baseball game. The programs that ranked lowest he proposed reducing.

Specifically, the provost recommended the elimination of the School of Library and Informational Science and the College of Public and Community Services (with the possible retention of its masters-in-social-work program). He also recommended major reductions in the College of Education, the College of Engineering, the School of Nursing, the College of Home Economics, and the School of Health Related Professions. In some cases the reductions would mean the elimination of one or more departments within those colleges.

All told, campus officials estimated that the cuts in academic programs would affect twenty-five hundred students and as many as two hundred faculty and staff members. Since tenure regulations require the university to give tenured faculty members thirteen months' notice of plans to eliminate their jobs, the reduction proposals would have little effect on the 1982–83 budget.

When university administrators announced their plans on April 2, those in the academic programs predictably provoked the greatest response.

'It Infuriates Me'

An ad hoc committee of faculty members and students was charged with reviewing the provost's recommendations and conducting hearings.

Individuals in the targeted programs have been outspokenly critical of Provost Bunn's judgment.

"We are the only accredited library-science program in Missouri, and it infuriates me—as a citizen as much as anything—that this campus, unilaterally, has made the decision to eliminate programs that exist nowhere else in the state," says Edward P. Miller, dean of the library school. "I don't think the provost could have done a worse job of abrogating the criteria for review if he tried."

Bob G. Woods, dean of the College of Education, who supported the idea of programmatic cuts, says he was prepared to reduce his budget by as much as $500,000, but when he learned that reductions of $1.2 million were required, he changed his mind. "I want the process to be refuted as unnecessary at this time," he says.

Officials in the College of Home Economics charge that the recommendations to eliminate two departments there were based on outdated information. "The decision regarding my program was based on a three-year-old internal-review document," says Kitty G. Dickerson, chairman of the department of clothing and textiles, who is in her first year at Missouri. "I was brought here to strengthen this department. There were thirty-five recommendations in that internal review, and we have already addressed all but three. But there was never an opportunity to let it be known that we have made this enormous progress."

Martha Jo Martin, assistant dean of home economics, says that eliminating the two departments would cost the college its accreditation and half of its enrollment.

Opposition was not limited to those in programs proposed for reduction. Says Andrew Twaddle, a professor of sociology, "My main concern is not with the actual targeting of programs but the fact that the administration made these decisions with little input from the faculty, except for a select group of its supporters.

"I honestly don't know what the university's real fiscal situation is—there are so many conflicting figures flying around, and no one is backing them up very well," he adds. "But according to the bylaws of this campus, the faculty is supposed to make academic policy, and when you're talking about what is or is not to be taught at the university, you're talking about policy."

Others are concerned about the impact of the proposals on women and minorities.

"We are assuming that the university is aware of its commitment to affirmative action," says W. L. Moore, an assistant professor of education and chairman of the Black Faculty and Staff Organization. "But we have not been kept informed, and we are very skeptical of all that is being done in this area."

Mr. Moore says his organization has determined that the proposed cuts would affect 63 percent of the black faculty members. The university's Office of Equal Opportunity says the figure is 33 percent. The discrepancy is due to the administration's inclusion of nonteaching blacks in its figures, says Mr. Moore. "But the precise number doesn't matter, because even 33 percent is too high a price to pay," he adds.

Of the campus's 620 black undergraduates, 255 are enrolled in targeted programs, says H. Richard Dozier, coordinator of minority-student services. "Blacks weren't admitted to this institution until 1950, and they make up only 3.7 percent of the student body," he says. "These cuts would be regressive."

Blacks on the campus have asked the administration for assurances that the university's five-year affirmative-action goals will be met.

There is also some feeling on the campus that faculty salary raises are being used as, in the words of one dean, "a smokescreen" for an attempt to change the institution from a multipurpose university to a research university. One reduction target, home economics, is, according to officials of that college, one of only two areas of study identified in federal farm-bill legislation as being part of the educational responsibility of a land-grant institution.

While some opponents of the proposals were testifying before the review committee, others were mustering support for them. Students, faculty members, and alumni mounted massive letter-writing and phone calling campaigns aimed at state legislators and the university's curators. Rallies were held, petitions circulated, press conferences staged. The Missouri State Teachers Association expressed outrage. The State Senate's Education Committee held a hearing.

On April 7, the Columbia campus's student senate passed a resolution denouncing the academic review.

On April 19, the faculty voted 237 to 70 to call for the resignations of the chancellor and the provost if the reduction proposals were not withdrawn. The vote, however, has been criticized—by, among others, Chancellor Uehling herself—for not being a true representation of the sentiments of the campus's 2,038-member faculty. Last November, when the faculty voted against mid-year salary increases if they were to come at the expense of campus jobs, more than eight hundred members cast ballots.

The 'Point Man'

The author of the resignation resolution, George V. Boyle, says he believes the vote was representative.

"We should not be cannibalizing ourselves in order to give people raises," says Mr. Boyle, director of labor education, a program not affected by the provost's proposal. "When you encounter heavy seas and the best plan the captain offers is to lighten the load by throwing crew members overboard, I think the crew has to try and come up with something better."

"Our approach to these reductions," says Provost Bunn, "required that I become the 'point man,' and the discussion stage has subsequently become an adversarial one: The source of the recommendations—me—has become as much a subject of debate as the recommendations themselves. It has also become a highly political one, and I think it's unfortunate that the debate has been brought to the legislature and the curators before we have completed the review process on campus."

Chancellor Uehling also came in for some personal criticism when the campus learned that she was among the final candidates for the chancellorship of the nineteen-campus California State University system. She took herself out of the running for that job last week and announced that she was committed to working for policies that would enable the Columbia campus "not simply to survive but to carry into the future even greater strength than before."

The chancellor says she is not surprised by the demonstrations of hostility. "It's a very frightening and painful process," she says. "I can understand the anger on the part of some, but I still think our greater obligation is to the institution as a whole."

Ms. Uehling says that while she will not review or comment on the recommended proposals until they come to her in their final form, she supports the process and is convinced of its necessity.

"For the past five years, the State of Missouri has provided the university with budget increases that have amounted to only one-half the rate of inflation," she says. "When I came, the faculty was already on the record in opposition to across-the-board cuts to provide salary raises, and we must bring salaries up to attract and retain quality people. We *have* lost some good people.

"We have no hidden agenda. Our only agenda is our determination to take charge of our own fate. We are trying to anticipate the future so that we won't have to engage in crisis kind of planning. There are enough signs of an impending erosion of our quality to make us want to get ahead and start doing what we do smaller and better."

There have also been signs that the state can't afford to support the university to any greater extent. Missouri voters in 1980 passed an amendment prohibiting the legislature from increasing appropriations unless there were corresponding growth in the state economy. In 1981, Missouri ranked forty-sixth in state-tax-revenue growth, one of the reasons the governor, on two occasions, withheld portions of the university's budget totaling 13 percent.

Nevertheless, some critics charge that salary increases—if they are essential now—could be provided for next year without eliminating programs, since there has been a slight increase in the state appropriation from what was originally expected, and a 17 percent hike in student fees.

"If you take a short-term view, it's possible to conclude that we could have an acceptable level of salary adjustment for the coming year," says Mr. Bunn. "That isn't the case if you're looking ahead. Some on campus feel that it isn't important for us to strengthen our salary structure, but in my judgment that is a very narrow view of the aspirations this campus should have for itself."

To be sure, there is faculty support for the administration. "I think the faculty who approved of this strategy previously ought to be heard from again," says John Kuhlman, a professor of economics. "I don't think we can afford to sit back and watch a few departments create this big fight with the provost."

Adds Sam Brown, chairman of the psychology department, "It would be difficult to find anyone to say they'd favor the cannibalization of their colleagues' jobs for the sake of a salary raise. But ignoring the source of funds, I can say as a department chairman that one of the major problems I face is insufficient salary increments for faculty."

Other Improvements Sought

According to Provost Bunn, when salary raises are given out, they will not be distributed uniformly but will be based on individual merit and the salary market in the particular field.

While salaries will have the highest claim on the "reallocated" funds, the provost also hopes there will be enough money to strengthen equipment and expense budgets—"to bring them back to at least the real-dollar level of three years ago."

The provost said he would consider seriously the advice offered by the committee reviewing his proposals. What is not an option, in his view, is to back away from the $7 million in savings that his proposals would provide.

When it reported to the provost May 6, however, the review committee announced that it had voted to weaken the effect of all but one of the proposed reductions. Mr. Bunn is expected to submit his final recommendations to the chancellor by the end of this week.

The Board of Curators, at meetings on May 6 and 7, conducted lengthy discussions of the reallocation process underway at the Columbia campus. The result, William T. Doak, president of the board, told the press, was that the curators were so divided on the question that had a vote been taken on the proposals they would have been rejected.

"We are trying to plan for a very uncertain future," says President Olson, "and I'm not sure we've yet found the mechanism for doing that. We are seeking it."

Chancellor Uehling is expected to submit her reallocation proposals to President Olson sometime in June. The curators are scheduled to vote on the proposals in July.

"The board's resistance to any program eliminations has certainly given those who favor such a course of action cause for pause," says the Faculty Council's David West, who has supported the process from the outset. "There has been much more visible and vocal opposition to the process in the past four weeks than there had been support for it up to that time."

On the Columbia campus, faculty members were circulating petitions calling for votes of confidence and of no confidence in the administration. Mr. West says he is advising those faculty members not to call for campuswide votes at this time.

"There has already been too much confrontation, and faculty votes would just prolong it," he says. "I think everyone should try to gather additional information and rethink his position. And try to find some means by which all of this division can be mitigated."

45

Political Processes in Organizations

The purpose of this exercise is to analyze and predict when political behavior is used in organizational decision-making and to compare participants' ratings of politically-based decisions with ratings of practicing managers.

Politics is the use of influence to make decisions and obtain preferred outcomes in organizations. Surveys of managers show that political behavior is a fact of life in virtually all organizations. Every organization will confront situations characterized by uncertainty and disagreement, hence standard rules and rational decision models can't necessarily be used. Political behavior and rational decision processes act as substitutes for one another, depending upon the degree of uncertainty and disagreement that exists among managers about specific issues. Political behavior is used and is revealed in informal discussions and unscheduled meetings among managers, arguments, attempts at persuasion, and eventual agreement and acceptance of the organizational choice.

In the following exercise, you are asked to evaluate the extent to which politics will play a part in eleven types of decisions that are made in organizations. The complete exercise takes about one hour.

Step I. Individual Ranking (5 minutes)

Rank the eleven organizational decisions listed on the scoring sheet below according to the extent you think politics plays a part. The most political decision would be ranked 1, the least political decision would be ranked 11. Enter your ranking on the first column of the scoring sheet.

Step II. Team Ranking (20 minutes)

Divide into teams of from three to seven people. As a group, rank the eleven items according to your group's consensus on the amount of politics used in each decision. Use good group decision-making techniques to arrive at a consensus. Listen to each person's

Thanks to Don Hellreigel for suggesting the idea for this exercise. The scoring sheet is based on Jeffrey Gandz and Victor V. Murray, "The Experience of Workplace Politics," *Academy of Management Journal* 1980, 23, 237–251.

ideas and rationale fully before reaching a decision. Do not vote. Discuss items until agreement is reached. Base your decisions on the underlying logic provided by group members rather than on personal preference. After your team has reached a consensus, record the team rankings in the second column on the scoring sheet.

Step III. Correct Ranking (5 minutes)

After all teams have finished ranking the eleven decisions, your instructor will read the correct ranking based on a survey of managers. This survey indicates the frequency with which politics played a part in each type of decision. As the instructor reads each item's ranking, enter it in the "correct ranking" column on the scoring sheet.

Step IV. Individual Score (5 minutes)

Your individual score is computed by taking the difference between your individual ranking and the correct ranking for each item. Be sure to use the *absolute* difference between your ranking and the correct ranking for each item (ignore pluses and minuses). Enter the difference in column 4 labeled "Individual Score." Add the numbers in column 4 and insert the total at the bottom of the column. This score indicates how accurate you were in assessing the extent to which politics plays a part in organizational decisions.

Step V. Team Score (5 minutes)

Compute the difference between your group's ranking and the correct ranking. Again, use the *absolute* difference for each item. Enter the difference in the column 5 labeled "Team Score." Add the numbers in column 5 and insert the total at the bottom of the column. The total is your team score.

Step VI. Compare Teams (5 minutes)

When all individual and team scores have been calculated, the instructor will record the data from each group for class discussion. One member of your group should be prepared to provide both the team score and the lowest individual score on your team. The instructor may wish to display these data so that team and individual scores can be easily compared as illustrated on the bottom of the scoring sheet. All participants may wish to record these data for further reference.

Step VII. Discussion (15 minutes)

Discuss this exercise as a total group with the instructor. Use your experience and the data to try to arrive at some conclusions about the role of politics in real-world organizational decision-making. The following questions may facilitate the total group discussion.

1. Why did some individuals and groups solve the ranking more accurately than others? Did they have more experience with organizational decision-making? Did they interpret the amount of uncertainty and disagreement associated with decisions more accurately?
2. If the eleven decisions were ranked according to the importance of rational decision processes, how would that ranking compare to the one you've completed above? To what extent does this mean both rational and political models of decision-making should be used in organizations?
3. What would happen if managers apply political processes to logical, well understood issues? What would happen if they applied rational or quantitative techniques to uncertain issues about which considerable disagreement existed?
4. Many managers believe that political behavior is greater at higher levels in the organization hierarchy. Is there any evidence from this exercise that would explain why more politics would appear at higher rather than lower levels in organizations?
5. What advice would you give to managers who feel politics is bad for the organization and should be avoided at all costs?

SCORING SHEET

Decisions	1. Individual Ranking	2. Team Ranking	3. Correct Ranking	4. Individual Score	5. Team Score
1. Management promotions and transfers					
2. Entry level hiring					
3. Amount of pay					
4. Annual budgets					
5. Allocation of facilities, equipment, offices					
6. Delegation of authority among managers					
7. Interdepartmental coordination					
8. Specification of personnel policies					
9. Penalties for disciplinary infractions					
10. Performance appraisals					
11. Grievances and complaints					

	Team Number						
	1	2	3	4	5	6	7
Team scores:							
Lowest individual score on each team:							

46

Honeywell in France

In November 1981, Edson Spencer, chairman and chief executive officer of Honeywell, Inc., was contemplating the start of negotiations between Honeywell and St. Gobain, the two principal joint venture partners in CII-Honeywell Bull (CII-HB). Spencer had become increasingly pessimistic about the general business climate in France since the election of Socialist Party leader Francois Mitterrand to the presidency in May 1981; however, he had also been recently informed by high French government officials that Honeywell's role in the Bull joint venture could yet be rewarding. This was possible in spite of the fact that St. Gobain was being nationalized and that the role of Honeywell in the joint venture would have to change as a result. Given these recent conversations, Spencer decided to explore the possibility of a mutually beneficial relationship through negotiations.

In this context, a number of questions were weighing on Spencer's mind: What should Honeywell's negotiating strategy be? What was the relative bargaining strengths between Honeywell and the French side? What were the intentions and options of French government officials, who were always in the background behind St. Gobain? How should Honeywell's negotiation effort be organized and what should its negotiating tactics be? Answers to these questions required analysis of Bull's importance to and position within Honeywell, the history of the computer industry in France, and the backgrounds of the individuals involved in the actual negotiations.

Honeywell, Inc.

Honeywell was formed as the Minneapolis Honeywell Regular Co., after a 1927 merger between Minneapolis Heat Regular Co. and Hon-

This case was written by Charles R. Kennedy, Jr., Associate Professor of Business Administration.

eywell Heating Specialties Co. (Its present name was adopted in 1964.) Originally, therefore, Honeywell was a specialist in thermostatic controls. Over time and through subsequent acquisitions, Honeywell broadened its activities into measuring instrumentation, pneumatic controls, and avionics. Control systems, however, remained its core business, comprising 46 percent of total sales and 59 percent of total profits as the company moved into the 1980s. Edson Spencer and past Honeywell chairmen, in fact, had all been the previous heads or executive vice presidents of Honeywell Control Systems.

Diversification into the computer business started in 1955 and was furthered by the 1965 acquisition of Computer Control Company. International activity followed immediately afterwards with the information of Honeywell Europe in 1966. Computers or information processing systems remained a minor part of Honeywell, however, until the 1970 purchase of General Electric's Information Systems Equipment Division. Nevertheless, Honeywell Information Systems (HIS) never surpassed control systems in relative sales or profits. As the company entered the 1980s, computers and information systems comprised 34 percent and 32 percent of sales and profits, respectively. Increasingly, however, Honeywell saw a major area of future competitive strength as being based in the synergy between control and computer systems, with one of the main battlefields focused on the rapidly growing office automation market.

Background of the Computer Industry in France: Pre-CII-HB

CII-HB had its roots in a French computer company called Compagnie des Machines Bull (CMB), which started as a small punch-card machine producer in the 1930s. By the late 1950s, CMB had become a relatively large and prosperous computer firm, with an average annual increase in sales of 25 percent between 1953 and 1960. In fact, by 1960, CMB employed 11,000 workers, making it one of the top thirty employers in France, and held about one-third of the French computer market, which was the largest share of any domestic firm. CMB also held about 10 percent of the computer market in Western Europe. CMB was such a success and stimulus to French national pride that it was often called "the Brigitte Bardot of French industry."

During the early 1960s, however, serious problems for CMB began to emerge, most notably the challenge posed by International Business Machines (IBM), who along with other U.S.-based computer firms expanded very rapidly in Europe during the post-World War II period. IBM in particular offered European computer customers new, technologically advanced mainframes that CMB lacked. In response, CMB had no choice but to develop a "state of the art" mainframe in order to compete with the Americans. Such product development, however, was difficult to achieve technologically and enormously expensive.

These obstacles to product development were greatly aggravated by CMB's relationship with the French "Gaullist" government. CMB was largely a family-owned and -managed corporation that had had strong ties to the Vichy government during World War II. As a result, the French government under the leadership of Charles de Gaulle refused to give CMB any financial support or special development contracts. In fact, several large loans to CMB that required Ministry of Finance approval were turned down during the early 1960s, a time in which research and development capital was critical. In order to survive in an increasingly competitive world, CMB was forced to look for other sources of capital.

General Electric had decided to enter the computer market in 1959 and began selling computers in France via limited export sales in 1962. Given GE's general lack of experience internationally, particularly in the computer business, they preferred to expand their operations in Europe through acquisitions or joint ventures with established firms. GE had offered to buy a 20-percent equity position in CMB in 1962 at the prevailing market price, along with promises of massive financial and technical support. CMB initially refused, but by the end of 1963, CMB's competitive position relative to IBM had deteriorated to such an extent that negotiations with GE were renewed. An agreement that largely duplicated the 1962 offer was then reached.

Before the deal could be consummated, however, Ministry of Finance approval, which in actuality meant President Charles de Gaulle's approval, was needed. The French president's decision, which came in early 1964, was an emphatic rejection of an "American solution" to CMB's problems, primarily because computers were perceived to be a vitally important strategic industry. Of course, de Gaulle was also generally concerned with the growing American business presence in Europe, which he felt was aided by the U.S. government's international monetary policies, but he was particularly angered by the U.S. government's recent embargo of computer sales to the French military-nuclear industry. In other words, U.S. business dominance of the computer industry had political-military implications that de Gaulle was unwilling to accept.

CMB was then forced to try a "French solution" by increasing its ties to domestic banking and electronic firms. This attempt proved futile, however, since French banks refused to back CMB with the funds it needed because of the company's weak financial and technological position. As a GE negotiator observed,

> *They [CMB] felt that even if necessary financing were forthcoming from French sources, this still wouldn't have been enough to make the company safe in the face of the onslaught of IBM competition. They had to have some stronger backing than that.*[1]

CMB still needed the capital and technical support that only a major firm like GE could offer.

By April 1964, the French government had apparently come to the same conclusion; it completely reversed the earlier decision, which it had termed "irrevocable," and now accepted "in principle" a GE-CMB joint venture. During the summer of 1964, a final agreement was struck and approved by the French government on terms much more favorable to GE then before. Instead of a 20-percent minority equity share, GE purchased 51 percent of the marketing and 49 percent of the manufacturing arms of GE-Bull (two separate corporate entities were created) for a price that was 25 percent less per share than had been offered six months earlier. Such a corporate structure and equity share were very much to the advantage of GE, for the company was mainly interested in CMB's extensive European marketing network (as was Honeywell six years later). Most of GE's computer manufacturing and product development would be centered in Phoenix, Arizona. As one GE executive stated about the 1964 merger,

> *The main point is that we are acquiring a first class distribution system. We will integrate production and distribution to make the best use of the strengths of both companies.*[2]

In spite of favorable entry terms, GE's computer business in France and worldwide did not prove very successful. Between mid-1964 and early 1967, for example, GE invested around $200 million in Bull's operations. Each and every quarter in that time period showed negative operating profits. GE's reaction was retrenchment: headquarters recommended a 25-percent reduction in Bull's labor force, or the layoff of 2,500 workers, and the dropping of the Gamma 140 computer line, which had been designed by CMB before the GE merger. French protests over "foreign domination" ensued and were aggravated by a renewed U.S. computer embargo to the French nuclear industry. The French government reacted to these developments by announcing that it no longer considered GE-Bull even a quasi-French computer firm (in fact, GE now held 66 percent of Bull equity as a result of capital contributions in the 1964–1967 period) and thus GE-Bull would no longer receive preferential treatment in government purchases or R & D assistance. Labor and product cuts were also implemented by the fall of 1967, and it was in this atmosphere that William R. Hart became managing director of Bull's operations.

GE-Bull's retrenchment policy proved financially successful under Hart's management. By 1969, Bull reported its first net profit, $650,000. Nevertheless, GE finally decided in February 1970 that the company should withdraw from the computer business worldwide and focus its resources on nuclear, jet engine, and other "core" electrical products instead. Although GE's chairman denied it, IBM simply proved to be too strong a competitor to warrant the risks and massive capital infusions required in the computer industry.

By May 1970, GE and Honeywell announced what many analysts regard as a "textbook" merger. It combined GE's mainframe technology and European marketing network with Honeywell's compatible computer line and management experience. Together, GE's and Honeywell's computer businesses held a 10-percent worldwide market share, making it the "undisputed No. 2" behind IBM. In France, Honeywell Bull had around 20 percent of the market versus IBM's 52 percent. Of course, French government approval was needed for the Honeywell arrangement. Such approval was quickly given after Honeywell agreed to merge much of its other European operations into Bull's orbit. In fact, such a merger was gladly accepted by Honeywell because Bull's marketing and manufacturing network dwarfed what Honeywell already had in place within the Common Market.

In October 1970, the GE and Honeywell merger was finalized with the creation of Honeywell Information Systems, 81.5 percent owned by Honeywell and 18.5 percent by GE. (GE's 18.5 percent was to be sold to Honeywell by 1980, which in fact occurred.) HIS represented the entire computer operations of both Honeywell and GE and included HIS's 66 percent ownership of Honeywell Bull.

HIS quickly proved a financial success. As Honeywell's *1971 Annual Report* stated,

> *Earnings of the company were up 12 percent on a sales increase of 1 percent . . . Improved earnings in our worldwide computer business contributed significantly to this performance. This was due in part to the fact that we have begun to realize the benefits we foresaw in merging GE's computer operations with ours.*

HIS revenue in 1971 had climbed to $950 million, or 47 percent of total Honeywell revenue, versus a pre-merger (1969) level of $763 million in computer-related sales and revenue, which was only 24 percent of the corporate total. Over half of 1971 HIS revenues, moreover, came from foreign computer operations, primarily those of Honeywell Bull. The French joint venture, in fact, marketed over half of its production in thirty-eight countries outside France.

Clearly Honeywell had taken a huge step toward establishing a major multinational presence. As Honeywell's *1970 Annual Report* stated,

> *We stepped up our evolution as an international company through the merger. We now employ 42,000 people outside of the U.S. (versus under 20,000 before 1970) and our volume there was $662 million, or 34 percent of total sales (versus under 20 percent in pre-merger years). About two-thirds of the computer operations that we acquired from GE are (in fact) overseas.*

The internationalization of Honeywell continued to bear fruit in subsequent years, although the recession years of 1974 and 1975 crimped sales and earnings for HIS and Honeywell in general, as revealed in Exhibits 46–1 and 46–2. It was within this financial backdrop that intensive negotiations concerning the future status of Honeywell Bull took place in France during 1975.

During the 1960s, in conjuction with the falling out between the French government and GE-Bull, another "national champion" in the computer industry had been created, Compagnie Internationale pour l'Informatique (CII). The French government had merged three small computer firms and provided CII massive infusions of capital and preferential purchases

EXHIBIT 46–1 ■ Total Revenue (millions of dollars)

	1972	1973	1974	1975
HIS	1061	1177	1233	1324
% Increase over previous year	12	11	5	7
Honeywell, Inc.	2125	2391	2626	2760
% Increase over previous year	9	13	10	5
HIS % of total	50	49	47	48

Sources: Honeywell, Inc., *10-K Annual Report,* 1973, p. 8; *10-K,* 1974, 1975, pp. 9–11.

EXHIBIT 46–2 ■ Earnings before Taxes (millions of dollars)

	1972	1973	1974	1975
HIS	54	75	53	57
Honeywell, Inc.	169	209	188	173
HIS % of total	32	36	28	33

Sources: Honeywell, Inc., *10-K Annual Report,* 1973, p. 8; *10-K,* 1974, 1975, pp. 9–11.

in the hope of challenging the American multinationals. By 1973, the effort was clearly faltering, as CII had not gained above 10 percent of the French market. There was some discussion within the Gaullist government of President Georges Pompidou to merge CII with Honeywell Bull, but an "all-European solution" was attempted instead. Consequently, with government prodding, CII in mid-1973 formed a French-German-Dutch combine called Unidata, with Siemens of Germany and Philips of Holland as partners.

Unidata did not meet French expectations or interests. CII sold virtually no machines in its partners' home countries, while Siemens and Philips made substantial inroads into the French market. As a result, the French government withdrew from Unidata and negotiated a merger of CII and Honeywell Bull by mid-1975, thus effectively ending the attempt for an all-European solution.

Honeywell's *1975 Annual Report* listed the benefits of this agreement: (1) a substantial increase in its share of the French computer market from around 20 percent to 25 percent; (2) French government subsidies of $270 million over four years; (3) French government promises of preferential purchases totaling $1 billion; and (4) a $58 million payment to Honeywell for decreasing its equity share from 66 percent to 47 percent in the newly merged company, which represented a net gain of $14.8 million.

Other benefits, which the *1975 Annual Report* did not mention, were significant as well. Honeywell retained certain specific management rights, including a veto power over capital increases, mergers, acquisitions, and other significant investments. Honeywell also had the right to appoint the chief executive officer, although the managing director would, by subsequent practice, always be a French national. In addition, Honeywell obtained a comprehensive set of security guarantees designed to protect the value of its equity share, namely a French legal commitment to buy Honeywell's 47 percent in CII-HB at book value in the event of nationalization. This provision was particularly important because in the 1974 presidential elections, Francois Mitterrand had campaigned for the nationalization of the French computer industry and lost by only 400,000 votes. The concept of a common product line was also agreed to and would be implemented by a Technical Committee, the chairmanship and majority of which were assigned to Honeywell. Common product line development was augmented by a royalty-free, cross-licensing agreement and by a "mirror-image" distribution system arrangement in which each party agreed to market each other's products based on the present status quo. From the view of Honeywell and the French government, the result of this merger was a big plus for both parties.

EXHIBIT 46–3 ▪ Selected Financial Records of CII-HB (millions of dollars)

	1976	1977	1978	1979	1980
Net assets	230	250	293	354	450
Total revenue	655	765	1486	1215	990
Net income	8.5	5.6	21.1	29.9	32.4

Sources: Honeywell, Inc., *Annual Reports,* 1977–80.

The Pre-1981 History of CII-HB: Finances, Product Development, and Politics

As the 1975 negotiations were underway, Bill Hart, the old managing director of the GE-Bull joint venture in the late-1960s, was lured away from GE to become HIS's senior vice president. One of his principal responsibilities was to oversee CII-HB relations.

Financially, CII-HB's performance and importance to HIS are reflected in Exhibits 46–3 and 46–4.

Moreover, Honeywell's earnings per share rose $1.60 in 1980. As Edson Spencer, Honeywell's chairman and CEO noted, "In 1980, our equity share in the French company's operating profit increased Honeywell earnings by $1.45 per share."

In the area of product development, a major dissimilarity between HIS and Bull was found in the large-scale mainframe business (memory capacity of over one million bytes or at least one megabyte). Bull's large mainframes were based on the old CII's Iris 80 line, which was a product development undertaken during Unidata days. As a replacement for the Iris 80, Bull was developing two new large mainframes, the so-called Y4 and Y5. These two large-scale systems, however, were viewed as a halfway state in the project to develop a completely common product line between HIS and Bull by the mid-1980s. Of course, politically and commercially, this temporary dissimilarity was seen as necessary. In the interim, however, potential product competition existed between Bull's large mainframes and HIS's.

At the medium-scale mainframe level, similar differences between HIS and Bull were present. Bull was the sole manufacturer of the Level 64 line, which had a memory size of between 192K bytes and 768K bytes, depending on the particular model. HIS produced instead a Level 66 line of machines that had a memory size that started at the upper end of the Level 64 but reached a top capacity of four megabytes. (The Level 66 thus included a large-scale and medium-size mainframe.) Potential competition, therefore, existed at the upper end of the 64s with the lower end of the 66s.

Attempts to avoid such competition leading to HIS-Bull conflicts were based on two policies or actions. First, Bull by 1980 was producing and marketing Level 66s as well as Level 64s within its own sales territory. Second, marketing guidelines were established to sell Bull 64s in the United States and other HIS markets. If a customer had a current memory capacity need in the 700K to 800K byte range, a Level 64 would be sold if that customer did not need greater expansion capacity in the future. If such expansion was highly probable, then Level 66s were sold instead.

The minicomputer business also experienced close cooperation. In 1975, the Level 6 system was introduced by HIS, with manufacturing extended to France in 1978. Although Bull called these the "mini-6s," they were the same machines as produced by HIS. These minicomputer systems were becoming increas-

EXHIBIT 46–4 ■ CII-HB Percentage of HIS and Honeywell, Inc., Net Income

	1976	1977	1978	1979	1980
CII-HB % HIS	40.7	15.1	38.6	36.0	31.2
CII-HJB % Honeywell, Inc.	7.5	3.9	10.5	11.5	11.0

Sources: Computed from Honeywell, *Annual Reports,* 1977–80.

ingly critical to HIS and Bull as add-ons to medium-scale and large-scale mainframes.

This high degree of product development and marketing cooperation can be seen in the relative R & D expenditures and product flows between HIS and Bull, which are demonstrated in Exhibits 46–5 and 46–6. All of these financial and product/market factors were critical ingredients of negotiating strategy between Honeywell and the French government in 1981–1982.

Political pressures on Honeywell's role in Bull had been mounting well before the 1981 presidential election. Protests had been heard since the inception of the 1975–1976 merger between CII and Honeywell Bull. The French Communist Party termed the deal "sabotage," while the Gaullist party (UDR) called it a deception. In large part, these criticisms were political posturing against President Valery Giscard d'Estaing and his UDF coalition, a French conservative but internationally liberal party. In another sense, however, these criticisms reflected a genuine debate over who, the French nation or Honeywell, had benefited most from the deal. Giscard and Honeywell naturally argued that both parties had benefited to a substantial degree—after all, IBM was the common threat to the aspirations of each side.

IBM certainly saw the Honeywell-French government relationship as a coalition formed against its interests. Since the CII merger with Honeywell, "IBM's share of government computer orders [in France] had dropped steadily from 37 to 26 percent, according to IBM officials. They attribute the decline to French government support of CII-Honeywell Bull." In addition to government controls, IBM asserted that it had lost some private contracts "because of government pressure." IBM decided not to protest this alleged favortism formally because, as an IBM spokesman remarked, "as they say in the French Foreign Legion, things could always get worse."[3]

In spite of possible Honeywell-French government collusion against IBM, the French political challenge to CII-HB increased substantially during the parliamentary elections of 1978, when Giscard's moderate-conservative coalition narrowly defeated the leftist alliance. As the Honeywell president stated afterwards, he "was very relieved" by the election results because "we would have lost our business" if Mitterrand and the leftists had won. The 1978 elections, however, did not end or reduce the threat to Honeywell's French operation. During 1979, for example, St. Gobain (with tacit government approval) bought out Compagnie General d'Electricite's 20-percent share in the French majority side of the computer group and began to negotiate the full or partial purchase of the government's 20-percent share as well. The threat to Honeywell was that St. Gobain would begin to "dominate the otherwise fragmented French side, achieving effective control of CII-HB."[4] These efforts continued into 1980 because "now the French want to squeeze out American Honeywell's remaining minority stake."[5]

In short, the potential threat to Honeywell's position in CII-Bull had a long history that predated the socialist election victory in May 1981 and was rooted in French national pride, which transcended the political ideologies of the right and left and had been hurt by the fact that 75 percent of the roughly $8 billion of

EXHIBIT 46–5 ▪ R & D Expenditures, CII-HB and HIS (millions of dollars)

	1976	1977	1978	1979	1980
CII-HB	69.4	91	108	127.9	129.6
Total HIS	331.5	397.7	431.7	551.4	720.6
% CII-HB to HIS total	20.9	22.9	25.0	23.2	18.0

Source: Honeywell, *1980 Annual Reports,* p. 7.

EXHIBIT 46–6 ▪ Intercompany Sales Between CII-HB and HIS (millions of dollars)

	1976	1977	1978	1979	1980
HIS sales to CII-HB	74.1	89.9	93.6	113.5	131.1
CII-HB sales to HIS	66.6	69.6	51.3	48.2	48.8

Source: Honeywell, *Annual Reports,* 1977–80

computers installed in France were sold by American companies. Many Gaullists, out of the nationalistic tradition of their founder, General Charles de Gaulle, had pressed for the nationalization of the French computer industry, and this conservative-nationalistic policy goal dovetailed quite nicely with the Socialist Party objective of "recapturing the domestic market."

The Post-May 1981 Environment

On May 10, 1981, Edson Spencer received a phone call from Roger Fauroux, head of St. Gobain, informing him that Mitterrand's election was imminent and that the nationalization of St. Gobain (now the majority French partner in CII-HB) was a near certainty. Its exact impact on Honeywell, however, was far less certain.

The Socialist government moved quickly on its election platform in all respects. Minimum wage and social security benefits were increased 10 percent and 20 percent, respectively. In addition, paid vacation benefits were extended, and the workweek was reduced from 40 to 39 hours. Presidential decrees also added 210,000 new jobs to the public sector. More fundamentally, a nationalization plan affecting eleven major industrial groups, including St. Gobain, was approved by the National Assembly in July 1981 by a 302-to-107 vote margin. Three firms with large foreign ownership (CII-HB, ITT-France, and Roussel-Uclaf) were targeted for intensive negotiations on their future status. The compensation bill flowing from the government to private stockholders of the eleven industrial groups was initially $5.5 billion, but it increased to $7 billion after pressure and rulings from French courts.

These policies had been implemented within an economic climate that had been deteriorating during the last year or two of Giscard's presidency. The primary cause of these economic reversals was not domestic policies but the consequences of the second oil shock, which followed the Iranian revolution. Many analysts were wondering if Mitterrand's domestic policies would help or aggravate the situation.

Spencer and other Honeywell executives visited Paris frequently to assess the situation. Commercially, CII-HB was suffering and on its way to a 1981 operating loss that would reduce Honeywell's corporate earnings by $14 million, or 61 cents per share, which represented 5 percent of Honeywell's total earnings per share in that year. Politically, Spencer found the overall business climate less than desirable. Thus, as Spencer commented, "Every indication was negative. We had only one viable option—to take our assets and get out."[6] Spencer's pessimism, however, obviously did not extend to all Honeywell business interests in France, because in July 1981, Honeywell expanded its French control systems subsidiary with an infusion of $6 million in cash. The sell-out option for Honeywell's stake in Bull was made possible by the 1976 agreement, which gave Honeywell the right to sell those assets at book value and be paid in dollars from an escrow account in a London bank if nationalization occurred. Based on the 1981 CII-HB balance sheet, Honeywell would be entitled to around $200 million, slightly more than the amount it had invested in 1970. With the nationalization of St. Gobain, CII-HB was also technically nationalized, which gave Honeywell the legal option to pursue or demand the implementation of the 1976 agreement.

Before taking this course of action, however, Spencer during an early November visit to Paris "began to hear from high Ministry of Industry officials that France was determined to become a world-class computer power and that Honeywell's role could be interesting and rewarding."[7] Shortly thereafter, Spencer was invited to the Elysee Palace for a discussion with Jacques Attali, Mitterrand's special counselor. Spencer reported that "Attali made it clear that he was speaking for the president and that *le president* wanted Honeywell to stay in France."[8] Spencer then decided to explore what possibilities existed between Honeywell and the French government.

Within days of the Attali-Spencer meeting, negotiations between Honeywell and the French were scheduled to begin. The French side was to be represented by executives of St. Gobain. The Honeywell negotiating team was to be cmposed of three individuals: William R. Hart, the senior vice president (second in charge behind the president) of HIS; David Louis, Honeywell's chief financial officer; and John Karis, Honeywell's assistant general counsel. Of the three, Bill Hart, of course, had the greatest experience with Bull and the French government. He had been involved with Bull since the late 1960s, was a Bull board member during the present negotiations, and had known many of the St. Gobain negotiators in that capacity for several years. The other two individuals had never been intimately involved in Honeywell-French relations.

The central questions for the negotiators remained: Given Bull's importance to Honeywell and the history of the computer industry in France, what should Honeywell's negotiating strategy be? And how should Honeywell's negotiating effort be organized?

Endnotes

[1] "Business Around the Globe," *Fortune,* September 1964, p. 59.

[2] *Ibid.*

[3] *Wall Street Journal,* April 7, 1980, p. 24.

[4] *Economist,* November 17, 1979, p. 81.

[5] *Economist,* April 5, 1980, p. 63.

[6] *Fortune,* June 28, 1982, p. 97.

[7] *Ibid.*

[8] *Ibid.*

47

Dover Municipal Hospital

I knew the hospital either made money or lost it based on its professional services. And I knew that you came in contact with the whole hospital through those services; so I said that's what I want to run. I also knew that professional services was filled with the biggest prima donnas on the staff—radiologists, biochemists, cardiologists—each more difficult than the others and that my predecessor, at age twenty-eight, had developed a bleeding ulcer and left.

Chuck Graham, Assistant Administrator
Dover Municipal Hospital

So thought Chuck Graham when he had accepted responsibility for professional services at Dover Municipal Hospital in Delaware. The past few months had given him a much better insight into just how difficult it was to manage those prima donnas, and now he had to decide whether or not, how, and how tightly to put the lid on this business of sending tests to outside laboratories.

The Dover Municipal Hospital

The Dover Municipal Hospital (DMH) was a complex of five buildings located in one of the poorest sections of Delaware's capital city. Constructed mostly in the 1930s, the physical plant was drab, and security was tight. After five o'clock in the evening, heavy chains and padlocks secured the doors to passageways leading from one building to another. Nearly all of DMH's patients arrived via the hospital's emergency room, and most of the remainder came through its ambulatory care unit. The Dover Police Department brought DMH most of the

This case was prepared by Professor John R. Russell of Boston University's Public Management Program with the help of Terrence Briggs, research assistant. Funds for its development were provided by a grant from the National Training and Development Service. The case is intended to serve as a basis for class discussion, not to illustrate either effective or ineffective handling of a managerial situation. Revised December 1977. Used with permission.
Names and locations have been disguised.

hospital cases it picked up, and other hospitals sent their "dump jobs"—indigent, uninsured patients that these hospitals were "too full" to accommodate.

Throughout its history, DMH had been a teaching hospital and was currently affiliated with Delaware University's medical school. The hospital was staffed entirely by residents and interns who worked under a salaried senior medical staff that provided both teaching and supervision. No physicians in private practice had staff privileges. All the senior medical staff committed only one-quarter to one-half of their time to the hospital. They were paid an "administrative" salary by the city, which was all that third-party reimbursers would pay for and which was only a fraction of what a doctor could earn in private practice or from a full-time job at a private hospital. Most of the physicians augmented their DMH salaries with teaching stipends from the university, salaries received as principal investigators on research grants, jobs managing outside laboratories, and other means. In addition, a special physicians' billing corporation culled the hospital's records to identify patients with third-party reimbursement resources, such as commercial medical insurance, that could be billed for the doctors' services. According to one observer, these arrangements created friction:

The city wants to pay for clinical care for indigent patients. It doesn't want to pay for research or teaching or try to make DMH a great research center. The medical staff, on the other hand, are the kind who are willing to give up the money available in private practice because they are researchers. And this is where they expect to do their research and their teaching.

The breakdown of billing for inpatient care was Medicare, 20 percent; Blue Cross, 3 percent; Medicaid, 40 percent; commercial insurance, 5 percent; and "self-pay," 35 percent. In practice, the hospital sent all its patients a bill, but did not expect to recover from any of the self-payers. Each year, DMH estimated the cost of the services it would deliver next year, subtracted the amount of third-party and self-paid reimbursements it expected, and submitted the remainder as its annual budget proposal to the city. The city usually cut several million from this proposal, and it was up to the hospital to determine how to absorb the cuts. The current city share of hospital expenses was about $10 million.

At one time, the hospital's capacity had been about 750 beds, but demand for its services had slackened when the advent of Medicaid and Medicare gave many indigents the option of going to other Dover hospitals. Eventually, over half of DMH's beds had been "delicensed." The staff currently numbered about 2,000, of whom approximately 150 were interns, residents, or senior medical staff, and the remainder were nurses, technicians, clerical help, maintenance people, messengers, orderlies, and so forth.

The *medical* staff was organized into two major departments—medicine (which included pediatrics, cardiology, gastro-intestinal, hematology, pulmonary, and other internal medicine subservices) and surgery (which included obstetrics/gynecology). There was also an outpatient department. The hospital's *administrative* staff reported to an associate director and three assistant directors—one for medicine, one for surgery, and one for professional services. The assistant director for professional services had administrative responsibility for the laboratories and other diagnostic services as well as various support services, such as medical records, admitting, social services, messenger, pharmacy, and transportation. (In a few instances, such as the biochemistry laboratory, these professional services subdepartments reported on medical matters to the department of medicine and on administrative matters to the assistant director of professional services.) Both the associate director and the heads of the two medical departments reported to the hospital director, who was hired by the city. The relative influence of the director, the associate director, and the medical staff depended on the individuals who occupied the various positions at a particular time.

Chuck Graham

In the spring of 1975, the old director of DMH retired and was replaced by Donna Breen. The two were a study in contrasts. Whereas her predecessor has been described as a wily and cautious civil servant who had managed, nevertheless, to alienate city hall, Breen was young, active, and had excellent relations with the city manager and his staff. She had just completed three years as Delaware's assistant commissioner for social services. Breen was without experience in medicine or the health system, but believed firmly that a hospital could be managed well by people who were good managers, but who were not necessarily doctors. She also believed in change and innovation. Good ideas should be tried and mistakes tolerated. Within a few days of Breen's arrival, the associate administrator resigned, and Breen, herself, decided to occupy the position until a suitable replacement could be found. In the weeks that followed, a great many junior administrators left DMH and others were shifted to new responsibilities. One of the latter was Chuck Graham.

Like Breen, Graham had no medical background. As an undergraduate, he had been a summer intern at DMH and decided he liked "working in health." After three years as a Peace Corps volunteer in South America, he returned to DMH, this time as unit coordinator for three wards and the intensive care unit. In this capacity, he was responsible for "administrative operations"—that is, making sure the units were properly stocked with supplies, dealing with the demands and complaints of the physicians and nurses, supervising the secretaries, and handling other administrative chores. Graham characterized the work as "middle management," which to him meant solving whatever problems came up in the wards and "doing what head nurses used to do but don't want to do anymore." After six months, he had been promoted to assistant manager for the unit coordination department and after a year, to head of the department. In a few months, he had been promoted again, to junior administrator in charge of twelve support service departments, including messenger, transportation, housekeeping, mail, central supply, laundry, and kitchen.

During the fall of 1975, Breen offered Graham any of the three assistant administrator slots, and Graham elected professional services:

I went from managing twelve departments to managing over twenty. They said I could give up transportation and messenger, but I decided to keep them. I knew if I wanted to make the labs work, I'd have to control the process from the time a specimen was drawn to the time the results were delivered back to the doctor.

The main additions to Graham's responsibilities were five large decentralized clinical laboratories and several small research labs that performed one or two tests of clinical importance to the hospital. The five were hematology, biochemistry, bacteriology, pathology, and the blood bank. They employed about two hundred people. A physician had medical responsibility for each of the labs, and as administrator, Graham would "more or less," as he put it, be in charge of personnel and budget.

If a lab wanted to buy a new piece of equipment, I'd have to sign off on it. On the other hand, if I wanted a lab to do a particular test, the doctor could say, "No, I won't do it." Or, he could say, "I'll do it, but it will cost you two technicians and $100,000 in equipment." In other words, the doctors controlled what went on in the labs. And I had to avoid practicing medicine.

Since the lab chiefs were there only part time, the day-to-day operations were run by chief technicians who ordered supplies, signed documents, scheduled work, and trained other technicians. Bringing outside work into the labs (except under a contract to which the city was a party) was against the law. While the lab chiefs had the final say on hiring technicians, Graham theoretically could fire anyone, including the lab chief himself. In practice, this was difficult, because replacing a lab chief for $15,000 to $20,000 meant finding someone in the area who had enough other activities to augment his DMH salary, but who still had enough time left to work one-quarter time for the hospital.

The Test List

During his early days on the job, Graham was plagued by his own ignorance of the labs and by a barrage of complaints from the doctors:

The physicians, when they're unhappy with the administration, think their best leverage is to complain. Donna (Breen) was moving strongly to shift the balance of who ran the hospital—from the physicians to the administration—and the physicians were fighting it. One thing they did was to complain about the service they were getting from the labs and other support departments. What really was bothering them was Donna's demands that they devote more time to clinical work and less to their research and teaching. She didn't want to support those activities with public funds.

One discovery Graham made was that no one in the hospital knew every test that was offered by the laboratories. His predecessor had tried to compile a list, but failed. Graham decided to try for himself and visited each lab chief:

They all said, "All we've got is a partial list." I said "May I see it?" and they said, "Sure, but it's outdated. We've added a few tests and dropped a few others. Also, I'm short a few people because of layoffs, and I really don't have time to put a list together for you now."

I began to think that most of the lab chiefs didn't want the administration to know what tests they could perform. It gave them more flexibility.

After two months of trying, Graham had virtually nothing of any value from biochemistry, pathology, or hematology. Bacteriology and the blood bank, on the other hand, had provided him with lists that he thought were complete.

What I did was design a form (see Exhibit 47–1). Then I said, "I want a completed form for every test you do. It's getting close to budget time; and if you give me ten tests, that's what I'll base your budget on. If you do fifty more on the sly, you'll have to find the funds on your own." Suddenly, I began to get a little cooperation, and the number of tests that everyone was doing began to go up.

I also began to call the chief lab technicians into my office and deal with them because the physicians were only there part of the time.

It took almost six months, but at the end of that time, Graham believed he had a collection of forms that represented quite accurately the tests currently being performed. He had also developed the following impressions of the five labs:

Hematology

The lab consisted of two units: the main hematology lab, where a staff of thirty technicians, blood drawers, and clerks provided round-the-clock service and performed the bulk of hematology testing, and an outpatient laboratory that ran simple tests on ambulatory patients. Little or no research was done in the lab.

The lab chief, who also ran the hematology lab at another Dover hospital, was extremely independent. Said Graham:

If he feels like doing a test, he does it. If he doesn't feel like it, you're out of luck. He's very difficult to get along with, but he's a very skillful hematologist, and he runs a quality lab. No matter what you want, though, it's push, shove, and toe-to-toe, and there's always a price attached to it.

He runs the lab like a dictator, and the techs do what he tells them to. But he sends them home two hours early if he thinks that's good for them. And he won't let his techs help with some of the chores that all the other lab techs share.

I've been told that he asks only for new equipment in his budget request, even when he

EXHIBIT 47–1 ▪ Dover Municipal Hospital: Sample of Completed Test Inventory Form

LAB: Central Hematology

1. *Lab test name:*
   White Blood Count (WBC)
2. *What it does (what is its purpose? What does it test for? What sample (blood, urine, etc.)? Is it a common test?):*
   Very Common Test
   Blood Sample
   Test for:
   Infection — Leukemia — Surgical conditions
3. *How many tests are done per year?:*
   85,000
4. *Is it part of a larger test (i.e., CBC, SMA 12)?:*
   Yes (CBC) — Usually done on Coulter Counter
5. *Charge of this test as of 8/25/76:*
   Manually — $ 4.00
   Coulter — $10.00
6. *Cost of the test as of 10/1/76:*
   $0.50
7. *Automated or manual test (batches or individual)?:*
   Either — Automated = 95%
   Manual = 5%
8. *How long does it take to perform?*
   Coulter — 45 seconds
   Manually — 10 minutes
9. *Emergency nature or routine (how quickly is it needed)?:*
   Either
10. *What reagents and equipment are used to perform this test?:*
    Reagents: 2% Acetic Acid - Manually (unopette)
    Isoton — Lyse S — Coulter
    Equipment: Microscope — coverglass — counting chamber — tally counter (manually)
    Coulter models
11. *The hours the test is offered (What is the turnaround time)?:*
    24 hours
    STAT Turnaround Time — 30 minutes or less
12. *Procedure used to perform the test (i.e., radioimmunoassay, etc.):*
    Manual unit count by hand
    Particle count on Coulter
13. *Who takes the specimen? What container is used? How is it transported?:*
    Phlebotomist — Lavender Top Tube (EDTA)
    By hand by tech — messenger service - pneumatic tube
14. *Amount of sample required:*
    At least half-filled Lavender Top Tube

knows some of the most vital older equipment will probably break down soon. Then when it does, you have to add money to his original budget so he can go on performing the tests.

Biochemistry

Staffed twenty-four hours a day, seven days a week, biochemistry was the largest producer of tests in the hospital. It was also the biggest money maker and the best equipped. Daily operations were supervised by a Ph.D. in chemistry who presided over a staff of about forty-five technicians and support personnel. There was also a consulting biochemistry lab that consisted of two people, on a normal forty-hour week, working on research grants and doing a few sophisticated clinical tests.

The chief of biochemistry was new at DMH. He had come to Graham with several requests from his technicians concerning longer lunch hours or shorter work days—all of which Graham had refused. He spent almost all his time either teaching or working on his research in the consulting biochemistry lab. The Ph.D. in chemistry appeared to run the laboratory.

Bacteriology

From a technical viewpoint, this was the showpiece laboratory. More than in the other labs, the work in microbiology—which involved planting specimens in culture media—was an art form. While the output of the hematology and biochemistry labs was sometimes criticized, the quality of microbiology's output was never questioned. The forty technicians and bacteriologists worked a five-day week, and because bacteriologists would not read anything that someone else had planted, delays sometimes developed over weekends.

The lab had a degree of fiscal independence that the other labs did not. Almost two-thirds of its budget came from a local foundation and another 15 percent from contracts to perform work for Memorial Hospital. DMH paid for only that part of the lab's budget that was not supported by these outside sources.

The lab chief was one of the DMH's medical "statesmen." He stayed out of hospital politics and hospital administration, seemed always to have a good word for everyone, and made few demands of his own. When he did ask for something—such as a new piece of equipment—the request was invariably reasonable.

Pathology

Pathology, with about ninety people, was concerned with the analysis of disease. Its lab chief, who was to retire at the end of 1976, had earned a national reputation in anatomical pathology research. His fund-raising efforts had paid for most of the equipment in the building where the lab was housed, and his continuing success at acquiring research grants kept more than a dozen physicians working at the hospital, providing services for which the city did not have to pay. In return for these benefits and the high quality of his work, he expected to be given a budget and then left alone. No one on the Dover University medical staff, except the senior surgeons, ever set foot in the laboratory. Graham visited the area once, but discovered that most of the doors were locked and that keys were not available.

Blood bank

The blood bank managed DMH's inventory of blood and performed the simple tests necessary to dispensing that inventory properly. Nominally, one of the staff surgeons was the lab chief, but the bank was actually managed by a very pleasant and capable nurse.

The Free T-4 Incident

As he was developing the list of tests and becoming more familiar with the laboratories, Graham learned that almost $150,000 in testing (10 percent of the total DMH lab budget) was being sent to labs outside the hospital. After securing a breakdown of these outside tests from the DMH accounting department (see

Exhibit 47–2), I he noted that over $20,000 was being spent annually just to perform Free T-4 tests at Memorial Hospital, Dover, where the biochemistry lab was run by a doctor who had recently left DMH. He asked several doctors why this was being done:

Their answer was something like, "Well, young man, this is a superior methodology being used by a superior laboratory. We've done it that way for three or four years, and it's really none of your business."

Rather than let the issue drop, Graham asked other doctors about the Free T-4 test. He discovered that there was a more advanced method of doing the test that could be set up in the DMH biochemistry lab for an initial cost of about $20,000.A

So, I went to my laboratory advisory committee (the group of doctors who advise me on the technical and medical aspects of the labs) and asked them if they thought it would be all right to switch to the new method. They said, "No." Then I went to biochemistry—since Free T-4s are basically biochemistry tests—and asked if he'd be willing to do them inhouse. I was told that it was none of my business, that I wasn't a physician, that Memorial's method was much better, and that biochemistry reported to the department of medicine anyway.

I didn't buy it. I called an out-of-state friend who was a hospital administrator and talked to his clinical pathologist, and he convinced me that the new method was not only better, it was cheaper. He also said the Memorial Hospital method cost a lot less than they were charging us, which made me think our money was being used to support teaching and research over there.

I went back to biochemistry and said, "Will you do it?" But he wouldn't. So I talked to hematology, and he said he'd do it provided I gave him another $15,000-a-year technician.

The Outside Testing Issue

In the midst of his efforts to resolve the Free T-4 issue and to compile a complete list of tests, Graham received a phone call from the city's auditor. The auditor, too, was concerned about the amount of outside testing. What was even more disturbing to him, many of the outside labs that DMH used were receiving more than $2,000 in business. The law required that dealings of this amount be covered by a contract and that these contracts be awarded on the basis of competitive bidding. None of DMH's outside sources were under contract.

In response to the auditor's prompting, Graham set out to learn, in detail, how the process worked. He found that physicians who wanted a test performed by an outside laboratory filled out a four-part form and delivered it (together with the specimen) to the secretary of one of the medical staff. (About ten or twelve secretaries throughout the hospital processed these requisitions.) The secretary sent a messenger, with one copy of the requisition, to the invoice office where the requisition was assigned an invoice number, authorizing payment for the test. The invoice number was filled in on the remaining three copies, the secretary obtained a cab voucher, and the messenger delivered the specimen and two copies of the requisition, via cab, to the outside lab. The remaining copy stayed with the secretary and was eventually filed in the patient's record. When it had performed the tests, the lab returned the results and one copy of the requisition to the DMH secretary (who transmitted the results to the doctor) and retained the second copy for its records. Periodically, the lab submitted a bill to the DMH invoice office, listing all the tests it had performed by invoice number. The invoice office matched the numbers with its copies of the requisitions, paid the outside lab, and sent the requisition copies to the hospital's billing office, so the costs could be billed to patients and third-party reimbursers.

The system seemed to work reasonably well except for several problems. First, messengers from the outside labs who delivered test results (and sometimes picked up requisitions and specimens) often got lost in DMH and delivered material to the wrong location. Second, the invoice office's copy of the requisition fre-

EXHIBIT 47–2 ■ Dover Municipal Hospital: Summary of Outside Laboratory Tests for January 1976

Test	Number of Tests	Price	Total
Ag Titer to Crystococcus	3	$ 20.00	$ 60.00
Alcohol Level*	42	16.00**	672.00
Alkaline Phosphatase—Fractionated*	2	10.00	20.00
Alpha Fetoglobin	2	11.00	22.00
Amino & Organic Acids	1	10.00	10.00
Aminophylline Level	1	23.00	23.00
Analysis of Kidney Stone	2	9.50	19.00
Analysis of Urinary Calculus	2	9.50	19.00
Anti-Mitochondrial Antibodies	1	16.50	16.50
Anti-Smooth Muscle Antibodies	1	16.50	16.50
Anti-Toxoplasma Antibodies	1	18.00	18.00
Australian Antigen (H.A.A.)	77	4.75	365.75
Barbiturate Level	3	16.50	49.50
Calcium*	64	6.50	416.00
Carcinoembryonic Antigen	11	30.00	330.00
Catecholomines	1	16.00	16.00
Chromosomes	1	100.00	100.00
Cortisol*	12	20.00	240.00
CPK — Fractionated*	1	8.00	8.00
CPK — Isoenzymes*	22	19.50	429.00
Digitoxin Level*	1	25.00	25.00
Digoxin Level*	19	21.00**	399.00
Dilantin Level*	20	25.00**	500.00
Dilantin & Phenobarb Level	1	25.00	25.00
Drugs of Abuse	1	35.00	35.00
Elavil & Thorazine Level	1	20.00	20.00
Estradiol Level*	13	38.00**	494.00
Fats*	1	6.00	6.00
Febrile Agglutinins	1	10.00	10.00
Fluorescent Treponema Antibodies	1	9.00	9.00
Free T-4	90	18.00	1,620.00
FSH*	15	22.00**	330.00
Gamma Glutamyl Transpeptidose	1	10.00	10.00
Gastrin Level	5	22.00	110.00
Histoplasma Compliment Fixation	1	29.25	29.25
Immonoglobulin E	1	15.00	15.00
17—Ketogenic Steroids*	1	18.00	18.00
17—Ketosteroids*	1	12.00	12.00
Lap Stain*	1	5.00	5.00
Latex Fixation*	1	11.00	11.00
Leucine Amino Peptidose	1	5.00	5.00
LH	15	22.00**	330.00
Lithium Level	1	9.00	9.00
Luteinizing Hormone	1	19.50	19.50

Mercury Level*	2	$ 6.00	$ 12.00
Metanephrine	1	20.00	20.00
Myoglobin	1	10.00	10.00
Mysoline Level*	2	18.00**	36.00
Parathyroid Hormone	13	49.50	643.50
Phenobarb Level*	2	16.50	33.00
Phenothiazine Screen	1	3.50	3.50
Phosphorus*	2	4.40	8.80
Pregnanetriol	13	23.00**	299.00
Progesterone*	15	24.00**	360.00
17—OH Progesterone	3	25.00	75.00
Prolactin Assay*	13	30.00	390.00
Protein Analysis*	1	38.50	38.50
Protein Electrophoresis	1	24.00	24.00
Rast Profile	1	70.00	70.00
Renin Level*	16	25.00	400.00
Rubella	18	8.00	144.00
Salicylate Level*	1	5.00	5.00
Semen Analysis	1	10.00	10.00
Sensitivity to 5 FC	1	15.00	15.00
Sub B Unit Level	1	21.00	21.00
Sweat Test*	1	35.00	35.00
Tegretol	1	18.00	18.00
Testosterone*	16	32.00**	516.00
Testosterone Doxycortisol	1	20.00	20.00
Theophylline Level	10	12.00	120.00
Toxic Screen (blood)	70	13.00**	910.00
Toxic Screen (urine, gastric)	35	13.00**	455.00
Valium Level*	2	15.00	30.00
Zarontin Level	1	15.00	15.00
	690		$11,634.30

*Can be performed at DMH.
**Average cost.

quently did not arrive in the billing office until long after the patient had been dismissed. Finally, there was no way for the invoice office to know if a test for which it was billed had actually been performed. It was standard practice for the invoice office to pay outside laboratory bills even if the invoice number could not be matched.

When a physician wanted a test done by one of the DMH labs, he obtained the specimen and filled out one of several different in-house, four-part requisition slips, depending on which lab did the test and what test it was. He then "stamped" the requisition with the patient's name and hospital number. One copy of the requisition stayed in the doctor's department for inclusion in the patient's record, and three copies, together with the specimen, were sent to the laboratory where the test was performed. The lab kept one copy of the requisition, sent one back with the test results, and sent the third to the DMH billing office so the patients and third-party reimbursers could be billed. (Instead of doing the work themselves, physicians could simply ask that a test be performed. In that case, a technician drew the specimen and a secretary filled out the requisitions.) The only substantial problem in this procedure occurred when a physician failed to provide the patient's name and number, or did so illegibly, so that subsequent billing was impossible.

Graham discovered several reasons why physicians sent tests to outside labs:

Sometimes the senior staff just decided that it made sense to use tests we couldn't or hadn't been performing. We also had some senior staff who ran laboratories outside DMH, and they might say to the house officers, "When you need an Australian antigen, send it to my lab, because I know they do it the way I like it done." They might even ask—as they made their rounds with the house staff—why Australian antigen tests hadn't been ordered for some patients and direct that they be ordered.

A lot of other tests went out because the physicians thought our labs did poor work or because they'd had a fight with the lab chief. The head of hematology had chewed out a lot of interns and residents for criticizing, so they tried to avoid his lab. Sometimes a fleeb (the person who draws the blood sample) would mix up specimens, so a physician would get wildly fluctuating results and conclude it was because the lab wasn't testing properly. Some of the newer interns and residents just didn't know what tests our labs could do.

Graham also discussed with several house physicians and lab chiefs the issue of contracting for outside laboratory services. They were all adamantly opposed to the concept.

City Hall had suggested that we give all the outside work to one laboratory, but there were some reasons why this didn't make sense. If you go to the lowest bidder, you may get someone with poor quality control. Then, once they've got your contract, they may begin to cut corners or reserve their fastest service for other customers. We also were using some small specialty labs that were doing work for us almost as a favor, and the price at a big lab under contract would almost certainly be much more.

I told all this to the auditor, but he wouldn't budge. He wanted everything over $2,000 under contract. He didn't care about the difficulties, and he didn't care if it cost more money. Those were my problems. He just wanted to satisfy the legal requirements for a contract.

V

VIEW FROM THE TOP

48

Palace Products Company

You are J. C. Kramer, executive vice-president of Palace Products Company. John Maguire, president of Palace Products, hired you from another company and you began work only one week ago. You were to train under Walter Hopkins, who was executive vice-president for one year until his retirement. You have twenty-two years of experience working in manufacturing companies, with ten years at middle and upper management levels. You have a bachelor of science degree in engineering.

Walter Hopkins is critically ill and will not be returning to work. You have not been with the company long enough to learn very much about the management system. You have just had time to learn the names of other managers. John Maguire wants you to assume full responsibility as executive vice-president because you are an experienced manufacturing executive. He told you that you are in complete control of internal operations. He does not want to interfere in your decisions because his role is to work with people in the environment and with International Controls Company, the company that purchased Palace Products two years ago.

History

Palace Products was started in 1948 by John Maguire and two other World War II veterans. They invented a flow control device and pooled their resources to develop and manufacture it. Palace Products grew rapidly and now produces control valves to regulate almost anything that flows through pipe. Palace originally

Prepared by Richard L. Daft. This case is adapted from several sources, including James B. Lau, "Crofts Products Company," *Behavior in Organization: An Experiential Approach* (Homewood, IL: Richard D. Irwin, 1975), 269–277; Harry R. Knudson, Robert T. Woodworth, and Cecil H. Bell, "Electronics, Incorporated," *Management: An Experiential Approach* (New York: McGraw-Hill, 1979), 128–138; E. Paul Smith, "You Are Bob Waters, Assistant Administrator at Unity Hospital," distributed by the Intercollegiate Case Clearing House, Soldiers Field, Boston, MA 02163; and the authors' own management experiences.

established a niche as an innovative new product leader in the field of control valves and flow control instruments. Over the last ten years, however, innovation has been less frequent. The products are rather standard. Other companies are gaining a new-product edge, and Palace has gradually experienced a decreasing market share. Palace Products was taken over two years ago by International Controls Co. in a friendly merger. To date, Palace has kept substantial autonomy from International.

The Situation

Palace Products is located in central Ohio. It has a capital investment in excess of $30 million, and produces seven major products for civilian (82 percent) and government markets (18 percent). Four products represent distinct types of control valves, and three products are instruments for flow control regulation. A control valve and instrument are typically combined to fit a specific flow control application. Palace also produces many valves on a custom order basis to meet unusual applications.

A fifth major product, called the 830 Butterfly Valve, is under development.

Flow control products have a variety of applications in refineries, pipelines, and utilities. Industrial applications represent 70 percent of Palace's business. Small control valves are used in virtually every home and building, and account for about 30 percent of total sales.

Palace's employees now include sixty-four engineers and thirty-eight technicians. There are approximately twelve hundred production employees who work two shifts. The manager in charge of production is Keith Malone. He has been in his current job for less than a year, but has been with the company about twenty-one years. His previous job included manager of quality control and manager of the machine shop. The marketing manager is Ray Thomas, who has been in his job four years. He was promoted from field sales manager into his present position. He is now responsible for the field sales manager (Mike McKay) and for the advertising and research manager (Bruce Parker). Marketing functions include promotion, merchandising, market research, market development, and direct sales to customers. Sixty-five employees work in the marketing department.

Pete Tucker is the manager in charge of research and development. Tucker has a Masters Degree in Electrical Engineering. Prior to his promotion thirty months ago, he was the manager in charge of electrical engineering. The Research and Development Department includes nineteen engineers and several technicians. Pete Tucker refuses to appoint anyone to supervisor roles because he believes his people should work as a team. Because of John Maguire's strong interest in research and development, nearly 8 percent of Palace's profits are allocated to this function.

The Engineering Department is managed by Bill Urban. Engineering typically implements the products created in Research and Development. Several engineering specialties are represented within the department, including electrical, mechanical, product, and systems engineering. The contracting specialist handles technical details involved in contracts with clients.

Al Wagner is in charge of employment and administrative services. His responsibility also includes community relations. This department has a staff of nineteen people. Wagner transferred from the corporate personnel department over eighteen months ago.

The finance manager is Ed Brock. He has been in his job about two years. Brock has an M.B.A. and is a specialist in management information systems. He is responsible for general and cost accounting, payroll, the computer unit, and accounts receivable and payable. Finance has a staff of about twenty people.

The demand for control valves has traditionally fluctuated with general business activity, especially construction. When construction and business activity is high, the control valve business booms. For the last two years, industry output has been stable, and the number of units shipped by Palace has declined slightly. Palace is not yet in financial trouble, but money is tight. High interest rates on short-term loans is drawing off cash.

Control valve innovation follows developments in electronics, metallurgy, and flow control theory. Developments in these fields are used by manufacturers to increase the sensitivity and efficiency of valves and instruments. Recent developments in electronics have led to new control valve applications based upon miniaturization and automatic controls. Palace has been working for three years on a new control valve design called the Butterfly. This design has the potential to regulate the flow of liquids at 75 percent of the cost of traditional designs.

Palace has a reputation for product quality and reliability. Engineering, research, and production have traditionally been important departments in the company.

In the single conversation you had with Walter Hopkins before he became ill, he confided to you that Palace should retrench for the next two years or so until economic conditions improved. He insisted that Palace's reputation for product quality would hold the customer base if the marketing department concentrated on servicing established customers rather than on finding new customers. Hopkins said that Maguire always wanted more money budgeted to R & D for new developments, but he disagreed. New products have been an enormous hassle, and Hopkins could not see their contribution to profit. He believed new products were more trouble than they were worth. Hopkins planned to concentrate on improving internal efficiencies. "Cutbacks now will leave us lean and strong for the economic upturn ahead." He also said, "One dollar saved in production is worth three dollars in sales."

Hopkins also confided to you that a staff member from International Controls Company headquarters suggested to President Maguire that a project or matrix form of structure be adopted at Palace. Maguire isn't sure whether that is a good idea, but most managers, including Hopkins, don't see any need to change organization structure. They are more concerned with human resources—finding and keeping good people.

Saturday, March 7

You were appointed executive vice-president on Thursday, March 5. On Friday morning you got word to all those reporting to you (see Exhibit 48–1) asking them to write you a memorandum if they had any issues to be discussed with you. By Friday night, your in-basket contained the memoranda below. You take these memoranda home for evaluation so you can plan your next week's activities.

Your Assignment

Study the memoranda and answer the following questions.

1. What are the four most important problems facing you? Specify and rank the problems in priority order of importance. What are the two least important problems facing you?
2. What techniques will you use to work on the problems during the coming week? Be specific. State exactly how you plan to approach and solve the problems listed in response to question 1.
3. What overall strategy should Palace Products adopt? Should the company cut back, retrench, and stress efficiency? Should it invest heavily in research and development in order to be innovative and reestablish itself as a product leader?
4. Based upon the information available to you, is a change in organization structure warranted? What would you recommend to Maguire?

EXHIBIT 48–1 ■ Organization Chart for Palace Products Co.

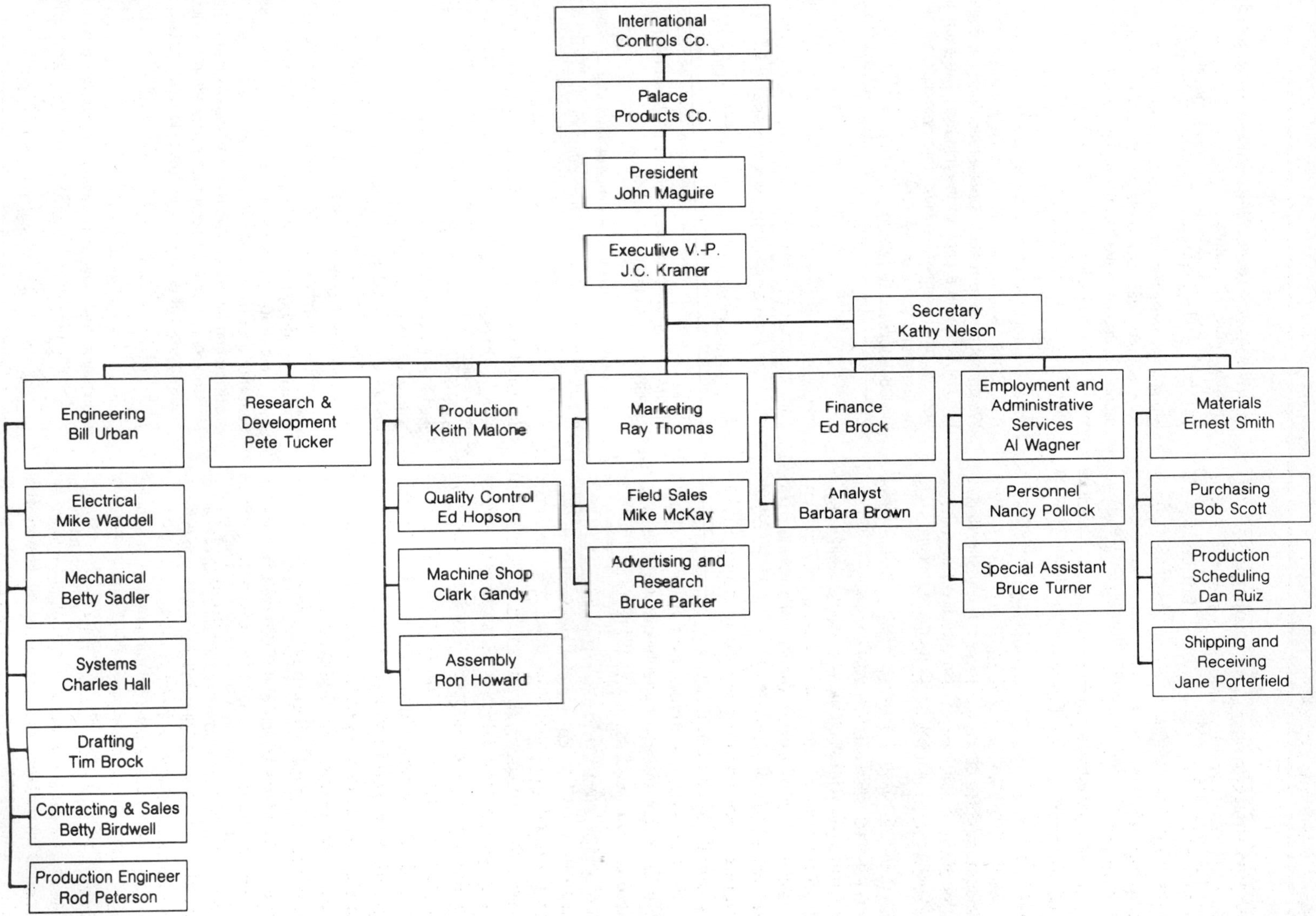

International Controls Co.
Palace Products Co.
President John Maguire
Executive V.-P. J.C. Kramer
Secretary Kathy Nelson
Engineering Bill Urban
Electrical Mike Waddell
Mechanical Betty Sadler
Systems Charles Hall
Drafting Tim Brock
Contracting & Sales Betty Birdwell
Production Engineer Rod Peterson
Research & Development Pete Tucker
Production Keith Malone
Quality Control Ed Hopson
Machine Shop Clark Gandy
Assembly Ron Howard
Marketing Ray Thomas
Field Sales Mike McKay
Advertising and Research Bruce Parker
Finance Ed Brock
Analyst Barbara Brown
Employment and Administrative Services Al Wagner
Personnel Nancy Pollock
Special Assistant Bruce Turner
Materials Ernest Smith
Purchasing Bob Scott
Production Scheduling Dan Ruiz
Shipping and Receiving Jane Porterfield

PALACE PRODUCTS COMPANY

OFFICE MEMORANDUM DATE: March 6, 1983

TO: J. C. Kramer
FROM: Kathy
SUBJECT: Your Meetings and Correspondence

Here are the memos that came in today. Mr. Maguire's memo is on top. Your luncheon appointments for the week are as follows:

Tuesday, March 10	11:30 A.M.–1:30 P.M.	Award lunch
Wednesday, March 11	12:00 A.M.–1:30 P.M.	Peter O'Reilly of O'Reilly Construction Co.
Thursday, March 12	10:00 A.M.–1:00 P.M.	Corporation meeting
Friday, March 13	12:30 P.M.–2:00 P.M.	Mrs. Rogers of the United Way

The following meetings were already scheduled by Mr. Hopkins.

Tuesday, March 10	8:00 A.M.–9:00 A.M.	Weekly staff meeting. This will include a discussion of new policies and procedures by Al Wagner and expanding opportunities for women by Nancy Pollock. A program for using less energy will be proposed by Bruce Turner.
Wednesday, March 11	9:00 A.M.–10:00 A.M.	Meet Chamber of Commerce representative.

See you on Monday.

PALACE PRODUCTS COMPANY

OFFICE MEMORANDUM DATE: March 6, 1983

TO: J. C. Kramer
FROM: John Maguire, President
SUBJECT: New Products and Corporate Meetings

J. C., let me welcome you aboard once again. I'm looking forward to working with you. I will be out of town for the next two weeks but will get together with you immediately upon my return.

I am quite concerned that Palace continues developing new control valve products and adding to our line. New developments have not been progressing very well, and decisions will have to be made in the near future for allocating funds and people to this endeavor. Could you get together right away with Pete Tucker and find out what new developments they would like to work on? We need to have these ideas consolidated and to select promising projects in the near future.

By the way, would you also check into the progress of our new model 830 butterfly valve? I've heard grumblings from two customers, but told them I didn't believe there was any problem. Where is the monthly report? It should have been on my desk by March 1. Would you please have that completed and bring it to my office?

One other thing. I'm scheduled to attend the International Controls Company meeting on Thursday at 10:00 A.M. Since I will be out of town, could you attend for me? We do not have to make a presentation and the corporation will send me a copy of the minutes. The executives from the other companies within International Controls will be there, and you can meet them.

I look forward to seeing you when I return.

PALACE PRODUCTS COMPANY

OFFICE MEMORANDUM DATE: March 6, 1983

TO: J. C. Kramer, Executive Vice-President
FROM: Ray Thomas, Marketing Department
SUBJECT: Model 830 Butterfly Valve

I understand that the new model 830 butterfly valve will not begin production for another two months. We have had repeated delays introducing this new system. It was originally scheduled to begin production last August, then January 1 of this year. Now the earliest date appears to be May 1. This is creating a serious problem for us, because we've been telling our customers about it and they want to have an opportunity to experiment with it. I anticipate a thirty- to sixty-day lag from the beginning of production before we will have products ready for delivery to customers. One of the salesmen heard from a customer that a small control valve company in Texas was about to introduce a new butterfly valve.

Another urgent matter is the model 820 retrofit. This should go on the market immediately. It also needs to be priced low or it could affect sales. Our retrofit is a small item, but it is badly needed because it will provide the precision control our competitior's products already have. Mr. Hopkins agreed with me that every effort should be made to have this product in the field immediately. We have promised our customers that the retrofit would be ready for delivery on April 1.

The sales forecasts for this year were based on the expectation that new products would go into production and sales as planned. Further delays in the introduction of the model 820 retrofit and the model 830 butterfly valve could seriously reduce sales forecasts for the year.

PALACE PRODUCTS COMPANY

OFFICE MEMORANDUM DATE: March 6, 1983

TO: J. C. Kramer, Executive V.-P.
FROM: Ernest Smith, Materials Manager
SUBJECT: Material Costs and Inventory Needs

I have been concerned for a long time about our steadily increasing materials costs. Due to the nature of our business almost 30 percent of our direct costs are materials related. Walter Hopkins agreed with me that we should do everything possible to increase efficiency at Palace Products. Reducing materials costs was a top priority for him. My people work hard to reduce costs and establish decent manufacturing schedules, but we can't do it alone. We always have to revise production schedules because of manufacturing problems, especially with the new models. My purchasing people don't get word on what to buy until the last minute, and then their materials need to be rush ordered and expedited. This increases costs at least 10 percent. By the time we get the materials, another design change may be underway, so the parts we rush-ordered may not be appropriate. Because of the way Engineering, Research, and Production work, our material costs are almost out of control.

Another important matter is the inventory problem. During the spring and summer we receive many small orders for one or two items. Setting up and manufacturing a special order is expensive. Sometimes after we complete the order the customer will decide they want one or two more of the same item. This means two setups for the same product and customer. For approximately $275,000, we could keep these small orders in inventory and fill orders much more efficiently. Ed Brock in Finance tells me he doesn't have $275,000 for inventory. Walter Hopkins agreed with me that this was another priority in our efforts to increase efficiency. An investment in inventory would be the best thing for this company right now.

The final problem are the designs for the model 830 butterfly valve. We need to get these designs finalized so we can establish decent manufacturing and purchasing schedules. The model 830 is supposed to go into manufacturing shortly, but as yet we have not been able to get a parts list that we can rely on. How can we go into production without acquiring parts? I wish the people in Engineering and Research would be more cooperative on this.

PALACE PRODUCTS COMPANY

OFFICE MEMORANDUM DATE: March 6, 1983

TO: J. C. Kramer
FROM: Barbara Brown
SUBJECT: Request for Appointment

Since you have an open door policy, I must see you. I am about to resign from the company and want to discuss it with you before I make the final decision. I have been here for six months. The assignments I am receiving from Mr. Brock simply are not challenging. I am not having any impact upon Palace Products Company. The projects I have been assigned are small and do not utilize the theoretical and analytical abilities I acquired during my M.B.A. training.

My mid-year progress report was excellent, which frustrates me even more. I would rather be rewarded for making a major contribution to this company than for doing small projects. I have tried to explain the problem to Mr. Brock, but he hardly has time to discuss it. He says he understands, but still hasn't assigned me to do anything really important. It is becoming clear to me that the Finance Department does not control anything here at Palace Products Company.

PALACE PRODUCTS COMPANY

OFFICE MEMORANDUM DATE: March 6, 1983

TO: J. C. Kramer, Executive Vice-President
FROM: Al Wagner, E. & A. S.
SUBJECT: Employment of the Disadvantaged

I received important information at a personnel meeting last night. The word is out that federal equal opportunity agencies will be looking at industrial plants in this area during the next six months. Currently, we have a very low ratio of disadvantaged employees. We may be in serious trouble.

I believe we should begin a crash program to employ fifty non-whites in all areas of the company. In order to save time, we should not use our normal testing procedures for these employees. Besides, our regular aptitude and intelligence tests may open us to charges of discrimination. Of course we can continue to use these tests for our normal employment of whites.

A crash program may involve some increased training and labor costs. Increased costs are better than losing government contracts. Besides, employing the disadvantaged is the right thing for Palace Products to do.

PALACE PRODUCTS COMPANY

OFFICE MEMORANDUM DATE: March 6, 1983

TO: J. C. Kramer, Executive V.-P.
FROM: Bill Urban, Manager, Engineering
SUBJECT: Engineering Activities

There is really not too much to report from here. Things are in good shape. I would like to give you a complete briefing on our activities and plans whenever your schedule will allow it. For now, I would like to call four things to your attention.

1. I heard a rumor that International Controls was planning to centralize many of the contracting and engineering activities to the corporate level. This would mean a transfer of people to corporate headquarters, and many of our activities would be done away from this plant. I think this is a terrible idea because centralized engineers wouldn't know the details of what we're doing here. The International people seem to think it would save money by consolidating engineers into a central facility and allow them to use up-to-date equipment. That would be a poor tradeoff in my opinion.

2. We continue to be short-handed by two engineers. Betty Sadler and Charles Hall both told me that some of their people have job offers from other companies. We may have to make counteroffers in the next few weeks.

3. A related item is the need to send five people to the American Engineering Society meeting in Las Vegas. Some of the engineering and research people want to report in a scientific paper some of the theoretical work behind the 830 butterfly valve. They will conduct a full-day session. This would be a great reward for them, but it will cost $7,500. We will need your approval because this will be well in excess of the travel budget.

4. The model 820 and model 830 developments seem to be coming along quite well. There is no urgency, but we do not have the most recent data and the final report from R & D. R & D claims we already have the data, but I think they are too busy to write the final report. We can't make the final decisions about production designs until we know the exact figures. I discussed this with Walter Hopkins last week, and he was going to see Pete Tucker about it.

PALACE PRODUCTS COMPANY

OFFICE MEMORANDUM DATE: March 6, 1983

TO: J. C. Kramer, Executive Vice-President
FROM: Nancy Pollock, Personnel
SUBJECT: Award Lunch

Don Jameson, a machinist, has been with the company thirty-five years and is being given an award as the most senior employee. He has been with the company since its founding, and a luncheon has been scheduled for him on Tuesday, March 10, from 11:30 to 1:30. It will be held in the luncheon room at the Townshire Hotel.

Walter Hopkins was going to present a company pin and give a brief talk. He always believed it was good human relations to emphasize the company's interest in those working here. Several of the senior production employees will attend the luncheon. Keith Malone agreed to substitute for Walter, but I'm sure you will also want to attend Don's luncheon.

PALACE PRODUCTS COMPANY

OFFICE MEMORANDUM DATE: March 6, 1983

TO: J. C. Kramer, Executive V.-P.
FROM: Al Wagner, E. & A. S.
SUBJECT: Reporting on the Model 820 and Model 830

I have attached a note from Bruce Turner, a bright young employee with the company. It reflects the problems he is having, and I have not been able to do much about it. The memo illustrates the lack of cooperation when we try to coordinate new product developments.

Dear Mr. Wagner:

One of my most important jobs is coordinating the monthly report for the Model 830 butterfly valve. In the initial meeting with you and Ed Brock from Finance, we worked out a monthly reporting plan for the 830 project. The plan was designed to record budget expenditures, and to keep upper management informed on the progress of each aspect of the development. We have tried to use a similar procedure for the Model 820 retrofit.

I'm getting no cooperation whatsoever. As it turns out, I am nothing but a pencil-pusher. I am having no influence at all on running and coordinating the 830 program. The departments are not taking this project seriously, no matter how many memos I write. R & D wants to do its own thing. Pete Tucker tells me that I give too much emphasis to reporting procedures and that I can expect the final report in a month or so. He says he is busy with important new developments, and the 830 is now old stuff. Keith Malone in Production says that they are having problems, and have not yet started production, but I don't know why. Marketing is pressing me to get the report moving, but they don't provide any useful information either. None of the departments bother to meet my deadline for a monthly report. As an administrative coordinator, I can't enforce compliance. What should I do?

Bruce Turner

PALACE PRODUCTS COMPANY

OFFICE MEMORANDUM DATE: March 6, 1983

TO: J. C. Kramer, Executive Vice-President
FROM: Edward Brock, Finance
SUBJECT: Integrated Management Information System

After a long struggle, we finally completed our computer-based integrated management information system last month. It cost $110,000, but will be well worth it. The new system will provide daily, weekly, or monthly information about sales, production scheduling, the status of customer orders, vendor deliveries, and the like. The system will also provide me with more detailed cost accounting data.

Unfortunately, although we debugged the computer software, the system is not working very well. One problem is that the managers are not providing the correct information and they are not using it. They are maintaining their own reports. They don't seem to want me to have the detailed figures I need for the cost-accounting reports. This system is important to the efficient operation of this company. Another problem is that we aren't using the most recent technical developments for data processing. I've set aside $60,000 for acquiring updated equipment. We will have the best MIS in the industry.

Walter Hopkins gave me his full backing to install the MIS. Would you talk to the other managers about adhering to the rules and procedures necessary to make the system work? Any assistance you can give me will be greatly appreciated. My staff and I have spent almost full time on this project for several weeks.

PALACE PRODUCTS COMPANY

OFFICE MEMORANDUM DATE: March 6, 1983

TO: J. C. Kramer, Executive V.-P.
FROM: Pete Tucker, Manager, Research and Development
SUBJECT: New Products

Our most pressing need is to get budgets approved for new developments. John Maguire has always supported new-product development in this company. Our people in R & D have a number of original ideas, and they are ready to start working on them. We will need a budget allocation of about $325,000 beginning April 1. We will have the people to allocate full time to the projects then. Would you contact Ed Brock about assigning the needed budget to us? He hasn't even responded to my memos. And please don't ask for a lot of formal plans and approvals. My people are very creative, which is their strength, and paperwork inhibits them. Palace Products has been a success because of new-product developments, and we need to maintain our momentum.

I also want to call your attention to problems in Production and in Engineering. The Model 820 retrofit has turned into a joke. We gave those people a perfect retrofit design, and somehow things have been screwed up so that it is not yet in production. It may be the people in production engineering or a lack of cooperation in the machine shop. Somebody was not able to follow through on an excellent design.

I have also heard that Engineering and Production are having problems with the new Model 830 butterfly valve. I want to assure you that everything is under control. We have completed the design work and the final report will be written as soon as we have some free time. Engineering has all the figures they need. I admit there were some slippages in the development of the 830. One hangup was due to the failure of the system to pass the high pressure flow control tests, but we anticipate no further difficulty. I don't see any reason why Engineering and Production should not be able to meet their schedules. By far the most important thing for us is to get the $325,000 so we can commit ourselves full time to new developments.

PALACE PRODUCTS COMPANY

OFFICE MEMORANDUM DATE: March 6, 1983

TO: J. C. Kramer
FROM: Keith Malone
SUBJECT: Model 820 Retrofit

I can't possibly make the production schedule for the Model 820 retrofit if I also have to be concerned about beginning production of the new Model 830 butterfly valve. The research, engineering, and marketing people are driving us crazy. Engineering keeps making design changes, and marketing people keep coming out to the shop to see when they can get their hands on the finished products. My people are working overtime to make production changes to meet design changes so the 820 won't be delayed any further. I strongly recommend that we stop all production activities on both the 820 and the 830 until all design issues are resolved once and for all.

I see that I made a mistake in accepting the 820 for production. The engineering people convinced me that there would be no more changes, but they did not have the final figures ready for me. It turns out they weren't clear about the final design. I won't make that mistake again.

By the way, can you get the Finance people off my back? They have installed a computer system and want to have us run everything into that computer. It creates a lot of extra work for us at a time when we don't need extra work. The computer has not been debugged, so my people still have to keep their own reports.

49

Panalba

The purpose of this exercise is to analyze the decision-making actions of an organization faced with conflicting responsibilities to its constituents and to society. This exercise may be conducted as a role-play, with members representing various constituents, or as an "unaffiliated" group decision process.

Strategic actions/planning in an organization may take into consideration constituents internal and external to its operations. Stockholders, employees, the board of directors, competitors, and government are a few of those to be considered. In the following exercise you will be challenged to determine the course of action to be taken by a major pharmaceutical manufacturer in the face of various demands.

Step I. Group Assignment (5 min.)

The class will be divided into groups of seven people. Each group will read the problem description below; the instructor will assign either the "Financial Accounting" or the "Social or Interest Group Accounting" to each group.

Step II. Group Decision (20 min.)

After reading the problem description each group will discuss and propose a course of action to be followed for the U.S. market. Select from the possible solutions A, B, C, D, and E.

Step III. Group Decision (5–10 min.)

Repeat step 2 for the foreign markets, again selecting from solutions A, B, C, D, and E.

Step IV. Class Discussion (20 min.)

Each group will briefly present its proposal and justification. The class will then discuss the relevant issues in relation to the theories and models that may have been presented earlier in classroom lectures and discussions. The following questions are provided to stimulate the discussion.

Abstracted from "Social Irresponsibility in Management," J. Scott Armstrong, *Journal of Business Research*, 5 (Sept. 1977), 185–213.

Discussion Questions

1. Which constituents and environmental factors must the company consider? Which are most important?
2. What role should the constituents play in the decision-making process? Should the company involve each in making a decision?
3. How would you describe the strategy of the Upjohn Corporation before the Panalba incident? What strategic shift, if any, would your course of action require?
4. What do you think are the internal cultural values of the Upjohn Corporation? How would these support the strategic goals of the company?
5. Can you cite other instances when an organization's cultural values conflicted with society's? How was this resolved?
6. Can organization theory teach managers to act ethically?

Background Information for Panalba

Assume that it is August 1969 and that Upjohn Corporation has called a Special Board Meeting to discuss what should be done with the product known as "Panalba."

Panalba is a fixed-ratio antibiotic sold by prescription, that is, it contains a combination of drugs. It has been on the market for over thirteen years and has been highly successful. It now accounts for about $18 million per year, which is 12 percent of Upjohn Company's gross income in the United States (and a greater percentage of net profits). Profits from foreign markets, where Panalba is marketed under a different name, are roughly comparable to those in the United States.

Over the past twenty years, there have been numerous medical scientists (e.g., the AMA's Council on Drugs) objecting to the sale of most fixed-ratio drugs. The argument has been that (1) there is no evidence that these fixed-ratio drugs have improved benefits over single drugs and (2) the possibility of detrimental side effects, including death, is *at least* doubled. For example, these scientists have estimated that Panalba is causing about fourteen to twenty-two unnecessary deaths per year, i.e., deaths that could be prevented if the patients had used a substitute made by a competitor of Upjohn. Despite these recommendations to remove fixed-ratio drugs from the market, doctors have continued to use them. They offer a shotgun approach for the doctor who is unsure of his diagnosis.

Recently a National Academy of Science—National Research Council panel, a group of impartial scientists, carried out extensive research studies and recommended unanimously that the Food and Drug Administration (FDA) ban the sale of Panalba. One of the members of the panel, Dr. Eichewald of the University of Texas, was quoted by the press as saying, "There are few instances in medicine when so many experts have agreed unanimously and without reservation" (about banning Panalba). This view was typical of comments made by other members of the panel. In fact, it was typical of comments that had been made about fixed-ratio drugs over the past twenty years. These impartial experts believed that while all drugs have some possibility of side effects, the costs associated with Panalba far exceed the possible benefits.

The Special Board Meeting has arisen out of an emergency situation. The FDA has told Upjohn that it plans to ban Panalba in the United States and wants to give Upjohn time for a final appeal to them. Should the ban become effective, Upjohn would have to stop all sales of Panalba and attempt to remove inventories from the market. Upjohn has no close substitute for Panalba, so consumers will be switched to close substitutes that are easily available from other firms. Some of these substitutes offer benefits that are equivalent to those from Panalba, yet they have no serious side effects.

The selling price of the substitutes is approximately the same as the price for Panalba.

It is extremely unlikely that bad publicity from this case would have any significant effect upon the long-term profits of other products made by Upjohn.

The following possible solutions were considered by the Board:

A. Recall Panalba immediately and destroy.

B. Stop production of Panalba immediately, but allow what's been made to be sold.

C. Stop all advertising and promotion of Panalba, but provide it for those doctors who request it.

D. Continue efforts to most effectively market Panalba until sale is actually banned.

E. Continue efforts to most effectively market Panalba and take legal, political, and other necessary actions to prevent the authorities from banning Panalba.

You, as a member of the board, must help reach a decision at today's meeting. The chairman of the board, Ed Upjohn, has provided this background information to each of the board members. He is especially concerned about selecting the most appropriate alternative for the U.S. market. (You must decide which of the possible alternatives is *closest* to your preferred solution.)

A similar decision must also be made for the foreign market *under the assumption that the sale of Panalba was banned in the United States.* This decision will be used as a contingency plan.

Financial Accounting

To assist with this decision, the chairman had asked the Controller's Office to make some quick estimates of what would happen as a result of each course of action. These estimates are summarized in the memo from the controller.

MEMO: To E. G. Upjohn, Chairman of the Board
FROM: Samuel Hardy, Controller (copies to Board of Directors)

The following estimates were prepared on very short notice by the Controller at Upjohn. As a result, these figures should be regarded as crude estimates as to what will happen. After-tax profits at Upjohn *prior* to this crisis have been predicted to be $39 million for 1969. The figures below are estimated losses from this prediction under each alternative. The figures represent only the financial losses to Upjohn stockholders.

Alternative	Estimated Losses* (In millions of dollars)
A. "Recall Immediately"	20.0
B. "Stop Production"	13.0
C. "Stop Promotion"	12.0
D. "Continue until Banned"	11.0
E. "Take Actions to Prevent Ban"	4.0

* This estimate represents present-value loss to Upjohn and covers all items (e.g., lawsuits, legal fees, expenses involved with recall). The losses would be spread out over a number of years.

Social or Interest Group Accounting

To assist with this decision, the chairman had asked the Controller's Office to make some quick estimates of what would happen as a result of each course of action. These estimates are summarized in the memo from the controller.

MEMO: To E. G. Upjohn, Chairman of the Board
FROM: Samuel Hardy, Controller (copies to Board of Directors)

The following estimates [see page 373] were prepared on short notice by the Controller of Upjohn. As a result, these figures should be regarded as crude estimates as to what will happen. After-tax profit at Upjohn *prior* to this crisis had been predicted to be $39 million for 1969. The figures below are estimated losses from this prediction under each alternative for each group. All other important effects from this decision have also been estimated.

Alternative	Estimated Losses* (in millions of dollars)			
	(1) Stock-holders	(2) Customers	(3) Employees	(1) + (2) + (3) Total Losses
A. "Recall Immediately"	20.0	0.0	2.0	22.0
B. "Stop Production"	13.0	13.6	1.8	28.4
C. "Stop Promotion"	12.0	16.8	1.2	30.0
D. "Continue until Banned"	11.0	19.6	1.0	31.6
E. "Take Actions to Prevent Ban"	4.0	33.8	0.2	38.0

* These estimates represent present-value losses to each group that is affected by this decision. The losses to customers represent deaths and illnesses caused by Panalba for which no compensation is received; losses to employees represent lost wages and moving expenses beyond those covered by severance pay and unemployment benefits.

50

Midwest Health System and Stuben Hospital

Laswell and Cumberland Counties in Illinois are divided both physically and socially by the Mosapecqua River that meanders from the north to south. Since 1934, Montpilier Hospital had been the primary medical facility for Laswell County (east side of the river) residents, while smaller community hospitals (e.g., Stuben, and St. Mary's) were the major secondary care providers in Cumberland County (west side). In 1974, the chief executive officer (CEO) of Montpilier Hospital, Milt Thompson, seeking a presence for the hospital on the opposite side of the river in Cumberland, began a series of informal, but ultimately nonproductive, conversations with Cleo Sutclif, R.N., CEO of Stuben Hospital. At the time, and for the next thirteen years, Thompson's vision of a vertically integrated health care delivery system encompassing the east and west shores of the Mosapecqua River was both misunderstood and threatening to Stuben's management and board of directors.

In 1983, the Midwest Health System (MHS) was founded with Thompson as its president. With the Montpilier Hospital as its flagship, MHS became the umbrella organization for a number of health-care delivery facilities and services, including the Montpilier Institute of Psychiatry, OutReach (a variety of home care programs and services), AmbuCare (ambulatory medical treatment centers), Midwest Health Products (a health products supply service), ALPHA (a preferred provider organization), and a network of family physician centers.

In that same year, Sutclif retired as CEO of Stuben Hospital. The board of directors conducted a nationwide search for a new top manager and ultimately settled on Alan Haverhill. Haverhill was viewed as a dynamic, progressive administrator who could successfully take the hospital into the 1990s. However, Haverhill's tenure at the hospital was cut short as he suddenly died in December 1985. The

Prepared by John S. Cramer, James B. Thomas, Linda K. Trevino, and William J. Lafferty, Jr. Used with permission.

board decided to contract for a temporary CEO while another search was conducted. Several bids for hospital management services were solicited from the area. One was from Logan Hospital and Health Services, Inc., another was from Acme Hospital, and a third from the Midwest Health System. As a result of the bid, and much to the surprise of Thompson, Ed Sutton from Logan Hospital and Health Services, Inc., was hired through a management contract to serve as CEO during the CEO search period, which was expected to be six months. At the time, Sutton was assistant administrator of Logan Hospital.

In June 1986, after decades of unwavering commitment to the idea of Stuben being an autonomous general-care hospital serving Cumberland County, the hospital's board began to consider the long-standing affiliation option offered by Thompson years earlier. An "agreement to discuss" affiliation was entered into between the board and Midwest Health System Discussions regarding the nature of such a relationship continued for almost a year.

In the fall of 1986, a new CEO, Richard Brown, was hired at Stuben Hospital. Over the next six months, the downward economic trend Stuben had been experiencing since 1981 continued. In March 1987, an independent health-care consultant was retained by Thompson, with the approval of the Stuben board, to conduct a management audit of Stuben. The audit revealed that:

> *Stuben Hospital is literally on a survival basis. However, there is little evidence to suggest that anyone is taking charge and really doing anything of a strategic nature. Everyone is looking to Midwest to rescue them from final disaster. Everyone is positive about Midwest. Stuben is a sinking ship without a captain. It will take a tremendous commitment of time, energy, patience, and resources to bring Stuben fully afloat. It can be done with the right leaders and support.*

On the verge of financial collapse, Stuben released Brown in March 1987. Dave Bluefield, the chief financial officer of the hospital since 1984, assumed the top manager position and picked up the reins of a hospital that was to continue to lose money for at least the next two years (see Exhibit 50–1).

In June 1987, Midwest Health System entered into a formal affiliation agreement with Stuben. Under the terms of the agreement, Stuben remained autonomous and Bluefield continued to report to the Stuben board. Assets, potential profit, and medical staff certification were all to remain within the purview of the Stuben board. Midwest Health System's role under the agreement seemed to be that of making program suggestions to which the board could respond yes or no—and it usually said no. By December, Stuben's financial situation required an influx of capital for the hospital to remain operational. MHS provided funding with the agreement that it would be considered "goodwill."

Stuben Hospital

At the time of the formal affiliation agreement, Stuben hospital was organized in a somewhat traditional manner (see Exhibit 50–2). A number of services were provided by outside contractors, including emergency room physicians, the pharmacy, housekeeping, maintenance, and social services.

The hospital operates out of three main buildings:

The "1985 building" is 18,000 gross square feet and is considered to be, at least structurally, the worst building in the complex. For example, the operating room vibrates because the ventilation system is mounted to the main support beams of the building. Further, the system's intake is mounted above the emergency room (ER) entrance, allowing fumes from ambulances and other traffic to enter the system and spread throughout the building. The ER itself is located above a basement garage, a code violation and an air pollution problem.

EXHIBIT 50–1 ■ Stuben Hospital Statements of Revenues and Expenses for the Years Ended June 30, 1988, 1987, and 1986

	1988	1987	1986
Patient service revenues	$4,838,868	$4,854,884	$4,502,187
Less contractual allowances and			
provision for doubtful accounts	897,713	925,057	789,794
Net patient service revenues	3,941,155	3,929,827	3,712,393
Other operating revenues	79,620	53,526	51,676
Total operating revenues	4,020,775	3,983,353	3,764,069
Operating expenses:			
Salaries and employee benefits	2,395,313	2,072,886	1,864,380
Supplies and other	2,038,360	2,068,742	1,947,749
Depreciation and amortization	257,811	216,500	189,931
Total operating expenses	4,691,484	4,358,128	4,002,060
Loss from operations	(670,709)	(374,775)	(237,991)
Nonoperating revenues:			
Investment income	53,896	47,309	50,694
Unrestricted gifts and bequests	31,626	10,030	17,779
Gain on sale of investments	11,270	71,199	19,976
	96,792	128,538	88,449
Deficit of revenues over expenses	$ (573,917)	$ (246,237)	$ (149,542)

The Smith Annex of the hospital was constructed in 1960 with additions completed in 1970. While considered by most at the hospital to be a "good" facility, this 32,000-square-foot building requires significant painting, grounding of receptacles, and general refurbishment in order to bring it up to standards.

The adjoining historic Winfeld House is used for nonpatient-related activities; however, it too requires considerable work, including a fire escape and other renovation.

In addition to these buildings, the hospital owns five residential rental properties adjacent to the main complex.

Competition

Several regional medical facilities provided services in competition with Stuben. The first of these, University Medical Center, had the best image in the region. It was in the middle of a $60-million, multiphase construction project that would last four more years. It had a medical education affiliation with several local hospitals, and a major nursing education program was relocating there over the next three years.

The next major competitor was Professional Medical Center, which also was engaged in a construction project that would cost over $25 million and would significantly improve its operating rooms and obstetric facilities. The center was known for its good medical staff and its operation of Mill Hollow Health Center, a well-respected outpatient treatment facility.

St. Mary's Hospital, another competitor, was engaged in a marketing program focused on its ophthalmology, podiatry, and obstetrics programs. Its ophthalmology program had the best state-of-the-art equipment, its podiatry program has captured 60 percent of the market in eighteen months, and its obstetrics program was promoting a "Birth Place Privacy Program." St. Mary's also had the only drug and alcohol

EXHIBIT 50–2 ■ Stuben Organization

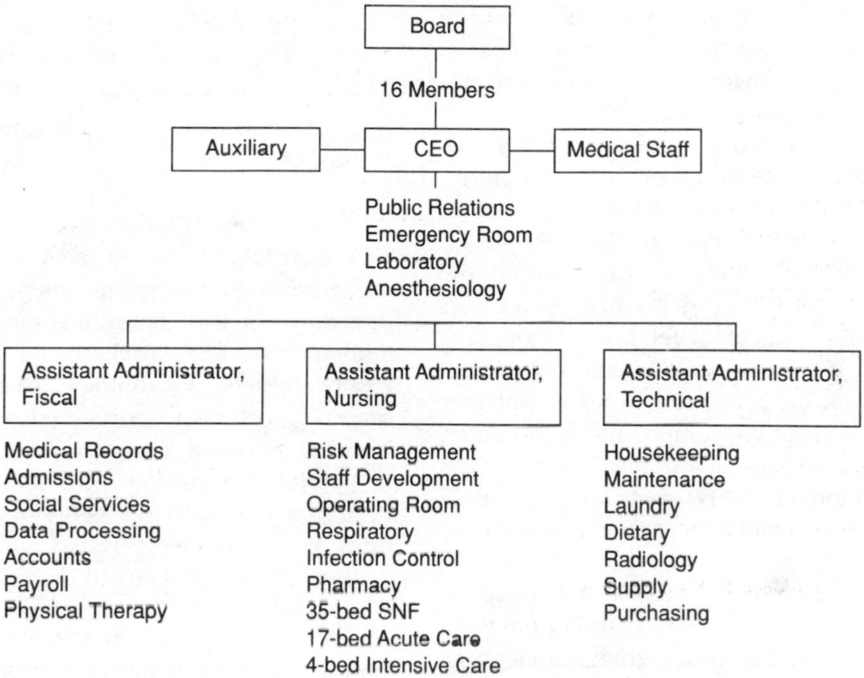

treatment program in its county and had recently worked out an agreement with the State Health Plan so that regulations would be modified in its favor.

Hilltop Surgical Center had just opened for business but was already known as a convenient, low-cost provider of outpatient surgical services. It was able to penetrate the local markets rapidly and was exacerbating an already acute shortage of nurses and other technical staff.

Oakmont Osteopathic Hospital was the last major regional competitor. Like the other local hospitals, it was in the midst of a building program, an $18 million program that was to be completed in 1989. Besides its excellent central location, it was building its market share by focusing on a cancer treatment program and the use of magnetic resonance instrumentation. It did have some problems in the community, however, from some consumer resistance to the osteopathic label.

John Little

In 1987, John Little replaced the retiring Thompson as MHS CEO. Little had been with Montpilier Hospital for twenty years, most recently as its strategic planner. Politics made up, in Little's opinion, about 60 percent of his job. He coped with politics by using group meetings and one-on-one encounters. Little adopted and promoted the view that, more than ever, affiliation with Stuben Hospital was a stepping stone to MHS's success in the area.

Little came to work as MHS's CEO with some very specific ideas about how hospitals should be run. In fact, he had written down the key points of his management philosophy and distributed them. That philosophy focused on two main areas: a focus on people and a sound set of business practices. He believed that teamwork, mutual respect, and a concern for fairness and equity coupled with a results orientation based on accountability could make any organization successful. He was well aware that the entire organization must accept these principles, so he set out through both formal and informal means to spread his message.

Multiple perspectives, however, were harbored by MHS and Stuben physicians, administrators, and boards of directors about the nature and resolution of the affiliation. Many key questions had to be addressed: How would the Stuben Board of Directors be made to alter its long-standing vision of Stuben as a full-care medical center? Would Stuben continue as a general care hospital, be converted to an ambulatory care center, become a women's specialty center, or be expanded into an extended care facility?

Little adopted the strategy of having face-to-face interactions and group meetings with the key players involved in the merger issue. In addition, at his request, reports generated by staff members were literally devoid of numbers and instead presented alternative perspectives and general guidelines for discussion and debate. In early 1988, MHS retained a consulting firm to organize and present the alternative strategies for affiliation. Again, at Little's insistence, data collection was secondary to providing a focus for discussion and sharing of ideas.

On October 13, 1988, the senior management staff of MHS, along with Bluefield and other key stakeholders, met to hear the consulting firm's presentation. Because most of the staff—and especially Bill Hagerty, assistant to the president—had worked with the consultants over the previous five months, the report was anticlimatic. Still, the presentation allowed for a convergence of ideas and facilitated the move toward consensus. The highlights of the presentation were as follows:

Consulting Report

The greatest challenge facing Stuben over the next few years was *survival*. In order to survive, several steps needed to be taken:

1. the Stuben board's perception of what the hospital was to be needed to be revised,
2. the role of Stuben in the west shore marketplace needed to be defined, and
3. medical staff that had been leaving Stuben because of its financial condition needed to be drawn back.

Several opportunities were available, but they were closely followed by a series of serious threats in the environment. Clearly one opportunity was coordinating services at Stuben with those offered by the Midwest Health System. Cardiology testing, a breast screening program, sports medicine, and physical therapy were also considered by many to be possible ventures at the hospital that would be well received by the community. Joint ventures with the medical staff could draw key medical personnel back to Stuben.

General threats that the hospital and MHS had to consider included the newly opened Hilltop Surgical Center, the lack of medical staff loyalty at Stuben, the inertia of the Stuben board, and MHS's inability under the current affiliation agreement to force needed change at Stuben.

Several strategic alternatives were presented. The first was to completely raze the building(s) and start over again. Given the problems with the present structures, some felt that this was a feasible alternative in spite of the financial implications of such a strategy. Indeed, in the long run, this could be the optimal strategy to follow since it might restore physician loyalty.

The second alternative was to convert the hospital and adjoining grounds into a long-term care facility. This alternative had several advantages:

1. the elderly market was expected to grow 25 percent over the next five years,
2. Stuben had an established and well-known name for this market niche,
3. it would round out the services offered by MHS, and

4. new sources of financing for this type of venture were very promising. However, given the fixed expenses needed for such an operation, this option could turn out to be unprofitable.

It might also be compounded by the nature of insurance reimbursement policies.

A third alternative was to establish Stuben as a women's health care center. This would allow MHS to build on its prominence in this market. The market of women between twenty-five and forty-four years of age was expected to grow 7 percent over the next five years. In general, this type of operation had been quite profitable in other areas of the state. Perhaps most importantly, this option was championed by Dr. William Chomski, a nationally known plastic surgeon who would be affiliated with the program. However, some expressed concern over this option because Stuben had a limited identity in the community in terms of these services and limited experience offering such services.

A fourth alternative was to position Stuben as an outpatient health center. This had a number of advantages, including the fact that it would establish a dedicated outpatient center for MHS on the west side of the river. It would also make Stuben into a smaller, focused, more responsive organization. Any excess capacity of the physical plant could be used for physician offices, special clinics, and other personnel. Disadvantages of this option included the inability to recruit the additional surgeons needed to operate such a facility and the political and emotional challenge that would probably come from the Stuben board. The problems with the physical plant could also be amplified if this option were selected.

Faced with these alternatives, Little and the top management team at MHS needed to make a decision on which strategy to pursue with Stuben.